Mastering XML

Mastering™ XML

Ann Navarro
Chuck White
Linda Burman

San Francisco • Paris • Düsseldorf • Soest • London

Associate Publisher: Cheryl Applewood
Contracts and Licensing Manager: Kristine O'Callaghan
Acquisitions & Developmental Editor: Kim Goodfriend
Editors: Benjamin Tomkins, Sally Engelfried
Technical Editors: Piroz Mohseni, Liam Quinn
Book Designers: Patrick Dintino, Catalin Dulfu
Graphic Illustrator: Tony Jonick
Electronic Publishing Specialist: Franz Baumhackl
Project Team Leader: Shannon Murphy
Proofreaders: Jennifer Campbell, Richard Ganis, Carrie Bradley, Amey Garber
Indexer: Mathew Spence
Companion CD: Keith McNeil
Cover Design: Design Site
Cover Illustrator/Photographer: Sergie Loobkoff, Design Site

Library of Congress Card Number: 98-86255
ISBN: 0-7821-2266-3

Manufactured in the United States of America

10 9 8 7 6 5 4 3

Software License Agreement: Terms and Conditions

The media and/or any online materials accompanying this book that are available now or in the future contain programs and/or text files (the "Software") to be used in connection with the book. SYBEX hereby grants to you a license to use the Software, subject to the terms that follow. Your purchase, acceptance, or use of the Software will constitute your acceptance of such terms.

The Software compilation is the property of SYBEX unless otherwise indicated and is protected by copyright to SYBEX or other copyright owner(s) as indicated in the media files (the "Owner(s)"). You are hereby granted a single-user license to use the Software for your personal, noncommercial use only. You may not reproduce, sell, distribute, publish, circulate, or commercially exploit the Software, or any portion thereof, without the written consent of SYBEX and the specific copyright owner(s) of any component software included on this media.

In the event that the Software or components include specific license requirements or end-user agreements, statements of condition, disclaimers, limitations or warranties ("End-User License"), those End-User Licenses supersede the terms and conditions herein as to that particular Software component. Your purchase, acceptance, or use of the Software will constitute your acceptance of such End-User Licenses.

By purchase, use or acceptance of the Software you further agree to comply with all export laws and regulations of the United States as such laws and regulations may exist from time to time.

Software Support

Components of the supplemental Software and any offers associated with them may be supported by the specific Owner(s) of that material but they are not supported by SYBEX. Information regarding any available support may be obtained from the Owner(s) using the information provided in the appropriate read.me files or listed elsewhere on the media.

Should the manufacturer(s) or other Owner(s) cease to offer support or decline to honor any offer, SYBEX bears no responsibility. This notice concerning support for the Software is provided for your information only. SYBEX is not the agent or principal of the Owner(s), and SYBEX is in no way responsible for providing any support for the Software, nor is it liable or responsible for any support provided, or not provided, by the Owner(s).

Warranty

SYBEX warrants the enclosed media to be free of physical defects for a period of ninety (90) days after purchase. The Software is not available from SYBEX in any other form or media than that enclosed herein or posted to *www.sybex.com*. If you discover a defect in the media during this warranty period, you may obtain a replacement of identical format at no charge by sending the defective media, postage prepaid, with proof of purchase to:

SYBEX Inc.
Customer Service Department
1151 Marina Village Parkway
Alameda, CA 94501
(510) 523-8233
Fax: (510) 523-2373
e-mail: info@sybex.com
WEB: HTTP://WWW.SYBEX.COM

After the 90-day period, you can obtain replacement media of identical format by sending us the defective disk, proof of purchase, and a check or money order for $10, payable to SYBEX.

Disclaimer

SYBEX makes no warranty or representation, either expressed or implied, with respect to the Software or its contents, quality, performance, merchantability, or fitness for a particular purpose. In no event will SYBEX, its distributors, or dealers be liable to you or any other party for direct, indirect, special, incidental, consequential, or other damages arising out of the use of or inability to use the Software or its contents even if advised of the possibility of such damage. In the event that the Software includes an online update feature, SYBEX further disclaims any obligation to provide this feature for any specific duration other than the initial posting.

The exclusion of implied warranties is not permitted by some states. Therefore, the above exclusion may not apply to you. This warranty provides you with specific legal rights; there may be other rights that you may have that vary from state to state. The pricing of the book with the Software by SYBEX reflects the allocation of risk and limitations on liability contained in this agreement of Terms and Conditions.

Shareware Distribution

This Software may contain various programs that are distributed as shareware. Copyright laws apply to both shareware and ordinary commercial software, and the copyright Owner(s) retains all rights. If you try a shareware program and continue using it, you are expected to register it. Individual programs differ on details of trial periods, registration, and payment. Please observe the requirements stated in appropriate files.

Copy Protection

The Software in whole or in part may or may not be copy-protected or encrypted. However, in all cases, reselling or redistributing these files without authorization is expressly forbidden except as specifically provided for by the Owner(s) therein.

For Dave—without your love and encouragement this project would not have been possible.

—Ann Navarro

To my wife, Eileen, and to my son, Lance, whom I rarely see, but think about every day.

—Charles White

To Lani—You were my source of inspiration and my guide.

—Linda Burman

ACKNOWLEDGMENTS

So many of these acknowledgment pages begin with "So many people contributed to the success of this book..." that it seems almost clichéd, but indeed, a good book takes an entire team to become a reality. For this book these people include my agent, David Rogelberg of Studio B Productions; the Sybex team: Acquisitions and Developmental Editor Kim Goodfriend, Associate Publisher Cheryl Applewood, Editors Ben Tomkins and Sally Engelfried, Technical Editor Piroz Mohseni, Project Team Leader Shannon Murphy, Electronic Publishing Specialist Franz Baumhackl, Proofreaders Jennifer Campbell, Richard Ganis, Amey Garber, and Carrie Bradley; and of course my coauthors Chuck White and Linda Burman.

Additionally, many individuals provided ideas, suggestions, answers, and other support during my work on this manuscript. Their contributions were invaluable, no matter how insignificant they may have seemed at the time. Thanks to each of you: Frank Boumphrey (HTML Writers Guild) for being my trail-guide through the DOM and EBNF; Shane McCarron (The Open Group) for serving as a general sounding board and for the many discussions on esoteric syntactical issues; Tim Berners-Lee (W3C) for a fascinating discussion on namespaces and schemas over lunch at the HTML WG meeting at MIT; Tim Bray (Textuality) for his insights on namespaces; Murray Altheim (Sun Microsystems) for his expertise on DTDs and his debating skills; and the many others I've undoubtedly missed mentioning here.

Finally, thanks to Dave—the most patient man on Earth, who loves having a wife that's just about as big a geek as he is.

—Ann Navarro

Thanks to my wife, Eileen, whose patience is more than could ever be asked for. Thanks to Denise Santoro and David Wall, who recommended me for this project, and Kim Goodfriend, who listened. Also, thanks to Barry Goldberg and Jeff Moore of Zedak for contributing the DTD and core XML files for several newspaper-related XML and XSL files originally developed for the *New York Times*. Thanks to Dave Hyatt of Netscape for some timely answers to questions about XUL and Chris Nelson of Mozilla zine for screen shots. I'd also like to thank James Clark and Stephen Deach, editors of the XSL specs, for their timely responses to several questions I posed to the public XSL-List, and to Tony Graham and Mulberry Technologies, Inc. for hosting the list. A special thanks is due Liam Quinn for some last minute technical editing on the XSL chapters.

Thanks especially to my agent, Chris Van Buren at Waterside, for all his help and efforts. And thanks to the many people at Sybex who made this book possible. And finally, thanks to my two coauthors, Ann Navarro and Linda Burman, for doing most of the work.

—Charles White

First, I'd like to thank Michael Sperberg-McQueen, Tim Bray, and Jean Paoli, the editors of the XML specification; Jon Bosack for his tireless pursuit of "doing it the right way" while chairing the XML Working Group; and Dan Connolly who played a major role in "making it all happen" at the W3C.

Many people have helped me with this book by providing feedback, insight, needed information, and just plain encouragement. Dianne Kennedy, in addition to contributing a chapter, was a constant source of guidance. Manish Sharma made it possible to include the chapter on SIF. Eric Freeze's and Chris Lilley's feedback is greatly appreciated. Kim Goodfriend lived up to her name, donating sage advice and encouragement, and Ben Tomkins showed amazing patience. I'd also like to thank Charles Goldfarb for personal inspiration and for inventing SGML without which XML never would have happened.

And finally I'd like to thank Ophar, Arakan, and Rasputin for helping me maintain a sense of humor throughout this process.

—Linda Burman

CONTENTS AT A GLANCE

Part VI The XML Toolbox

Part VII XML Applications

Part VIII Using XML to Solve Real Business Problems

Appendices

TABLE OF CONTENTS

INTRODUCTION

Although there are many books about XML on the market, this one is a bit different. *Mastering XML* is a technical resource aimed at teaching you how to construct XML data, but it is also much more. The rich framework of information surrounding the technical detail provides depth and breadth not usually found in purely technical computer books. For that reason, *Mastering XML* is a necessary addition to your library, whether or not it already includes books on XML.

Is This Book for You?

Are you a newcomer to XML, hoping to learn about all the excitement? If the answer is "Yes," you will not be disappointed. By the time you have finished reading *Mastering XML*, you will have an excellent grasp of the critical elements of XML and probably be writing XML code. You'll also have learned about each member of the XML family, how the standards are developed, and how XML is being used in the real business world.

Do you already have experience with XML? If you do, you will also find a wealth of useful information in *Mastering XML*. It will fine-tune your XML skills and bring you up-to-date on advances in the XML world. You'll find that this book will expand your knowledge beyond the basics and take you on to the challenges of producing DTDs and schemas, developing your own namespaces, and integrating powerful XML-based applications into your repertoire.

For those with a background in HTML, you'll learn how to transition your content and why HTML is great for display but XML is right for data. If you're already familiar with SGML, but want to add XML to your portfolio, you'll find *Mastering XML* to be a valuable resource, and it will tell you all about SGML for the Web.

Mastering XML makes no assumptions about your computing background. It will provide you with the knowledge necessary to step into the intriguing world of XML!

How This Book Is Organized

This book is organized into eight parts containing 30 chapters in total.

Part I, *Getting Started with XML*, introduces you to the thrilling history behind the creation of XML. You'll learn what XML really is, what it's good for (the business case), and what organizations are tasked with its continuing development. You'll also learn where the future is likely to lead—both on the standards front and in the industry. It also includes an XML Web resource guide.

Part II, *The Building Blocks of XML Document Creation*, walks you step-by-step through the process of creating your own XML documents. It provides the basic syntax common to all XML documents as well as the rules for XML grammar. You'll learn how to create your own elements, attributes, and entities. You'll also learn when to use each and how they come together into the Document Object Model.

Part III, *Designing Your Data*, focuses on the design decisions that must take place before you create your XML data or documents. You'll learn how to evaluate information you want to repurpose or interchange and choose how it should be defined for others to use. You'll look at the differences between DTDs and schemas, and learn when you might choose one over the other for constraining data.

Part IV, *Putting It All Together*, takes you through the each phase of parsing and processing XML. Different types of tool functions are examined, allowing you to evaluate which systems and approaches will work best for you. You'll be introduced to more advanced issues such as linking documents and information together using XLink and XPointer and controlling the display of XML documents with CSS or XSL.

Part V, *Converting to XML*, gives you a look at an exciting proposal from the W3C: the eXtensible HyperText Language (XHTML). XHTML is a conforming XML vocabulary, and thus the two standards converge. Advanced features such as modularization of XHTML and extended forms processing are covered in this section.

Part VI, *The XML Toolbox*, gives you an inside tour through the world of XML development tools, XML-enabled browsers, and XML-enabled server technologies. Learn from brief examples how both large and small businesses are taking advantage of XML on the Web today.

Part VII, *XML Applications*, explains the meaning of "standards" and looks inside the world of standards organizations. It then provides a number of examples of these applications and vocabularies—commonly used implementations of XML that serve a specific purpose such as displaying mathematical computations in MathML, rendering scalable vector graphics with SVG, and more.

Part VIII, *Using XML to Solve Real Business Problems*, highlights how XML-based solutions can solve mission critical business problems. The developers of XML solutions provide a glimpse of the endless possibilities for XML and discuss case studies of real-world XML business applications.

In addition, you'll also find appendices at the back of the book. Appendix A provides a comprehensive resource for XSL properties and their values—a must-have for anyone working with the styling and display of XML documents. Appendix B details the abstract modules used to build extensible documents with XHTML. Finally, the *Mastering XML* companion CD provides valuable XML development utilities that will aid you in your XML projects.

Conventions Used in This Book

Mastering XML uses several distinct conventions to help you find the information you need as quickly as possible. Tips, Notes, and Warnings, shown here, are used to highlight important topics

TIP

Here you'll find insider tips, shortcuts, or interesting bits of information that will aid you in your exploration of XML.

NOTE

A note represents details that the authors are calling to your attention.

WARNING

Warnings indicate that extra caution should be used when working with the subject at hand. Your decisions could have widespread impact on your success!

This Is a Sidebar

Interesting but somewhat tangential information that deserves more than a note will appear as *sidebars*.

In this type of box, you might find background information on a company or technology that is mentioned within the main text or an expansion of some topic that deserves a second look.

Ready to Dig In?

When HTML was introduced we thought that nothing could be more amazing, but soon we realized that although we could go wonderful places and see a huge amount of new information, we had no control over the data with HTML.

A new era has begun for the Web now that XML is real. We can still have a lot of fun, but we can also get real work done. Are you ready to join in? Turn the page and head down the path toward *Mastering XML*.

PART I

Getting Started with XML

CHAPTER

ONE

1

The Road to XML—The Evolution of Markup Languages

- Early text processing systems
- The road to XML
- GML and SGML
- The birth of HTML
- From HTML to XML

If you've read much about the Web recently, you've undoubtedly heard about XML (and that was probably one reason you purchased this book). In this chapter, we'll introduce you to XML, the Extensible Markup Language, which is best described as a means of structuring data. XML provides rules for placing text and other media into structures and allows you to manage and manipulate the results.

Before you can fully understand what XML is and why it was developed, it's helpful to understand where it came from. To do that, we need to go back to the roots of markup languages in general, beginning with the text processing solutions of the early computer age.

Early Text Processing Systems: In the Beginning, We Wrote on Paper

In the beginning, there was the word. Well, not just one word, but lots of them—thousands, millions, and billions of them. What to do with them quickly became a problem. How could they be managed so that their intended meaning would be clear? The world's first *text processing* systems involved recording words with pen and paper (or perhaps chisels and rock?). In the computer age, text processing encompasses not only original document production, but document storage, formatting, manipulation, publishing, and other tools that parse, render, fold, spindle, and mutilate text.

The advancements made over the past decade in word processing and desktop publishing systems mask the complexity of the text formatting tasks that go on behind the scenes. Documents written in popular word processing programs such as Microsoft Word or Corel's WordPerfect have the same look on-screen as they will on the printed page. This has been given a mouthful of an acronym: WYSIWYG (pronounced "wizzy-wig"), or What You See Is What You Get.

While they're certainly convenient, WYSIWYG document handling tools are also quite deceiving. The user is shielded from the instructions given to the computer that generate the look and layout of the page. Prior to these technological advancements in word processing, this formatting was done by human typesetters who followed written *markup* instructions. The term "markup" is taken literally from the practice of writing formatting instructions on a printed copy of the text—"marking it up." Today, that same markup process occurs in Word and in other text processing environments, including XML.

The Road to XML Also Began with Pen and Paper

The process of transitioning between paper and pen–based markup and today's electronically marked up versions went through several general phases. When the markup process was first transferred to the computer, the same types of instructions were provided, e.g.: "Make this section bold." "Set font style to 12 pt. Garamond." These lists of instructions were referred to as *procedures* for the document-rendering agent to perform, thus the origin of the term *procedural markup*.

Unfortunately, procedural markup still suffered from many of the same pitfalls as handwritten markup. The focus was on presentation rather than structure. Two passages that may have the same visual treatment aren't necessarily related in structure: one might be an address, the other a footnote. Changes to the desired presentation required a second pass of the markup process. Additionally, since the focus was on the visual result, the process often relied on assumptions about the capabilities of the printer, computer screen, or paper involved in the final product.

Consolidating Instructions with Macros

The next phase of markup techniques was the introduction of *macros*. A macro is a list of commands and/or a sequence of keyboard strokes that is represented by a unique name or tag symbol. That tag is then inserted into a document where that set of instructions should be executed. This *generic code* is then passed to a secondary formatting application before final display.

TIP

The formatting application isn't necessarily a second distinct program, it's often just another component of the larger program, as in most word processing packages.

Generic coding can save significant amounts of time when an author wants to change the way structures within the document are processed. To change how an A-level heading is presented, the instruction only need be edited in a single place: that is, you only need to change the macro defined for A-level headings rather than change each occurrence of an A-level heading within the document. Because formatting instructions are defined only once for a given macro tag, they also act as an authoring shorthand.

Moving beyond authoring aids, generic coding provides a means for automated processes to interact with the document. An editor could be instructed to find all lists defined in a bulleted style and reformat them as numbered lists. More complex processes could be used to extract and compile outlines from a large document or any number of other post-authoring manipulation tasks.

GML: Presentation Follows Structure

In the late 1960's, three researchers at IBM, Charles Goldfarb, Ed Mosher, and Ray Lorie, began working on the global problem of dealing with thousands of legal documents created on disparate systems that used proprietary formats. Portability across the company was difficult to impossible because of these constraints. Their research brought to light three primary requirements for any interoperable system:

- The document processing programs needed to support a common document format.
- The common format needed to be specific to their domain—i.e., legal documents.
- To achieve a high degree of reliability, the document format would have to follow specific rules.

This system of document formatting was named the *Generalized Markup Language (GML)*.

NOTE It's no coincidence that GML also represents the initials of the three researchers: Goldfarb, Mosher, and Lorie.

A Common Document Format

The first requirement of GML is that the systems involved must support a common document format. Then-current practices for document creation included text-formatting instructions, so it was a logical step to base GML on the model of document markup. The semantics of that markup would, however, be universal across implementations for the first time.

Domain-Specific Formatting

The problem Goldfarb, Mosher, and Lorie were trying to solve dealt with the world of legal documents. Anyone who has been exposed to a legal contract knows that they belong to a world entirely of their own. Latin phrases and very specific and obscure phraseology are commonplace. If they had chosen to create a generic language, the unique needs of legal documents would not have been represented in the feature set of the language. Specialization then, was a good thing, and this became their second requirement: that their language apply specifically to their needs.

Rule-Based Formatting

Goldfarb, Mosher, and Lorie's final requirement recognizes that for successful computer processing of a document, there must be some means of verifying that the markup conforms to the common document format of the first requirement and that any domain-specific formatting constraints were followed.

This last requirement may not be as obvious as the other two. That a new system should be portable and address the specific problem at hand is clear. But think for a moment about how those two requirements could be met and, most importantly, how the domain-specific issues could be dealt with.

To better understand this concept, take a simple document style, the memorandum, and look at the common elements it contains, as shown in Figure 1.1.

FIGURE 1.1:

A simple office memorandum

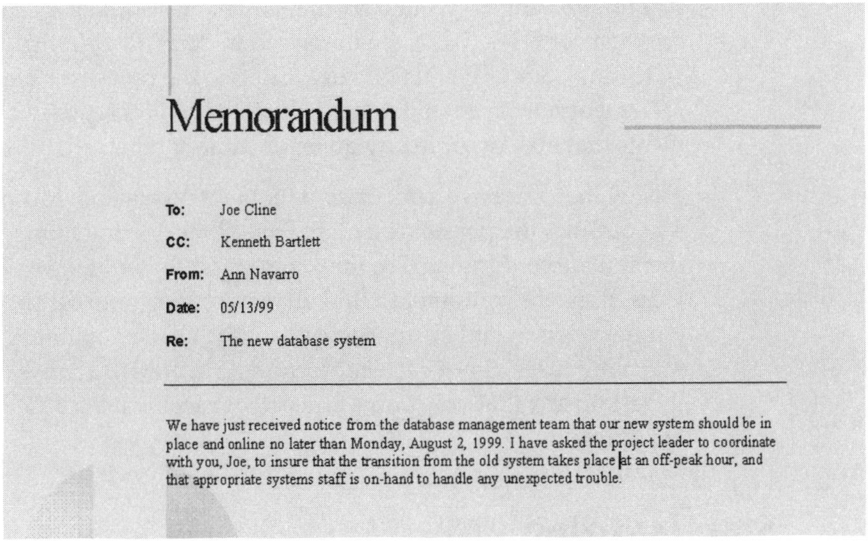

Memorandum

To: Joe Cline

CC: Kenneth Bartlett

From: Ann Navarro

Date: 05/13/99

Re: The new database system

We have just received notice from the database management team that our new system should be in place and online no later than Monday, August 2, 1999. I have asked the project leader to coordinate with you, Joe, to insure that the transition from the old system takes place at an off-peak hour, and that appropriate systems staff is on-hand to handle any unexpected trouble.

The formatting you're concerned with is the *structural* formatting of the document, not the visual presentation. It doesn't matter to the document system that this memo uses 30-point Times New Roman type for the "Memorandum" label, nor does it matter that it includes visual elements such as the horizontal rule. What does matter is that there are six major elements that are included in every memo:

- Who the document is intended for (the "To:" field)
- Who has been sent a copy of the document (the "CC:" field)

- Who sent the document (the "From:" field)
- The date the document was written (the "Date:" field)
- The subject matter (the "Re:" field)
- The document body

If you were to create a markup language for memos, its structure would certainly include elements that contained each of these six elements. Standardizing the methodology even further, you'd give labels to each element that remain the same, no matter where or by whom the document is created. For example, whom the document is intended for will always be prefaced by the To: notation. The subject matter will always use the Re: notation.

These rules for the memoranda document type give a computer a basic vocabulary for working with our documents. This set of rules is called a *document type definition*, or DTD. DTDs are discussed in detail later in this book, and Chapter 8: "Creating Your Own DTD" is dedicated to the process of creating your own XML DTDs. For now, it should suffice to say that DTDs represent the collection of elements that may occur in any given document type.

Now that you have a standard document type and a document type definition that outlines the possible elements that your document may contain, you can manipulate conforming documents in any number of ways. For instance, if you were to ask the computer to find all memos that were directed to Joe Cline, the query system could be instructed to search each document's To: field to find matching cases. Since each conforming memo will always have that To: field, there's no risk that you won't find a document just because the memo is formatted differently.

Standardizing GML

Over the next eight years, Goldfarb continued work on the Generalized Markup Language and acted as technical leader of an international group of developers that fine-tuned his creation. They finally agreed upon what would be called the *Standard Generalized Markup Language*, or *SGML*, and final adoption of SGML was approved by the International Organization for Standardization (ISO), in 1986.

NOTE

The name ISO isn't intended as an acronym for International Organization for Standardization (which would make it IOS). Instead, it was derived from the Greek *isos*, meaning equal. An apt name for an international standards body, don't you think?

ISO is an international consortium of standards bodies from over 130 countries, with one representative per member nation. The organization was founded in 1947 to promote cooperation in scientific and academic endeavors and to facilitate global commerce and information exchange.

SGML is currently overseen by many of the same participants that first brought about its creation. However, it now belongs to a new subgroup known as JTC1/SC34 (International Organization for Standardization/International Electro-Technical Committee, Subcommittee 34). In addition to work on SGML, this group has produced standards for related works such as HyTime, which deals with the representation of hyperlinks, and DSSSL (Document Style Semantics and Specification Language), which standardizes the creation of style sheets and served as a reference point for the World Wide Web Consortium (W3C). (See the sidebar "Managing the Web: The World Wide Web Consortium" for more information on the W3C.)

Managing the Web: The World Wide Web Consortium

The World Wide Web Consortium (W3C) was formed in late 1994. Its top priority was to guide the structure and growth of HTML. The W3C has published an activity statement that summarizes its involvement in the standards process and defines its goals and directional vision for the future. You can find this document online at `http://www.w3.org/MarkUp/Activity`.

Today, more than 350 member companies work together to produce specifications governing nearly every aspect of the Web, from HTML and XML to methods of describing resources, including RDF (Resource Description Framework), privacy practice guidelines with P3P (Platform for Privacy Preferences), and even digital signatures.

The Consortium is hosted across three academic institutions: the Massachusetts Institute of Technology Laboratory for Computer Science (MIT/LCS) in the United States, Institut National de Recherche en Informatique et en Automatique (INRIA) in Europe, and the Keio University Shonan Fujisawa Campus in Asia. Funded by member organizations, the W3C brings key industry players to the same table to produce specifications that may be used by everyone on the Web.

SGML

SGML might best described by what it isn't:

- It does not promote a specific document structure.
- There is not a limited tag set that must be used.
- It will not constrain the potential of creating new document standards.

SGML provides the common framework necessary to describe documents and to create new measures of conformance. Almost all languages that have been created to manipulate documents can trace at least a portion of their roots back to SGML. Indeed, the Web as we know it today would not exist had this standardization of description not been performed.

SGML itself is used by many large organizations, such as the United States Department of Defense, to handle complex electronic document exchanges. Avoiding the presentational features common to other document formats like PDF—or even Word documents—SGML concentrates on the structure of the information. As we noted previously, it does not promote one specific structure, but instead allows for the customized containment of data.

By bounding data only by structures and not with presentation, it can be quickly compiled, indexed, sorted, transformed, or brought together in any fashion desired for delivery to almost any media, whether it's print, screen, audio, or something else.

However, the extreme freedom offered by SGML did present drawbacks when researchers first began to form the ideas that led to HTML and the Web. HTML, of course, started the Web on its way. As the Web matured, users found that HTML went a little too far in simplifying SGML, and they needed a means of exchanging content using a broader structural form. But before we go there, let's take a look at the beginnings of the Web.

How the Web Was Born

It's not surprising that today's most popular markup language was born of the same sort of problem-solving effort as that which created SGML. In 1989, Tim Berners-Lee, a British researcher working in Geneva, Switzerland, at CERN (*Conseil European pour la Recherche Nucleaire*, now known as The European Laboratory for Particle Physics), was frustrated by the lack of portability and compatibility in the vast quantities of research materials stored at the center. Additionally, many of the projects undertaken at the facility were enormous in scope and inevitably brought about the question, "How would we manage so much information?" Not only did they need to deal with compatibility of document types—SGML, CERNDOC, VMS/Help, Unix file systems, and more—but they also faced the challenge of organizing and linking the entire catalog of material available at the facility. None of the existing formats provided a mechanism to do that. In his original proposal describing what would later become the World Wide Web, Berners-Lee wrote:

> The actual observed working structure of the organization is a multiply connected "web" whose interconnections evolve with time. In this environment, a new person arriving, or someone taking on a new task, is normally given a few hints as to who would be useful people to talk to. Information about what facilities exist and how to find out about them travels in the corridor gossip and occasional newsletters, and the details about what is required to be done spread in a similar way. All things considered, the result is remarkably successful, despite occasional misunderstandings and duplicated effort.
>
> A problem, however, is the high turnover of people. When two years is a typical length of stay, information is constantly being lost. The introduction of the new people demands a fair amount of their time and that of others before they have any idea of what goes on. The technical details of past projects are sometimes lost forever, or only recovered after a detective investigation in an emergency. Often, the information has been recorded, it just cannot be found." —Tim Berners-Lee, *Information Management: A Proposal*, March 1989, CERN, Geneva, Switzerland

In addition to the troubles encountered in simply *locating* the information, researchers also had to deal with the requirement of using different types of terminals and different terminal software to access the data based on what system was used to create it. Sounds familiar, doesn't it?

Berners-Lee envisioned a world in which access to data would be a simple task, accomplished in a consistent manner regardless of the terminal or program in use. The concept of *universal readership* was formed, embracing the idea that any individual on any type of computer in any location should be able to access data using only one simple and common program.

As he began to expand upon the universal readership concept, Berners-Lee realized that the traditional ways of thinking about information in linear or sequential order wasn't necessarily the best way to present that information across these disparate systems. This realization eventually led to the use of the now-familiar concept of *links* on the Web.

Linked Information Systems

Most of the information storage and retrieval methods that you're familiar with are probably *hierarchical* in nature. This means that each bit of data is sorted in a structured manner. The files on your computer are sorted in such a way by default, that is, files that begin with numbers come first as a group, followed by files that begin with letters. Within each group, files are sorted from lowest value (*0* in the numbers group, *A* in the letters group) to highest value.

A linked information system doesn't require such order or structure. You can travel from the number *1* to the letter *Q* and back to the number *9*, all the while having the information in each bit of data relate appropriately. This is the basic structure—perhaps better stated as a nonstructure—of the World Wide Web. Documents are stored on thousands of computers, or *nodes*, around the world. Despite the unordered nature of the storage system, a document on a server in California can provide an entry point, or *link*, to a document stored on a server in Finland. Furthermore, you can link directly to the pertinent information; your users won't have to search through the entire site to locate what you are referring to.

This fluidity, combined with the programming efforts that brought about what we now know as browsers, fulfills the vision that Tim Berners-Lee had way back in the virtual "dark ages" of the Internet: The World Wide Web.

The Birth of the Web at CERN

At first, the idea of the Web being born of one man at a facility many of us have never heard of seems a bit far-fetched. But by visiting the CERN Web site (`http://www.cern.ch`), you'll learn that it was actually a natural place for such a collaborative effort to begin.

CERN was founded in 1954 as one of Europe's first joint ventures between 12 member nations. Nineteen nations now hold membership, and over 6,500 scientists are involved in research there, representing over 500 universities based in 80 countries.

The CERN Web site has extensive information about the history of the Web, as well as details on how the Web works. If you're ever in a position to visit CERN, you'll see that they have the first original Web server on display (see Figure 1.2)!

FIGURE 1.2:

The original Web server, on permanent display at CERN in Geneva, Switzerland

From Links to Hypertext: HTML

When Berners-Lee began laying out his plan for a linked information system, he was unaware that a term already existed for the process—*hypertext*—which was coined in the 1950's by Ted Nelson. Hypertext can be defined as "human readable information linked together in an unconstrained way."

In the beginning, these systems often used proprietary interfaces. Work was being done as early as the late 1980's to standardize hypertext systems. These efforts converged in the Internet arena with the development of the Hypertext Markup Language, or HTML, established by Berners-Lee. This original version is now known as HTML 1.

NOTE

The original version of HTML was based on the default SGML tag syntax and the SGML idea of platform independence. Berners-Lee wanted to keep it simple. He did not want people to have to understand SGML in order to use his tag set, so a DTD was not created for HTML 1. Therefore, HTML 1 was not a true application of SGML. Only with HTML 2, in which a DTD was specified, could HTML be considered a true SGML application.

In 1993, a young student named Marc Andreesen at the National Center for Supercomputing Applications (NCSA) at the University of Illinois, Urbana-Champaign, created a graphical user interface for the Web known as Mosaic. It was originally developed on the X Windows platform, a Unix-based environment. (At the time, Unix was the most common operating system for Internet-connected computing systems.)

Later that year, the Mosaic programmers began devising custom extensions to HTML to expand on the capabilities of the Mosaic browser. Little did they know the trend that they would set in motion!

These advances, along with suggestions from other individuals and institutions, were combined into an updated version of HTML, HTML 2, under the supervision of the Internet Engineering Task Force (IETF) in mid-1994.

From HTML to XML

The most recent W3C-approved recommendation for HTML was published in late December 1997 as HTML 4. This recommendation presented us with three distinct versions of HTML:

HTML 4 Strict—Presentational elements and attributes are no longer allowed within the HTML—those attributes should be addressed by using Cascading Style Sheets.

HTML 4 Transitional—Continues to allow presentational elements and attributes within the HTML markup.

HTML 4 Frameset—Used with all documents that make use of the FRAME element.

The move to HTML 4 Strict, the preferred implementation of HTML, was intended to steer Web developers back to the original course for HTML: that of a structural markup language. Like SGML, HTML elements describe discrete blocks of data, such as the HEAD or BODY elements. Further granularity in structure is provided by elements that can appear inline within a block or that may be nested.

NOTE

The full HTML 4 recommendation may be found online at `http://www.w3.org/TR/REC-html40/`.

In 1994 through 1996, the years between HTML 2, as published by IETF, and HTML 3.2 (the predecessor to HTML 4), the Web saw an explosion in popularity from the business and individual user communities. It was no longer strictly the domain of academia. With this change in audience came the desire to make Web pages look more like print media with added colors, fonts, alignment, and all the layout features that are now associated with desktop publishing.

Though these presentational attributes were incorporated into the HTML recommendations in full strength with HTML 3.2, it quickly became apparent that trying to put too much "look" into what was supposed to be a structural language was creating problems for developers and users alike. Developers and their clients were dismayed when their creations didn't look the same from one browser to another, and users were frustrated by the varying levels of browser support for these new features and the associated plug-ins that were often required.

By separating presentational markup from structural markup in HTML 4 into HTML Strict, the W3C not only got back to the roots of traditional markup languages, but also positioned itself well for introducing XML to the world's Web scene.

NOTE

By no means is XML intended to wholly replace HTML. The Web currently consists of millions upon millions of documents written in HTML. Those pages won't go away any time soon, if at all! Instead, XML will bring to the Web the freedom of structure found in SGML. (We're already seeing major advancements in that arena from electronic commerce and data interchange companies.) Both HTML and XML will have many uses for years to come.

Transitioning from HTML to XML

In May of 1998, the W3C sponsored a workshop in San Francisco, California, called "The Future of HTML." Nearly 100 participants spent two days discussing the current needs of the Web community and what new work, if any, the W3C should take on within the HTML domain.

By the end of the workshop, it was quite clear that the consensus pointed toward the W3C providing a means of smooth transition between HTML and XML, and that any future HTML work by the W3C should facilitate that change. As a result, the W3C issued an activity statement outlining the suggested course of action agreed upon at the workshop. This document is still online and may be found at `http://www.w3.org/MarkUp/Activity.html`.

A new W3C Working Group was formed and, as of this writing, has produced a draft of XHTML 1—the Extensible Hypertext Markup Language—which serves as a transition between HTML and XML. This new draft forms the basis from which a proposed recommendation was issued just as this book went to press. The W3C membership will consider granting this draft full Recommendation status, and that may very well have taken place by the time you read this. Chapter 17: "Advanced XHTML" discusses this new language in detail.

As pointed out previously, neither XML nor XHTML is intended to fully replace HTML. Instead, XHTML serves as a bridge between the two languages, effectively allowing them to peacefully coexist.

Why Must We Switch to XML?

There's no doubt about it, HTML will be around for a very long time. Nothing in the W3C's plans to transition the Web's "state of the art" will preclude developers from using HTML—the W3C has simply declared that its work on HTML, save for the transitional XHTML, is done. The consortium's focus on XML will remove a major roadblock from the path of continuing growth of the Web.

HTML is inflexible in that it cannot allow domain-specific tag sets to be created and used without formally introducing them into the HTML DTDs. XML, on the other hand, is designed for that express purpose, allowing these communities to serve their own needs without resorting to lobbying for inclusion in what would only be a horribly bloated new HTML.

It is also important to point out that HTML is designed for Web publishing. It does this well and will serve this function for the foreseeable future. XML, on the other hand, provides a mechanism for the interchange of structured information on the Web. This sort of data is required to transform the Web from a publishing media to an application-processing environment.

Why Not Go Back to SGML?

If HTML is limiting and SGML provides a means for describing document structures, why not simply go back to SGML?

SGML is a language for creating languages. With SGML, you can create tag sets—for example, the Air Transport Association used SGML to create a tag set for aircraft maintenance documentation, and the Society of Automotive Engineers used SGML to create a tag set for automotive service manuals.

Think about building a model airplane. If that airplane were a document, a markup language would be used to put it together. SGML would be used as the basis for the assembly instructions, not the assembly process itself.

SGML is an incredibly rich meta language. It is completely configurable—for example, you can change the symbols for tagging from angle brackets (`<tag>`) to curly braces ({tag}). You can change the tag name lengths from 8 characters to 88 characters. All this flexibility takes computing power on the part of tools that interact with SGML. However, for the Web you need lightweight tools and processes. As a subset of SGML, in many ways XML serves as a lightweight, Web-compatible version of SGML. The differences between XML and SGML, while often described as additional constraints, actually make XML more suitable for the distributed environment of the Web. A very detailed paper comparing the two, written by noted XML expert James Clark, can be read on the W3C's Web site at `http://www.w3.org/TR/NOTE-sgml-xml-971215`. The actual differences are fairly technical, having to do with the manner in which tags are formed and abbreviated, character and entity references, the structure of comments, and other delimiters. You may want to take a look at the paper after you've worked through the first three parts of this book.

Up Next

In this chapter, you reviewed the starting point for today's Web markup languages, SGML. You learned how HTML evolved with the birth of the World Wide Web and discovered how XML relates to each of these technologies.

In the next few chapters, you'll get better acquainted with XML by looking at the original design goals and learning how the standard has evolved into a whole family of standards. You'll then begin examining the basic building blocks of the XML language and explore the future of XML.

CHAPTER

TWO

2

Getting Acquainted with XML

- What is XML?
- Design goals for XML
- XML and its relatives—a family of standards
- How the XML family is developed
- The basic building blocks and features of XML
- Why choose XML?
- The future of XML
- A list of XML resources

Now that you know the history of markup languages and how XML compares to its nearest relatives, SGML and HTML, we can explore what XML actually is, how it came to be that way, and what its future may bring.

What Is XML?

What, precisely, *is* XML? What made its designers so passionate about it and why has learning about it become *de rigueur* for anyone creating applications for the Web?

Let's start with the most visible definition—the abstract from the XML 1 Specification V1 of February 1998.

> "The eXtensible Markup Language (XML) is a subset of SGML that is completely described in this document. Its goal is to enable generic SGML to be served, received, and processed on the Web in the way that is now possible with HTML. XML has been designed for ease of implementation and for interoperability with both SGML and HTML."

In other words, XML *is* SGML. In fact, the Version 1 specification states that

> "XML is an application profile or restricted form of SGML, the Standard Generalized Markup Language (ISO 8879). By construction, XML documents are conforming SGML documents."

By defining XML as SGML it appears that the editors of the XML Specification wanted to leverage the benefits of SGML but streamline it for Web delivery. You might also infer that they recognized an SGML implementation can be time-consuming, so they specified that XML must be easy to implement.

One of the advantages of SGML that the editors wanted to preserve is the concept of "abstract" data that can be separated from a particular presentation, enabling "write once; deliver many," i.e., media-independent publishing. They also wanted to make use of "content tagging," which is using descriptive element names to describe the content within a document to facilitate precise search and retrieval, component recomposition, and reuse.

But the W3C Working Group also realized that since the delivery medium for XML is the Web, it has to have features that do not exist in SGML. Let's look more closely at the design goals for XML to see if these assumptions are true.

NOTE XML is definitively not an extension of HTML. XML is a language like SGML—it defines tag languages or what are now called *vocabularies* and *XML applications*.

Design Goals for XML

XML was developed by the XML Working Group, which started out as "the SGML Editorial Review Board," formed by the World Wide Web Consortium (W3C) in 1996 and chaired by Jon Bosak. The development was also strongly influenced by an XML Special Interest Group that evolved from "the SGML Working Group" also organized by the W3C. The design goals, as they are listed in the specification, are as follows, along with a brief explanation of why they were adopted. We are indebted to Tim Bray, the co-editor of the XML specification, for some of the information in these explanations.

XML shall be straightforwardly usable over the Internet The designers were anxious to have XML become the major interoperability standard, not only for data that is exchanged over the Net, but also within the enterprise. Therefore, they wanted it to transparently interact with HTTP and other major communications protocols that are already in place.

XML shall support a wide variety of applications The designers wanted to encourage the development of all kinds of tools that would create and interact with XML, not just tools that live on Web servers. (Although this is really not a design goal for the language, it conveys the intent of the working group in terms of XML adoption.)

XML shall be compatible with SGML This may sound like an obvious goal but, in fact, it was fairly difficult to achieve according to Tim Bray. Creating a true subset means that all XML must also be valid SGML; it also means you have to keep enough SGML to make documents interoperable.

It shall be easy to write programs which process XML documents This was clearly a priority for both tool and data developers. The goal was to make the language small enough to enable the development of good tools in a reasonably short amount of time. Tools that did not have to rely on reading a DTD would also be easier to create. Thus the idea of a "well-formed" XML document was born to hasten the development of tools which would, in turn, speed adoption of XML.

The number of optional features in XML is to be kept to the absolute minimum, ideally zero This was to avoid one of the challenges of SGML. While options make the language more flexible and powerful, they can also prove troublesome and interfere with data interchange, since all processors may not be able to read all documents. The goal was to ensure that any XML processor could read any XML document.

XML documents should be human-legible and reasonably clear This goal makes sense since most of the original W3C Working Group came from a document markup background. But it is useful in a more general sense as well, because if the markup is human-readable, you can modify it in something as basic as a text editor.

The XML design should be prepared quickly The group understood that the time was right to launch XML into the world and if they spent too much time developing the standard, the effort might get sidetracked. Companies who couldn't wait might start extending the draft specs with their own proprietary tags, and we'd be back to the infamous "browser wars."

The design of XML shall be formal and concise This would make the language programmer-friendly.

XML documents shall be easy to create This goal refers to authoring tools. The group wanted to encourage the development of a wide variety of creation tools for all types of users and not limit them to either very specialized tools or plain text editors used by expert markup "hackers."

Terseness in XML markup is of minimal importance This emanated from the desire to avoid some of the complexity of SGML. In order to be as terse as possible, a feature called "minimization" can be used in SGML that allows the creator to omit pieces of markup, like end tags. The W3C Working Group chose clarity over cleverness, making all XML markup very explicit.

There were also two goals that did not appear in the formal specification. The first had to do with internationalization, which resulted in the Unicode mandate, an aspect that was considered critical from the very beginning. The second was to design the language to be cleanly structured enough so that someone could apply an easy scripting facility.

Thus, these goals do substantiate the premise that the W3C Working Group wanted to preserve the scalability and elegance of SGML but at the same time ensure that software developers could create a critical volume of XML tools and XML data in a reasonably short amount of time.

TIP

The entire text of the XML v1 Specification, which includes these design goals, can be found at the W3C site: `http://www.w3.org/TR/REC-xml`. However, we recommend reading the specification with the assistance of Tim Bray's annotated version at `http://www.xml.com/axml/testaxml.htm`. Bray clarifies the language of the specification and provides a texture and personal context for the design process.

Introducing XML and Its Relatives—A Family of Standards

As you know, XML is not one technology but rather a group of technologies. We refer to these technologies as a "family of standards." This family consists of the following specifications:

- eXtensible Style Language (XSL)
- XML Linking Language (including Xpath, Xlink, and Xpointer)
- XML Namespaces

In this book, we add XML Schemas to this list because it is has become as important as the technologies listed above, although it is not yet a W3C Recommendation.

The following sections serve as an introduction to these key XML technologies. Each is analyzed in more depth in later chapters.

NOTE

It should be noted that the lack of XML Querying in this group of key family members is acknowledged as a rather glaring gap in the XML technology suite, especially for electronic commerce. However, there is only so much that the W3C can do at once. A workshop on XML Querying was held in December 1998 by the W3C, which was extremely well attended and at the time of writing, a W3C Working Group is in the process of being formed. In our opinion, this technology is key to the overall success of XML.

eXtensible Style Language (XSL)

At first, the world was so excited to have HTML that they were happy with just having it rendered. Then the "browser wars" ensued, and Web designers began to resent the amount of work it took to create separate documents (and to update them) for each browser. They wanted easier control over the look and feel rather than being dictated to. They needed a *standard language* for describing presentation. Thus, Cascading Style Sheets (CSS) were born. Cascading Style Sheets made it possible for the same HTML content to be easily formatted in multiple ways.

XSL works with XML data similar to the way CSS works with HTML. XSL is the style language for rendering XML that was derived from a combination of Document Style Semantics and Specification Language (DSSSL), the style sheet language designed for presentation of SGML data, and CSS. XSL, like DSSSL, is based on the premise that data or content should be an abstraction and, therefore, should not include any presentation information directly, as it does in HTML. In other words, the rules created with the style language—the style sheet—should define how the content will appear; the formatting shouldn't appear in the content itself. Like XML, XSL is extensible. At the time of this writing, a number of tools already support it, and many more are expected to become available as soon as it becomes a Recommendation (which will probably be very soon). See Chapter 14: "Displaying XML: Introducing XSL" and Chapter 15: "Displaying XML: Advanced XSL," for more information.

TIP

If you want to learn more about DSSSL, go to **www.oasis-open.org/cover/kennDSSSLInt.html**. This Web page also references several DSSSL tutorials and the actual specification.

XML Linking

When you think about the Web, you immediately think about easily accessing related pages. Hyperlinking is what makes the Web compelling. However, HTML linking only goes in one direction—transporting you from the page you're on to the page you'd like to go to. There's no way, for instance, to link to a specific *part* of a page and no way to easily create links between external pages if the links don't already exist. There are an infinite number of other exciting possibilities as well. The XML Linking Working Groups are exploring some of these today.

XML linking and addressing mechanisms are specified in three W3C Working Draft documents: XML Path Language (XPath), XML Pointer Language (Xpointer), and XML Linking Language (XLink). See Chapter 12: "Using XML Linking," for complete information on XML Linking.

XPath

The primary purpose of XPath is to do the actual addressing of parts of rather than the whole XML document. The name XPath comes from "path notation," which is used for navigating through the hierarchical structure of an XML document.

XLink

XML Linking Language (XLink) uses XML syntax to create structures to describe both the simple unidirectional hyperlinks of today's HTML as well as more sophisticated multiended and typed links. The important part of XLink is that is defines the relationship between two or more data objects (or portions of objects) as opposed to a whole document.

XPointer

XPointer builds on XPath to support addressing into the internal structures of XML documents. Thus, you can use the XML markup to link to specific parts of another document without supplying an ID reference.

NOTE

The XML Linking Working Group has benefited from work done on *HTML*, *HyTime* (an ISO standard for hyperlinking) and the *Text Encoding Initiative Guidelines (TEI P3)* which provides a concise syntax for specifying complex links.

XML Namespaces

The humans mind can distinguish context. If you're told to address a package to 23 Technology Drive, you aren't going to confuse that with being asked to address a group of shareholders at a meeting next week. However, given the state of natural language recognition technology today, a computer software program is challenged to make that distinction.

The simplest way of describing XML Namespaces is that they are a way of assigning unique names to document constructs so that software can operate correctly and avoid collisions. Since there are vocabularies under development, DTD/schema writers may want to take applicable pieces from several DTDs. The problem that might arise is that there might be elements with the same names but with different semantics or different contexts. Namespaces allow context to be given to element names, which allows them to remain unique and thus processable. See Chapter 11: "Understanding Namespaces," for more information.

XML Schemas

The XML 1 specification supplies a mechanism for "declaring constraints"—defining the rules—which governs the structure and the content relationships within a document. That mechanism can be referred to as a *schema.* This term is borrowed from the relational database world and simply means the model that a particular set of information conforms to. (Actually, it usually defines the model for a whole class of documents.) The type of schema provided in the XML specification is a Document Type Definition (DTD). DTDs come to us from SGML and, since XML is a subset of SGML, they also are used for XML documents.

DTDs work very well for document centric applications. (See the section "Why Choose XML? The Business Case" later in this chapter and Chapter 26: "Looking at Real World Examples," for more explanation of *document centric.*) However, a more extensive schema language based on XML syntax is needed so that software applications can process XML documents automatically. For that reason, several schema definition languages have been submitted to the W3C, and a W3C Working Group was formed to develop a superset of the capabilities found in XML 1 DTDs. See the section "The W3C Organizer" for more information about the XML Schemas Working Group. For more information on XML Schemas in general, see Chapter 9: "Creating Other Types of XML Data Schemas."

More XML Family Members

In addition to the specifications that make up the family of standards discussed in the previous sections, other related standards are briefly described in the following sections, "Document Object Model (DOM)" and "Scalable Vector Graphics (SVG)."

Document Object Model (DOM)

The DOM was developed to provide a standard platform- and language-neutral application interface for manipulating HTML and XML data. Thus, a software program can write to the DOM rather than having to manipulate the XML directly. You can learn more about DOM in Chapter 10: "Parsing and Processing XML."

Scalable Vector Graphics (SVG)

SVG is an XML application for describing the rendering of two-dimensional graphics objects. These include three types: vector graphic shapes, images, and text. The goal of the SVG Working Group is to produce a specification that can be easily implemented in browsers and authoring tools and that will result in widespread adoption by content creators. Three proposals to this effect have already been submitted. More information on SVG is available at `http://www.w3.org/Graphics/SVG/`.

The W3C Standards Process: How the XML Family Is Developed

We know that the W3C is responsible for the release of the XML V1 specification as a W3C Recommendation. But how does that process work? How does a proposal get from being just a proposal to being a recommendation? What are the steps that it goes through? Does every good XML idea submitted to the W3C eventually become a recommendation?

Since this progression seems to be a mystery to many people, we provide an overview here. For more detail, see Chapter 23: "Introducing XML Standards, Applications, and Vocabularies."

The W3C XML Activity

To really understand what happens at the W3C in terms of XML, it's necessary to examine how the XML Activity, led by Dan Connolly, is organized. The XML Activity is composed of the following groups:

The XML Coordination Group Made up of the chairs of all of the individual W3C Working Groups, as its name suggests, this group's role is to coordinate the activities of the working groups to avoid conflicts. It also suggests policy changes, maintains liaisons outside the W3C, and maintains the W3C document that describes the XML Activity.

The XML Schemas Working Group Started after various proposals were submitted to develop a schema language that would be more extensible than DTDs. This group is charged with crafting a standard with input from proposals that is much more than the lowest common denominator. The thorny issue of how to plug-in a vocabulary, DTD, or schema at a particular point in another vocabulary, DTD or schema, is one type of challenge that the XML Schema Working Group is addressing.

The XML Linking Working Group According to the W3C Draft Specification, the objective of this working group is to design "advanced, scalable, and maintainable hyperlinking and addressing functionality for XML."

The XML Information Set Working Group The task of this group is to determine how the physical representation of XML documents can be described in more abstract ways than they are in the XML 1 Recommendation. The goal of this group is to develop a common reference set that other specifications can use and extend so that complete interoperability among various XML-based specifications and tools will be more easily achieved.

The XML Fragment Group This group's task is to define a way to send fragments of an XML document without having to send all or part of the parent document with it. The challenge is how to provide the recipient of the fragment with enough information about the fragment's context to make it usable. This group is building on work that was done by SGMLOpen Consortium, now called OASIS (Organization for the Advancement of Structured Information Standards).

XML Syntax Working Group This group is concerned with topics like XML Style Sheet Linking, Cascading Style Sheets, XSL, defining an XML Profile (which would provide a standard way for a device or application to publish the fact that it supports a particular subset of the Recommendation), and XML Canonicalization. This group also is looking into aspects of digital signature technology, internationalization developments, and errata in the XML 1 Specification.

OASIS (Organization for the Advancement of Structured Information Standards)

SGMLOpen was originally formed as a vendor-only consortium dedicated to furthering SGML education in the marketplace and technical work to increase interoperability. Over time, it added user members as well, to contribute primarily to the technical work of the consortium such as the specification for Fragment Interchange.

As the consortium evolved, it made sense to accommodate related technologies such as CGM (Computer Graphics Metafile), and of course, XML. Since many of the companies in the consortium were in the forefront of XML development but also wanted to maintain association with SGML, the members adopted the idea of a consortium that would be an umbrella for SGML, XML, CGM, and related technologies of the future. OASIS has now become the home of XML.org, a repository for XML DTDs, schemas, and vocabularies.

XML-Related Activities

In addition to the XML Activity described previously, the following is a list of other W3C Activities that are closely related to XML or contain certain XML technologies within them:

- **Hypertext Markup Language (XHTML)** Development of HTML as a suite of XML tag sets so specific XML vocabularies like MathML can be used.
- **Resource Description Framework (RDF)** A framework for Metadata.
- **Document Object Model (DOM)** See Chapter 10 for more information.
- **Mathematical Markup Language (MathML)** See Chapter 25: "Using XML Applications," for more information.
- **Style Sheets (CSS, XSL)** See the chapters on displaying XML for more information: Chapter 13: "Working with Cascading Style Sheets," Chapter 14, and Chapter 15.
- **Synchronized Multimedia Integration Language (SMIL)** See Chapter 25 for more information.
- **Scalable Vector Graphics (SVG)** SVG is described in slightly more detail in Chapter 23.

The Standards Progression

What follows is an overview of the standards progression process. Chapter 23 includes a more detailed examination of each step.

Submissions

Typically, one or more W3C member companies submit a proposal of new technology. If it is properly submitted in HTML and is about an appropriate topic, the W3C liaison (for XML submissions it's Dan Connolly) must acknowledge receipt of the submission with some kind of commentary. However, there is no definite connection between a submission and the *recommendations* track. A *note* can be one result of the submission.

NOTE

Many companies submit proposals with the full understanding that no additional work will (or should) be pursued by the W3C on that topic. They submit these proposals hoping they will become W3C Notes, for the commentary that the W3C provides, and to have their work acknowledged on the W3C Web site. Often, this type of note documents a specific industry vocabulary. If you are not overly familiar with this term and would also like to know the relationship of "vocabularies" to "standards," see Chapter 23 for more detail.

Notes

A Note can be a submission of new technology or it can be a discussion written by an active W3C Working Group for the clarification and integration of existing standards. There is no implied commitment on the part of the W3C to do anything.

Working Groups and Drafts

If the W3C decides that a submission is critical to its mission of creating interoperable standards across the Web, it will create a W3C Working Group to study the submission and others on the same topic. The working group then creates W3C Working Drafts of its work in a particular area.

Depending on how desperate developers are for information and direction on a particular topic, the release of a working draft can generate a considerable amount of excitement. For instance, the recent release of the first working draft from the XML Schema Working Group caused quite a stir because developers had been waiting for direction for a very long time.

Proposed Recommendation

When all the members of the working group have agreed that the current working draft meets the goals and requirements of the group—a process which is described in detail in Chapter 23—the working draft goes through a *last call* and can then become a W3C Proposed Recommendation, depending on the opinion of the Director of the Advisory Committee.

NOTE

The W3C is committed to localization. At this point in the process, all documents must contain a statement about how the technology relates to international standards and other relevant standards activities.

Recommendation

All of the members of the W3C Advisory Committee must reach consensus on the proposed recommendation before it can become a W3C Recommendation. Even then, it is up to the director whether or not it becomes an actual recommendation. It is important to note that the W3C Process Document does not call a recommendation a "standard." In fact, it clearly states that a W3C Recommendation can be submitted to a formal standards body (such as ISO) if desired.

Status of the XML Working Groups

Now you know the (sometimes tortuous) path that brought the XML V1 Specification into the world. The following is a list of the key technologies and XML Working Groups that are currently being considered by the W3C. To get up-to-the-minute information on the status of any working group or submitted note, check the W3C Web site at `http://www.w3.org/xml/`.

- Namespaces in XML
- The XML Linking Group
- The XML Information Set Group
- The XML Fragment Interchange Group
- XML Syntax Group
- XML Schema Group
- Scalable Vector Graphics (SVG)
- Resource Description Framework (RDF)

- XHTML 1.0 (eXtensible Hypertext Markup Language)
- Document Object Model (DOM)

The Basic Building Blocks and Features of XML: Overview

Now you know more about what XML is and how XML technologies become W3C Recommendations. But what are its components? How do you use it?

The following section introduces the parts that make up XML without going into the nitty-gritty. Part II: *The Building Blocks of XML Document Creation,* delves into all of these concepts in great detail.

The Critical Components: Pieces and Parts of XML

How do you start building XML documents and systems? First, you need to analyze all the important documents and data structures and then create one or more DTDs, right?

Well, if we were discussing an SGML implementation, the answer would always be "right." However, XML has the concept of both *well-formed* and *valid*, meaning that a DTD (or, in the future, an XML Schema) is not required in every case.

NOTE The XML Schema Working Group is still in the working draft stage of defining a schema language. Currently, DTD is the only specified XML schema.

Well-Formed and Valid

You may have heard the term *well-formed* or *valid*. This phrase is incorrect. *Every* XML document is well-formed; otherwise, it isn't XML. Describing a document as being well-formed means that it conforms to basic rules of XML such as:

- It must have start and end tags for every element.
- It must have one, and only one, root element.
- Empty elements are formatted correctly.

- The case of start and end tags can be either uppercase or lowercase, but they must match.
- Elements must nest correctly.
- Attribute values must always be in quotes.

A *valid* document is well-formed and has also been validated against a DTD (or other specified XML Schema). This means that an XML parser has determined that the document conforms to the rules of the schema associated with the document.

Document Type Declaration

The XML Document Type Declaration points to the Document Type Definition (DTD) and other external *entities* (physical storage units).

An XML document can't be valid unless it contains a `<!DOCTYPE` Declaration which declares a DTD. On the other hand, a document with a `<!DOCTYPE` Declaration can still be read by an XML processor that doesn't check DTDs. As Tim Bray explains in the Annotated Specification:

> "There is a whole class of XML processors, called non-validating processors, which, as their name suggests, do not check the document against the contents of the DTD, whether or not it is provided."

TIP

It's very easy to use the term *DTD* incorrectly. Remember, it means Document Type Definition, not Document Type Declaration.

Document Type Definition (DTD)

The Document Type Definition (DTD), as we discussed in Chapter 1: "The Road to XML," and in this chapter's previous section "XML Schemas," defines the *grammar* of the document. In other words, it specifies the structure of the document and how content is nested.

You may ask, "If you don't absolutely need a DTD, why bother? Doesn't the parsing process result in a substantial performance hit? And don't DTDs take a long time to create?"

Clearly, performance is an issue. For that reason, applications like indexing, displaying or interchanging known data, may not require a formal DTD or XML Schema. However, your application may require a DTD (schema) to operate successfully. See Chapter 8: "Creating Your Own DTD" and Chapter 9 for more discussion on this topic.

Logical and Physical Structures

An XML document can be described in terms of logical structure or physical structure.

Logical Structure The logical structure of a document includes elements and attributes (defined in the sections below). It also includes cross-references, which are links to other parts of the document or links to external objects. This linking is built into the basic XML language and is not dependent on XML Linking Language. This type of linking is useful when you want to insert a graphic, a footnote, or a bibliographic reference at a particular place.

Elements As you know by now, every XML document, whether it has a DTD, schema, or is merely well-formed, has some kind of predefined structure or model. The structural components are called *elements*. Elements contain information or content and can also contain other elements. (They can also contain both or they can be empty).

There is one element that contains all the other elements called the *root element*. As you learned in Chapter 1, XML documents must have one root element. (Root elements can also be called document elements, depending on whether you want to think of the tree structure of the document or the fact that the whole document is a series of layers within the document element.) *Tags* show the beginning and end of an element. Tags and elements are not synonymous, although they are often used that way.

Attributes Some elements have additional information that is added by using *attributes*. Attributes can be compared to labels or adjectives. They can also supply *Metadata*—data about the data. For instance, if you were writing about various types of cars, the attributes might define the colors, engine power, and so on. Attributes may be required or may be optional depending on the document's DTD or XML Schema.

TIP

In XML, all attribute values must be in quotes, unlike in HTML and SGML, where the quotation marks are optional.

Physical Structure While the logical structure refers to the conceptual document, the physical structure describes the actual bits and where they are stored. According to the XML Specification, "An XML document may consist of one or many storage units. These are called *entities*."

Entities The naming convention of entities is similar to that of elements and attributes in the logical structure. There is one entity that contains the whole XML document, which is called the *root* or *document* entity.

An XML processor sees an XML document as a series of characters, which it reads in sequential fashion. When it sees something called an *entity reference*, it reads the name of the entity and replaces the entity reference with the actual chunk of text (characters), graphic, or other type of media that is referred to. An entity can be anything from a single character to a huge file, but authors often break documents up into small chunks of data to form entities that are easier to operate on. Entities can be any type of media (a graphic, a sound clip, an animation, and so on), and they can be stored anywhere—for example, in a database, in a flat file on a remote server, or on a Web site.

NOTE If this is your first exposure to this terminology, don't worry. There is much more detail about all of these terms in the upcoming chapters.

Why Choose XML? The Business Case

Now you've learned where XML originated from and what its basic pieces and parts are. We've also examined how it came to be a Recommendation. But we haven't talked about *why* people want to use it. There must be strong business drivers or companies wouldn't be hurling large amounts of money at developing XML tools and implementations, the number of XML conferences wouldn't be mushrooming, and you wouldn't be reading this book. In this section, we'll explore why XML makes such good business sense.

What Is XML Good For?

Some people immediately reply that XML is good for documents. Others are adamant that its purpose is for data. Others say that it's good for both. You may ask, "Don't documents contain information? And isn't information data? So how can there a difference between documents and data?"

The answer depends on how you define *document* and, more importantly, what kind of implementation you want to accomplish. In Chapter 26, "Looking at Real World Examples," we examine the issue of *document centric* versus *data centric* in detail. In this chapter, we are going to consider the functions and applications where XML shines, a few of which are explored in more detail below and others which will be covered in more detail in Chapters 23 and 26. Clearly, any application of XML will include many functions working together.

As you can see from the extensive yet still incomplete list that follows, XML enables many kinds of applications both over the Web and within an enterprise. The point to always keep in mind is that a standard interchange language makes it possible to easily exchange data and therefore enables applications that we're just beginning to imagine.

- Global media-independent publishing
- Search and retrieval of precise data using element names and Metadata
- Post processing
- Increased performance
- Component/media management
- Web site management
- Accessibility
- Custom publishing
- Personalized publishing
- Event-driven database interaction
- Interapplication communication
- Data aggregation
- Electronic commerce
  - Shopping applications
  - Supply chain management
- Electronic Document Interchange (EDI)

Of course, as we've said previously, you need more than just raw XML and you need more tools and stability in the other related standards. But any application will either understand XML directly or be able to contact a transformation engine that does. Thus data will be exchanged more or less transparently, making operations that are currently expensive, slow, and labor-intensive much less so. In business, change should only be made to create new revenue vehicles or to save money on existing ones. It appears that XML-based systems will be able to accomplish both of those goals.

Global Media-Independent Publishing

When publishing meant only putting ink on paper, a publisher's challenges were to find the best authoring and composition systems and a great printer. Those challenges still exist, but now print is only one medium. Publishing online to multiple media is the norm. However, even today, content is usually created first for print and then repurposed for online vehicles like CD-ROMs, hand-held devices, or the Web.

What are the implications of this process? If the initial output is print, there is a reasonable likelihood that the content is being designed for print composition. Therefore, repurposing the content for another medium is anything but easy and breaking it into components to be stored in a repository for eventual recombination and reuse is next to impossible.

However, if the publisher uses a format-neutral language like XML combined with a powerful style sheet language like XSL, the content can be created without a particular composition system or delivery medium in mind. Then, when the medium is chosen, the content is formatted and delivered using a template that is appropriate for the output medium.

Thus, the same content can produce multiple different presentations of the data resulting in "write once, publish many" capability. Also, once content has been "tagged," the individual components can be managed separately in a content management system and recombined as desired in another content vehicle. Or, since Unicode is mandated by XML, certain elements could be localized for a particular country and easily inserted at the appropriate place in the content.

The benefits of XML for media-independent publishing extend beyond lower production costs for existing and new content vehicles. If all products incorporate the same XML vocabulary, publishers are no longer hostages of particular vendors—at least, not for content interchange.

NOTE

You may have heard a number of phrases that sound almost the same—media-neutral publishing, cross-media publishing, platform-independent publishing, and media-aware publishing—and wondered if they are actually different technologies or the same thing described in different ways. A rule of thumb seems to be that the terminology depends on the latest branding message and also on the focus of the speaker. In other words, these terms can all be used to mean the same thing but sometimes a particular vendor will choose one phrase to describe a particular solution that may not be standards-based.

Post Processing

It seems pretty clear that HTML is not going away. It will continue as the main delivery mechanism for Web content for a long time to come. However, because it produces static content that is not always reliably tagged, a browser can't do anything with it today except display it. But if content is written in XML, an XML-aware browser can sort and filter the data. For instance, if the results of a search are delivered in a format (tagged attributes) that can be manipulated by the browser without round trips to the Web server, precise information can be displayed and performance will be increased.

Search and Retrieval of Precise Data

The ability to actually find what you are looking for is a great concept but not easily achieved with Web technology that relies on HTML. Everyone has had the experience of fashioning a query using every available feature of all the different search engines and still only getting long lists of hits that only sometimes include the piece of information being searched for. Search engines tout their ability to find every reference in the world, but in reality they aren't always able to filter through the millions of references to find what you want. In the early days of the Web, the idea of finding new information through serendipity was regarded as a feature, but today the novelty has worn off. No one has time to follow a bunch of links with the hope of finding something relevant at the other end.

The reason for this imprecision on the part of the search engines is that most HTML that exists today has been coded for visual presentation, for example, bold, italic, and indented. HTML also has a simple concept of structure: a heading, a paragraph, or a list. HTML does not include elements, such as author, price, or title, cannot assign specific attributes to those elements, and cannot provide consistency of structure. XML solves this problem with an extensive set of coding tags for identifying specific information within text. Thus precise data is retrieved, eliminating the endless search through long lists of hits.

> **NOTE**
>
> Remember that XML is an enabling set of technologies, not a solution by itself. It is also useful to keep in mind that these solutions could be and have been developed with proprietary software. The drawback is that if it's proprietary, it's not based on a standard that other software can recognize. Therefore, additional software—usually in the form of scripts—has to be written to translate each piece of data for each system that it is going to. And each of these scripts has to be updated every time there is an update, change, or addition to the software on either side. The management and maintenance of such systems is a nightmare that most companies have been living with since the beginning of electronic interchange.

The Future of XML

How will XML and its related standards evolve over the couple of years? And what is happening in the XML industry in the areas of tools, vocabularies, consortia, adoption, and so on? In this section, we'll discuss the future of XML and whether or not it will replace HTML.

Immediate Future: Evolution of XML Standards

The W3C expects that over the next six months there will be considerable stabilizing of the XML Working Group Drafts and that many will become W3C Recommendations. Some of this information is reflected in the following list, but to keep up-to-date, you must consult the W3C site and Robin Cover's page on the OASIS site at `www.w3.org/xml`, and `www.oasis-open.org/cover` respectively.

- The XML Linking Working Group is expecting to reach Recommendation very soon.
- The XML Information Set Group plans to have a Proposed Recommendation by Fall 1999.
- The XML Fragment Group is in last call on the working draft and is expecting to submit a proposed recommendation by Summer 1999.

- The XML Syntax Group plans to deliver the following in 1999:
  - Proposed Recommendation for the XML Style Sheet Linking Version 2
  - Proposed Recommendation for the XML profile
  - Proposed Recommendation for Canonicalizing XML
  - An update to XML 1 Errata
- The XML Schema Group's work has proceeded very rapidly up to this point, as evidenced by the two working drafts, which have already been released. The goal is to reach a proposed recommendation on data typing and schema language in 1999. However, the group is dealing with some very thorny issues, which may slow it down.
- There is no question that a standard XML Query language is absolutely crucial for development of e-commerce applications. Thus, the newly formed working group is expected to move rapidly to consider the three existing submissions.

Will XML Replace HTML?

In the earliest days of XML, most people in the Web world had either never heard of XML or thought it was an extension to HTML. A great deal of media coverage was given to the debate about whether XML or HTML was better when they were simply two different things. The question is not as pressing now, but for those of you that would like an answer to the question, "Will XML completely replace HTML as the data format for Web content?" we say, emphatically, "No!" There is absolutely no chance that all of the content that has already been produced for the Web will be converted to XML or even have XML Metadata wrapped around it (although the latter is somewhat more likely), and there is no reason that this should happen. What is most probable is that some people will continue to create HTML as they do now since it is very easy. Others will take advantage of XHTML, which, as you learned in Chapter 1, provides a more transitional approach. But HTML will be with us in some form for many years to come.

The Future of the XML Industry

We've looked at the actual standards, but what about the industry? Initially, the only available XML tools were developer tools—mostly parsers—and SGML tools that had been adapted for XML. Bleeding edge developers could experiment and build prototypes but that was about it. Companies with existing SGML implementations began to think about switching to XML, but real business tools were completely lacking.

However, over the last few months, a huge number of new Web tools have come on the market, and almost every one—particularly business-to-business tools—has claimed that it "does XML." Some of this functionality is internal to the particular tool or toolset, and some is very rudimentary, but a trend has been clearly established. We predict that over the next two years, almost every tool will have the capacity to process XML data—whether the functionality is part of the tool itself or provided via an engine called for that purpose. Thus, data integration from disparate sources will become transparent.

Today, there are still only a few complete XML implementations. Some of these are described in Part VIII: *Using XML to Solve Real Business Problems*. However, most companies are still at the prototyping stage using the tools and standards that exist and are waiting for more to come.

Some of the facilitating tools that will soon be released will be XSL editors that make it easy to create style sheets so you don't have to code them in XSL. Some companies have produced early versions of these tools, but most are waiting until the specification reaches recommendation. You will also see browser plug-ins that take advantage of all the features of XSL while the browsers themselves catch up. In the same vein, when the querying specification becomes solid, you will see small tools released that can be used to write queries, in addition to the XML Querying facility that will be added to the large databases. These are just two of the many areas where tool developments will take place.

One of the big barriers to business adoption of XML has been the lack of industry-specific XML vocabularies, both for data within the document, and for Metatdata to describe the data object or document. Recently, these vocabularies have begun to pop up with dizzying speed, especially for e-commerce, but they haven't been extremely useful except to the people who already knew about them. There was no way for a developer to find out which ones existed without spending many hours poring through all the submissions on the W3C site and reading all of the industry news.

Now, finally, two repositories have been announced, `XML.ORG` and `BizTalk.com`. (Both of these are referenced in the section "XML Resources" later in this chapter). When these repositories are completely operational, it should be possible to query them to find out if a vocabulary already exists for the various aspects of your implementation. The easy availability of this information will speed the development of new tools and of XML adoption, which in turn will encourage the development of still more vocabularies.

With the development of tools and Metadata vocabularies, companies will be able to realize the benefits of XML that we described earlier in the chapter. From a revenue-generating or cost-savings point of view, these benefits are so compelling that most implementations of e-commerce and enterprise computing are expected to use XML-enabled technology in some way.

There is little doubt that XML will become ubiquitous. At that time, XML will stop being a hot topic of conversation for everyone except the people who are actively involved with extending the standards and developing new products based on those extensions. XML will become a *checkmark*. Almost all products, including the leading word processors, will be able to save documents as XML, although we can't predict exactly *when* this will happen.

XML Resources

There are many excellent XML resources available. The following list is not exhaustive, but it includes the major Web sites. Many of these sites also contain resource lists pointing to even more XML information. Also, most of the vendors of XML products have resource lists and white papers on their sites. You will not be surprised to learn that the typical URL is `www.companyname.com/xml`.

- Tim Bray's *Annotated XML Specification* (`http://www.xml.com/axml/axml.html`) is a very useful companion to the XML V1.0 specification, as noted earlier.
- One of the most comprehensive sources for all that is happening in the SGML and XML worlds is Robin Cover's page on the OASIS Web Site (`http://www.oasis-open.org/cover/xml.html`).
- Microsoft's XML site contains a variety of great XML articles and reports (`http://msdn.microsoft.com/xml`). You can also find scenarios, written by one of our authors, Linda Burman, that describe how XML can be used at `http://msdn.microsoft.com/xml/c-frame.htm#/xml/default.asp`.
- You can find excellent coverage of XML industry news and analysis from Seybold and O'Reilly at `http://www.XML.com`.
- The official World Wide Web Consortium site contains all of the specifications and much more, including links to articles and talks given by W3C activity leads (`www.w3.org/xml`).

- The Graphic Communications Association site (`http://www.gca.org`) is an excellent resource for general information about XML, XML conferences, the XMLFiles, an online newsletter, and XML industry initiatives sponsored by GCARI, the standards arm of the GCA, including:
    - XML and EDI
    - Information Content and Exchange (ICE)
    - Publishing Requirements for Industry Standard Metadata (PRISM)
- The OASIS Web site gives a comprehensive list of providers of XML products and services (`www.oasis-open.org`)
- Portals to the XML industry (new repositories for registration and retrieval of XML DTDs, Schema and vocabularies) include:
    - XML.ORG, under the auspices of OASIS (`www.xml.org`)
    - BizTalk.com, which belongs to Microsoft (`www.biztalk.com`)
- Web Developer's Virtual Library provides a very comprehensive set of articles, tools listings, and much more (`http://wdvl.internet.com/`). Ken Sall is to be congratulated for creating and keeping up this site.
- xml-dev is a list for W3C XML developers. To subscribe, mail to majordomo@ ic.ac.uk the following message: subscribe xml-dev. To subscribe to the digests, mail to majordomo@ic.ac.uk the following message: subscribe xml-dev-digest.

Up Next

In this chapter, you learned the history of markup languages and gained a basic understanding of what XML is and how it came to be, its basic building blocks, and how it continues to evolve. You were also introduced to the business drivers for XML and how they will affect its future adoption.

Now it is time to move into the specifics. In Chapter 3: "Creating XML Documents" we'll discuss basic XML documents and the components that go into building them, as well as touching on the additional technologies, such as XLink, XPointer, and XSL, that allow a complete document solution.

PART II

The Building Blocks of XML Document Creation

CHAPTER THREE

3

Creating XML Documents

- Mastering basic syntax
- Building a complete XML document
- Rules of XML grammar
- Managing logical structure
- Choosing between a DTD and a schema
- Introduction to XML Namespaces

What exactly constitutes an XML document has never been simply defined. Most people would identify a document that is named with the file extension `.html` as an HTML document, but formally there's more to it than that. Similarly, many lay people will likely think that documents that have the XML extension are XML documents—but they'd be incorrect.

The W3C XML Recommendation simply states that "XML documents are conforming SGML documents." If we turn to the SGML Specification, we find that a document is "a collection of information that is processed as a unit." It's all rather nebulous, isn't it? To make it even more confusing, XML discussions tend to be abstract, which can be confusing to the average user who's simply trying to put this new techno-wonder to use.

In this chapter, we'll introduce the basic concepts that must be mastered in order to produce simple XML documents, using as many concrete examples as possible. For purposes of this chapter only, we'll refer to a document as the contents of a single file.

Mastering Basic Syntax

The process of writing an XML document is no more difficult than writing an HTML document. You have tags, attributes for those tags, and the content that goes in between. In many ways, XML documents are even easier to author than HTML documents, in that you get to make up your own tags!

The Document Prolog

The first item that should appear in any XML document is the *XML declaration*, which appears in the document's *prolog* or opening section. Like an HTML document's <DOCTYPE> declaration, an XML declaration identifies the language the document is written in (XML) and provides a version number. A sample of each is shown below, with the XML declaration listed first, followed by the HTML declaration.

```
<?xml version="1.0"?>
<!DOCTYPE HTML PUBLIC "-//W3C//DTD HTML 4.0//EN">
```

The first thing you might notice is that the XML declaration is, to the human eye, considerably less complicated. The only unusual aspect to it is the ? characters that appear just inside the opening and closing element angle brackets (< and >). This construct is known as a *processing instruction*, a type of information passed to the XML processor, discussed in detail in the section "Processing Instructions" later in this chapter. The next important difference is that the HTML doctype is written in uppercase letters, while the XML declaration appears in lowercase. This case-sensitivity is an important aspect of XML grammar.

XML Is Case-Sensitive

In HTML, authors have the freedom to choose how they write most elements and attributes. `<HTML>` is the same as `<html>`, which is the same as `<HtMl>` or any other combination. This treatment, *case folding*, or conversion from lowercase to uppercase and vice versa, carried forward from SGML.

In XML, however, case *does* matter. The overriding reason that the authors of the XML Recommendation had for choosing this narrower path was for simplicity's sake. A text processor that must interpret differences in case must make complex decisions when converting from one case to another. In the English alphabet, it's straightforward: *a* always capitalizes to *A*. However, in languages where *diacritic* (accent) characters are used, the rules for conversion aren't always that simple. Rather than requiring the text processor to learn an increasingly large set of semantic rules for conversion, the problem simply goes away when the characters represented in different cases are treated as different characters. Therefore, in XML `<element>` is not the same as `<ELEMENT>` and neither is the same as `<Element>`.

The Document Type Definition (DTD)

In Chapter 2: "Getting Acquainted with XML," we discussed the differences between well-formed XML documents and those that are valid. To be considered valid, an XML document must survive review of the document when compared against the rules set forth for the document in the Document Type Definition (DTD). Before a validating parser can perform that check, it must know where to find the DTD that should be used.

DTDs can be written internally to the document, that is, written right inside the doctype declaration statement, or they may be referenced using a URL (or a combination of the two). The treatment of DTDs in XML is much the same as the usage of style sheets in HTML documents, with both external style sheets and the `<STYLE>` element.

The most simple doctype declaration is that which references a URL:

```
<!DOCTYPE memo SYSTEM "FooCorp-Memo.dtd">
```

All doctype declarations begin with the <!DOCTYPE construct. The second term is the name of this doctype—its semantic name, not its filename. In this case, we're using the "memo" doctype. The third segment is the URL of the file that contains the DTD: FooCorp-Memo.dtd.

The Document Element

Every XML document must have a single element that contains all other elements. This all-encompassing element is known as the *root element* or the *document element*. In HTML, the root element is <HTML>. All other content is found within the bounds of the opening and closing HTML tag.

In XML, there is no single required document element: in other words, all XML documents don't start with <XML>. In fact, they can't, because the string XML is reserved. In Chapter 1: "The Road to XML: The Evolution of Markup Languages," we worked with a memorandum. When expressed in XML, the document element was <memo>, and all other elements and content were contained within that document element, as seen in Listing 3.1.

LISTING 3.1

```
<?xml version="1.0"?>
<!DOCTYPE  MEMO SYSTEM "www.foo.com/memo.dtd">
<MEMO>
<TO>Joe Cline</TO>
<CC>Kenneth Bartlett</CC>
<FROM>Ann Navarro</FROM>
<DATE>03/16/99</DATE>
<RE>The new database system</RE>
<BODY>We have just received notice from the database management team
that our new system should be in place and online no later than Monday,
August 2, 1999. I have asked the project leader to coordinate with you,
Joe, to insure that the transition from the old system takes place at
an off-peak hour, and that appropriate systems staff are on-hand to
handle any unexpected trouble. </BODY>
</MEMO>
```

Document Content

What comes next is what we traditionally think of as "the document"—that is, the actual content. XML content is typically expressed using one of four methods:

- Elements
- Attributes
- Comments
- Processing instructions (sometimes referred to as the *document instance*)

Elements

Elements are the primary logical components of a document. They are bound by *start tags* and *end tags*. It's important to distinguish between the tag sets that delimit elements and the element itself, especially because the terminology is used somewhat differently in HTML.

An XML element is composed of the CDATA, bound by the start tag and end tag, that *describes* the element. Therefore, in the following element:

```
<lunch>Today's special includes a cup of potato-cheese soup, a chicken
salad sandwich, and your choice of soft drink.</lunch>
```

`<lunch>` isn't the element, it's a part of the tag set that describes the element. The actual element is the entire chunk, known as a *document component*.

If you were discussing the markup for the `lunch` element, the appropriate reference would be "the lunch element tag," which might be abbreviated to "the lunch tag."

Certain elements may not have any content. These are known as *empty elements*. Empty elements you may be familiar with from HTML include `<IMG>` and `<BR>`. It's important to recognize that "empty" refers to the fact that no content is present between the opening and closing tags. It does not mean that the element cannot contain additional information in the form of attributes. For instance:

```
<img src="mycat.jpg">
```

is just as empty as this element:

```
<br>
```

One small change needs to be made to these elements before they can be used in an XML document. XML requires that all elements be complete. That is, they have an opening and a closing tag. Since empty elements have no content, writing

```
<img src="mycat.jpg"></img>
```

or

```
<br></br>
```

seems rather redundant. To handle this, an abbreviated syntax was developed for empty elements, where the tag could be opened and closed at the same time by inserting the forward slash immediately before the > character, as follows:

```
<img src="mycat.jpg"/>
```

or

```
<br/>
```

Creating elements is discussed in more detail in Chapter 4: "Understanding and Creating Elements."

Attributes

An *attribute* is a property of an element. Attributes are expressed as information within an element's start tag. For example, the lunch element of the previous section may be given an attribute that defines the day on which that meal would be served written as:

```
<lunch day="Wednesday"> …element content… </lunch>
```

As with HTML attributes, XML attributes are composed structurally as a *name=value* pair, where *name* is the name of the attribute and *value* is the value the attribute is to assume for this instance of the element. You could think of attribute values as variables in algebra. In the expression x=7, x correlates to the attribute name, and 7 is the value of x in that instance.

Deciding whether information should be stored in an attribute or as element content can be confusing, especially when it's easy to create child elements for finer granularity in your data. A general guideline to follow is to store information in an attribute if the information describes the element. Information that provides the actual data, on the other hand, should be a part of the element content. This decision-making process, as well as other information on attributes, is covered in more detail in Chapter 5: "Understanding and Creating Attributes."

Suppose you need to create an element that describes a book. You could write it with several child elements.

```
<book>
     <title>Effective Web Design: Master the Essentials</title>
     <author>Ann Navarro, Tabinda Khan</author>
     <publisher>Sybex</publisher>
     <ISBN> 0782122787</ISBN>
</book>
```

This information could easily be written as attribute name=value pairs since each child element contains short strings of characters, as shown here:

```
<book title="Effective Web Design: Master the Essentials" author="Ann
Navarro, Tabinda Khan" publisher="Sybex" ISBN="0782122787"/>
```

If the data included a review or synopsis of the book, that text would be more appropriately stored as element content, as shown here:

```
<book title="Effective Web Design: Master the Essentials" author="Ann
Navarro, Tabinda Khan" publisher="Sybex" ISBN="0782122787">
     <synopsis>A skills-based guide to Web design based on current W3C
     HTML 4 standards, "browser-safe" graphics techniques, and advanced
     multi-media features in site designs, this text will appeal to all
     levels of Web users who are looking for design techniques based on
     the newest standard of HTML (version 4).</synopsis>
</book>
```

Comments

In almost any markup or programming language, it's possible for authors to leave comments inside a document for later reference by themselves or other human readers. In fact, it's good programming practice to be liberal with comments so that when you refer to a document written weeks or even months or years ago, you'll remember what you were thinking at the time.

A comment written in XML is syntactically equivalent to those found in HTML and SGML: it begins with a *markup declaration open delimiter* (`<!`) and a *comment open delimiter* (`--`). Combined, these delimiters appear as `<!--`.

You close a comment with a *comment close delimiter* and a *markup declaration close delimiter*, or `-->` when combined. Any character data may be contained within an XML comment except the > character or double hyphens (`--`), as they may be mistakenly interpreted as part of the markup declaration close delimiter or the comment close delimiter. A full XML comment appears like the following:

```
<!-- I am a valid XML comment -->
```

Comments may appear anywhere in a document, provided they are outside other markup and not immediately prior to the XML declaration.

Though comments are most often used for human reference, there's nothing inherent in their structure that prevents them from being passed to an application by the XML parser. In fact, the XML Recommendation states that "…an XML processor may, but need not, make it possible for an application to retrieve the text of comments."

Processing Instructions

Processing instructions, or *PIs*, are defined as markup that provides information to be used by software applications (as opposed to markup that is used to describe the document). Where an XML parser may or may not pass comments on to applications, a conforming parser *must* pass on processing instructions. A sample PI is written as:

```
<?noisemaker noise="sound.wav" ?>
```

As mentioned when introducing the XML declaration, processing instructions are bound by the <? and ?> character sets. The next entry is known as the *processing instruction target*, or *PITarget*. PITarget refers to the application the instruction is intended for, in the above case, an application named `noisemaker`. The attribute `noise` and its corresponding value of `sound.wav` indicate that the noisemaker application should make the noise contained within that sound file. While this is a rather nonsensical example, it demonstrates how easy it is to pass instructions on to applications.

Building a Complete XML Document

Now that you've been introduced to each section of a well-formed XML document, you can begin putting together documents of your own.

Say, for example, you need to create a document that represents an itinerary for a recent business trip. Table 3.1 outlines the information that must appear in the document.

TABLE 3.1: Itinerary Data for a New XML Document

Flight Data					
Date	**Origin**	**Destination**	**Flight**	**Departure**	**Arrival**
05/09/99	Fort Myers, Fla.	St. Louis, Mo.	TW751	09:00	10:43
05/09/99	St. Louis, Mo.	Toronto, Canada	TW314	13:01	15:58
05/14/99	Toronto, Canada	St. Louis, Mo.	TW671	16:50	18:04
05/14/99	St. Louis, Mo.	Fort Myers, Fla.	TW480	18:54	22:33

Accommodations			
Hotel	**Address**	**Arrival**	**Departure**
Crown Plaza Toronto Centre	225 Front Street West Toronto, Canada	5/09/99	05/14/99

To begin, you need to start with the document prolog. For this example, use `trip.dtd`.

```
<?xml version="1.0"?>
<!DOCTYPE itinerary SYSTEM "trip.dtd">
```

Remember that the doctype name is taken from the name of the document element, in this case, `<itinerary>`.

From Table 3.1, you know that you have two primary types of data to include in the itinerary document: flight data and accommodation data. These two logical components should have corresponding elements, for example, `<flight>` and `<accommodations>`.

The flight data includes short strings that denote the date of the flight, departure city, arrival city, flight number, departure time, and arrival time. This concise data lends itself well to attribute name=value pairs, so you can create flight elements as empty elements, one for each flight segment:

```
<flight date="05/09/99" origin="RSW" destination="STL" number="TW751"
   departure="09:00" arrival="10:43"/>
```

You may have noticed that the flight number data combines the airline identifier (TW for TWA) and the flight number. Expand that into two variables: airline and number.

```
<flight date="05/09/99" origin="RSW" destination="STL" airline="TWA"
   number="751" departure="09:00" arrival="10:43"/>
<flight date="05/09/99" origin="STL" destination="YYZ" airline="TWA"
   number="314" departure="13:01" arrival="15:58"/>
<flight date="05/14/99" origin="YYZ" destination="STL" airline="TWA"
   number="671" departure="16:50" arrival="18:04"/>
<flight date="05/14/99" origin="STL" destination="RSW" airline="TWA"
   number="480" departure="18:54" arrival="22:33"/>
```

NOTE The fact that the origin and destination values are expressed as three-character airport codes is something that can be established in the DTD. A discussion of how to constrain attribute values when creating your own DTD can be found in Chapter 9: "XML Data Schemas."

The next logical component of the itinerary document is the accommodations element, which, as shown in Table 3.1, includes the hotel name, a street address, and arrival and departure dates.

The street address contains enough information that placing it in an attribute name=value pair could become awkward. For this element, then, use a mix of attributes and child elements to hold the details.

```
<accommodations type="hotel" arrival="05/09/99" departure="05/14/99">
     <hotel>Crown Plaza Toronto Centre</hotel>
     <address>225 Front Street West
                 Toronto, Ontario, Canada
                  M5V 2X3</address>
</accommodations>
```

If you wanted to, you could further refine the information about this property by defining attributes so that the `hotel` element contains data such as its star rating or to what hotel chain it belongs, if any. For now, leave it as is. Now, if you put each of these logical components together, you'll have your completed document:

```
<?xml version="1.0"?>
<!DOCTYPE itinerary SYSTEM "trip.dtd">
<itinerary>
<flight date="05/09/99" origin="RSW" destination="STL" airline="TWA"
   number="751" departure="09:00" arrival="10:43"/>
```

```
<flight date="05/09/99" origin="STL" destination="YYZ" airline="TWA"
   number="314" departure="13:01" arrival="15:58"/>
<flight date="05/14/99" origin="YYZ" destination="STL" airline="TWA"
   number="671" departure="16:50" arrival="18:04"/>
<flight date="05/09/99" origin="STL" destination="RSW" airline="TWA"
   number="480" departure="18:54" arrival="22:33"/>
<accommodations type="hotel" arrival="05/09/99" departure="05/14/99">
     <hotel>Crown Plaza Toronto Centre</hotel>
     <address>225 Front Street West
                  Toronto, Ontario, Canada
                   M5V 2X3</address>
</accomodations>
</itinerary>
```

From a design perspective, you didn't necessarily have to place all of the flight elements before the accommodations element. You could have organized them in date sequence, where they would appear as:

```
<flight date="05/09/99" origin="RSW" destination="STL" airline="TWA"
   number="751" departure="09:00" arrival="10:43"/>
<flight date="05/09/99" origin="STL" destination="YYZ" airline="TWA"
   number="314" departure="13:01" arrival="15:58"/>
<accommodations type="hotel" arrival="05/09/99" departure="05/14/99">
     <hotel>Crown Plaza Toronto Centre</hotel>
     <address>225 Front Street West
                  Toronto, Ontario, Canada
                   M5V 2X3</address>
</accomodations>
<flight date="05/14/99" origin="YYZ" destination="STL" airline="TWA"
   number="671" departure="16:50" arrival="18:04"/>
<flight date="05/14/99" origin="STL" destination="RSW" airline="TWA"
   number="480" departure="18:54" arrival="22:33"/>
```

How you arrange the elements is completely up to you.

Rules of XML Grammar

Though authors have quite a bit of freedom in how they create XML documents, there are a few rules that must be followed. Since we work with XML as a language, these rules are called XML grammar.

Introducing the Extended Backus-Naur Form (EBNF)

In order to dig down into the formal grammar of XML, you'll need to be able to understand how it's written. XML and many other W3C Recommendations are written in a style known as *Extended Backus-Naur Form* (EBNF).

NOTE EBNF was created in 1960 by John Backus and Peter Naur as a formal notation for describing the syntax of a computer language, ALGOL60. Since that time, it has served as the model for nearly every other description of syntax for new programming languages.

EBNF is primarily intended for machine consumption, though it's been said that it was designed for humans as well. For nonpropeller-heads, that may—at least on the surface—be a bit of a stretch. We'll attempt to demystify XML grammar by breaking down the notation piece by piece.

Basic Notation

Every grammar rule defined in XML is written in the same form:

```
symbol ::= expression
```

The characters `::=` represent the phrase *is defined as*. If you were to define a new symbol `vowels` to represent the lowercase letters *a*, *e*, *i*, *o*, and *u*, you could write:

```
vowels ::= [aeiou]
```

This translates to "The symbol `vowels` is defined as the letters *a*, *e*, *i*, *o*, and *u*."

Rules can also refer to *ranges* of sequential characters so you don't have to write out each character in a set as you did with `vowels`. For instance, if you were to define the symbol "FirstFive" as the first five lowercase letters of the alphabet, a range could be placed in the expression:

```
FirstFive ::= [a-e]
```

This translates to "`FirstFive` is defined as the letters *a* through *e*."

Note that so far these definitions have been limited to lowercase letters. Remember, XML is case-sensitive, and `a` is not the same as `A`. This applies to grammar rules, too. If you wanted to define `vowels` as either upper- or lowercase, the rule would have to be written as:

```
vowels ::= [aeiouAEIOU]
```

Grouping Characters

EBNF allows for more complex expressions as well. For instance, *white space* is defined in XML as one or more of a space, a tab, a newline character, or a linefeed character. Using EBNF, you can write an expression that allows you to say "one or more of any of these options," as follows:

```
S ::= (#x20 | #x9 | #xD | #xA)+
```

S is the symbol used to represent white space. `#x20` is the hexadecimal number 20 (equivalent to ASCII 32), which represents the space character produced by your keyboard's spacebar. `#x9`, `#xD`, and `#xA` represent the tab, newline, and linefeed characters, respectively. The pipe character | between each item means "or" or "alternately." The + character placed immediately after the set parentheses indicates "one or more." Thus, this grammar rule is read as, "White space is defined as one or more of the space, tab, newline, or linefeed characters."

Excluding Characters

There may be times when the most succinct expression involves excluding a few members from a set. Consider the alphabet again. Consonants can be defined as all the letters in the lowercase alphabet except the vowels. An XML grammar rule for consonants written in EBNF could appear as:

```
consonants ::= ( [^aeiou] | alphabet)
```

This would be read as "Consonants are defined as the alphabet, except the letters *a*, *e*, *i*, *o*, and *u*." In this instance, the pipe character is used to separate the subject of the expression (alphabet) from the exclusion set.

NOTE This rule for consonants presumes, of course, that `alphabet` has been previously defined.

One But Not the Other and Either/Or

As an example, say that a college student is quite driven. To this student an acceptable grade is an A, not a B (and certainly not anything else). If you were to express that in EBNF, you could write:

```
AcceptableGrade ::= A - B
```

This says, "An acceptable grade is defined as the character *A*, but not the character *B*."

However, if this student were to relax their standards a bit and decide that Bs were OK after all, you could rewrite the expression to read, "An acceptable grade is defined as the character *A* or the character *B*," or:

```
AcceptableGrade ::= A | B
```

Remember the old *Saturday Night Live* skit where the new product named Shimmer could be used as either a floor wax or a dessert topping? You could translate that into this either/or instance:

```
Shimmer ::= FloorWax | DessertTopping
     !
```

Managing Logical Structure

To write XML documents that are immediately well formed and/or valid, it helps to be able to visualize the document's logical structure.

Remember the sample XML memo shown in Listing 3.1? Figure 3.1 is a tree diagram that represents the logical structure of the memo.

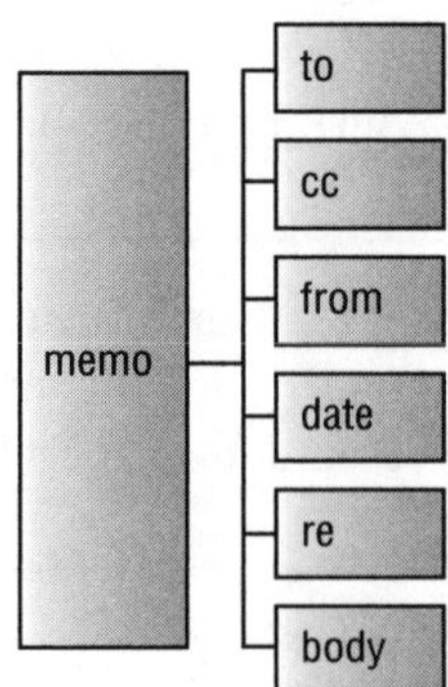

FIGURE 3.1: Listing 3.1 represented as a tree diagram

Notice how each element inside the <memo> element in Listing 3.1 is drawn as an object that branches off the root memo object (now you can see where these organic terms such as *root* come from!). If you were to expand the memo to include a second paragraph and a signature inside the <body> element, as shown below, the tree would expand as well, as shown in Figure 3.2.

```
<body>
    <p>We have just received notice from the database management team
    that our new system should be in place and online no later than
```

```
        Monday, August 2, 1999. I have asked the project leader to coordi-
        nate with you, Joe, to insure that the transition from the old
        system takes place at an off-peak hour, and that appropriate sys-
        tems staff are on-hand to handle any unexpected trouble.</p>
        <p>Please notify me if you have any difficulty during this transi-
        tion.</p>
        <sig>Best,<br/>
               Ann</sig>
</body>
```

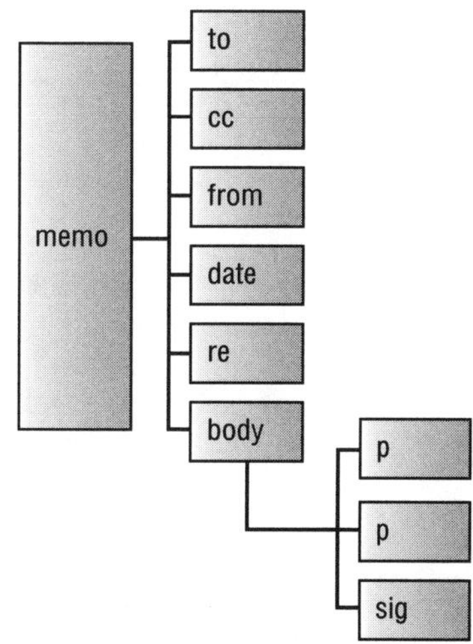

FIGURE 3.2:

Additional branching occurs when a branch has more than one element.

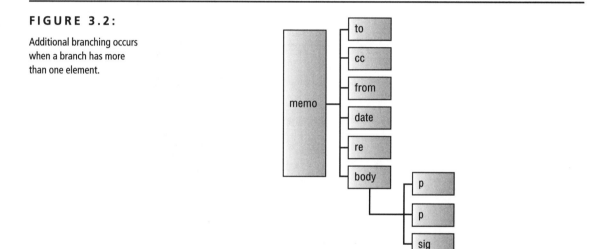

> **NOTE** Some members of the SGML community refer to terminal branches in a tree diagram, such as the `<sig>` element in our example, as *leaves*.

A well-drawn diagram can help you organize your thoughts when it's time to write the DTD for your document.

Choosing between a DTD and a Schema

The term *schema* most often refers to a description of the tables and fields (along with their relationships) found in a relational database system. This type of description can be classified as a conceptual schema, as it represents ideas and relationships. Figure 3.3 contains a simple diagram that outlines the schema of a database stored in Microsoft Access.

FIGURE 3.3:

A schema diagram produced by Microsoft Access

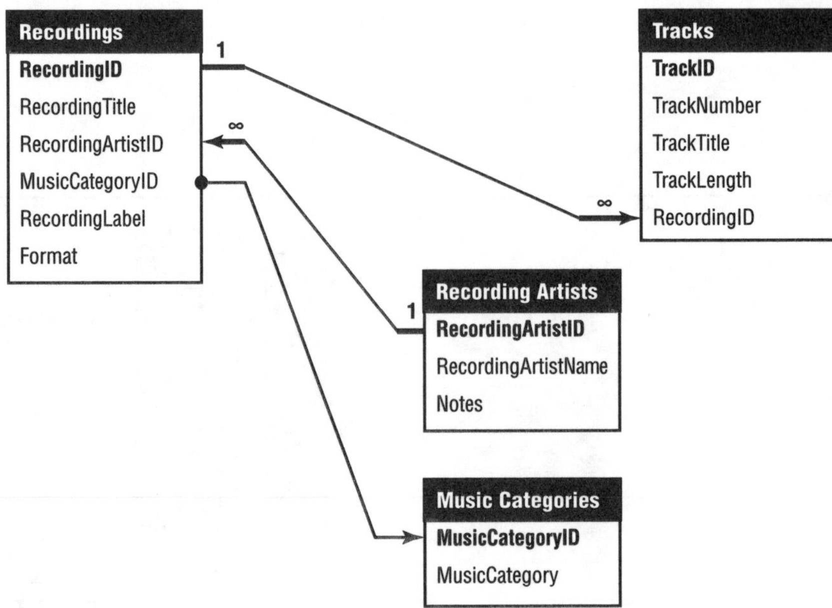

In XML, the description of the document contents is in terms of elements and attributes rather than database tables and fields, and it takes place in the DTD. However, DTDs are admittedly difficult to write well, and they are not particularly reader-friendly. Further, they lack support for using namespaces internally and are very limited in their descriptive powers based on the use of EBNF syntax.

Quite a few proposals have surfaced that make use of XML-like syntax for producing schemas for XML documents. Two major proposals were submitted to the W3C: XML-Data, produced by representatives from Microsoft, DataChannel, ArborText, Inso Corporation, and the University of Edinburgh; and the Schema for Object-oriented XML (SOX) from Veo Systems, Inc.

NOTE Both the XML-Data and SOX submissions, as well as others addressing this problem space, are available on the W3C's Web site at `http://www.w3.org/Submission/`.

The W3C, as part of its reorganization of their XML activity, approved an XML Schema Working Group to review ideas for improving the ability to automate XML document processing by using enhanced descriptive techniques (that is, schemas).

Authors who feel their needs aren't served by DTDs will be able to use schemas to help process and constrain their data. The solution the XML Schema Working Group develops may include the ability to use both techniques, providing not only for well-formed documents that refer to schemas, but also for well-formed and valid documents that likewise behave according to constraints laid out in a schema.

At the time of this writing, the XML Schema Working Group had not yet published a first working draft. The XML-Data, SOX, and others' proposals are discussed in more depth in Chapter 10: "Parsing and Processing XML."

Introduction to Namespaces

One of the greatest strengths of XML has the potential also to be one of its greatest weaknesses: the ability to create custom tags. Say you decide to create a catalog of all your music CDs. In doing so, you use tags such as `<artist>`, describing the band or singer's name, and `<title>`, for the name of the CD.

Meanwhile, your next-door neighbor has been working on a catalog of his modern art collection. He too uses the tag `<artist>`. But instead of `<artist>` bounding the element for a band or musician's name, it refers to the sculptor or painter, and `<title>` refers not to a music CD, but to a painting or statue.

Much to you and your neighbor's dismay, one day when you're both at work someone slips past the doorman and burglarizes all the apartments on your floor. The police arrive that evening and ask you to provide a list of items that were taken. Back at the precinct house, they'll be composing their own document of all items taken in this spree of burglaries—and there's the dilemma. How will they deal with at least two different sets of objects being described with the same tag sets?

The solution to this and the countless similar situations that will arise when blending documents is the concept of *XML Namespaces*. The W3C defines an XML Namespace as "a collection of names, identified by a URI reference, which are used in XML documents as element types and attribute names."

TIP

Don't be intimidated by the *space* in *namespaces*. *Space* is used by members of the SGML community in a manner that is synonymous with *domain* or *arena*. For example, you might say, "Protecting the President of the United States is the domain (or the arena) of the Secret Service." In SGML, you'd be talking about spaces.

In order to blend the common element types of you and your neighbor's documents, the combined document will first need to identify a URI reference for each namespace. This is formally known as *declaring* the namespace. Suppose the detective's stolen-property list report has a document element of `<property>`. Both namespaces can be declared in the document by adding two attributes to that element as follows:

```
<property
xmlns:ann="http://www.foo.com/music.xml"
xmlns:dave="http://www.google.com/art.xml">
```

The first attribute, `xmlns:ann`, identifies this as a namespace declaration (by virtue of the `xmlns:`), with `ann` as the namespace prefix—a shorthand method of referring to the namespace elsewhere in the document. The actual namespace URI is the value of this attribute, or `http://www.foo.com/music.xml`, where you've stored your music catalog document.

WARNING

Keep in mind that the namespace URI is not intended to represent a dictionary-style document that defines each element you use in your namespace. Instead, it represents a usage instance where that namespace may be found.

The second namespace to be used for this blended document has the same structure: the attribute is made up of the reserved string `xmlns:` and a prefix, this time `dave`, to identify your neighbor. His art collection document is found at `http://www.google.com/art.xml`, which serves as his namespace URI.

Now, when compiling the list of stolen property, the namespace prefix is used to identify whose instance of `<artist>` and `<title>` is being used at any given time, e.g.:

```
<item24>
     <object>music CD</object>
     <ann:artist>Sarah McLachlan</ann:artist>
     <ann:title>Surfacing</ann:title>
</item24>
...
```

```
<item43>
     <object>sculpture</object>
     <dave:artist>Maurice Fallon</dave:artist>
     <dave:title>Contemplation</dave:title>
</item43>
```

Namespaces may also be declared inline to address single or infrequent use instances.

```
<action>
<fingerprinting xmlns:scl='http://statecrimelab.gov'>
yes
</fingerprinting>
</action>
```

The addition of the `xmlns` attribute to the `fingerprinting` element indicates that it is taken from the namespace belonging to the State Crime Lab, which uses the `scl` prefix. The detective on the case makes use of the state's required action elements to describe his activities on the scene.

XML Namespaces are discussed in more depth in Chapter 12: "Using XML Linking."

Up Next

In this chapter, we covered the basics of XML document creation, and you now know that you'll need to include a document prolog, a root element that contains all further elements and content, and any pertinent processing instructions in your XML documents.

Now you're ready to move on to the next chapter and dig further into the process of creating elements and defining their attributes, child elements, and content models. In the remainder of Part II, you'll also learn to create attributes and entities.

CHAPTER FOUR

4

Understanding and Creating Elements

- Structuring element tags
- Creating your first elements
- The role of elements in the DOM
- Writing valid element markup
- Getting an element from a database

One of the chief characteristics of XML's extensibility is the power for you to create your own elements. Elements have a long tradition in HTML because they are the central building blocks of HTML markup. An HTML element, such as the body element, might contain a number of other elements within it, such as a number of paragraph elements (the p element), or several link elements (the a element).

In HTML, you must use elements that the target browser will recognize. In other words, you can't make up elements as you go along. If you create markup that looks like the following, the browser will ignore it:

```
<FAKEELEMENT>Here is some content</FAKEELEMENT>
```

Nothing bad will necessarily happen, but if you hope to achieve something by creating the element and the browser ignores it, your efforts are wasted.

NOTE Technically, you *can* create elements for use in Microsoft Internet Explorer 4 (IE4) and 5 (IE5), the latter of which handles XML. This exception is beyond the scope of this chapter, but you still need to tell IE5 what to do with these new elements, generally through a scripting language such as JScript, a Microsoft-specific implementation of JavaScript.

What is possible with the power to create your own elements? Although in theory you're limited only by your imagination and the resources of your development team, there are several uses that come quickly to mind:

- In publishing environments, you can use elements to manage wide varieties of information. Such information might track author names, book titles, ISBN numbers, colophons, synopses, and just about anything else you might think of that is relevant to the publishing world.
- Accounting and other business departments might use custom elements to map relational databases to XML documents. Imagine, for example, a database of products. Each product name in the database could be assigned an element name automatically by specialized software that converts database tables into XML documents. By assigning each Product ID in the database an ID attribute within each element, you can manipulate the document in any number of ways, creating endless possibilities for you and your customers.

- The scientific community is already making substantial use of XML by creating shared Document Type Definition (DTD) within specific scientific fields for a vast range of purposes. The Chemical Markup Language (CML) is one example of a vocabulary that has taken XML's element-creation power and refined it for use in practical ways.
- You could develop elements for home use that track recipes, bank accounts, your rotisserie baseball leagues, birthdays, and any number of other personal needs.

The list of possible uses for elements is endless. You can probably think of some of your own right now. In this chapter you'll master the art of creating elements, and learn how they are accessed with scripting and programming languages. Specifically, you'll learn what an element is, how to create your first element, the fundamental rules associated with XML element creation, the role of elements in the Document Object Model (DOM), and how to validate XML elements against a DTD.

What Is an Element?

As you learn XML markup, it is important to know exactly what an element is. An element is a component of a document. Elements can be made up of other elements, other types of data, or a descriptive representation that tells the XML parsing application about a resource that exists elsewhere than within the document itself.

Elements can consist of content. Their purpose is generally to organize the structure of a document. An easy way to think about how this works is a book chapter outline in a technical publication. A chapter outline usually consists of several top-level headings. Within each top-level heading are subheads. Sometimes, these subheads have their own subheads. It would be silly to have a subhead outside the scope of a level-one head, because it would interrupt the flow of the text within the document.

XML elements work in much the same way as a chapter outline. They must combine to create a document with good structure in order to work properly. As XML usage grows, people will find that there is a true art in creating well-structured XML documents. You'll discover that there is a good reason for XML's nesting requirements (you'll be examining those requirements later in the chapter), as you can probably guess by thinking about how a chapter outline is structured.

A simple XML element based on a typical chapter would have as its root element the information that tells the reader a new chapter has begun:

```
<CHAPTER>
<!-- SOME CONTENT GOES HERE -->
</CHAPTER>
```

As you can see, the CHAPTER element is fairly generic. An element should begin by describing its contents in the broadest possible terms, then drilling down to reveal more information. Which chapter is it? This markup tells you more:

```
<CHAPTER>
<CHAPTERNUMBER>Five</CHAPTERNUMBER>
<CHAPTERTITLE> Understanding Computers</CHAPTERTITLE>
<LEVELONEHEAD>Computers Aren't as Smart as They Look</LEVELONEHEAD>
</CHAPTER>
```

You can think of each of these elements as containers. All XML documents have a central container, within which resides every other container. This container is the *root element*. Remember, there are four rules to always keep in mind with root elements:

1. There is always only one root element in an XML document.
2. Following any opening declarative statements, the root element is always the first element in an XML document.
3. The root element's closing tag is never followed by another element's closing tag.
4. Like any other element, there must be case agreement between the opening and closing tags.

You can see, then, why it would be folly to name the first element of the fictitious book: XML document CHAPTERTITLE. You would not want to include the actual content of the chapter within that element, which you would need to do if it had been named as your root element. You'll learn more about the role of a root element in a document's hierarchy later in this chapter.

Structuring Element Tags

Now that we've gone over the basics, let's move into the actual structure of elements. One rule that must be hardwired into your conscience is this: All elements in XML documents must contain both an opening and a closing tag. There are never any exceptions to this rule, and any violation of this rule will, unequivocally, result in a parsing error. In the HTML world, many browsers forgive markup errors and inconsistencies fairly readily. An HTML parser will often simply try its best to parse invalid markup. This is not so with an XML parser. An XML parser will typically generate some type of error message when it encounters malformed markup. Some parsers, such as Internet Explorer 5, will even tell you where the error occurred, as shown in Figure 4.1.

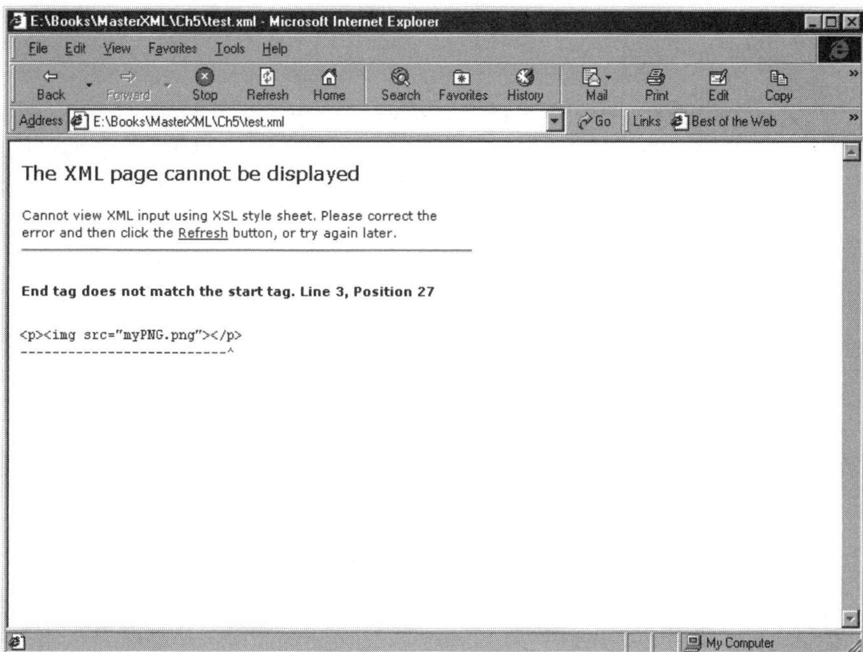

FIGURE 4.1: Internet Explorer 5 generates helpful error messages. Such as this one which is generated because the `img` element was not closed.

Understanding the Difference between Tags and Elements

To understand the structure of an element, and eventually how to create an element, you first must understand the difference between a tag and an element.

You've already seen what an element looks like. A tag helps create the markup for an element—it's inherently part of the element. These tags provide a descriptive framework for the element. Let's take apart the following example:

```
<p>p</p>
```

The < and > symbols are called *delimiters* and are used to separate tags from a document's character data.

TIP

In programming practice, delimiters can take various forms, as long as they are used to separate data. For example, oftentimes you will see delimiters in databases. A simple database table might use commas as delimiters. For example, 1, 2, 3, 4, 5, 6 could be considered a database.

These delimiters also separate tags from an element's *generic identifier* (in this case, the `p` encased between the two delimiters: `<p>`). The generic identifier is also called the element name. If you put the delimiters together with the generic identifier, you have part of a tag. The `<p>` in this example is an opening tag. In order for it to be part of a valid XML tag, it must have a closing tag: `</p>`. To avoid confusing a tag with an element, just remember that a tag is the markup that is used to identify the element.

An element's opening and closing tags can take one of two forms, depending on whether or not an element has content. If an element has content, it should have an opening tag, followed by its content, followed by its closing tag:

```
<myelement>some content</myelement>
```

An element with no content has its opening and closing tag all within its two delimiters. So the preceding element, without content, would look like this:

```
<myelement/>
```

The important thing to remember when considering empty elements is the closing backslash. Leave it off, and the XML document won't parse. It is also legal to write the closing tag after the opening tag, with no content between the two, like this:

```
<myelement></myelement>
```

Remember that XML is not like HTML, and therefore XML parsers won't even try to parse markup that isn't well formed. They'll just give up. Most pages on the World Wide Web today will not parse if they are opened by browsers that follow such strict conformance guidelines. Therefore, it is best to pay heed to XML conformance issues early in your XML development career.

Following the Basic Rules

Now that you've learned the difference between tags and elements, and before we move into the actual creation of elements, there are a few rules associated with element creation in XML that are important to remember. Remembering and applying these rules will go a long way toward producing error-free XML documents. In fact, breaking any of these rules will result in a parsing error:

- Use case consistently when referring to the same element. For example, `<TITLE>` is not the same as `<title>`, ever.
- Always include single or double quotation marks around any attribute value. This would be acceptable in an HTML document: `<img width = 10>` (which is not well-formed markup in XML). It is not acceptable in XML. Instead, you must include quotes: `<img width = "10">`.
- All elements must consist of opening (<) and closing (>) tags. Thus, depending upon whether or not you are using content, the element should look like either `<myelement>mycontent</myelement>` or `<myelement/> or <myelement> </myelement>`.
- All elements must be nested within one root element, and the XML document must have the root element's closing tag as the final closing tag of the document, because the root element contains every element within the document. You'll learn more about that in the next section.
- Element names must consist of XML name tokens (discussed in Chapter 5: "Understanding and Creating Attributes") and cannot begin with any variation of "XML", digits, hyphens, or a period, although these can appear after the first character in the name.

That's it. There are not many rules to follow, and they're logical. That's one of the beauties of XML. It consists of a remarkably logical set of rules that make few demands on your interpretive powers. What's more, you'll never hear another argument about whether it's better to include quotes around attributes, because you don't have a choice; or whether to close a paragraph tag (all tags must close). The reason for this is that XML is all about data, and so it must be used accordingly, and its rules must have a logical structure.

Creating Your First Elements

As you learned earlier, there are two kinds of elements—those with content and those without. Often, the way you create an element in XML documents will be dictated to you either by a DTD or a schema. Chapter 8: "Creating Your Own DTD," and Chapter 9: "Creating Other Types of XML Data Schemas," teach you how to write DTD and schemas. It's important to understand these chapters because even if you never write your own DTD, you'll often need to read one. You can't build robust XML documents if some kind of DTD or schema isn't used; you'll never get beyond static, text-only pages without a schema or DTD.

If an element does not have a corresponding element-type declaration within a DTD, it may result in an invalid document. This depends on whether the XML document containing the element has a DTD associated with it.

TIP You can use an internal DTD to provide declarations about elements that are not handled in external DTD, or for those occasions when you are working without any DTD at all. Sometimes in the early phases of XML application development you may find yourself starting off handling your declarations in an internal DTD, then transferring everything to an external document when everything seems to be in order.

This section concentrates on developing elements without relying on a DTD. That way you can concentrate on the structure of elements and the few rules that must be followed in order to end up with a well-formed XML document.

Using Content Models

Most often, XML element content is guided by *content models*. Content models are declarative statements in DTD that govern what kind of content an element can possess. These declarative statements can include information about:

- The nesting rules of each element. In other words, which elements, if any, an element can have as content, and the order in which they must appear. A DTD content model might, for example, forbid the `order` element from containing a `product` element.
- The number of times one element can be nested within another.

Content models are just one facet of a DTD you'll come to know as you create elements that follow a formal DTD. Content models fall under a larger group of four types of content that a DTD will dictate to you if you are writing a DTD-compliant XML document. The types of content that can be used in an element are:

- `EMPTY`
- `ANY`
- Mixed
- Elements

Chapter 5: "Understanding and Creating Attributes," goes into more detail about how DTDs will affect your document creation. Specifically, you'll see the importance attributes play in document creation.

Creating Elements without Content

The first kind of element to examine is an *empty* element. An empty element is an element that doesn't contain any content or data. An element might be empty for any number of reasons. It may contain only properties (represented by attributes) that reference other files or help characterize what the element is about.

The HTML element `img` is an example of an empty element. The newest flavor of HTML, XHTML, is an HTML specification using an XML DTD. Because XHTML is based on XML, you need to remember to use closing tags when developing empty elements.

As all elements in XML must have an opening and closing tag, it is easy, if you're familiar with HTML, to guess where the opening tag in the `img` element must be. But what about the closing tag? You place the closing tag just after the generic identifier that names the element (in this case, `img`), as follows:

```
<img src="myhome.png" />
```

To ensure proper rendering in browsers that don't read XML, it's important to add the space after any attribute value and before the closing slash mark. You could also simply create two separate sets of tags, like so:

```
<img src="myhome.png"></img>
```

Comparing HTML and XML Empty Tags XML rules are simple, and, as you'll discover, quite logical. Unlike HTML, XML is not plagued by inconsistencies.

This means that when you hear that all elements must have opening and closing tags, there are no exceptions. Empty elements are not an exception to this rule; they are just handled a bit differently than elements with content. For example, the following snippet of code will generate an error in Internet Explorer 5:

```
<?xml version="1.0"?>
<body>
<p><img src="myPNG.png"></p>
</body>
```

In fact, as you saw in Figure 4.1, IE5 generates an error message that actually helps you debug the application with this simple message: "End tag does not match the start tag. Line 3, Position 27." This message tells you two things:

1. Not everyone refers to opening and closing tags in the same way.
2. You must use closing tags, even with empty elements.

Chapter 16: "Converting from HTML to XML" goes into much more detail about how to transition HTML documents to XML. The point here is to emphasize the importance of closing the empty tags, whether they are from legacy HTML files or new XML documents.

TIP

If you use HTML markup as XML, such as within the XHTML namespace, you might find yourself in a bit of a quandary when attempting to use the `br` element. You could use `<br></br>`, but then the browser will interpret it as if you had created your markup like so: `<br><br>`. This gives you two line breaks when you most likely wanted one. The reason for this is that early browser implementations did not foresee the advent of XML. The workaround is to use the abbreviated version: `<br />`. It is absolutely vital to include that extra space preceding the closing slash mark when writing markup for Mozilla-based browsers like Netscape, and some versions of Internet Explorer. Including the extra space is a good habit to get into for all such abbreviated elements.

Determining Empty Element Structure An empty element can consist of no more than the name of an element. This is referred to as an element-type name, or generic identifier. So at its simplest, an empty element looks like this:

```
<anEmptyElement/>
```

Most likely, your empty elements will have some kind of attribute attached, but there is no requirement for this. An attribute is that part of an element that describes the element's properties. Expanding on the previous example, you might have this:

```
<anEmptyElement reason="none"/>
```

Generally you'll find empty elements in documents that are bound to some kind of DTD or schema. There's not much use for empty elements if a parser doesn't have a set of declarations from which to interpret their meaning from a scanned document.

Creating Elements with Content

There will be numerous occasions for including content in your element.

TIP

When you develop XML code using a text editor, the easiest way to guarantee that you nest elements properly is to input both the opening and closing element tags, like so: <tag></tag>. You can then input your content: <tag>content</tag>. This works if an element has content, but not for empty elements, that appear like this: <tag/>.

In simplest form, an XML element consists of an opening and closing tag, and the generic identifier describing the element name. A typical element looks like this:

```
<title>My Favorite Book</title>
```

You can also create an element with other elements as content:

```
<title><chaptertitle>The Blank Look</chaptertitle></title>
```

Or, you can create an element with an entity as content:

```
<title>&chaptertitle;</title>
```

These previous lines of codes are examples of the content model at work. You'll remember that the content model consists of four types of content: `EMPTY`, `ANY`, Mixed, and Elements. Of these, the last three types of content are used to determine the kinds of content used by an element.

Creating Elements with `ANY` Content An element declaration in a DTD may allow for either an element or parsed character data as allowable element content. This gives the document creator more leeway in creating the element, but can lead to a loss of structure. A DTD containing such a declaration would include a line that looks like this:

```
<!ELEMENT MYELEMENT ANY>
```

You'll likely not run across this kind of declaration too often in a DTD, and if you do, the chances are that the author of the DTD will recover control over document structure by defining a strict series of attributes for the element.

Creating Elements with Mixed Content A DTD author might limit the structure a bit more than with an ANY declaration by allowing for mixed content. By allowing for mixed content, the DTD author will permit an element to consist of a mix of other elements and parsed character data. This is much like the ANY content model, but it's different because in this scenario the DTD author may specify which elements are allowed. There is no specific DTD declaration for mixed content. Mixed content is a generic term used to define what type of content an element declaration defines in its declarations.

Take the following example, which is an example of mixed content. This declaration, using the mixed-content model, is one you'll see frequently.

```
<!ELEMENT MYELEMENT (#PCDATA)>
```

This tells the document author that the element MYELEMENT can contain mixed content of any XML-compliant parsed character data. The #PCDATA type means parsed character data, and can contain any amount of parsed character data, including none at all. There are two important considerations when thinking about mixed-content models using parsed character data:

1. Although the elements do not need to actually contain any character data (because the #PCDATA declaration allows for zero or more characters), the elements do need to appear in the document.
2. PCDATA-type content is always part of a mixed-content model, even if there is no other kind of content involved, such as other elements.

The DTD author can go a step further by declaring that in addition to parsed character data, it is okay to include a few other specific elements, in any order:

```
<!ELEMENT MYELEMENT (#PCDATA) | MYOTHERELEMENT | ANOTHERELEMENT>
```

In the preceding line of code, the elements MYOTHERELEMENT and ANOTHERELEMENT can appear within the element MYELEMENT in any order. All three of the following lines of code are valid according to this content-model declaration:

```
<MYELEMENT>Here is <MYOTHERLEMENT>another way</MYOTHERELEMENT><ANOTHER-
   ELEMENT>.</ANOTHERELEMENT></MYELEMENT>
<MYELEMENT><ANOTHERELEMENT><MYOTHERLEMENT>Here
   </MYOTHERELEMENT></ANOTHERELEMENT>is another way. </MYELEMENT>
<MYELEMENT><MYOTHERLEMENT> Here is another way.
   </MYOTHERELEMENT><ANOTHERELEMENT>Shall we add some more character
   data just for fun?</ANOTHERELEMENT></MYELEMENT>
```

The | operator is used to separate content-model options in the element's declaration. The options can occur in any sequence, which is unlike the content model that follows, the elements content model.

Creating Elements with Elements as Content This could be called the child-content model, because this model dictates that any element content must contain another element. Because XML has stringent nesting rules, by necessity these elements must be descendents of the containing element. The elements contained in this content model must appear in the sequence specified. The sequence is specified in the DTD in a comma-delimited list:

```
<!ELEMENT MYELEMENT (MYCHILD, YOURCHILD, HERCHILD)>
```

In the preceding line of code, the element MYELEMENT must have the following nesting order:

```
<MYELEMENT><MYCHILD/><YOURCHILD/><HERCHILD/></MYELEMENT>
```

Note that in this example, the MYCHILD, HERCHILD, and YOURCHILD elements are empty. However, these elements will also be defined by the same DTD that declared the MYELEMENT element, and so would need to follow whatever content model was declared for those elements. They may or may not have been declared empty, but assume in this case, for the sake of clarity, that they were.

Summarizing the Content Model

To enhance your ability to view a DTD and determine how to develop an element according to the rules of that DTD, look at Table 4.1, which lists the content types you'll find in a typical DTD. Don't worry much about the syntax you see in Table 4.1 just yet. As you learn to write a DTD in upcoming chapters, reading one will come as a matter of course.

TABLE 4.1: Content Types Used in DTD

Content Type	Description	DTD Syntax
EMPTY	The DTD is telling you that no content is allowed. Empty elements can have attributes, however.	<!ELEMENT myelement EMPTY>
ANY	The DTD allows any kind of content in an element.	<!ELEMENT myelement ANY>
Mixed	The DTD allows you to mix content so that character data and other elements can coexist within the element.	text-only: <!ELEMENT myelement (#PCDATA)> text and element content: <!ELEMENT myelement (#PCDATA | elementName | elementName)*>
Elements	This part of the DTD governs content models and dictates that specific elements must be nested within an element in a specific way (see the preceding discussion).	<!ELEMENT myelement (mysubelement | yoursubelement)>

When you learn to read a DTD, you'll make decisions about element content based on the declarations you see within the DTD, like those in the far-right column of Table 4.1. These will act as rules that will provide direction as to where different types of content are placed. As XML matures, XML editing software will likely validate your documents on the fly as you write them. In the meantime, you need to do it yourself, and to do so you need to be able to read a DTD. In the next chapter, you'll learn that there's much more to element content than what you see in Table 4.1, because element attributes also have a separate set of content rules that can be applied through a DTD.

Understanding Nesting and Hierarchy

As important as all the syntactical aspects you've learned are, probably no rules of element creation are more important than the rules about *nesting*. Nesting refers to the way a group of elements resides within the structure of a document. Document elements in XML all have one thing in common, no matter what their root element. This is true if you're using a content model or not, and no content model is allowed to change that rule. The root element is always the first element in an XML document, and always contains every other element in the document.

This makes it easy to recognize an XML document. Take a look at the following snippet:

```
<book>
<title>Mastering XML</title>
<publisher>Sybex</publisher>
</book>
```

Note how the two elements, `title` and `publisher`, are contained, or *nested* within the `book` element. This is a hierarchy of elements, which is based on an old concept in computer science of nodes and abstract data that you'll be looking at in the next section.

Nesting properly is a fairly simple process, and you'll quickly find yourself able to detect mistakes. Look at the following code and see if you can tell what is wrong with it:

```
<?xml version="1.0"?>
<book>
<title>Mastering XML</title>
</book>
<publisher>Sybex</publisher>
```

Can you tell which of the elements in the preceding lines of code is the root element? In other words, which element contains all the other elements? There isn't a root element, so, assuming the preceding lines of code represent the entire document, then the document is not well formed, and will generate a parsing error.

Understanding Nodes

The hierarchy of elements is based on the concept of *nodes* and abstract data structures. Nodes play a big role in the DOM, which plays a big role in the use of dynamic XML, so it helps to know something about their history. They're an essential part of understanding the hierarchy at the root of XML documents (no pun intended).

NOTE

We'll be discussing the DOM in greater length later in this chapter, but for now, know that the DOM is a set of interfaces that helps manage XML nodes programmatically.

Nodes describe information about the data structures that are common to modern programming languages. These descriptions are considered abstract by computer scientists because they can be applied across a variety of different computer languages, such as C, Pascal, and Java. In XML, these data structures are called trees. Computer languages might call them something else, such as lists or collections. Whatever they are called, each individual instance of data within that tree (or list or collection) that gets processed is a node.

Generally, any time you have an abstract data structure, it must be traversed in a specific, definable way. This is a very important concept in XML, particularly when considering some of the more complex tasks associated with scripting involving the DOM. You traverse the nodes of an XML document tree following a very specific pattern, a hierarchical one defined by parents, children, and siblings. It's important to understand nodes because as you progress in your mastery of XML, you'll likely encounter them often. It is easy to make the assumption that a node object is by definition an element, but that is not the case. A node can be an element attribute, or even the text content of an element. In other words, it is any instance of data within a document tree that gets processed.

About Parents and Children

The hierarchy of XML is based on the way elements are nested within one another. But it is also based on the relationship of each node in the tree, which, as you now know, means that each instance of data has a relationship with the others. Because XML is structured as a parental hierarchy, the relationships that nodes have with one another are based on each element's position in relation to the root element. The root element of an XML document is always considered the parent of any other object that immediately follows its position in the document. If another child is nested within the root element's child, then that element is a child of the first child. If an element has two subelements that are not nested within each other, they are siblings of one another.

This notion of parents and children is prevalent within the DOM. It can be confusing, too, as most documentation referring to the structure of XML documents refers to trees, leaves, and branches. Rather than getting bogged down by the semantics, try to keep in mind these general ideas:

- All XML documents begin at the root level with a root node followed by a root element. The root node represents the document itself. You won't be worrying about the root node in this chapter, which focuses on the hierarchical relationship among elements.

- The root element is referred to in a scripting or programming environment as a `documentElement`. This is its representation in the DOM. Its properties and methods, the key programmatic constructs of DOM properties, are all inherited by the root element's descendants.
- Any other elements that exist must be contained within the root element.
- The first element contained within the root element is considered a child of the root element. If there is more than one child element and that child element is not nested within the first child element, then those child elements are both children of the parent, and siblings to one another.
- The child element of the root element may itself contain elements. If so, those elements, also called *subelements*, are children of the child.
- Elements containing subelements are called branches, and elements without any subelements are called *leaves*. They have no child elements of their own.

Diagramming the Hierarchy If you look at Figure 4.2, you can get a better handle on how it all works. In the diagram, you can see that every element in the document `myXML.xml` is contained within the root element (called `rootElement`). This root element contains three children: `childA`, `childB`, and `childC`. Each of these child elements of the root element also has children. Note, however, that I did not name these children in a way that implied they were grandchildren of the root element. The reason is that the direct relationship between elements ends with the first child. This is an important consideration because if you use a scripting language, such as ECMAScript, to manipulate an XML document, you will traverse the tree one node at a time.

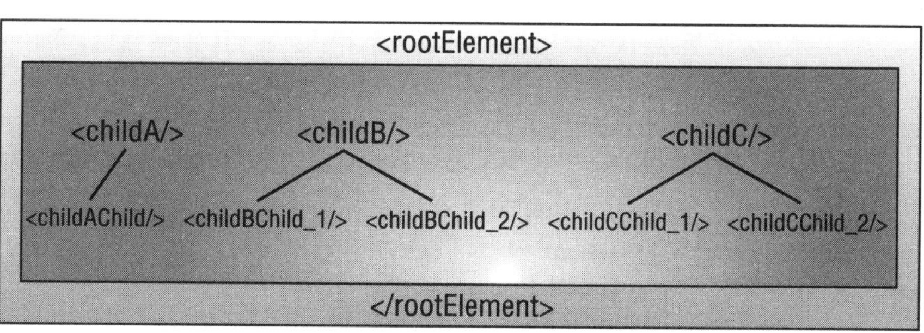

FIGURE 4.2: Looking at XML element hierarchy

NOTE

ECMAScript is the newest standard for JavaScript, which has taken on a new name to reflect a more standardized methodology. ECMAScript is equivalent to JavaScript as implemented in Netscape Navigator 3. Any flavors of JavaScript beyond that you may encounter, such as the JScript implementations found in Netscape Navigator 4 and IE4 and 5, are extensions to that model and not standardized in any way, at least not yet.

To get at the element `childBChild_1` in Figure 4.2 (using JScript in Internet Explorer 5), you would write the following line of script:

```
myXMLdoc.documentElement.childNodes.item(1).childNodes.item(0)
```

In the preceding line of code, `myXMLdoc` is the name of the XML document, in this case accessed by a unique identifier using the ID attribute within another document. Don't worry if you're not sure what we are talking about here. Just know that one document can access another, and once it does, you refer to it often by its ID in the top level of a script. Such references are made from the top level down, beginning with the document, then moving on to the root element, and then the root element's child.

Understanding Dot Syntax Don't be too concerned if the preceding line of code is completely unfamiliar. There are a few things worth mentioning about it, however, from a purely illustrative standpoint. Notice, for example, the dot syntax that is used. The dots are used in much the same way as slashes and backslashes are used to name a path within a computer's directory structure, or when accessing a Web site. `myXML` represents the actual XML document (also called the root node). The next node in the hierarchy is the root element, represented by the `documentElement` property. The `documentElement` property is part of the document interface within the official DOM as specified by the W3C. The first `childNodes` property refers to the `childB` element, and the second `childNodes` property refers to the `childBchild_1` element. Listing 4.1 shows how the entire document looks as a complete XML file.

LISTING 4.1 Understanding How to Traverse a Document Tree Using Dot Syntax

```
<?xml version="1.0"?>
<rootElement>
     <childA>
             <childAChild/>
     </childA>
```

```
    <childB>
            <childBChild_1/>
            <childBChild_2/>
    </childB>
    <childC>
            <childCChild_1/>
            <childCChild_2/>
    </childC>
</rootElement>
```

Matching the Document Hierarchy to the DOM If you're confused about the relationship between Listing 4.1 and the line of script it's associated with, look at Figure 4.3. The diagram in Figure 4.3 matches the hierarchy as used in script with the actual XML document. Don't get too hung up right now on grasping the way the script works. The idea is to keep in mind the importance of hierarchy and nested elements, not only as they pertain to the structure of an XML document, but also as they pertain to the scripting languages that manipulate their data.

FIGURE 4.3: Matching elements with their corresponding DOM objects

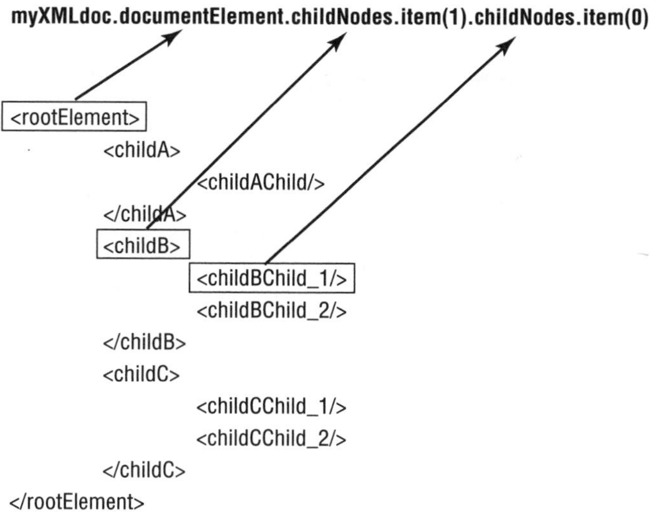

Each node in an XML document can be accessed in script by traversing the XML document tree using the parent-child hierarchy. You can't get to a node without first accessing the top-most element in the tree (unless you're working with document fragments, but that's beyond the scope of this discussion). This is the same hierarchy that has been used since the introduction of JavaScript. The document model used in the earliest implementations has been made more robust for XML, but the concept is the same.

If you're familiar with scripting, you'll find accessing XML nodes (elements and their attributes and content) a breeze. If you're not familiar with scripting, and all of this seems a bit perplexing, don't worry about it too much.

NOTE Scripting will be covered in richer detail in Chapter 22: "Java and XML."

For now, focus on understanding the role of elements relative to one another, and why it is so important to nest them properly. In our view, it's not quite enough to properly nest elements because the XML Specification says you must. It is also important to understand why this logical structure exists in the first place. One reason is the role of the DOM and its interface with scripting and even programming languages such as Java and C++.

The Role of Elements in the DOM

The DOM is a set of interfaces that provides programming access to the nodes of a document, beginning with the document's root node, in a language-independent way. The DOM is a recommendation from the W3C (`www.w3.org/TR/REC-DOM-Level-1/`) that is supported in IE5 and is being targeted by Netscape Navigator 5. Additionally, it is receiving wide support in the Java community as a viable interface between Java and XML. You can also use a number of other languages to access the DOM and work with XML. Some of the computer and scripting languages you might consider while working with the DOM and XML may include, but not be limited to:

- ECMAScript (JavaScript)
- JScript (Microsoft's implementation of JavaScript, which contains numerous extensions to the original specs)
- Java
- Visual Basic
- VBScript (a scripting language used primarily for IE5–specific Web pages and ASP (Active Server Pages)

- Python
- UserTalk (a scripting language used by Userland Frontier)
- Perl
- C
- C++

Thinking about Objects

An element is made accessible to scripting languages like JavaScript and object-oriented programming languages like Java because every element is also an object.

An element doesn't need to contain any data to be considered a legitimate object. The `img` element is a good example of a familiar element from HTML that doesn't contain any data. Rather, it contains properties in the form of attributes such as `src`, which describes where the object is located. An image's actual data is contained in a separate file that is referred to via the `src` attribute. The `img` element, or object, always remains the same, but it can contain different properties, and these properties can be changed on the fly through scripts.

Try inputting the following code within an HTML file:

```
<img src = " " />
```

If you load this HTML file into a browser, you'll get a broken-image icon. That's because you're dealing with an object that has properties that mean nothing to the browser. In fact, its properties refer to a resource that contains no data. It's still an object, though, and thus, it is also an element. You might want to change the `src` attribute value to something that makes sense to a browser, such as `src="http://www.myplace.com/home.gif"`. This is why the Document Object Model (DOM) is so important to XML. The DOM consists of object interfaces and their properties you can manipulate with script.

Objects have become extremely important in the computer world. By manipulating them in script, you can turn static Web pages into dynamic Web pages. To better understand how an element can be considered an object, review the following tag:

```
<p style="font-family:serif">This is a paragraph</p>
```

In the preceding tag, the `p` element consists of a number of parts that help describe it as an object. This element consists of data made up of a string ("This is a paragraph"). A *string* is computer-talk for a series, or string, of one or more text characters. This element also consists of an attribute, `style`, which has the value `font-family:serif` assigned to it.

You'll learn more about the DOM and scripting techniques in Chapter 21: Java and XML.

Within the DOM, the most commonly used interface is the element interface. Table 4.2 shows the various properties and methods associated with it. The element interface contains properties and methods that make it possible to access an element's attributes. From a technical perspective, an attribute isn't a child of anything. Because of that, the developers of the DOM built a series of interfaces within the DOM that contain properties and methods developers can use to access element attributes. Table 4.2 contains just one such interface, the element interface. There are actually several other interfaces, but they're beyond the scope of this chapter. If you're not familiar with scripting or programming, Table 4.2 won't mean much to you. Don't worry about that. We've included it as both an aid for programmers and a way to show non-programmers how the DOM is used to access elements and change their properties on the fly.

TABLE 4.2: The Element Interface in the DOM

Attribute	Description
tagName	This interface attribute can be used as an element object property to retrieve the name of a specified element.
Method	**Description**
getAttribute(*name*)	This interface method can be used to return a string value containing the name of an attribute.
removeAttribute(*name)*	This interface method makes it possible to dynamically remove an attribute from an element.
setAttribute(*name*, *value*)	This interface method makes it possible to dynamically add an attribute to an element. The value in the parameter is a string value, so the method needs to be used carefully because any markup set by the method will be interpreted as literal text, not as markup. As you progress in your XML development, you'll learn how to escape specific characters, as they are set by programming methods or by other processing mechanisms.
getAttributeNode(*name*)	This interface method makes it possible to retrieve a specific attribute, which is named in the parameter.

Continued on next page

TABLE 4.2 CONTINUED: The Element Interface in the DOM

Method	Description
getElementsByTagName(*name*)	This interface method can be used to retrieve the names of all the elements that are descendants of the element the method is being operated on, and that have the name given in the parameter.
normalize()	This interface method makes it possible to combine an element's text nodes in one normalized form to make it easier to manage the saving of documents.
removeAttributeNode(*oldAttribute*)	This interface method can be used to remove an attribute from an element's attribute, by naming the attribute you want to remove in the list method's parameters.
setAttributeNode(*newAttribute*)	This interface method makes it possible to add an attribute to an element's attribute list.

Writing Valid Element Markup

Now that you know all the rules about creating elements and how they fit into the document, we are going to look at ways of making sure your documents are well formed. We'll also take a look at how to manage your element content through validation.

Comparing Well-Formed against Not-Well-Formed

A well-formed document is a document that follows the core rules of XML. A valid document is a document that follows the core rules of XML, *and* adheres to a DTD or schema assigned to that document. Before you tackle document creation using a DTD, it might be worthwhile to review some of the concepts of what makes a well-formed document.

Take a look at Table 4.3 to see why some elements are well formed, and some are not. Remember, though, that you're looking at elements not bound to any DTD or schema. A DTD or schema might require an element to consist of specific attributes or data types. In those cases, even though an element may consist of well-formed markup, the markup may result in an invalid document, because it didn't adhere to the declarations in the associated DTD or schema. You don't need to worry about that right now, however. For now, just think about why the elements in Table 4.3 are well formed or not.

TABLE 4.3: Well-Formed Elements vs. Not-Well-Formed Elements

Well-Formed	Not-Well-Formed (and why)
<number>1</number>	<number = “1”><1></number>
<number=1></number>	<number=1></number>
<analysis><type>psychological</type></analysis>	<analysis><type>psychological</analysis></type> *these elements are not properly nested*
<title>Mastering XML</title>	<title>Mastering XML</TITLE> *case usage is not consistent*
<book> <title>Mastering XML</title> <publisher>Sybex</publisher> </book>	<book> <title>Mastering XML</title> </book> <publisher>Sybex</publisher> *there is no root element*

Managing Data Content within Elements

As you have learned, elements can take content comprised of other elements, or specific data represented by text characters. Elements can also have extra information attached to them through attributes. There are two ways to manage element content. One way is through DTD validation. Another way is through the use of a schema.

Using DTD Validation

Early in the chapter we mentioned that there are four specific types of content models to which elements can adhere. These four types of content models are dictated through the use of a DTD. You'll recall that these four types are the `EMPTY`, `ANY`, Mixed, and Elements content models.

A DTD as a separate document is called an external DTD. It needs to be declared in the prolog of an XML document if that XML document is to be validated against it. You can also make your declarations within the XML document itself. This is called an internal DTD. You'll be learning how to create a DTD in Chapter 8.

When creating XML document elements that are validated against a DTD, the elements must follow the rules as specified by the DTD, whether that DTD is an internal or external DTD. If there is no DTD, then the elements only need to be well formed within the XML vocabulary.

But a document that does not have an associated DTD or schema is not a valid document. This may seem like a confusing statement, so let's examine it further. After all, saying a document is not valid seems like a strong statement. It implies that the document is no good, and that it has no validity within the XML environment, which is not the case. When a document is not valid, it just means that no DTD or schema is available against which to validate it. There are, in other words, no rules for the document to follow. The document might still be perfectly well formed XML, which means an XML parser should parse it. A DTD provides document authors a chance to maintain a set of rules XML documents should follow. Using a DTD (or a schema) will make it easier to maintain consistency of structure, but there is no requirement that an XML document be valid, or, in other words, follow a set of rules according to some DTD that is out there or that you create.

What you have learned in this chapter regarding when and how to recognize the various parts of the content model should serve you well as you embark on the mission of creating your own DTD. Chapter 8 provides greater detail on how to develop and interpret DTD.

Validating against Schemas

Another area that will grow as XML matures is the validation of XML documents against *schemas*. Schemas are XML documents that contain content-type definitions, much like a DTD does. An XML document that wishes to validate against a schema generally uses what is called a *namespace*. The namespace provides a mechanism through which the XML processor handling the XML document being validated knows about the schema being used for validation.

There have been several proposals before the W3C regarding schema specifications. Each of them has focused on a specific aspect of document creation. Among the types being considered have been the following:

- Document Content Description for XML (DCD)
- Schema for Object-oriented XML (SQX)
- Document Definition Markup Language (DDML) Specification, Version 1
- XML Data

The W3C has narrowed its focus somewhat to two working drafts on schemas. One focuses on structure, the other on data types. The first is called XML Schema Part 1: Structures. You can find it at `http://www.w3.org/TR/xmlschema-1/`. The other is called XML Schema Part 2: Datatypes. You can find it at `http://www.w3.org/TR/xmlschema-2/`. The working draft that focuses on schema structure describes the syntax and elements that are allowed when creating schemas. There is a DTD that must be adhered to. The working draft that focuses on datatypes focuses on the types of data that are allowed. This is where the difference between DTD and schemas really comes into play. Schemas allow for a much larger set of datatypes than DTDs allow. You can specify integers and other numbers, dates, and Booleans (true-false datatypes). To validate against these schemas, you need to declare a namespace and then adhere to that namespace declaration when using the elements that are validated against the schema.

Schemas are validated against a document when the document gains access in some way to the validating schema. The current working draft does not specify how a document must gain access, but generally documents will use namespaces to do so. The only requirement is that a schema must be identified by a Uniform Resource Identifier (URI). This is not the same as the more familiar URL. A URI acts as an identifying mechanism that doesn't require a physical presence on a network. The following is an example of a namespace that declares the use of Microsoft's schema that works in IE5:

```
<MYROOTELEMENT xmlns="mySchema: theValidatingSchema.xml">
<MOREELEMENTS>
...<!-- More content here -->
</MOREELEMENTS>
</MYROOTELEMENT>
```

IE recognizes schemas, but not those written using the current specification (in working draft stage as this book went to press). Microsoft has its own set of schema elements, which are used to develop schemas that are then used to validate documents and access the rich data types afforded to content authors who chose to use them instead of a DTD.

You can also generally include the namespace prefix with the element name. This is a good idea especially if you are using multiple schemas. Consider the following code snippet:

```
<MYROOTELEMENT
   xmlns:schema1="http://www.mydomain.com/schemas/schema1.xsd"
```

```
xmlns:schema2="http://www.mydomain.com/schemas/schema2.xsd"
xmlns:schema3="http://www.mydomain.com/schemas/schema3.xsd">
<schema1:CHILDELEMENT>some content here</schema1:CHILDELEMENT>
<schema2:CHILDELEMENT>some content here</schema2:CHILDELEMENT>
<schema3:CHILDELEMENT>some content here</schema3:CHILDELEMENT>
</MYROOTELEMENT>
```

The preceding lines of code create a way to access what seems to be one element (CHILDELEMENT) three different ways. Of course, because the prefixes `schema1:`, `schema2:`, and `schema3:` were added they in fact create three different elements. However, CHILDELEMENT may have originated with one definition. Schemas might then evolve to handle that same element differently, depending on the circumstances. Perhaps CHILDELEMENT referenced the same object from three different vendors. Substitute `car` for CHILDELEMENT, and the three prefixes for GM (`GM:car`), `Ford` (`Ford:car`) and Honda (`Honda:car`), and you can see why namespaces and schemas might come in handy. You might build a generalized DTD to handle cars, then create a more specific schema for each make of car, which have the same general properties (or attributes) but have many vendor-specific features.

The `xsd` extension of the URI in the preceding code refers to each schema. This follows the convention of the most recent working draft.

One drawback to schemas is that in order for an XML processor to validate against a schema, it needs to have an instruction set built into the parsing software. An example of a schema-aware XML processor is Internet Explorer 5. Internet Explorer 5 knows about the element types made possible through the XML Data schema. The XML Data schema allows you to create your own schema for more robust datatypes than what the XML Specification allows, thus making it possible to use integers, floats, and other numeric entities within elements and their attributes. That's the strength of schemas; they allow a more open model than DTD validation. The real question over time will be whether schemas become vehicles for software vendors to continue creating compatibility woes over the Web, or whether schemas rally around their promise of providing access to rich datatypes.

NOTE

You'll learn more about schemas in Chapter 9: "Creating Other Types of XML Data Schemas." You'll learn about namespace in Chapter 11: "Understanding Namespaces."

Getting an Element from a Database

Now that you know the basics of how to create an element, let's take a quick look at an example of an element at work. As an example we'll use a hypothetical database.

In the hypothetical database, you might find a category called `order`. You could then create an XML document that contains an XML element with the same name. The `order` element within the XML document may in turn have an ID number corresponding to the product's order number within the database. Such an element may look something like this:

```
<order id = "10249">
<product>tofu</product>
<product>Manjimup Dried Apples</product>
</order>
```

Figure 4.4 shows a sample database from the Microsoft Access database program. The order field in the database was converted into an order element in the preceding line of code. Thanks to the flexibility of XML, you're not confined to sorting your data in any one specific way. In the preceding example, several fields were left out from the originating database. Using a scripting or programming language, or XSL (a style-sheet language for XML), you can filter data and records in just about any manner you choose.

You can see from the preceding code that elements can take different kinds of content. The order element, for example, contains other elements. The product element has an ID attribute attached to it, and contains descriptive text for its value.

You don't need to rely on an existing database to create elements. You can simply invent your own as long as you follow the rules of well-formed XML markup. You could have an element called `<extrasillybutIlikeitwheresthespam/>`, as long as it is structured correctly.

FIGURE 4.4:

A sample database from Microsoft Access

Order Details : Table

Order ID	Product	Unit Price	Quantity	Discount
10248	Queso Cabrales	$14.00	12	0%
10248	Singaporean Hokkien Fried Mee	$9.80	10	0%
10248	Mozzarella di Giovanni	$34.80	5	0%
10249	Tofu	$18.60	9	0%
10249	Manjimup Dried Apples	$42.40	40	0%
10250	Jack's New England Clam Chowder	$7.70	10	0%
10250	Manjimup Dried Apples	$42.40	35	15%
10250	Mishi Kobe Niku	$16.80	15	15%
10251	Gustaf's Knäckebröd	$16.80	6	5%
10251	Ravioli Angelo	$15.60	15	5%
10251	Louisiana Fiery Hot Pepper Sauce	$16.80	20	0%
10252	Sir Rodney's Marmalade	$64.80	40	5%
10252	Geitost	$2.00	25	5%
10252	Camembert Pierrot	$27.20	40	0%
10253	Gorgonzola Telino	$10.00	20	0%
10253	Chartreuse verte	$14.40	42	0%
10253	Maxilaku	$16.00	40	0%
10254	Guaraná Fantástica	$3.60	15	15%
10254	Pâté chinois	$19.20	21	15%
10254	Longlife Tofu	$8.00	21	0%
10255	Chang	$15.20	20	0%
10255	Pavlova	$13.90	35	0%
10255	Inlagd Sill	$15.20	25	0%
10255	Raclette Courdavault	$44.00	30	0%
10256	Perth Pasties	$26.20	15	0%
10256	Original Frankfurter grüne Soße	$10.40	12	0%
10257	Schoggi Schokolade	$35.10	25	0%
10257	Chartreuse verte	$14.40	6	0%
10257	Original Frankfurter grüne Soße	$10.40	15	0%
10258	Chang	$15.20	50	20%
10258	Chef Anton's Gumbo Mix	$17.00	65	20%

Record: 8 of 2155

Up Next

In this chapter, you learned how to create an element. Overall, you'll probably find that elements are fairly simple to develop. By themselves, however, they wouldn't be particularly robust objects. In order to make them more robust, you must explore their attributes, which you'll do in Chapter 5: "Understanding and Creating Attributes."

CHAPTER

FIVE

5

Understanding and Creating Attributes

- What is an attribute?
- Understanding attribute syntax
- Understanding attribute types
- Putting it all together

If you're familiar with HTML, you've seen attributes many, many times, even if you've never given them much thought. The nature of HTML is such that you can use an attribute without thinking much about it. You don't need to even understand that much about the syntax involved, or even, for that matter, if it's correct. Browsers tend to simply ignore attributes that aren't structured properly.

One example of an HTML attribute is the `src` attribute. The `src` attribute belongs to the `img` element, which exists in just about every Web page in existence. In HTML, a `src` attribute within an `img` element looks something like this:

```
<img src = "http://www.mySite.com/myGif.gif">
```

Attributes play a key role in XML development, just as they do in HTML. If you're not familiar with HTML, the definition of an attribute is still easy. An attribute in XML is the part of an element that contains additional information about an element. This chapter explores the key concepts behind attributes, will help you understand the syntax behind attribute development, and show you how to manage attribute types, particularly their relationship to DTD.

What Is an Attribute?

To better understand attributes let's take a look again at a line of HTML code:

```
<img src = "http://www.mySite.com/myGif.gif">
```

The `src` attribute in the line of code acts as a modifier to the `img` element. It's a bit like grammar. A cat is nice, but a big, fancy, fluffy, splendiferous cat is nicer. The adjectives big, fancy, fluffy, and splendiferous are all modifiers; they help give the noun (cat) attributes. Whether or not you agree that these kinds of cats are indeed nicer, you most likely will agree that the description is more specific than just cat.

So, as mentioned previously, an attribute in XML is the part of an element that contains additional information about an element. Attributes are especially useful for managing the kinds of content that you encountered in Chapter 4: "Understanding and Creating Elements." You'll remember that elements consist of four kinds of content with various combinations of other elements and character data. Attributes break these kinds of content down further and allow you to specify how they are managed.

Attributes can consist of ten specific types of content. When a DTD is being followed or written, attributes are said to be one of these ten types. Each of these types is described later in this chapter, but it is useful to run down the list quickly so that you can begin to become familiar with them. Any attribute value must consist of one of the following ten types of attributes available to an XML document:

CDATA Used to indicate that an attribute value can consist only of character data that won't be interpreted as markup.

ENTITY Used to indicated that the attribute value will represent an external entity in the document, which when referenced by that document will match the name of the attribute value.

ENTITIES Same as ENTITY, except you can name more than one, and separate them by white space in a list.

Enumeration An enumerated list of values that the attribute value must match.

ID Used to establish a unique identifier for an element. If there is more than one ID with the same value, the parser will throw an error.

IDREF Used to allow an element to reference an ID that has been named for another element.

IDREFS A list of white-space delimited ID references.

NMTOKEN Similar to CDATA, but the character usage is limited to letters, digits, underscores, colons, periods, and dashes.

NMTOKENS A white-space delimited list of NMTOKEN values.

NOTATION Used as a way to map a reference to a NOTATION declaration that exists elsewhere in the DTD.

There are a number of other new phrases in the preceding list, such as IDREFS and NOTATION. Don't worry if you don't recognize them. We'll be addressing this terminology as the chapter proceeds.

Generally, although the nomenclature may be new to you, if you've worked with HTML you'll be comfortable with the various types of content involved with XML. If your programming background doesn't include HTML, you'll still be comfortable, because XML structure borrows heavily from a number of different programming concepts. Strings, for example, are used by almost all modern object-based programming languages.

NOTE

Wondering about the difference between CDATA and #PCDATA? #PCDATA is *parsed character data*. The # character is used so that **#PCDATA** could never be mistaken in a DTD element declaration as a name, because the # character can't be used in an element name. Parsed character data is a reference from SGML that in XML means that the XML processor will read a document's text and search for telltale markers that indicate markup—particularly the < and & characters. CDATA is *character data*. A CDATA attribute contains PCDATA, but the parser strips all entity values. This means that the attribute values **<** and **&** will be returned by the processor as < and &, respectively.

Don't let yourself get thrown by words such as *entities*. If you've used img elements or used < to represent the < character in HTML, you'll certainly be comfortable with entities. If you haven't used HTML, but have worked with objects, you'll also be comfortable working with entities. If you've never worked with any kind of computer programming, for now, think of entities as placeholders that act as shortcuts to larger pieces of information. XML allows a much broader scope of objects to be used in an XML file than HTML has traditionally made room for, hence the use of entities. The surprising thing about the way XML makes room for so many different kinds of content is how efficiently it does so. A key reason for this efficiency is the way attributes can be used to manage many different things.

Understanding Attribute Syntax

One of the joys of XML is its lack of a massive set of rules of syntax, and nowhere is this more apparent than with attributes. All you really need to keep in mind are these few simple things:

- Within the tag containing an element name and any of that element's attributes, the element name comes first.
- An element attribute's value must always be in either double or single quotes. No exceptions.
- As with elements, you must use case consistently when referring to an attribute matched against a declaration. For example, <TITLE fiction="yes"> is never the same as <TITLE FICTION="yes">.

The following code shows what a typical attribute looks like. As with most XML document fragments, you'll usually be writing against a DTD or schema, but don't worry about that yet:

```
<BOOK type = "digital">
<TITLE fixed = 'yes'>Freedom's Dream</TITLE>
<REVIEW comments = "entertaining and clever"/>
</BOOK>
```

In the preceding lines of code, there are two attributes. One, `type`, belongs to the `BOOK` element, and the second, `fixed`, belongs to the `TITLE` element. If the attributes in the preceding lines of code were written without quotes, an XML parser could not parse the containing document because the containing document would not be well formed.

You can also mix double quotes and single quotes. Be sure to use ASCII apostrophe and quotes, rather than "smart quotes" (such as those created in word processing programs and desktop publishing software for stylistic reasons), which map out to different character values in Unicode. A situation when you might encounter single and double quotes and when the distinction between attribute values can be important is within the context of XSL (Extensible Style Sheet Language):

```
<xsl:if test="false"> <!- really means that the test is false ->
<xsl:if test="'false'"> <!- false is a string value, not a Boolean. The
test is for the actual string value 'false' ->
```

Understanding Attribute Types

Attributes and their content types are managed most easily through a DTD or schema. This discussion will be focused on DTD, because the schema specifications at the time this chapter is being written are still being fleshed out by W3C working groups. If you're not using a DTD to develop attributes, and are just assigning arbitrary names and values, things will become more difficult as you build bigger and more complex documents. Even if you're using an XML document strictly as a document for holding data (in which case you may think you don't particularly need a DTD), you'll find that, essentially, attributes don't really mean much without a DTD to communicate their meaning to applications and external definitions. You'll learn how to create your own DTD in Chapter 8: "Creating Your Own DTD."

NOTE

One notable exception to the preceding statement is projects that use XSL with XML documents. You can accomplish quite a bit with XSL without a DTD for the source document.

Without a DTD or schema, you generally won't be able to do as much with your document. You also won't be able to add objects like binary files to your document, because you need to declare your entities in the DTD attribute lists (which you'll learn about in Chapter 6: "Understanding and Creating Entities"). Of course, you can easily add images and objects using XHTML to develop XML-compliant HTML. You can also view the latest W3C recommendations at `http://www.w3.org/TR/xhtml1/`.

NOTE

You may want to check out `http://www.w3.org/TR/xmlschema-1/`, and `http://www.w3.org/TR/xmlschema-2/`, for proposals on standardized schema vocabularies that provide richer options for data types such as dates and integers. These are the latest working drafts for a W3C recommendation. You can also view the Microsoft proposal (which IE5 conforms to) at `www.w3c.org/TR/1998/NOTE-XML-data-0105/`. Note that the working drafts are the direction standards are going, not the Microsoft proposal. However, IE5 will not recognize schemas built on the standard unless Microsoft releases a component for IE5 that recognizes them.

Learning about Attribute Lists

When you encounter a DTD, you'll see element declarations followed by what are called attribute lists. Within a DTD you'll be able to recognize an attribute list easily enough through the `ATTLIST` keyword. A typical attribute list in a DTD might look something like this:

```
<!ELEMENT book (#PCDATA)>
<!ATTLIST book title "fixed">
```

You may not be familiar with DTD declarations yet, so let's review what is happening in the preceding two lines of code. The first line declares the element and the content it can contain (`#PCDATA` is parsed character data). It is the next line you'll be most interested in as you're reading DTD requirements on attributes. When validating an XML document this line, you must provide the attribute list declarations that determine what constraints, if any, the validating DTD has on the attributes you want to use in an element. The ATTLIST references first the element to which the attribute list applies. An element's attribute list can be as long as the DTD author wants it to be. In the preceding example, the ATTLIST declaration is for the book element, and it describes the title attribute. The declaration says that the default attribute is fixed. An attribute list in a DTD consists of three parts: The first part is the name, the second part is a type, and the third part is something called the default. You'll find out more about these three parts in Chapter 8.

Using Default Attribute Values

As you develop attributes you may be constrained by a DTD that governs their use. One such constraint involves *default* values for attributes. A default value is the value given to an attribute when the document author (as opposed to the DTD author) declines to specify a value by leaving the attribute off an element's tag. It should be noted that an attribute value of " " is not in conformance with a DTD attribute list declaration unless the declaration somehow specifies this as an acceptable value. To leave an attribute out of a tag you simply do not include it in the tag, but remember, you can only do that if the attribute is not required.

Recognizing Default Values You can recognize a default attribute by looking at the attribute list declaration in a DTD. Remember the order of the parts within attribute list declarations, because they will always occur in the same order. In the following line of code, the default value is paperback:

```
<!ATTLIST BOOK BINDING CDATA "paperback">
```

This means that if a document writer includes a BOOK element in an XML document and they leave off the attribute, the BOOK would automatically be a paperback, as far as the XML document is concerned. Consider the following line of code:

```
<BOOK>Mastering XML</BOOK>
```

Based on the attribute list declaration that preceded this line of code, the book *Mastering XML* would be a paperback, because paperback was named as the default value of the BINDING attribute, and the XML document author didn't include the attribute value paperback when building the element tag.

Using the #IMPLIED Keyword Another default type is indicated by the #IMPLIED keyword. This keyword can cause some confusion. An #IMPLIED keyword shows up in a DTD when the author wants to make it known that an attribute is allowable for a particular element, but that it doesn't need to be there. Such an occasion exists when you see an attribute list declaration that looks something like this:

```
<!ATTLIST BOOK BINDING CDATA #IMPLIED>
```

Technically, what happens here is that an XML parser will pass a blank value to the processing XML application, which may or may not enter its own default value.

Using the #REQUIRED Keyword Sometimes a DTD author will want an element to have a required attribute. Let's say a document contains sound files. More than likely, any element used to describe the sound will need an attribute to help locate the sound file.

You'll know an attribute is required because the attribute list declaration will contain a keyword named #REQUIRED. This occurs in the default part of an attribute list declaration. The following line of code demonstrates what an attribute list containing a requirement looks like. The following declaration merely says that the URL attribute must be used within the SOUND, or any document instance associated with the DTD will be invalid:

```
<!ATTLIST SOUND URL CDATA #REQUIRED>
```

Managing Attribute Types

There are three general categories under which the ten attribute types listed earlier in the chapter fall. These are as follows:

Enumerated types Enumerated types are attribute values named specifically within the DTD (either as optional choices or as a reference to a notation named elsewhere in the document).

String types String types consist of any kind of character data not parsed by the XML processor.

Tokenized types Tokens are basically XML datatypes that provide a way for naming and identifying node instances.

You can see how to categorize the ten attribute types in Table 5.1.

TABLE 5.1 Attribute Type Categories

String Types	Tokenized Types	Enumerated Types
CDATA	ENTITY	NOTATION
	ENTITIES	Enumeration
	ID	
	IDREFS	
	IDREF	
	NMTOKEN	
	NMTOKENS	

TIP Attribute types are crucial, but only if you are validating against a DTD. If you're not validating against a DTD, you can safely avoid them. Additionally, the attribute types discussed here are fairly primitive. Much work is being done on data typing that goes beyond what is shown here.

Before getting into the specifics of the various attribute types you might encounter in a DTD, you'll want to understand one important concept within XML, normalization.

About Normalization

Normalization is used to manage white space effectively. You've encountered it if you've ever put in more than one space between words in an HTML document and seen that only one space shows up. This is the standard way XML handles white space. A detailed explanation of this is a bit beyond the scope of this chapter, but it helps to think of normalization as a process that strips out extra white space and attaches character and entity references appropriately, depending on the circumstances.

Learning about Enumerated Types with Enumeration and Notation Attributes

A notation declares that an element will be referenced to a notation declared elsewhere in a document. It assists helper applications to process unparsed entities. The information isn't as much for the XML parser as it is for outside applications that must recognize and work with the entity being called. You won't want to work with these much unless you have a clear idea on how to tie everything together. To do that, you'll need to understand how to work with entities, which is covered in the next chapter. Unparsed entities rely on notation declarations to identify them so that the application processing the XML document knows what kind of entity is being used and what to do with it. The use of the system identifier (SYSTEM in the notation declaration) is required, and it must be a URI. The syntax for a notation declaration that appears in a typical DTD would look like this:

```
<!NOTATION PNG SYSTEM "http://myDomain.com/MYGRAPHICSPROGRAM.EXE">
```

Then, the DTD author refers to that declaration in an associated NOTATION attribute declaration:

```
<!ATTLIST IMAGE src NOTATION (PNG)>
```

Here, the attribute declaration refers directly to the notation that was declared previously (PNG). The name of the notation, PNG, was arrived at arbitrarily, but now must be referred to correctly in the attribute list declaration. Within the XML document instance itself, the final element might look something like this:

```
<IMAGE src ="PNG">
```

Remember not to get too involved in the syntax of the DTD here if there seems to be too much new information. You'll be learning how to develop DTD syntax in Chapter 8. The important thing to remember is that if you develop attributes with notation values, be very sure they have been declared in the DTD appropriately using both a notation declaration and a NOTATION attribute declaration. In the next chapter you'll discover another caveat to working with unparsed entities (and their associated notations) is that processors are not obligated to handle them. This means they don't need to pass them off to another application, even if you name that application in your notation declaration.

Notations aren't limited to referencing binary files as in the preceding example. You can also use them to refer to literal notations that are publicly available or made available privately (perhaps through a corporate intranet) so that specific formatting rules can be handed off in certain situations. You might, for example, want to specify the way a date is formatted, using an internationally accepted encoding.

Managing String Types with *CDATA* Attributes

The CDATA keyword in a DTD indicates that any string of non-markup characters is legal when you create your attributes in the XML document instance. A typical attribute list declaration for character data (CDATA) looks like this:

```
<!ATTLIST BOOK CHAPTER CDATA #REQUIRED>
```

The preceding line of code indicates that the CHAPTER attribute is required within the BOOK element, and that it can take any character data other than markup. Specifically, you cannot include any of the following in CDATA: <, >, ", ', or &.

Therefore, if you create an attribute value pair from the previous attribute declaration, you might have something like this:

```
<BOOK CHAPTER="Chapter One"/>
```

In fact, thanks to the #REQUIRED keyword, you definitely need to include the CHAPTER attribute while developing a <BOOK> element, although what value you include is up to you, as long as it is legal XML character data.

You can use the following entity references in place of markup when you need markup in attribute values. The XML processor strips out the entity references and returns them as the following markup:

- < can be replaced with < or <
- > can be replaced with > or >
- " can be replaced with " or "
- ' can be replaced with ' or '
- & can be replaced with & or &

Tokenized Types

A token is the means by which XML provides a way to name a node instance. There are different ways to achieve this, and some node-naming procedures are more specific than others are. Some tokenized types will be used in situations that require unique qualifiers. In those cases, you would use ID and IDREF attributes. Other occasions will warrant an identifier that focuses on providing a naming scheme, in which case you might use only a name token. Still other occasions will require the naming of entities.

Using Name Tokens Name tokens are qualified strings that have limits on what kind of character data they can contain. If there is only one allowable NMTOKEN attribute type, the NMTOKEN keyword is used, and if more than one is allowed, the NMTOKENS keyword is used. Name tokens are restricted to letters, numbers, and the following special characters:

- . (a period)
- - (a dash)

- _ (an underscore)
- : (a colon)

The DTD syntax you'll want to look for will resemble the following line of code:

```
<!ATTLIST STATISTIC NUMBER NMTOKEN #REQUIRED>
```

Understanding Entity Attributes You manage objects with entity attributes. If you're familiar with HTML, you probably have used the `img` element, which helps you work with graphic objects. You may not be aware that the `img` element has been deprecated in HTML, which in W3C parlance means it will be phased out over time, and that although it is still valid during a transitional period, it is no longer part of the official recommendation. The `img` element will be replaced by the `object` element, which achieves the same thing as an `img` element, but is more robust because it can be used to link multimedia files such as sounds and movies in addition to images. Entities both are and are not a big deal. They're a big deal because they have the potential to become a major source of activity as XML grows, and are not a big deal because they are easy to use.

Like HTML objects, entities are generally referenced through a Uniform Resource Identifier (URI). Typically, the DTD syntax will look something like this:

```
<!ENTITY CHAPTERSOURCE SYSTEM "http://www.javertising.com/book1.htm">
```

Be aware that you can't use entities without declaring them in an internal or external DTD. Entities are parsed according to either a style sheet or how the parsing application typically processes the type of file referred to by the entity. You'll recognize an entity type within an attribute list when you see in a line of code like the following:

```
<!ATTLIST CHAPTER SOURCE ENTITY #REQUIRED>
```

Then, you would include it in the markup of the XML document instance like so:

```
<CHAPTER source = "CHAPTERSOURCE">
```

Using ID and IDREFS Many databases have fields labeled ID, where information such as customer number are stored. Unique identifiers make it easy to access elements as objects, which is an important consideration when developing scripts. The reason this is such a fundamental process to the world of scripts and object-oriented programming languages like Java is that the unique identifier, by allowing access to individual elements as unique objects, makes it easy to transform those objects.

Consider one of the Web's most basic and popular script mechanisms, the image rollover. An image rollover is accomplished by loading an array, or set, of images into a document so that the browser is aware of them when the document has loaded. Then, a specific `img` element is targeted as the rollover. When an `onmouseover` event occurs as a result of a user's mouse hovering over an image (just before clicking), the image changes because the `img` element's `src` attribute value has changed. In an HTML document, a single line of script causes this action:

```
Img001.src = "myNewImage.gif"
```

The ID attribute value in the preceding line of code is `Img001`. Here, it might help to look at the corresponding HTML:

```
<img id="Img001" src="someDomain/myNewImage.gif"><!-- Remember, if this
was XML-compliant HTML, there would be a closing slash before that last
bracket -->
```

This value identifies a specific `img` element as the element that should be changed (when called to action by an event such as `onmouseover` and its associated function). Figure 5.1 and Figure 5.2 show how this works.

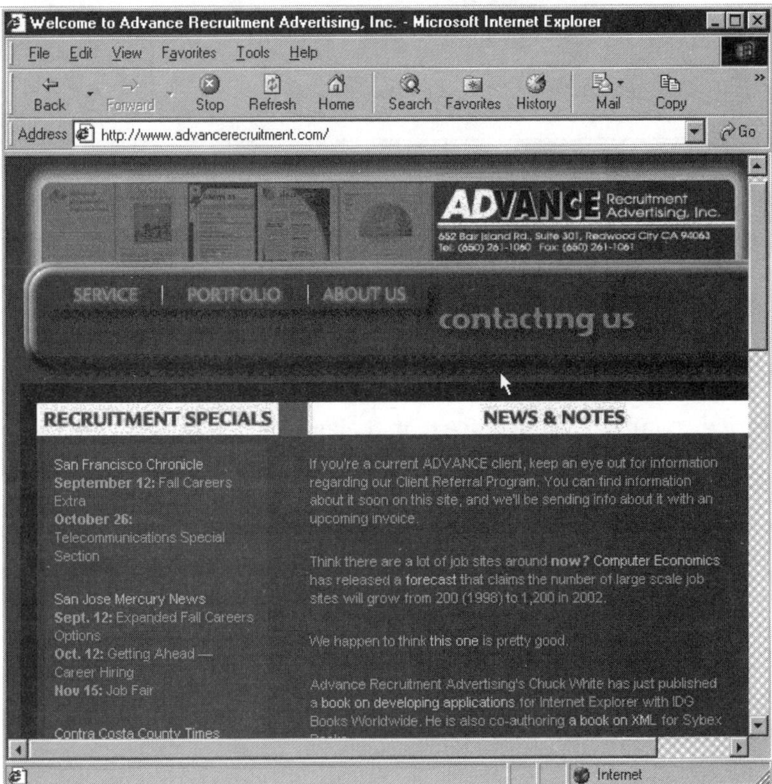

FIGURE 5.1:

An image rollover—here just prior to the `onmouseover` event

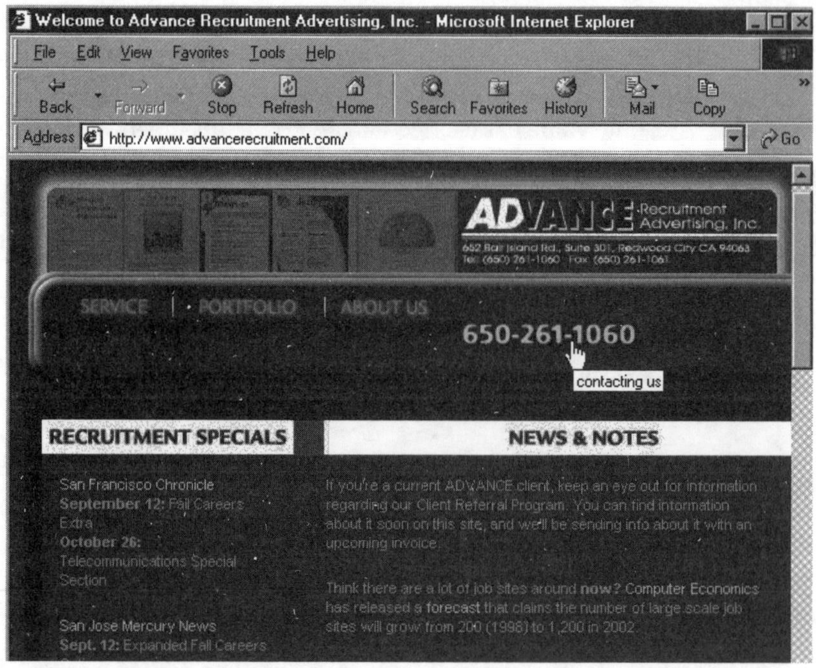

FIGURE 5.2:

An image rollover—here just after the `onmouseover` event

TIP

See Chapter 21: "Java and XML" for a more thorough discussion on scripting and object-oriented programming techniques for XML.

IDs are also a key part of many database tables. A DTD mapped out from a database table will often include an ID attribute for certain kinds of elements (like those used in customer databases) and declare that attribute to be an ID type. ID type attributes act as unique identifiers, meaning any reference to an element's ID must be a reference to that element. This means that an element is thus uniquely identified. IDREF and IDREFS attribute values must point to a corresponding ID value. That, in fact, is what IDREF values do. They point to a unique ID previously referred to in a document. If you see an ID declaration in an attribute for a declared element, you know that the element must possess a unique identifier in order for the document to be valid against the DTD. Here's an example of an ID attribute declaration within a DTD:

```
<!ELEMENT MYELEMENT (#PCDATA)>
<!ATTLIST MYELEMENT myID ID #REQUIRED>
```

The corresponding attribute in an XML document instance might then look like this:

```
<MYELEMENT myID="109912">
```

Then, you might want to simply refer to that ID using an IDREF attribute. The declaration would look something like this:

```
<!ATTLIST MYELEMENT_REF myIDref IDREF #REQUIRED>
```

The attribute that appears in the XML document would refer to an ID. Consider an e-commerce site and you can quickly figure out how this might come into play. You might want to reference this ID in a shopping cart. So you simply refer to it like so, using, of course, the rules supplied in the DTD:

```
<MYELEMENT_REF myIDref="109912">
```

Two elements cannot have the same unique identifier. If they did, they wouldn't be unique. But IDREF attribute values allow you to refer to an ID. You might want to refer to more than one, in which case you'll use an IDREFS attribute value, assuming a declaration was made in a DTD:

```
<!ATTLIST MYELEMENT_REF myIDrefs IDREFS #REQUIRED>
```

Then, in your XML document instance, the actual attribute value pair might look like this:

```
<MYELEMENT_REF myIDrefs="109912 109913">
```

This way, you can add as many references to the unique identifier as you wish.

Putting It All Together

In the last two chapters, you learned the basics about elements, attributes, and the kinds of content they can deliver. Don't worry if you don't understand everything yet, especially in relation to the DTD, because you'll be learning more as you continue with the book. The samples included in the following sections are intentionally basic. The key to following them is to try to understand how the XML document follows the DTD element and attribute list declarations.

Taking a Look at a DTD

Now let's take a look at how the various topics we've covered in this chapter fit together. To do that, we'll examine a DTD, and see how to put together an XML file based on the rules from that DTD. We're not going to cover every kind of element and attribute content type here. Rather, we'll demonstrate the basics of how to read the DTD so that you can put together a valid XML file. Listing 5.1 shows a DTD for a classified ad system.

LISTING 5.1 A Simple DTD—output.dtd

```
<!ELEMENT AD (NEWSPAPER, (INCOLUMN | DISPLAY))>
<!ENTITY ADTEXT SYSTEM "adText.txt">
<!ATTLIST AD id ID #REQUIRED>
<!ELEMENT NEWSPAPER (#PCDATA)>
<!ELEMENT INCOLUMN (INCOLUMNSIZE, INCOLUMNCONTENT)>
<!ELEMENT INCOLUMNSIZE (#PCDATA)>
<!ELEMENT INCOLUMNCONTENT (#PCDATA)>
<!ATTLIST INCOLUMNSIZE lines NMTOKEN #REQUIRED>
<!ATTLIST INCOLUMNSIZE width (1 | 2 | 3 | 4 | 5 | 6 | 7) #REQUIRED>
<!ELEMENT DISPLAY (DISPLAYSIZE, DISPLAYCONTENT)>
<!ELEMENT DISPLAYSIZE (#PCDATA)>
<!ELEMENT DISPLAYCONTENT (#PCDATA)>
<!ATTLIST DISPLAYSIZE lines NMTOKEN #REQUIRED>
<!ATTLIST DISPLAYSIZE width (1 | 2 | 3 | 4 | 5 | 6 | 7) #REQUIRED>
```

A DTD will always lead off with the root element. The filename for this DTD is `output.dtd`. The root node of the XML document that is validated against the DTD is the XML document instance. In other words, if the name of the file that uses this DTD is `myXML.xml`, then that is the document instance, and thus, the root node. Remember that the root node is not the same as the root element. The root element is `AD`, which means any other element that exists within the document must be nested within `AD`. Furthermore, this particular declaration for the root element states that it must include two elements: `NEWSPAPER`, and either `INCOLUMN` or `DISPLAY`. You'll learn more about goodies such as occurrence indicators in Chapter 8, but for now, refer to the simple chart in Table 5.2 to explore them. They provide an opportunity for DTD authors to lay down specific guidelines about when and how often an element may occur.

TABLE 5.2 DTD Occurrence Indicators

Symbol	Occurrence Description
|	Represents `or`, which means one *or* another named element may occur.
,	A delimiter that separates required elements.
?	An indicator that allows a named element, but does not require the named element, and which allows no more than one instance of that same named element.
*	An indicator that allows any number of a named element to occur.
+	An indicator that requires the named element to occur at least once or as often as the document creator wishes, so long as the minimum requirement of one appearance is met.
()	These symbols group elements that are placed within them.

As you can see in Listing 5.1, the `AD` element must have the `NEWSPAPER` element, and, as a comma follows the `NEWSPAPER` in the DTD declaration, you know that more elements are required. These elements are grouped together by the `()` symbols, but the elements within these symbols, `INCOLUMN` and `DISPLAY`, are separated by the `|` symbol. This means as the XML document author, you have a choice between those two elements, but you must use one of them because they are grouped together and appear after the comma. The line of code referenced from Listing 5.1 is as follows:

```
<!ELEMENT AD (NEWSPAPER, (INCOLUMN | DISPLAY))>
```

The next item you'll notice in Listing 5.1 is an entity declaration. Forget that for now, because you'll be taking a closer look at this same listing, and this entity, in Chapter 6.

After the entity declaration you find an attribute list declaration for the `AD` element. See if you can tell what is going on in that declaration based on what you read in the previous sections:

```
<!ATTLIST AD id ID #REQUIRED>
```

In this example the DTD is being written for an advertising agency that wants to be able to output classified advertisement text and easily sort the advertisements by ID number for use within an invoicing and confirmation database. The DTD author decided to make the ID attribute a requirement within the AD element. Thanks to the content model XML offers the author was even able to insist that the ID attribute content act as a unique identifier. This makes it easier to process the document as a content-management system, and also allows for easy integration into invoicing and job-tracking systems.

The next element, NEWSPAPER, is a simple declaration that states it can contain any parsed character data. Note that if the DTD author does include a declaration for the NEWSPAPER element, the DTD will fail:

```
<!ELEMENT NEWSPAPER (#PCDATA)>
```

If you are in the situation where a DTD author hands you a DTD that includes element declarations that include other elements, make sure that the declarations are made for the elements later in the DTD, or you'll have problems.

TIP

XML editing software tools that take some of the tedium out of the process are emerging. SoftQuad's Xmetal, for example, generates an error when you try to create a new XML document matched against a malformed DTD. The software even specifies the location and type of error in the DTD. This saves you the trouble of starting a document that is being written against an improperly designed DTD. Xmetal is available on this book's companion CD-ROM.

The next line of code in Listing 5.1 is a declaration for one of the two kinds of elements that can be a child of the AD element. Let's take a look at this line:

```
<!ELEMENT INCOLUMN (INCOLUMNSIZE, INCOLUMNCONTENT)>
```

The preceding line of code indicates that two elements must reside within the INCOLUMN element. The next four lines of code declare these elements and their attributes:

```
<!ELEMENT INCOLUMNSIZE (#PCDATA)>
<!ELEMENT INCOLUMNCONTENT (#PCDATA)>
<!ATTLIST INCOLUMNSIZE lines NMTOKEN #REQUIRED>
<!ATTLIST INCOLUMNSIZE width (1 | 2 | 3 | 4 | 5 | 6 | 7) #REQUIRED>
```

Notice the NMTOKEN keyword in the INCOLUMNSIZE element's lines attribute list declaration? As was mentioned in an earlier section, the NMTOKEN keyword limits you to certain kinds of characters (letters, digits, dashes, underscores, periods, or colons). The second attribute list declaration for the INCOLUMNSIZE element describes the width of the newspaper ad in number of columns. As the newspapers used for this DTD have no more than seven columns, the specific value options are listed. One of these values must be used, and the attribute, like the lines attribute, must be included with the element. The rest of the declarations follow patterns similar to those just described.

Writing against a DTD

This brings us to the XML document itself, which is written against the DTD. Judging from the DTD, you know that the first element will be the AD element. Take a look at Listing 5.2 to see how the document looks.

LISTING 5.2 Validating against a Simple DTD

```
<?xml version="1.0"?>
<!DOCTYPE AD SYSTEM "output.dtd">
<AD id="001">
<NEWSPAPER>San Francisco Chronicle</NEWSPAPER>
     <INCOLUMN>
     <INCOLUMNSIZE lines="50" width="1">
     </INCOLUMNSIZE>
     <INCOLUMNCONTENT>&ADTEXT;</INCOLUMNCONTENT>
     </INCOLUMN></AD>
```

Figure 5.3 shows how this document looks as parsed by Internet Explorer 5. Notice that the entity &ADTEXT; is replaced by some actual text in the browser window. Don't worry yet about how this works; you'll learn more about it in Chapter 6. For now, focus on how the document in Listing 5.2 adheres to the DTD. Because the DTD is found on a local machine, the keyword SYSTEM is used to access the URI. Sometimes, you'll see the keyword PUBLIC used here, which makes it a public identifier. This is not a sufficient mechanism if you are looking for any kind of portability, because it refers to a specific identifier. This identifier may or may not be stored in a way that can actually be accessed by the document. The rules contained by the DTD may even be stored by a processing application. Whatever the case, they're used primarily by previously established SGML documents for compatibility with XML.

FIGURE 5.3:

An XML document rendered in Internet Explorer 5

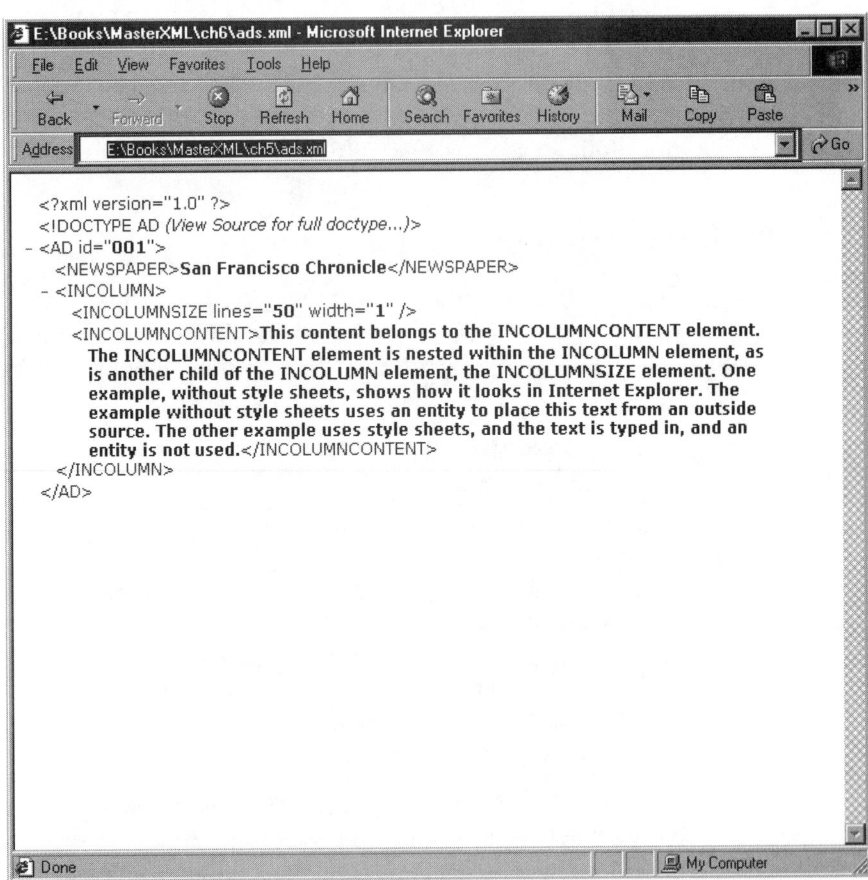

Figure 5.4 shows the same document with one line of code added: a link to a style sheet. You can use Cascading Style Sheets (CSS) to present elements in XML-aware applications such as IE5. Notice where the link to the style sheet is and the way the entity is replaced with actual text in Listing 5.3.

FIGURE 5.4:

An XML document with a linked style sheet

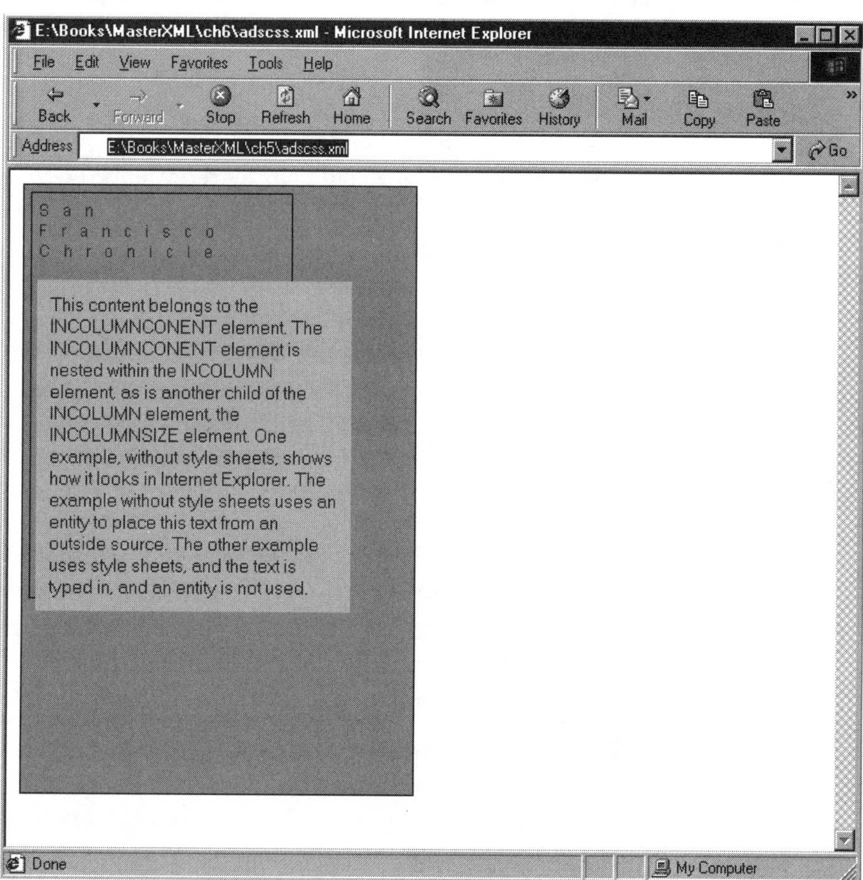

LISTING 5.3 **Linking a Style Sheet to an XML Document**

```
<?xml version="1.0"?>
<?xml-stylesheet href="adcss.css" type="text/css"?>
<!DOCTYPE AD SYSTEM "output.dtd">
<AD id="001"><NEWSPAPER>San Francisco Chronicle</NEWSPAPER><INCOLUMN>
<INCOLUMNSIZE lines="50" width="1"></INCOLUMNSIZE>
<INCOLUMNCONTENT>This content belongs to the INCOLUMNCONENT element.
The INCOLUMNCONENT element is nested within the INCOLUMN element, as is
another child of the INCOLUMN element, the INCOLUMNSIZE element. One
example, without style sheets, shows how it looks in Internet Explorer.
The example without style sheets uses an entity to place this text from
```

```
an outside source. The other example uses style sheets, and the text is
typed in, and an entity is not used.</INCOLUMNCONTENT>
</INCOLUMN>
</AD>
```

We included the link to the style sheet to demonstrate the nesting concept in a more visual manner. The outside border represents the root element AD, which contains two other elements NEWSPAPER and INCOLUMN (remember from your DTD that you could have chosen DISPLAY instead). You can see from Figure 5.4 that because INCOLUMN is not nested within NEWSPAPER, the borders for the NEWSPAPER element fall beyond the borders of the INCOLUMN element. Both elements, however, fall within the root element's borders.

Up Next

This chapter took a closer look at attributes and how to interpret DTD so that you can write valid documents. The truth is, anyone can master the simple art of writing an attribute. All you need to do is remember those quote marks. The real skill will come in interpreting how DTD attribute lists describe the rules you must follow. Hopefully this chapter has provided some insight into the matter.

In the next chapter, we'll look at entities. Entities are powerful, easy-to-use mechanisms that allows for complex data and document management. We'll finish up that chapter with a further look at a DTD and how an XML document follows the declarative rules to manage validity.

CHAPTER

SIX

6

Understanding and Creating Entities

- Learning the basics about entities
- Learning how to use entities
- Making sure your entity markup is legal
- Understanding general entities
- Using parameter entities
- Harnessing the power of entities

If you've developed HTML-based Web pages you probably have used entities quite often, even if you've done most of your development with WYSIWYG editors. If you use the < symbol in a WYSIWYG editor and look at the source code, you'll find that the actual HTML code used to represent the < looks like this:

```
&lt;
```

This is an example of an entity. An entity is markup that should not be parsed according to the normal syntax rules for the parsing processor. The < symbol needs to be represented as an entity, because the parser would confuse < symbols with < tags. For example, if an HTML document contains HTML code examples, entities provide a simple way to represent HTML tags without confusing the parser.

XML uses a few of the same entities as HTML to represent markup that should not be parsed by XML syntax rules. However, XML considerably extends the power of entities because you can define them just as easily as you can define elements. This means that entities can consist of a broad range of objects. These objects can include just about any programming-based object that comes to mind including binary graphics, word processing files, or multimedia applets. This chapter will look at entities and guide you through the process of understanding and creating them. Specifically, we'll examine:

- What entities are
- When to use entities
- The different types of entities available to XML authors
- How to use internal and external entities
- How to use parameter and general entities
- How to be sure your entity markup is legal
- The use of system and public identifiers
- Ways of harnessing the power of entities by learning from examples that demonstrate how entities are defined in DTD for referencing in a document instance

Learning the Basics about Entities

An easy way to understand entities is to review the examples in Chapter 5: "Understanding and Creating Attributes." However, you won't need to flip back to that chapter, rather, you'll revisit parts of those listings in this chapter. You may recall from the listings in that chapter an odd bit of code featuring an ampersand (&), followed by a word and a semicolon. Chapter 5 included a listing that contained the following bit of markup:

```
<INCOLUMNCONTENT>&ADTEXT;</INCOLUMNCONTENT>
```

The parser—in that example Internet Explorer 5 (IE5)—displayed a document showing something that looked considerably different from the entity. In fact, it showed an entire paragraph of text, instead of the entity itself. `&ADTEXT;` is an entity that acted as a sort of placeholder for a larger fragment of text. Entities can be used as a kind of shorthand that allows you to embed blocks of text or even entire documents and files into an XML document. This makes updating documents across networks very easy. Entities also allow you to represent special characters like markup. You can even use entities in a DTD to cut down on the amount of code.

There are two kinds of XML entities: general entities and parameter entities. The HTML entities described in this chapter's opening paragraphs are a type of general entity called predefined entities. Within the scope of general entities and parameter entities are four other types of entities, which can be considered subsets of general and parameter entities:

Internal entities These are entity references that refer to entities whose definitions can be found entirely *within* a document's DTD.

External entities These are entity references that refer to entities whose definitions can be found outside of a document.

Parsed entities These are entities that the XML processor can and will parse.

Unparsed entities These are entities that are not parsed by the XML processor, but instead are handed off to another application for processing and are often described by binary mechanisms, such as those in image files.

Learning How to Use Entities

Have you ever run a mail merge function in a word processing program? In a mail merge, you develop a database of names and addresses and bind them to a word processing document with some markup. The markup tells the word processor where in the word processing document the address information from the database should go. If you've used mail merges, you've seen the concept of entities at work. Instead of character data, such as an address block, XML allows a wide variety of data to be used as an entity.

Entities operate on a similar principle to mail merge functions in the sense that an entity acts as a replacement mechanism. That's why entities are such great shorthand for XML documents. Some of the uses for entities include:

- Denoting special markup, such as the > and < tags.
- Managing binary files and other data not native to XML.
- Reducing the code in a DTD by bundling declarations into entities.
- Offering richer multi-language support.
- Repeating frequently used names in a way that guarantees consistency in spelling and use.
- Providing for easier updates—by using entities in your markup for items you know will be changed later, such as sports scores or software version changes, you greatly improve dynamic document automation.
- Managing multiple file links and interaction.

Making Sure Your Entity Markup Is Legal

Entity syntax rules vary depending on the kind of entity you are using, but like everything else in XML, they're pretty straightforward. When you use an entity within an XML document, you must make certain of five things:

1. The entity must be declared in the DTD or a schema. If you're creating an XML document that is not being validated against a DTD or schema, then

you need to create enough of a DTD yourself within the XML document to at least declare the entity that you are using. The exceptions to this rule are the predefined entities of XML, but there are only five of them, so they're easy to remember (you'll visit these a bit later).

2. A general entity referenced within an XML document must be surrounded by the & character on one end and the ; character at the other (`&myEntity;`).
3. The name of an entity must begin with a letter or underscore (_), but can contain letters, underscores, whole numbers, colons, periods, and/or dashes.
4. An entity declaration cannot consist of markup that begins in the entity declaration and ends outside of it.
5. A parameter entity must be declared with a preceding percentage sign (%) with a white space before and after the percentage sign, and be referenced by a percentage sign with no trailing white space.

Understanding General Entities

The jargon and semantics involving XML can be overwhelming, and one example of this is entities. There are external general parsed entities and external general unparsed entities, as well as parameter entities and internal general entities. This all can get pretty confusing. Our advice is to keep it simple and focus on the two kinds of entities that have a clear difference in usage. Those two kinds of entities are general entities and parameter entities. The underlying concepts are the same in that they both act as a kind of shortcut.

General entities are easier to describe by what they are not than what they are. If it's not a parameter entity, then it's a general entity. Parameter entities can only appear in DTD. General entities appear in the main XML document (called the document instance) that begins with the root element. It's actually more accurate to say that the entity *reference* appears in the document instance, whereas the entity definition is found in the DTD. In fact, you can't create an entity reference within a document instance without validating it against a declaration made in either an internal or external DTD or schema.

Using Predefined Entities

XML has several predefined, or built-in, entities that can be invoked without any special declarations. These are the simplest kinds of general entities and are the only kinds that require no declarations within a DTD or schema. These are listed in Table 6.1.

TABLE 6.1: Predefined XML Entities

Entity	Corresponding Character
<	<
>	>
'	'
"e;	"
&	&

If you've worked much with HTML, you've no doubt encountered these entities or their numerical equivalents. Whether you've worked with HTML or not, it's important to know that the purpose is somewhat different with these entities than others. They're not really so much shortcuts as they are a means for preventing the XML processor from throwing an error or refusing to parse your XML document. If you look at the symbols in Table 6.1 you can see that they are symbols that might often be encountered in XML markup, and thus act as a means for representing these characters when you don't want them interpreted as markup. Using an entity from Table 6.1, you could write the following line of code, without worrying about DTD validation (see Figure 6.1 to see how this is rendered in IE5):

```
<MYELEMENT>1 &lt; 2.</MYELEMENT>
```

These are the easiest kinds of entities to use. But they don't offer much beyond a few very simple, specific tasks. XML provides a method for declaring entities in a DTD for reference later in your document instance.

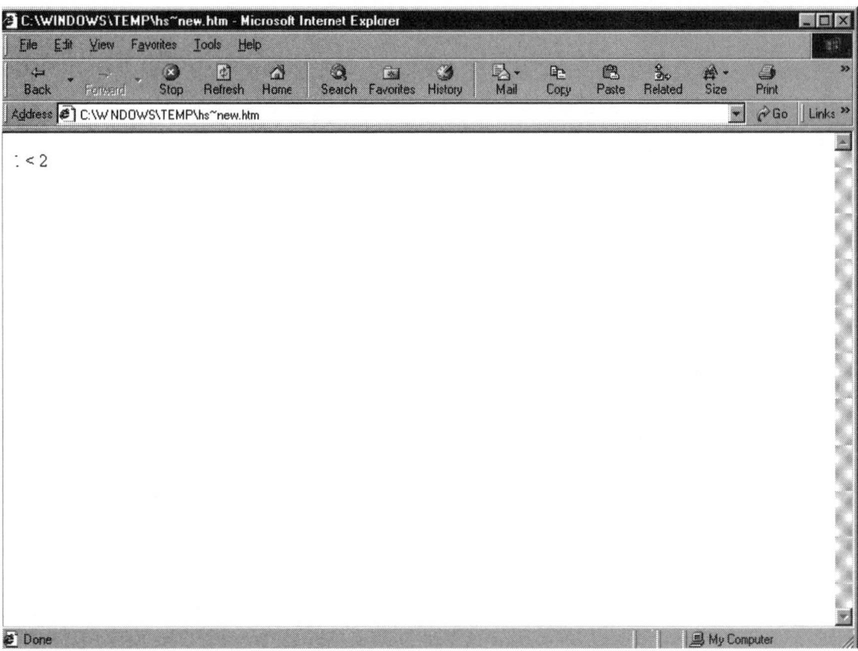

FIGURE 6.1:

A predefined entity rendered in IE5

Working with Character References

You can include special kinds of references within your XML documents with *character references*. Character references are similar in look to entity references, but they aren't declared and refer to specific characters (such as accented letters) using a special numbering system called Unicode. Unicode is an encoding system that maps character data across the world's language boundaries. You can use a character reference in your XML document as long as you know the corresponding Unicode reference, but some developers might choose to create an entity reference to it in your DTD so that others know what you're trying to do.

The default character set for XML is the ISO-Latin-1 character set, which is what most English-speaking and Western European developers will use. There are numerous other character sets that can be included, but they need to be declared in the DTD. If you use ISO-Latin-1, you don't need to declare either the character set or the character references from that set. However, there are many languages of the world, and attempts are being made to include the capacity to manage these languages.

NOTE

The XML 1 specification requires XML processors to support character references mapped to the ISO/IEC 10646 character set, which is a Unicode encoding. To gain access to the world of Unicode and the character sets available for non-Western European languages, visit `http://charts.unicode.org/Unicode.charts/normal/Unicode.html`. This web site provides an extensive series of charts for a variety of languages, and the corresponding hexadecimal code to include in entity and declarations and references. For the most recent Unicode specification, visit `www.unicode.org/unicode/reports/tr8.html`.

Using Parsed Entities

Another kind of entity reference are those that refer to a declaration made within a document and can be parsed by the XML processor. These are called parsed entities, which some people refer to as text entities because their definitions are represented as a string of text within quotation marks in the validating DTD. For example, consider the following lines of code:

```
<!ENTITY ADTEXT "This content belongs to the INCOLUMNCONTENT element.
The INCOLUMNCONTENT element is nested within the INCOLUMN element, as
is another child of the INCOLUMN element, the INCOLUMNSIZE element. One
example, without style sheets, shows how it looks in Internet Explorer.
The example without style sheets uses an entity to place this text from
an outside source. The other example uses style sheets, and the text is
typed in, and an entity is not used.">
```

The preceding line of code may look familiar from the previous chapter on attributes, where you learned that one of the valid attribute types was `ENTITY`. The preceding lines of code are an example of an internal parsed entity declaration. Such a lengthy declaration is also a good example of why external entity references are convenient. The XML processor will parse this entity when it is referred to in the XML document instance:

```
<MYELEMENT>&ADTEXT;</MYELEMENT>
```

When the XML document is processed, the entity `&ADTEXT;` is replaced by the definition that is contained between the quotation marks (see Figure 6.2). If an entity can be used in such a way, it is considered a parsed entity. An entity either is parsed or it is not parsed, and if not, it called an unparsed entity, which means the processor will pass it on to another application for processing.

FIGURE 6.2:

The entity reference is replaced by the actual defining text.

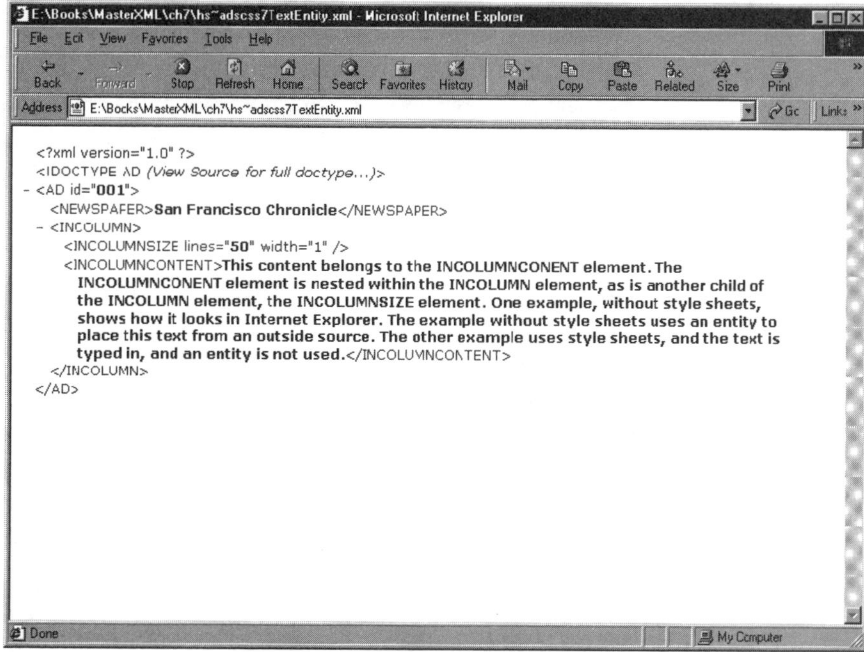

Imagine, now, that the text in the entity declaration changes for some reason. Perhaps a new version of software has come out and the descriptions change. Or, in our case, some general silliness ensues. Thus the preceding example becomes:

```
<!ENTITY ADTEXT "This content has been completely changed in accordance
to Best Practices, because it was best to do so.">
```

Figure 6.3 shows the result of this change. These kind of changes become even more significant when external DTDs are used instead of internal DTDs, because global changes could be made to multiple documents: one edit, many changes.

NOTE

Note that Figures 6.2 and 6.3 shows a tree representation of the XML document, which is how IE5 renders XML documents not attached to style sheets. Although, technically, a default XSL style sheet is always used by IE5 to render the tree if a style sheet is not named for the XML document that is parsed by IE5's XML processor.

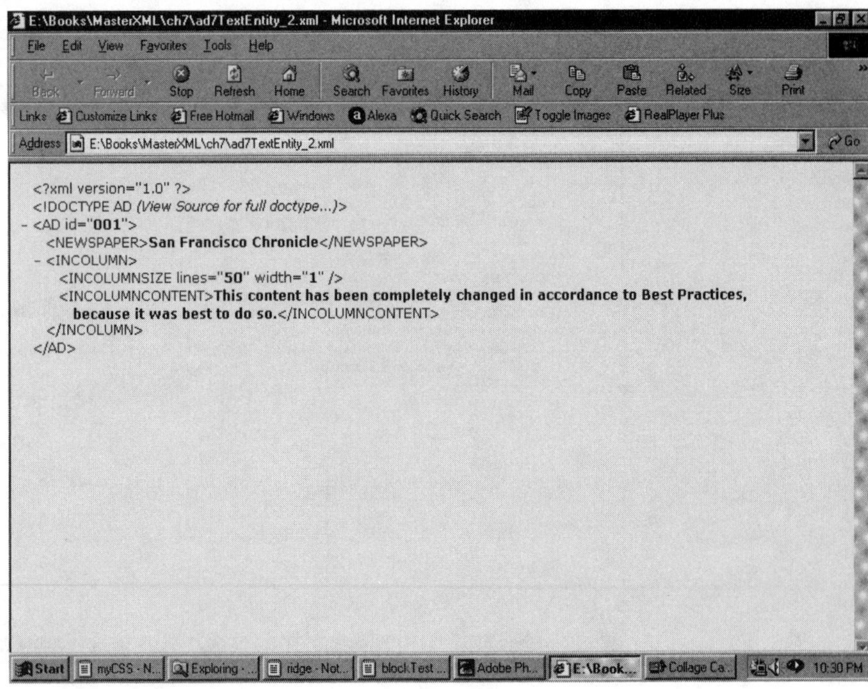

FIGURE 6.3:

The XML processor interprets changes in entity definitions.

Managing Unparsed Entities

Whereas parsed entities can be referenced within an element, an unparsed entity must appear as an attribute value. Processors need to know what to do with these entities, so the instructions must be laid out in the DTD. These instructions appear in the form of an ENTITY declaration that includes the file type of the entity the processor can expect. In addition, the DTD is required to include a NOTATION declaration that indicates to the processor what software will be handling the request.

The interesting thing about such NOTATION declarations is that the processor doesn't really care too much about it. If an invalid path is declared as part of the notation, the XML parser simply moves on to the next order of business. Consider the following line of code:

```
<!ENTITY ADGRAPHIC SYSTEM "border.png" NDATA PNG>
<!NOTATION PNG SYSTEM "MYGRAPHICSPROGRAM.EXE">
```

Without getting too bogged down by the intricacies of DTD authoring, think about the ENTITY declaration in the preceding lines of code as being part of a larger DTD. The ENTITY declaration is declared using, first, the ENTITY keyword, then the name of the entity (ADGRAPHIC in the preceding example). NDATA is an identifier and PNG is the file type. The NDATA keyword and a value indicating the file type (PNG in this case) are required.

Next, you see the NOTATION declaration. This declaration simply tells the XML processor where it can find a program to which it can pass along the information. The XML processor can choose to process the information itself if it wants to, but the DTD author needs to give the XML processor the choice. In other words, the DTD author must include the name (and path) of the software that should process the binary. Figure 6.4 shows what happens when the XML processor in IE5 doesn't encounter the NOTATION element in an XML document's DTD.

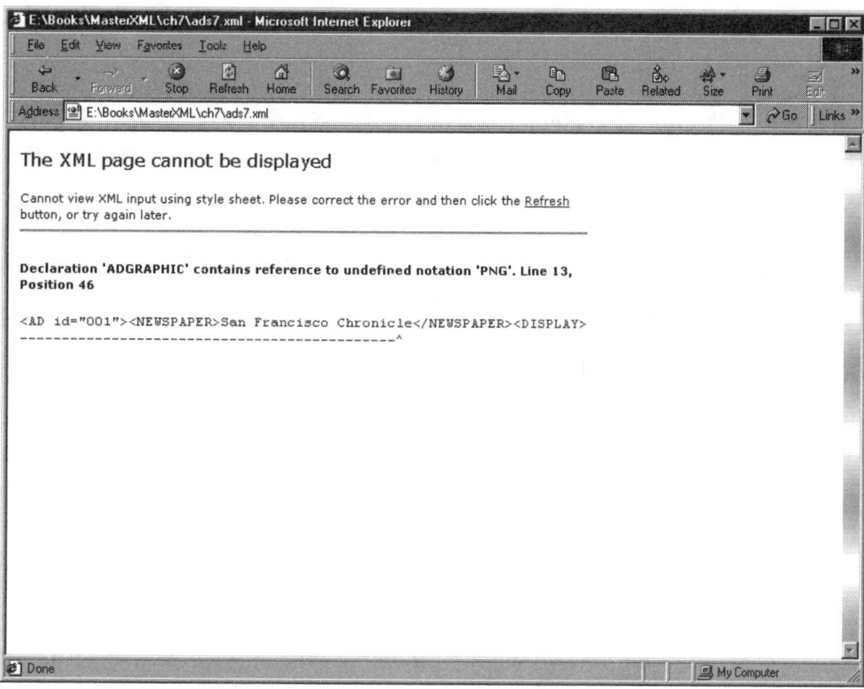

FIGURE 6.4:

IE5 will protest if you don't include a NOTATION declaration for an unparsed entity.

There is no requirement whatsoever that an XML processor actually process an unparsed entity, but it can if it wants. This is true even if that unparsed entity is an external XML document. The main thing to remember about unparsed entities, as they are often binaries of some kind (like images, music, and even Excel or Word documents), is that you're not really looking for a way to render them within an XML browser. Really, there is no such thing as an XML browser. XML, after all, is not a presentation markup language. An XML processor doesn't care what you do with the image or multimedia entity described in your XML document.

The processor is concerned with helping to manage your entities, make them searchable, easy to update, add structure to the whole process of document creation, and pass along the entity reference to a processing application that can handle it. This doesn't mean that no errors will be generated when the entity is processed, but if you encounter an error message and are certain it's related to an unparsed entity, the message is likely being generated by the application that is handling the entity, not the XML processor. This is an important consideration when diagnosing problems associated with XML documents and their entities.

An unparsed entity is not referenced in the document instance the same way as other entity references—with a beginning & character and ending ; character. In the earlier example, in order to reference the ADGRAPHIC entity, you need to include it as an attribute value. Unparsed entities aren't, and and can't be, referenced in elements. They must be referenced as attribute values and in order to be referenced as an attribute value, the attribute that references the unparsed entity must be declared in the DTD as able to work with entity types. This means that when you're looking at a DTD, it needs to have one more line of code than what you encountered a bit earlier. So add that line of code to your DTD as follows:

```
<!ENTITY ADGRAPHIC SYSTEM "border.png" NDATA PNG>
<!NOTATION PNG SYSTEM "MYGRAPHICSPROGRAM.EXE">
<!ATTLIST DISPLAYCONTENT src ENTITY #REQUIRED>
```

For the time being, let's assume that an element declaration was made for an element named DISPLAYCONTENT a bit earlier in the DTD. The attribute list declaration for the DISPLAYCONTENT element states that there is a src attribute, and that the attribute type is an entity. Now all you need to do is name the entity as the value of the attribute in the DISPLAYCONTENT element's src attribute as follows:

```
<DISPLAYCONTENT src="ADGRAPHIC"/></DISPLAY>
```

Notice that when you include the entity as an attribute value, there is no preceding & and no ending ; character surrounding the entity. You're not restricted to using binary graphics as the entity file format. However. You can use any number of file formats. The only limitation is the ability of the XML processor to pass it on to an application that can do something with the entity.

Using Internal and External Entities

Not only is every entity either parsed or unparsed, but every entity is also either internal or external. These are not mutually exclusive concepts. For instance, you can have an external parsed entity or an external unparsed entity.

An internal entity is one that is defined locally within a DTD, such as the earlier example, which is repeated as follows:

```
<!ENTITY ADTEXT SYSTEM "This content belongs to the INCOLUMNCONTENT
element. The INCOLUMNCONTENT element is nested within the INCOLUMN ele-
ment, as is another child of the INCOLUMN element, the INCOLUMNSIZE
element. One example, without style sheets, shows how it looks in
Internet Explorer. The example without style sheets uses an entity to
place this text from an outside source. The other example uses style
sheets, and the text is typed in, and an entity is not used.">
```

Generally, you want to avoid writing long definitions, like the previous, in your DTD. You also may want to develop a system by which it's easier to manage a large group of entities. One way to do this is with external entities. For instance, in the preceding example, you could include a string of text within the quotation marks in a separate text file, call it `adText.txt`, and then refer to that file in a Uniform Resource Identifier (URI) in the DTD entity declaration as follows:

```
<!ENTITY ADTEXT SYSTEM "adText.txt">
```

The preceding line of code accomplishes the same thing as the lines of code before it, but makes for a more compact DTD. The end result in the document instance, however, will be the same. When the entity reference is made in the document instance, the actual rendering of the document displays the replacement text contained in the file `adText.txt`. The result is the same screen that you saw in Figure 6.2.

Let's examine the line of code a bit more closely.

```
<!ENTITY ADTEXT SYSTEM "adText.txt">
```

The code, which is an entity declaration within a DTD, begins with the keyword `ENTITY`. The next word, `ADTEXT`, is the name of the entity. The keyword `SYSTEM` is called an *external identifier*, which can take the value of either `SYSTEM` or `PUBLIC`. The external identifier `SYSTEM` refers to a URI. In the preceding example, `"adText.txt"` is a relative URI and could just as easily been an absolute URI such as `"http://www.myDomain.com/adText.txt"`.

Generally you'll see the *public identifier* for entities with either built-in processor support or with some other kind of special retrieval mechanism. They're designed for intranet or extranet use—or any kind of a situation where the entity is common knowledge among the systems accessing its use.

NOTE You'll learn more about *public identifiers* and *system identifiers* in Chapter 8: "Creating Your Own DTD."

You've already seen an unparsed external entity when how to use the `ADGRAPHICS` entity was demonstrated a bit earlier in the chapter. You can't have an unparsed internal entity because XML rules forbid it. To include an unparsed internal entity, you'd have to include the actual code in the definition that lies between the quote marks in the entity declaration, which isn't particularly realistic.

To review the syntactical difference then, between internal and external entities:

- Internal entities are declared without any external identifiers (the `SYSTEM` or `PUBLIC` keywords) in the DTD.
- External entities must be declared with an external identifier (the `SYSTEM` or `PUBLIC` keywords) in the DTD.
- External unparsed entities must have the `NDATA` keyword included in their DTD declarations.
- External unparsed entities must have a `NOTATION` declaration indicating to the XML processor what application should handle the entity.

Using Parameter Entities

You'll actually encounter parameter entities in more detail in Chapter 8, because parameter entities are used exclusively in DTDs. You should become familiar with parameter entities now, if only to begin the process of keeping the syntactical differences between parameter and general entities clear in your head.

Parameter entities accomplish the same thing as other entities that act as shortcuts. Using parameter entities, you can include element and attribute list declarations as groups and refer to them easily as single entities. You can even include an entire DTD in a parameter entity.

You can probably imagine, even if your knowledge of DTD development is still in an early stage, that quite a bit of time can be saved by using parameter entities in a DTD. Of course, it can be difficult to hard code an XML document in a text editor if you have to validate it against a DTD that uses other DTDs, but in the long term that shouldn't be a major problem. This is because text editors that make developing against DTD much easier are beginning to appear, and these tools will help you develop elements that follow the rules set forth in the DTD, and in turn reduce the amount of time you spend manually searching through DTD.

NOTE Chapter 18: "XML Development Tools," provides a complete examination of XML editors and other XML development tools.

Parameter entities distinguish themselves from general entities by the inclusion of one simple character, the percentage sign (%), in the entity declaration:

```
<!ENTITY % myParameterEntity "myElement | myElement2 | myElement3">
```

Notice there is nothing else on either side of the percentage sign. When a parameter entity is referenced, you simply place the percentage sign next to the entity that is being referenced followed by a semicolon:

```
<!ELEMENT ANELEMENT  (%myParameterEntity; |anotherElement)*>
```

A parameter entity is only referenced through another declaration within the DTD, never within the document instance. So you won't see anything like this:

```
<MYELEMENT>%anIllegalParameterEntity</MYELEMENT>
```

Actually, that's not entirely true. You may see something like the preceding line of code, but it won't mean anything as far as entities are concerned. An XML processor would simply parse the preceding code like it would any other character data.

A parameter entity can be defined with any valid DTD markup. This makes it very useful for large groups of entity declarations. You could catalog those entity declarations as part of a separate DTD, or within a text file, and include them using an external identifier like a *system identifier* or *public identifier*, like so:

```
<!ENTITY % myParameterEntity "http://www.myDomain.com/
someEntities.txt">
```

The preceding line of code is an example of an external parameter entity. You could use such a parameter entity to manage large amount of language encoding, for cataloging a library of images, or for e-commerce purposes. There are no limits.

TIP

Be kind to others. As your parameter entity references grow and the complexity of your DTD increase, comment on the code you use to develop the parameter entities in your DTD as well.

Harnessing the Power of Entities

Now that you've had a chance to look at entities from a conceptual standpoint, it's time to see how they work in the guts of an XML document. If you're uncomfortable with all the DTD jargon, don't worry too much yet. By the time you're finished with Chapter 8, you'll have a good grasp of DTD development. Unfortunately, in the meantime it's not really possible to discuss entities without at least taking a glimpse into their DTD syntax.

Developing General Entities

We'll focus our practical examination of general entities by looking more closely at two kinds of general entities: parsed and unparsed. We'll start by taking a look at an XML document with its DTD included (this is called an internal DTD) to make it easier to see how entities are referenced. Take a look at Listing 6.1 and see if you can track down the entities in the listing's internal DTD. The DTD starts with the [character and ends with the] character. What follows after that is the document instance, which is the main part of the XML document that you would have if you split Listing 6.1 into two listings, one with the DTD and one with the document instance.

LISTING 6.1 Incorporating Entities into an XML Document Using an Internal DTD

```
<?xml version="1.0"?>
<!DOCTYPE AD [
<!ELEMENT AD (NEWSPAPER, (INCOLUMN | DISPLAY))>
<!ENTITY ADTEXT_1 "Check out this entity:">
<!ENTITY ADTEXT_2 SYSTEM "adText.txt">
<!ATTLIST AD id ID #REQUIRED>
<!ELEMENT NEWSPAPER (#PCDATA)>
<!ELEMENT INCOLUMN (INCOLUMNSIZE, INCOLUMNCONTENT)>
<!ELEMENT INCOLUMNSIZE (#PCDATA)>
```

```
<!ELEMENT INCOLUMNCONTENT (#PCDATA)>
<!ATTLIST INCOLUMNSIZE lines NMTOKEN #REQUIRED>
<!ATTLIST INCOLUMNSIZE width (1 | 2 | 3 | 4 | 5 | 6 | 7) #REQUIRED>
<!ELEMENT DISPLAY (DISPLAYSIZE, DISPLAYCONTENT)>
<!ELEMENT DISPLAYSIZE (#PCDATA)>
<!ELEMENT DISPLAYCONTENT (#PCDATA)>
<!NOTATION PNG SYSTEM "D:\Program Files\Photoshop 4.0 LE\Photosle.exe">
<!- The processor does not actually
care where the program that executes the binary lies, although the
binary won't
run if the path isn't set correctly ->
<!ATTLIST DISPLAYCONTENT src ENTITY #REQUIRED>
<!ENTITY ADGRAPHIC SYSTEM "border.png" NDATA PNG>
<!ATTLIST DISPLAYSIZE lines NMTOKEN #REQUIRED>
<!ATTLIST DISPLAYSIZE width (1 | 2 | 3 | 4 | 5 | 6 | 7) #REQUIRED>
]>
<AD id="a001"><NEWSPAPER>San Francisco Chronicle</NEWSPAPER><DISPLAY>
<DISPLAYSIZE lines="636" width="2">
</DISPLAYSIZE>
<DISPLAYCONTENT src="ADGRAPHIC"/></DISPLAY>
<INCOLUMN><INCOLUMNSIZE lines="2" width =
"2"/><INCOLUMNCONTENT>&ADTEXT_1; &ADTEXT_2;</INCOLUMNCONTENT>
</INCOLUMN>
</AD>
```

Did you find the entity declaration ADTEXT_1 in the DTD in Listing 6.1? You can see that a string of text defines the ADTEXT_1 entity. Note that no external system or public identifier was used. The reason for this is that if you use an external identifier, the processor will attempt to find an external entity. But the first entity is an internal parsed entity consisting only of a string. So you leave out the identifier and simply define the entity with the string between quotes. If you use an external identifier with a parsed entity, when you load the XML document the XML processor will return an error like this:

```
Error while parsing entity 'ADTEXT_1'. Could not load 'Check out this
entity:'. The system cannot locate the resource specified. Line 25,
Position 1
```

The reason is that the system or public identifier tells the processor to look for that string of text as a URI.

Now take another look at Listing 6.1 and see if you can find the next entity. This one is called ADTEXT_2. Notice how this entity is defined with the system identifier, which tells you you're dealing with an external entity. Now it makes sense for the XML processor to look for something external, in this case a text file named adText.txt.

Next, you should find an external entity called ADGRAPHIC, which is defined by a relative URI. The graphic is called border.png. The .png extension refers to the Portable Network Graphics (PNG) format, which is a graphic format somewhat akin to a high powered GIF file (lots of color and transparency options). So the processor will look for the graphic and pass it on to another application for processing.

Now that you've located the three entity declarations in the internal DTD of Listing 6.1, it's time to see how they're referenced in the document instance. Remember that entities are referenced in different parts of the document instance, depending on their type:

- Parsed entities— either internal or external—such as those similar to the ADTEXT_1 and ADTEXT_2 entities are referenced exclusively in elements.
- Unparsed entities are referenced exclusively through an element's attribute.

In Listing 6.1 you can track down the first entity, ADTEXT_1, and see that it is referenced using the following notation: &ADTEXT_1;. The giveaway is the ampersand (&) and semicolon (;) on either side of the entity name. When the XML processor encounters &ADTEXT_1;, it replaces the entity reference with the actual text used to define the entity (see Figure 6.5). The same holds true for the next entity, &ADTEXT_2;, which is also a parsed entity. The last entity, ADGRAPHIC, is referred to as a value for the src attribute in the DISPLAYCONTENT element. The rules of XML state that in order to use an unparsed entity in this way, not only must you declare the entity in the DTD, but you must declare that the attribute whose value will consist of the entity be declared as being an ENTITY type in the DTD. In the example in Listing 6.1, the following line of code accomplishes this in the internal DTD:

```
<!ATTLIST DISPLAYCONTENT src ENTITY #REQUIRED>
```

NOTE

The examples used here are for the humble beginnings of a hypothetical markup language for newspaper advertising. For a more robust, and real-world, example of a classified advertising DTD, see http://www.zedak.com/admarkup. The URL points to a system being developed by the *New York Times* and the Zedak Corporation for newspapers wishing to incorporate XML markup into older, more traditional classified advertising markup systems. The DTD is being considered as a standard by the Newspaper Association of America and a portion of it appears in the next example.

FIGURE 6.5:

The &ADTEXT_1; entity is replaced by a text file when displayed in IE5.

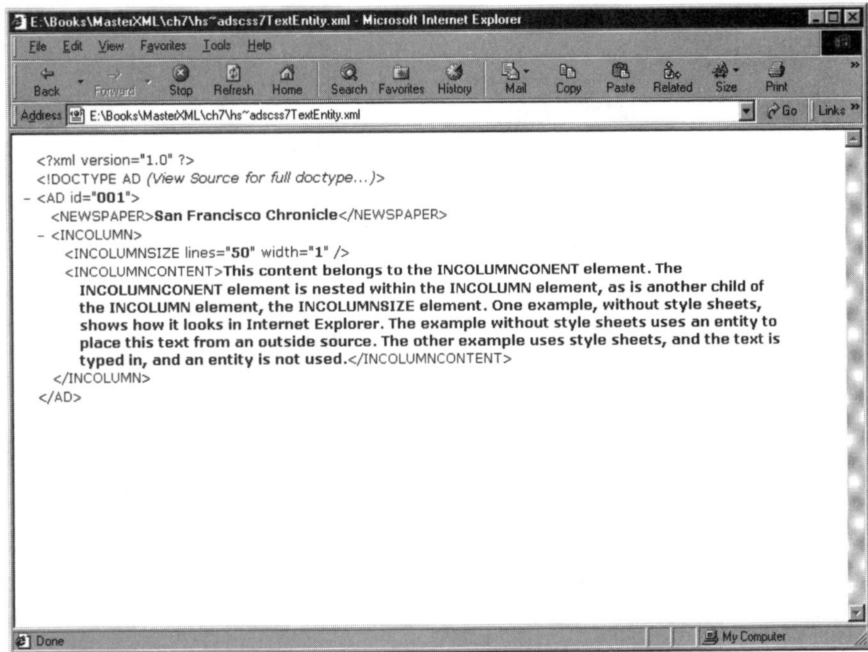

Developing Parameter Entities

Parameter entity development is a bit beyond the scope of this chapter, as you haven't yet learned how to develop DTD, but it's worthwhile to have a look at how they work in a real world scenario. Listing 6.2 shows a portion of a DTD that manages a classified ad system for the *New York Times.*

LISTING 6.2 Portions of a Classified Advertisement System for the *New York Times*

```
<!- Copyright 1998, The New York Times.->
<!-                         AD TEXT                          ->
<!ENTITY % inline "#PCDATA|font|glyph|image|keyword|mailbox|margin">
<!ENTITY % spacer "space|tab">
<!ENTITY % flow   "center|left|line|right">
<!ELEMENT text    (%inline;|%flow;|reply)*>
<!ELEMENT center  (%inline;|reply)*>
```

```
<!ELEMENT font     (%inline;|%flow;|reply)*>
<!ATTLIST font
  size (agate|5|6|10|12|13|14|18|24|30|31|36|48|60|72) "agate">
<!ELEMENT glyph    EMPTY>
<!ATTLIST glyph
  name (en|em|thin|figure|dash|open|close|1-8|3-8|5-8|7-8|1-4|3-4|1-
3|2-3|1-2) #REQUIRED
>
<!ELEMENT keyword (#PCDATA)>
<!ATTLIST keyword
  format  CDATA    ""
  name    CDATA    #REQUIRED
  punct   CDATA    ""
  scale   CDATA    ""
>
<!ELEMENT left     (%inline;|reply)*>
<!ELEMENT line     (%inline;|%spacer;|reply)*>
```

Listing 6.2 shows a small portion of a much larger DTD. Without getting too hung up on the all the semantics of this DTD, see if you can find the way parameter entities are used. Let's go through that process step by step.

First, you can see an entity declaration early on in the listing for an `inline` entity. The code for this first entity declaration looks like this in Listing 6.2:

```
<!ENTITY % inline "#PCDATA|font|glyph|image|keyword|mailbox|margin">
```

Notice the use of the percentage sign (%), which tells the XML parser that the associated entity is a parameter entity. Also, notice there's a space between separating the percentage sign from any other content. This is important, because it tells the XML processor that the entity is being declared and defined, not referenced. The declaration states that any element declared with the `inline` entity as part of its definition (either required or optional) would thus also consist of either PCDATA, or the font, glyph, image, keyword, mailbox, or margin elements.

To better understand this, take a look at an instance where the `inline` entity is actually used. You'll note that the `text` element declaration includes the `inline` entity in its definition:

```
<!ELEMENT text     (%inline;|%flow;|reply)*>
```

As you can see, the `inline` entity is used as part of the `text` element's definition, along with another entity and the `reply` element. This means that the text element could contain the `font` element, because the `font` element is declared in the `inline` definition. Unto itself `Inline` is not an element. It's an entity, and acts as a shortcut to gather a bunch of other declarations together for a more compact DTD.

Up Next

As you've seen in this chapter, entities can be a powerful tool. They provide a convenient mechanism for managing large amounts of content. You can use them to protect your XML content from being interpreted as markup, or for adding multilingual capability to your document. You can also use them as powerful shortcuts that can cut endless hours of coding. Databases may use them extensively to manage large catalogs of images, legal documents, technical specifications, and the like.

The next chapter will examine how to design your documents. XML, after you get comfortable with it, is not as complicated as it first seems. But designing documents for XML is an art unto itself. The next chapter will offer some insight into the XML document design process.

PART III

Designing Your Data

CHAPTER

SEVEN

7

XML Design Principles

- Selecting a design methodology
- The functional specification
- Design meetings
- Structure charts
- Document analysis
- Evaluating usability
- Well-formed vs. formal XML schema

XML provides a mechanism for the interchange of structured content on the Web. This structured content is tagged in XML with tag sets that are designed to serve a particular function and convey a particular meaning either to a human or to a software application. For example, some tag sets merely provide an extension of HTML to code content that provides specialized metadata to facilitate advanced search and retrieval techniques. Other tag sets may be much more sophisticated and actually provide a direct map to database fields. What makes an XML tag design appropriate? How do you decide where to begin and how to design the right tag set? This chapter will help you select a design approach, write a functional specification, recruit your design team, and develop your own XML tag set using structure charts as a design aid.

Selecting a Design Methodology

Before you begin your tag set design, it is important to select the appropriate methodology. The methodology you select primarily depends upon the type of XML creation environment because this is where tags are first entered. There are three main sources of XML data:

- Software designed to automatically tag XML data from structured sources such as databases
- Editors that update existing tagged XML data sources
- Authors that create original material and tag that data in XML as they author

In cases where software automatically tags XML data, a highly complex tag set may be used with little impact on staff or schedules because the program does the tagging. In cases where existing data is updated and supplemented, the number of tags and ease-of-use is a concern, but not critical. The number of tags and their ease-of-use is most critical when an author must "tag" data in XML as text is created. In this case the usability of the tag design is paramount and the design approach you select for your project will be influenced by which XML source is at the heart of your design.

NOTE

Selecting nomenclature that is familiar to authors and editors is a major factor in usability. XML designers assign tag names. XML tag names do not have to be complex; simple, easy-to-understand tag names are best!

Depending upon your XML authoring environment, you may select one of the following XML design approaches:

Chief Engineer Approach The design is created by a single designer.

Facilitated Team Approach The design is created by a project team assisted by an XML design expert.

Informed Partnership Approach The design is created by an XML design expert with guidance from a project team.

The Chief Engineer Approach

The *Chief Engineer Approach* is based upon employing the expertise of a chief engineer to create the XML design (typically an XML DTD). The Chief Engineer may be an internal staff resource or an outside XML design consultant may be employed. In this approach, an XML designer, or chief engineer, spends time gathering both requirements and data samples and then develops a tag design that meets the project requirements. Typically the chief engineer documents the DTD and may even present a review of the new XML tag set and its proposed usage to the implementation and/or authoring staff. Often the chief engineer hands the XML DTD off to an internal user, technology group, or integration group that will use the DTD as the basis for developing their XML system.

NOTE

You can find a listing of independent XML consultants by linking to the Independent Consultants Cooperative (ICC) logo on the home page of the Graphic Communications Association (GCA) at `http://www.gca.org/` as in Figure 7.1. Consultants are one of many technical resources listed at this site.

FIGURE 7.1:

Independent XML Design Consultants do not represent or sell specific products.

Graphic Communications Association's

Independent Consultants Cooperative

The Graphic Communications Association Information Technologies Independent Consultants Cooperative is an organization of independent industry XML/SGML consultants who work in cooperation with GCA to provide services for GCA members. All ICC members are vendor independent, have a proven track record, and are known as top quality providers of XML/SGML services. Give the GCA/ICC consultants a call! Work with the best in the industry!

Advantages

The *Chief Engineer Approach* has several advantages. First, if the XML consultant assuming the role of chief engineer is the expert that he or she purports to be, the XML design will be elegant. That is, you should not find beginner errors in the design. Perhaps the largest benefit is that the DTD will be developed with little impact on the resources of the your organization. If one is looking at the bottom line in terms of development dollars only, this approach provides a high quality solution and incurs the least overall cost.

Disadvantages

The *Chief Engineer Approach* has disadvantages as well. Perhaps the biggest disadvantage is the lack of participation by eventual stakeholders and users in creating the XML design. When document-type designs are handled "off-line," the project sponsors typically do not have a clear understanding of the design decisions that were made and why these are the best decisions. Likewise, end users typically have little or no participation when the *Chief Engineer Approach* is employed. The *Chief Engineer Approach* has little negative impact when the XML data is tagged automatically as it is extracted from a structured database.

However, handing editors or authors who use tags in an authoring environment a de facto tagging scheme, to which they must conform, can be disastrous. The support and buy-in of end users in a direct XML editing/authoring environment is key. If end users have no ownership of the development process, they may revolt. Revolt can run the gamut from a very slow learning and adoption curve to simply walking away from the project. In such environments, the *Chief Engineer Approach* is likely not the best choice.

Facilitated Team Approach

The *Facilitated Team Approach* to XML design represents the exact opposite philosophy of the *Chief Engineer Approach*. Using the Facilitated Team Approach methodology, the XML designer serves as a facilitator to a project team and begins by identifying all stakeholders. This group typically includes technology staff, editorial staff, production staff, trainers, and representatives from management. The facilitator works with the group to introduce the principles of XML modeling to the team and to guide the team through the development of each and every model. The designer must continually balance design decisions made by the team, based upon their knowledge of the data, with solid XML design practices. Design participants become owners of the XML design and understand the design decisions that are made.

Advantages

Clearly, developing an XML design utilizing the *Facilitated Team Approach* takes more time and internal organization resources than does the *Chief Engineer Approach*. Depending upon the complexity of the data or document being modeled, a design session may run from several days to several weeks and will require the involvement of not only the XML design expert, but of the project staff as well. However, the XML expertise gained by the staff and the design that results from user-centric development may be worth the increased expense. When using the *Facilitated Team Approach* it is important to deploy the XML design throughout the organization using the same approach.

Disadvantages

The *Facilitated Team Approach* may require a greater commitment of organizational resources than are justified by the benefits or return on investment for the project. This approach has more value when authors and editors are directly involved in XML tagging. It has little positive impact in the automated XML tagging environment and therefore may not be the best design methodology for that environment.

TIP

Before committing to a *Facilitated Team Approach*, you should be sure that you have the necessary corporate resources as well as development time.

Informed Partnership Approach

A third XML design methodology is the *Informed Partnership Approach*. Using this methodology, an organization employs an XML designer to help them define project specifications. As in the *Facilitated Team Approach*, the designer involves all stakeholders and leads the process of defining initial requirements, followed by a brief design session. Rather than work through every detail of the design, the team defines general data models for certain data constructs and then the designer completes these objects at a later time.

Following the initial team design sessions, the designer continues to work on and takes responsibility for refining the document model as well as creating and validating an XML DTD, or schema, off-line. The designer continues holding review meetings with project staff along the way to maintain close communication. During the final stakeholders meeting, the DTD is given a formal review and signoff by all project members. Using this methodology, all participants become owners of the DTD just as they do using the *Facilitated Team Approach*. Stakeholders understand the design decisions that were made and can help foster adoption of the design.

Advantages

The *Informed Partnership Approach* works well to provide the insight and consensus that is required to provide the ease-of-use that is required when XML tagging must be done by authors or editors without imposing undue burden on corporate resources. It also is appropriate when translating a structured database design into data that will be automatically tagged in XML because staff will understand the design decisions and be able to support the design as it evolves over time. This approach provides significant design benefits and minimizes the cost in staff resources and decreases development time.

Disadvantages

The *Informed Partnership Approach* has few disadvantages. While being less expensive than the *Facilitated Team Approach*, this approach will be more costly and take more time than the *Chief Engineer Approach*. The costs and benefits must be carefully weighed when deciding if XML will be created by automatic tagging.

The Functional Specification

Imagine that you have just hired a new programmer. You want the programmer to design and write a JavaScript or a C++ program. You would never tell the programmer to just write the program without giving instructions about what the program must do. In fact, the thought of writing a script or program without a clear specification of intended functionality is ridiculous.

Creating an XML design is similar to designing any kind of software. An XML design is developed to facilitate encoding data in such a way that it can be processed to provide required functionality. Developing a clear specification of the functionality of the XML design is the starting point for creating XML designs.

NOTE The functional specification need not be lengthy, although it can be. The basis of functional specification is simply a set of statements about the expected functionality the XML-tagged data.

Examples of statements from a functional specification include:

- The tag set will support three levels of indexing.
- The tag set will enable searching on both part and model numbers.
- The tag set will support production of both the print and on-line format.
- The tag set will adopt the nomenclature found in the SPEEDE/Express industry data standard.
- The tag set must conform to the requirements set forth by the SAE J2008 Standard for the interchange of automotive service information.
- The tag set must identify a security classification for each procedure, illustration, and technical overview.

The functional specification that you develop will be used as your guide to creating an XML design. The resulting XML tag set should support all requirements in your functional specification.

TIP

You should be careful not to introduce a level of complexity in your tagging that is not required by the end users of the data. A common design error is to design a tagging scheme that is more complex than the project actually requires, which places undue burden on application software developers and authors and editors as well.

When your design is complete, you should evaluate it against the specified functional requirements for XML data to ensure that it meets all your requirements. Note that requirements may change during the design process. Changes to your functional specification are acceptable, but should be documented so that the final design and functional specification match one another.

Design Meetings

If you are using either the *Facilitated Team Approach* or the *Informed Partnership Approach* you will work with a team to create your XML design. Although some members of the team may have an understanding of XML, many may not, so it is important to begin your design meetings with a kickoff session. At this session members of the team should be introduced to one another and their individual areas of expertise highlighted. Basic XML concepts, including elements and attributes, should be explained in a brief opening tutorial so that all team members share the same level of understanding and nomenclature. It is also helpful to review the business requirements that are driving the XML design project so that all team members understand both the necessity and the goals of the project.

Following the XML tutorial, a review of the functional specification for the design should be conducted. Functionality should be discussed and updated by the team if any shortcomings are discovered. Oftentimes team representatives each bring functional requirements that provide benefits to their particular area within the organization. It is important to recognize that each viewpoint is valuable and should be reflected in the final design. As you might guess, compromises are often required.

TIP

It is often a good idea to hold an off-site design session. This prevents interruptions and reduces the chance that critical personnel will be pulled away to solve day-to-day work problems. It also sends a message that the XML design session is important to the organization.

Using Structure Charts

While working with your team, it is important to remember that you are working primarily with subject-matter experts. These people understand the data being modeled, but are not XML experts. XML designs are now formalized with an XML DTD. The XML DTD is a type of schema that provides definition and constraints for the data objects that make up the design. The syntax for the XML DTD is outlined in each XML Specification.

NOTE At this time, the XML DTD is the only way to formalize and record the constraints of your XML Design. The W3C Schema Working Group is developing a robust schema language that will provide an alternative to the XML DTD for future designs. See `http://www.w3.org/NOTE-xml-schema-req.`

Experience shows that steering clear of XML DTD syntax, and instead using a graphical approach, provides a level of comfort for those team members who are subject-matter experts, but know little about DTD. This approach enables both the designer and the team to concentrate on data modeling rather than getting hung up on the syntax.

NOTE You can create structure charts using flip charts or overhead transparencies. Software tools designed specifically for this function are also available.

When using structure charts, it is important that you adopt a clear syntax for representing structures that will later be translated into the XML DTD. For example, there must be a way to show that an element is made up of subelements. There must also be a way to express the frequency of elements and their order in the model.

A common format for structure charts is the graphical interface developed by Microstar Software Ltd. for their Near and Far® Designer 3, an XML design development tool. In Figure 7.2, you will see structure chart output by this tool that demonstrates the syntax for expressing both frequency and sequence of elements in an XML design.

FIGURE 7.2:

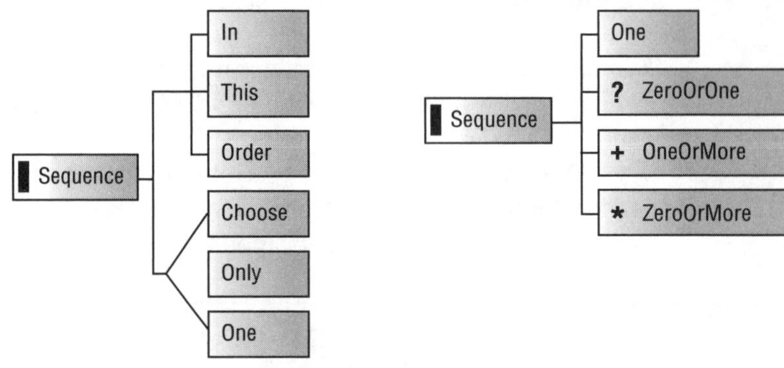

Sequence and frequency indicators for XML design structure charts by Near & Far® Designer™3 from Microstar Software Ltd.

Document Analysis

By this point, you have selected your design methodology and design tools. You have also selected your design team and gathered any relevant specifications and data samples. You are now ready to begin the work of data analysis. So where do you start?

Using Reference DTDs and Vocabularies

In the early days of document-data modeling, every model was unique. But since document data modeling began in the early 1980's, experts in many disciplines have conducted quite extensive data modeling efforts, bringing the best minds and most experienced subject-matter experts into play. Today, data models, or DTDs, have been developed for more than 16 industries. From manufacturing and telecommunications, to airlines and railways; from the Department of Defense, to automotive and heavy trucking; from computer systems to electronics; from pharmaceutical to medical and legal; from newspapers to multimedia, entertainment, and commercial publishing; cross-industry groups have built industry-specific tag designs.

When you begin your own data design, it is imperative that you begin by examining existing models to determine if a good base, or reference model, already exists for the type of data you wish to tag in XML. Starting from a reference DTD enables you to take advantage of design, development, testing, and documentation done by others. It might well be that application software is already available for the standard you choose. This will save you and your organization time and money.

To find the right reference model you might look in your industry. The "standard" DTD in you industry is usually a good starting point. It may have many of the data structures that you have in your own documents. It also may share a nomenclature that is specific to your industry. You may even have legislative or business requirements to conform to the industry standard model. If there is no specific industry standard DTD, you may find an existing general-purpose DTD, such as HTML, that you can enrich for your own purposes. Table 7.1 shows a number of existing DTDs that you may find useful.

TABLE 7.1: Reference DTDs by Discipline

Reference DTD	Use or Discipline
MIL38784B (CALS)	Military Specification; Technical Documentation.
ATA Spec 2100	Specification for Airframe/Engine Documentation.
DocBook	Specification for Software Documentation; some use for hardware as well.
SAE J2008	Specification for documentation of Vehicle Service Information; some use for other service information as well.
ISO 12083	Electronic Manuscript Standard; used for journals, articles, serials and books. Some use for magazine articles as well.
HTML	Hypertext Markup Language; used for Web publishing; some extend it for simple publications that will be used be used on the Web.
TEI	The text encoding initiative is a book oriented structure for documents, has additional features to support software documentation.
HL7	Health Level 7; for use in the medical community for charting and diagnosis.
SIF	Schools Interoperability Framework; defines the interchange objects in the K-12 school software interoperability environment. Based on SPEEDE/Express data structures.
TCIF	Telecommunications Industry Forum standard; defines major structures that comprise a data sheet.

NOTE You can find the HTML 4 reference data at the W3C site at `http://www.w3.org/TR/REC-html40`. An XML version of the SAE J2008 reference DTD is at `http://www.xmlxperts.com/saexml.htm`. The DocBook reference DTD can be accessed at `http://www.oasis-open.org/docbook/`.

If you find a reference DTD to use as the basis for your XML design, you must decide whether to use it directly or to modify it for your own use. The advantage of using a reference DTD directly as it was written is that you can also use off-the-shelf applications that were written for that DTD. This will save you development time and cost. On the other hand, the reference DTD may contain many structures that you do not need and that writers and editors will not use. These structures will most likely be confusing to your authors if you do not take the time to eliminate them.

NOTE

Reference DTDs were was developed for use by all organizations within a vertical industry. This means that everyone has contributed structures to the DTD. Reference DTD tends to have more elements and options than any DTD that has been developed for specific use within any of the contributing organizations.

If you decide to modify the reference DTD you have selected, begin by reviewing the DTD and deleting any structures that you do not use in your documents. For example, the DocBook DTD contains a number of very specific content elements such as *MouseButton, ReturnValue, UserInput, Literal, Command, Key,* and *Function*. You may not need writers to identify each of these kinds of data in order to meet your functional requirements. Rather than asking writers to tag data to this level of granularity, you may choose to delete these specific content elements from the reference DTD. Deleting elements from a reference DTD is often called *pruning*.

Next, review your documentation samples and the functional requirements for the project against the reference DTD to determine if the reference DTD meets all the requirements. Suppose that you want to search on ModelNumber but ModelNumber is not an element in the reference DTD. This means that you must add the new element ModelNumber to the DTD so that it can serve the intended business function.

TIP

Many reference DTDs are only available in SGML. If you want to use an SGML DTD as your reference DTD, you must first convert that to an XML DTD. This includes removing all inclusions, exclusions, and connectors. Once the reference DTD is a valid XML DTD, you can begin the process of pruning the DTD and adding your own unique extensions.

In addition to using complete industry-standard DTDs, you may use new XML vocabularies as the basis for your own design. An XML Vocabulary is an XML tag set. A vocabulary may be a complete XML DTD but because XML does not require a DTD, an XML Vocabulary may simply be a set of tag definitions upon which you can base the tag names in your DTD.

Basic Design Decisions

Before you begin document analysis, it is important that you make some conscious design decisions. Making design decisions up front can speed the overall process of analysis. In addition, having a clear design philosophy means that the resulting XML design will be consistent and much more usable.

NOTE Basic XML design decisions must be made no matter which design methodology you have selected. The methodology (Chief Consultant, Facilitated Team, or Informed Partnership) does not dictate actual XML design decisions.

Content-Based Model vs. Structure-Based Model

The first decision you are likely to face will come as you model high-level elements. These are the major logical divisions of the XML design. Let's suppose you are modeling a service manual made up of the following sections:

- Introduction
- Operation
- Electronic Parts
- Mechanical Parts
- Hydraulic Parts
- Troubleshooting
- Wiring Diagrams

You are immediately faced with two choices for modeling the service manual. It could be modeled based on its content as:

```
<!ELEMENT ServiceManual (Introduction, Operation, ElectricParts,
MechanicalParts, HydraulicParts, Troubleshooting, Wiring)>
```

When you model the manual based on content, you have a way to immediately zero in on the content that you want to retrieve or reuse by the element type. However, you have created many more tags for your authors and editors to learn. You also create a very prescriptive environment with this sort of model. You cannot alter the order of the content types that make up the manual. Nor can you add new content types to the manual without changing the XML DTD.

An alternate way that you could model the service manual is based on generic structures that make up the manual:

```
<!ELEMENT ServiceManual (Section+)>
```

Here you have a design with fewer tags for authors and editors to learn. You also have a much more flexible, general-purpose model. You are free to change the order of the sections and even to add new sections without updating the XML DTD. However to locate specific content in a service manual tagged to this model, you would need to search on section titles.

The choice here must be guided by the functional specification for the project as well as the method of tagging. If tagging is applied automatically by a program (perhaps during a database extract process), then the number and specificity of the tags is of little concern. If your functional specification indicates a highly controlled authoring environment (authors/editors) or that there is some end requirement for data in sections to be specifically identified, then the content approach is warranted as well.

NOTE

In either case, making this design decision before beginning the data analysis and development of the XML design can be most helpful.

Rigid Model vs. Flexible Model

Another design decision that must be made is the rigidity or flexibility of the model. In XML, you must precisely enumerate all possible ordering of elements in your DTD. You do not have the ability to list elements and specify that they can occur in any order, but you do have the ability to specify options for any element in a model and the ability to offer alternatives.

NOTE

XML does not allow for the AND connector (&) as does ISO 8879 (SGML). This occurrence specification has been dropped from the XML subset of SGML.

In the service manual example, the content-based model of the service manual is very rigid; it specifies elements that must occur in an exact sequence. You could add flexibility to that model by making the elements optional. This would allow you to specify the order, but not mandate the presence of each and every element:

```
<!ELEMENT ServiceManual (Introduction?, Operation?, ElectricParts?,
MechanicalParts?, HydraulicParts?, Troubleshooting?, Wiring?)>
```

Another way you could add flexibility to this model is to create a repeating OR group. In this way the writer could select just the sections that are appropriate, in the order the writer determines is best:

```
<!ELEMENT ServiceManual (Introduction, (Operation | ElectricParts |
MechanicalParts | HydraulicParts | Troubleshooting | Wiring)*>
```

In this model, note that is possible for a writer to include two sections of Operation. There is nothing in XML that says pick one of each of these in any order, which was the function of the AND connector in SGML.

The selection that the XML designer makes must be based on both the functional specification and the tagging mechanism. Again, if data is being automatically tagged (from a database), then specifying a prescribed element order is sensible. If authors and editors are involved, and if data is subject to variability, a more flexible approach makes good sense.

Inline Content vs. Metadata

The functional requirement to identify content for purposes of retrieval or reuse requires you to make a choice as to how the content will be tagged to facilitate retrieval. In some cases it makes sense to identify the content inline as data is authored. In other cases it is more reasonable to identify metadata or keywords at the beginning of the document or for major logical document structures.

Suppose, for example, you are creating a design for the documentation of a specific kind of hardware (like an engine or a gasoline pump). The data is to be authored by technical writers and engineers. It is critical that part numbers and model numbers are identified within each procedure. If you are working in an environment where writers use XML editing software, it is not unreasonable to expect writers to identify the content as each paragraph is authored:

```
<!ELEMENT Para (#PCDATA | PartNbr | ModelNbr )*    >
```

If, on the other hand, the writers are not using an XML-aware editing tool, identifying inline content becomes much more difficult. In such an environment, some tagging could be automated based on scanning text for key words. The limits of automated tagging should be your guide in designing in-line content tags.

Even in the XML-aware editing environment, identifying each model and part number within a paragraph may be too burdensome for the engineers and technical writers. If you judge this to be the case, you can move the specification of content to a higher level of the XML design. In fact, in many cases it is placed at the document level. At this level, content identification is considered to be metadata; it is really *data about the data* within the document:

```
<!ELEMENT ServiceManual (ModelNbrs,PartNbrs,Introduction,(Section)+ )>
```

If you decide to include XML tags to identify content, either inline or as metadata, be sure that the content tags in your XML design provide the functionality required in your initial specification. You must account for all business requirements in your design, but not get carried away and place an undue content tagging burden on authors and editors.

Recursive vs. Specified

Many times you will find that certain structures repeat within themselves. For example, you might have a list within a list. Or you might have subprocedures within a major procedure. Or you may have subsections within a section. How you will model these cases is a basic design decision. Making that decision before you create the model will lead to consistency across the models you create.

One way to model structures that repeat within themselves is to simply model them in that way:

```
<!ELEMENT list (item | list)+
```

This is called a *recursive model*. A recursive model is very elegant. It enables elements to nest inside each other infinitely. There is no real concern that you would exceed the nesting level for lists with such a model. It is often difficult to develop software that will handle an infinite level of nesting. In addition, allowing many levels of nesting often confuse writers who loose track of what level they are authoring.

TIP

Ask yourself, "Can my authors keep track of the level of writing when each element that is nested has the same tag name?" (i.e. <list>. . .<list>. . .<list>. . .)

An alternative to creating a recursive model is to specify the level of nesting and to clearly indicate the nesting level in the tag name:

```
<!ELEMENT List (item | List2)+    >
<!ELEMENT List2 (item | List3)+   >
<!ELEMENT List3 (item)+  >
```

In this model, there are only three levels of lists. Using this sort of model it is much easier to configure XML software, and writers always know at which level they are writing. The downside is that it is possible to exceed the nesting level. In that case, the DTD would need to be updated to allow an additional level of lists, and all related XML software would need to be reconfigured as well.

TIP

The standard HTML heading tags (H1, H2, H3, H4, H5, and H6) have numbers that may seem to indicate levels of headings. But the HTML DTD is not designed in nested levels as discussed here. The numbers in these tag names simply indicate the relative "size" of the heading format and do not imply level of nesting!

What About Exclusions?

In some cases one develops a general model that works almost everywhere. For example, let's consider the following model for a paragraph. It allows for text entry as well as identification of part numbers, model numbers, internal cross references, and footnotes:

```
<!ELEMENT Para (#PCDATA | PartNbr | ModelNbr | Ftnote | IntXref )*    >
```

Now suppose you model a footnote. In a footnote you want to allow paragraphs and lists. But you do not want to allow a footnote within a footnote, so you create the following model:

```
<ELEMENT Ftnote (Para | List1)+ >
```

In XML there is no easy way to exclude the footnotes that are allowed within a paragraph (see the paragraph model) when the paragraph occurs within a footnote. Handling situations like this require a basic design decision to be made and used consistently throughout the design.

NOTE

Handling exclusions is the most difficult decision facing industry standard organizations that want to convert their SGML DTD to XML DTD. You can see how this was handled by ISO 12083 (Electronic Manuscript Standard) by referring to `http://www.xmlxperts.com/12083.htm`.

One of two approaches may be taken. The first is to simply leave the model as it is shown above. The philosophy here is that a writer or editor would never put a footnote inside a footnote and that one must trust them to use good judgement.

The second approach is to create a special paragraph model for the footnote that does not allow a footnote. Because you cannot have two elements with identical names in an XML design, you must give the paragraph in the footnote a unique name.

```
<!ELEMENT Ftnote.Para (#PCDATA | PartNbr | ModelNbr | IntXref )*    >
<ELEMENT Ftnote (Ftnote.Para | List1)+ >
```

Note that while taking the approach of creating special elements provides a great deal of control over our XML models, it also adds a great number of tags for authors and editors to use. This is often not an easy choice to make.

Modeling High-Level Structures

Once you have formalized the design approach, you are ready to begin by modeling high-level structures. The process of document analysis is basically a top-down breakdown in which you begin to divide the document into logical units beginning with one *root element*. All other elements must nest within the root element. Look at Figures 7.3, 7.4, and 7.5 to see examples of high level structures modeled in the HTML, ISO 12083, and SAE J2008 reference DTD. You will find one root element at the highest level and then several other high level elements that indicate the logical units that nest within the root element.

FIGURE 7.3:

HTML DTD high level structures

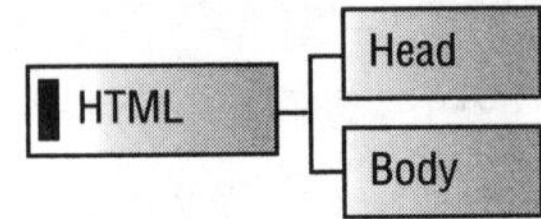

<!ELEMENT HTML (Head, Body)>

FIGURE 7.4:

ISO 12083 article DTD high level structures

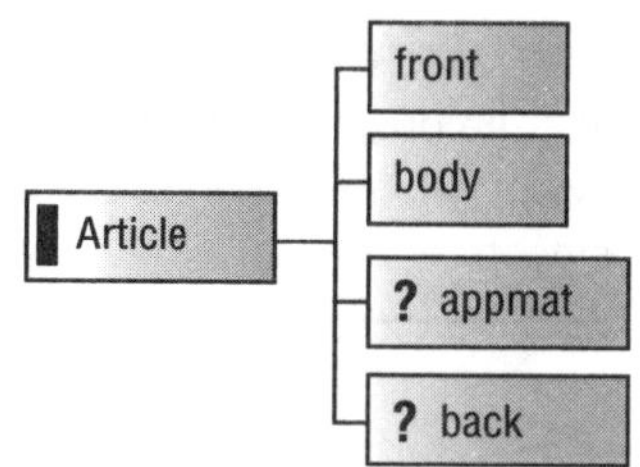

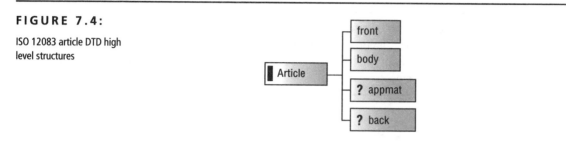

<!ELEMENT article (front, body, appmat?, back?)>

FIGURE 7.5:

SAE J2008 DTD high level structures

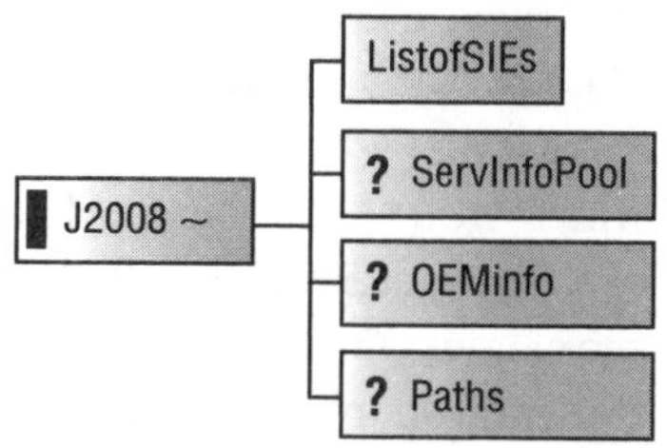

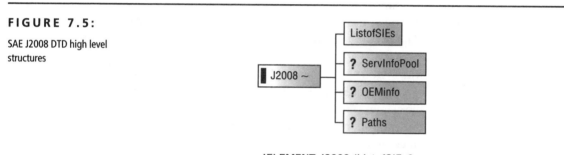

<!ELEMENT J2008 (ListofSIEs?, ServInfoPool?, OEMInfo?, Paths?)>

Creating Building-Block Elements

Once high-level structures have been modeled, you are at the text level of the document. Here you enter text using familiar structures such as titles, paragraphs, lists, and tables. Many designers call these the *text building-block elements.* Typical text building-block elements include headings and titles, paragraphs, procedures, different kinds of lists, footnotes, cross references, tables, figures, and graphics.

Text building-block elements can be borrowed from a reference DTD, even if the high-level document structures cannot. Again, the advantage of borrowing models from a reference DTD is that the work has already been done, tested, and documented. Even borrowing models at this level can save you time and money.

TIP

While the HTML DTD is not particularly useful in situations when defining a hierarchical structure or specific content tagging is required, using text building-block elements from HTML may make sense because so many people already know these elements.

Using Element Classes

Some text building-block elements can be grouped into element classes. For example, one class of building-block elements is those elements that are used for identifying inline content. A second class is elements that define paragraphs. A third class is those elements that make up phrases. The advantage of creating an element class is that you can define the class once and then use the entire class (group of elements) wherever appropriate. To form element classes you use *parameter entities* in your XML design. The following example shows the definition and use of a parameter entity called `%chardat` (character data) in the SAE J2008. First, all the elements that can appear at the character level are grouped and given a parameter entity name (`chardat`). This group is then used, or called, when writing an element definition.

```
<!ENTITY % chardat  "Emph| Sub |Sup |Ftnote |Intxref |Figureref |
                     Tableref | Diagref |Extxref | Symbol" >
<!ELEMENT Title   - - (#PCDATA | %chardat;)*>
<!ELEMENT SubTitle  - - (#PCDATA | %chardat;)*>
```

Classes of attributes may also be designed using the parameter entity mechanism. For example, you could design an attribute set called `%ids` to be used in any attribute list that has the ID/IDREF attributes. You could also design an attribute set called `%meta` that is made up of metadata attributes to be used with many element types.

XML Usability

When your XML design is complete, it is time to review the design to determine its usability. This is a time to make edits that will significantly improve implementation, training, and use of the design.

Begin by reviewing the tag names (generic identifiers). If authors or editors will be doing the tagging review the tag names with an end user. Some important questions to ask are if the names are intuitive and would any change in nomenclature make this tag set user-friendlier? If the answer to either is yes, make the changes now.

TIP

If you are using an industry standard DTD in order to interchange with others or to meet legal/contractual requirements you have little control over the tag names. Creating a mapping table from current or accepted names to the standard tag names will be a useful addition to the documentation you create for the tag set.

Next, examine the capitalization of tag names, how the tags are constructed, and how abbreviations are used. Consistency is critical to the usability of the tag set.

The tag set on the left side of the following list adheres to consistent capitalization rules (XML tags are case sensitive). The tag set on the right side does not.

<ServiceManual>	<ServiceManual>
<Section>	<section>
<Title>	<title>
<WiringDiagram>	<Wiringdiagram>

The tag set on the left side of the following list is consistent in the way tag names are constructed. The tags set on the right is not consistent:

<service.manual>	<ServiceManual>
<section>	<Section>
<title>	<Title>
<wiring.diagram>	<Wiring.diagram>
<ftnote.para>	<ftnotepara>

TIP

Never use a colon (:) in a tag name. The colon is reserved to indicate the *namespace* of the tag and has a special meaning to XML processors.

The tag set on the left side of the following list uses standardized abbreviations. The one on the right side does not. Review the tags in your design and make sure that abbreviations are standardized wherever used.

<ServiceManual>	<ServiceManual>
<PartNbr>	<PartNumber>
<ModelNbr>	<ModelNbr>
<ChapterNbr>	<ChapNum>

Next, you should examine the tag set for consistency in design. The design for elements in a class should be parallel. This means that similar elements should have similar designs for both the elements and attributes.

In this example there are three kinds of lists. Note the similar design.

```
<!ELEMENT alphalist (item,item+) >
<!ELEMENT numlist (item, item+)  >
<!ELEMENT bullist (item, item+)  >
```

In the following example, the lists do not have a similar design. This can be confusing to writers and tend to compromise the usability of the different kinds of list tags.

```
<!ELEMENT alphalist (item,item+) >
<!ELEMENT numlist (numitem+)     >
<!ELEMENT bullist (bul,item)+    >
```

A final consideration that affects the usability of the tag set is the sheer number of tags. A large number of tags affect usability the most when authors or editors are responsible for tagging data, but can also affect the complexity of programs designed to apply tags automatically. Count the number of tags in your design and see if you can use a generalized structure in place of unique structures (which require more tags). If possible, replace specific structures with general-use structures. This may not be an option for high-level elements, but is often easy for text building block elements.

Look back to the example of the three list types. Why are there three list types? If it is so that the formatting of each list type will be different, you could combine the lists into one model and differentiate the formatting by using a type or role attribute. Be sure to constrain the number of types so that you limit the possibilities for both the end user and the software developer. Using this approach the three list models can be consolidated into this model:

```
<!ELEMENT list (item, item+)>
<!ATTLIST list   type  (bul | alpha | num) "bul" >
```

Now Throw the DTD Away!

Throughout this chapter we have discussed the principles of XML Design. We have consistently discussed that the outcome of the XML design process is an XML DTD. Now you may wonder why we talk in these terms when one of the attractive features of XML is its well-formedness and the fact that XML does not require a DTD.

The XML Specification clearly allows for two levels of conformance—valid and well-formed. Well-formed means that the data coded in XML is properly nested and all entities are declared. Valid XML is not only well formed, but also has a DTD and conforms to the constraints expressed within the DTD.

XML is designed so that data coded in XML is self-describing by virtue of being well-formed. As such, XML without a DTD can be processed. This provides you with extraordinarily flexible data-delivery capabilities. You can, for example, sort and filter information to deliver well-formed and personalized processable XML information sets on the Web.

It is important to understand that delivery of well-formed XML does not mean that a DTD was not used when the data was created. It simply means that the DTD is not required for this use of the data. An XML DTD may be used where validity is important, such as during the authoring process. At other times, such as when viewing the data, the constraints imposed by a DTD are not required and may, in fact, slow processing.

Up Next

Now that you know how to select a design approach, write a functional specification, and recruit your design team, you're ready to move on to the next step: learning how to actually write the DTD. The next chapter will carefully guide you through that process.

CHAPTER

EIGHT

8

Creating Your Own DTD

- The grammar of XML
- Element attributes
- Establishing entities
- Defining elements
- Creating attribute lists
- Tools for building a DTD

One of the greatest benefits to XML is the flexibility it gives you in creating documents. To take maximum advantage of that flexibility, however, XML authors must understand the Document Type Definitions (DTDs) used in a document's creation.

DTD: The Grammar of XML

A DTD describes the grammar expected of documents that use its vocabulary. Just as English grammar helps writers form proper sentence structure, XML grammar helps authors create properly structured documents. The expected XML grammar is recorded in the DTD. In previous chapters, we have talked about an XML document being *valid*; the DTD provides the means to verify the document's conformance: that is, its validity.

To help identify the components of a DTD, in this chapter you'll build one to be used in creating a college course catalog.

Gathering Data

Before you begin deciding what elements or attributes you might include in the DTD, you need to document just what kind of data will need to be described in a catalog document. The first pass at the list of data objects to be included is shown in Table 8.1. We call these data objects because we haven't yet decided if they'll become elements or attributes or if they'll be included in the DTD at all.

TABLE 8.1: Data Objects to Be Included in the Catalog

Course	Identifies an individual course
Name	Contains the course name
Length	Describes how long the course runs
Instructor	Identifies who's teaching the course
Ta	Indicates the presence of a teacher's assistant

Continued on next page

TABLE 8.1 CONTINUED: Data Objects to Be Included in the Catalog

Taname	Identifies the teacher's assistant if one is used
Description	Provides a description of the course
Prerequisite	Lists any other courses that students must complete first
Textbook	Identifies any required texts
Title	Identifies the title of a required text
Author	Identifies the textbook author's name
Isbn	Identifies the unique ISBN number of the textbook
Publisher	Identifies the book publisher's name

You need to further refine this list by identifying which objects are related to each other. For instance, the object name describes the object course, so those are related. You could do this by drawing a tree diagram, as shown in Figure 8.1, or by using a table (see Table 8.2).

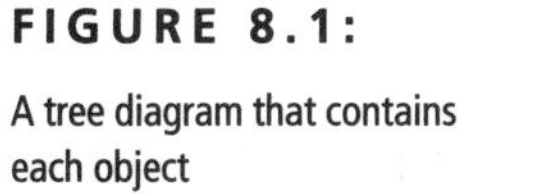

FIGURE 8.1:

A tree diagram that contains each object

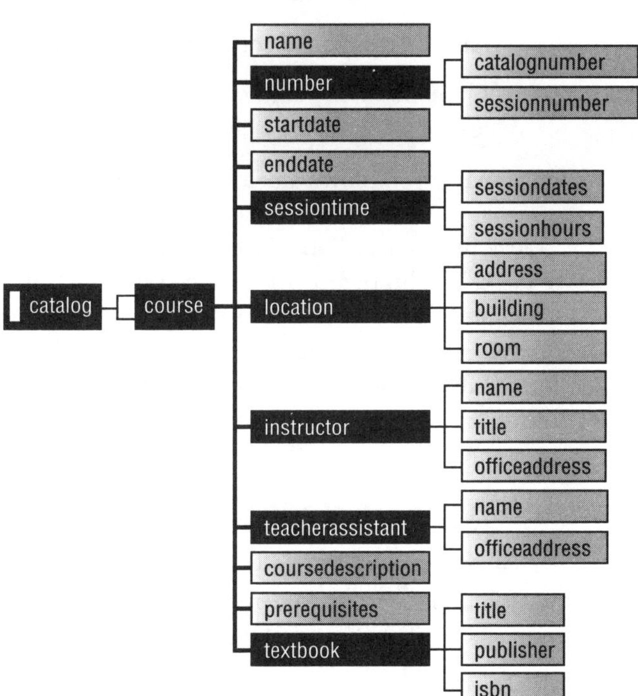

TABLE 8.2: Major Objects and Their Related Objects

Object	Related Objects
course	name, start, length, instructor, ta, taname, description
textbook	title, author, isbn, publisher

Using either the tree diagram or table method of visualizing the data, it's clear that course and textbook are primary objects that are described by several other data objects. That property is important when determining how to express the *content model* for each element in the DTD.

The content model is part of the element declaration and defines what kind of content may be found within an element. Note that this doesn't mean what kind of attributes an element might have, but instead what kind of content may appear between the element's tag set. Should it be just character data? Can it also include other elements?

XML describes four different types of content:

Empty No content is allowed.

Any Any type of content is permitted.

Element Only content that consists of other elements is permitted. No text-based data may be included.

Mixed Allows an element to contain both data and element content.

Once these characteristics have been determined, you can begin to write the actual DTD. But before you begin assigning data objects to element or attribute status, let's review the syntax used in making these declarations. In Chapter 3: "Creating XML Documents," you were introduced to Extended Backus-Naur Form (EBNF), the syntax used to produce DTD. You'll learn more EBNF throughout the rest of this section.

Element Type Declarations

Each element in a DTD must be declared. XML grammar has very specific syntax rules. The element declaration must begin with the string `<!ELEMENT`, which, of course, identifies it as an element declaration.

TIP

Note the consistency in starting syntax with the doctype declaration: both begin with the <! characters and a string that states the declaration's purpose.

Next, the element is given a *generic identifier*, more commonly referred to as the element name. The last piece of information included in the declaration is the *content specification*, where a list of allowed elements, attributes, or content model information is provided.

Putting these pieces together, if you wanted to create an element named "fruit" that had an empty content model, the element declaration would be written as:

```
<!ELEMENT fruit EMPTY>
```

In the same manner, the any content model, though rarely used, would be written as:

```
<!ELEMENT fruit ANY>
```

When you move into element and mixed content models and optional and repeating elements, the declaration becomes a bit more complicated, as explained in the next few sections.

Element Content Model

The simplest example of an element content model is an element that must contain one and only one element of a given name. If apples were the only occurrence of fruit possible, then the element declaration for fruit would be:

```
<!ELEMENT fruit (apples)>
```

The parentheses indicate the generic identifier within them is a contained element. More than one element may be declared by using a comma-delimited list such as:

```
<!ELEMENT fruit (apples, oranges)>
```

This comma-delimited list is known as a *sequence*. In a sequence, each subelement is required to be present when the element declared is used. Therefore, in this example, when fruit appears in a document, both apples and oranges must appear within the element `fruit`.

If a document author is allowed a choice of subelements, rather than being required to use all possible subelements, the list is delimited with the vertical bar character |, as seen here:

```
<!ELEMENT fruit (apples | oranges)>
```

The two options can even be combined, using nested sets of parentheses. The declaration:

```
<!ELEMENT sundae (icecream, whippedcream, nuts (fudge | caramel))>
```

describes the basic structure of an ice cream sundae: it has ice cream, whipped cream, and nuts, with a choice of fudge or caramel toppings.

Optional and Repeating Elements

So far, our element declarations have dealt with subelements that must occur; that is, none have been optional (although you had the choice of fudge or caramel in the previous example, you did not have the choice of having neither), nor have they explicitly been able to occur more than once. In order to indicate a subelement's optional or recurring status, you need to add an *occurrence indicator* to the element declaration. Occurrence indicators are single character symbols that appear immediately after the generic identifier name or sequence of names. For instance, if you chose to make the nuts in the ice cream sundae optional, you would write:

```
<!ELEMENT sundae (icecream, whippedcream, nuts? (fudge | caramel))>
```

The ? symbol in this declaration indicates that the subelement is optional and may occur zero times or once within the parent element.

This indicator, along with the two other occurrence indicators that are available, is shown in Table 8.3.

TABLE 8.3: Symbols Used as Occurrence Indicators

Indicator	Represents...
?	Optional (zero or one occurrences)
*	Optional and repeatable (zero or more occurrences)
+	Required and repeatable (one or more occurrences)

Optional and repeatable means that a subelement doesn't have to occur, but if it does, it can do so more than once. An example might be:

```
<!ELEMENT pizza (vegetables*, pepperoni)>
```

This means that pepperoni will always be present and zero or more vegetables may be. So you could have just a pepperoni pizza; one with pepperoni and onions; or one with pepperoni, onions, green peppers, and jalapenos.

Required and repeatable means that the subelement will appear at least once and maybe more. To show an option for extra cheese on your pizza, you could declare:

```
<!ELEMENT pizza (cheese+, pepperoni, vegetables*)>
```

Occurrence indicators can also apply to sequences and choices. If vegetables were listed individually, you might say:

```
<!ELEMENT pizza (cheese+, pepperoni, (onions | peppers | jalapenos |
tomatoes)*)>
```

This declares that the pizza will consist of one or more instances of cheese, plus pepperoni and zero or more choices of the listed vegetables.

Mixed Content Models

A mixed content model, as its name implies, provides a mix of character data (terminal content) or subelements that are allowable inside the current element, or a combination of both.

The paragraph element in HTML has a mixed content model. It can contain text (character data) as well as other elements, such as an emphasis element and its contents:

```
<P>The content of this paragraph is of a <em>mixed content model</em>
because it contains both character data and subelements</P>
```

Element Attributes

Attributes allow document authors to provide additional information about an element. It may be information that will impact the rendering of the element, such as establishing an alignment in a paragraph with the align attribute:

```
<P align="center">This text should be centered by the parser</P>
```

On the other hand, attributes often hold succinct bits of information that help further describe an element. If you wanted to include information about the size of the pizzas defined previously, you could do so by creating a `size` attribute.

In this section, we'll explore how to define an attribute, the type of data it can hold, and its possible values.

Attribute-List Declarations

Like elements, attributes must be declared in the DTD. Rather than being declared individually, attributes for each element are declared in an *attribute list*. The attribute-list declaration contains the opening string `<!ATTLIST`, the element's generic identifier, the attribute name, and its default value.

If you were to create a required **breed** attribute for the element **dog**, the ATTLIST declaration would look like:

```
<!ATTLIST dog breed CDATA #REQUIRED>
```

When creating a document that uses the **dog** element, you could supply any character string (CDATA) you desired as the value of the **breed** attribute, such as:

```
<dog breed="newfoundland"> or
<dog breed="lab/collie mix">
```

See the section "Attribute Types" later in this chapter for more information on CDATA.

A list of attributes may be declared at the same time. You could add color and sex to the attributes for **dog**, such as:

```
<!ATTLIST dog breed CDATA #REQUIRED
                  color CDATA #REQUIRED
                    sex CDATA #REQUIRED>
```

The `REQUIRED` keyword on each of these attributes means that each one must appear in each instance of the dog element. If you were to use:

```
<dog breed ="schnauzer" color="salt & pepper">
```

leaving out the `sex` attribute, it would not be a valid use of the **dog** element, since all three attributes are required.

Information stored in attributes often comes from a limited set of possible values. For instance, the sex attribute only has two possible values: male or female. In order to formally limit the potential values of the sex attribute using a group of choices, you could rewrite the dog attribute list as:

```
<!ATTLIST dog breed CDATA #REQUIRED
              color CDATA #REQUIRED
              sex (male | female) #REQUIRED>
```

When a limited set of values is declared, it is no longer necessary to declare that the value must be CDATA, since the only two options provided meet the definition of CDATA already.

Attribute Value Types

There are four forms of attribute types:

- String types
- Tokenized types
- Enumerated types
- Entities

String Types

A string datatype is probably the simplest form of datatype to understand: it simply means "a string of characters." In the previous section, we used the attribute type of CDATA to represent character data. CDATA is the simplest form of attribute string type and means *character data*. Character data is simply any string of characters, so "hello" can be classified as CDATA, as can "abc123."

Tokenized Types

A tokenized type refers to a group of types that the parser has normalized to reduce intermediate white space to a single character, completely discarding any leading or trailing white space.

NMTOKEN A token is a type of label. When the value of an attribute is intended to act as a name for the element instance, the NMTOKEN attribute type is used. The

NMTOKEN attribute type means *name token*. A common example of NMTOKEN is the name attribute for the anchor element in HTML:

```
<a href="foo.html" name="myanchor">
```

The strings that make up a name token are restricted. First, they must begin with a letter, so

```
<a name="1a">
```

is illegal, but

```
<a name="A1">
```

is acceptable.

The additional characters may only include letters, digits, and the punctuation characters dash (-), underscore (_), colon (:) and period (.).

Finally, name tokens may not begin with the series xml in any case variation (e.g., XML, XmL, etc.).

ID and IDREF Two other tokenized attribute types are ID and IDREF. In many situations, document authors will find it necessary to refer to a specific occurrence of an element. For instance, the popular technique in HTML-based Web pages of creating mouseover image changes using JavaScript requires that each image have a unique label that can be referred to in the script. These labels are created using an attribute of the type ID. Attribute values of type ID are considered tokenized types because they provide a distinct identity or label.

To preserve the ability to refer to one specific instance of an element, the value of all ID attributes occurring within a document must be unique.

A common usage of ID attributes in XML documents is to provide cross-referencing capabilities. This requires a pair of attributes: the ID attribute, which is applied to the target portion of the reference, and the IDREF attribute, which is found in the referring portion of the reference.

For example, an XML-based thesis document will have plenty of footnote and bibliographic references. The designer of the thesis DTD would create a footnote element and a corresponding reference element, as seen here:

```
<!ELEMENT footnote (p*)>
<!ATTLIST footnote noteid ID #IMPLIED>
<!ELEMENT reference EMPTY>
<!ATTLIST reference target IDREF #REQUIRED>
```

When used, these elements might appear as:

```
<p>This text is going to have reference to a footnote at the end of the
paragraph<reference target="A1"/>
```

Then later, when the footnotes appear, you'd find:

```
<footnote noteid="A1"><p>This is the text that makes up the
footnote</p></footnote>
```

The strings used as the `ID` attribute values are considered XML names and must conform to the same rules.

TIP

Remember that an XML name must begin with a letter, and it continues with additional letters, numbers, or the punctuation marks hyphen, underscore, colon, or periods. They may not begin with the string `xml`.

Enumerated Types

An enumerated attribute type occurs when authors may only choose from a fixed set of possible attribute values. For example, if an attribute that holds the gender of an individual were named `sex`, it would be an enumerated attribute type, as the author has only two possible values to choose from: male or female.

Entities

Entities are discussed in greater detail in the section "Establishing Entities," later in this chapter. For now, think of them as references to additional content, either as abbreviations or files and objects.

An entity can also be referred to as an *unparsed entity* or an *external unparsed entity*. Essentially, unparsed entities are objects that are left alone by the XML parser. These objects could be graphics, spreadsheets, word processor documents, HTML files, or any other type of file-based data that should not be parsed into XML.

As you might suspect, the IMG element in HTML takes an entity attribute of SRC. The ATTLIST declaration would be written as:

```
<!ATTLIST IMG SRC ENTITY #REQUIRED>
```

NOTE

Discussing entities as a datatype vs. entities as a "thing" can be somewhat confusing. What's important to understand is that designers can specify that the value of a particular attribute will be an entity (as defined elsewhere).

Setting Default Values for Attributes

Often an attribute will have a particular value that is used more than others are. This value would be a good candidate for a *default* value. You should be familiar with working with default attribute values in HTML. For instance, the form-reset button has `reset` as its default value string.

Setting a default value for an attribute allows document authors to save time when producing markup. Additionally, it gives the DTD designer a means to express the expected or traditional behavior of the attribute.

Providing the default value in the ATTLIST declaration is quite simple; it is placed immediately after the possible values as seen here:

```
<!ATTLIST LOCATION STATE "FL">
```

This statement defines the attribute `state` for the element `location`. The DTD designer has chosen to provide the default value of `"FL"` for the U.S. state of Florida, as the form it belongs to is used in a document that is geographic-specific to that region.

Normalizing Attribute Values

As you begin to work with attributes and potential values, you may soon realize that the strings used for attribute values can be written in many ways and still have the same semantic meaning. That is, "Small", "SMALL", "SMall", "smaLL", etc., all represent the word *small*. In addition to the issue of letter case, the string may have variations in white space, such as " small " and "small ".

To avoid these pitfalls, the XML Working Group built *attribute normalization* into the XML Recommendation. An attribute is considered normalized when these four conditions are met:

- Any embedded character entity references have been resolved into the characters they represent.

- General entity references are fully resolved.
- Carriage return/line-feed characters are replaced with spaces.
- Leading, trailing, and multiple contiguous white-space characters are condensed to a single space.

Consider the following markup:

```
<couple names=" Dave
&amp; Ann  ">
```

NOTE

An element this short wouldn't normally be written in such an awkward manner, but, with particularly long elements or attribute values, an author may continue the element on a new line for ease of reading in the editor.

The XML parser begins by finding the entire attribute value by locating the pair of enclosing quote characters. Next, the character entity reference `&` is resolved to the ampersand character &. You're then left with:

```
" Dave
& Ann  "
```

The next step is replacing the carriage return/line-feed character(s) into a single space, changing the string to:

```
" Dave & Ann  "
```

Finally, the leading and trailing white-space characters are removed, resulting in the normalized attribute value of:

```
"Dave & Ann"
```

Establishing Entities

In the simplest of terms, an entity is a storage container like a virtual box or Tupperware container. It can hold anything from an expanded definition of an abbreviation to large segments of XML markup that might be used repeatedly in different places in large documents. The different types of entities are:

- General entities

- SYSTEM and PUBLIC identifiers
- External entities
- Unparsed entities
- Parameter entities

General Entities

Entities are declared in the DTD much in the same way that elements are. A general entity declaration for an abbreviation might look like:

```
<!ENTITY tv "television">
```

The entity declaration is opened and the entity name is given, followed by the expanded definition for the entity.

The abbreviation example here is what's known as a *parsed entity*. This means that when the XML parser processes the document, it parses the entity by replacing the entity name with the previously referenced value. For instance, the copyright symbol © is an entity. Its unparsed state is `©`. If you were to declare a fixed value for an attribute that was to use the copyright symbol, you'd use © rather than the parsed version © that is in the attribute list definition.

System and Public Identifiers

Identifiers for information found external to a document come in two distinct types: system and public. System identifiers refer to information based on a URI. You might think of it as which system the resource is located on.

A system identifier uses the SYSTEM keyword in the entity declaration. For example:

```
<!ENTITY myinfo SYSTEM "http://www.my.com/info.xml">
```

Declares the entity `myinfo` and indicates that it may be located at the URI provided.

Public identifiers, on the other hand, use a widely agreed upon name to represent the information. They are used frequently in DOCTYPE declarations. One you may be familiar with from HTML is:

```
<!DOCTYPE HTML PUBLIC "-//W3C//DTD HTML 4.0 Transitional//EN">
```

The quoted string is the agreed upon name for the World Wide Web Consortium's HTML 4 Transitional Recommendation. Since public identifiers are by definition widely agreed upon and well-known, the system running the processing software will generally have the entity installed along with it or will know from where to download it. To guard against a system not knowing where to retrieve information for a public identifier, authors will often include the default URI, such as:

```
<!DOCTYPE HTML PUBLIC "-//W3C//DTD HTML 4.0 Transitional//EN"
 "http://www.w3.org/TR/REC-html40/loose.dtd">
```

TIP

Adding the URL to the declaration isn't required, but it is considered good practice.

External Entities

An external entity is one where the defined contents are found outside of the current document. For instance, a company that publishes hundreds of individual documents online may have the same copyright statement that needs to be included in each document. Rather than defining the copyright statement entity in each document, an external entity can be referenced to pull in the data from elsewhere on the system.

TIP

External entities work on the same premise as server-side includes found in many large HTML-based Web sites.

The external entity is formatted as:

```
<!ENTITY copyright SYSTEM "http://www.foo.com/copyright.xml">
```

The copyright entity would then be used in the document in the following manner:

```
<ARTICLE>
…article content…
&copyright;
</ARTICLE>
```

When the XML processor parses the document, it recognizes the copyright entity as it was previously defined in the DTD. The processor then retrieves the replacement text from the specified URL and places it where `©right;` appears in the source document.

Unparsed Entities

Not every bit of data an author includes in a document should be parsed by the XML processor. For instance, images are not files that will be parsed. Instead, they're passed on as is by the parser and placed in a specified location within the document, for example:

```
<!ENTITY image SYSTEM "http://www.foo.com/pix.gif" NDATA GIF>
```

Two new items are found in this declaration, `NDATA` and `GIF`. NDATA declares that the entity is unparsed data. GIF, of course, represents the file type that will be found.

Parameter Entities

Up until now, we've focused on entities that are used in the document space. XML provides for another type of entity, a *parameter* entity, which is used only within the DTD itself. Just as you use general entities to import data into the document, you use parameter entities to import content into the DTD.

Syntactically, parameter entities are very similar to general entities. What sets them apart is the inclusion of the % character between the opening entity declaration string `<!ENTITY` and the entity name. As with a simple general entity, parameter entities are most often used as DTD shorthand, relieving the DTD designer from typing in attribute lists or other common elements repeatedly.

For example, the XHTML 1.0 Transitional DTD makes considerable use of parameter entities. The entity `TextAlign` is created to hold the string describing potential alignment values of left, center, and right:

```
<!ENTITY % TextAlign "align (left | center | right) #IMPLIED">
```

Later in the DTD when an element can take the align attribute, instead of writing out `"align (left | center | right) #IMPLIED"` each time, the DTD designer only needs to use `%TextAlign;`, and the previously defined information is replaced when the XML processor reads the DTD. This can be seen in the element declaration for the paragraph element, where the `%TextAlign;` parameter entity is used along with several others:

```
<!ELEMENT p %Inline;>
<!ATTLIST p
     %attrs;
     %TextAlign;
>
```

Parameter entities don't always have to be local. Consider, for example, the content of a large corporate intranet. The human resources division has specific needs for their documents, while the help desk has their own requirements. Yet each department is also required to maintain an overall corporate standard for the elements and attributes that make up copyright statements, revision tracking information, and other details that must be present in each document on the system.

Rather than each DTD used on the intranet having to rewrite the element, attribute, and entity declarations used in those common segments, the information systems division can create a standard DTD segment that can be incorporated into additional DTD using an external parameter entity.

The DTD fragment would be created as an independent object, such as the basic sample in Listing 8.1.

LISTING 8.1 standard.ent

```
<!ENTITY tracking (#PCDATA)>
<!ATTLIST tracking
…attribute list content…
>
<!ENTITY copyright (#PCDATA)>
<!ATTLIST copyright
…attribute list content…
>
```

The individual DTD designer then needs only to declare the external parameter entity by making reference to the URI for the file `standard.ent`:

```
<!ENTITY % standard SYTEM "http://www.company.com/standard.ent">
```

Then simply they would use the entity reference

```
%standard;
```

when they want that segment dropped into the DTD.

Putting It All Together

Now that you've learned how elements, attributes, and entities are written in DTD, it's time to refer back to Figure 8.1, the tree diagram built at the beginning of this chapter of the course catalog document.

The diagram shows the root element of `catalog` and one major element, `course`. The task at hand is to determine which items in the branches of this diagram will become elements in the DTD and which should become attributes of the `course` element.

Categorize Your Content

One of the easiest ways to pick out which pieces of information should become elements rather than attributes is to look at how much data is going to be present. A good candidate for an attribute is a short string such as dates, numbers, single words, or very short phrases. If there is the potential for sentences or even paragraphs, then that data is best categorized as content for the element.

Looking at the first level of objects in the tree diagram, two should catch your eye as potential containers for larger amounts of data: `course-description` and `prerequisites`. For the moment, consider these elements and start building a new tree diagram (see Figure 8.2).

FIGURE 8.2:

Two elements added to the new tree diagram

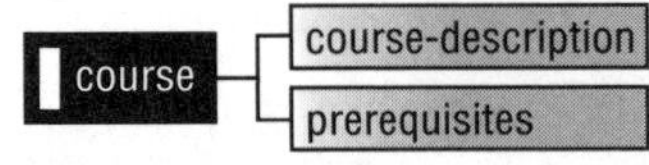

The next category of content is those pieces of data that have potential subelements or attributes of their own. These candidates are identifiable as the objects that continue to have branches below them in the tree diagram, such as `number`, which has `catalog-number` and `session-number` branching off it. In this group you'll find number, session-time, location, instructor, teacher-assistant, and textbook.

Just because these objects have subobjects doesn't automatically make them ideal candidates for being elements. You may find that while the data is related, the whole branch of information is better suited to individual attributes on the element further up the diagram. For now, set this group aside.

Finally, there are three remaining objects: name, start-date, and end-date. Each of these objects will contain short text strings and are good candidates for attributes to the course element.

Defining Elements

So far, you've determined that the root element catalog will have one or more occurrences of the course element. To express this in an element declaration, you'll need to use the + occurrence indicator to represent one or more possible instances of the course element. Begin building the DTD with the catalog element declaration:

```
<?xml version="1.0" encoding="ISO=8859-1"?>
<!DOCTYPE catalog [
<!ELEMENT catalog (course+)>
```

Next, you've determined that course-description and prerequisites should be subelements of course. Logically, each course will need a description, so that element will have an occurrence indicator of "one."

What isn't yet apparent is whether you should require that each course have information about prerequisites. Will it be understood that there are no prerequisites if the information is not present, or should that information always be present, even if it has the content of none? For the purposes of the sample DTD, you should require the element. Therefore, the element declaration for course will look like this:

```
<!ELEMENT course (course-description , prerequisites*)>
<!ELEMENT course-description (#PCDATA)>
<!ELEMENT prerequisites (#PCDATA)>
```

The prerequisites element has an occurrence indicator of one or more (*) because advanced courses may have several criteria for successful participation.

NOTE

The elements are declared as having the #PCDATA content model, as you only want them to include text data. Designing a DTD means that you require the document author to remember both what elements and attributes are optional and which elements or attributes must always be included. Balancing these two aspects of authoring can be difficult and may require tweaking the DTD after it has been tested by the end user.

Now it's time to look again at the group of data objects that had their own subobjects: `number`, `session-time`, `location`, `instructor`, `teacher-assistant`, and `textbook`. Each object must be evaluated for suitability as an element or set of attributes.

The Number Element

The `number` object had two children in the original tree diagram: `catalog-number` and `session-number`. The catalog number is the course's primary identification number, such as English 101. The session number indicates the specific instance of the English 101 course: perhaps Spring 2000 semester, session 1. The information may be stored in a more concise way, such as E101 for the course number, with a suffix identifying the session: E101.4. Using that method of identification, just a single `number` element or attribute might be appropriate. The design of the DTD can be greatly impacted by the form of existing data.

How information is to be used can also impact the decisions made when designing a DTD. A school may have a general course catalog that describes the full line of course offerings, but they may not list specific class sessions, instead presenting that information in a separate course schedule document. To accommodate both uses, you could create the `number` element as having two attributes: `catalog-number`, which is required, and `session-number`, which is optional. Since both the catalog number and session number are small strings of identifying information, they're perfect candidates for attributes.

Since you're only working with the element declarations right now, you can simply remember that thought process for when you are ready to assign attributes to the elements. For now, the `number` element declaration becomes an empty element:

```
<!ELEMENT number   EMPTY >
```

The `course` element will now need to be updated since you've chosen to make `number` a subelement:

```
<!ELEMENT course (number , course-description , prerequisites*)>
```

The Session Time Element

The session time information is similar in scope to the session number information, in that this information would appear in a course schedule document but not the general catalog document.

The decision here, then, is whether to create a `session-time` element with two attributes (`session-dates` and `session-hours`), or to simply create two attributes to the course element that cover both details. Since the occurrence of both pieces of information is based on usage, we'll turn this information into attributes of `course` and implement them in the DTD shortly.

The Location Element

Where a class is held may vary with each specific class session. Therefore, this shouldn't be a required element of `course`, since the general course catalog doesn't address session specific information. The subobjects do contain a lot of information, however, so it's probably best to classify `location` as a subelement of `course` with a zero-or-one occurrence indicator. The `course` element then becomes:

```
<!ELEMENT course (number , course-description , prerequisites+ , location?)>
```

The location element now has three data objects that will be either subelements or attributes: `address`, `building`, and `room`. The items `building` and `room` are definitely short strings appropriate for attributes, but `address` can be a bit more cumbersome to format in that manner. The best solution may be to create a subelement of `address`, allowing free-form entry of the data and retaining `building` and `room` as attributes. Doing so would create a location element declaration of:

```
<!ELEMENT location (address)>
```

The Instructor Element

The `instructor` data object also has three subobjects: `name`, `title`, and `office-address`. These objects are similar to that of location, with `office-address` requiring a fairly loose manner of entering data. Use the same structure here by creating an instructor subelement to course that will have attributes of `name` and `title` and a subelement of `office-address`. The instructor element appears as:

```
<!ELEMENT instructor (office-address)>
```

The course element is updated as:

```
<!ELEMENT course (number , course-description , prerequisites+ , loca-
tion?, instructor+)>
```

TIP

The `instructor` element has an occurrence indicator of one or many (+) since it is possible to have a course that is taught by a team of instructors rather than a single individual. The + indicator provides for that possibility.

The Teacher-Assistant Element

The `teacher-assistant` object follows the same model as `location` and `instructor`, though it only has two data objects to deal with. The `office-address` object will become a subelement, and `name` will be an attribute:

```
<!ELEMENT teacher-assistant (office-address)>
```

Courses may also have more than one TA (or none at all), so the course element declaration is updated as:

```
<!ELEMENT course (number , course-description , prerequisites+ , location?
, instructor+ , teacher-assistant*)>
```

The Textbook Element

The last data object to evaluate is the `textbook` object. It has three subobjects: `title`, `publisher`, and `isbn`. Each of those objects may be expressed as short strings of data and are good candidates for attributes. Create an empty textbook element to hold them:

```
<!ELEMENT textbook EMPTY>
```

The final update to the course element is:

```
<!ELEMENT course (number , course-description , prerequisites+ , location?
, instructor+ , teacher-assistant* , textbook+)>
```

Again, the textbook element is shown with an occurrence indicator of one or more, since a course may use multiple textbooks.

Address Subelements

Three subelements of `course` will also have subelements of their own: `location`, `instructor`, and `teacher-assistant`. You'll need to create the element declaration for each of those.

```
<!ELEMENT address (#PCDATA)>
<!ELEMENT office-address (#PCDATA)>
```

To summarize, the new DTD now has the following declarations:

```
<!ELEMENT catalog (course+)>
<!ELEMENT course (number , course-description , prerequisites+ , loca-
tion? , instructor+ , teacher-assistant* , textbook+)>
<!ELEMENT number EMPTY>
<!ELEMENT course-description (#PCDATA)>
<!ELEMENT prerequisities (#PCDATA)>
<!ELEMENT location (address)>
<!ELEMENT instructor (office-address)>
<!ELEMENT teacher-assistant (office-address)>
<!ELEMENT textbook EMPTY>
<!ELEMENT address (#PCDATA)>
<!ELEMENT office-address (#PCDATA)>
```

The corresponding tree diagram appears in Figure 8.3. Next, you'll begin working on the attribute list declarations for each element.

FIGURE 8.3:

A tree diagram of the elements in your DTD

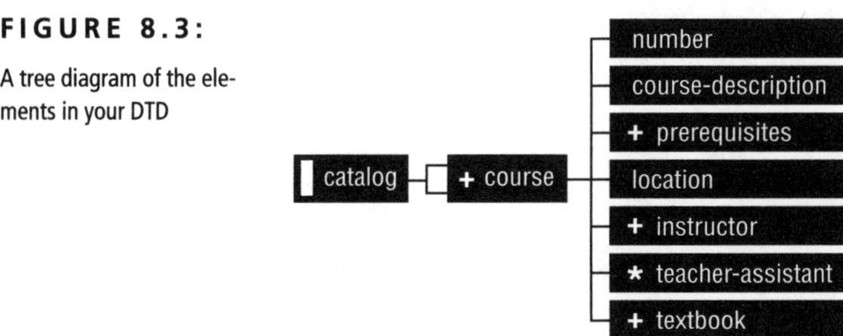

Creating Attribute Lists

When you categorized the data to be included in your course document, you set aside three data objects as candidates for attributes on the course element: `name`, `start-date`, and `end-date`.

The first object, `name`, will be necessary when describing the course both in a general catalog and in a course schedule. Therefore, it should be a required attribute of the course element. `Start-date` and `end-date` only apply to scheduling documents, making them optional. The `#IMPLIED` keyword will be used in the attribute list to denote this.

Based on this data, the attribute list declaration for the **course** element would be written as follows:

```
<!ATTLIST course name CDATA #REQUIRED
        start-date CDATA #IMPLIED
          end-date CDATA #IMPLIED>
```

This declaration is placed immediately after the course element declaration in your DTD:

```
<!ELEMENT catalog (course+)>
<!ELEMENT course (number , course-description , prerequisites+ , loca-
tion? , instructor+ , teacher-assistant* , textbook+)>
<!ATTLIST course name CDATA #REQUIRED
        start-date CDATA #IMPLIED
          end-date CDATA #IMPLIED>
<!ELEMENT number EMPTY>
<!ELEMENT course-description (#PCDATA)>
<!ELEMENT prerequisities (#PCDATA)>
<!ELEMENT location (address)>
<!ELEMENT instructor (office-address)>
<!ELEMENT teacher-assistant (office-address)>
<!ELEMENT textbook EMPTY>
<!ELEMENT address (#PCDATA)>
<!ELEMENT office-address (#PCDATA)>
```

Additional attribute lists are created in the same manner: information that has previously been noted as optional will take an #IMPLIED attribute. Required information should be so noted. So far, you have not defined any specific value options for any of your attributes, so each will take the CDATA attribute type.

The resulting DTD is shown in Listing 8.2.

LISTING 8.2 **catalog.dtd**

```
<?xml version="1.0" encoding="ISO=8859-1"?>
<!DOCTYPE catalog [
<!ELEMENT catalog (course+)>
<!ELEMENT course (number, course-description , prerequisites+ , loca-
tion? , instructor+ , teacher-assistant* , textbook+)>
<!ATTLIST course name CDATA #REQUIRED
              start-date CDATA #IMPLIED
             end-date CDATA #IMPLIED>
```

```
<!ELEMENT number EMPTY>
<!ATTLIST number
catalog-number CDATA #REQUIRED
session-number CDATA #IMPLIED>
<!ELEMENT course-description (#PCDATA)>
<!ELEMENT prerequisities (#PCDATA)>
<!ELEMENT location (address)>
     <!ATTLIST location
            building CDATA #REQUIRED
            room CDATA #REQUIRED>
<!ELEMENT instructor (office-address)>
     <!ATTLIST instructor
            name CDATA #REQUIRED
            title CDATA #REQUIRED>
<!ELEMENT teacher-assistant (office-address)>
     <!ATTLIST teacher-assistant
            name CDATA #REQUIRED>
<!ELEMENT textbook EMPTY>
     <!ATTLIST textbook
            title CDATA #REQUIRED
            publisher CDATA #REQUIRED
            isbn CDATA #REQUIRED>
<!ELEMENT address (#PCDATA)>
<!ELEMENT office-address (#PCDATA)>
]>
```

As we've purposefully kept this DTD simple, there are no entities or notations to declare. The final tree diagram is shown in Figure 8.4.

FIGURE 8.4:

The final tree diagram for catalog.dtd

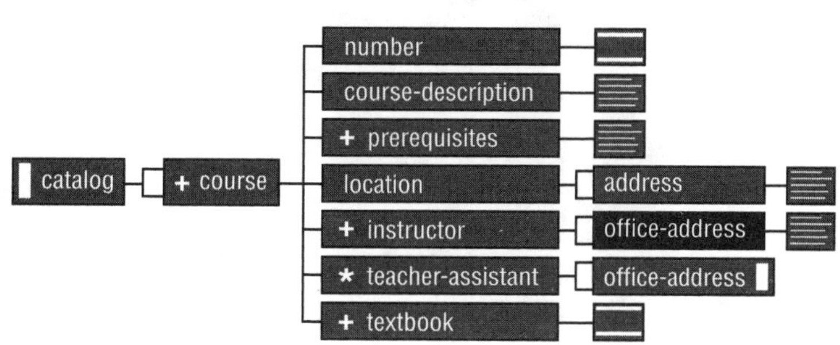

Tools for Building DTD

Writing DTDs is considered a rather difficult art form, even for the experts. To assist us mere mortals in this task, several software programs have been released. They range in complexity from simple outline aids to fully developed visual modeling tools.

Trial versions of the software packages introduced here, Visual XML and Near and Far Designer, are available on the CD for this book.

Visual XML

This Java-based application provides a full array of XML editing tools. When creating DTDs, you have the option of working in the DTD/Schema view or the source view. The DTD/Schema view incorporates a familiar folder and document style structure in one pane, with a panel of radio buttons, select boxes, and other tools that guide you through each step of the element or attribute declaration process (see Figure 8.5).

FIGURE 8.5:

The Visual XML Data/Schema design view

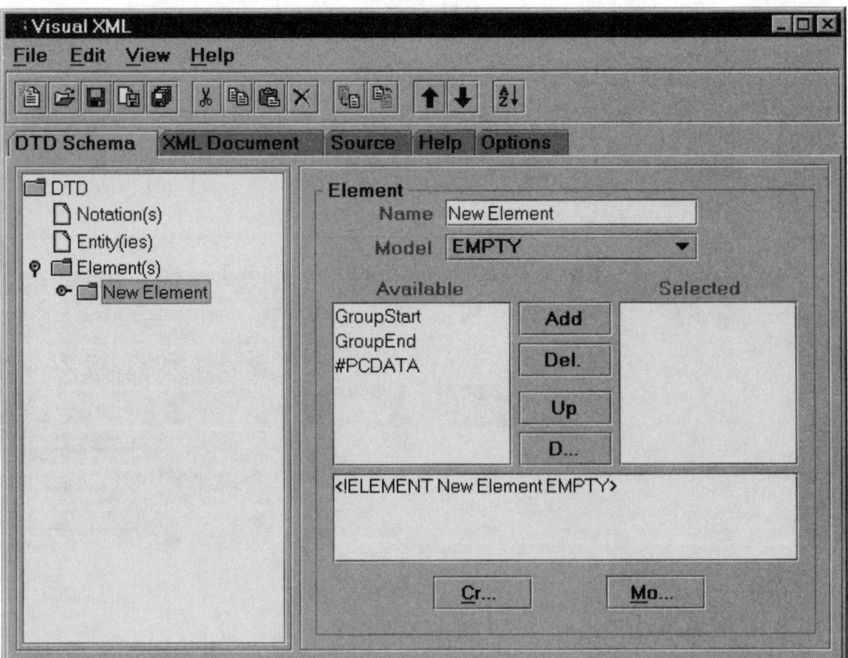

Near and Far Designer

Our personal favorite visual modeling tool is Near and Far Designer 3 from Microstar Software Ltd. As well as being available on the CD at the back of this book, you can download a demo version from the company's Web site at `http://www.microstar.com`. It comes in two versions: an XML-only version and an SGML or XML product. Unless you plan to do serious SGML authoring, the XML version should suffice.

The Near and Far Designer application window begins with a generic root element at the head of what will become a tree diagram (see Figure 8.6).

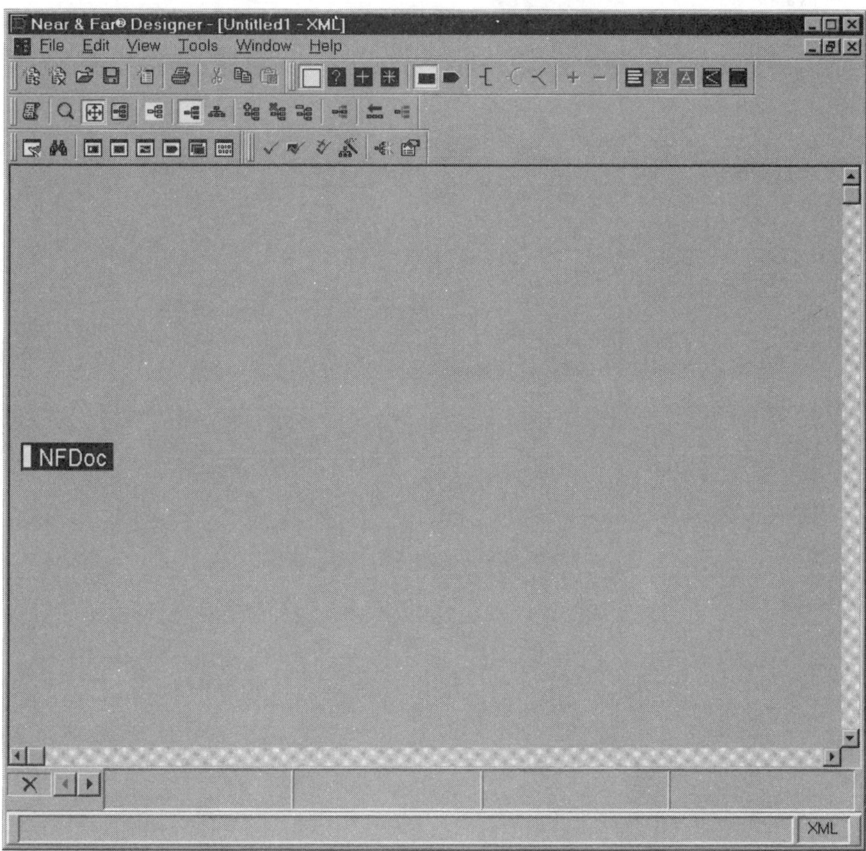

FIGURE 8.6: The Near and Far Designer application window

The tree may be oriented horizontally or vertically, and it grows as new elements are dragged and dropped into the structure, as shown in Figure 8.7.

Full details necessary to create a working DTD can be added to the element, such as attribute lists, content models, and more. The Attribute dialog, shown in Figure 8.8, guides you through the process of completing the attribute declaration providing the list of possible attribute types, default value options, and room to express groups of potential values and default value settings.

FIGURE 8.7:

The tree expands as new elements are inserted.

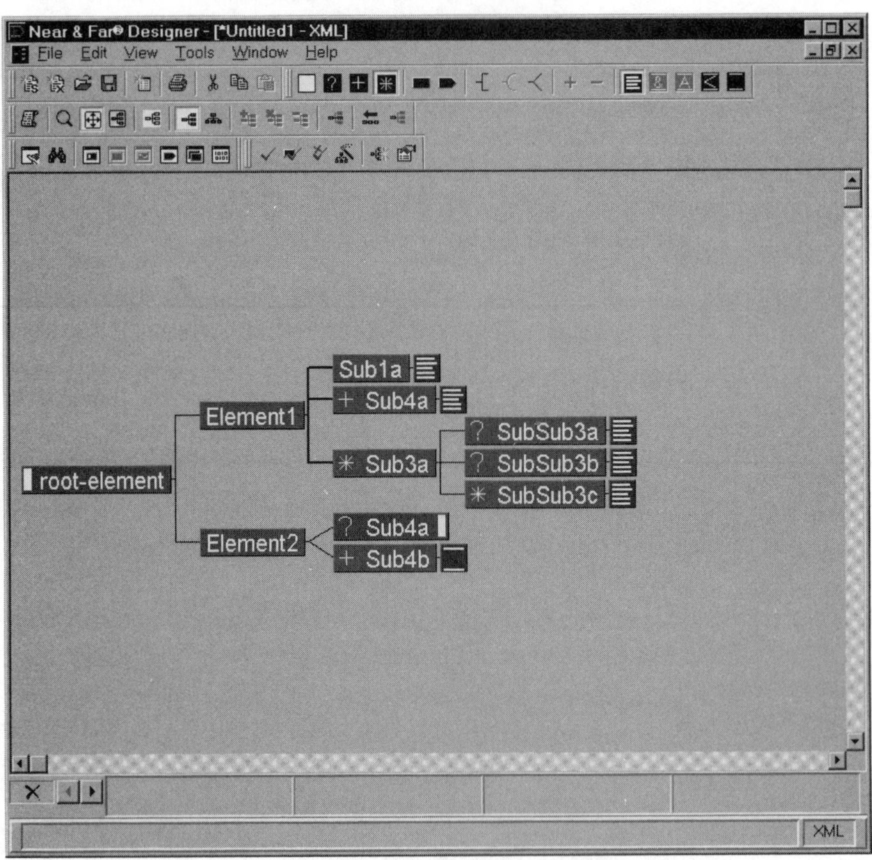

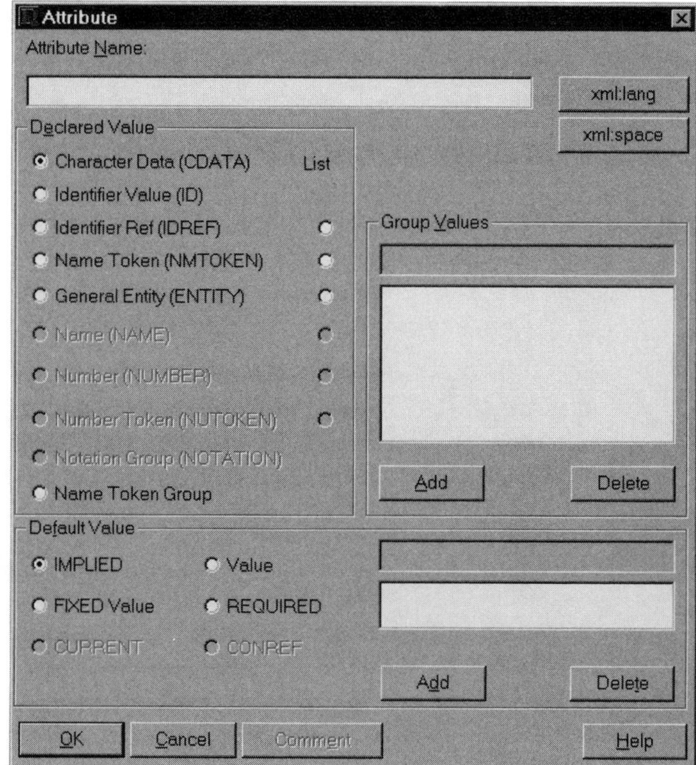

FIGURE 8.8:

Every attribute detail can be adjusted in a single dialog box.

Up Next

In this chapter, you learned the skills necessary to write your own DTD, including gathering data about the type of document the DTD is to describe and categorizing that data into potential elements and attributes. Once your data is organized, you also learned how to define elements and declare lists of attributes. You were introduced to several tools that may be used to pull all of this information together into a working DTD.

Next, you'll be introduced to another type of document description, the XML Schema. You'll learn the differences between DTD and schemas, and you'll learn how to choose which one will work best for you.

CHAPTER

NINE

9

XML Data Schemas

- What is a schema?
- How do schemas differ from DTD?
- Available datatypes
- Building a simple schema

From the early days of XML implementation, many users found that they had great freedom in creating highly structured documents, but they had trouble sufficiently limiting the content of those structures. Other existing technologies, such as database management systems and programming languages, have supplied means to constrain data, so it would certainly follow that a way could be found for XML to do the same thing. Some point out that DTDs can provide some of this functionality, but the XML community has generally accepted that they don't go far enough and their syntax is unapproachable to many. This chapter explores these issues.

What Is a Schema?

You are probably familiar with the term *schema* if you've done any work with databases. In the world of database management systems, the schema is a formal description of the database structure. It defines internal structures such as tables and fields and the relationships between those items.

Schemas are most often described as a *model* for the content of documents. The term is actually taken from the database world, where the schema describes the tables and the fields within tables that make up the data being stored.

Models and schemas are defined by their *constraints*. A constraint is a limit on what may appear in the document at any given point. There are two basic types of constraints within XML schemas: *content* constraints, which determine where and when elements may be used, and *datatype* constraints, which govern what types of data may appear in an element.

The datatype constraint can be instrumental in the success of a document. For instance, using an XML DTD, an element for `zip-code` could only realistically be constrained as PCDATA, as in:

```
<!ELEMENT zip-code #PCDATA>
```

Unfortunately, this situation sets up the possibility that:

```
<zip-code >ABC-125433-fbX</zip-code >
```

is both well-formed and valid, even though ABC-125433-fbX certainly doesn't represent a zip code in any form that we normally think of them.

The datatype constraints available in schemas can allow the schema designer to limit the content of the `zip-code` element to either a five-digit number or a nine-digit number that's broken between digits 5 and 6 by a hyphen.

Comparing Schemas with DTDs

The difference between schemas and DTDs is a point of confusion for many people working with XML, not just newcomers. While both systems provide structure for documents, they do have several key differences, as listed here:

Language DTDs are written using formal EBNF (Extended Backus-Naur Form) notation. Schemas are written in XML itself.

Data Constraints DTDs have minimal data constraints available. For example, a `<telephone>` element could be defined to contain `CDATA`, but it could not, using a DTD, be constrained to just numerals. Schemas allow more specific constraints to be placed on data.

User-Defined Types When working with DTDs, designers are limited to a fixed set of content models. Schemas provide for archetypes, which allow greater flexibility in limiting and expressing content.

While this list may look like it favors schemas over DTDs, we don't necessarily feel that schemas are better. Which method you use to define your document structure is a personal choice that you will base mostly on the type of data you will be working with and partly on preference. These issues will be explored in greater detail throughout this chapter.

Working with Datatypes

The content models available to XML DTD authors provide some measure of control over what can appear in any given element. Attributes can be further constrained by the use of enumerated values. However, when it's impractical to provide the author with every potential value choice, even the most restrictive attribute type can only be limited to strings of letters, digits, and a minimal set of punctuation characters.

In many cases, the value of attributes or the terminal content of elements should be even further constrained. For instance, an element for a date is often found in memo documents. In XML, there is no way to constrain the content of that element to a specific date format. Therefore, a validating parser could only check for content, not for content that consists of an actual date.

In other fields of computing, such as programming languages or database operations, there is the ability to constrain data to basic units known as *datatypes*. The XML Schema Working Group's requirements document (found at `http://www.w3c.org/TR/NOTE-xml-schema-reg`) identifies the following requirements that must be addressed:

1. Provide for primitive datatyping, including byte, date, integer, sequence, SQL and Java primitive datatypes, etc.
2. Define a type system that is adequate for import/export from database systems (e.g., relational, object, OLAP).
3. Distinguish requirements relating to lexical data representation vs. those governing an underlying information set.
4. Allow creation of user-defined datatypes, such as datatypes that are derived from existing datatypes and which may constrain certain of its properties (e.g. range, precision, length, or mask).

We'll look at each of these requirements in more detail throughout the rest of this chapter.

The Value Space

Before we can begin defining different datatypes, we need to review the definition of datatype as it pertains to the XML Schema: Datatypes Working Draft. The Datatypes Working Draft defines datatype as follows:

> *A datatype has a set of distinct values, called its value space, and is characterized by facets and/or properties of those values and by operations on or resulting in those values. Further, each datatype is characterized by a space consisting of valid lexical representations for each value in the value space.*

So, conceptually, if there were a datatype known as "English," its value space could be any word in the English language. It could be constrained by a facet that indicates the word must appear in a specific dictionary.

The term *lexical representation* refers to the appearance of the data. U.S. residents know that a zip code can be written either as a five-digit string or as five digits, a hyphen, and four more digits. In terms of a zip-code datatype, that means there are two valid lexical representations of the data.

Primitive Datatypes

The XML Schema Working Group understood that many uses for data are so generic that the datatypes are understood nearly universally. Rather than requiring each schema designer to reinvent the wheel for each of these, the Working Group chose to include 14 primitive datatypes in the specification for public use. Table 9.1 contains the full list, which will be discussed in further detail in the rest of this section.

TABLE 9.1: Datatypes Built-in to XML Schema

Built-in Datatypes	
ID	NOTATION
IDREF	string
IDREFS	boolean
ENTITY	number
ENTITIES	dateTime
NMTOKEN	binary
NMTOKENS	uri

The first eight datatypes were introduced in Chapter 8: "Creating Your Own DTD." They remain the same when working in schemas. The remaining six may be familiar to you if you've done any programming.

string A string is a group of characters. The word *string* is, in and of itself, a string of six characters. They may include any combination of UCS or Unicode characters.

boolean The mathematical representation of true or false (sometimes written as yes/no or 0/1).

number Self-explanatory. Numbers are not limited to whole numbers but may also include real numbers, rational numbers, etc.

dateTime A specific time on a given date, written as a single string, e.g., "1999-07-05 14:48:38" could be considered a dateTime string.

binary Strings of binary data. These could be graphics files, executable programs, or any other binary data.

uri A universal resource identifier.

Additional types are generated from these 14 basic built-in datatypes in the *schema for schemas* that each user-generated schema references. Each generated datatype has a *basetype* (one of the 14 built-in datatypes) from where the new type was generated. Those datatypes include:

integer As defined in mathematics, the sequence of numbers from negative infinity through positive infinity (e.g., –1, 0, 1, 2, 3, etc.). Number is the basetype for integer.

decimal Also of basetype integer, decimals may have exact fractional parts, e.g., 4.25 would be a valid decimal representation.

real Sometimes referred to as scientific notation in other programming languages. These are numbers with a significantly large number of digits after the decimal point, which are traditionally written in exponential notation, e.g., 10E6, or –2.54E5. The basetype for real is number.

time The time portion of the dateTime datatype. The default representation is written as 15:33:33 or 153333.

timePeriod A distinct period of time with a starting dateTime and an ending dateTime.

User-Generated Datatypes

A user-generated datatype takes ones of the built-in datatypes and, by adding additional constraining facets, creates a new datatype. For example, schools assign value to individual courses expressed in the number of units earned upon completion of the course. The basetype for the new units type would, of course, be number. However, just any number won't do. Units can't be a negative number. Though individual courses don't earn a student more than five units, an enrolled student may currently posses zero units when they begin their first term and may hold several hundred units of credit when they are nearly finished with advanced degrees.

The units type will need a constraining facet that defines the minimum value of zero, and a maximum of positive infinity, since there is no practical identifiable limit to the number of units a student might earn.

Further granularity can be achieved when appropriate. For instance, the numeric marks given in competitive figure skating range from 0.0 to 6.0. A mark datatype could be described as having the basetype of decimal, with a minimum value of 0.0 and the maximum value of 6.0. Though the minimum and maximum values are expressed using tenths, the potential values in that range are not as limited.

The *precision* and *scale* of a number can impose those limits. In the skating example, the precision will always be 1, since the value is limited to being between 0 and 6. The scale is the number of decimal places acceptable. In this example, only one is allowed. Therefore the scale of our mark datatype would be the value 1.

Syntax for Building a Schema

In this section, you'll build a schema that could be used for a local XML users group. The group leadership wants to build a member directory that contains the following information about each group member:

- member number
- last name
- first name
- e-mail address
- postal address
- telephone number
- date joined
- adult or youth member

To begin, you need to start with the required formalities of every XML Schema, the preamble.

The Schema Preamble

As with XML DTDs, or any XML document for that matter, each schema instance has a set of required identifying information at the beginning of the file, known as the *preamble*. The preamble consists of the W3C Doctype for schemas:

```
<!DOCTYPE schema PUBLIC '-//W3C//DTD XML Schema Version 1.0//EN' SYSTEM
'http://www.w3.org/1999/05/06-xmlschema-1/structures.dtd'>
<schema xmlns='http://www.w3.org/1999/05/06-xmlschema-
1/structures.xsd'>
```

WARNING

The XML Schema specification is still a W3C Working Draft, meaning it's not yet finalized. As such, the URI used as the SYSTEM identifier in the DOCTYPE declaration will change as the specification moves from Working Draft to Proposed Recommendation to full Recommendation. Refer to the W3C Web site at `http://www.w3.org/` or the support Web site for this book for updates.

Logically, the first element you will declare is the larger container element that will wrap around an entire member record. The simplest declaration would be to write:

```
<elementType name="record">
     <mixed/>
</elementType>
```

This declares that there is an element type named `record` and that it has a mixed content model, meaning it can contain other elements or character data.

It should be noted that elements cannot appear within a mixed content model element type unless they are specifically declared. Therefore, the typical representation of an element type that will only contain character data is still </mixed>. The absence of other element declarations is the indication of only character data.

If you begin working down your list of proposed data, the member number is the next element to be defined. Since it is a number, its datatype will certainly either be the built-in datatype number or a generated type that has constraining facets.

In order to keep proper track of membership records, the member number needs to be a unique number for each individual. The club assigned its founder the member number "1" and gives out new numbers sequentially. This indicates that the possible values of a member number element should be whole numbers equal to or greater than 1. Looking at the generated datatypes, you can see that integer would serve this purpose well, if you constrain it to have a minimum value of 1. You need to create this datatype before we can declare the member-number element.

You first need to give the new datatype a name; in this example, it will be NumType.

```
<datatype name="NumType">
     <basetype name="integer"/>
     <minInclusive>1</minInclusive>
</datatype>
```

This states that you have created a datatype referred to as NumType, which uses integer as its basetype. It has a minimum inclusive value of 1 (meaning it must be 1 or greater).

Now you can define the member-number element type:

```
<elementType name="MemNum">
     <datatypeRef name="NumType">
</elementType>
```

This says that your new element type is named MemNum, and its possible values are determined by the datatype being referenced, specifically the NumType datatype.

The element types for the member's name are quite simple:

```
<elementType name="FirstName">
     <mixed/>
</elementType>
<elementType name="LastName">
     <mixed/>
</elementType>
```

Next, you'll need to create an archetype that will govern the data for the user's address:

```
<archetype name="address">
     <sequence>
           <elementTypeRef name="street" minOccur="1" maxOccur="1">
<elementTypeRef name="apt" minOccur="0" maxOccur="1">
     <elementTypeRef name="city" minOccur="1" maxOccur="1">
     <elementTypeRef name="state" minOccur="1" maxOccur="1">
     <elementTypeRef name="zipcode" minOccur="1"
maxOccur="1">
     </sequence>
</archetype>
```

By creating an archetype, you can reuse the sequence given for more than one element. For instance, though the club only tracks mailing addresses now, they may want to differentiate between residence, mailing, and shipping addresses later. With the address archetype in place, you only need to reference it when defining the element types for the other addresses, for example:

```
<elementType name="residence.address">
     <archetypeRef name="address">
</elementType>
```

The elements referenced inside the archetype still need to be declared, of course, and you can do that simply with the following section:

```
<elementType name="street">
     <mixed/>
</elementType>
<elementType name="apt">
     <mixed/>
</elementType>
<elementType name="city">
     <mixed/>
</elementType>
<elementType name="state">
     <mixed/>
</elementType>
<elementType name="zipcode">
     <mixed/>
</elementType>
```

The telephone number element needs to be constrained to a particular format: three digits, a hyphen, three digits, a hyphen, and four digits.

NOTE

When working with international addresses or phone numbers, changes need to be made to the default formatting. For purposes of this example, we'll assume all members are residents of the United States.

Begin by creating a `phone` datatype of basetype `string` because, although telephone numbers are certainly made up of numeric digits, they aren't numbers on which you might perform mathematical operations. The presence of hyphens in them also prohibits them from being strictly numeric presentations and makes them more appropriate as strings.

```
<datatype name="phone">
     <basetype name="string"/>
```

```
        <lexicalRepresentation>
                <lexical>999-999-9999</lexical>
        </lexicalRepresentation>
</datatype>
```

The `lexicalRepresentation` element acts as a wrapper around the potential methods of expressing the data. For simplicity's sake, your schema will require full 10-digit telephone numbers. If you had chosen to make the area code optional, you could provide two potential expressions:

```
<lexicalRepresentation>
        <lexical>999-9999</lexical>
        <lexical>999-999-9999</lexical>
</lexicalRepresentation>
```

The element type would then be declared as:

```
<elementType name="telephone">
        <datatypeRef name="phone">
</elementType>
```

Finally, the complete schema appears as follows:

```
<!DOCTYPE schema PUBLIC '-//W3C//DTD XML Schema Version 1.0//EN' SYSTEM
'http://www.w3.org/1999/05/06-xmlschema-1/structures.dtd'>
<schema xmlns='http://www.w3.org/1999/05/06-xmlschema-
1/structures.xsd'>
<elementType name="record">
        <mixed/>
</elementType>
<datatype name="NumType">
        <basetype name="integer"/>
        <minInclusive>1</minInclusive>
</datatype>
<elementType name="MemNum">
        <datatypeRef name="NumType">
</elementType>
<archetype name="address">
        <sequence>
                <elementTypeRef name="street" minOccur="1" maxOccur="1">
<elementTypeRef name="apt" minOccur="0" maxOccur="1">
                <elementTypeRef name="city" minOccur="1" maxOccur="1">
                <elementTypeRef name="state" minOccur="1" maxOccur="1">
                <elementTypeRef name="zipcode" minOccur="1"
maxOccur="1">
        </sequence>
```

```
</archetype>
<elementType name="street">
     <mixed/>
</elementType>
<elementType name="apt">
     <mixed/>
</elementType>
<elementType name="city">
     <mixed/>
</elementType>
<elementType name="state">
     <mixed/>
</elementType>
<elementType name="zipcode">
     <mixed/>
</elementType>
<datatype name="phone">
     <basetype name="string"/>
     <lexicalRepresentation>
            <lexical>999-999-9999</lexical>
     </lexicalRepresentation>
</datatype>
<elementType name="telephone">
     <datatypeRef name="phone">
</elementType>
```

Up Next

In this chapter, you learned about the limitations of DTDs in the newly robust world of XML and how schemas can help authors constrain content of elements in ways that DTDs cannot. You explored the built-in and generated datatypes available for your use, and you stepped through the process of creating your own datatypes and archetypes.

Next, you'll explore what happens when an XML document is processed by an XML parser and then displayed in an XML compatible browser.

PART IV

Putting It All Together

CHAPTER

TEN

10

Parsing and Processing XML

- The challenge of displaying XML
- Transforming XML
- Java and XML
- The basics of programming for XML
- SAX and DOM

Until this point, we've talked about what an XML document is, how it's constructed, and producing a DTD or schema to support documents, but we haven't yet touched on actually viewing them. It sounds like a simple task: you just load an XML document into an XML browser, and view it, right? Well, it's not quite that simple. This chapter will introduce you to the processes involved in parsing and displaying XML documents.

The Challenge of Displaying XML

A browser that is going to display XML documents has a significant challenge: how to interpret the *semantics*, or intended meaning and representations, of user-defined elements. Consider what happens in today's Web browsers when displaying the following HTML, as shown in Figure 10.1.

```
<h1>This is a heading</h1>
<P>This is a paragraph.
<P>This is another paragraph.
..
```

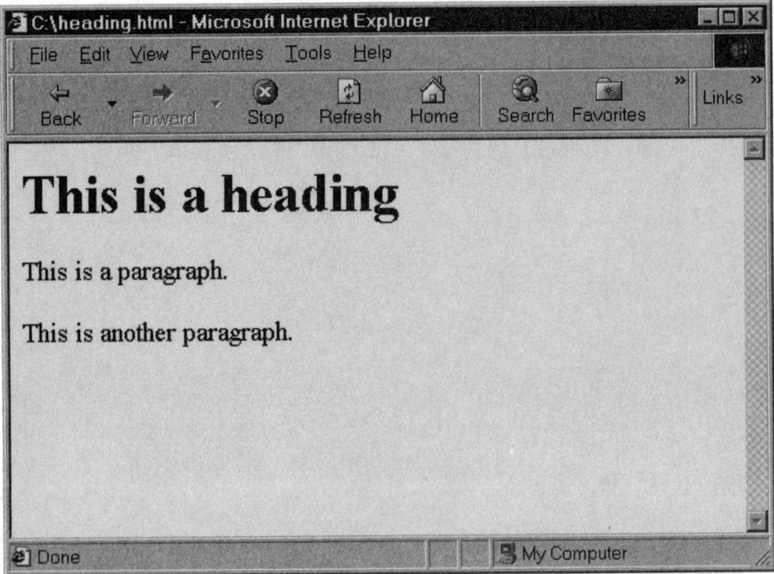

FIGURE 10.1: Standard HTML presentation of headings and paragraphs

A heading and paragraph look like a heading and paragraph based on the arcane knowledge of HTML and the intended results that were built into the Web browser when the programming team created it. The browser knows that a heading is a phrase that marks a specific section of text, and it provides a general label of the same. The contents of a paragraph are contained in a single block of text, which is separated from other paragraphs of block elements by a blank line.

However, if a browser were supplied with the following XML, it has no arcane knowledge of the meaning of these tags:

```
<heading>This is a heading</heading>
<paragraph>This is a paragraph.</paragraph>
<paragraph>This is another paragraph.</paragraph>
```

The use of descriptive names for the tags certainly enables a human to infer their meaning. The browser, on the other hand, doesn't have sufficient intelligence to extract the semantic simply by reading the word used as the element name.

For the XML document author to properly pass semantics and display information to the XML-enabled browser, a style sheet is required. In this section, we'll give a quick overview of what a style sheet is and how it's put to use with XML. See Chapter 13: "Displaying XML: Working with Cascading Style Sheets," Chapter 14: "Displaying XML: Introducing XSL," and Chapter 15: "Displaying XML: Advanced XSL" for more information on style sheets and the Extensible Style Sheet Language (XSL).

Building a Parse Tree

The first task any XML processor must perform is to read a document and construct a hierarchy of elements and content. Just how that process takes place depends on how the programmer designed the processor to work, but there are three basic models: linear, tree, and object. Working from the top down, at the top of the parse tree is the list of primary elements; the next level contains attributes, followed by content. What order these occur in depends on the model chosen.

Linear Document Processing

As its name implies, a processor using a linear document model simply reads through the file, character by character, line by line. Very specific portions of the document can be targeted by using linear descriptions, such as the fourth letter of the fifth word of the second paragraph in the first chapter.

This kind of addressing only holds up well if the document remains stable, and if you're intimately familiar with the content and placement of the content within the document. To give an example of how rare this is, even the authors of this text would be hard-pressed to tell you what the fourth letter of the fifth word of the second paragraph in the first chapter is! So, rather than using a linear model, most processors use one of the remaining two options, the tree or object model.

The Tree Model

Figure 10.2 is a tree diagram that you originally saw in Chapter 8: "Creating Your Own DTD" to help illustrate the process of building XML DTDs. When an XML processor uses the tree model for processing an XML document, the results are very similar.

FIGURE 10.2:

A tree diagram that describes an XML document

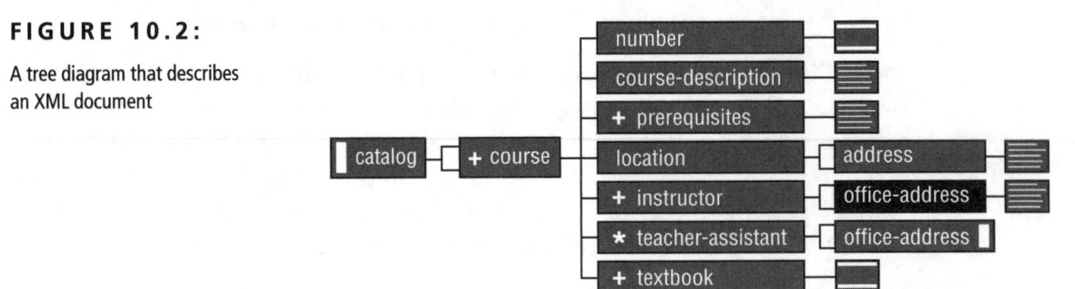

The processor starts at the root element, since it is the first one found within the document, and then follows the paths formed by each branch it encounters. In the example, the first element found is `catalog`, which is the root element. Next, the processor retrieves one of the `course` elements (assuming there is more than one). That course element is referred to as a *node* and also as a *branch* in the "tree" terminology. The processor continues to traverse the branch until it no longer has any subbranches—*twigs* or subelements—to follow and then until it finds no more *leaves*, which are the final elements on any branch or twig.

Looking at the example diagram, you can see that the processor might begin with the `number` element and determine that there are no twigs or leaves (subelements) appended to it and then backtrack up the branch until the next branch is encountered: the `course-description` element. It will continue that process until it has traversed the final branch found within `course`.

Presuming there are additional `course` elements in the document, once the processor is finished with the first course, it moves on to the second and repeats the process all over again.

TIP

Notice that both the linear and tree models of document processing look at the document as a whole, passing through it taking different paths.

The Object Model

When an XML processor uses the object model to look at a document, it's like someone opening up a traveler's suitcase. The suitcase is the container, which represents the root element of the document. When you open the suitcase, as illustrated in Figure 10.3, you will find a number of different objects such as a pair of shoes, several shirts, a skirt or two, some underclothes, and a toiletry bag.

FIGURE 10.3:

The object model is like the contents of a suitcase

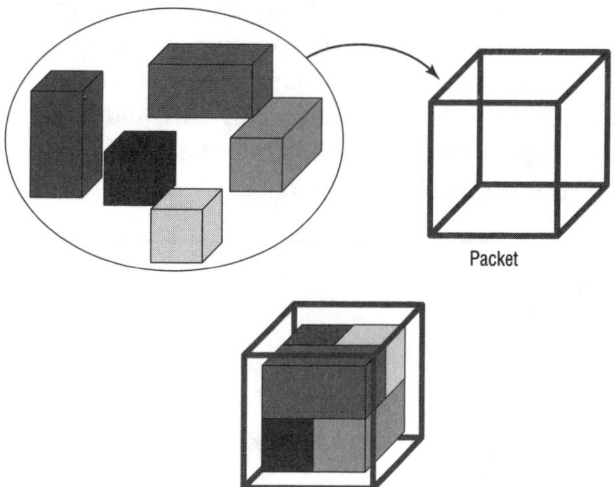

Just like a customs officer inspecting a suitcase, the XML processor will inspect each object (the elements of the document) individually, making note of their properties. This includes any descriptive information (attributes) and whether the objects contain other objects (subelements).

When an object is encountered that is also a container, that fact is noted as a property of the object. Later in processing, that container will be opened and the objects found within it will go through the same inspection the container object went through. For instance, a toiletry bag may contain a toothbrush, a tube of toothpaste, a bar of soap, a razor, and a pillbox. The processor dumps the contents of the bag onto its virtual counter and looks over each new object. It notices that the pillbox is also a container, and it will eventually empty that as well, inspecting the smaller items kept inside.

NOTE Whether the processor stops and inspects the contents of containers first, before inspecting other objects found at the same level, depends on how the processor was built. In an object model, the processor is not required to act like the tree hierarchy that uses a recursive model of inspection.

Transforming XML

XML works very well as a generic storage mechanism for data content. You don't, however, have to be constrained to displaying that content as "pure" XML. Once the XML is delivered to an application, that application may choose to transform the data from XML into another document type that better suits its internal display properties. For example, Microsoft's Internet Explorer 5 Web browser can receive content marked up in XML and then transform it into appropriate HTML display. Figure 10.4 illustrates the path an XML document might take when being transformed in this manner.

FIGURE 10.4: A possible transformation path for XML content

XML in Internet Explorer 5

Microsoft has equipped the IE5 Web browser to process XML using two methods: by creating *XML islands* or through ActiveX controls.

Creating XML islands simply means that an XML fragment or document is inserted into an HTML file. Two techniques for doing this are available, and both make use of the IE-specific <XML> tag. Version 1 of a basic XML island is shown here:

```
<html>
<body>
<xml id="hello">
     <phrase>Hello World - in XML!</phrase>
</xml>
</body>
</html>
```

WARNING Don't be surprised if you try to load this file and get a blank page. Since the island is loaded as an object and you haven't yet told IE5 how to display it, the "blank page" is actually what you *should* see!

You can add a short bit of scripting to the sample that will alert you to any error conditions found in the XML code. If one is found, the alert box will pass through the reason for the error. The HTML file is adjusted as follows:

```
<html>
<body>
<xml id="hello">
     <phrase>Hello World - in XML!</phrase>
</xml>
<script>
     thisDoc=hello;
     if(thisDoc.parseError.reason !="")
            {
            alert(thisDoc.parseError.reason)
            }
</script>
</body>
</html>
```

If you made a typo in the XML island, perhaps closing the <phrase> tag with </Phrase> instead of using all lowercase, then the alert box would appear when you attempt to load the document, as shown in Figure 10.5.

FIGURE 10.5:

Error capturing in IE5

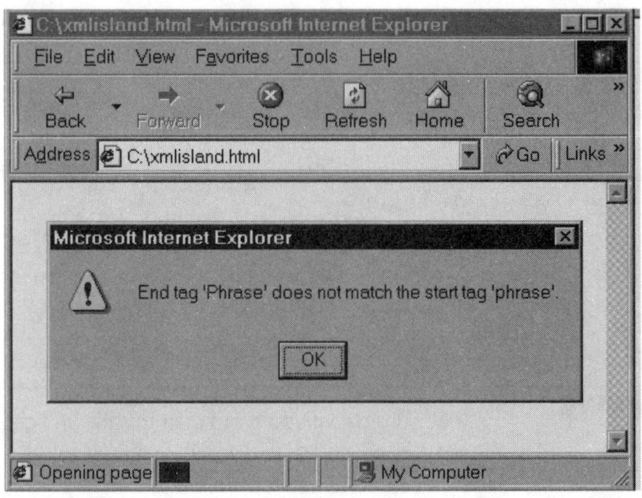

Rather than incorporating all of the XML inside the HTML document, authors can import the island using a SRC attribute on the XML element:

```
<html>
<body>
<xml id="hello" src="island.xml">
</xml>
<script>
     thisDoc=hello;
     if(thisDoc.parseError.reason !="")
             {
             alert(thisDoc.parseError.reason)
             }
     alert(thisDoc.documentElement.nodeName)
</script>
</body>
</html>
```

Figure 10.6 shows the alert box that bears the name of the node (the element included in your island).

FIGURE 10.6:

The node name appears on the alert box as a result of the script.

XML via an ActiveX Control

The HTML file used to load the XML object via an ActiveX Control makes use of a few more lines of scripting:

```
<html>
<script>
var myFile = new ActiveXObject("microsoft.XMLDOM");
myFile.load("island.xml ");

if(myFile.parseError.reason !="")
     {
     alert(myFile.parseError.reason)
     }
Alert(myFile.documentElement.nodeName)
</script>
</html>
```

Java and XML

It's often been said that Java is the natural language of XML. After all, Java is a platform-neutral programming language, and XML is a platform-neutral markup language—it seems a perfect fit!

Indeed, most of the parsers, processors, and development tools for XML available on the market today are written in Java. In this section, we'll take a look at a popular Java-based programming interface known as SAX.

The Basics of Programming for XML

XML is a terrific mechanism for storing all kinds of data. Because XML is so standard, it can be used for everything from a small program configuration file to an enterprise-wide database. But when you have to store data, you generally need to process it in some way. That's where the programming comes in. In this section, we'll introduce you to the fundamental concepts of programming for XML data.

When programmers get together, they frequently speak of Application Programming Interfaces (APIs). They compare APIs the way chefs compare spices and other ingredients, which makes sense because they serve a similar function. An API lists the kinds of procedures (functions) that are available in a function library. In the same way that a chef combines ingredients to create a dish, a developer combines functions (using procedure calls) to create a program.

NOTE

To finish the analogy: The "recipe" for the program, the underlying logic that describes how it works, is known as an *algorithm*.

Introducing SAX and DOM

With the background covered, we can launch into an explanation of the two basic APIs for programming XML: SAX and DOM. The Standard API for XML (SAX) was developed as a collaborative effort between programmers who frequent an Internet mailing list known as XML-DEV (XML developers). SAX requires the least memory and tends to run fast, so you'll frequently see it used for server-side applications. Servers tend to use the SAX API because they have to be fast and may have thousands of desktop client systems attached to them.

However, the speed of the SAX interface comes at a price. With SAX, the program sees the XML only once as it goes whizzing by. The program has to figure out what to do with the data right away, do it, and then get ready to handle the next item. That's fine for most server-side applications. On the client side, however, the situation is frequently a bit different. There, you may be sitting with your desktop computer and want to create a document that is stored in XML. As you create the document, you might go back to the top to change the title, then insert some text in the middle, then add a sentence at the end. For this kind of processing, where you need to move around the structure and make adjustments to it, a developer would use the Document Object Model (DOM).

The DOM is more memory-intensive than the SAX, because the entire document must be kept in memory at one time. But because the document is available in memory, you can move back and forth in the document and make changes to it. SAX, on the other hand, is a one-way proposition—it lets you move forward through the document, but never back.

In the remainder of this section, you'll gain more insight into how SAX and DOM APIs work. (See the sidebar "The Functionality Gap" for an interesting oversight in these specifications.)

The Functionality Gap

One interesting difference between SAX and DOM is that the SAX API lets you read an XML document but does not include any functions for writing one. DOM, on the other hand, lets you manipulate XML structures and write them but says nothing about how to read them in.

At the moment, that situation forces developers to understand both APIs if they want to both read and write XML structures. However, future versions of these APIs may well remedy the functionality gap. In the meantime, most XML libraries provide some mechanism to solve the problem. However, since this functionality is not covered by any existing standards, libraries from different vendors tend to solve the problem in different ways.

SAX

When a human reads an XML data structure, they can make sense of it right away. For a program, it's not that easy because the program only sees one character at a time. It's the job of the SAX implementation to put those characters together in the most meaningful way, breaking up the data stream into useful chunks of information that can be delivered to your program.

NOTE

Remember that SAX is an API, which is an abstract specification for the kinds of procedure calls the program can make. To actually *use* the API, you need someone's implementation of it. Implementations are available from Sun, IBM, and many other vendors.

How SAX Works The process of breaking up data into manageable chunks is known as *parsing*. When you use the SAX API, your program interacts with a SAX *parser*. Here's an example of what the SAX parser does with a simple e-mail message coded in XML:

```
<message>
     <to>
     you@yourPlace
     </to>
     <from>
     me@myPlace
     </from>
     <subject>
     First Contact
     </subject>
     <content>
     This is a message for <b>you</b>
     </content>
</message>
```

As it inspects the characters one at a time, the SAX parser might carry an on internal dialog like this:

```
"Let's see. I see a left angle bracket ("<"). OK. This must the
     beginning of a XML tag."
"Now I see an "m". It wasn't a slash, so this isn't an end tag."
"I've got "e", "s", "s", "a", "g", and "e". All parts of the tag name.
     What's next?"
"Ah. I've got a right angle bracket (">"). I recognize it now! Now I
     know it's not an empty tag. What I have here is a start tag named
     "message". I'll send that to the application."
```

The SAX parser then delivers that little package of information to the application. (The SAX API tells the programmer how to set things up so the parser can do that.) What the application sees is a series of information packages. The SAX parser operates like a scanner moving through the XML document, identifying logical chunks of information and delivering them to the application. That process is illustrated in the following series of diagrams:

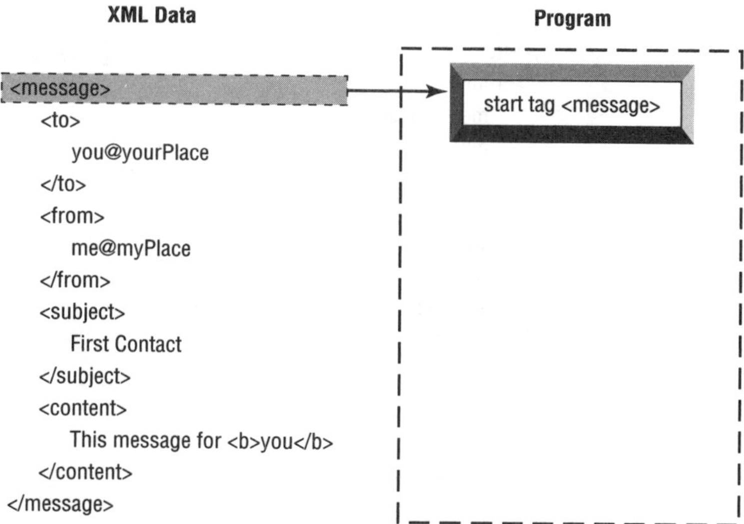

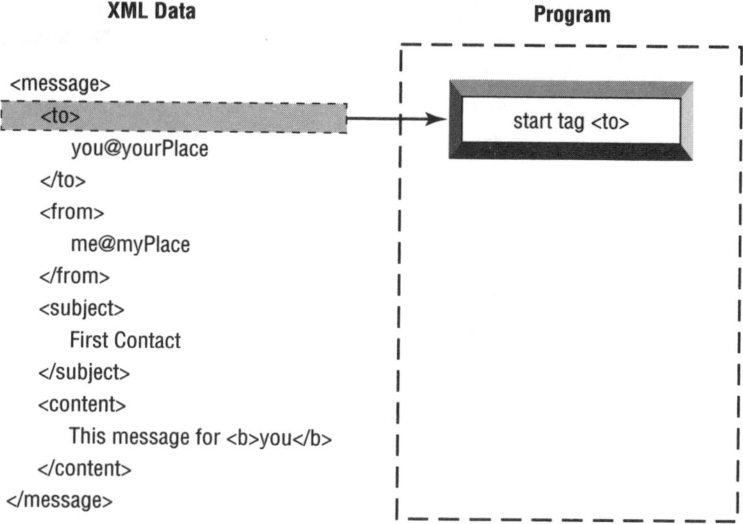

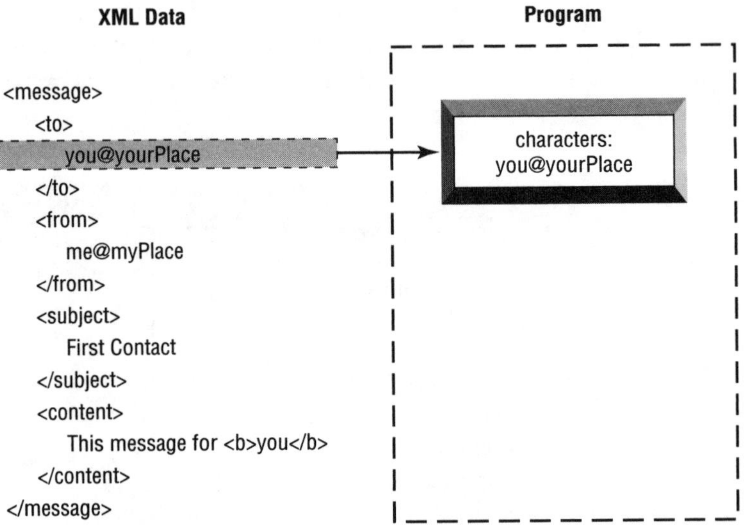

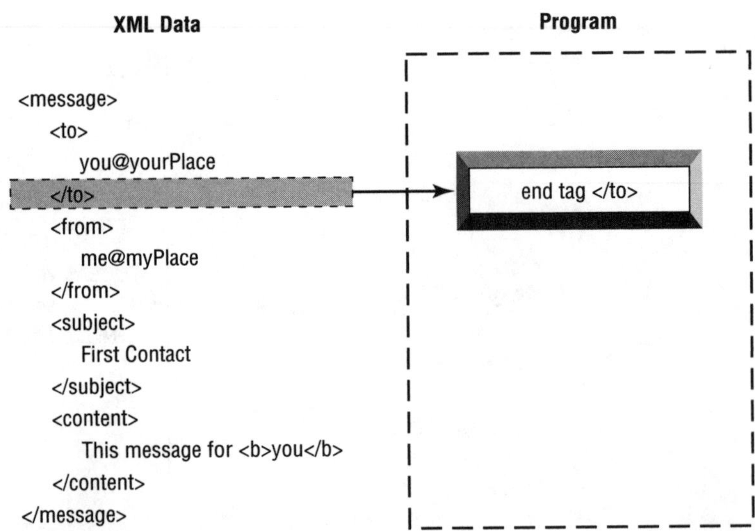

Documents and Data Before we move on to the DOM API, there are some additional aspects of the SAX example that need to be examined. Note that the `content` element contains an HTML-like tag for boldface: <b>. That's perfectly fair—because you can define any tags you want to in XML, you might as well define some of the tags you are used to from HTML.

From the way the message is written, it's clear that there is a difference between a tag like `<to>` and one like <b>. You can think of `<to>` as a structure tag that identifies a particular piece of information. The <b> tag, on the other hand, is a presentation tag that is embedded within a chunk of text.

That's great for you, but that distinction is lost on the SAX parser. What the parser sees is:

```
start tag:  <content>
characters: This is a message for
start tag:  <b>
characters: you
end tag:    </b>
characters: .
end tag:    </content>
```

You can see here that there are multiple packages of characters intermixed with the start and end tags. It is this feature that makes XML useful for documents. The difference between XML data and XML documents consists entirely of what the XML is representing. When the XML contains characters intermixed with tags, as above, they're usually called an XML document.

XML data, on the other hand, usually means the kind of structure where, once you see characters, you won't be seeing any more start tags. For example, the `<to>`, `<from>`, and `<subject>` elements of the e-mail message meet the criteria for a classic data structure. In this part of the message structure, the tags identify the data elements and the characters constitute the data. See the sidebar "Ignorable White Space" for more information on this subject.

Ignorable White Space

In reality, the spaces on the line before each tag are characters. Why doesn't the SAX parser pass them to the program, too? The answer is that it will do exactly that, unless there is a DTD for the XML structure.

In this section, we have been assuming the existence of a DTD that tells the parser something like this: "A `<message>` element contains `<to>`, `<from>`, `<subject>`, and `<content>` elements. Each of those elements, in turn, contains text, and the `<content>` element may contain some additional tags, as well."

Because the specification for the message element does not include text, the SAX parser knows that the spaces preceding the `<to>` element are insignificant. They fall under the heading of *ignorable white space* and the SAX parser ignores them.

If the DTD were not present, the spaces would be sent to the program as characters because the parser would have to assume that every character is significant.

DOM

Although there is no standard method for creating a DOM from an XML structure, most XML processing libraries include some mechanism to do so. The resulting in-memory data structure is known as a *tree*. The XML message example is shown here as a tree:

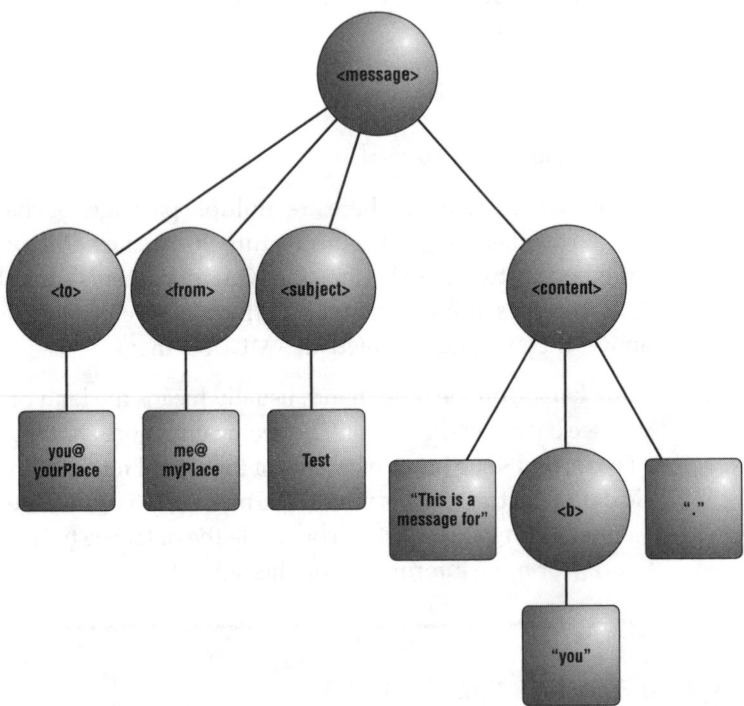

In general, a tree contains one or more *nodes*, which are arranged to make the structure. The lines in the tree show which nodes are contained and which are containers for other nodes. For example, the diagram shows that the `message` node contains the `to`, `from`, `subject`, and `content` nodes. Each of the nodes contains an `object`. For convenience, text objects are shown as rounded squares, while nodes that contain element-identifier objects are shown as circles. In reality, they are all simply nodes in the tree. Together, all of the objects form a model. Since the model describes the structure of a document, this structure is known (naturally enough) as a Document Object Model.

The tree can be created one piece at a time, or it can be created from an existing XML structure. Once the tree exists in memory, you are free to perform a variety of operations on it.

When you are editing a document at your terminal, for example, the cursor tells you where your current position is. In the same way, the DOM keeps track of your current position in the tree. The current node in the tree is the one you are visiting. To visit a different node, you traverse to it by invoking one of the positioning functions in the XML-processing library. Other functions let you create and add a new node to the tree, remove a node, move a node to a new position, or modify the contents of a node.

When you are done making changes to the tree structure, you can invoke the DOM library's print function to produce XML output. The result of printing the message tree, for example, would be very similar to the XML you saw at the beginning of this section.

The tree that is created by printing from the DOM may not be 100 percent identical to the tree that was read in. The differences, however, will be entirely cosmetic. All of the data will be preserved.

NOTE

In reality, an XML structure can contain comments and other elements of syntax that are not ordinarily reflected in the DOM, unless the developer takes special pains to do so. By default, the DOM contains just the data that is encoded in XML, not syntactical elements like comments. To print out an XML structure that contains the original syntax, the developer needs to create a DOM that includes them. This mechanism is not part of the current standard, although it may well be defined by a future standard. Until a standard is defined, the mechanism you use to create the extended tree will depend on which library you are using.

Up Next

In this chapter, you learned that XML processors may take one of three approaches to parsing a document: the linear model, the tree model, or the object model. XML may also be transformed into other outputs such as HTML, and Microsoft's Internet Explorer 5 can transform XML using either XML islands or an ActiveX Control. You explored how both SAX and DOM can be used in the interpretation and processing of XML content and you were introduced to some of the programming techniques associated with both methods.

Next, you'll begin working with XML Namespaces, the mechanism used to differentiate elements and attributes created by two different individuals or organizations in their own XML DTDs or Schemas.

CHAPTER

ELEVEN

11

Understanding Namespaces

- What is a namespace?
- How are namespaces applied to XML documents?
- Blending different namespaces in a single document
- Setting a default namespace

One of the most important requirements of successful communication is being sure that both parties are using the same common vocabulary. If you and a friend are discussing having a car sent to meet your friend at the airport, and your friend considers a "car" to mean a limousine, and you consider a "car" to mean your secretary in her Geo Metro subcompact, your friend would likely be disappointed with the results.

A namespace provides context for names that aren't particularly unique. Having a point of reference as to where an instance of a name originated allows the semantics of the name to be carried over from that world. In this chapter, you'll learn how namespaces address this issue and master the necessary skills to apply them in your XML documents.

Why Do You Need Namespaces?

The flexibility that XML brings to creating documents can also be the cause of conflicts when sharing or blending documents. Where one document has defined an element named `record` pertaining to a music collection, another may use `record` to store data about vehicle registration or an instance of a doctor-patient consultation. This conflict in an element name is sometimes referred to as a *collision* in namespaces.

The project of resolving the problem of formally managing these collisions—perhaps more aptly, *preventing* these collisions—was assigned to the newly formed XML Namespaces Working Group. The result, as you'll see throughout the rest of this chapter, is a very simple albeit abstract concept that greatly enhances the ability of programmers and the applications they create to work with multiple documents and their inherent namespaces in a seamless manner.

What Is a Namespace?

A namespace is an abstract and science-fiction–sounding label for a sphere of influence or jurisdiction. That space may be as limited as only incorporating a single instance of a document or as broad as "anything produced in the state of Florida."

The formal definition, found in the W3C Namespaces in the XML Recommendation is, "An *XML Namespace* is a collection of names, identified by a URI reference [RFC2396], which are used in XML documents as element types and attribute names."

To be a little more concrete, you could define a namespace for the Finance and Education office of the HTML Writers Guild, for example. It will be decreed that any time they discuss an "application," they're specifically referring to a Guild membership application and not a software program or a job request. When they speak or write about certificates, they're not talking about gift certificates, certificates of deposit, or some form of coupon; instead they're talking about the certificates of completion offered by the Online Education program to students who successfully complete one of our courses.

This *common vocabulary* is an important abstract collection of terms, so everyone can discuss "applications" and "certificates" without any confusion as to what those words represent.

However, when the postman comes in and asks someone to sign the certificate that accompanies the overseas letter he's about to deliver, it would be a good bet that he's not talking about Writers Guild certificates of completion. Instead, he's talking about the "certified mail" slip that proves that someone took possession of the letter.

In order to formalize an understanding of a vocabulary, it needs to be labeled as such, and have a reference point. In the next section, you'll learn how to cover both of these needs.

Namespace Notation

To begin using a namespace, you must first publicly declare it, or in more pioneering terms, stake your claim to it. XML has many instances of declarations: document type declarations, entity declarations in DTDs, etc. The namespace declaration is similar to these other XML syntaxes.

The namespace declaration occurs with an element. It can be applied to just a single element, or it can be applied to an entire document by placing the declaration within a document's root element.

Using the hypothetical office namespace, our root element might be `<office>`. The declaration takes the form of:

```
<office xmlns:hwgf="http://www.hwg.org/services/classes/">
```

The first item is the element name, `office`. Next is the namespace attribute. The `xmlns:` acts as a prefix, identifying the attribute as an XML Namespace. The letters `hwgf` comprise the name that you're giving to the namespace (`hwgf` stands for the HWG office in Florida). The attribute value is the URI reference noted in the formal definition for a namespace.

Namespace URIs: Why Is There No "There" There?

A common complaint heard about the namespaces in the XML Recommendation is that the URI used to reference a namespace doesn't necessarily contain meaningful content to help define that namespace. In other words, if you had a namespace declaration of:

```
<root xmlns:foo="http://www.foo.com">
```

the namespace URI reference that points to `http://www.foo.com` cannot be expected to hold a dictionary style list of all element types and attributes that will be used in the `foo` namespace. Instead, its *only* semantic meaning is to provide a unique and world-accessible means of identification. URIs were chosen based on their worldwide accessibility over the Internet.

The key to remembering the purpose of a namespace is to think of it only as a label. It is not required to travel to the URI given.

Now that you've defined what the namespace value represents, it's time to put one to use in a short document.

Declaring Namespaces

In Chapter 3: "Creating XML Documents," you created a very basic XML document that takes the form of a memo, as seen here:

```
<?xml version="1.0"?>
<!DOCTYPE  MEMO "http://www.foo.com/memo.dtd">
<MEMO>
<TO>Joe Cline</TO>
<CC>Kenneth Bartlett</CC>
<FROM>Ann Navarro</FROM>
<DATE>03/16/99</DATE>
<RE>The new database system</RE>
<BODY>We have just received notice from the database management team
that our new system should be in place and online no later than Monday,
```

```
August 2, 1999. I have asked the project leader to coordinate with you,
Joe, to insure that the transition from the old system takes place at
an off-peak hour, and that appropriate systems staff are on-hand to
handle any unexpected trouble. </BODY>
</MEMO>
```

To declare a namespace for the memo, just add the namespace declaration to the root element:

```
<?xml version="1.0"?>
<!DOCTYPE MEMO "http://www.foo.com/memo.dtd">
<MEMO xmlns="http://www.foo.com">
...content...
</MEMO>
```

Namespaces are *inherited*, meaning that unless additional namespace ownership is indicated, elements are a part of the namespace declared in the previous parent (or grandparent, etc.) element.

Blending Namespaces

A document can use elements from more than a single namespace. The following schedule entry blends the primary scheduling namespace of Foo Corporation and an entertainment namespace used by a local entertainment schedule publication:

```
<?xml version="1.0"?>
<!DOCTYPE SCHEDULE "http://www.foo.com/schedule.dtd">
<SCHEDULE xmlns="http://www.foo.com">
<appt type="personal">
<date date="08/02/99"/>
<time time="19:30"/>
<with person="Dave Navarro"/>
<event>
<film xmlns="http://www.e-guide-swfl.com">
<title>Star Wars Episode I: The Phantom Menace</title>
     </film>
</event>
</appt>
</SCHEDULE>
```

In this sample, the Foo Corporation namespace applies to the `schedule` element, as does `appt`, `date`, `time`, `with`, and `event`. A new namespace, for E-Guide

Southwest Florida, is declared on the `film` element. Since `title` is contained within `film`, `title` is used in the context of the e-guide namespace.

There may be times when namespaces need to be blended in a document, but the usage isn't as compartmentalized as in this simple example. To provide assistance to document authors facing this problem, the XML Namespaces Recommendation provides a solution known as *qualified names*.

Using Qualified Names to Represent Namespaces

As you might imagine, having to write `xmlns="http://www.blah.com"` as an attribute to nearly every element when working on a complex blended namespace document could be problematic. The idea of a qualified name provides authors with shorthand to represent previously declared namespaces.

One technique involves declaring multiple namespaces in the root element. Taking another look at the schedule example, that would appear as:

```
<?xml version="1.0"?>
<!DOCTYPE SCHEDULE "http://www.foo.com/schedule.dtd">
<SCHEDULE xmlns:foo="http://www.foo.com"
     xmlns:eguide="http://www.e-guide-swfl.com">
```

Notice that the two namespace declarations use a modified attribute name. Instead of just `xmlns`, the attribute now has three parts: `xmlns`, a colon, and another string of characters. The `xmlns` is known as the *prefix*, and the string after the colon represents the *local part*. When the namespace is used later in the document, the local part is used as a prefix to the element in use to identify the namespace it belongs to. To demonstrate:

```
<?xml version="1.0"?>
<!DOCTYPE SCHEDULE "http://www.foo.com/schedule.dtd">
<SCHEDULE xmlns:foo="http://www.foo.com"
          xmlns:eguide="http://www.e-guide-swfl.com">
<foo:appt type="personal">
<foo:date date="08/02/99"/>
<foo:time time="19:30"/>
<foo:with person="Dave Navarro"/>
<foo:event>
<eguide:film>
<eguide:title>Star Wars Episode I: The Phantom Menace</eguide:title>
     </eguide:film>
```

```
</foo:event>
</foo:appt>
</foo:SCHEDULE>
```

In this model, each element carries the prefix for its assigned namespace.

NOTE

Notice that the element name is actually changed from `appt` to `foo:appt` for purposes of tag creation. The closing tag must also use the namespace prefix.

This model can work well when elements from different namespaces are intermixed almost at random, but it can be nearly as cumbersome as fully declaring namespaces on elements when large or predictable sections of a document use a single namespace.

To temper the burden, the infrequently used secondary namespaces can be introduced in the elements they do the most work in, rather than in the root, requiring all elements to then be qualified. For example:

```
<?xml version="1.0"?>
<!DOCTYPE SCHEDULE "http://www.foo.com/schedule.dtd">
<SCHEDULE xmlns:foo="http://www.foo.com">
<appt type="personal">
<date date="08/02/99"/>
<time time="19:30"/>
<with person="Dave Navarro"/>
<event>
<film xmlns="http://e-guide-swfl.com">
<title>Star Wars Episode I: The Phantom Menace</title>
     </film>
</event>
</appt>
<appt type="networking">
<date date="08/04/99"/>
<time time="20:00"/>
<event>
     <fundraiser xmlns="http://www.charityinfo.com">
            <title>Black and White Ball</title>
            <benefiting>Children's Hospital</benefiting>
     </fundraiser>
</event>
</appt>
</SCHEDULE>
```

Remember that all child elements within an element that has a namespace declaration inherit that new namespace. Therefore, `title` and `benefiting` are within the namespace applied to the `fundraiser` element, whereas `title` is in the namespace applied to the `film` element.

Using Namespaces with Attributes

Elements aren't the only data objects that can belong to namespaces. Attributes from one namespace can be used in elements from a second namespace. Sound confusing? The notation helps keep things straight. Let's say you wanted to add an HTML-style attribute to the film title in the previous example. Before you can use HTML, you'd have to declare that namespace, which could be done in the root element:

```
<SCHEDULE xmlns:foo="http://www.foo.com"
xmlns:eguide="http://www.e-guide-swfl.com"
xmlns:h="http://www.w3.org/TR/REC-html40">
```

Then the style attribute is prefixed with the h-qualified name:

```
<eguide:film>
<title h:style="color : blue">Star Wars Episode I: The Phantom Men-
  ace</title>
  </eguide:film>
```

The scope of the element remains in the `eguide` namespace, but it can import the style attribute found in the html (`h`) namespace by using a qualified name for the attribute.

Namespace Scoping and Defaulting

The behavior of inheriting a namespace, which you saw in the previous section's samples, is referred to in the W3C Recommendation as *scoping*. The *scope* of a namespace is the element in which it occurs, along with any contained child elements. You might think of a scope as a "sphere of influence."

As you saw in the `event` element, which falls in the scope of the `foo` namespace, a second namespace can be declared and have its *own* scope:

```
<event>
<film xmlns:eguide="http://e-guide-swfl.com">
```

```
<title>Star Wars Episode I: The Phantom Menace</title>
     </film>
</event>
```

The `title` element, as a child of the `film` element, is within the scope of the `eguide` namespace and not the `foo` namespace of the grandparent `event` element. Once the `film` element closes, the scope reverts back to `foo`.

The idea of namespace *defaulting* may at first sound similar to scoping, but it is different in a very key manner. First, to define defaulting, a *default namespace* is the namespace that applies to the element where it is declared and any child elements contained within *that do not have prefixes of their own.*

Let's look back at the first time you introduced two namespaces to the schedule document:

```
<?xml version="1.0"?>
<!DOCTYPE SCHEDULE "http://www.foo.com/schedule.dtd">
<SCHEDULE xmlns:foo="http://www.foo.com"
          xmlns:eguide="http://www.e-guide-swfl.com">
<foo:appt type="personal">
<foo:date date="08/02/99"/>
<foo:time time="19:30"/>
<foo:with person="Dave Navarro"/>
<foo:event>
<eguide:film>
<eguide:title>Star Wars Episode I: The Phantom Menace</eguide:title>
     </eguide:film>
</foo:event>
</foo:appt>
</foo:SCHEDULE>
```

Instead of providing a qualified name for both, you can declare the `foo` namespace as the default namespace. The root element would then be written as:

```
<SCHEDULE xmlns="http://www.foo.com"
xmlns:eguide="http://www.e-guide-swfl.com">
```

Notice that in this instance, you have not declared a qualified name for the `foo` namespace. It is, instead, the default namespace. Then when the `eguide` material is presented, you can use the prefix only on those elements:

```
<eguide:film>
<title>Star Wars Episode I: The Phantom Menace</title>
  </eguide:film>
```

The `title` element does not require the `eguide` prefix because, as a child element of `film`, it falls within the scope of the `eguide` namespace.

TIP

Though the `eguide` prefix on the `title` element in this usage isn't required, it's never wrong to include it.

Up Next

In this chapter you learned that namespaces provide a point of reference or a "sphere of influence" for element and attribute names. By declaring namespaces in elements, you can differentiate your names from similar names of others. In addition, you learned that blending namespaces is easily done by declaring multiple namespaces in the document and using qualified names where possible to clarify markup.

In the next chapter, you'll be introduced to XML's expanded linking capabilities, allowing you to provide new mechanisms for transport between documents.

CHAPTER

TWELVE

12

Using XML Linking

- Syntax for constructing locators
- Implementing simple links
- Building extended links
- Linking to portions of resources with XPointers

The XML 1 Recommendation provides authors with a way to describe their documents. However, one item not fully addressed in XML is how to link various documents and subdocuments together. Rather than depending on the simplistic linking ability of HTML, those working on XML chose to expand the possibilities for linking by creating its own language: XML Linking.

At the time of this writing, XML Linking was still very much a work in progress. Changes will no doubt be made to the information presented here. However, the general ideas and potential described in the current XLink Working Draft and in this chapter should remain true.

Locator Syntax

The locator for a resource is provided by a URI. That URI may be refined by the presence of an XPointer to identify a specific subresource, or through fragment identifiers or queries.

Locator grammar is written in Extended Backus-Naur Form (EBNF), which is covered in depth in Chapter 3: "Creating XML Documents." A locator is expressed as:

```
Locator ::= URI | Connector (XPointer | Name)
| URI Connector (Xpointer | Name)
Connector ::= '#' | '|'
```

meaning a locator is defined as one of the following:

- A URI
- A Connector, which is composed of an XPointer or a Name
- A URI and a Connector

A Connector may be either the hash (#) or pipe (|) character, which prefaces an XPointer or fragment identifier. As the third locator option indicates, a locator can also be composed of both a URI and fragment bound by the Connector.

A link is asserted by a *linking element*. A familiar linking element is HTML's anchor element, <a></a>. With an author's ability to create unique elements and therefore unique tag sets in XML, being able to identify immediately what is or isn't a linking element isn't always possible. The authors of the XLink Working Draft had several options of how they could deal with this problem:

- Linking elements could be required to be limited to certain reserved element type names.
- Linking elements could be required to use special reserved attributes.
- Link recognition could be left to the application and/or style sheet to handle.

The first option, requiring linking elements to use a limited set of element type names, limits an author's ability to create their own elements, something the XML Working Group does not like to do.

The third option, while the most permissive, is also the most impractical. Experience has taught the Web community that if application behavior is not clearly mapped in the language, the resulting functionality across applications is uneven, at best.

That left the working group with the second option: requiring linking elements to use reserved attributes for proclaiming their linking abilities. The attribute selected for this use was `xml:link`.

TIP Notice the reserved linking attribute uses the XML Namespace identifier.

Two types of linking elements are defined by the XLink language, and their type is used as the value of the `xml:link` attribute. The names of these values are `simple` and `extended`.

A simple link is always one-directional, meaning you can only use that link to travel from point A to B; you can't travel from point B to point A. A simple link is also usually an *inline* link. An inline link is defined as a link where the content of a linking element serves as a participating resource—that is, a resource that belongs to the link.

For example, an anchor is an inline link. It takes the general form of:

```
<a href="http://www.foo.com/bar.html">The Ultimate Foo Bar document</a>
```

The resource `http://www.foo.com/bar.html`, identified by the anchor element as "The Ultimate Foo Bar document," is a part of the linking element <a>. That makes it a participating resource, which in turn defines the link as an inline link.

An extended link, as its name implies, can handle more than a simple link. It may connect to an unlimited number of resources. We'll take a closer look at extended links in the section "Working with Extended Links."

Practical Implementations of Simple Links

With the technical discussion out of the way, implementing simple links is quite, well, simple! Summarizing the last section, a simple link is an inline link that connects a local resource to a single remote resource. That is, you go from point A on the current document to document B.

Note that we said from *point* A to *document* B. A simple link will always connect to a resource, which is a whole piece. If you wanted it to connect to a subresource, an XPointer would be required, and that means it's not a simple link anymore.

In its most basic form, a simple link element must have two attributes that deal with the link: `href` and `xml:link`. The `href` attribute works just as it does in HTML: it contains the URI of the remote resource the link will take you to. The `xml:link` attribute is used to declare what type of link you are creating, in this case, a simple link. So, the usage becomes `xml:link="simple"`.

If an XML document were to describe this book, we might see links from the three `<author>` elements that take the reader to a bio about each of the three authors. Such elements would be constructed as:

```
<author name="Ann Navarro" href="anavarro.html" xml:link="simple"/>
```

NOTE The presence of the link attributes doesn't limit the ability of the element to contain other attributes. Instead, it simply takes on the added functionality of the link when the author chooses to use it as one.

Describing a Simple Link's Purpose: The Role Attribute

Software applications that process XML documents will have a wide variety of abilities: they won't necessarily be confined to a "read and display" function. To enhance the interaction between application and XML document, additional element attributes provide authors with the means to include information intended specifically for the application and not the end user.

For example, a cookbook written as an XML document would have many links: links to recipes, descriptions of ingredients, definitions for cooking terms, etc. By providing a description of a simple link's purpose, the application can distinguish a request for resources that contain a description of the spice saffron from the recipes that make use of it.

These semantic differences are stored in the `role` attribute. The value of this attribute may be anything the author chooses; there are no strict rules for its content. Consistency, however, is important. The application must be able to make sense of the values assigned and process them in the manner the author intended.

Using the cookbook scenario, roles may be defined as follows:

```
<element href="saffron.html" xml:link="simple" role="spice/origin">
saffron</element>
```

This element serves as a simple link to the document `saffron.html` and provides the application with the note that a linked resource deals with the origin of a spice.

NOTE The role of many elements may be indicated to humans by the names that we choose for them, since we now have so much freedom in XML. However, those semantics are not passed on to the application: software places no meaning on element names beyond the unique label they provide for themselves.

Humans may be provided with additional descriptive information about the resource by using the `title` attribute. The application may pass on the title value through a ToolTip or other means native to the individual application.

```
<element href="saffron.html" xml:link="simple" role="spice/origin"
title="The origins of Saffron">saffron</element>
```

Directing Content Display for Simple Links

XML Linking gives authors additional flexibility in where the content contained in the linked resource should be displayed. With HTML links, the content is usually displayed in the browser, replacing the content from the resource that originated the link. The only other option available is to open a new window or frame by naming a new target.

By using the show attribute, you can direct the application to follow either of these familiar behaviors or—and this is the most exciting option—the application may be instructed to embed the content within the local resource. In essence, this creates a new document comprised of the original resource and the linked resource, which is now fully contained within the original document.

The show attribute then, takes one of three values:

replace The traditional link behavior where the new resource content is displayed by the application, replacing the original view.

new The new resource content is displayed in a new window or frame.

embed Content from the linked resource is displayed inline, effectively becoming a part of the original document.

Figures 12.1 and 12.2 demonstrate this embedding technique displayed in an HTML file as the result of some fairly serious scripting using Active Server Pages (ASP).

FIGURE 12.1:

An embedded display before links have been activated

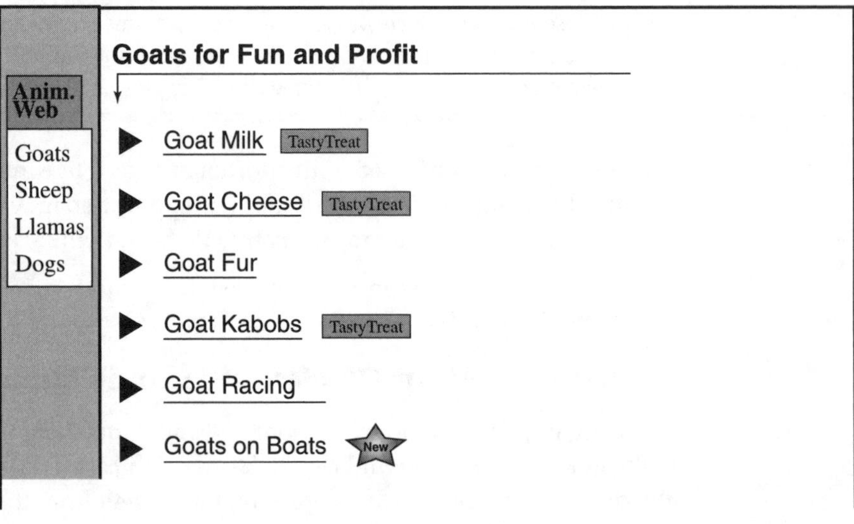

FIGURE 12.2: An embedded display after the link has been activated

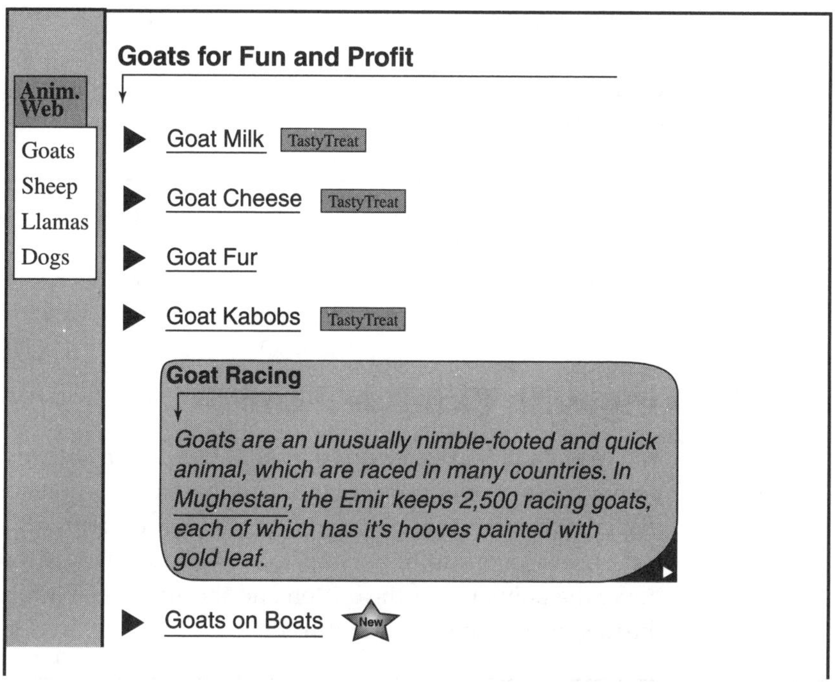

Under XML, this task would be easily accomplished just by using the `show` attribute, rather than the ASP scripting required to serve up this example.

User-Activated or Automatic Linking

A final attribute used in simple links is one that controls when a link is traversed, either at the request of the user or automatically. Automatic link traversal may at first seem rather silly; after all, why would you want to display a document only to immediately surf off to the next? But remember the new display option of embedding new resources that is available by using the `show` attribute. By embedding several resources and then directing the application to automatically traverse the links, authors can build complex documents that are dynamically generated at load time without the overhead of databases or difficult-to-use middleware applications required for such flexibility today.

These link-activation options are defined by the `actuate` attribute, using one of two values: `user` or `auto`. The value `user` will of course, perform as traditional HTML links do: it's only activated when the user proactively follows it. Alternatively, by setting the value to `auto`, the resource is, as you'd suspect, loaded automatically.

NOTE

Of course, embedding isn't the only possible scenario for using an actuate value of auto. It could be used to transport users from an outdated document to a new one or for any number of reasons that unique situations might present.

Working with Extended Links

You're already familiar with several techniques in software design that allow the author or developer to provide additional information about an object yet only display that information when it's requested. ToolTips are a good example of this: if the user wants additional information about a button's functionality, simply hover the pointer over the button and the additional information (the tip about the tool) is displayed (see Figure 12.3).

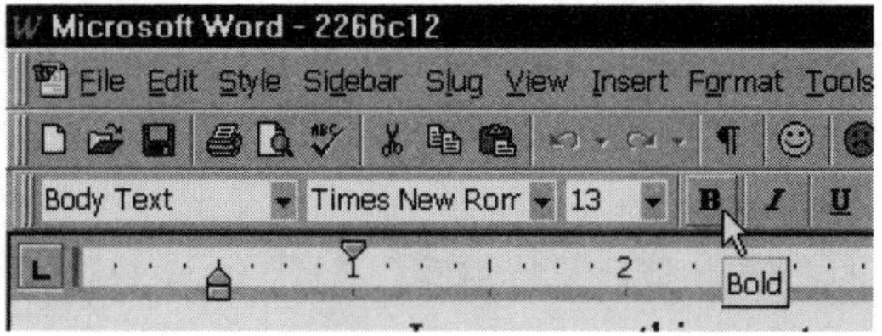

FIGURE 12.3:

A ToolTip in action in Microsoft Word

The same concept has been incorporated in several popular Web browsers to display the contents of an image's ALT attribute as a ToolTip (see Figure 12.4).

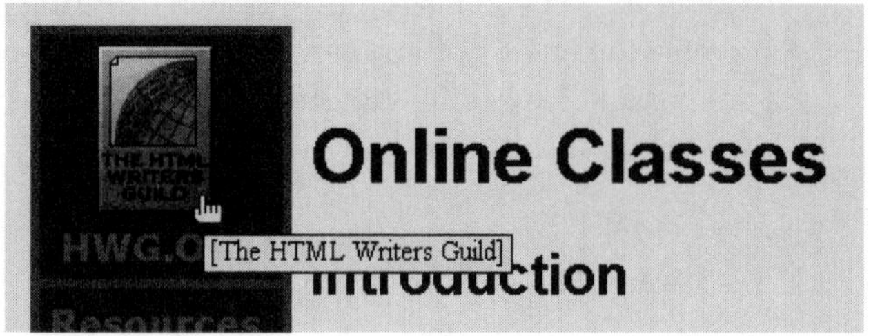

FIGURE 12.4:

ALT text displayed as a ToolTip in Netscape Navigator

Now, what if you could extend that idea and place your own notes on software or Web documents just as you might mark up a textbook in a college course or put a Post-It note on a memo from your boss? The ability to annotate other documents in that manner is available now through XLink's extended linking behavior.

Using Extended Linking to Review a Manuscript

In computer book publishing, manuscripts such as the one that served as the basis for this book are often reviewed by as many as four or five people before the final copy is approved. Whether the document is passed from one reviewer to another on paper or in electronic form, keeping track of comments from that many people can get confusing, even with the "revision marks" feature available in popular word processing software.

By using XML and XLink's extended linking feature, you can keep a "clean" copy of the original manuscript, and each reviewer's comments can be accessed through links instead of writing comments in the margins of a paper document or crowding out original text in electronic form.

Consider that two reviewers might wish to comment on the same passage in the document, say, in this section under the heading "Using Extended Linking to Review a Manuscript." Both sets of comments would need to share the same source link. This situation is referred to as a *link with more than two link ends*. To distinguish between the link to Reviewer A's comments and the link to Reviewer B's comments (in this example, Fred and Joe, respectively), you'll need to put *locator subelements* within the extended link element. This looks like:

```
<comment xml:link="extended">
     <locator href="fred-1.xml" role="Fred">
     <locator href="joe-1.xml" role="Joe">
<h4>Using Extended Linking to Review a Manuscript</h4>
…additional manuscript content…
</comment>
```

Each locator references a unique resource. As in a simple link, the role attribute provides machine-usable semantic information for the user-agent to use when processing the link.

More than one locator may have the same role. Remember that roles are not unique identifiers. If Fred had two distinct comments to make about this passage, a third link could be added:

```
<comment xml:link="extended">
     <locator href="fred-1.xml" role="Fred">
```

```
    <locator href="fred-2.xml" role="Fred>
    <locator href="joe-1.xml" role="Joe">
<h4>Using Extended Linking to Review a Manuscript</h4>
...additional manuscript content...
</comment>
```

When displaying the links, the user agent could refer to a style sheet or preprogrammed behavior to differentiate between links that represent Fred's comments and those that belong to Joe. Figure 12.5 is an artist's representation of how a user agent might render such an extended link.

NOTE

We've used an artist's rendering here, since current browsers haven't yet implemented XLink. Remember that at the time of this writing, XLink was still very much a work-in-progress at the W3C.

FIGURE 12.5:

An artist's rendering of extended linking

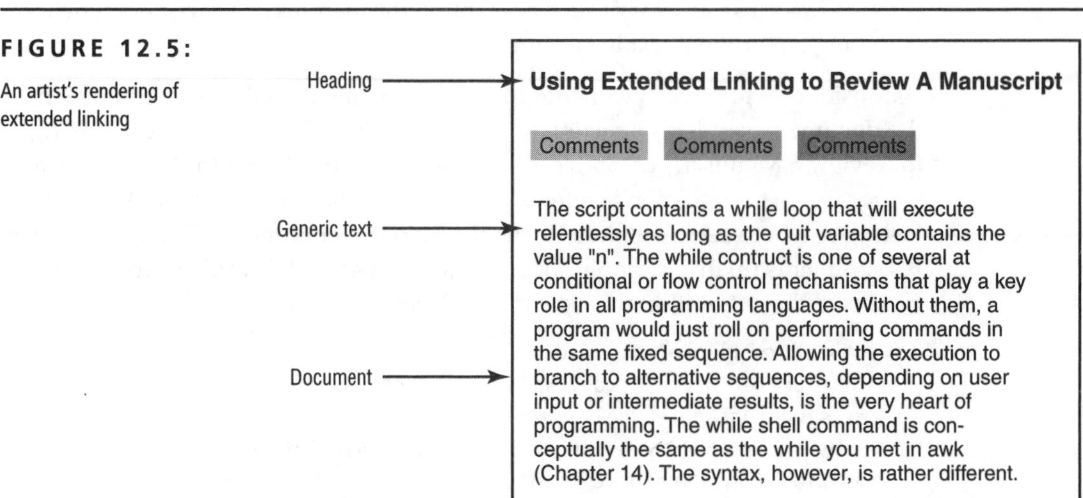

Locators, as with simple links, may take the additional attributes described previously in this chapter, `actuate` and `show`. Indeed, locators are nearly identical in syntax to simple links. Remember that a simple link combines the link attribute and the locator into a single element.

The major implementation hurdle that must be overcome for extended links is how an application will locate and process the links when they do not appear in the primary participating resource—that is, when the link appears in a document other than the one where the hotspot will be found. To deal with this, the concept of *extended link groups* was defined to allow applications to identify documents that contain links relevant to a given resource. See the section "Extended Link Groups" for more information.

Link Attribute Collisions

The flexibility of XML and XLink that allows an author to use any element as a linking element can also create some problems. The attributes that govern link semantics and behavior may have names that are already in use by the element an author might wish to use as a linking element. What happens then?

The solution for this *collision* of attributes is provided in XLink by *attribute remapping*. In other words, a mechanism is provided to sort out the conflict.

In the following example, you'll be working with a document that described the participants of a workshop. You have a chairperson, several presenters, and quite a few attendees. Each individual is described using a `<participant>` element, and their role in the workshop is described using a role attribute within `participant`, such as:

```
<participant role="chairperson">Murray Davis</particpant>
<participant role="presenter">Geoff Winters</participant>
<participant role="presenter">Susan Stanley</participant>
<participant role="attendee">Gina Santos</participant>
<participant role="attendee">Andre Veloti</participant>
<participant role="attendee">James Sullivan</particpant>
```

If you then wanted to make the `participant` element a link in order to provide access to a short bio on each individual, you find yourself with a conflict: `participant` already has a role attribute. Does this mean you have to rework your document to use a different attribute to describe the role of each participant in the workshop? No! Simply remap the attribute in the DTD.

The existing DTD entry for the participant element may look like:

```
<!ELEMENT PARTICIPANT ANY>
<!ATTLIST PARTICIPANT
role CDATA  (chairperson | presenter | attendee) #IMPLIED
    >
```

To remap the role attribute, an internal subset of attributes would need to be added containing:

```
<!ATTLIST PARTICIPANT
     xml:attributes CDATA
                    #FIXED "role xl-role"
>
```

This syntax uses pairs of attribute names. The first of each pair is the default XLink name, in this case, the role attribute. Next is the new name that the XLink attribute will be mapped to: `xl-role`.

TIP

The `xl-` prefix is not required, though it's a good idea to follow similar syntax for better readability and quick interpretation by humans.

When finally written into the document, the participant elements would now assume this syntax:

```
<participant xml:link="simple" role="chairperson" xl-role="bio"
   href="davis.xml">Murray Davis</particpant>
<participant xml:link="simple" role="presenter" xl-role="bio"
   href="winters.xml">Geoff Winters</participant>
<participant xml:link="simple" role="presenter" xl-role="bio"
   href="stanley.xml">Susan Stanley</participant>
<participant xml:link="simple" role="attendee" xl-role="bio"
   href="santos.xml">Gina Santos</participant>
<participant xml:link="simple" role="attendee" xl-role="bio"
   href="veloti.xml">Andre Veloti</participant>
<participant xml:link="simple" role="attendee" xl-role="bio"
   href="sullivan.xml">James Sullivan</participant>
```

Should the participant element have several attributes that conflict with default attributes for link elements, you'd map each of those as well. The internal subset declaration in the DTD can take a space-delimited list of remapped attribute names:

```
<!ATTLIST PARTICPANT
     xml:link       CDATA  #FIXED "simple"
     xml:attributes CDATA
                    #FIXED "role xl-role title xl-title show xl-show"
>
```

Extended Link Groups

Consider again the manuscript that is being reviewed by Fred and Joe. When comments are made on a specific block of prose, the reader will need to be alerted by the presence of a hotspot. When using a simple link, the hotspot is generated by the presence of the link. But with out-of-line extended links, Fred and Joe aren't marking up the manuscript itself; they're writing their own XML document that contains each of their comments. Therefore, if the application used to read the manuscript is to create hotspots where Fred or Joe has made a comment, the application must know where these documents are and be aware of the links contained within. This information can be provided to the application with an *extended link group element*.

An extended link group element is a special form of an extended link. It is used to store a list of links to other documents that need to be applied to another participating resource, such as a read-only manuscript document. A special locator element is also used within the extended link group element, the *extended link document element*.

A link group element with the element name `reviews` is expressed as:

```
<reviews xml:link="group" steps="1">
     <reviewer xml:link="document" href="fred.xml" role="Fred">
     <reviewer xml:link="document" href="joe.xml" role="Joe">
</reviews>
```

The first element, `reviews`, sets up the group using the `xml:link` value of `"group"`. The attribute `steps` are optional. When used, this attribute alerts an application that the extended link group will be directing it to a document that will contain another extended link group (see Figure 12.6).

The value of steps is numerical, allowing the author to indicate how many times the application should expect to be sent out to locate additional documents. The number of steps a group can traverse is unlimited.

NOTE

Well-written applications will still be able to traverse additional steps and locate documents referenced by additional extended link groups, even if the `steps` attribute doesn't appear in the initial extended link group element.

FIGURE 12.6:

How an application might traverse steps of extended link groups

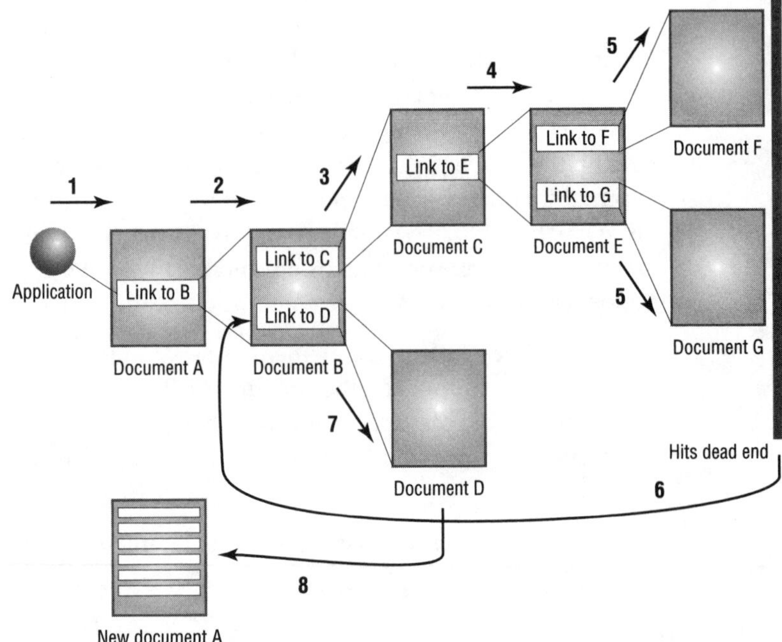

Advanced Uses of Extended Links

The W3C XLink Working Draft suggests several tasks that could be well-suited for the additional capabilities of extended links. These include:

- Enabling outgoing links in documents that cannot be modified to add an inline link
- Creating links to and from resources in formats with no native support for embedded links (such as most multimedia formats)
- Applying and filtering sets of relevant links on demand
- Enabling other advanced hypermedia capabilities

Just exactly how these scenarios should be implemented is beyond the scope of the XLink Working Draft—and for good reason. Application developers can choose how they wish to represent the semantics attached to each resource or subresource. This built-in flexibility allows for growth in terms of new devices or clients that may be traversing these links; it also allows for new forms of media to be developed without requiring backward compatibility to an enforced semantic interpretation.

Getting Specific: XPointers

As discussed previously in this chapter, links refer to entire resources. If you wanted to be more specific, such as referring to a paragraph out of a chapter resource, the paragraph is referred to as a subresource. In order to link to a subresource, you must have a way of pointing to that specific portion of the larger resource. That ability is available through XPointers.

The basic addressing unit of an XPointer is known as the *location term*. When location terms are combined, they represent a precise location.

In HTML, specific points in a document can be referenced using fragment identifiers. The URL is composed of the full resource file, as in `http://www.foo.com/myfile.html`, as well as the fragment name appended to the URL with the # character serving as a *connector*. The final URL would appear as `http://www.foo.com/myfile.html#fragment-name`.

Figure 12.7 shows a Web page that includes a link to a subresource. Note that in the status bar the URL has the # connector construct. When followed, this link will result in the browser displaying the new resource content from the subresource point onward (see Figure 12.8).

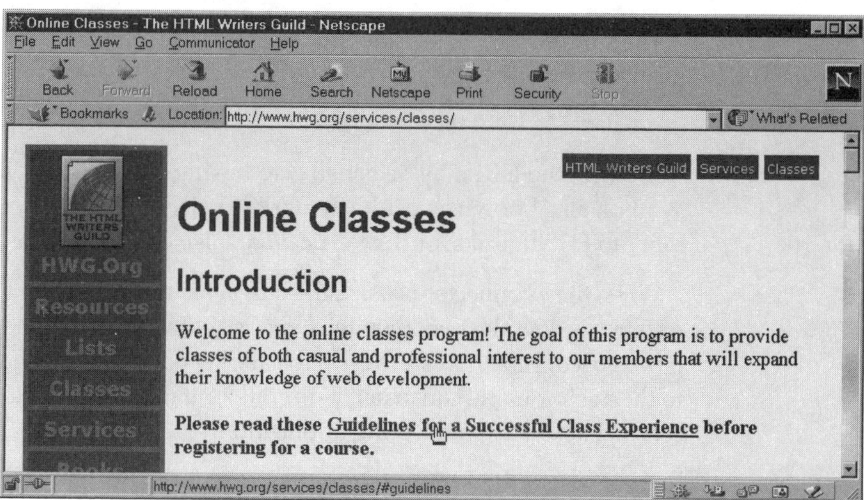

FIGURE 12.7:

An HTML link that refers to a subresource

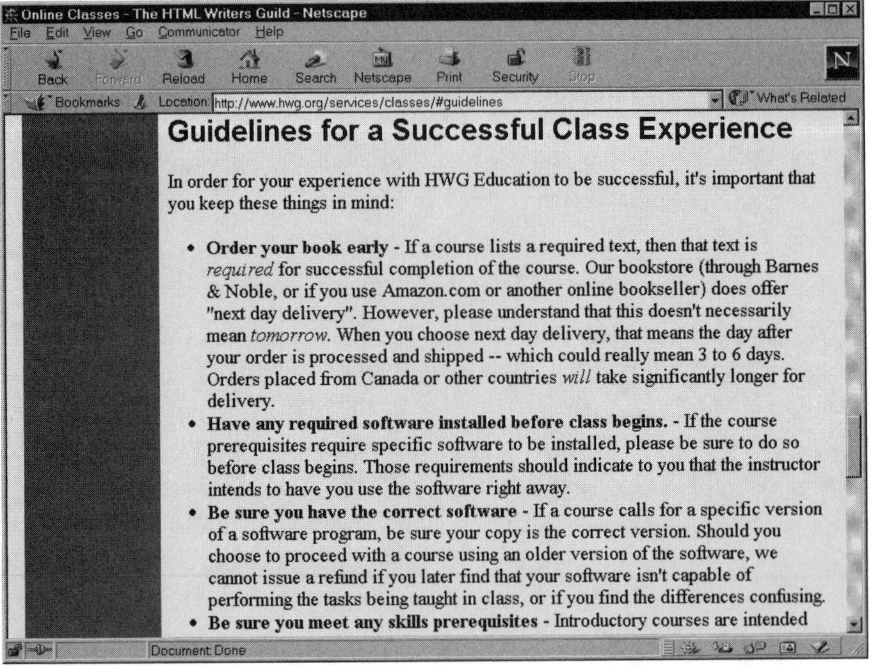

FIGURE 12.8: Display after a subresource link is followed

The subresource is identified in the HTML document by using the name attribute in an anchor element:

```
<a name="guidelines">
```

In XML, the URI may be constructed using one of two connectors: the pound symbol, also known as the hash mark (#), used in HTML for backward compatibility to HTML links, or the vertical bar, also called the *pipe* character (|).

When the # connector is used, the link behavior is as with HTML: the entire linked resource is downloaded, then the focus is shifted to the named fragment. When the pipe is used, behavior is left up to the application. As subresources are not confined to the anchor name construct, a discrete unit of markup could be retrieved and served back to the requesting application.

For instance, the XML 1 Recommendation has a healthy set of references in Appendix A of the document. Rather than downloading all 174K of the document simply to display the less than 200 characters involved in a single definition list term and definition that make up the subresource, you can download only the subresource:

```
ISO 639
(International Organization for Standardization). ISO 639:1988 (E).
```

```
Code for the representation of names of languages. [Geneva]: Interna-
tional Organization for Standardization, 1988.
```

This ability is an incredible boon for the conservation of bandwidth and the connection costs associated with Internet connectivity, to name just one important factor behind this prescribed behavior for XPointers.

TIP

The pipe construct can be used for intraresource links just as # references can. Any variances in behavior are determined by the application.

Pointing to IDs

The simplest example of an XPointer is written in XML by referencing an `ID` attribute in the element you want to point to. For example, a menu document may use the element `<meal>` in this manner:

```
<menu>
<meal id="friday.breakfast">
     <entree>French Toast and Sausage</entree>
     <beverage>coffee</beverage>
</meal>
<meal id="friday.lunch">
     <entree>Chicken Fajitas</entree>
     <beverage>Iced Tea</beverage>
</meal>
<meal id="friday.dinner">
     <entree>New York Steak</entree>
     <beverage>Wine</beverage>
</meal>
</menu>
```

If a link was to point specifically to Friday's lunch, the pointer would be expressed as `#id(friday.lunch)`, or in a full URL as `http://www.foo.com/menu.xml#id(friday.lunch)`.

Traversing the Element Tree Using Location Terms

The syntax expressed in the menu example requires that an element have an `ID` attribute before an XPointer can refer to it. When you're attempting to link to a resource that you don't control, however, it's quite possible—if not probable—that the element you want to use as a resource doesn't have an `ID` attribute.

To get around this limitation, authors can traverse the element tree starting with the root element. This process is referred to as using a *location ladder* (climbing the tree by using a ladder, get it?).

When a starting point has been given using `ID` or `root`, it is called an *absolute* location term. Once you step down to a branch of the root element, you're looking at a *child* location term. A child location term is also a relative location term.

TIP

Think of relative terms using the same family nomenclature. You can have child, parent, and sibling location terms.

Using the previous menu sample, assuming menu is the root element, you could write a URL of:

```
http://www.foo.com/menu.xml#root().child(2, meal)
```

This means that within the document found at `http://www.foo.com/menu.xml`, you are pointing to the second child element of `menu` (the root element), of the element type `meal`. Looking at the markup again, you'll find the second child element of menu highlighted in Figure 12.9, where the XPointer is referring to the element for Friday's lunch.

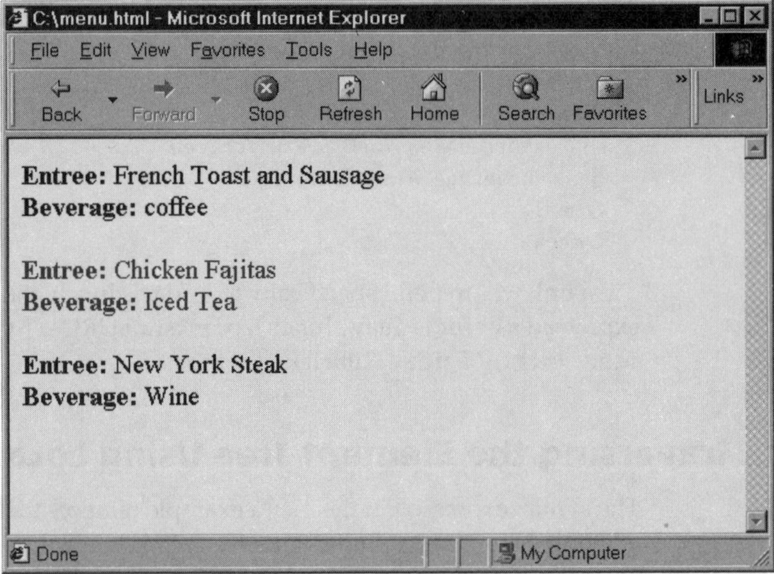

FIGURE 12.9: Traversing the element tree using the root as a starting point

Any element or node on an element tree can be accessed using relative location terms. Table 12.1 lists the types of relationships that can exist between terms, as defined in the current XPointer Working Draft.

TABLE 12.1: Relationships between XPointer Terms

Term	Description
child	Identifies direct child nodes of the location source
descendant	Identifies nodes appearing anywhere within the content of the location source
ancestor	Identifies element nodes containing the location source
preceding	Identifies nodes that appear before the location source
following	Identifies nodes that appear after the location source
psibling	Identifies sibling nodes (sharing their parent with the location source) that appear before the location source
fsibling	Identifies sibling nodes (sharing their parent with the location source) that appear after the location source

Spanning Location Terms

When describing relative location terms, we said that any element or node could be accessed using relative location terms. One might think that such an addressing system would cover all possibilities.

But what if you want to refer to a portion of a document that covers more than one discrete element? Perhaps, using the previous example, someone is interested in the meals for Tuesday through Thursday (assuming the document covered that much data), but not for Monday or Friday. The subresource would then need to span nine meal elements from `id tuesday.breakfast` to `id thursday.dinner`.

To do this, you can introduce two subresource arguments to the location term, resulting in a *spanning location term*. To select the means using relative location terms, you would write:

```
http://www.foo.com/menu.xml#root().span(child(4),child(13))
```

This means the resources found beginning with the 4th direct child element of menu (the root of this document), through the 13th child element, inclusive. In other words, Tuesday's breakfast through Thursday's dinner.

Additional Locator Term Types

Table 12.2 describes all five locator term types, including those we haven't covered in detail.

TABLE 12.2: Locator Term Types

Term Type	Usage
absolute	Establishes a location source.
relative	Dependent on a location source. Provides means for traversing the element tree from the original source location.
spanning	Contains two location arguments that, when spanned, create the location.
attribute	Location referenced by matching attribute name.
string	Matches the location based on character strings rather than element and node names or attributes.

Up Next

In this chapter, you learned how links are constructed using the XML Linking language. You explored ways that subresources may be referenced in very specific ways, and how links may be applied to documents that you do not control.

In the next couple of chapters, you'll be introduced to several methods used to display XML. Since XML has no representational semantics of its own, additional instructions must be provided before an application can appropriately render a document. Cascading Style Sheets (CSS) and the Extensible Style Language (XSL) are two languages that are used for just that purpose.

CHAPTER THIRTEEN

Displaying XML: Working with Cascading Style Sheets

- What is CSS?
- Using style sheets in XML
- Learning about Style rules
- CSS formatting properties
- Other CSS media types
- Looking at CSS3

XML is designed to separate a document's structure from the way it is presented. The creators of XML had no intention of including formatting capabilities within XML markup syntax. Still, there are plenty of times you will want to display an XML document, so a way needs to be found to manage that process. Style sheets offer such a way.

Currently, there are two types of style sheets available for displaying XML: Cascading Style Sheets (CSS) and the eXtensible Style Language (XSL). There are huge differences between the two. CSS will display an entire XML document by traversing the XML document tree from the root element to the last element of the tree. It follows the tree in the order of the elements' appearance in the tree. Basically, it provides a means to add a style to each element as they appear within the structure of the document.

XSL, on the other hand, is not so much a language used for dressing up a tree as it is for transforming a tree. In fact, XSL takes the original document tree and creates a new one based on a potentially complex set of instructions that the developer provides.

There is little question as to which of the two style-sheet languages is more robust. XSL allows you do things such as search for strings of text and display certain elements or attributes under certain conditions of your choosing. CSS offers none of this power.

Nevertheless, CSS can be a good starting point if you're determined to view some XML documents in a Web browser like IE5. In addition, CSS is the only way to view XML files using Gecko, the newest version of Netscape Navigator (although the organization dedicated to bringing out Netscape Navigator 5 is trying to incorporate XSL into the final release). This chapter will explore the fundamentals of CSS development. CSS is growing in power. With the advent of CSS2, which is the newest version of CSS, you can now have the browser generate content, such as list numbering and text strings. The newest version also supports paged media (distinct pages with explicit page breaks, rather than a continuous form as in most Web pages), and the most recent working draft expands on this significantly. In addition, the prerelease version of Netscape Navigator uses CSS extensively not only to interpret and display documents, but to describe its user interface. You'll find out more about that in Chapter 19: "XML-Enabled Browsers." This is not expected to change when the final release comes out.

What Is CSS?

CSS, short for Cascading Style Sheets, was invented as a way to make Web pages more attractive without forever adding formatting tags to the HTML standard. Currently, there are two versions of CSS available as official standards, CSS1 and CSS2. Anything CSS1 can do CSS2 can do better, so we'll focus our attention on style sheets as implemented by CSS2 recommendations. Therefore, all references to CSS in this chapter refer to CSS2, which is analogous to CSS, version 2. At the time of this writing, CSS3 was in working draft stage. CSS3 focuses primarily on extending the functionality of paged media and user interface issues.

This chapter will cover many of the rules and properties of CSS2, but not all of them. CSS rules have become quite extensive, and an entire book could easily be devoted to them. Hopefully you'll learn enough about them that by the end of this chapter you'll be able to easily apply style sheets to an XML document and have a good grasp of how they work.

At the end of the chapter, you'll learn about some features of the emerging rules of CSS3. As this book went to press, CSS3 was not yet enjoying much browser support, but things change quickly in the style sheet world, so you may be interested in learning how to harness the power of these new rules.

NOTE

You can view the latest reference on CSS2 from the authoritative source on CSS—the W3C—at `http://web1.w3.org/TR/REC-CSS2/`.

WARNING

At the time of this writing, the only browser support for CSS in XML is IE5, and even IE5 is not fully compliant with CSS2, much less CSS3.

Using Style Sheets in XML

To include a style sheet in an XML document, simply include a processing instruction in the XML document's prolog, like so:

```
<?xml-stylesheet type="text/css" href="myCSS.css" ?>
```

A processing instruction provides instruction to another computer software system outside of the XML processor. So it isn't the XML processor that will be handling your style sheets, but rather a software program capable of rendering the XML elements according to the prescriptions offered up by the CSS rule set contained in the processing instruction. In the example in the preceding line of code, the CSS rule set the style sheet processor will process is a file called `myCSS.css`. You can give an external file name any name you want as long as you are sure the file name of the style sheet you create is the same as the style sheet you reference. For example, you might have a style sheet with only one rule (see Figure 13.1):

```
MYELEMENT {font-size:10px}
```

If your style sheet only has one rule you need to create a valid CSS file in a text editor. The next step would be to save it with a file name of your choice—in this case, `myCSS.css`—and link it in the XML file:

```
<?xml-stylesheet type="text/css" href="myCSS.css" ?>
```

FIGURE 13.1:

There's only one line of code, but it's a valid CSS file.

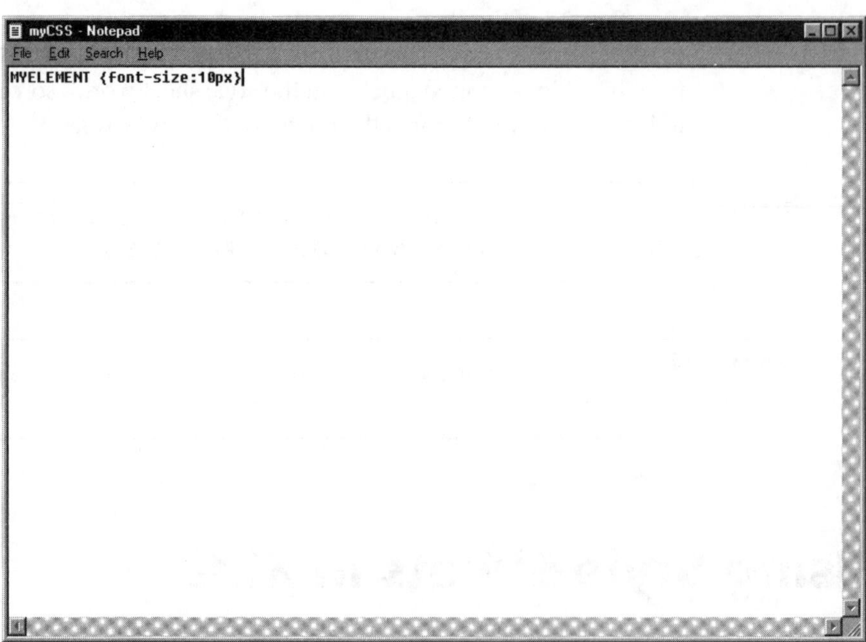

Of course, where you go after saving the CSS file is up to you. You can get as complicated as you want. CSS is very accessible, but allows for a fairly high degree of formatting complexity.

Learning about Style Rules

When developing style sheets you work within rules. When you have finished developing a complete set of rules, you save that set as a style sheet with a `.css` extension. Rules, in turn, consist of two main sections:

- The selector
- The declaration

The selector names the element to which a style property will be applied. The declaration describes those properties. In the example below, the element `MYELEMENT` is the selector. The selector always sits outside of the right curly brace. The right curly brace indicates that the declaration is being made, and the left curly brace terminates the declaration:

```
MYELEMENT {font-family: Helvetica}
```

There are two additional aspects of the declaration in the preceding code. The declaration between the curly braces consists of a *property* (`font-family`) and a *value* to be assigned to the property (`Helvetica`).

Learning about Selectors

The simplest kind of selector, a type selector, applies a style sheet property to a specific element. If you've ever worked with CSS in HTML, the syntax will look familiar:

```
P {font-family: Arial}
```

In the preceding example, the `P` character is a selector that applies to the `P` element. You can use any element in your XML document, or any element you anticipate using in your XML document, as a selector:

```
MYLOOKATMYGOOFYNAMEELEMENT {font-family: Helvetica}
```

It doesn't matter if you never actually use that element in an XML document. The CSS file will still be valid. A CSS processor searches a CSS rules set and looks for matches against the XML document it is trying to format.

You can also group selectors together to create more compact code:

```
P, A, TD, SPAN {font-size: 12px}
```

When you group selectors together like this, you use a comma to separate each element that is defined as part of the selector.

There are several other kinds of selectors you can use in CSS besides the element selector, such as the following:

- The class selector lets you assign a `class` attribute value as a selector.
- The ID selector lets you use a unique identifier as a selector.
- The attribute selector lets you match elements by their attributes.
- The universal selector, indicated by the * operator, acts as a wildcard, which means that all elements within its scope will be selected.
- The descendent selector lets you include an element's descendent.
- The child selector lets you name a specific child (but not its parent).
- The adjacent sibling selector lets you name a specific sibling that shares a parent element with another element.

Generally, you'll use class and ID selectors when creating HTML for XML. XHTML is a form of HTML that follows the syntactical rules of XML (all start tags have end tags, attribute values in quotes, etc).

NOTE You'll learn more about XHTML in Chapter 16: "Converting from HTML to XML."

Using Class Selectors

The class selector is declared with a period preceding the name of the `class` attribute value that is being used. You might have a class selector like this one:

```
.myClass {font-size: 10px}
```

Notice the period preceding the selector name. The class selector would then apply to any element containing that name as a `class` attribute:

```
<p class = "myClass">here is a paragraph</p>
<div class = "myClass">this is a block of text</div>
```

Notice in the preceding lines of code that the `class` attribute is used within two different elements, and that the period is no longer there. You can create more finely tuned instances for such class selectors by declaring that only certain elements with that class name will be formatted according to your declarations:

```
p.myClass {font-size: 10px}
```

In the preceding example, only `P` elements with the `class` attribute value set to `myClass` would receive the indicated formatting.

Using ID Selectors

An ID selector is a selector that defines how a unique identifier should be formatted. A unique identifier is what you might suspect it to be based on its name: it uniquely identifies an element with the `id` attribute:

```
<p id="myID">Here is a paragraph</p>
```

When creating an ID selector, you mark it as an ID selector by including a pound sign before the name of the selector:

```
#myID {font-size: 10px}
```

This is an excellent way to access an element as an object and apply scripting mechanisms using whatever object model the target browser supports. Hence, in IE5, you might have a script that manipulates the `myID` object like so:

```
<p id="myID" onmouseover="myID.style.fontSize='12px'">
```

Using Attribute Selectors

You can also choose elements by their attributes. This means you could add a certain color to all a elements that have an `href` attribute:

```
a[href] {color:blue}
```

You can even find a match based on the value of an attribute, rather than merely the name of the attribute. This is accomplished with the use of the equal sign:

```
a[href=mySite.com] {color:red}
```

You can combine your efforts so that more than one attribute value is selected for an element. All you need to do is add the second selector. You don't need any kind of operator. This is called using a multiple attribute selector:

```
a[href=mySite.com][name="myName"] {color:red}
```

Using Universal Selectors

The programming world has long used an operator called a *wildcard*. The operator is an asterisk and looks like this: *. Think of wildcards as analogous to the word "all" and you'll have a good idea about how they work. In CSS, they're called universal selectors, and they allow you to choose all the elements within their scope. This makes it easy to define rules for XML documents:

```
* {font-size: 14px}
```

The preceding line of code acts almost like a template, as now all the elements in your document will default to a font size of 14px.

NOTE For a chart containing browser support information for specific CSS selectors, visit `http://webreview.com/wr/pub/guides/style/mastergrid.html`.

Using the Descendent Selector

You can select the descendent of an element using the descendent selector for those occasions when you want to name a specific element whenever it occurs somewhere within another element. If you were developing an XHTML document, you might want every a element that occurs within a p element to consist of some specific styling. You would then create the following:

```
p a {text-decoration: none}
```

Using Child Selectors

Sometimes you might want specific children of an element. In those cases, you can create the following line of code:

```
p > a {text-decoration: none}
```

Using the preceding line of code, the selector would not match if the a element was not a child of the p element. You can take this a step further by using the *first-child* pseudo class. This limits the choice to the first child of an element, allowing for greater refinement of your style sheets:

```
p > a:first-child {font-size:1.2em}
```

In the preceding line of code, all a elements that are the first-child elements of the p elements will have a font size of 1.2 em.

Using Adjacent Sibling Selectors

If you want to select the latter of two elements that share a parent, you use the + operator. The following selects the a element if it is a sibling of the span element, and they share the same parent:

```
span + a {font-size: 8px}
```

Learning about Declarations

All declarations are contained in curly braces ({ }). Within a declaration, a property is separated from its value by the colon (:). So the basic syntax of a style sheet rule goes like this:

```
SELECTOR {property: value}
```

The property is any valid CSS property, and the value is any valid CSS unit of measure. Remember, though, that a selector is much more complicated than the one word shown in the preceding line of code.

Managing Block-Level Formatting

If you've used CSS in HTML, you may be familiar with terms like *block level formatting* to describe the way some elements are formatted. A typical block level element in HTML is the DIV element, which is used to separate blocks of text. When applying style sheets to XML, you'll generally be working with block level elements because CSS formats elements in the order of the their appearance in the document (unless you use absolute positioning).

To get an idea of how block level formatting works, take a look at the following small XML file:

```
<?xml version="1.0"?>
<?xml-stylesheet href="adcss8.css" type="text/css"?>
<AD id="a001"><NEWSPAPER>The Grand Gazette</NEWSPAPER><DISPLAY>
```

```
<DISPLAYSIZE lines="636" width="2">
</DISPLAYSIZE>
<DISPLAYCONTENT>Here is some content</DISPLAYCONTENT>
<INCOLUMNCONTENT>Here is some more content</INCOLUMNCONTENT></DISPLAY>
</AD>
```

Now, without worrying too much yet about what each rule means, take a look at the following rules:

```
AD {display:block;
background-color:#FF9900;
padding:10px;
border: black 1px outset;
width: 600px;
height: 450px;
}
NEWSPAPER {display:block;
letter-spacing: 10px;
font-family: sans-serif;
height: 30px;
font-size: 12px;
color: #333333;
width: 500px;
height: 300px;
border: black 1px outset;
padding:5px;
}
DISPLAY {display:block;
position: absolute;
top: 50px;
left: 10px;
width: 440px;
background-color:#660099
}
DISPLAYCONTENT {display:block;
padding: 10px;
color: #003300;
background-color: #CCCC99;}
INCOLUMNCONTENT {display:block;
padding: 10px;
color: #003300;
background-color: #CCCC99;}
```

You can see in Figure 13.2 how the XML is rendered in IE5 when the style sheet is applied to the document. Now, try switching a couple of elements around, like so:

```
<?xml version="1.0"?>
<?xml-stylesheet href="adcss8.css" type="text/css"?>
<AD id="a001"><NEWSPAPER>The Grand Gazette</NEWSPAPER><DISPLAY>
<DISPLAYSIZE lines="636" width="2">
</DISPLAYSIZE>
<DISPLAYCONTENT>Here is some content</DISPLAYCONTENT>
</DISPLAY>
<INCOLUMNCONTENT>Here is some more content</INCOLUMNCONTENT>
</AD>
..
```

FIGURE 13.2:

XML document as rendered by IE5 using a style sheet

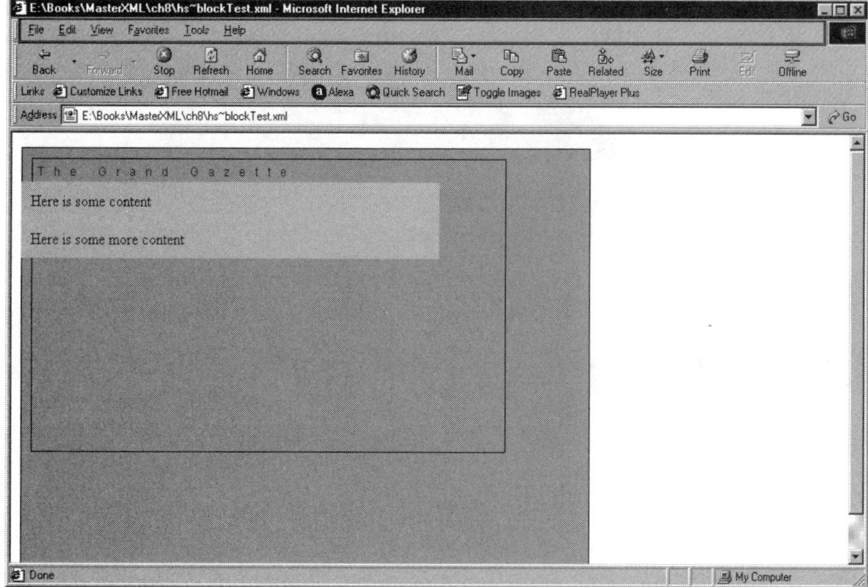

Figure 13.3 shows how the newly structured XML file looks in the browser. This is also a good example of one of the drawbacks of CSS within regular XML documents. In order to move an element's position within the block-level-formatting scheme you need to change the actual of the position of the element within the XML document.

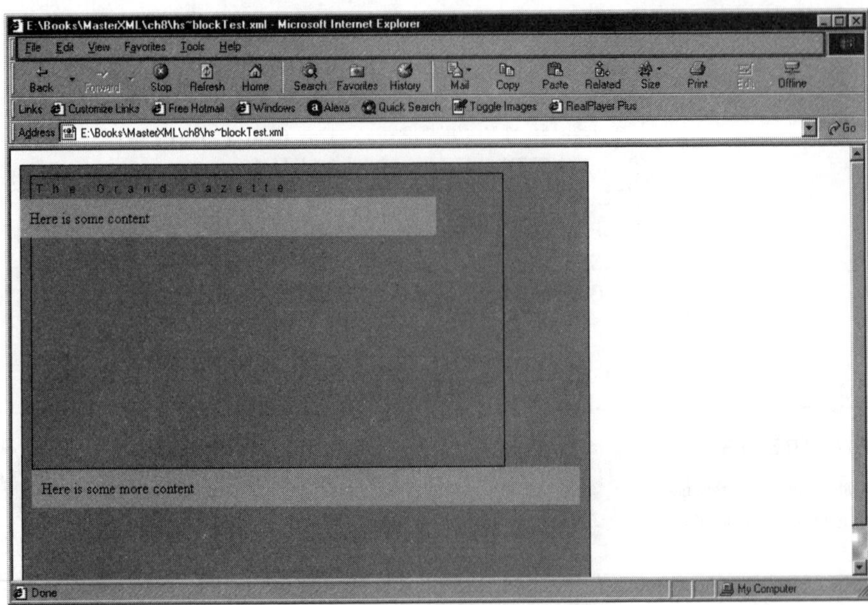

FIGURE 13.3:

The XML document as it appears after moving the elements around

Now, let's examine some of the specific properties available through CSS.

Examining CSS Formatting Properties

Now it's time to take a more thorough look at individual CSS formatting properties. What follows is not a definitive guide, because the CSS2 Recommendation, upon which the following sections are based, is quite extensive. You will find, however, most of the CSS properties you'll want to use in your XML development.

CSS Properties

The following several pages will take a closer look at several CSS properties. First, we'll provide the name of the property, then briefly describe what it does. We'll give a short example, then list the values that you can use in the declaration.

position

You can use positioning to manipulate the positions of elements, although trying to manage positioning on large XML documents could be somewhat nightmarish until some very good style editors appear on the scene. An element's positioning properties are set using the `position` property.

This property tells the rendering engine how to display an element relative to other elements. A value of `absolute` means the element should be placed exactly in the position described in the `top`, `left`, and/or `right` properties, without any regard to the position of any other elements. A declaration using a `position` property can be used like so:

```
MYELEMENT {position: absolute}
```

Possible Values

```
absolute
relative
fixed
static
inherit
```

top, *left*, and *right*

These properties tell the rendering engine where to display an element along the *x* (`left` and `right`) and *y* (`top`) axes of an *x* and *y* coordinate system. This coordinate system starts at the top left of a user agent window, unless the element being positioned resides within another element, in which case that parent element's top-left corner is the point of origin. If using the `right` property, the *x* axis begins at the right edge of the parent. If you look at Figure 13.4 you can see a box and the numbers 0, 0. The arrow points to the location where these coordinates lie. The lower left-hand portion of the box points to two other coordinate numbers, 300, 300. These are arbitrary, since a real browser window may be bigger or smaller, but essentially this means that the box's left-hand corner is 300 pixels from the top and 300 pixels from the left of the point of origin.

Here is an example of how a `top` property might appear in a style sheet rule. In this example the element appears 10 pixels from the top and 10 pixels down from the top of the containing window or parent element:

```
MYELEMENT {position:absolute; top: 10px; left: 10px}
```

Figure 13.5 shows how the XML document you looked at earlier in the chapter appears when absolute positioning is used. Absolute positioning does not make it terribly different, but you do have more control over the placement of objects. Listing 13.1 shows the style sheet used with an XML document.

FIGURE 13.4:

The 0 coordinates of the x and y axes are in the upper-left corner of a browser window using the left and top properties.

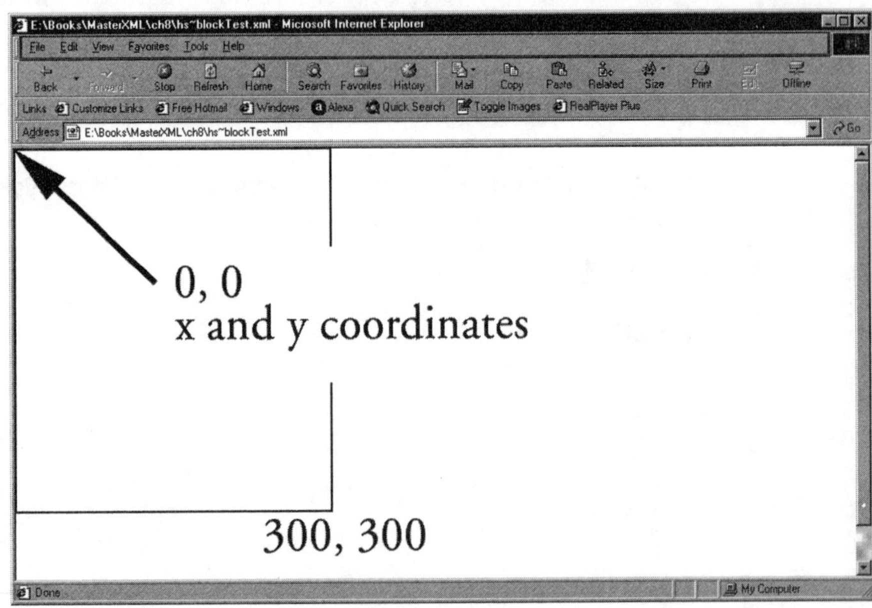

FIGURE 13.5:

Rendering an XML document using absolute positioning

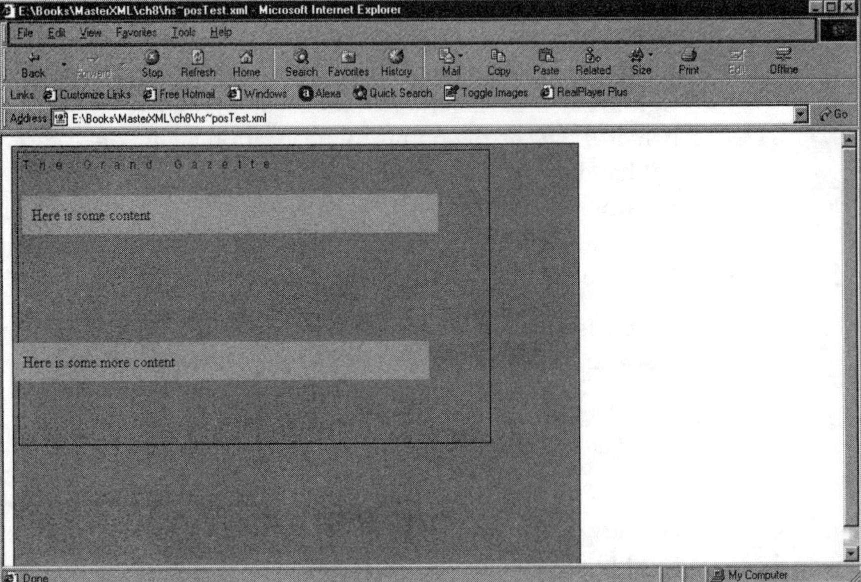

LISTING 13.1 A Style Sheet with Absolute Positioning

```
AD {display:block;
position: absolute;
top: 10px;
left: 10px;
background-color:#FF9900;
padding:10px;
border: black 1px outset;
width: 600px;
height: 450px;
}
NEWSPAPER {display:block;
position: absolute;
top: 5px;
left: 5px;
letter-spacing: 10px;
font-family: sans-serif;
height: 30px;
font-size: 12px;
color: #333333;
width: 500px;
height: 300px;
border: black 1px outset;
padding:5px;
}
DISPLAY {display:block;
position: absolute;
top: 50px;
left: 10px;
width: 440px;}
DISPLAY {position: absolute;
top: 50px;
left: 10px;
}
DISPLAYCONTENT {display:block;
position: absolute;
top: 0px;
left: 0px;
width: 440px;
padding: 10px;
color: #003300;
```

```
background-color: #CCCC99;}
INCOLUMNCONTENT {display:block;
position: absolute;
top: 200px;
left: 0px;
width: 440px;
padding: 10px;
color: #003300;
background-color: #CCCC99;}
```

If you've used CSS in HTML documents, the selectors probably look familiar to you, except that they're not the traditional `P` and `BODY` selectors based on HTML elements. Instead, they're selectors based on elements you can create yourself. Note in Listing 13.1 that there can be a space between the declaration and selector, but it is not required.

Possible Values

```
length
percentage
auto
inherit
```

display

This property tells the rendering engine how, or if, to display an element. Because an XML document might feature a number of elements you may not want to display, you can choose to hide them using this feature. The browser should collapse elements around the items that don't display, and expand those elements' containers if the display is turned back on dynamically through a script.

Possible Values

```
inline
list-item
none
white-space
normal
pre
nowrap
block
run-in
compact
```

```
marker
table
inline-table
table-row-group
table-header-group
table-footer-group
table-row
table-column-group
table-cell
table-caption
inherit
```

font family

This font family name property is used for a specified element. The `family-name` value can be a list of fonts. The rendering engine will then look for those fonts in the order of their appearance in the list. For example, in the code that follows, a rendering engine will search first for `Arial`, then `Helvetica`, then a `sans-serif` font:

```
MYELEMENT {font-family: Arial, Helvetica, sans-serif}
```

A `font-family` value is a known font name, such as Helvetica or Times, whereas a generic family represents a general font type, such as Serif or Sans Serif. The browser searches for what is generally the system default font for the type of font indicated. Note that there must be a comma between each listed font.

The generic fonts can be useful when combined with the `font-weight` property (see "Font Weight") when intelligent user agents are properly using the CSS2 font matching algorithms.

Possible Values

```
inherit
family-name
generic-family: serif | sans-serif | cursive | fantasy | monospace
```

font style

This property indicates whether a font should be bolded (`oblique`) or italicized (`italic`). If neither is indicated, the value is `normal`. A typical instance of its use might look like this:

```
MYELEMENT {font-style: oblique}
```

Possible Values

```
normal
italic
oblique
inherit
```

font weight

Using a value of 100–900 is the way to make the most of this property. Font weight is different from font style in that the property examines entire font families and chooses the best one according to the value you give. Some font families are rather extensive. For example, a computer system may have Futura installed with a number of different font *faces* associated with the name.

For instance, if you wanted to access Futura Bold, you would assign a font weight of 700, because that is how bold faces map out. Medium maps out to 500, and Book maps out to 400. There is no hard and fast rule on how fonts are supposed to map out. Rather, the system is based on a font specification known as `OpenType`. There aren't many `OpenType` fonts around, so generally the rendering engine will do the best it can with the fonts on the system. An example of using `font-weight` might look like this:

```
MYELEMENT {font-weight: 300}
```

In the preceding line of code, the font would render at (hopefully) a little lighter than normal.

Possible Values

```
normal
bold
oblique
100, 200, 300, 400, 500, 600, 700, 800, 900
inherit
```

font size

This property contains a value of an element's font size. You can choose to name the value in a variety of ways, including using either absolute or relative units of measurement. A typical example might look like this:

```
MYELEMENT {font-size: 10px}
```

In the preceding line of code, a font size of 10 pixels is given. You can use any valid CSS unit of measurement to name an absolute size. Or you can use any number of predefined sizes (xx-small, x-small, small, medium, large, x-large, xx-large).

Possible Values

```
absolute-size
xx-small - xx-large
relative-size (larger | smaller)
length
percentage
```

font

You can group numerous font properties together with this property. That way, you can avoid writing code like that shown in the following:

```
MYELEMENT {font-family: Helvetica; font-weight:300; font-size: 30px}
```

You can wrap everything up in one declaration:

```
MYELEMENT {font: Helvetica 300 30px}
```

The rendering engine is supposed to be smart enough to deduce from the type of unit of measurement what each unit is referring to, so there's no special order of appearance for each separate attribute.

Notice how there are no commas or other delimiters other than spaces between the attributes. All global declarations behave this way in CSS.

New in CSS2 is the ability to configure font styles on the system level to manage the styles of fonts in the status bar (using the `status-bar` property), controls like buttons and drop-down menus (`caption`), label icons (`icon`), menu lists (`menu`), and various smaller controls (`small-caption`).

Possible Values

```
font-family
font-style
font-variant
font-weight
font-size
line-height
caption
icon
```

```
menu
message-box
small-caption
status-bar
inherit
```

color

This property paints an element's character data, using a value you provide in the declaration. In the lines of code that follow, any text within the MYELEMENT element would be painted black:

```
MYELEMENT {color:#000000}
MYELEMENT {color: black}
MYELEMENT {color: rgb(0,0,0)}
```

Any of the previous nomenclatures is correct in naming the color value. Regardless of how you choose, the color is based on an RGB color space. CSS3 proposals are suggesting color profile support, as well, but the spec was not fully defined as this book went to press.

Possible Values

```
color
inherit
```

background-color

This property paints an element's background. This can be very helpful in XML because it helps you differentiate elements in a visual way. The background of the element MYELEMENT in the following line of code, for example, would be painted a light shade of yellow:

```
MYELEMENT {background-color:#FFFFCC}
```

You can also choose to have a transparent background, which is, incidentally, the default.

Possible Values

```
color
transparent
inherit
```

background-image

CSS also allows you to use an image as a background. You can use either an absolute URL as a value or a relative path:

```
MYELEMENT {background-image: url(wowwattapicture.jpg)}
```

Possible Values

```
uri
none
inherit
```

background-repeat

This property indicates whether an image should repeat, and, if so, what axes the image should repeat along. This controls what HTML authors will recognize as the tiling mechanism. Back in the days before CSS, the only way to use a background image was within the HTML body element. There was no way to control the fact that the image tiled, meaning that the image repeated itself throughout the page background. With CSS, you can use the background-repeat property to prevent or manage the tiling. The background can repeat along either the y axis or the x axis, or both, or not repeat at all:

```
MYELEMENT {background-image: url(myLogo.gif); background-repeat:
repeat-y}
```

Possible Values

```
repeat
repeat-x
repeat-y
no-repeat
inherit
```

background-attachment

An image doesn't have to scroll when a window does. You can set the background-attachment property to `fixed` to keep an image in a fixed position while the containing window scrolls up or down:

```
MYELEMENT {background-image: url(myLogo.gif) background-attachment:
fixed}
```

Possible Values

```
scroll
fixed
inherit
```

background-position

This property names the position of a background image relative to the top left of the element to which the property is applied:

```
MYELEMENT {background-image: url(myLogo.gif) background-position: left
bottom}
```

Possible Values

```
percentage
length
top
center
bottom
left
right
```

background

This is another global property that manages a number of other properties for more compact code, similar to the way the `font` property is used. Instead of using individual declarations for background color, background image, etc., you can develop one declaration, like so:

```
MYELEMENT {background: url(myLogo.gif) repeat-y fixed}
```

Notice how there are no commas or other delimiters other than spaces between the attributes. All global property declarations behave this way in CSS.

Possible Values

```
background-color
background-image
background-repeat
background-attachment
background-position
inherit
```

word-spacing

You can add spaces between words using this property. Any valid CSS unit of measurement can be used to describe the values:

```
MYELEMENT {word-spacing: 20px}
```

Possible Values

```
normal
length
inherit
```

letter-spacing

This property acts as sort of a low-rent kerning mechanism by allowing you to expand the amount of space between letters. Any valid CSS unit of measurement can be used to describe the values:

```
MYELEMENT {letter-spacing: 2px}
```

This results in output that looks like this, depending on how you set your positive values: `k e r n i n g`. Used judiciously, this property can add a nice touch to headlines, especially when combined with a Sans Serif font.

Possible Values

```
normal
length
inherit
```

text-decoration

The `text-decoration` property has gained popularity in HTML circles because it can be used to remove the underline effect from the <a> element. You can also employ a variety of other utilitarian text effects, such as strike-through (`line-through`), and the dreaded `blink`.

Possible Values

```
none
underline
overline
line-through
blink
```

vertical-align

This property is more complex than it appears at first glance. It governs the position of an element within a container, or character data within an element. When you want to apply the property to the way text is aligned within an element, choose one of these values: `top`, `middle`, or `bottom`. If you want to manage the way an element is positioned within a parent element, choose one of these values: `baseline`, `sub`, `super`, `text-top`, or `text-bottom`. In the latter case, the element will be placed relative to the parent element's text baseline. A text baseline is the imaginary line that would be drawn under a line of text that had no descending characters (like a `g`). An example of this property would look like this:

```
MYELEMENT {vertical-align: baseline}
```

Possible Values

```
baseline
sub
super
top
text-top
middle
bottom
text-bottom
percentage
length
inherit
```

text-transform

You can name a property that declares if an element's containing text is capitalized or not by using this property:

```
MYELEMENT {text-transform: uppercase}
```

Possible Values

```
capitalize
uppercase
lowercase
none
inherit
```

text-align

You can also format text by making it flush right, flush left, centered, or justified:

```
MYELEMENT {text-align: justified}
```

A string is used only with table cells for which you specify how to align text within the column of a table. This is useful for aligning the cells of a table for currency, or some other occasion that warrants specific character-based alignment requests. To style currency, you might do something like this:

```
td {text-align: "."}
```

The preceding line of code would align all the cells within a column with the decimal point for a more elegant rendering of a table containing currency. This functionality is not limited to currency, but can be used for any number of reasons you might have for wanting alignment based on a specific character.

Possible Values

```
left
right
center
justify
string
inherit
```

text-indent

You can indent paragraphs using this property, using any valid CSS unit of measure or a relative value:

```
MYELEMENT {text-indent: 1em}
MYELEMENT2 {text-indent: line-height}
```

When you use `line-height` as a value, the rendering engine uses the current `line-height` property of the element.

Possible Values

```
length
percentage
line-height
normal
number
length
percentage
```

margin

This is a global property for managing the `margin-top`, `margin-right`, `margin-bottom`, and `margin-left` properties in any combination. The possible values are all the same, so they are grouped at the end of the list of properties related to margins. Each of the other margin-related properties refers to specific margin areas.

The `margin` property is different than the `padding` property in that the margin is the amount of space existing outside the edge of an element. A typical use of this property might look like this:

```
MYELEMENT {margin: 5px 9px}
```

Multiple values in this global property work as follows:

- If there is one value, all four margins take the named value.
- If there are two values, like in our example, the top and bottom margins take the first value and the left and right margins take the second value.
- If there are three values, the top margin takes the first value, the right and left margins take the second value, and the bottom margin takes the third value.
- If there are four values, the order is top, right, bottom, and left.

Margin properties can be broken down into top, right, bottom and left margins. Each of these has its own property, which you can use in any combination:

`margin-top` This property refers to the top margin of an element.

`margin-right` This property refers to the right margin of an element.

`margin-bottom` This property refers to the bottom margin of an element.

`margin-left` This property refers to the left margin of an element.

Possible Values

```
length
percentage
inherit
```

padding

This is a global property for managing the `padding-top`, `padding-right`, `padding-bottom`, and `padding-left` properties in any combination. The possible values are all the same, so they are grouped at the end of the list of properties related to element padding. Each of the other padding-related properties refers to specific padding areas.

This property is useful for adding space between elements, and is especially useful when you want to add some space between paragraphs of text.

Padding is different from margins in that the padding is the amount of space between the edge of an element and the beginning of the element's content on any or all sides of the element. A typical use of this property might look something like this:

```
MYELEMENT {padding: 5px 9px 2px}
```

Multiple values in this global property work like this:

- If there is one value, all four padding sides take the named value.
- If there are two values, the top and bottom padding sides take the first value and the left and right padding sides take the second value.
- If there are three values, like in our example, the top padding side takes the first value, the right and left padding sides take the second value, and the bottom padding side takes the third value.
- If there are four values, the order is top, right, bottom, and left.

Padding properties can be broken down into top, right, bottom and left padding properties. Each of these has its own property, which you can use in any combination:

`padding-top` This property refers to the padding between the top of an element and the beginning of that element's content.

`padding-right` This property refers to the padding between the right side of an element and the beginning of that element's content.

`padding-bottom` This property refers to the padding between the bottom of an element and the beginning of that element's content.

padding-left This property refers to the padding between the left side of an element and the beginning of that element's content.

Possible Values

```
length
percentage
inherit
```

border-width

This property is a global value for the `border-right-width`, `border-bottom-width`, and `border-left-width` properties. Here is an example of this property in action:

```
MYELEMENT {border-width: 5px 9px 2px}
```

The order of values acts the same as the `padding` and `margin` properties as follows:

- If there is one value, all four borders take the named value.
- If there are two values, the top and bottom borders take the first value and the left and right borders take the second value.
- If there are three values, like in our example, the top border takes the first value, the right and left borders take the second value, and the bottom border takes the third value.
- If there are four values, the order is top, right, bottom, and left.

The other border-related properties take the same kinds of values as the border-width property, but they can only take one value each.

Border width properties can be broken down into top, right, bottom, and left border areas. Each of these has its own property, which you can use in any combination.

border-top-width This property refers to the top border of an element.

border-right-width This property refers to the right border of an element.

`border-bottom-width` This property refers to the bottom border of an element.

`border-left-width` This property refers to the left border of an element.

Possible Values

```
thin
medium
thick
length
inherit
```

border-color

This property names the color of a border. Here is how it might look:

```
MYELEMENT {border-color: #FFFF33}
```

Possible Values

```
color
```

border-style

You can create graphic effects for your borders with this property. The `ridge` and `groove` values, for example, can be used to create boxes for an application's splash page, or to set off an element in some other distinguishing way. Or you can use the `outset` value to drop a border just offset from an element's edge:

```
MYELEMENT {border-style: outset}
```

Possible Values

```
none
dotted
dashed
solid
double
groove
ridge
inset
outset
inherit
```

border-top, border-right, border-bottom, and *border-left*

Use one of these global properties to manage the particulars of a border's style:

```
MYELEMENT {border-top: groove 4pt blue}
```

Possible Values

```
border-width
border-style
color
inherit
```

border

This is another global property, this time for managing the full range of border attributes. You can use any valid CSS unit of measure or a relative unit. A typical example of this property would look quite similar to the `border-top`, `border-right`, `border-bottom`, and `border-left` properties:

```
MYELEMENT {border: groove 4pt blue}
```

Possible Values

```
border-width
border-style
color
width
length
percentage
inherit
height
length
```

float

This property is used for text-wrapping content around elements. It provides a way for you to describe whether an object should float to the left or right of another container, or not float at all. You can't combine this property with absolutely positioned elements. If you do, the browser will ignore the request:

```
MYELEMENT {float:right}
```

In the preceding line of code, the object will actually float to the right of its containing block, and surrounding content will float to the left.

Possible Values

```
left
right
none
clear
inherit
```

Generating Content

CSS2 makes it possible to generate content that doesn't originate from the document tree emanating from the XML source document. You can generate string content using two new pseudo elements, the `:before` and `:after` pseudo elements.

As this book went to press, browser support for these pseudo elements was limited to Netscape 5. Taking advantage of these features is a simple procedure requiring the same basic syntax mechanisms as the rest of CSS.

Using *:before* and *:after* Pseudo Elements

The two pseudo elements used for content generation, `:before` and `:after`, are used in the same way. As their names imply, each is used before or after an element's beginning or ending content. For example, if you want to provide a flag to a reader that a paragraph features a description before the paragraph's contents actually begin, you would create a rule using the `:before` element. Or perhaps you want to number a list. Again, you can use the `:before` element to accomplish this:

```
p:before {content:description}
p:after {content: thank-you}
li:before {content:
```

Most likely, you'll want to get more specific than this, because you may not desire generated content before every paragraph. In that case, you can associate a class name with the content you want to generate. For instance, if you have a class named `describe`, you would associate the class with the pseudo element and the target element (the `p` element) like so:

```
p.describe:before {content:description}
```

That way, the following line of code would find itself with generated content using style sheets containing the preceding lines of code:

```
<p class= "describe">A small, round mammal that makes unpleasant noc-
turnal hissing noises</p>
```

Whereas the following paragraph would not generate any content:

```
<p>The Three Toed Sloth</p>
```

The engine that really drives this process is the `content` property. This property takes any number of values to guide you in generating your content.

content

To generate the type of content you want, you can use the `content` property with `:before` and `:after` pseudo elements. You can name a string value, a URI, a counter for number generation, quote specifications, and even attributes. You use the `display` property to manage the flow of the elements, such as whether or not the content is placed in a box or whether it should be inline. You can also use the `display` property to set the content in something called a *marker box*, which is a box drawn around only the generated content, rather than all of the content, which is the default.

Possible Values

```
string
uri
counter
open-quote and close-quote
no-open-quote and no-close-quote
attr()
```

counter-increment

The `counter-increment` property helps you manage automatic numbering. You use it within the `:before` and `:after` pseudo elements to assist you in providing a more automated structuring process for your style sheets. This is a great tool for generating chapter and section titles, or any other structuring or outlining mechanism for which automatic number generation would be helpful. The syntax looks like this:

```
MYELEMENT:before {
content: "some string" counter(identifier_1)
counter-increment: identifier_1;
}
```

Possible Values

```
identifier
integer
none
inherit
```

counter-reset

Like the `counter-increment` property, the `counter-reset` property helps you manage automatic numbering. You also use this property within the `:before` and `:after` pseudo elements. The syntax looks like this:

```
MYELEMENT:before {
content: "some string" counter(identifier_1)
counter-increment: identifier_1;
counter-reset: identifier_2
}
```

In the preceding example, the `counter-reset` property resets the counter to 0. You can then start it up again as you see fit.

Possible Values

```
identifier
integer
none
inherit
```

Length Units

Valid units of measurement in CSS are as follows:

em A unit of measurement based on the pitch size of the font whose size is being measured

ex A unit of measurement based on a font's lowercase `x` character

px The size in number of pixels

in The size in inches

cm The size in centimeters

mm The size in millimeters

pt The size in points

pc The size in picas

Valid Color Units

Valid color units for CSS properties are as follows:

- #000000 (hexadecimal)
- RRR,GGG,BBB (RGB expressed in units from 0–255)
- R%,G%,B% (RGB expressed in percentages)
- colorName (The actual name of the color)

NOTE The newest CSS3 Working Draft includes support for color profiles. See Color Profiles for CSS3, found at `http://www.w3.org/TR/css3-iccprof`, for the latest W3 activity in that area.

Examining Other CSS Media Types

If you were already familiar with CSS, then you'll be interested in some of the new properties that have found their way into CSS2. For example, there are four new properties that apply to page breaks for printing purposes: `page-break-before`, `page-break-after`, `orphans`, and `widows`.

In addition, there are numerous audio-related style sheet properties (called aural style sheets). For example, `speech-rate` regulates how fast a page should be read, and you can apply speech-related formatting by using such properties as `pitch`, `pitch-range`, `stress`, and `richness`.

Looking at CSS3

As this book went to press, the W3C Working Group was beginning to issue a series of working drafts regarding the newest iteration of CSS, CSS3. Most of these will not be supported in any browsers for some time. We're providing a glimpse ahead. By the time you read this book, they may be much closer to final adoption.

Using the @namespace at Rule

With the advent of XHTML, the W3C is recognizing the need for some namespace support within CSS. So a new *at rule* has been proposed that, as this book went to press, was part of a new working draft emerging that would be part of CSS3. The syntax would look something like this:

```
@namespace prefix namespace
```

The prefix is optional, but if it's not used, then any selector without a prefix defaults to the named namespace in the declared at rule. Namespace at rules follow the same rules as other cascading style sheets, which means that if a namespace is declared more than once within a document, the last one wins.

To declare an XHTML namespace within an at rule, you would include the following in your style sheet:

```
@namespace html url(http://www.w3.org/Profiles/xhtml1-strict)
```

Or

```
@namespace html url(http://www.w3.org/Profiles/xhtml1-transitional)
```

If you want to declare the XHTML namespace throughout the document as your default—a good idea if you're using XHTML—you can just leave off the HTML prefix:

```
@namespace url(http://www.w3.org/Profiles/xhtml1-transitional)
@namespace url(http://www.w3.org/Profiles/xhtml1-strict)
```

To access these namespaces, you can include them in your selectors. This introduces a new operator, the `|` operator, which is called the namespace separator. The characters preceding the namespace separator make up the *namespace component*, in W3C jargon. So the syntax will look something like this:

```
myNameSpace|myElement { font-size:14px }
```

You can also use universal selectors specified by the * operator. Thus, `mynameSpace | * {font-size:14px}` would result in all elements within the declared namespace (the `mynameSpace` namespace) to have a font size of 14 pixels. Of course, cascading style sheets being what they are, this can be overridden by a more localized style rule that applies style to a specific element.

You can also apply the @namespace at rule to attribute selectors. The syntax should look like the following:

```
myNameSpace | myElement [myAttribute] {font-size: 14px}
```

The preceding rule would look for a match of any element named `myElement` that contained an attribute called `myAttribute`, and apply the font-size definition that we declared. The rules about default namespaces and universal selectors apply to attribute selectors just as they do element selectors. Take a look at the following rule and see if you can tell what the match would be:

```
[* | [myAttribute] {font-size: 14px}
```

In the preceding line of code the CSS processor will search for all the elements that have an attribute named `myAttribute`. What's more important is that this match will occur no matter what the namespace, because the universal selector was used to say, "all namespaces, please." This kind of matching capability greatly extends the reach of CSS, if browsers are developed to support it.

The syntax of all CSS3 is subject to change until a final recommendation is drawn up. When this book went to press, there were several working drafts available for CSS3, each focusing on a different aspect of cascading style sheets. These included:

- CSS Namespace Enhancements, found at `http://www.w3.org/TR/css3-namespace`
- Color Profiles for CSS3, found at `http://www.w3.org/TR/css3-iccprof`
- Multi-column Layout in CSS, found at `http://www.w3.org/TR/css3-multicol`
- Paged Media Properties for CSS3, found at `http://www.w3.org/TR/css3-page`

Whether or not the W3C will combine these into one document is not yet clear. The W3C is generally reliable for the way it handles its links, though, and you should be able to find the spec by going to one of the aforementioned sites.

Up Next

Generally, you'll find most of your XML-related CSS development within the confines of XHTML. XHTML is well suited for CSS because CSS was designed with the HTML model in mind. In the future, it is expected that CSS and XSL will converge to some degree, and share formatting objects and other qualities. CSS is an excellent way to leverage older HTML documents against new XHTML, and will greatly enhance your transition efforts. In the next chapter, we'll examine a much more complex style sheet language, XSL. There, you'll find that the basics of XSL are fairly simple. The learning curve is a bit steeper than what you may be used to in the world of style sheets and Web development because the level of complexity grows quickly as you move on.

CHAPTER

FOURTEEN

14

Displaying XML: Introducing XSL

- Introducing XSL
- Creating an XSL document
- Understanding transformations
- Learning about XSL formatting
- Mastering templates

If you're looking for methods to display XML, this is where things begin to get interesting. XSL, which stands for eXtensible Style sheet Language, is a very powerful tool for transforming XML documents into other formats by transforming an XML document into a separate tree structure. Currently, XSL is used primarily to transform XML semantics into a display format, such as the kind of display you're used to seeing in Web browsers. Despite considerable debate about semantics within the XML/XSL development community, XSL has moved along rapidly as a viable XML presentation language.

In this chapter you'll learn about the first of two main parts of XSL transformations. These determine which part of an XML document will actually be rendered. The nice thing about XSL is that you can process as much or as little of an XML document as you want. With very long XML documents you may, in fact, end up with only one line that actually is rendered in a browser or processed by an XSL processing agent. You'll find that there are very practical reasons for this. In the next chapter you'll learn about *formatting objects*, which is a term used to describe the formatting vocabulary of XSL, and is considered the second main part of XSL.

Some of the concepts behind pattern matching may be a little tricky if you don't have a programming background, so we recommend concentrating on the basics in this chapter, and exploring advanced XSL topics later. By the end of this chapter, if you can develop HTML files with some degree of comfort, you shouldn't have any problem creating XSL documents. Some of the specific concepts you'll explore in this chapter include:

- Fundamental XSL concepts such as transformations and pattern matching, templates, and a review of key XSL transformation elements.
- How to combine CSS style sheets with XSL.
- The basics behind the available formatting options.

Introducing XSL

In this book, we use XSL to paint a picture of what in reality are three separate languages in various stages of development at the W3C. When we refer to XSL in this book, we are referring to any one of the following languages, which can be used in various combinations for XSL development:

- The XML vocabulary describing the formatting objects portion of XSL. The syntax in this book is based on the April 21, 1999 W3C Working Draft. The most current working draft can be found at `http://www.w3.org/TR/WD-xsl/`. If you follow the W3C links for XSL, this is where you'll end up. Formatting objects can be inserted into a result tree created by another part of XSL, called XSLT, or XSL Transformations.
- XSL Transformations is a markup vocabulary describing the transformation part of XSL. Most of the syntax in this book is based on the August 13, 1999 W3C Working Draft, although the namespaces reflect the October 8, 1999 W3C Proposed Recommendation, which was released as this book went to press. The most current syntax can be found at `http://www.w3.org/TR/WD-xslt`. XSLT takes an XML document—called a source document—and outputs a completely different version of the document—called a *result tree*—based on a series of filters and patterns that you include within a style sheet.
- The XML Path language (XPath), although not technically XML, is a language used to address XML document fragments, which are portions of an XML document. This language is used by XSLT (also XPointer and XLink) to describe the expressions and location paths (which you'll learn about later) that allow you to create expressions to manage the selection of nodes for more advanced XSL transformations, which we'll cover more extensively in the next chapter. The syntax in this book is based on the July 9, 1999 W3C Working Draft on XPath, which can be found at `http://www.w3.org/TR/xpath`.

Keep in mind that all of these vocabularies were still in the *working draft* stage at the time this book went to press. That means that their specifications as developed by the W3C have not been finalized and are subject to change, and could, potentially, be abandoned altogether. Before taking on XSL in a production environment, be sure you are aware of the status of these vocabularies by checking the appropriate sites for each as listed in this section.

NOTE

Some of these languages may move out of W3C Working Draft stage into W3C Recommendation status by the time you read this. Review `http://www.w3.org/Style/XSL/` for the most current links and the status of all the documents relating to XSL.

TIP

Many of the formatting properties used by XSL can be found by referencing CSS and CSS2 (the Cascading Style Sheet languages) at `http://www.w3.org/Style/css/`.

Introducing Transformations

If you've used CSS style sheets with HTML, you're familiar with the way selectors are used to apply styling to HTML elements. If you haven't used CSS before, don't worry, because XSL is a different type of process. The only advantage CSS users have is their familiarity with some of the specific properties of CSS that we reviewed in the previous chapter.

XSL takes a different approach than CSS. An XSL processor looks at an XML document and calls it a source document. Then it examines the XML and makes decisions based upon the way you write the XSL document. You may, for example, tell the XSL processor to render only the `text` element (not to be confused with a text node in general) in an XML document that may in fact be loaded with many more elements. You can tell the XSL processor to do this in an XSL document by employing transformation mechanisms such as *patterns*. It may remind you somewhat of a mini-search engine. The process for developing patterns will look somewhat familiar to anyone who has worked with SQL, which is a common database querying language. The XSL processor searches for a pattern, and a series of one or more *templates* that match these patterns to return a *result tree*. The result tree is a third document instance that is derived from the application of the style sheet document to the source tree. You'll find out exactly what templates and patterns are just a bit later in the chapter.

Consider a situation in which you only want one small portion of an XML document to be transformed. Much of an XML document may be dedicated to information that you're not interested in showing to anyone else. If you are developing for a newspaper, you may want your classified advertising to have XML constructs, but you don't want to display or send to the client items such as run dates or client names. XSL allows you to simply choose which elements you want to display (see Listing 14.1) or send. The XML document is so large that it wouldn't be prudent to include it all in this book. The `<!-- more xml content here in production document -->` comment near the end of Listing 14.1 indicates the areas of the document that are snipped. The XSL document that will actually be applied to Listing 14.1 will attempt to match only *one* element for transformation. It will create a result tree out of that element and leave the rest of the original document and elements alone.

LISTING 14.1 A Fragment of a Larger XML Document for XSL Pattern Matching

```
<?xml version="1.0" ?>
<?xml-stylesheet type="text/xsl" href="helpwanted.xsl" ?>
<advertisement action="update">
     <!-- more xml content here in production document-->
          <address>
               <address_line>Northpoint Communications</address_line>
               <address_line>80th Floor</address_line>
               <city>San Francisco</city>
               <state>CA</state>
               <postal>10000-1234</postal>
               <country>USA</country>
          </address>

     <text>
          <font size="10">
               <center>
                    <keyword name="empl_category" punct=" ">Computers
                    </keyword>
                    <keyword name="empl_title" punct=" ">Director of
                    Information Technology </keyword>
               </center>
          </font>
          <keyword name="empl_experience">Northpoint Communications is
          seeking a proven and dedicated IT professional with at least
          5 years experience in enterprise, systems and network manage-
          ment and administration</keyword>

          <keyword name="empl_skills">Must have experience in COBOL,
Y2K, PBX systems, Novell, Networking, and be able to manage large-scale
enterprise systems.</keyword>
          <center>
               <keyword name="phone">
                    no calls please
               </keyword>
          </center>
     </text>
     <!-- more xml content here in production document-->
</advertisement>
```

If you look through Listing 14.1 you'll find a `text` element. This is the element that will be matched by the XSL processor. Figure 14.1 shows the result in an XSL-enabled Web browser. There is quite a bit of information in the XML source document, but not much is pertinent to our task at hand, which in this scenario is just to be able to show the ad in a browser. Most of the other information in the XML document, though important from an administrative standpoint, isn't of significance to someone who just wants to display the advertising copy that is embedded in the document. So an XSL document is created that, in effect, matches the `text` element and displays its contents (including any of its child elements).

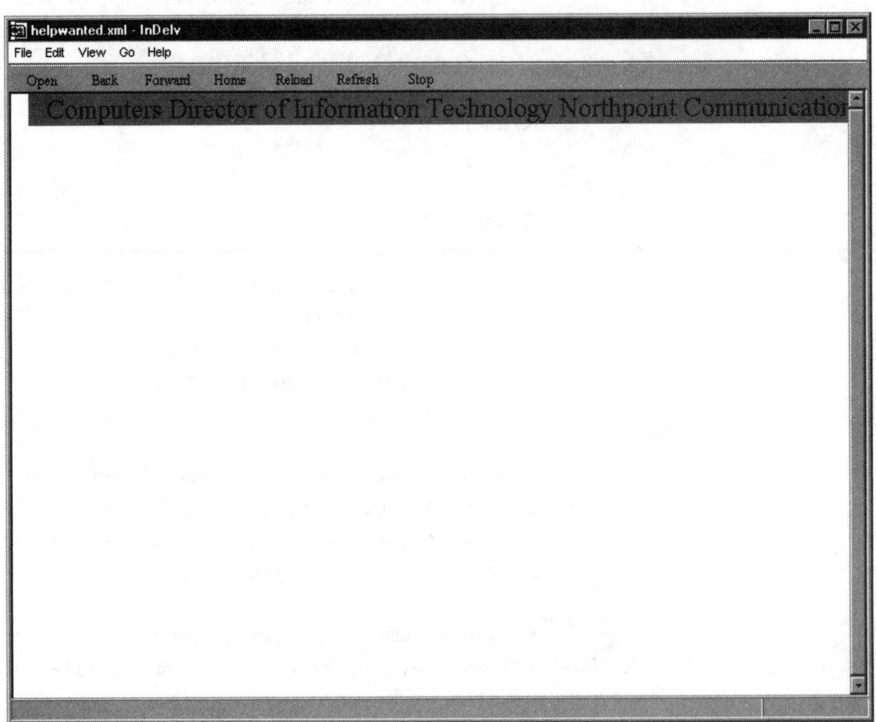

FIGURE 14.1: The XSL Processor displaying XML elements based on a pattern match

If you look at the following snippet from the actual style sheet, you can get an idea of how it works, as long as you don't worry about the details yet. The initial match is made on the root node of the XML document, which is always the document itself (not the root element, as one might suspect).

NOTE

Remember this important point: The root node of the XML source document is always the document instance, which is a node. The patterns that are matched against this node are matched to the children of the root node, and do not include the node itself.

```
  <xsl:template match="/">
  <fo:block
   font-size="40pt"
   background-color= "#ff6600"
   border-color="#000033"
          start-indent="12pt">
    <xsl:apply-templates select="advertisement/text"/>
  </fo:block>
</xsl:template>
<xsl:template match="advertisement/text">
  <fo:block
   font-size="20pt"
   border-color="#000033"
          start-indent="12pt">
    <xsl:apply-templates/>
  </fo:block>
</xsl:template>
```

Note that in the preceding code we left out the XML prolog and `xsl:stylesheet` element, but otherwise it is a complete style sheet. The key ingredient to this code is this fragment: `xsl:template match="advertisement/text"`. You'll revisit this element later, but for now you should know that this element is used to create templates. In this case, a template was made for the source document's `text` element. The `advertisement/text` value in the `match` attribute is a location process that searches for matches that you will learn shortly.

Deciding on a Formatting Model

The transformation process is basically the same no matter what your result tree looks like. Even the IE5-based XSL transformation syntax is very nearly the same thing as the W3C's standards, although the syntactical differences that exist are fatal to a compatible, write-once run-anywhere approach. The formatting model you choose for the result tree, however, can vary significantly. Among the possibilities:

- You can use an HTML-based formatting model, meaning you can end up with a result tree consisting of HTML markup (either XML-compliant or not).

- You can use formatting objects based on the W3C's official recommendation for XSL, which are a series of markup tags developed by the W3C that describe a paged media similar to what you might find in print media layout programs but can also be displayed in browsers.
- You can output the result tree as raw text or byte streams.
- You can output the result into any number of other XML-based vocabularies, such as SVG (Scalable Vector Graphics), an emerging vector graphics Web standard.
- Theoretically, you can probably even output the result tree as PostScript, RTF (Rich Text Format), or some other non-XML language or markup, but the difficulties encountered doing so probably wouldn't make it worth the bother (although never underestimate the resilience of determined programmers).

Even though there is a W3C-defined standard for formatting objects, you are not bound to it, and the W3C XSLT specs have a number of examples showing several formatting options. There are no formal official requirements or restrictions on what to use as your result tree-formatting model. This is true even though the Web site you are taken to when looking up the latest W3C Working Draft for XSL is a site that describes formatting objects markup (`http://www.w3.org/Style/XSL/`).

No matter what form your formatting takes, you are likely to add what are called *literal elements* to your result tree. A literal element is an element you hard code into your output yourself, and isn't part of the XSLT namespace. This acts as the formatting information for the data that is inserted into a result tree from the source document. In our previous example, you may have noticed some strange-looking syntax within the template:

```
<fo:block
     font-size="40pt"
     background-color= "#ff6600"
     border-color="#000033"
            start-indent="12pt">
      <xsl:apply-templates select="advertisement/text"/>
    </fo:block>
```

The `fo:block` element is an example of a literal result element found in templates. It is also a formatting object. You use this to add to a template in your style sheet and use it as a formatting container of sorts for the data from the XML source document that needs to be formatted. The XML data can't format itself. So you need to give it some help. You do this by adding these literal result elements to a template. In the preceding code, the data in the `text` child element of the `advertisement` element will take on the formatting characteristics of the surrounding literal result elements.

Letting Built-In Transformations Take Over

XSL provides a default mechanism so that there is always *something* rendered when a style sheet is created. These are "built-in" and recognized by the XSL processor (although IE5 has its own defaults that you'll learn about in Chapter 19: "XML-Enabled Browsers."). Any template you create overrides these defaults, but they do exist and result in text being placed into a result tree.

Built-In Element Transformations

The simplest default transformation involves the way elements are handled. If you had no definitions of your own, then the XSL processor would handle elements as if you had written the following:

```
<xsl:template match="*|/">
     <xsl:apply-templates/>
</xsl:template>
```

You'll learn about operators later, but for now just be aware that the preceding code covers everything, because if you translate the search pattern to English it would mean "any element node or the root node." The forward slash (/), or virgule, always represents the root node when it is by itself.

A built-in transformation also exists for modes (which you'll learn about when you learn more about template matches later in the chapter):

```
<xsl:template match="*|/" mode="m">
     <xsl:apply-templates mode="m"/>
</xsl:template>
```

Built-In Text and Attribute Transformations

There is also a built-in transformation for text and attributes. This transformation copies the text and attribute values from the source document to the result tree:

```
<xsl:template match="text()|@*"
     <xsl:value-of select="."/>
</xsl:template>
```

Additional Built-In Transformations

There are also built-in transformation rules for processing instructions and comment nodes. They tell the processor to go ahead and do nothing. This means that when no rule is matched no processing instruction or comment node is created in the result tree from the source.

Creating an XSL Document

An XSL document uses namespaces to enable XML documents to pass transformation and formatting instructions to an XSL processor. The style sheet is then accessed with a processing instruction in the XML source document:

```
<?xml-stylesheet type="text/xsl" href="myXSLdoc.xsl" ?>
```

Note the difference with the `type` attribute value when you are processing an XML document for display using CSS instead of XSL:

```
<?xml-stylesheet type="text/css" href="myXSLdoc.css" ?>
```

The processing instruction for a style sheet can take a number of pseudo-attributes. The same pseudo-attributes are used whether you're linking an XSL style sheet or a CSS style sheet. All but the `alternate` pseudo-attribute behave like the HTML 4 `LINK` element (`<LINK REL="stylesheet">`). The `alternate` pseudo-attribute behaves like (`<LINK REL="stylesheet">`. The available attributes are shown in Table 14.1.

TABLE 14.1: Pseudo-Attributes Used with the `<?xml-stylesheet ?>` PI

Pseudo-attribute	Description
`href`	A required pseudo-attribute that gives the location of the style sheet as a URI string
`type`	A required pseudo-attribute that names the kind of style sheet being linked
`title`	An optional pseudo-attribute that names the style sheet
`media`	An optional pseudo-attribute that names the target media
`charset`	An optional pseudo-attribute that names the character set associated with the style sheet
`alternate`	Available values for this pseudo-attribute are **yes** and **no**, with a default of **no**

The XSL style sheet itself is an XML document. Like all XML documents, you can create an XSL style sheet in any text editor. Rather than saving the file with a `.xml` extension, however, you give it a `.xsl` extension.

The style sheet's elements all have a leading prefix that matches the namespace prefix declared at the beginning of the style sheet. Technically, in some implementations, you don't need to use the `xsl:` prefix you'll find throughout this chapter and the next, but you should use it anyway. However, the latest W3C Working Draft requires the use of the `xsl:` prefix.

NOTE You'll learn about where and how to declare your namespace later in the chapter when you learn about the `xml:stylesheet` element.

It is possible (though doubtful) that by the time you read this, the spec will change again about requiring the `xsl:` prefix. You should use it anyway. The reason you should use the `xsl:` prefix is that some XSL processors are not namespace aware, or, if they are, they interact with other programs that aren't. These kinds of XSL processors use elements like the `xsl:element` element as fixed elements, so giving the element a different prefix based on a different namespace won't work. Besides, it's just the generally accepted practice. Chances are, people won't recognize what you're doing if you use a different namespace and prefix name.

Understanding Transformations

Transformations in XSL can involve a number of different processes, but generally they are all centered on the notion of a special kind of addressing process based on pattern matching and selecting. This is really a pretty simple concept, although the implementation of XSL addressing can be quite complex. If you were to translate the syntax of XSL into English, a typical addressing mechanism in XSL at its most basic level would go something like this: "I'm looking for every Siamese cat in your data base. Please return each match as you find it." You can push these types of queries into just about any direction imaginable. You won't necessarily get a response to queries of this type, but you might, and nothing really bad happens by asking. For example, figuratively speaking, you could say something like, "I'm looking for every Siamese cat in your data base that has green ears and speaks Esperanto."

Chances are, you'll come up empty. XSL lets you try however, using the syntax that is designed for XSL pattern matching.

You might be wondering, then, why transformations are not called queries. The reason is that XSL (or more correctly, XSLT, which is what the transformation part is called) doesn't truly respond to queries, at least not in the typical sense of a database query via SQL or some other well known database querying mechanism. XSLT transforms a source document into a new *result tree*, based on a pattern of matches you develop. Each element in the source document is matched against the matching elements in the XSL document as the source document is read: this process is known as *ordering*. The result tree is often written out as an HTML document, but it can also be written as a group of formatting objects. In other words, it *transforms* an XML source document, or tree, into something else.

The important thing to remember about the whole transformation process is that it is quite separate from the formatting process. The transformation vocabulary (specifications as implemented by the W3C Working Group) makes no demands about *how* your documents should be formatted.

NOTE A thorough discussion of namespaces can be found in Chapter 11: "Understanding Namespaces."

Learning about Pattern Matching and Selecting

One key tool that drives the transformation engine is pattern matching. Perhaps the easiest way to understand pattern matching is by returning to the search for Siamese cats. Let's say you have a small database of all the Siamese cats in your town. If you maintained this information in XML it might look something like this:

```
<CATS>
<SIAMESE>
<NAME>Maurice</NAME>
<NAME>Felica</NAME>
<NAME>Fred</NAME>
<NAME>Tom</NAME>
<NAME>Elroy</NAME>
<GREENEARED>Elroy</GREENEARED>
<YELLOWEARED>Tom</YELLOWEARED>
<NOEARS>Maurice</NOEARS>
</SIAMESE>
</CATS>
```

Using pattern matching, rather than doing a search for all the cats, you create a matching pattern that each incoming element from the source XML document is matched against. If you were sure they all had a name, you could match each instance of a cat whose name was represented in the XML source file as a value for the `NAME` element. Forget for a moment how this pattern would be formatted in a result tree. For now, you know that the following values would show up if the result were to appear in a comma delimited text file: `Maurice`, `Felica`, `Fred`, `Tom`, and `Elroy`.

Understanding the Concept of Pattern Matching

Often in any search there is a process called drilling down. This just means that you want more specific information from the results that you've already retrieved. Pattern matching works in a similar way. In the current matching attempt for cats you want to match any cat that has green ears. That would be `Elroy`. In XSL, this is handled by specific elements that are part of the XSLT vocabulary. Without worrying yet what exactly the following element means, just know that to get your first result, you merely wrote the following line of code:

```
<xsl:template match= "NAME">
```

The preceding line of code matches any element called `NAME`. This particular pattern is not particularly effective, though, if your XML document has multiple elements with `NAME` children. You might have a bunch of dogs (with names) in the same database, or maybe different kinds of cats other than Siamese, so you need to find a way to filter out the stuff you don't want. XSLT provides convenient syntax for filtering called *location paths*.

NOTE

The semantics behind all this gets kind of strange if you've neverencountered this kind of syntax, so don't get too bogged down in it. The more you read about XSLT, the more you'll hear about XPath, and the way it is used to manage *expressions*. Generally, expressions use the XPath language to refine the search capabilities of elements that use the `select` attribute, whereas the `match` attribute uses a subset of the expression capabilities described by XPath. This subset of XPath is incorporated into the XSLT language.

Using Location Paths

Remember the line of code that was used to match Siamese cats (`xsl:template match="NAME"`)? You'll remember it wasn't specific enough, and that you needed to filter out the other cats and dogs that might be in the database. You can create a *location path* to help you address your match properly. The structure of a location path will remind you of the kind of paths you see for URLs in your Web browser. To make your addressing specific, you just traverse the XML document tree, following its structured hierarchy to your destination:

```
<xsl:template match= "CATS/SIAMESE/NAME">
```

It might be natural to assume based on what you know about XML that it would be incorrect to write this:

```
<xsl:template match= "NAME">
```

After all, you haven't included the root element. The preceding code isn't invalid, however, because XSLT lets you simply ask the XSL processor to find a match against a specific element. Whatever additional information you supply is up to you (as long as it's legal syntax according to XSLT or XPath). One form of information you can add comes in the form of operators that describe an element's relationship relative to the current node being worked from. You'll learn more about these later in the chapter.

Both of the examples cited are examples of patterns. They form the core of the XSL transformation language. What *is* similar to the way Web addresses work is the way you drill down, not along a directory structure as on the Web but along the XML source document's hierarchy. It would be invalid to write something like this based on the way the CATS XML source document is structured:

```
<xsl:template match= "CATS/GREENEARS">
```

The reason this kind of match would not be successful is that in this case, the GREENEARS element is a child of the SIAMESE element, not the CATS element. A pattern matching sequence must use a very specific pattern matching procedure that strictly follows the hierarchy of an XML source document in order to be successful. You'll find that expressions deviate from this rule to some extent, but even complex expressions require a context from which everything else is referenced. In a nutshell, this procedure dictates that patterns must use what is called a *context node* from which XSL processors initiate their search. A context node is the first instance of a match within a transformation element. If there is no value named in an XSL element's match attribute, and then the context node is always the root node. In the preceding example, the context node was CATS. The only way to drill down is to work with:

- The element's children.
- The element's attributes.

- The element's siblings (if expressions are used).
- The element's parents (if expressions are used).

TIP

Much XSL matching will be done without the knowledge you have here. In other words, you already know there is no `GREENEARS` element that is a child of the `CATS` element. But what if you don't know whether there is or not? There are two possible solutions. One, XSLT allows for extremely sophisticated filtering, so you might be able to accomplish a satisfactory match using more sophisticated patterns. Two, this is a good reason why DTDs should be used whenever possible. A DTD will tell you whether or not such an element is permitted, and you can then manage your patterns based on the rules in the DTD.

These rules are managed by *location match patterns,* which guide the process of identifying the way location paths are traversed. In the example, you established your context node using the `match` attribute of the `xsl-template` element. Then you focused on getting to specific children of that element. All XSL transformations follow this basic concept. It can all get pretty complex, but just remember that no matter how extravagant some of the XSL code you run into may seem, it is all based on this general matching or selecting mechanism that is designed to help you filter out specific information.

Using Pattern Operators

There are a number of operators that are important because they help manage the way patterns are managed. In particular, they help manage the scope of patterns. Technically, they're shortcuts to more complex descriptions of XSLT patterns, but they have an advantage because they're easy to use and make for shorter code.

The `@` Operator The `@` is an attribute operator that locates the named attribute within a given element. To use it, you place the operator in front of the name of the attribute you're searching for within the search pattern string:

```
xsl:value-of select="keyword@name"
```

If you're trying to perform a pattern match for a specific attribute value, you can use brackets to set it off:

```
xsl:value-of select="keyword[@name='auto_exterior']"
```

The * Operator The * mimics a wildcard, which means it can find all instances of a named node's children. It's not really a wildcard in a true programming sense, but is instead an operator for managing the syntax of abbreviated axis identifiers you encountered earlier. Nevertheless, you will see it referred to often as a wildcard in XSL documentation, so we'll follow that convention in the examples in this chapter. To see this operator at work, take a look at the following two snippets of code. Both of them are used to format the XML document fragment that appears at the beginning of this chapter. The first snippet, written for IE5, demonstrates what happens when one element is selected within a template match pattern:

```
<?xml version='1.0'?>
<xsl:stylesheet xmlns:xsl="http://www.w3.org/TR/WD-xsl">
     <xsl:template match="/">
          <HTML>
               <BODY>
     <xsl:for-each select="advertisement">
               <p style="font-family:sans-serif; color:#003300; font-
     size:12pt">
<xsl:value-of select="*"/>
               </p>
     </xsl:for-each>
          </BODY>
          </HTML>
     </xsl:template>
</xsl:stylesheet>
```

Figure 14.2 shows how IE5 renders the document. The only element that has any formatting displayed is the `advertisement` element. You can quickly amend your document to display all the `advertisement` element's children by simply adding a wildcard after a backslash:

```
<xsl:for-each select="advertisement/*">
```

So now your new style sheet looks like this:

```
<?xml version='1.0'?>
<xsl:stylesheet xmlns:xsl="http://www.w3.org/TR/WD-xsl">
     <xsl:template match="/">
          <HTML>
               <BODY>
                    <xsl:for-each select="advertisement/*">
                         <p style="font-family:sans-serif;
     color:#003300; font-size:12pt">
<xsl:value-of select="*"/>
                    </p>
```

```
        </xsl:for-each>
                </BODY>
            </HTML>
        </xsl:template>
    </xsl:stylesheet>
```

It's the same style sheet, with that one exception of a new wildcard operator. As you can see within the `xsl:value-of` element, you can also use the operator by itself as an attribute value. In both uses of the wildcard operator's use in the preceding code, it is used as part of an abbreviated location path.

FIGURE 14.2:

Formatting one element in an XML document

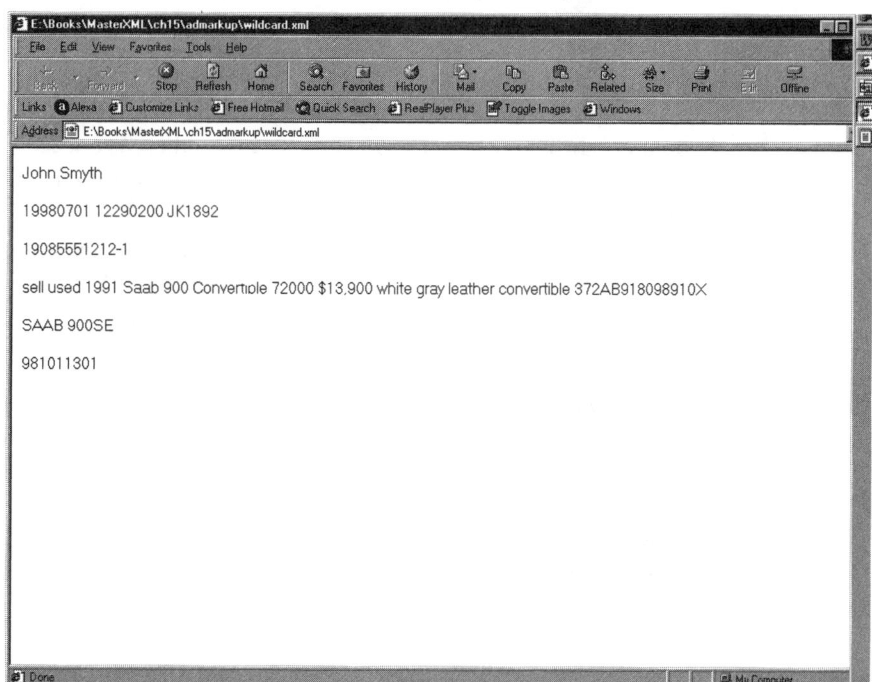

NOTE You'll be examining what elements, such as the `xsl:for-each` and `xsl:value-of`, do a bit later in this chapter.

Using / and // Operators You can manage your pattern selection process by using a / or // operator to tell an XSL processor how to navigate a source document's hierarchy. The forward slash (/) operator tells the processor where a named node lies in relation to its child or parent. If a node is on the left side of the slash, it is a parent of whatever is on the right side of the slash. If a node is on the right slide of the slash, then it is a child of whatever is on the left side:

```
xsl:value-of select ="PARENTELEMENT/CHILDELEMENT"
```

Another selection operator is the double forward slash (//). This is called the recursive descent operator, which tells the processor to search for every node named on the right of the operator that is below the node named on the left of the operator. Thus, //MYELEMENT would result in every instance of MYELEMENT being returned, because it is acting on the root element (by default, since there is nothing to the left of the element, the processor assumes it must be the root element). In other words, it looks for all the descendents of the named node, and doesn't care where in the hierarchy they are located.

The ., or current context operator, tells the processor to look for the pattern named on the right within the current context. When there is one slash following the current context operator (./), the XSL processor searches within the current context. When the current context operator is followed by two slashes (.//), the same thing is accomplished, only in a strictly descending order. For example, ./TEXT, would generally mean the same thing as /TEXT. However, .//TEXT would result in all TEXT elements that are descendents, or below, the current context node (the current element) being selected.

The | Operator Also called the union operator, this operator is used to allow your pattern to take an either/or search. You can use it in a match pattern, like so:

```
<xsl:apply-templates match="MYELEMENT | YOURELEMENT"/>
```

Using Grouping Operators You can also use grouping operators to manage hierarchy navigation. The grouping operators include parentheses (), brackets ([]), and braces ({}).

Generally, brackets are used for filtering operations, such as the following, where you search for a Siamese cat with yellow ears:

```
SIAMESE[EARS="YELLOW"]
```

In the preceding code, you searched for a child element of the SIAMESE element called EARS, then drilled further down by checking that the content of EARS was YELLOW. The corresponding XML fragment would look like this:

```
<SIAMESE>
<EARS>YELLOW</EARS>
</SIAMESE>
```

Learning about XSL Node Types

XML documents consist of what are called trees, which are examined by XSL processors to determine how to output results. You begin with a source tree, and end with a result tree. Central to the concept of trees is the concept of nodes, which are, in effect, data objects that can be categorized in one way or another. When talking about a tree, or an XML hierarchy, we are talking about the way an XML document's nodes are navigated, named, sorted, and output. There are seven node types used in XSL:

Root nodes There can only be one root node because it represents the document's root, of which, by definition (the XML spec requires a tree), there can only be one. That is because this node represents the document itself. Its value is the same as the document element in the Document Object Model (DOM), and can be referred to in any number of ways depending on what you are reading. Generally it is called a document instance. The first child of the document instance, or root node, is the root element.

Element nodes An element node represents an element and can include an URI reference and can have comment nodes and processing instruction nodes as a child. The document order is determined by the order of appearance of the elements within the root node. Any entity references are expanded, character references are resolved, and a unique identifier can only exist if the XML document containing it is validated against a DTD that declares that element, as an `ID`. If there is no DTD declaration, then there are no unique identifiers. The value of this node consists of all the character data within the element. If the element has children, then the character data is concatenated (think of two strings of text strung together) in document order.

Text nodes Text nodes consist of groups of one or more instance of character data, including character data in a `CDATA` section. Comments and processing instructions content is not considered character data.

Attribute nodes These are nodes consisting of attributes. If a DTD includes an `#IMPLIED` attribute but the XML source document does not name that attribute, there is no associated node for it. There are also no attribute nodes associated with namespace declarations.

Namespace nodes Each element also has a namespace node corresponding to its namespace prefix and the default namespace prefix (such as `xsl:` and `xmlns`, respectively).

Processing instruction nodes Any processing instruction appearing in the document has a corresponding node consisting of the name, which is the target of the processing instruction, and the value, which is a string that appears after the target but doesn't include the ?> termination delimiter. A processing instruction node is not included in the processing tree.

Comment nodes A comment's value is that part of the comment that falls within the `<!--and-->` characters. The nodes are associated with the comment's value.

Each node has a corresponding string value that is either an inherent part of that node or can be ascertained from the value of the node's descendents. Because of the normalization rules of XML, it's possible that white space will be stripped during the transformation process. XSL provides ways to control this, including the `xsl:text` element and the `xsl:space` attribute. Neither the processing instruction node nor the comment node is included in an XSL processing tree.

Understanding Templates

An XSL template governs the way specific elements are matched and transformed. These specific elements can include the entire XML source tree or only a small portion of it. The choice is made through the use of templates. Templates are matched up against source tree elements, and formatting elements are inserted into them by another part of the style sheet. The core process underlying the use of XSL templates is a programming trick called recursion. In the programming world, recursion occurs when a function calls itself, which in some languages can be a dangerous thing if you don't include a way to stop it from calling itself (the function may just repeat forever). In XSL this isn't a problem. XSL templates are able to apply themselves within their own definitions, and the action elements that apply templates (surprisingly enough called `xsl:apply-templates` elements) can search recursively for templates that are defined later in the style sheet.

XSL Template Elements

To understand how templates are used, let's get right into the elements that are used to manage them. In the next few sections we'll look at three key elements:

The `xsl:stylesheet` element Used as the parent for your style sheet.

The `xsl:template` element Used to define a template.

The `xsl:apply-templates` element Used to apply templates.

There are other ways to add content to templates besides the `xsl:apply-templates` element, but they will be covered in later sections, as well as in Chapter 15.

Using the *xsl:stylesheet* Element

The `xsl:stylesheet` element is always the first element you'll encounter in a style sheet. You can create a template, then apply it as needed. The `xsl:stylesheet` is where you specify any namespaces for the style sheet. If you use formatting objects, for example, you can say so within the `xsl:stylesheet` element using the `result-ns` attribute:

```
<?xml version='1.0'?>
<xsl:stylesheet
version="1.0" xmlns:xsl="http://www.w3.org/1999/XSL/Transform"
     xmlns:fo="http://www.w3.org/1999/XSL/Format"
     result-ns="fo">
```

The preceding code tells the XSL processor that it should format the result tree using formatting objects. There are other formatting procedures available to the processor. The key question will be whether or not the processor will honor your request. The extensibility of the language means that there is considerable discretion in declaring result namespaces, as long as they don't conflict with the namespace (or its prefix) assigned for your style sheet. You'll be reviewing this next.

Managing Namespaces within the `xsl:stylesheet` or `xsl:transform` Element Early in this chapter you learned about how you can use different formatting models in your result tree. Namespaces can be confusing, especially if you're not really interested in namespaces and just want to write style sheets. Namespaces are important, however, because they manage the way XSL and XML documents interact with one another. One way this management occurs is when you use namespaces to define the formatting model. There are several namespaces that can be used within the `xsl:stylesheet` element. Some of these define the formatting model; others provide information about the transformation process. Some of these namespaces include the following:

- `xmlns:xsl="http://www.w3.org/1999/XSL/Transform"`: This is the official standard transformation namespace used as part of the W3C Recommendation (in working draft as this book went to press). You should use this for XSL style sheets you expect to follow the most current standards. It is not supported by IE5.

- `xmlns:xsl="http://www.w3.org/TR/WD-xsl"`: This is the namespace you must use for style sheets processed by IE5. The bad news is that IE5 won't process style sheets with the `xmlns:xsl="http://www.w3.org/1999/XSL/Transform` namespace, and most processors that can render the `xmlns:xsl="http://www.w3.org/1999/XSL/Transform` namespace won't process IE5-compliant style sheets. This is, of course, because IE5 doesn't use a standards-based namespace.

- `exclude-result-prefixes`: This attribute is used in the `xsl:stylesheet` element for those occasions you want to include style sheet elements in your result tree without confusing the XSL processor. You can use the `xsl:exclude-result-prefixes` attribute in literal result elements (non-XSLT elements) to achieve the same effect. The value of each of these two attributes should contain prefixes of the namespaces you want to exclude from the processor's XSL interpretation. These prefixes are separated by white space if there is more than one prefix.

- `xmlns:axsl="http://www.w3.org/1999/XSL/TransformAlias">`: This namespace allows you to create an "alias" transformation namespace. This allows you to place XSLT elements into literal elements, without the XSL processor actually processing them as XSL elements. They are merely written into the result output. In your style sheet such an element might look something like this: `<asxl:template match="someElement"><!-- some result elements here --></asxl:template>`.

Managing Result Trees with Namespaces You can describe how you want your result formatted by including namespace attribute values within the `xsl:stylesheet` element. Note that the result namespace tells the processor what method it *should* use for transforming the source tree. The processor is not required to do so, however. In fact, the XSL processor is not required to use *any* specific formatting vocabulary. A result namespace attribute can only offer a recommendation, or preference, for how the source tree should be transformed.

You can define the result to be formatting objects by using the following namespace:

```
xmlns:fo="http://www.w3.org/1999/XSL/Format"
```

Currently, this namespace is only supported in the browser world by the InDelv XML Browser, which can be found at `http://www.indelv.com` (although it is supported by several XSL processors). You should use this in conjunction with the `result="fo"` attribute name/value pair, but this is not a requirement. Thus, to make a fully compliant, standards-based XSL style sheet using formatting objects, you would use the following style sheet element:

```
<?xml version="1.0"?>
<xsl:stylesheet
version="1.0"
xmlns:xsl="http://www.w3.org/1999/XSL/Transform"
xmlns:fo="http://www.w3.org/1999/XSL/Format"
result-ns="fo">
...
</xsl:stylesheet>
```

Use this namespace to declare your result tree as being HTML 4–compliant:

```
xmlns="http://www.w3.org/TR/REC-html40"
```

This means that the XSL processor should (but is not required to) output the result tree in a way that is compliant with HTML 4. Empty elements can thus end up in the result tree with no closing slash mark (`<br>`). If you don't use this namespace, the XSL processor will transform empty elements by including closing slash marks (`<br/>`), according to XML rules.

NOTE

An exception to this is when you use the **`xsl:output`** element, which also allows you to name your result output formatting. You'll explore this element in Chapter 15.

You can also use the following for those occasions you are working with XHTML. This namespace declares the result tree to be in compliance with XHTML, an XML-based version of HTML under development at the W3C:

```
<xsl:stylesheet xmlns:xsl="http://www.w3.org/TR/xhtml1">
```

If you know your style sheet will contain only one template for the root node, you can use a simplified form of syntax for managing HTML:

```
<html xmlns:xsl="http://www.w3.org/1999/XSL/Transform"
    xmlns:xsl=http://www.w3.org/TR/xhtml1
    xsl:version="1.0">
    ...
```

The preceding code is the same as using this:

```
<xsl:stylesheet
     version="1.0"
     xmlns:xsl="http://www.w3.org/1999/XSL/Transform"
                    xmlns:xsl="http://www.w3.org/TR/xhtml1">
```

You can use a processor-specific namespace, if you know the XSL processor will support the namespace you're using in your attribute value. The following namespace is used by XT, James Clark's XSL processor (more on this in Chapter 15) to output raw text:

```
xmlns="java:com.jclark.xsl.sax.NXMLOutputHandler"
```

SVG is a vector based imaging markup language in development at the W3C. This namespace declares the result to be in SVG format:

```
xmlns="http://www.w3.org/Graphics/SVG/svg-19990412.dtd"
```

NOTE

Note that the SVG DTD declared in the preceding code is a specific working draft. Any future processor that supports SVG will probably use a different namespace. This example is used for illustrative purposes only. Remember that namespaces require processor support in order to work.

As you might have surmised from this review of formatting namespaces, it's not the prefix assigned to the namespace that is important. An XSL processor won't recognize a namespace by its prefix. It will (or won't) recognize the URI assigned to that prefix. You can write your own processor in Visual Basic, put it on your NT server so that it works with ASP, and have it output XHTML. The key for creating an XSLT 1–compliant program will be, aside from programming skills, making sure the processor recognizes the URI and processes the result accordingly.

Learning about `xsl:stylesheet` Child Elements and Attributes Children of the `xsl:stylesheet` element (except for result child elements) are shown in Table 14.2. The child elements of these elements are also shown, thus giving you a summary of many of the elements available to you as an XSL developer. They are based on the August, 1999 W3C Working Draft. These child elements can appear in any order you want. The one exception to this rule is if you use the `xsl:import` element, which must always be the first child element of the `xsl:stylesheet` element.

NOTE You can also use the `xsl:transform` element in place of the `xsl:stylesheet` element—the two elements are interchangeable and are defined in precisely the same way in the XSLT DTD.

TABLE 14.2: Child Elements of the `xsl:stylesheet` Element and Their Child Elements

Element	Children
xsl:import	none
xsl:include	none
xsl:strip-space	none
xsl:output	none
xsl:preserve-space	none
xsl:key	none
xsl:functions	none
Xsl:namespace-alias	none
xsl:decimal-format	none
xsl:attribute-set	xsl:attribute, xsl:use
xsl:variable	xsl:processing-instruction, xsl:comment, xsl:element, xsl:attribute, xsl:apply-templates, xsl:call-template, xsl:apply-imports, xsl:for-each, xsl:value-of, xsl:copy-of, xsl:number, xsl:choose, xsl:if, xsl:text, xsl:copy, xsl:variable, xsl:message
xsl: param	xsl:processing-instruction, xsl:comment, xsl:element, xsl:attribute, xsl:apply-templates, xsl:call-template, xsl:apply-imports, xsl:for-each, xsl:value-of, xsl:copy-of, xsl:number, xsl:choose, xsl:if, xsl:text, xsl:copy, xsl:variable, xsl:message
xsl:template	xsl:processing-instruction, xsl:comment, xsl:element, xsl:attribute, xsl:apply-templates, xsl:call-template, xsl:apply-imports, xsl:for-each, xsl:value-of, xsl:copy-of, xsl:number, xsl:choose, xsl:if, xsl:text, xsl:copy, xsl:variable, xsl:message, any result elements

You'll learn more about these elements in this and the next chapter. Table 14.3 summarizes the attributes that are available to the `xsl:stylesheet` element.

TABLE 14.3: `xsl:stylesheet` Attributes

Attribute	Description
`xml:space`	Tells the XSL processor what to do with white space. The values are `preserve` and `preserve`.
`id`	The style sheet's unique identifier.
`xmlns:xsl`	Declares a namespace for the style sheet; for the current specification (at the time of this writing), the DTD for XSLT indicates that this is a fixed attribute with the value of `http://www.w3.org/1999/XSL/Transform`.
`extension-element-prefixes`	Supplies a white space delimited list of additional namespaces that can be used as extensions.
`exclude-result-prefixes`	Supplies a white space delimited list of namespaces that should not be processed as XSL transformation elements.

xsl:template

A template is a structured container that manages the way a source tree or a portion of the source tree is transformed. Generally, when you build a style sheet, you'll build a series of templates that match elements you'd like to attach some style to. The `xsl:template` defines a set of rules for transforming nodes in a source document into the result tree. This is handled by the `match` attribute, whose value provides the pattern. You might have an element named CATS in your XML source document (document instance).

In the example that follows, the XSL processor will search for CATS elements and insert the corresponding content into an HTML `DIV` element:

```
<xsl:template match="CATS">
     <div>
            <xsl:apply-templates/>
     </div>
</xsl:template>
```

The preceding example is rudimentary. Most likely, you'll want to be more specific about what you want to do. As it stands now, the template applies its children, which means that given this XML file:

```
<?xml version='1.0'?>
      <CATS>
      <SIAMESE>Sam</SIAMESE>
      <PERSIAN>PETE</PERSIAN>
      </CATS>
```

You'll end up with this in your result:

```
<div>Sam Pete</div>
```

Table 14.4 shows the attributes available to the `xsl:template` element, and provides a brief description of their use.

TABLE 14.4: `xsl:template` Element Attributes

Element	Attribute
`mode`	Identifies the processing mode and matches it against an `apply-templates` element that has a matching mode value
`name`	Gives a name to the template so that it can be accessed by the `apply-templates` element
`priority`	Used to prioritize among duplicate matches
`match`	Identifies the template to be processed. A value of / indicates that the root node should be processed

xsl:apply-templates

This element tells the processor to process a named template (which means the children of the named template are processed) that has been defined using the `xsl-template` element. Child elements of the `apply-templates` include:

- `xsl:sort`
- `xsl:with-param`

The possible attribute values for `xsl:apply-templates` are listed in Table 14.5. The attribute you'll use the most is likely to be the `select` attribute, which tells the processor which template to return into the output.

TABLE 14.5: xsl:apply-template Attributes

Attribute	Description
mode	Identifies the processing mode and selects only those **template** elements that have a matching mode value
select	Identifies the node to be processed—if this attribute is not used, then the processor will process the template of the current node in the order of their appearance in the source document

In the example that follows, the template for the P element is applied within the same context as its description. In this case the child template of an XML source file's P element are applied to the result tree. It gives the result tree the following formatting instructions "Apply all templates that match child elements of the P element from the source document and insert into the result tree as instructed by those templates."

```
<xsl:template match="P">
          <fo:block
                font-size="12pt">
                <xsl:apply-templates/>
          </fo:block>
    </xsl:template>
```

The `xsl:apply-templates` element tells the processor to look for any other templates that match the `xsl:apply-templates select` attribute `in` the style sheet and apply them here if they match child elements of the context node. Note that in creating this template, you don't have to use the `apply-templates` element within the `xsl:template` element to make it work. You could choose to apply the template somewhere else:

```
<xsl:template match="P">
          <fo:block
                font-size="12pt">
</fo:block>
    </xsl:template>
<xsl:template match="DIV">
          <fo:block>
                <xsl:apply-templates select="P"/>
          </fo:block>
    </xsl:template>
```

In the preceding block of code, the template is defined in one place, and applied in another. In the previous lines of code, the processor will insert P children of any DIV element into the result tree.

If you use the xsl:apply-templates element without the select attribute, be aware that you may inadvertently be applying default templates. In other words, you might be inserting text nodes (or some other node), even though that is not your intent. Consider the following XSL:

```
<?xml version='1.0'?>
<xsl:stylesheet
version="1.0" xmlns:xsl="http://www.w3.org/1999/XSL/Transform">
<xsl:output method="text" indent="no"/>
  <xsl:template match="nodeTester">
    <xsl:apply-templates/>
</xsl:template>
<xsl:template match="text">
<xsl:variable name="myPositionVariable"
         select="position()"/>
NodeList position = <xsl:value-of
        select="$myPositionVariable"/>
</xsl:template>
</xsl:stylesheet>
```

Now take a look at the source document:

```
<?xml version='1.0'?>
<?xml-stylesheet type="text/xsl" href="position.xsl" ?>
<nodeTester type="referral">
  <function>
    <name>position() function</name>
  </function>
  <text>This function helps find the position of a node in the node
list
   </text>
 </nodeTester>
```

The result document that would be created by this style sheet would look like this:

```
position() function
NodeList position = 4
```

Forget for a moment some of the unfamiliar XSL elements. The main point of this exercise is to point out that because the xsl:apply-templates element is used without the select attribute in the nodeTester template, the default rules take over until they're told otherwise. As an experiment, try adding a `select` attribute to this `xsl:apply`-templates element:

```
<xsl:template match="nodeTester">
    <xsl:apply-templates select="text"/>
</xsl:template>
```

If you run the new code through your XSL processor you'll find that it bypasses the default rules and applies the specific templates you ask it to.

There are many variations on how to manage the way you apply a template. The main point to remember about this element is that it calls on the processor to apply any templates (if they are child elements of the source element) that appear in a given style sheet. Or, if the `select` attribute is used, the processor is instructed to apply all the child templates of the named template.

Understanding Selection Patterns

Pattern matching involves quite a large number of possible addressing routines, and the sections that follow don't come close to covering them all. But to get a handle on the concept it's best to take a look at the simplest transformation elements first.

The one important point is to remember the difference between what is called pattern matching and selection patterns. As we mentioned previously, selection patterns use XPath expressions to greatly expand your pattern's filtering capabilities. Pattern matches are limited to templates, numbering (XSLT has automatic numbering capabilities), and keys (which offer a kind of cross-referencing capability to XSLT).

NOTE Numbering and keys are covered in Chapter 15: "Displaying XML: Advanced XSL."

Pattern matches are also limited in the patterns that can be constructed. You can only match nodes or perform simple tests on the following:

- element names
- child elements
- descendents
- attributes

Selection patterns, however, have the full vocabulary of XPath expressions at their disposal. This means that in addition to what pattern matches can accomplish, expressions give you access to parent and sibling elements.

Another big difference between pattern matches and selection patterns is that pattern matches only generate node lists, whereas selection patterns can generate the following data types:

- strings
- numbers
- Booleans

NOTE The truth is, in your day-to-day XSL development you often won't notice the semantic differences between pattern matching and selection patterns. But you'll find that this knowledge comes handy during those occasions where you run into trouble generating result trees you expect.

Using the *xsl:for-each* Element

The `xsl:for-each` element makes it possible to get more specific with your selection patterns. Actually, the use of this element is only the tip of the iceberg in the selection process. Things can get pretty complex when managing pattern searches. Your filtering options are quite extensive, but they're easiest to understand when you start with this most basic of search patterns. When using the `xsl:for-each` element, you are in effect saying: "For each instance of the element I am naming, do this…" Table 14.6 lists the attributes of the `xsl:for-each` element.

TABLE 14.6: Attribute of the `for-each` Element

Attribute	Description
`select`	Identifies the node to be processed.
`xml-space`	Indicates whether or not white space should be preserved—takes two values: `default` and `preserve`.

If you examine the code that follows, you can see how specific you can get when selecting a node. The `xsl:for-each` element names the element you want the subsequent node test to apply to. It says, "For each `text` element that is a child of the advertisement element (note the use of the backslash for an abbreviated location path), find the first name instance of a keyword element that has a name attribute and that name attribute must have a value of auto-year. If the search is successful, insert the value of the auto-year attribute into an HTML p element, and style it as shown by the included style attribute." Whew! That's a lot of information to take in. You'll learn a bit more about the xsl:value-of element in the next section.

TIP

It's worth noting here, even though you haven't yet encountered the value-of element, that it only returns the first instance of the element that matches the selection. We'll reemphasize this point when we visit this element more formally, but it is an important consideration. It's easy to make the mistake of thinking xsl:value-of will return every instance of the matching element, but that's not the case (in fact, that's what the xsl:for-each element is for).

```
<?xml version='1.0'?>
<xsl:stylesheet xmlns:xsl="http://www.w3.org/TR/WD-xsl">
    <xsl:template match="/">
          <html>
                <body>
                <xsl:for-each select="advertisement/text">
                      <p style="font-family:sans-serif;
    color:#ff6600; font-size:100pt">
<xsl:value-of select="keyword[@name='auto_year']"/>
                      </p>
    </xsl:for-each>
                </body>
          </html>
    </xsl:template>
</xsl:stylesheet>
```

Generally, this element is used in place of apply-templates during those occasions that you are familiar with an XML source document's specific hierarchy. If you know there is a text element that is a child of the advertisement element, it is safe to use this element. If you don't know whether this is the case, however, it's best to use apply-templates. Figure 14.3 shows the result in a browser. It's also a good element to use for repetitive tasks that involve traversing a tree in document order, especially when inserting source XML data into an HTML table.

Did you notice the namespace attribute name/value pair (xmlns:xsl="http://www.w3.org/TR/WD-xsl")? This is the namespace used by the IE5 XSL processor.

If you use the XSL standard namespace, the associated XML file won't show up in IE5 (but of course can still be processed by standards-compliant XSL processing software).

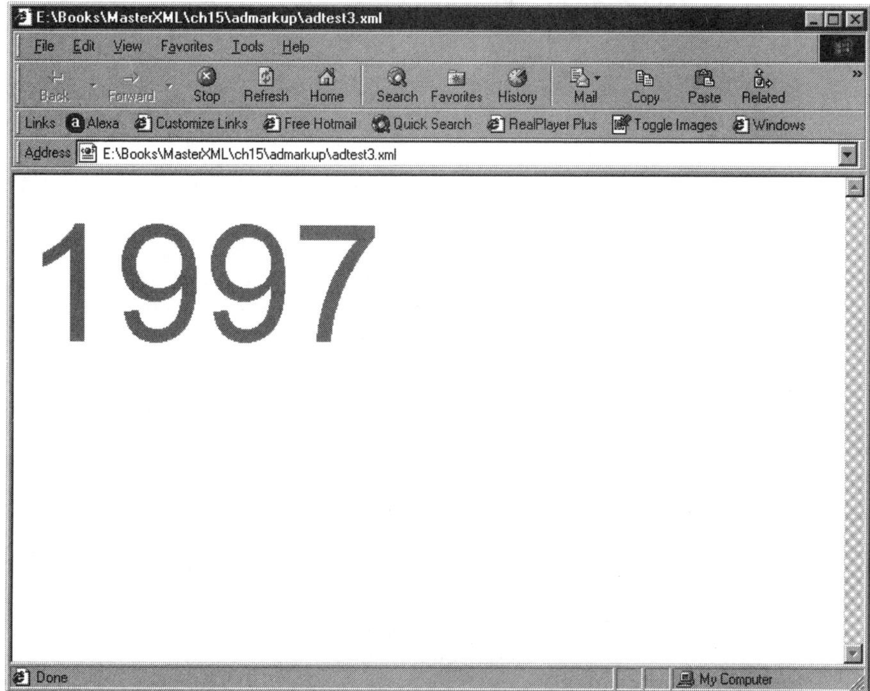

FIGURE 14.3: Using the `xsl:for-each` element

Using the *xsl:value-of* Element

This element evaluates a node and returns its value as a string into the source tree. This is an easy, convenient way to format a specific element by using HTML. Consider the snippet of code that follows:

```
<xsl:for-each select="advertisement/text">
     <p style="font-family:sans-serif; color:#ff6600; font-size:12pt">
<xsl:value-of select="keyword[@name='auto_year']"/>
<span style="font-size:12pt; color:black;">
<xsl:value-of select="keyword[@name='auto_exterior']"/>
<!--make sure there is one white space between each element->
<xsl:value-of select="keyword[@name='auto_body']"/>
```

```
<xsl:value-of select="keyword[@name='auto_mileage']"/></span>
    </p>
    </xsl:for-each>
```

At this point it may be helpful to look at the XML source tree this document is transforming. What follows is a small fragment from the XML document:

```
<text>
        <font size="10">
            <center>
                <keyword name="auto_make" punct=" ">SAAB </keyword>
                <keyword name="auto_model" punct=" ">900SE </keyword>
            </center>
        </font>
        <keyword name="auto_year" punct=" ">1997 </keyword>
        <keyword name="auto_exterior" punct=" ">yellow </keyword>
        <keyword name="auto_body" punct=", ">convertible, </keyword>
        <keyword name="auto_mileage" format="9'k miles'" scale="1000"
                      punct=", ">14k miles, </keyword>
        Auto, PL, PW, AC, power leather Seats
        Showroom cond. Assume lease.
        <center>
            Call
            <keyword name="phone" format="T999-999-9999" punct=" ">
                212-333-3333
            </keyword>
        </center>
    </text>
```

Can you tell what the XSL style sheet is doing? Keep in mind that the XML source tree's root element is an unseen `advertisement` element. So the location path for reaching the `text` element is `advertisement/text`, because `text` is not nested within any other element in the source document.

You can view the entire document on the CD-ROM that comes with this book. The file is called `listing14.1.xml`. The XSL processor is told that for each `advertisement/text` instance, or for every instance that a `text` element is a child of an `advertisement`, it should do something. See if you can tell what the XSL processor is told to do for each instance it encounters the `advertisement/text` combination. Basically, the XSL processor is told to narrow down the search—or more correctly, refine the pattern. Using your `xsl:value-of` element, the XSL processor is told to look not only for specific elements nested within the `text` element, and not only specific attributes within that element (using the `@` operator). It is told to look for specific values for those attributes. This allows for extremely powerful processing. Table 14.7 shows the attributes that are available to the `xsl:value-of` element.

TABLE 14.7 `xsl:value-of` Attributes

Attribute	Description
`select`	Identifies the node to be processed

Other Selection Elements

There are additional selection elements you can use, which we'll look at in Chapter 15. We'll also look at an assortment of sorting and conditional elements that help you define your patterns with as much precision as you care to apply.

Learning about XSL Formatting

The notion of separating transformation from formatting is the main difference between the CSS and XSL style sheet models. Keeping transformations separate from formatting means you can pick how to format the XML documents you are trying to display, by choosing a namespace that your target XSL processor understands. Chances are that if you're using a Web browser like Internet Explorer or Netscape, if it supports XSL at all it will support the namespace that outputs HTML.

In this section you'll learn about the various formatting options available using XSL. You'll do this by examining the following formatting topics:

- First, you'll compare the way HTML and formatting objects are inserted into a result tree using the same XSL element, the `xsl:value-of` element.
- Then, you'll explore how to combine XSL and CSS.
- Finally, you'll take a look at a brand new way to render, or display, XML elements in a browser by learning about formatting objects, which can be easily converted into files for print.

Comparing Formatting Output Options

As you saw earlier in the chapter, a transformation can send a result tree to a formatting namespace that tells the XSL processor how to format the result tree. Recall that one way to apply formatting is to use HTML.

Obviously, the namespace issue discussed earlier in this chapter is a large one when you're writing to a wide audience. Even if Internet Explorer is updated to handle the recommended namespace used by the W3C, there are numerous early versions of IE5 lurking about, which will make it impossible to be sure your audience will be able to view your documents. If that sounds like a familiar lament regarding browser conformance issues, it is.

The most obvious answers are to create your result trees on the server, and send out HTML from there. Any browser can then read these files. Or, use an autodetect script to redirect browsers to the correct page.

What happens when XSL outputs HTML? There are two key operations taking place:

- The XSL processor inserts a requested XML source document node or HTML literal result elements into a named HTML element so that it can be rendered as HTML in a Web browser.
- Unless you include a namespace declaration that indicates the HTML 4 Specification (using the `xmlns="http://www.w3.org/TR/REC-html40"` namespace attribute/value pair), or use the `xsl:output` element, the HTML that is output *must* be valid XML, because you are working with an XML document (the XSL formatting document).

Outputting XML Document Fragments

Let's get right down to it, then, and see how this all works. Consider an XML document for a classified ad. The goal is to render the advertisement in a browser. Although the document contains all of the ad copy you need, it also contains a number of elements you don't want to display. For example, the run dates, the name and contact information of the client, and a host of other internal administrative records are all things you would rather not display to the public at large. Actually, because of privacy concerns, you probably wouldn't want this kind of information to be available semantically through a "view source" browser menu command, either, but let's forego that concern for now. Listing 14.2 shows the XML source document you'll use with your XSL file.

Let's consider the following XML document, which contains some elements we don't want processed by the XSL processor:

LISTING 14.2 An XML Source Tree for XSL Processing

```
<?xml version ="1.0"?>
<?xml-stylesheet type="text/xsl" href="Ad0915HTML_3.xsl" ?>
```

```
<!-- href="Ad0915FO_3.xsl" for FO -->
<advertisement><!-- (id , rundate , text )-->
     <id>001</id>
     <rundate>09/09/99</rundate>
     <text>
     <headline>Career Opportunities at Northpoint</headline>
          <font size="agate">
               <center>
NorthPoint Communications, Inc. is a competitive local exchange carrier
(CLEC) focused exclusively on delivering dedicated data to growing
businesses nationwide through wholesale agreements with service
provider partners. Our rapid deployment of DSL service and incredible
growth and success have created an excellent opportunity for a select
group of experienced, self-motivated team players to join us as we
chart the future of the rapidly evolving data communications and
telecommunications industry. If you would like to speak with our
recruiters in person, come see us at the WorkWorld High Tech Career
Expo in San Francisco (Hyatt Embarcadero Pacific Concourse) on May 3rd
and 4th from 10 am to 7 pm.

We offer competitive salaries and benefits, attractive stock options,
and an excellent opportunity for personal and professional career
growth. The preferred method to apply is via our Web site. Please visit
www.northpointcom.com to review complete job descriptions and for spe-
cific instructions on how to email your resume. If you are unable to
attend the Career Expo, please forward your resume, cover letter and
salary history to: NorthPoint Communications, Human Resources Depart-
ment, 222 Sutter Street, 7th Floor, San Francisco, CA 94108; fax: (415)
273-2660. EOE
               </center>
          </font>
     </text>
</advertisement>
```

If you know that the part of the document you want to display is all contained within the preceding document fragment, you can start with the simplest kind of pattern match that exists. By calling on the `xsl:value-of` element, you can insert a node into a block-level element (valid as XML, incidentally). Take a look in the following style sheet at where the `xsl:value-of` element is. Notice in Listing 14.3 that it is placed between the beginning and ending `H1` tags.

LISTING 14.3 **Inserting an `xsl:value-of` Element into an HTML Literal Result Element**

```
<?xml version='1.0'?>
<xsl:stylesheet
     version="1.0"
     xmlns:xsl="http://www.w3.org/1999/XSL/Transform"
     xmlns="http://www.w3.org/TR/REC-html40">

  <xsl:template match='/'>
    <html><body>
            <xsl:apply-templates/>
                </body>
            </html>
  </xsl:template>
<xsl:template match="advertisement">
  <xsl:apply-templates select="text"/>
  </xsl:template>
  <xsl:template match="text">
  <H1>
     <xsl:value-of select="headline"/>
  </H1>
</xsl:template>
</xsl:stylesheet>
```

If the code in Listing 14.3 seems at all confusing to you, remember that all you're doing is placing some content into a result element, the `H1` element. It's just that the content is an XSL formatting element that has an attribute value matching a node in the XML source document. Basically, it's a content mechanism that retrieves a node from the XML document and inserts it into the content area of the HTML `body` element. The main template is matched against the root node:

```
<xsl:template match="/">
```

You'll find a more structured explanation of how templates work a bit later in the chapter. For now, focus on what the `xsl:value-of` element does. The action takes place in the `text` template, which consists of a literal result element (`H1`), and a node inserted from the XML source file (the text node child of the `headline` element). The text node is inserted between the `H1` element's start and end tags.

The `xsl:value-of` element only picked up the first `headline` child it encountered (in this case it is the only instance, so it doesn't matter), because that's what it does by definition. This element doesn't pick up every instance of an element's children, only the first.

Wait a second, you may wonder. There are no child elements within the `headline` element. Indeed, it is true that there are no child *elements*. But the `xsl:value-of` element doesn't select the child *element* of the `headline` element. It selects the `child` of the headline. In other words, it selects the child *node*, which happens to be a *text* node in this case (remember that nodes aren't only elements—they consist of a number of other types of data). This happens to be the character data we are after. It is displayed in the browser in Figure 14.4.

FIGURE 14.4:

Applying the `xsl:value-of` element using HTML

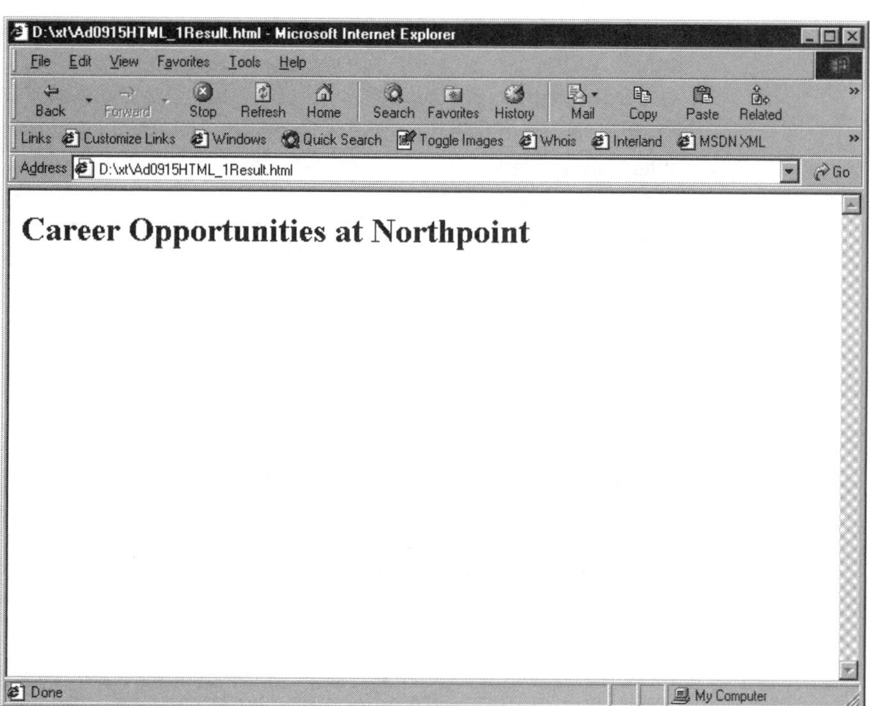

As you can see in Figure 14.4, the following text node is inserted into the result tree: `Career Opportunities at Northpoint` between the `H1` start and end tags. To experiment, try using the same code but adding some literal result elements. For example, you could add a link to the `text` template:

```
<xsl:template match="text">
  <H1>< ahref ="http://www.myDomain.com/jobs">
     <xsl:value-of select="headline"/></a>
  </H1>
</xsl:template>
```

By using the preceding code, you would end up with a link for your headline. This is by no means the only way to format this document fragment, nor even the best way. The best way to get a feel for XSL formatting is to experiment. The possibilities are rather endless, and you can have a lot of fun with it.

Outputting Formatting Objects

Now let's take that very same XML source document, and the same basic XSL style sheet, and create a different kind of result. You'll see that the concept is exactly the same. You wrap your `xsl:value-of` element inside a formatting container. In this case, the formatting container is a formatting object based on the XSL formatting objects specifications created by the W3C (still in W3C Working Draft at the time this book went to press). Listing 14.4 shows a simple formatting object result tree.

LISTING 14.4 Inserting an `xsl:value-of` element into a Formatting Object Literal Result Element

```
<?xml version='1.0'?>
<xsl:stylesheet
     version="1.0"

     xmlns:xsl="http://www.w3.org/1999/XSL/Transform"
 xmlns:fo="http://www.w3.org/1999/XSL/Format"
     result-ns="fo">
  <xsl:template match='/'>
    <fo:display-sequence
        start-indent='6pt'
        end-indent='6pt'
        font-size='12pt'
             font-family='sans-serif'
             >
             <xsl:apply-templates/>
                 </fo:display-sequence>
  </xsl:template>
<xsl:template match="advertisement">
  <xsl:apply-templates select="text"/>
  </xsl:template>
  <xsl:template match="text">
  <fo:block
     font-size='18pt'
     color="red">
     <xsl:value-of select="headline"/>
  </fo:block>
```

```
</xsl:template>
</xsl:stylesheet>
```

Once again the `xsl:value-of` element is placed between the beginning and ending block-level tags of your formatting markup, but in this case your formatting markup takes the form of formatting objects. You might be able to guess that the `fo:block` element is a block-level element that operates in a similar way to paragraphs on a page. In this case, the text contained in the XML source document's `headline` element is inserted into the result tree.

The root template contains a page sequence element that adds some general formatting properties that may later be inherited by some child elements (don't worry about this yet). Then an `apply-templates` element is placed so that all the remaining templates in the file are applied. The next template to be applied is the template written for the `advertisement` element. This element only contains a description for one template, which is a template for the `text` element. This, in turn, contains the `xsl:value-of` element, and nothing else. The result can be seen in Figure 14.5.

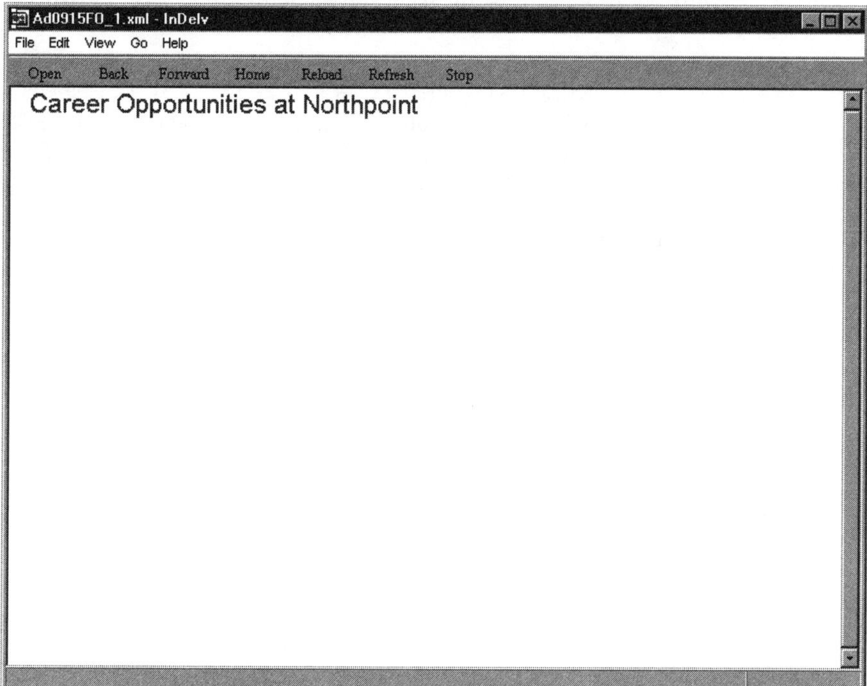

FIGURE 14.5:

Applying the `xsl:value-of` element using formatting objects

Combining XSL and CSS

Things could get pretty boring if you could only format in strict HTML (HTML 4 doesn't feature much presentation-rich capability, and relies on style sheets to render styles). So you can add CSS style elements or attributes to your HTML output in your result tree.

In Chapter 13, you learned how to create CSS style sheets for XML documents. CSS has been in use now for a few years in the HTML world, and one easy way to apply them is by using what are called inline style sheets. These are created using the HTML `style` attribute, which is available to nearly every HTML element. The value of the `style` attribute takes the form of the style sheet syntax you learned about in Chapter 13:

```
<body style = "font-family:sans-serif; font-size:10px">
some html content here
</body>
```

Instead of defining the style using the more formal selector syntax described earlier in this chapter, you create your definitions in the `style` attribute. If you've used inline cascading style sheets before, this won't be anything new.

TIP

Generally, it's considered safer to use CSS in a STYLE element in the HEAD element with the value/attribute pair text/css rather than line, in case CSS is not the default style. This example is written for IE5, and works well for that browser.

Let's go back to the previous example and just apply some very simple CSS styling to a small portion of the document you are displaying. Figure 14.6 shows how the XML document looks after applying a style sheet designed for IE5 based on the code that follows:

```
<?xml version='1.0'?>
<xsl:stylesheet xmlns:xsl="http://www.w3.org/TR/WD-xsl">
     <xsl:template match="/">
                    <xsl:apply-templates select="//text"/>
</xsl:template>
<xsl:template match="text">
     <html>
          <body>
          <p style="color:#330033; font-family:sans-serif">
```

```
<xsl:value-of select="//text"/>
                </p>
           </body>
           </html>
     </xsl:template>
</xsl:stylesheet>
```

FIGURE 14.6:

Outputting HTML through XSL

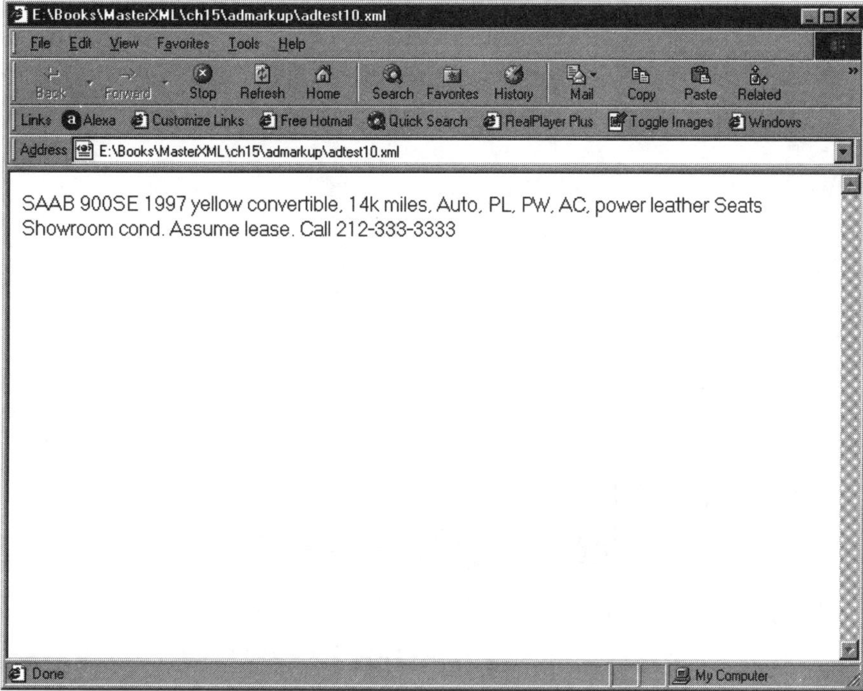

The preceding code fragment added a style attribute to the HTML p element. Adding some CSS is as easy as that. Generally, you won't need to worry about including the `display` property like you do with CSS style sheets you link to XML documents, because the display architecture is already handled by the HTML. Adding borders and background colors is the same as it would be adding it to HTML:

```
<p style="color:#330033; font-family:sans-serif;
border: 3px thin outset;
background-color:red;">
<xsl:value-of select="//text"/>
     </p>
```

Figure 14.7 shows how the preceding lines of code would appear in a browser implementing the full style sheet.

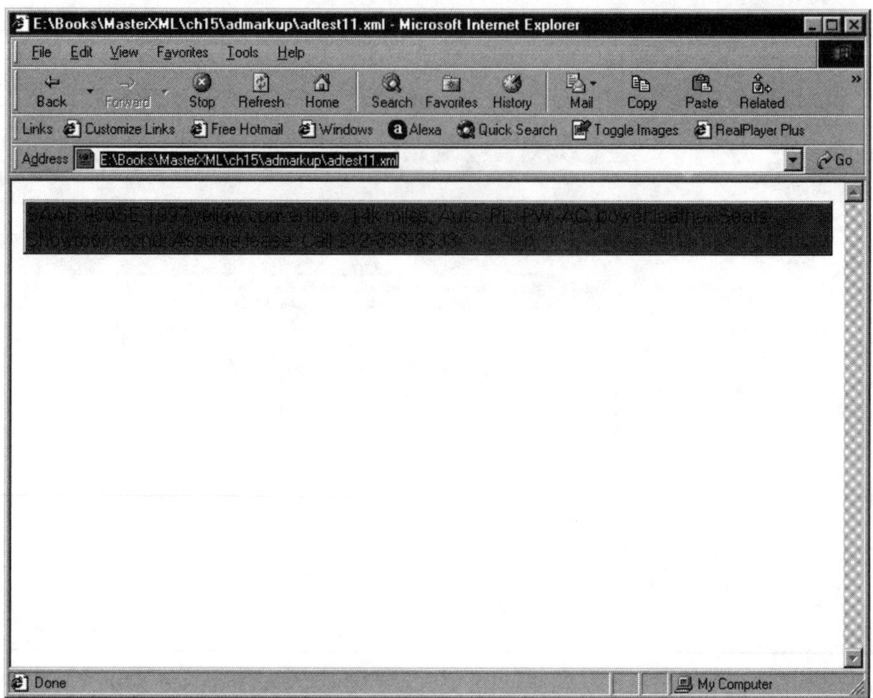

FIGURE 14.7: Adding CSS style to XSL style sheets

Practical Application of CSS/XSL Combinations

To improve your understanding of CSS/XSL combinations, you'll take a look at a way to format a story using a step by step approach. You'll start with the most basic XSL style sheet elements, then expand on their complexity.

To gain a solid understanding of the processes at work, you'll need to lead off with two XML files. You'll be referring to those files throughout the rest of this section. The first XML file you'll be applying style sheets to is Listing 14.5. This will be your source tree. From there, you will develop several result trees.

LISTING 14.5 The Source XML File `introXSL.xml`

```
<?xml version="1.0"?>
<?xml-stylesheet type ="text/css" href="story.xsl"?>
<!DOCTYPE story SYSTEM "storyxsl.dtd">
<story>
<title>Freedom's Dream</title>
<author>by Charles White</author>
<copyright>Copyright 1996, 1999 by Charles White</copyright>
<section>
<para>Had it been a dream, Antron Crimea's memory of the clenched fist
   piercing the sky of a tumultuous, thundering crowd would have been
   bearable solitude. As it was though, the reality brought him to
   another place, to a distance only something like a dream could take
   him.</para>
<para>&quot;The crowd forgot everything,&quot; is how Antron described
   the situation to his psychiatrist, <link id="ChesapeakeLink">
   Chesapeake Alert.</link>
   Antron remembered the rhythm, the pulse, everything. After all this
   time the energy of the crowd still seemed to reverberate through his
   head.</para>
<para>Chesapeake Alert was nothing but a large bulbous mass of jelly-
   like flesh; a brain plopped down on an empty, expensive slice of
   carpet. And though he had no legitimate locomotive capabilities of
   his own, he was aware of the movements of a billion others.</para>
<para>Antron's hundred legs crawled around what was left of the carpet
   in the kind of pace unknown to you or I. His earlier confusion had
   long ago been dissolved by the righteous events of what he had seen
   during the course of events Billy Freedom had ignited.</para>
<para>&quot;Sometimes betrayal is a necessity,&quot;said Chesapeake.
   &quot;Startling. And expensive. It must be weighed
   carefully.&quot;</para>
</section>
     <auto-link
            xml:link="simple"
            actuate="user"
            href="sec_2.xml"
            show="replace">this is a link</auto-link>
</story>
```

There is also a DTD for the source tree shown in Listing 14.5. This DTD appears in Listing 14.6. This is a pretty basic DTD file.

LISTING 14.6 A DTD for introXSL.xml

```
<!ELEMENT story (title*, author*, copyright*, section+, auto-link*)>
<!ATTLIST story id ID #IMPLIED>
<!ENTITY quot "&#34;">
<!ELEMENT title (#PCDATA)>
<!ELEMENT author (#PCDATA)>
<!ATTLIST author id ID #IMPLIED>
<!ELEMENT copyright (#PCDATA)>
<!ELEMENT section ((graphic*, para*), list*)>
<!ATTLIST section
reference ENTITY #IMPLIED>
<!NOTATION PNG SYSTEM "Iexplore.exe">
<!NOTATION GIF SYSTEM "Iexplore.exe">
<!ELEMENT graphic (#PCDATA)>
<!ATTLIST graphic
src ENTITY #REQUIRED
id ID #IMPLIED>
<!ELEMENT para (#PCDATA | link)*>
<!ATTLIST para id ID #IMPLIED>
<!ELEMENT link (#PCDATA)>
<!ELEMENT list (#PCDATA)>
<!ATTLIST link id ID #IMPLIED>
<!ELEMENT auto-link ANY>
<!ATTLIST auto-link
xml:link CDATA #FIXED "simple"
href CDATA #REQUIRED
inline (true | false) "true"
role CDATA #IMPLIED
title CDATA #IMPLIED
show (replace | new | embed) #IMPLIED
actuate (auto | user) #IMPLIED
behavior CDATA #IMPLIED
content-role CDATA #IMPLIED
content-title CDATA #IMPLIED
>
```

Now you're ready for the first style sheet. This style sheet, written for IE5, is basic and just captures all the text and runs it all together in one continuous line. The first style sheet is shown in Listing 14.7.

LISTING 14.7 A Basic Style Sheet for `introXSL.xml`

```
<?xml version='1.0'?>
<xsl:stylesheet xmlns:xsl="http://www.w3.org/TR/WD-xsl">
     <xsl:template match="/">
            <HTML>
                   <BODY>
                          <xsl:value-of />
                   </BODY>
            </HTML>
     </xsl:template>
</xsl:stylesheet>
```

You can't get much more basic than the style sheet in Listing 14.7, and obviously you're going to need more style than what is shown in Figure 14.8.

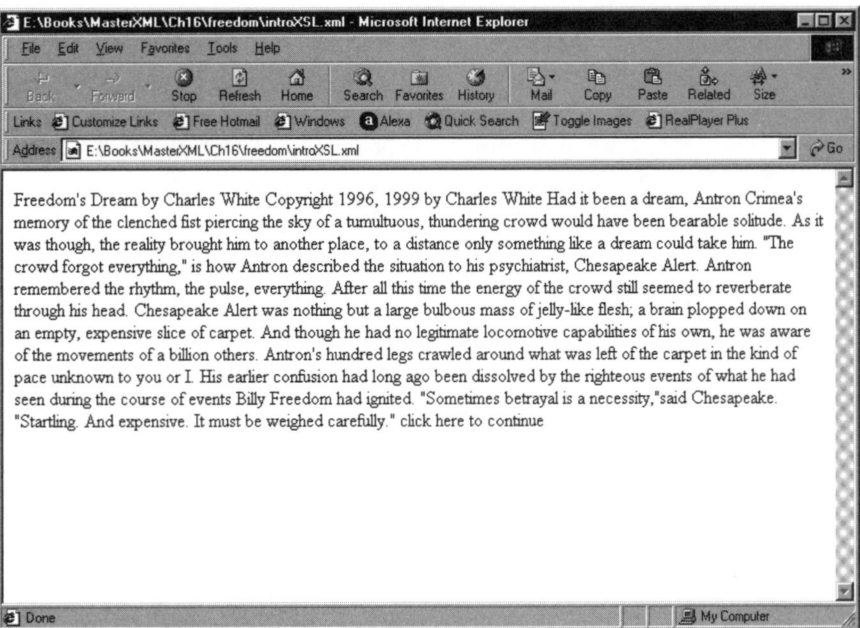
E:\Books\MasterXML\Ch16\freedom\introXSL.xml - Microsoft Internet Explorer
File Edit View Favorites Tools Help
Back Forward Stop Refresh Home Search Favorites History Mail Copy Paste Related Size
Links Customize Links Free Hotmail Windows Alexa Quick Search Toggle Images RealPlayer Plus
Address E:\Books\MasterXML\Ch16\freedom\introXSL.xml
Go
Freedom's Dream by Charles White Copyright 1996, 1999 by Charles White Had it been a dream, Antron Crimea's memory of the clenched fist piercing the sky of a tumultuous, thundering crowd would have been bearable solitude. As it was though, the reality brought him to another place, to a distance only something like a dream could take him. "The crowd forgot everything," is how Antron described the situation to his psychiatrist, Chesapeake Alert. Antron remembered the rhythm, the pulse, everything. After all this time the energy of the crowd still seemed to reverberate through his head. Chesapeake Alert was nothing but a large bulbous mass of jelly-like flesh; a brain plopped down on an empty, expensive slice of carpet. And though he had no legitimate locomotive capabilities of his own, he was aware of the movements of a billion others. Antron's hundred legs crawled around what was left of the carpet in the kind of pace unknown to you or I. His earlier confusion had long ago been dissolved by the righteous events of what he had seen during the course of events Billy Freedom had ignited. "Sometimes betrayal is a necessity,"said Chesapeake. "Startling. And expensive. It must be weighed carefully." click here to continue
Done
My Computer

FIGURE 14.8: The most basic of style sheets

WARNING

Although the `xsl:value-of` element works without an attribute in IE5, a standards-based XSL style sheet must include the `select` attribute. Generally, in instances similar to Listing 14.7, you can simply select the context node to make it conform: `xsl:value-of select="."`.

Adding Some CSS Style Listing 14.8 shows how to add a bit more pizzazz to the style sheet by adding some CSS style sheet properties to the result tree. It doesn't do much more than that, but it's a start.

LISTING 14.8 Adding CSS Properties to the Style Sheet

```
<?xml version='1.0'?>
<xsl:stylesheet xmlns:xsl="http://www.w3.org/TR/WD-xsl">
     <xsl:template match="/">
<html>
     <head><title>A test</title></head>
     <body>
<xsl:for-each select="story/section">
     <p style =
     "font-family:sans-serif;
padding-top:7px;
font-size:13px"><xsl:value-of />
</p></xsl:for-each>
</body>
</html>
     </xsl:template>
</xsl:stylesheet>
```

Note the way the selection process has been narrowed down somewhat. In this case, we're looking for each `section` element that appears as a direct descendent of a `story` element. Note also how there is a bit of CSS added to the result tree. It's all as simple as writing some HTML and adding some inline CSS style sheets, but you need to remember that XML is much less forgiving than HTML. Some browsers may render your CSS style if you leave off an end quote (although they're likely to behave unexpectedly). You won't catch any breaks with XSL, however. The result is shown in Figure 14.9.

Selecting Content for the Result Tree In Listing 14.9, some of the character data in the XML source tree is purposely omitted by choosing the content within the `para` element.

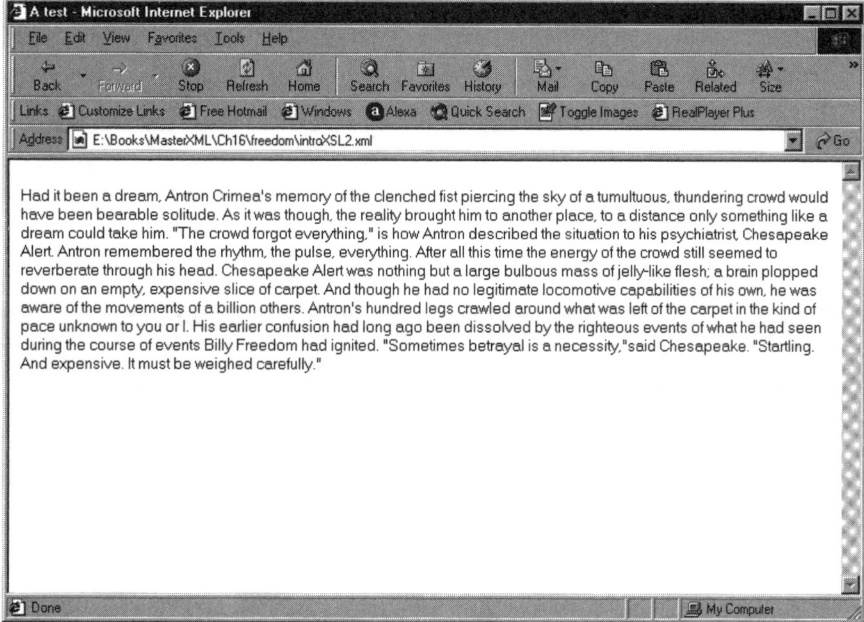
A test - Microsoft Internet Explorer
File Edit View Favorites Tools Help
Back Forward Stop Refresh Home Search Favorites History Mail Copy Paste Related Size
Links Customize Links Free Hotmail Windows Alexa Quick Search Toggle Images RealPlayer Plus
Address E:\Books\MasterXML\Ch16\freedom\introXSL2.xml Go
Had it been a dream, Antron Crimea's memory of the clenched fist piercing the sky of a tumultuous, thundering crowd would have been bearable solitude. As it was though, the reality brought him to another place, to a distance only something like a dream could take him. "The crowd forgot everything," is how Antron described the situation to his psychiatrist, Chesapeake Alert. Antron remembered the rhythm, the pulse, everything. After all this time the energy of the crowd still seemed to reverberate through his head. Chesapeake Alert was nothing but a large bulbous mass of jelly-like flesh; a brain plopped down on an empty, expensive slice of carpet. And though he had no legitimate locomotive capabilities of his own, he was aware of the movements of a billion others. Antron's hundred legs crawled around what was left of the carpet in the kind of pace unknown to you or I. His earlier confusion had long ago been dissolved by the righteous events of what he had seen during the course of events Billy Freedom had ignited. "Sometimes betrayal is a necessity,"said Chesapeake. "Startling. And expensive. It must be weighed carefully."
Done
My Computer

FIGURE 14.9:

Adding style with CSS properties

LISTING 14.9 Selecting an Element

```
<?xml version='1.0'?>
<xsl:stylesheet xmlns:xsl="http://www.w3.org/TR/WD-xsl">
     <xsl:template match="/">
<html>
     <head><title>A test</title></head>
     <body>
     <xsl:for-each select="story/section">
     <p style =
     "font-family:sans-serif;
padding-top:7px;
font-size:13px">
<!--BE SURE TO NOT TO DELETE THE CLOSING TAG WHEN ADDING THE SELECT
ATTRIBUTE -->
<xsl:value-of select="para"/>
</p></xsl:for-each>
</body>
```

```
</html>
    </xsl:template>
</xsl:stylesheet>
```

You need to be careful here and be sure to add the closing tag in the `xsl:value-of` attribute. Although it's very nice to be able to select the `para` element and add some style to it, choosing the element this way is somewhat limiting, because it only selects the first instance of it (Figure 14.10). There is more than one `para` element to be formatted as discussed in the next section.

FIGURE 14.10:

Singling out the contents of the first `para` element using XSL and CSS

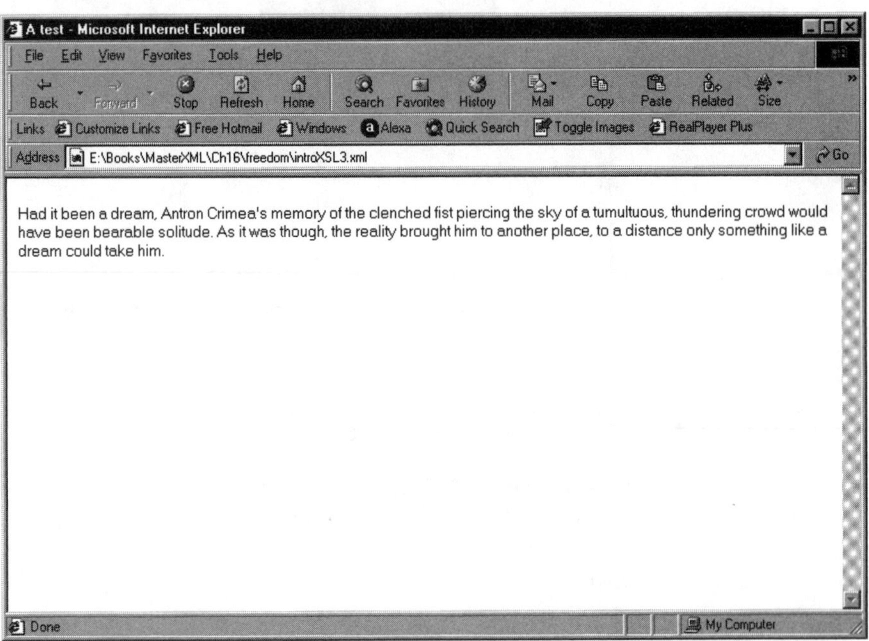

Selecting Additional Elements for Formatting First, we'll add a title and author element to the result tree. In Listing 14.10 HTML is used to begin the result tree construction process. The HTML begins as the first output element within the source tree. From there, the `head` and `title` elements are added. After reaching the body element, it must be rendered, but how? You could just type in the text, but that defeats the purpose of XML. So insert a node based on the XML source element `story`. Then you can begin adding some real CSS style. Note in particular the use of the CSS `letter-spacing:5px;` property and value. This is used to mimic the print world's letter spacing technique (usually called tracking and kerning in desktop publishing environments, depending on how the process is used). Of course, a typographer who takes the art seriously would be severely traumatized by this kind of treatment, but it works for the Web, which from a designer's point of view has always been about compromise. Figure 14.11 shows the results.

LISTING 14.10 Applying Font Styles in CSS

```
<?xml version='1.0'?>
<xsl:stylesheet xmlns:xsl="http://www.w3.org/TR/WD-xsl">
     <xsl:template match="/">
<html>
     <head><title>Freedom's Dream</title></head>
     <body>
     <xsl:for-each select="story">
     "font-family:sans-serif;
padding-bottom:1px;
font-size:18px;
text-align:center">
<xsl:value-of select="title"/>
</p></xsl:for-each>
     <xsl:for-each select="story">
     <p style =
     "font-family:sans-serif;
padding-bottom:7px;
font-size:12px;
letter-spacing:5px;
text-align:center">
<xsl:value-of select="author"/>
</p></xsl:for-each>
<xsl:for-each select="story/section">
          <p style =
          "font-family:sans-serif;
padding-top:7px;
font-size:13px">
<xsl:value-of select="para"/>
</p></xsl:for-each>
</body>
</html>
     </xsl:template>
</xsl:stylesheet>
```

FIGURE 14.11:

Applying font styles in CSS for display in IE5

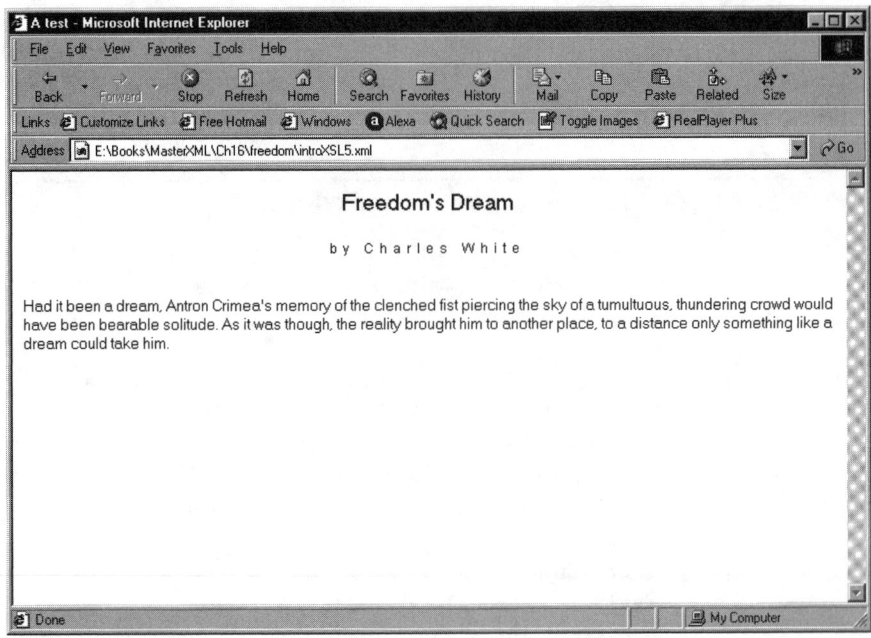

Using Operators to Improve Pattern Matching The next step is to output all of the `para` elements, not just one. So you use an operator to seek out all the `para` elements that exist below the root node. Listing 14.11 shows how to do this, and Figure 14.12 shows the results.

LISTING 14.11 Outputting the Rest of the para Elements

```
<?xml version='1.0'?>
<xsl:stylesheet xmlns:xsl="http://www.w3.org/TR/WD-xsl">
     <xsl:template match="/">
<html>
     <head><title>Freedom's Dream</title></head>
     <body>
            <xsl:for-each select="story">
     <p style =
     "font-family:sans-serif;
padding-bottom:1px;
font-size:18px;
text-align:center">
<xsl:value-of select="title"/>
```

```
</p></xsl:for-each>
     <xsl:for-each select="story">
            <p style =
            "font-family:sans-serif;
padding-bottom:7px;
font-size:12px;
letter-spacing:5px;
text-align:center">
<xsl:value-of select="author"/>
</p></xsl:for-each>
     <xsl:for-each select="//para">
            <p style =
            "font-family:sans-serif;
padding-top:7px;
font-size:13px">
<xsl:value-of/>
</p>
</xsl:for-each>
</body>
</html>
     </xsl:template>
</xsl:stylesheet>
```

FIGURE 14.12:

Adding the rest of the `para` elements and displaying them in the browser

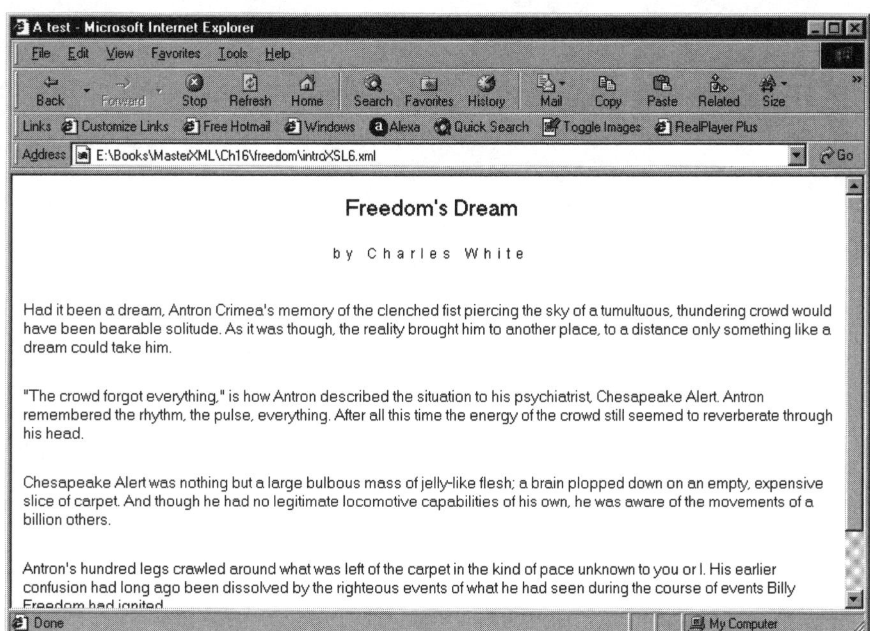
A test - Microsoft Internet Explorer
File Edit View Favorites Tools Help
Back Forward Stop Refresh Home Search Favorites History Mail Copy Paste Related Size
Links Customize Links Free Hotmail Windows Alexa Quick Search Toggle Images RealPlayer Plus
Address E:\Books\MasterXML\Ch16\freedom\introXSL6.xml
Go
Freedom's Dream
by Charles White
Had it been a dream, Antron Crimea's memory of the clenched fist piercing the sky of a tumultuous, thundering crowd would have been bearable solitude. As it was though, the reality brought him to another place, to a distance only something like a dream could take him.
"The crowd forgot everything," is how Antron described the situation to his psychiatrist, Chesapeake Alert. Antron remembered the rhythm, the pulse, everything. After all this time the energy of the crowd still seemed to reverberate through his head.
Chesapeake Alert was nothing but a large bulbous mass of jelly-like flesh; a brain plopped down on an empty, expensive slice of carpet. And though he had no legitimate locomotive capabilities of his own, he was aware of the movements of a billion others.
Antron's hundred legs crawled around what was left of the carpet in the kind of pace unknown to you or I. His earlier confusion had long ago been dissolved by the righteous events of what he had seen during the course of events Billy
Done
My Computer

Adding Basic Functionality The last thing to do is add a link. This is accomplished by merely adding an HTML a element to the result tree. Listing 14.12 shows how this is done.

LISTING 14.12 Adding a Link to Result Tree Elements

```
<?xml version='1.0'?>
<xsl:stylesheet xmlns:xsl="http://www.w3.org/TR/WD-xsl">
     <xsl:template match="/">
<html>
     <head><title>Freedom's Dream</title></head>
     <body>
            <xsl:for-each select="story">
     <p style =
     "font-family:sans-serif;
padding-bottom:1px;
font-size:18px;
text-align:center">
<xsl:value-of select="title"/>
</p></xsl:for-each>
     <xsl:for-each select="story">
            <p style =
            "font-family:sans-serif;
padding-bottom:7px;
font-size:12px;
letter-spacing:5px;
text-align:center">
<xsl:value-of select="author"/>
</p></xsl:for-each>
     <xsl:for-each select="//para">
            <p style =
            "font-family:sans-serif;
padding-top:7px;
font-size:13px">
<xsl:value-of/>
</p>
</xsl:for-each>
<xsl:for-each select="//auto-link[@href ='sec_2.xml']">
     <p style =
     font-family:sans-serif;
padding-top:7px;
```

```
font-size:13px">
<a href="sec_2.xml" style="font-family:sans-serif;
font-size:13px">
<xsl:value-of/>
</a>
</p>
</xsl:for-each>
</body>
</html>
     </xsl:template>
</xsl:stylesheet>
<!-- need to show the last part of the XML source doc for this example
-->
```

There's also a bit added to the original XML source tree, just to show what is happening. Several instances of the `auto-link` element are added, but the XSL file only chooses the one you want. Note that the fragment that follows is part of a different XML source document. Although some is left out the rest to save room, it's the same as the one in Listing 14.11, except this has several more links. Why did we use HTML to create a link when XML has a much more powerful linking mechanism? Adding a link using an HTML element improves the likelihood the link will work.

```
<auto-link
     xml:link="simple"
     actuate="user"
     href="sec_2.xml"
     show="replace">this is a link</auto-link>
     <auto-link
     xml:link="simple"
     actuate="user"
     href="sec_3.xml"
     show="replace">this is a link</auto-link>
     <auto-link
     xml:link="simple"
     actuate="user"
     href="sec_4.xml"
     show="replace">this is a link</auto-link>
     <auto-link
     xml:link="simple"
     actuate="user"
     href="sec_5.xml"
```

```
        show="replace">this is a link</auto-link>
        <auto-link
        xml:link="simple"
        actuate="user"
        href="sec_6.xml"
        show="replace">this is a link</auto-link>
</story>
```

Here's the portion of Listing 14.12 that applies to the preceding code:

```
<xsl:for-each select="//auto-link[@href ='sec_2.xml']">
     <p style =
     "font-family:sans-serif;
padding-top:7px;
font-size:13px">
<a href="sec_2.xml" style="font-family:sans-serif;
font-size:13px">
<xsl:value-of/>
</a>
</p>
</xsl:for-each>
```

Look at the preceding code fragment more closely and you'll see a selection that tries to first match the `auto-link` element, then an attribute within that element named `href` whose value is `sec_2.xml`. Then that element is wrapped around an anchor element to assure the link will work in browser that doesn't support the XML-based link used.

Mastering Templates

Earlier in this chapter you learned the basics behind using templates with XSL style sheets when you were introduced to the `xsl:template` and `xsl:apply-templates` elements. You didn't, however, get much of an opportunity to see how they really work. Here, we'll take a closer look at the concepts behind the `xsl:template` and `xsl:apply-templates` elements. These are key ingredients to XSL, so understanding their underlying principles is an essential part of mastering XSL.

On a purely tactical level, templates are much like the master pages in page layout programs like Quark Xpress and Adobe PageMaker. These print publishing software programs allow you to create a master page that you can apply to a newly created page. When you apply a master page to a page, the master page automatically inserts all its objects into the page. A similar concept works with XSL templates. The structure of a multiple template XSL document looks something like this:

```
ROOT TEMPLATE
template a
template b
template c
template d
template e
template f
```

Then you apply `template` `a`, `b`, `c`, `d`, `e`, or `f` to the root template using one of several processing elements. These elements include:

- `xsl:apply-templates`
- `xsl:for-each`
- `xsl:sort`
- `xsl:copy-of`

These elements manage node processing. They don't insert any text data, which is the responsibility of the `xsl:value-of` element.

The easiest way to go about managing templates is to define each template for each node you want to process. Will an element named `myelement` have a large typeface? Then define your template for that element `myelement` by using either a formatting object with a large type face or an HTML object with CSS styling and a large type face type defined using CSS. Define each node one by one until you have a series of defined templates. Then you can develop your style sheet easily by adding the template(s) as the need arises.

TIP

If you're wondering about the difference between the `xsl:apply-templates` and `xsl:for-each` elements, consider their context. Use `xsl:apply-templates` when mixing content. Use the `xsl:for-each` element for repeating data with the same structure. A table of baseball statistics, for example, might be more efficiently transformed using the `xsl:for-each` element than the `xsl:apply-templates` element, although there is nothing inherently wrong with using the `xsl:apply-templates` element in those cases. Overall, though, you'll find it more efficient to use the `xsl:for-each` element for managing repeated data.

Creating Templates

To get the most out of your template designs, generally you'll follow a specific sequence as you begin the design process. This sequence will typically go something like this:

1. First develop some design goals—take into consideration such matters as your audience and what kind of functionality you expect to generate via the data within the source document.
2. Next, think in terms of how you'd want the page to look in HTML (or some other formatting mechanism). It's not even a bad idea to set up an HTML page that looks like the output you expect to send to your XSL result tree, at least when you're first getting the feel for XSL.
3. Then, create a template for each node you expect to appear in your output. Remember you won't necessarily want to display all nodes in the XML source document. And even if you do, chances are nodes will be styled differently based on their relationship to other nodes or data.
4. Next, determine where in the result tree you want each new template that you've just created to appear.

Let's walk through these steps with a specific example. This example takes a "help wanted" classified advertisement and displays the appropriate information, depending on the functions that you need. In this case, the design goals can be summed up as follows:

- Display information about the ad to an operator who is inputting text into a browser that sends the information via a form to a server so that the ad copy can be updated.
- Enable the operator to view relevant information about the ad. Some of this information may change on the fly in future iterations.
- The style sheet will be written using the IE5 namespace so the operator can view it the XML file in IE5.

To begin the exercise, you'll need to take a look at the original source document, which is an XML file called `helpwanted.xml`. This source file is shown in Listing 14.13. Pay the most attention to the bolded elements within the source document. From that point on, we'll develop a root template that will in turn access other templates as needed.

LISTING 14.13 XML Source Document for Help Wanted Style Sheet

```
<?xml version="1.0"?>
<?xml-stylesheet type="text/xsl" href="helpwanted.xsl" ?>
   <advertisement action="create"> <!--root element -->
   <id version="2">
      SJMN.101899.40011
   </id>
   <status value="accepted">
      accepted</status>
   <expiration>12-05-99</expiration>
    <reference>
       Northpoint Communications Recruitment Ad
    </reference>
    <comment>
        Rateholder
   </comment>
   <contact id="contact1">
      <name>
         Ellis Jones III
          </name>
      <address>
         <address_line>Northpoint Communications</address_line>
         <address_line>80th Floor</address_line>
         <city>San Francisco</city>
         <state>CA</state>
         <postal>10000-1234</postal>
         <country>USA</country>
      </address>
      <phone>
         14159899999
      </phone>
      <fax>
         14159899999
      </fax>
      <email>
         jones@northpoint.com
      </email>
      <url>
         http://www.northpointcom.com
      </url>
   </contact>
```

```
<source>
   <updated>
      <timestamp>
         25864782 55698254
      </timestamp>
      <userid>
         NP011
      </userid>
   </updated>
   <created>
      <timestamp>
         25864781 55698250
      </timestamp>
      <userid>
         JK1892
      </userid>
   </created>
   <base version="1">
      SJMN.101899.40011
   </base>
</source>
<advertiser>
    <account type="agency">
   12090875867-ADV
</account>
<contact_ref link="contact1"></contact_ref>
   <payment>
      <invoice>
         40011-1349857098
      </invoice>
   </payment>
</advertiser>
<coding>
   <employment>
      <empl_side value="offered">
      </empl_side>
      <empl_category>Computers</empl_category>
      <empl_title>
         Director of Information Technology
      </empl_title>
      <empl_experience>Northpoint Communications is seeking a proven
      and dedicated IT professional with at least 5 years experience
      in enterprise, systems and network management and administration
```

```
        </empl_experience>
        <empl_salary>
          100,000
        </empl_salary>
        <empl_skills>Must have experience in COBOL, Y2K, PBX systems,
        Novell, Networking, and be able to manage large-scale enter-
        prise systems.</empl_skills>
        <empl_benefits>Stock options, health insurance, health club
membership
        </empl_benefits>
      </employment>
      <contact>
        <name></name>
        <phone>14155551212</phone>
      </contact>
    </coding>
    <text>
      <font size="10">
        <center>
          <keyword name="empl_category" punct=" ">Computers</keyword>
          <keyword name="empl_title" punct=" ">Director of Informa-
tion Technology </keyword>
        </center>
      </font>
      <keyword name="empl_experience">Northpoint Communications is
      seeking a proven and dedicated IT professional with at least 5
      years experience in enterprise, systems and network management
      and administration
      </keyword>
      <keyword name="empl_skills">Must have experience in COBOL, Y2K,
      PBX systems, Novell, Networking, and be able to manage large-
      scale enterprise systems.
      </keyword>
      <center>
        <keyword name="phone">no calls please
        </keyword>
      </center>
    </text>
    <publication name="sjmercurynews">
      <pub_alias>12588421
      </pub_alias>
      <pub_price>$828.00
      </pub_price>
```

```
            <pub_options>
               <claim>7
               </claim>
               <columns>1</columns>
               <forwarding collect="email">Please email replies to
                  <mailbox>hr</mailbox>@sjmn.com
                  <rate basis="Email forwarding service charge--Full run"
                  unit="ad">$25.00
                  </rate>
               </forwarding>
               <tearsheet>
                  <rate basis="Tear sheet service charge" unit="recipi-
                  ent">$20.00
                  </rate>
               </tearsheet>
               <shading>
                  <rate basis="Shading premium" unit="standard">20%</rate>
               </shading>
            </pub_options>
            <class>adv-SJMNEMP
               <title>Employment/Computers</title>
               <classword>Professional Recruitment</classword>
               <classword>Help Wanted</classword>
               <lines>40</lines>
               <sortkey>ADV-NP40011</sortkey>
               <zone>
                  ALL
                  <title>Rate Holder</title>
               </zone>
               <rundate>
                  19980719
                  <rate basis="Rateholder" unit="line">$5.70
                  </rate>
                  <instance>
                     <edition>BASE</edition>
                     <section>12</section>
                     <page>22</page>
                     <column>9</column>
                     <offset>17.85</offset>
                  </instance>
               </rundate>
            </class>
         </publication>
      </advertisement>
```

Okay, so now what do you do with this? First, decide about some design goals. These design goals are arbitrary in this case, and are based more on how to demonstrate XSL in a book than on how it might actually be useful in a practical setting. Nevertheless, demonstrating XSL is in and of itself a design goal.

Developing Individual Templates

The ultimate goal on our agenda is developing the root template. This template will access other templates, and insert them as needed into the result tree. So first you need to build those templates. You might want to start off by creating an input mechanism so that an operator, customer, or ad agency can input text associated with the ad. They might, for example, wish to update an existing ad. The source file has a lot of information, some of which will be of interest to the individual typing text into the text input, and some of which will not be. So your first goal is to filter out any unwanted information.

Template 1: The `text` Template For the sake of brevity, let's focus on the first several elements of the source tree. You'll also want to keep your eye on the `text` element, which appears much later in the code but contains the ad copy. The fragment you're interested in, minus the nodes contained in the `text` element, looks like this:

```
<?xml version="1.0"?>
<?xml-stylesheet type="text/xsl" href="helpwanted.xsl" ?>
   <advertisement action="create"> <!--root element -->
   <id version="2">SJMN.101899.40011</id>
   <status value="accepted">accepted</status>
   <expiration>12-05-99</expiration>
    <reference>
       Northpoint Communications Recruitment Ad
    </reference>
    <comment>
        Rateholder
   </comment>
   <contact id="contact1">
      <name>
         Ellis Jones III
          </name>
      <address>
         <address_line>Northpoint Communications</address_line>
         <address_line>80th Floor</address_line>
         <city>San Francisco</city>
         <state>CA</state>
         <postal>10000-1234</postal>
```

```
      <country>USA</country>
   </address>
   <phone>
      14159899999
   </phone>
   <fax>
      14159899999
   </fax>
   <email>
      jones@northpoint.com
   </email>
   <url>
      http://www.northpointcom.com
   </url>
     </contact>
<!-- rest of document -->
</advertisement>
```

The first element is the root element, advertisement. This element contains some information in its attribute that we'll look at later in this chapter. For now, know that some of the result tree is chosen as the result of a matching process that says, in effect, "If this advertisement is an update, show this result, otherwise, show something else." You do this because you want to include the text input area no matter what, but you want it labeled differently depending on whether the ad is new or an update. If the ad is an update, you want the text input area label to say, "Enter new ad copy in the space below:". Otherwise, you'll assume the ad is new, in which case the label should say: "To create your ad, enter ad copy in the space below:".

In addition, if the ad is an update, you might want an interactive display mechanism that shows the ad copy as it might look styled for a Web page while operators or customers edited it. Actually, you might want this anyway, but for this example, let's say you just want the display to appear when an updated ad is being worked on.

It wasn't too long ago that the only way to create this kind of conditional was by using a scripting language such as JavaScript, but XSL has a number of conditional elements you'll be exploring in the next chapter that make the process considerably easier. For now, let's develop the two templates that this conditional will access, depending on what the condition is. If the ad is an update, then you'll create the following template:

```
<xsl:template match="text"><!--If an update-->
<div id="adDisplayBox"
style="position:absolute;
top: 80px;
```

```
        left:300px;
        width: 270px;
        color:#FFFFCC;
        font-family:sans-serif;
        border: 3px thin outset;
    background-color:#663300;padding:3px">
    <span style="font-weight:800">
    <xsl:value-of select="font/center/keyword[1]"/></span><br/>
    <xsl:value-of select="keyword[0]"/><p>
    <xsl:value-of select="keyword[1]"/></p>
    </div>
    <div id="textAreaLabel" style="padding-top:12px;
    position:absolute;
    top:25px;
    left:10px;
    font-family:serif;
    font-weight:800;
    font-size:14px">
    Enter new ad copy in the space below:</div>
    <div id="textAreaContainer" style=
    "position:absolute;
    top:50px;
    left:3px;
    width:290px;
    padding-top:6px">
    <textarea name="adfiller" style="width:280px;
    height:280px;" wrap="virtual" id="210011"></textarea></div>
    </xsl:template>
```

There's a lot here, so let's break it down. The first fragment of the template merely establishes the fact that you're looking to create a style sheet template for the `text` element:

```
<xsl:template match="text"><!--If an update-->
```

Next, define what you want the node to look like. Start by defining the styles for the box that will display the advertising copy. In this case, HTML and CSS is used to accomplish this. Because you'll be inserting specific child nodes of the `text` element into HTML objects, you create a `div` element, which in HTML can act as a container. To that container, you apply some CSS style sheets. You want the text display box off to one side, so that the user of the Web page can input ad copy into a text-input area on one side and view the copy as it looks styled on the right. So you use absolute positioning to set the text display box off from the text area box.

CSS also lets you style the text area box itself so that you don't have to use text area sizing attributes, `rows` and `cols`, to define the text area size. This is in line with the emphasis within HTML away from presentation and toward structured display, with presentational aspects defined by style sheets. The same is true of the choice of using absolute positioning instead of tables. Tables were not meant for positioning display elements of Web pages, but old habits die hard, and most examples of XSL use tables to render stylistic display. If you want to stay true to the spirit of current HTML development, you'll want to veer away from using tables for designing and use positioning instead (unless your output is being generated server-side for all kinds of browsers).

The key to using absolutely positioned elements is the HTML `div` element, which can be used as a containing object. In the preceding code fragment, the `div` element identified by its unique identifier (through its `ID` attribute) as `textAreaContainer` has a width of 290 pixels and is 3 pixels to the left of its parent, which in this case is the Web page. So then you know it is safe to place the text display container 300 pixels to the left of the page's left side. Take a look at the code fragment that follows to see where in the template this styling mechanism appears:

```
<xsl:template match="text"><!--If an update-->
     <div id="adDisplayBox"
     style="position:absolute;
     top: 80px;
     left:300px;
     width: 270px;
     color:#FFFFCC;
     font-family:sans-serif;
     border: 3px thin outset;
background-color:#663300;padding:3px"><span style="font-weight:800">
<xsl:value-of select="font/center/keyword[1]"/></span><br/>
<xsl:value-of select="keyword[0]"/><p>
<xsl:value-of select="keyword[1]"/></p>
</div>
```

Notice the `div` element `adDisplayBox`. This is the text display that you want to appear to the right of the text area input. You gave it a background and a border more as a way to set it off and make it easy to see in a printed figure for a book than for any other reason. See Figure 14.13 to see how this looks in a Web page. The template matches the source document's `text` element because you're trying to display the nodes within that element, because it contains the ad copy. However, the XML source document is structured in a way that makes it necessary to choose specific child elements of the `text` element. If you didn't, all the text characters in the `text` element would show up as concatenated text, and some copy you don't want to appear would show up, as well.

First you create the object you want to use as the container, which is the `div` element `adDisplayBox`. You give it some CSS style, then select the nodes you want to display within your container. You didn't need to use the pattern to select child nodes of the `text` element. You chose to use an indexed selection system, but you could have chosen child nodes by attribute name or some other mechanism. You really can choose quite a large number of ways to create selection matches, and you'll discover the ways that work best for you as you continue to develop XML and XSL documents. In the preceding example, you looked for the second instance of the `keyword` element that was a child of a `center` element that was a child of a `font` element that was a child of the context node, which in this case is the `text` element. The second two matches addressed the first and second instance of a `keyword` element that was a child of the context node. Look at the XML source fragment below to see the process in action:

```
<text>
      <font size="10">
         <center>
            <keyword name="empl_category" punct=" ">Computers</keyword>
            <keyword name="empl_title" punct=" ">Director of Informa-
tion Technology </keyword>
         </center>
      </font>
      <keyword name="empl_experience">Northpoint Communications is
      seeking a proven and dedicated IT professional with at least 5
      years experience in enterprise, systems and network management
      and administration
      </keyword>
      <keyword name="empl_skills">Must have experience in COBOL, Y2K,
PBX systems, Novell, Networking, and be able to manage large-scale
enterprise systems.
      </keyword>
      <center>
         <keyword name="phone">no calls please
         </keyword>
      </center>
        </text>
```

The finished product needs to display the text in a more structured format than in Figure 14.13. A good exercise would be to continue reading the following descriptions of template development, which do show how to structure and style text nodes, and apply what you learn to this text node.

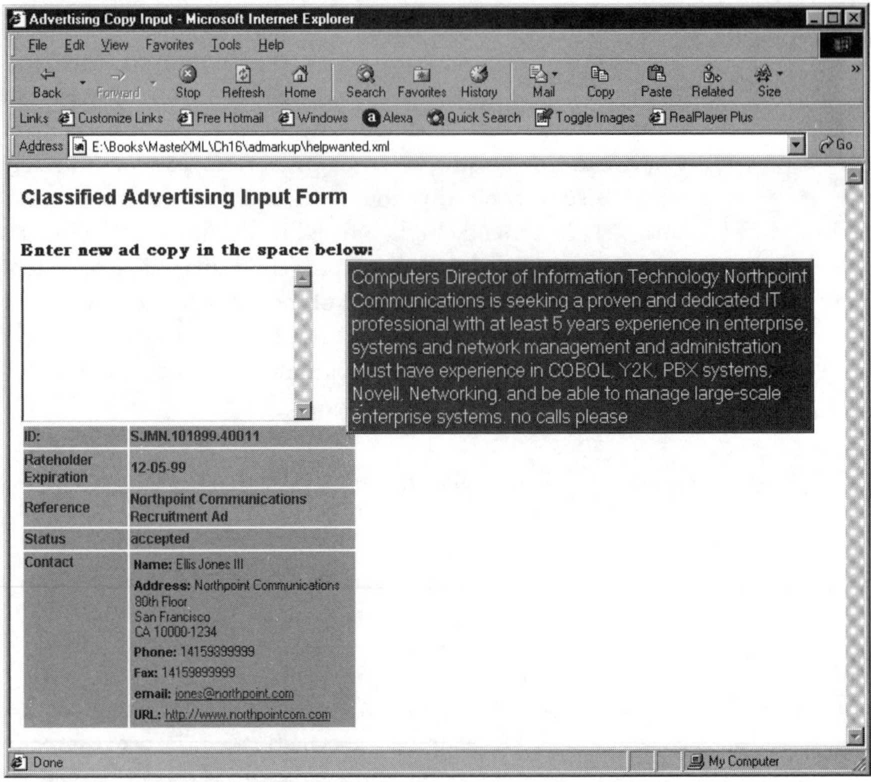

FIGURE 14.13: The text display appears next to the text area input courtesy of CSS absolute positioning.

Templates 2, 3 and 4: The `id`, `reference`, and `status` Templates So now you've developed your first template. You'll want to build more, so your next design goal is that information about the ad should be made available to the operator. Just what information is made available depends greatly on what the needs are and who the operator is. For your purposes, you'll just assume that only a fraction of the information available in the source document will need to be displayed. You'll put this into a table to make it easy for the operator to view the information, especially if some of it is likely to change. The information you're looking for is all quite similar, so you'll probably be using an `xsl:for-each` element to build the table within the root template. First, gather all the data you want into a series of table cells by developing a template for each node you wish to output into the result tree:

```
<xsl:template match="id">
<td>ID:</td>
<td>
<xsl:value-of select="//id"/></td></xsl:template>
```

That takes care of the `id` element. This is a very simple little template that will output all the text character data that is contained in the `id` element into a table cell. It also creates a table cell with the values you've given. These values act as a label for the data. Now you can add a few more templates that do the same kind of thing. Adding the next element down on the list, create a small template for the `reference` element. The principle is the same as for the previous template. After that, create a template for the `status` element. The two templates look as follows:

```
<xsl:template match="reference">
<td>Reference</td>
<td><xsl:value-of /></td>
</xsl:template>
<xsl:template match="status">
<td>Status</td>
<td><xsl:value-of />
</td>
</xsl:template>
```

All of the preceding small templates will be accessed in the root template by using an `xsl:for-each` element, which is a good way to work with repeating elements (in this case the selected child elements of the root element advertisement—`id`, `expiration`, `reference`, `status` and `contact`).

Template 5: The contact Template This next template is a bit more complicated because you want to add more than just the node you referenced into a table cell. The contact information is contained within the `content` element, which contains a number of child elements. If you just insert the `content` node into the result tree, you'll end up with a bunch of character data. In fact, you'll end up with all the character data within the content node, which will result in a string that looks like this:

```
Ellis Jones III Northpoint Communications 80th Floor San Francisco
CA 10000-1234
    USA 141598999991 4159899999 jones@northpoint.com http://www.north-
    pointcom.com
```

This is fine if all you want is the data, but you want to format it in a way that is pleasing to the eye and easy to read. In fact, why not go a step further and take advantage of the fact that you're using HTML for formatting, and create some links with the `e-mail` and `URL` elements. The first part of the `contact` template may look familiar to you, based on your previous code fragments:

```
<xsl:template match="contact">
<td style="vertical-align:top">Contact</td>
```

```
<td>
<table>
```

Let's just stop right here for a moment. You've added another table into a table cell. You're mirroring the structure of the XML source document somewhat by plunking the `contact` element's children into their own cells within a separate table within the cell that holds the parent `contact` element. You'll apply some fine-tuning to the CSS as well, so that the contact info will be more distinct within the framework of the overall design:

```
<tr>
<td style="font-size:11px; font-weight:800">Name: <span style="font-
size:11px; font-weight:300">
<xsl:value-of select="name"/></span></td></tr>
```

Note that you haven't inserted the actual child nodes yet. For this, you can use a very handy little tool called the `xsl:for-each` element, which acts as a kind of loop. It basically says that for each instance of the `address` element, add each of its children according to the definitions that follow. So add the `xsl:for-each` element, like so:

```
<tr>
<td style="font-size:11px; font-weight:800">Address: <xsl:for-each
select="address">
<span style="font-size:11px; font-weight:300">
```

Notice that you've added an HTML `span` element, which is wrapped around a series of `xsl:value-of` elements:

```
<xsl:value-of select="address_line"/>
<br/>
<xsl:value-of select="address_line[1]"/>
<br/>
<xsl:value-of select="city"/>
<br/>
<xsl:value-of select="state"/>
<xsl:value-of select="postal"/>
<br/>
</span>
</xsl:for-each>
</td></tr>
```

The `address` element was special because it had a number of child elements, but the rest of the children of the `contact` element are easy, because they don't have any children, so you only need to worry about outputting their character data:

```
<tr><td style="font-size:11px; font-weight:800">Phone: <span
style="font-size:11px; font-weight:300"><xsl:value-of
select="phone"/></span></td></tr>
<tr><td style="font-size:11px; font-weight:800">Fax: <span style="font-
size:11px; font-weight:300"><xsl:value-of select="fax"/></span></td></tr>
<tr><td style="font-size:11px; font-weight:800">email: <span style=
"font-size:11px; font-weight:300"><a
href="mailto:jones@northpoint.com">
<xsl:value-of select="email"/></a></span></td></tr>
<tr><td style="font-size:11px; font-weight:800">URL: <span style="font-
size:11px; font-weight:300"><a href="www.northpointcom.com">
<xsl:value-of select="url"/></a></span></td></tr>
</table>
</td></xsl:template>
```

The concept of inserting XSL elements as output is demonstrated in a clear way in the preceding code fragment. Notice how, for example, the HTML `span` element is used to change the weight of the font of the `phone` element. The `phone` element contains a phone number, from its label, which was hard coded using HTML as part of the table cell contents. You can write in anything you want to add content to the style sheet output, as long as it makes sense from an HTML standpoint, and as long as your tree is XML-compliant. Another area where insertion of XSL elements as output is easy to see is the use of the HTML `a` element, which is used here to create a live link for the `e-mail` and `URL` elements. In this case, the `a` element was added, with the appropriate `href` attributes, and insert the desired element was inserted into the element's contents. You could have just as easily written the text in yourself, but that defeats the purpose of XSL, as you know that the URL may change, and any changes should be taken care of in the source document.

When you break this template down, it's not quite as complex as it first appears. It uses the same general concept as the previous templates. The only complication arises when you decide to process some of its children.

Developing the Root Template

Now it's time to put together the root template for your XSL style sheet. This is where you'll take a look at all the various templates and decide which ones you want to actually use. You don't need to use them all, and any that you don't use will not show up in the result tree. In this case, you'll use all the templates you developed. Using them is just a matter of inserting them into the part of the output elements that you want them to appear. Listing 14.14 shows the entire root template and the various templates used throughout. The templates being applied are highlighted in bold text.

LISTING 14.14 The Root Template

```
<?xml version='1.0'?>
<xsl:stylesheet xmlns:xsl="http://www.w3.org/TR/WD-xsl">
<xsl:template match="/">
<html><head><title>Advertising Copy Input</title></head>
<body>
<div
style="font-family:sans-serif;
font-size:18px;
font-weight:800;
padding-bottom:14px;
color:#333333">Classified Advertising Input Form</div>
 <xsl:choose>
<xsl:when test = "advertisement[@action='update']">
<xsl:apply-templates select="//text"/>
</xsl:when><!--which one?-->
<xsl:otherwise>
<xsl:apply-templates select="advertisement"/>
</xsl:otherwise></xsl:choose>
<div><table style="width:300px">
<xsl:for-each select="advertisement">
<tr style="background-color:#66cccc;
height:18px;
font-family:sans-serif;
font-weight:700;
color:#333300;
font-size:12px;
vertical-align:middle">
     <xsl:apply-templates select="id"/>
     </tr>
     <tr style="background-color:#66ccff;
height:18px;
font-family:sans-serif;
font-weight:700;
color:#333300;
```

```
font-size:12px;
vertical-align:middle">
     <xsl:apply-templates select="expiration"/>
     </tr>
     <tr style="background-color:#66ccff;
height:18px;
font-family:sans-serif;
font-weight:700;
color:#333300;
font-size:12px;
vertical-align:middle">
     <xsl:apply-templates select="reference"/>
     </tr>
            <tr style="background-color:#66cccc;
height:18px;
font-family:sans-serif;
font-weight:700;
color:#333300;
font-size:12px;
vertical-align:middle">
     <xsl:apply-templates select="status"/>
     </tr>
     <tr style="background-color:#66cccc;
height:18px;
font-family:sans-serif;
font-weight:700;
color:#333300;
font-size:12px;
vertical-align:middle">
     <xsl:apply-templates select="contact"/>
     </tr>
</xsl:for-each>
</table>
</div>
</body>
</html>
     </xsl:template>
```

You probably noticed within this root template how the table row begins and end with no table cells contained within them. Let's take a look at the last instance of this to see why. Notice the `<xsl:apply-templates select="contact"/>` element. This is used to insert the contents of the named template into the table row.

The table cell markup isn't included because the table cell markup was included in the `contact` template, and you'd end up with some seriously wrong markup in the result tree.

You'll also notice the use of what is called a conditional (the `xsl:when` element) discussed in the next chapter. Don't worry about this element quite yet. You'll learn more about that in the following chapter on advanced element syntax. The template additionally contains some unfamiliar filtering syntax, such as `advertisement[@action='update']"`. This selects an advertisement element that has an action attribute with a value of update. You'll learn more about this kind of selecting in the next chapter.

Up Next

XSL takes a very different approach than what you are used to seeing if you used CSS, but still draws heavily from that language for formatting. The best way to really understand how to work with XSL is to practice, practice, and practice. Open a style sheet in your text editing program and load its associated XML file in a browser and watch what happens when you save your changes to the style sheet and click the browser's reload button. You'll find that you'll be able to quickly apply the many concepts you learned in this chapter. Among those concepts were:

- Understanding transformation, including pattern matching and templates.
- Learning about XML formatting, including how to output to HTML and use formatting objects to create displayed XML.

In the next chapter, we'll explore XSL more deeply, and explore some of the nuances of expressions more deeply. By now, you can probably develop some rudimentary style sheets. By the time you finish the next chapter, you will be able to develop much more powerful style sheets.

CHAPTER

FIFTEEN

Displaying XML: Advanced XSL

- Understanding the data model
- Using advanced element syntax
- Conditional processing
- XSL variables
- Using expressions
- XSL functions
- Extending XSL

After you become familiar with the basics, you'll need to decide how far you want to go with XSL. In particular, XSLT, the transformation side of XSL, is quite complicated. XSLT has numerous built-in functions and expressions that allow you to manipulate data types and create very specific results. This chapter will introduce some of the more complex transactions available through the XSL model.

The bottom line on XSLT is that for all its complexity, it isn't much more than a sophisticated addressing mechanism designed to transform a set of XML elements into a result tree. It's important to remember that the XSLT output is a result tree and not a stream of characters especially when you start managing some of the more complex transformations available through XSL. String management, the strength of the Perl programming language is powerful in XSL. Loops and counters, as seen in JavaScript and Java, have no match in XSL. Still, XSL flirts with these concepts, and programmers have had the most success to date understanding and applying XSL to real-world problems. If you have developed in HTML, you should be able to manage XSL, but some of the more complex transformations will take a bit of extra effort.

NOTE

During much of XSL's development, computer scientists debated the question of whether XSL was "Turing complete." A Turing-complete language has iteration or recursive calls and arithmetic that make it possible to index across two states (not geographic states, but rather abstract mathematical states formulated by Alan Turing in the 1930s). Turing machines can read tapes filled with As and Bs and change their state from 0 to 1. This is an abstract concept, but some felt that if XSL was Turing complete, then it was a full-fledged programming language rather than a markup language.

Using XSL Tools

The easiest way to develop a valid XSL result tree and a feel for data models is to use a tool that outputs the result tree for you and generates an error message when you've gone astray. Using IE5 is one way to accomplish this, but has the following limitations:

- It's not strictly standards based and thus calls into question whether or not your documents are portable (i.e., whether or not they will work across different platforms).
- You can't view the result tree that is generated without add-on tools.
- It won't handle FOP output.

Despite these limitations, Internet Explorer is a great place to start using XSL. Many of the examples in Chapter 14: "Displaying XML: Introducing XSL" were generated for IE5.

XT

For more complicated result trees that take advantage of the newest versions of XSL you need a more powerful tool than Internet Explorer, such as XT. XT is easy to use, but if you're not familiar with Java and the way class paths work it can be fairly intimidating at first. XT is an XSL processor written by James Clark, a legendary XML guru who has been developing XML and SGML applications for years. XT is available on the *Mastering XML* companion CD-ROM or can be downloaded at `http://www.jclark.com`.

XT makes understanding the tree structure of a result document easy because the file you want to turn into a result tree is the name of the last parameter. XT creates this file after processing the first two parameters: the source document and the style sheet document. If you leave off the last parameter—the name and location of your result tree file—XT generates the file on-screen.

FOP, an XSL-to-PDF Converter

FOP is a program that converts XSL formatting object result tree files to `.pdf` format, a popular prepress and Web format used by the print publishing industry that was developed by Adobe Systems. FOP is a Java 1.1 application that reads a formatting object tree, which can be in the form of an XML document or can be passed in memory as a DOM document or a SAX event. FOP is available on the *Mastering XML* companion CD-ROM or can be downloaded at `http://www.jtauber.com/fop/`.

Using Advanced Element Syntax

In Chapter 14, you learned about the simplest of XSL tasks including inserting nodes, text, or result elements into a result tree and building templates. The elements that you'll be reading about next enhance the capabilities of XSL. Some, like `xsl:output`, control the type of result; other elements, like the `xsl:element` element, insert nodes into the result tree, or help you create cleaner code (`xsl:variable`).

Deciding on Output Requirements

XSL does not limit you to creating only XML result trees. For instance, your result trees can be another kind of text or a sequence of bytes. Although this means that the result isn't necessarily a "tree" in the true XML sense, we will refer to output as result trees for consistency.

You control the way your result tree is output by using the `xsl:output` element. This element must be a top-level element, meaning that it must appear as a child of the `xsl:stylesheet` element or the `xsl:transform` element (these are synonymous with each other).

The type of output generated depends on the output chosen using the `method` attribute. This attribute takes one of three values: `html`, `text`, or `xml`. If the value is `html`, the output is generated as HTML (the old fashioned kind that doesn't care about case-sensitivity). If the value is `text`, every text node is generated in document order without any escaping. If the value is `xml`, then the output is generated as a well-formed XML general parsed entity.

An example of how to use this element is in the section describing the `xsl:text` element. The attributes for the `xsl:output` element are listed in Table 15.1.

WARNING One caveat regarding the `xsl:output` element is that the XSLT processor is not required to honor your request.

TABLE 15.1: `xsl:output` Attributes

Attribute	Required	Possible Values, Description
`method`	No	Can be `html`, `text`, or `xml`, or a name with a prefix that is expanded into a URI using namespace declarations in scope on the `xsl:output` element (in which case, the handling of the output is dependent on the namespace and the processor handling the output).
`version`	No	Version of the output method.
`cdata-section-elements`	No	A list of XML qualified names whose text node children are output as CDATA sections.
`indent`	No	A **yes** value indicates that the processor can add white space to indent the results, and a **no** value indicates that it should not.
`media-type`	No	Names the media type (MIME type).

Continued on next page

TABLE 15.1 CONTINUED: `xsl:output` Attributes

Attribute	Required	Possible Values, Description
`doctype-system`	No	Names the system identifier for use in the Document Type Declaration.
`doctype-public`	No	Names the public identifier for use in the Document Type Declaration.
`omit-xml-declaration`	No	`yes`, `no`; specifies whether the processor should omit an XML declaration.
`standalone`	No	`yes`, `no`; specifies whether the processor should output a stand-alone document declaration.
`encoding`	No	Describes the encoding of the byte sequence (e.g. UTF-16, ISO8859-1, etc.).

Managing Forwards Compatibility

The `version` and `xsl:version` attributes can be used to manage compatibility. Currently there is no version 2 of XSL, but if there were, you would identify it using these attributes: the `version` attribute with the `xsl:stylesheet` or `xsl:transform` element and the `xsl:version` attribute with literal result elements.

Creating Elements and Attributes

There are two special XSL elements you can use to create elements and attributes on the fly. The `xsl:element` is used to create elements, and the `xsl:attribute` is used to create attributes.

Creating Elements with *xsl:element*

You can create an element using the `xsl:element` element. This element has a required attribute—`name`—that is used to provide the element's new name. The newly created element acts as a template for any children or attributes that you create with the new element. This element is useful for a number of reasons. One simple application you might want to try is adding a link:

```
<xsl:element name="a">
<xsl:attribute name="href">http://myDomain.com/
myFancy.htm</xsl:attribute>
<xsl:text>This is a link</xsl:text>
</xsl:element>
```

This produces the following result:

```
<a href="http://myDomain.com/myFancy.htm">
This is another link</a>
```

The `xsl:text` element (discussed later in the chapter) allows you to insert element content into your element, but one nice thing about XSLT is that many of its element names are self-explanatory. There is also a `namespace` attribute for providing a namespace for your new element. All the attributes for this element are listed in Table 15.2.

TABLE 15.2: `xsl:element` Attributes

Attribute	Required	Possible Values, Description
`name`	Yes	`yes`, `no`; used only when copying element nodes, this attribute references attribute sets that are named in a separate `xsl:attribute-set` element and is interpreted as an attribute value template (described later in the chapter)
`namespace`	No	Provides a namespace for the attribute and is interpreted as an attribute value template
`use-attribute-sets`	No	`yes`, `no`; used only when copying element nodes, this attribute references attribute sets that are named in a separate `xsl:attribute-set` element and is interpreted as an attribute value template
`xml:space`	No	`default`, `preserve`; used to manage white space

Creating Attributes with *xsl:attribute*

You can create an attribute using the `xsl:attribute` element and then nest it within the applied element. This element has a required attribute—`name`—that is used to provide the attribute's name. The value of the attribute is placed within the `xsl:attribute` element's contents. The following short example shows how to create a simple element and its associated attributes.

```
<xsl:element name="PARA">
<xsl:attribute name="ALIGN">LEFT</xsl:attribute>
<xsl:attribute name="TYPE">FOOTNOTE</xsl:attribute>
Output some contents here
</xsl:element>
```

Attributes must be created in such a way that none of the following guidelines are violated:

- An attribute can't be added after any of the new element's children within the tree structure.
- An attribute can't have a duplicate name.
- An attribute can only be added to an element node.
- An `xsl:attribute` element's content can contain only character data during its instantiation, and the XSL processor should insert a closing /> tag as soon as non-attribute content is encountered. The attributes for this element are listed in Table 15.3.

TABLE 15.3: `xsl:attribute` Attributes

Attribute	Required	Possible Values, Description
`name`	Yes	`yes`, `no`; used only when copying element nodes, this attribute references attribute sets that are named in a separate `xsl:attribute-set` element, and is interpreted as an attribute value template.
`namespace`	No	Provides a namespace for the attribute.
`xml:space`	No	`default`, `preserve`; used to manage white space.

Using the *xsl:text* Element

You can output the text of selected nodes by using the `xsl:text` element, which outputs the content within its tags. This text-generating element improves the management of white space on those occasions when you want to trim white space. It also improves the management of special characters, such as `<`, which is the character reference for the < character. You might want to create non-XML code of some kind within a text file.

Take a look again at the `xsl:output` element you saw a bit earlier in this chapter, and see how both it and the `xsl:text` element might be useful. Given the following XML document fragment, you can construct newspaper markup that can be read by a classified advertising markup system. The target classified advertising system doesn't use XML, but that doesn't matter because you can use the `xsl:output` element's `method` attribute to output text (`method="text"`). The following is a fragment from a source document:

```
<text>
   <headline>Career Opportunities at Northpoint</headline>
   <para fontsize="agate" justify="flushleft">NorthPoint Communications,
   Inc. is a competitive local exchange carrier (CLEC) focused exclu-
   sively on delivering dedicated data to growing businesses nationwide
   through wholesale agreements with service provider  partners. Our
   rapid deployment of DSL service and incredible growth and  success
   have created an excellent opportunity for a select group of experi-
   enced, self-motivated team players to join us as we chart the future
   of the rapidly evolving data communications and telecommunications
   industry. If you would like to speak with our recruiters in person,
   come see us at the WorkWorld High Tech Career Expo in San Francisco
   (Hyatt Embarcadero  Pacific Concourse) on May 3rd and 4th from 10 am
   to 7 pm.
   </para>
</text>
```

And here is the XSL file:

```
<?xml version='1.0'?>
<xsl:stylesheet xmlns:xsl="http://www.w3.org/1999/XSL/Transform">
  <xsl:output method="text" indent="no"/>
  <xsl:template match='/'>
<xsl:apply-templates select="advertisement/text"/>
</xsl:template>
   <xsl:template match="text">
   <xsl:apply-templates/>
   </xsl:template>
   <xsl:template match="headline"><xsl:text>\F4</xsl:text>
   <xsl:value-of select="text()"/></xsl:template>
   <xsl:template match="para">
   <xsl:if
test="self::para[@fontsize='agate']"><xsl:text>\F1</xsl:text><xsl:value
-of select="text()"/></xsl:if>
   <xsl:if test="self::para[@justify='flushleft']">
                <xsl:text disable-character-
escaping="yes">&lt;</xsl:text></xsl:if>
   </xsl:template>
</xsl:stylesheet>
```

Take note of the last `xsl:text` element in bold. You'll see the `<` character reference, which the XSL processor returns as the less than character (<). The target markup, which is designed for a non-XML classified newspaper advertising markup system, requires the less-than character to declare text to be flush left, but using this character can cause problems in the XML world. The combination of the `xsl:output` and `xsl:text` elements eliminates this problem. The result looks like this:

```
\F4Career Opportunities at Northpoint
\F1 NorthPoint Communications, Inc. is a competitive local exchange
   carrier (CLEC) focused exclusively on delivering dedicated data to
   growing businesses nationwide through wholesale agreements with
   service provider partners. Our rapid deployment of DSL service and
   incredible growth and success have created an excellent opportunity
   for a select group of experienced, self-motivated team players to
   join us as we chart the future of the rapidly evolving data communi-
   cations and telecommunications industry. If you would like to speak
   with our recruiters in person, come see us at the WorkWorld High Tech
   Career Expo in San Francisco (Hyatt Embarcadero Pacific Concourse)
   on May 3rd and 4th from 10 am to 7 pm.<
```

Keep in mind that it's illegal to have an end tag without a start tag, and vice versa, so don't create this kind of markup if you are generating XML elements. Also, if you are outputting XML, you shouldn't get a < character, anyway, but the character reference (`<`) instead. If you are generating elements that *are* well-formed, you don't need to use `xsl:text`; you can just create the elements using the `xsl:element` element or literal result elements because that is what the XSL processor expects.

> **TIP**
>
> White space is among the more vexing issues with XSL, because it may or may not be stripped out of the source document or the style sheet. In addition, it's possible that white space will be added to a result tree. Generally, a text node is never stripped unless it contains nothing but white space characters. It also won't get stripped if the text node's parent has a white space–preserving attribute or if the closest ancestor of the text node contains a `preserve` value in an `xml:space` attribute.

You can also use the `xml:space` attribute (despite its name, this is an attribute, not an element) to preserve white space using a value of `preserve`. This attribute is basically the same as the `xml:space` attribute made available through the XML 1 specification.

The `xsl:text` element takes one possible attribute: `disable-output-escaping`. The default value is `no`. If the value is `yes`, character references are not escaped. The attributes for this element are listed in Table 15.4.

TABLE 15.4: `xsl:text` Attributes

Attribute	Required	Possible Values, Description
`disable-output-escaping`	No	`yes`, `no`; used to declare if character references should be escaped in the output

Using the *xsl:processing-instruction* Element to Create Processing Instructions

You use the `xsl:processing-instruction` element when you want to output a processing instruction. Any special characters occurring within the element's contents will not be escaped. A processing instruction invoking XML 1 looks like this:

```
<xsl:processing-instruction name="xml">version="1.0"</xsl:pi>
```

This element can appear anywhere within the `xsl:template` element. The attributes for this element are listed in Table 15.5.

TABLE 15.5: `xsl:processing-instruction` Attributes

Attribute	Required	Possible Values, Description
`name`	Yes	Any valid XML character data; provides the name of the processing instruction
`xml:space`	No	`default`, `preserve`; used to manage white space

Copying with the *xsl:copy* Element

You can copy an element from the XML source document into the result tree by using the `xsl:copy` element. Whether or not you copy the character data, child elements, or attributes of a node depends on how you direct the `xsl:copy` element. You can include the `xsl:apply-templates` element as a child element to include other information, such as character data and attributes.

This is different than using the `xsl:value-of` element, which specifically inserts text from an element into the output tree. The idea behind `xsl:copy` is to copy the beginning and end tags of the matched element, and optionally, its character data, children, and attributes (by using, for example, `xsl:apply-templates`). The syntax for this element looks like this:

```
<xsl:template match="myElement">
<xsl:copy>
     <xsl:apply-templates select="@myElement"/>
     <xsl:apply-templates/>
</xsl:copy>
</xsl:template>
```

Taking the `myElement` element, you may want to simply add that element without any of its content, children, or attributes:

```
<myElement someAttribute="myAttribute">myElement data</myElement>
```

You would then add `<myElement/>` to the result tree by creating a very simple template that does nothing more than add the element:

```
<xsl:template match="myElement">
<xsl:copy/>
</xsl:template>
```

But what if you want to copy more than just the element's tags? The following template will add `<myElement someAttribute="myAttribute"/>` to the result tree.

```
<xsl:template match="myElement">
<xsl:copy>
     <xsl:for-each select="@*"><xsl:copy/></xsl:for-each>
</xsl:copy>
</xsl:template>
```

The following template will add `<myElement someAttribute="my-Attribute">myElement someContent</myElement>` to the result tree:

```
<xsl:template match="myElement">
<xsl:copy>
     <xsl:for-each select="@* | text()">
<xsl:copy/>
   </xsl:for-each>
</xsl:copy>
</xsl:template>
```

Because the context node is an element, attributes and children are not automatically copied; if you want to copy them, you need to create additional markup. The two preceding snippets of code enhance the match step-by-step. First, the `xsl:for-each` element is used to address any attributes of the matched node. Then, the `text()` function is used to copy any text that exists as content within the `myelement` element. You'll learn more about the `text()` function later in this chapter. The attributes for this element are listed in Table 15.6.

TABLE 15.6: `xsl:copy` Attributes

Attribute	Required	Possible Values, Description
`use-attribute-sets`	No	`yes`, `no`; used only when copying element nodes, this attribute references attribute sets that are named in a separate `xsl:attribute-set` element.
`xml:space`	No	`default`, `preserve`; used to manage white space.

Using the *xsl:comment* Element

Traditionally programming and markup languages have always used comments to add clarity to programs, scripts, or markup. In markup languages, comments are often used to hide functionality from a processor or browser that might not understand the syntax of the functionality. Consider the way a style sheet document is added in HTML, as follows:

```
<head>
<title>My Title</title>
<style type= "text/css">
<!--
.mystyle {font-size:10px}
-->
</style>
</head>
```

The style sheet in the preceding lines of code is hidden from view from lower-level browsers that can't understand style sheet element content. Browsers that recognize the `style` element will ignore the comment tags (`<!--` and `-->`). XSL comments accomplish the same thing as comments in other languages, such as HTML. Three main uses for the `xsl:comment` element follow:

- Adding comments to an XSL style sheet

- Adding a script
- Debugging your code

A typical code fragment using this element might look like this:

```
<script language="JavaScript">
<xsl:comment>
<![CDATA[
function myfunction() {
     //function statements here;
}]]>
//</xsl:comment>
</script>
```

Using the CDATA section, you can be sure that you can include markup within your script fragments without worrying about whether the markup is well-formed. So it's good programming practice to include it, even if you suspect any script-related markup *will* be well-formed. So if you're developing for a result tree for the HTML 4 namespace and want to include a simple function, you might do something like this:

```
<script>//<xsl:comment>
<![CDATA[
document.write("<P>This is<B>great</B>!")
]]>
//</xsl:comment></script>
```

The `]]` characters together are not legal anywhere within an XML document unless they denote an end to a CDATA section. This makes it easier to debug XSL documents containing script. The attributes for this element are listed in Table 15.7.

TABLE 15.7: `xsl:comment` Attributes

Attribute	Required	Possible Values, Description
`xml:space`	No	`default`, `preserve`; used to manage white space

Using the *xsl:import* Element

The `xsl:import` element imports other style sheets into your style sheet document. When you import a style sheet, you add all the nodes and content of that style sheet to the imported style sheet document. Unlike most XSL style sheet elements, the `xsl:import` element is governed by strict rules about where it can appear in the style sheet: it must always be the first child of the `xsl:stylesheet` element.

The `xsl:import` element defines the value for the element's `href` attribute. The value of the `href` attribute consists of a URI where the imported style sheet is located. If the style sheet being imported is being referenced through a relative URI, the base URI is always the importing style sheet:

```
<xsl:stylesheet xmlns:xsl="http://www.w3.org/1999/XSL/Transform">
<xsl:import href="myimport_1.xsl"/>
```

Of course, you can also use an absolute URI:

```
<xsl:import href="http://www.mydomain.com/myimport_2.xsl"/>
```

If you're wondering which elements take precedence in this scenario, the rule is pretty simple: the elements in the style sheet containing the link to the imported style sheet take precedence over the elements in the imported style sheet. The attributes for this element are listed in Table 15.8.

TABLE 15.8: `xsl:import` Attributes

Attribute	Required	Possible Values, Description
`href`	Yes	Any valid URI

Using the *xsl:apply-imports* Element

The `xsl:apply-imports` element is similar to the `xsl:apply-templates` element. The difference is that the `xsl:apply-imports` element is used to apply an imported style sheet to a template.

The rules for imported style sheets dictate that the oldest style sheet always takes precedence. You might have a style sheet with an imported style sheet, which in turn may have an imported style sheet of its own. What happens to precedence then?

The result nodes simply appear in the order of appearance within the various imports. The `xsl:apply-imports` element cannot have other elements nested within it and is always an EMPTY element; it also has no attributes.

Using the *xsl:include* Element

This element works the same way as the `xsl:import` element, except that the elements included within the included document replace the `xsl:include` element. Consider an included document that looks like this:

```
<xsl:stylesheet xmlns:xsl="http://www.w3.org/1999/XSL/Transform">
<xsl:template match="MyElement">
<MyElement1><xsl:apply-templates/></MyElement1>
</xsl:template>
</xsl:stylesheet
```

If this style sheet is named `myStyleSheet_1.xsl`, and you include it in another style sheet, its elements will replace the `xsl:include` element in memory:

```
<xsl:include href="myStyleSheet_1.xsl"/>
```

The preceding line of code becomes:

```
<xsl:template match="MyElement">
<MyElement1><xsl:apply-templates/></MyElement1>
</xsl:template>
```

If this included style sheet contained any `xsl:import` elements, those elements would move into their place in the tree, right under any other `xsl:import` elements already there. Any imported style sheets already been in place within the root template will take precedence over any imported style sheets from within an included style sheet. So far, there has been very little field testing of these features. The attributes for this element are listed in Table 15.9.

TABLE 15.9: `xsl:include` Attributes

Attribute	Required	Possible Values, Description
`href`	Yes	Any valid URI

Using the *xsl:message* Element

An XSL processor can send a message to a user whenever the `xsl:message` element is invoked. How the message is actually sent to a user is dependent on the XSL processor. The lone attribute for `xsl:message` is shown in Table 15.10.

TABLE 15.10: xsl:message Attributes

Attribute	Required	Possible Values, Description
`xml:space`	No	`default`, `preserve`; used to manage white space

Using the *xsl:key* Element

The `xsl:key` element is similar to the concept of unique identifiers, except that these elements are more generalized in nature. If you've ever searched through a database by keyword, you have an idea of how this element works. The `xsl:key` element acts similar to a cross-reference. Consider the short snippet that follows:

```
<xsl:key name="somekeyword" match="myElement" use="keyword"/>
```

You could then use a `key()` or `keyref()` function with a pattern to search for any elements containing the `somekeyword` value of the `xsl:key` element's `name` attribute. There are no requirements forcing you to make this a unique identifier, so you can create more powerful sorting features with this element. In the code fragment that follows, you can determine there are 10,000 red delicious apples available without directly accessing the information. This is accomplished by using a key reference. Take a look first at the following source:

```
<!--this is a source code fragment -->
<FRUIT>
<APPLES>Red Delicious</APPLES>
<QUANTITY>10,000</QUANTITY>
<AVAILABILITY spring="yes"/>
</FRUIT>
<FRUIT>
```

```
<APPLES>Fuji</APPLES>
<QUANTITY>20,000</QUANTITY>
</FRUIT>
```

Now take a look at the following fragment from an imaginary XSL style sheet:

```
<xsl:key name= "crossRef" match="FRUIT" USE="APPLES">
```

To set up a cross-reference, create a template and use a `keyref` function to access the spring (you'll learn more about functions a bit later in the chapter):

```
<xsl:template match="AVAILABILITY">
<xsl:value-of select="key ('crossRef', QUANTITY')"
```

Although a "function" handles this transformation, it is nothing more than an advanced matching process. The `xsl:key` element tells the processor to use the `APPLES` element to establish the cross-reference. Then the processor references the key `crossRef` in the `AVAILABILITY` template. The key takes it from there and selects nodes that match the pattern named in its definition (the `FRUIT` element). From that information, the processor can tell that the specific `APPLES` being searched are "Red Delicious Apples," so it returns the content of the `QUANTITY` element based on that result. The attributes used by `xsl:key` are shown in Table 15.11.

TABLE 15.11: `xsl:key` Attributes

Attribute	Required	Possible Values, Description
`name`	Yes	A name token; specifies the name of the key
`match`	Yes	Any valid character data; names the pattern to match against the key
`use`	Yes	Any valid character data; node set expression that denotes the set that the key should use

Using the *xsl:decimal-format* Element

Table 15.12 includes `xsl:decimal-format` attributes that indicate what characters are allowed to appear during the interpretation of format patterns during the process implemented by the `format-number()` function.

TABLE 15.12: `xsl:decimal-format` Attributes

Attribute	Character Specified
`decimal-separator`	Decimal sign
`grouping-separator`	Grouping separator
`percent`	Percent sign
`per-mill`	Per mill sign
`zero-digit`	Zero digit
`digit`	Digit
`infinity`	A string representing infinity
`NaN`	A string representing a value that can't return a number
`minus-sign`	A string representing the default minus sign

Conditional Processing

One advantage of XSL is that you can create tests to manage your matches. The match succeeds if it meets a certain condition. In XSL you manage the way you want matches to be made, but conditional processing makes it possible to offer precise definitions regarding these matches.

Using *xsl:if* to Test Conditions

To see how conditionals work, take a look at Listing 15.1. The root element for the source document in Listing 15.1 is the `advertisement` element. This element has an attribute (`action`) that can take one of several values. The XML document and its style sheets are designed to manage a real world situation, so one thing the XSL document allows you to do is decide when and what objects are displayed.

WARNING

You never want to make confidential information publicly available in your XML document, even if you "hide" it using XSL. If the document is not on a secure server, anyone with something as simple as Telnet can see it.

In Listing 15.1, the `advertisement` element's `action` attribute takes on a value of `create`. According to the DTD, this attribute is allowed several values. For the purposes of this exercise, assume that there are only two options: `create` or `update`. Let's also assume the design goal calls for a text area input to be displayed. Thus you would write XSL choosing the text that labels the text box according to the value of the `action` attribute. Listing 15.1 shows how this works using XSL implemented in IE5.

LISTING 15.1 How to Develop Style Sheets Based on Conditions

```
<?xml version='1.0'?>
<xsl:stylesheet xmlns:xsl="http://www.w3.org/TR/WD-xsl">
<xsl:template match="/">
            <xsl:apply-templates />
</xsl:template>
<xsl:template match="/">
<html>
     <body><xsl:for-each select="//advertisement">
<xsl:if match = "advertisement[@action='update']"><div
style="font-family:sans-serif;
font-size:18px;
font-weight:800;
padding-bottom:14px;
color:#333333">Classified Advertising Input Form</div><div
style="color:#FFFFCC; font-family:sans-serif; border: 3px thin outset;
background-color:#663300;padding:3px">
<xsl:value-of select="//text"/></div>
<div style="padding-top:12px;
font-family:serif;
font-weight:800;
font-size:14px">
Enter new ad copy in the space below:</div>
<div style="padding-top:6px">
<textarea name="adfiller" cols="30" rows="8" wrap="VIRTUAL"
id="210011"></textarea></div></xsl:if>
            </xsl:for-each>
     </body>
     </html>
</xsl:template>
</xsl:stylesheet>
```

The attributes for the `xsl:if` element are listed in Table 15.13.

TABLE 15.13: xsl:if Attributes

Attribute	Required	Possible Values, Description
test	Yes	The test that should be used for applying, whether or not the process should be implemented.
xml:space	No	default, preserve; used to manage white space

Using *xsl:choose* to Make Selections

The xsl:when and xsl:otherwise elements are used to help manage the conditional testing of nodes processing. In Listing 15.2, the xsl:choose element is used as the main conditional wrapper. JavaScript and other programming languages use similar conditionals to manage functions. If you compared the xsl:choose to a similar JavaScript statement, the xsl:choose element would be equivalent to the if statement. Listing 15.2 shows how this element works in IE5.

LISTING 15.2 Using the xsl:choose Element to Choose Output

```
<?xml version='1.0'?>
<xsl:stylesheet xmlns:xsl="http://www.w3.org/TR/WD-xsl">
<xsl:template match="/">
            <xsl:apply-templates />
</xsl:template>
<xsl:template match="/">
<html>
     <body><xsl:choose>
<xsl:when test = "advertisement[@action='create']"><div
style="font-family:sans-serif;
font-size:18px;
font-weight:800;
padding-bottom:14px;
color:#333333">Classified Advertising Input Form</div><div
style="color:#FFFFCC; font-family:sans-serif; border: 3px thin outset;
background-color:#663300;padding:3px">
<xsl:value-of select="//text"/></div>
<div style="padding-top:12px;
font-family:serif;
```

```
font-weight:800;
font-size:14px">
Enter new ad copy in the space below:</div>
<div style="padding-top:6px">
<textarea name="adfiller" cols="30" rows="8" wrap="VIRTUAL"
id="210011"></textarea></div></xsl:when>
<xsl:otherwise><div
style="font-family:sans-serif;
font-size:18px;
font-weight:800;
padding-bottom:14px;
color:#333333">Classified Advertising Input Form</div>
<div style="padding-top:12px;
font-family:serif;
font-weight:800;
font-size:14px">
To create your ad, enter ad copy in the space below:</div>
<div style="padding-top:6px">
<textarea name="Newadfiller" cols="30" rows="8" wrap="VIRTUAL"
id="210011"></textarea></div>
</xsl:otherwise></xsl:choose>
            </body>
     </html>
</xsl:template>
</xsl:stylesheet>
```

The template in Listing 15.2 simply states that when the `advertisement` element has an `action` attribute value of `create`, as stated in the `xsl:when` element, a series of actions should take place. The attributes for the `xsl:choose` element are listed in Table 15.14.

TABLE 15.14: `xsl:choose` Element Attributes

Attribute	Required	Possible Values, Description
`test`	Yes	The test that should be used for applying, whether or not the process should be implemented
`xml:space`	No	`default`, `preserve`; used to manage white space

Managing Numbers and Sorting

One way to add precision to generating result output and refine your matches is to use numbering elements and sorting elements.

Using *xsl:sort*

You can sort elements by naming a sorting pattern as children of the `xsl:apply-templates` and `xsl:for-each` element. This prevents the processor from processing elements in the order they appear in the document, and instead processes them according to the order named using `xsl:sort`. You can use more than one `xsl:sort` element, but the first appearing in the template takes order precedence over the next. The attributes for the `xsl:sort` element are listed in Table 15.15.

TABLE 15.15: `xsl:sort` Element Attributes

Attribute	Required	Possible Values, Description
order	No	`ascending`, `descending`; default is `ascending`; denotes whether the sort should occur in ascending or descending order.
lang	No	Same values as `xsl:lang`; describes the language used for the sort keys.
data-type	No	`text`, `number`; default is `text`; this attribute specifies the data type of the strings that are being sorted.
case-order	No	`upper-first`, `lower-first`; signals whether upper- or lowercase strings should be ordered first.
select	No	Any node; default is `.` and the value of the current node denotes which node should be sorted.

Formatting Numbers with the *xsl-number* Element

You can number elements automatically using the `xsl:number` element, which rounds a numerical attribute value into an integer and then inserts the number as text into the result tree. The architecture behind this mechanism relies on the construction of a list that is based on a number of different factors each controlled by attribute values specified at design time. The resultant list is converted into a string and inserted into the result tree. The attributes for the `xsl:number` element are listed in Table 15.16.

TABLE 15.16: `xsl:number` Element Attributes

Attribute	Required?	Description/Possible Values
`level`	No	Names the level of the source tree that the element applies. Three possible values: `single`, `multiple`, and `any`. If the value is `single`, the processor counts starting with the current node and continues to count all the preceding siblings of the current node that match the pattern defined in the `count` attribute. If the value is `multiple`, the processor constructs a list of the current node's ancestors in the order of their appearance in the document hierarchy and begins counting the preceding siblings of each member of the list. If the value is `any`, the processor begins to count at the current node and includes any preceding elements that are matched to the `count` attribute.
`count`	No	The default value is the element type name of the current node. It can also have a specific value defined for it that names the element that should be counted.
`from`	No	A value that names a pattern for starting the counting. When this attribute is used, the counting facilities initiated by the `level` attribute are begun at the element named in the `from` attribute (whether the count goes to preceding or ancestor elements depends on which `level` attribute value is named).
`format`	No	Allows you to choose from several numbering styles; a value of `i` results in lowercase Roman numerals, a value of `I` results in uppercase Roman numerals, a value of `a` results in lowercase letters, and a value of `A` results in uppercase letters.
`lang`	No	This attribute specifies the language used.
`letter-value`	No	Allows you to choose between `alphabetic` or `other` values in determining how the numerals should be represented. If the value is `other`, the sequence of results is numeric, but if the value is `alphabetic` the sequence of results are letter characters.
`grouping-separator`	No	Specifies how digits are separated (some countries use spaces instead of commas for 1,000,000).
`grouping-size`	No	Denotes the number of digits in a group.

XSL Variables

If you're not a programmer, you might assume that introducing variables into a markup language is not fair, but variables in XSL are not much different than entities in XML. If you can think of them that way, you should still have no trouble with them. There are two kinds of variable elements, the `xsl:variable` element, and the `xsl:param` element. Both are allowed at the top level (a global variable) and in individual templates of the style sheet. An element is considered a top-level element if it is a child of the `xsl:stylesheet` element. There are a few general rules to bear in mind when developing style sheet variables:

- There can't be more than one top-level variable with the same name and level of importance. An XSL processor will either deliver an error message or choose the variable that it deems most important.
- The value of a variable can be any object returned by expressions or the contents of the element that creates the variable (`xsl:variable` or `xsl:param`).
- Variables are always called by other elements with a `$` symbol. This symbol is not used anywhere else within the XSL vocabulary, so whenever you see a reference to anything with `$` as a leading character within an expression such as `<fo:block font-family ="{$fontFamilyVariable}` the reference is a variable.
- Unlike programming language variables, variable values cannot be changed dynamically by some function within XSL. This can be disconcerting to programmers accustomed to statements such as `a= if x then b else c`, but makes it easier to conditionally change variable values.
- When variables aren't declared in a document's top level, but rather in a template, the variable is available to all siblings and their descendents, not including the `xsl:variable` or `xsl:param` elements themselves.
- A variable can be bound to one of the four XPath data types: Boolean, string, number, or node set.
- A variable can be bound to a data type exclusive of variable elements, such as a result tree fragment. You can only perform string operations on result tree fragments and you can't use the `/`, `//`, or `[]` operators on them. Any

action performed on a variable has the same effect as it would on the equivalent node set.

- Result tree fragments can only be returned by variable expressions if the variables are result tree fragments, if they are the results of expression functions that create result tree fragments, or the result of a system property whose result is a result tree fragment.

Binding with the *xsl:variable* Element

The `xsl:variable` element is the simplest type of variable: a simple construct that holds a value that can be referenced somewhere else in a document. An `xsl:variable` element has one required attribute—`name`—that you can use to name your variable:

```
<xsl:variable name="colorIt">color</xsl:variable>
```

The element content is the value of the variable. You can reference the variable somewhere else in your document, such as within a template, as follows:

```
<xsl:template match="lesPommes">
<xsl:element name="APPLE"><xsl:attribute
name="{$colorIt}">red</xsl:attribute></xsl:element>
</xsl:template>
```

The preceding example creates a new element, called `APPLE` and an attribute for that new element. Note how the attribute takes its name from the value of the previous variable. This creates an attribute—`color`—that is then assigned a value of `red`. The value of the variable doesn't involve the content of the attribute, however, and won't change if you maneuver the various conditional elements, as a programmer might do with JavaScript or Java. Rather, the value of the variable is exactly as you assign it, in this case `color`. You could name the value of the variable within the element name that was created instead and use the `$colorIt` variable as the value of the `xsl:element` element's `name` attribute. If you're familiar with programming, you might even think that XSL variables work the opposite way programming variables work, in that variables with a constant value are referenced by objects rather than objects with values that vary. The attributes for the `xsl:variable` element are listed in Table 15.17.

TABLE 15.17: xsl:variable Element Attributes

Attribute	Required	Possible Values, Description
name	Yes	Name token that is the name given to the variable
select	No	An expression that provides the value of the variable

Using Attribute Value Templates

The key to using variables involves *attribute value templates*. Simply put, these make it possible for you to use the values of attributes as expressions, as in the following code:

```
<xsl:template match="lesPommes">
<xsl:element name="APPLE"><xsl:attribute
name="{$colorIt}">red</xsl:attribute></xsl:element>
</xsl:template>
```

The attribute value assigned to the new element APPLE was assigned through the variable `$colorIt`. This is an example of an attribute value template in action. An attribute value template is created by an expression in a template. Take a look at the following source document fragment that uses a variable in the attribute value template:

```
<APPLE>
<color>red</color>
</APPLE>
```

If you want to create an attribute value template with color as an attribute rather than a nested element, you can do this:

```
<xsl:template match="APPLE">
<APPLE color="{color}"/>
</xsl:template>
```

Here you're using a literal result element, which may not help much with automation, so you may instead want to create your elements using the `xsl:element` and `xsl:attribute` elements. So taking that same information from that source document fragment, you might end up with this:

```
<xsl:template match="APPLE">
<xsl:element name="APPLE"><xsl:attribute
name="{color}">red</xsl:attribute></xsl:element>
</xsl:template>
```

The important thing to remember about attribute value templates is that they can use any expression. So they can get just as complex as any expression you are capable of creating.

Using the *xsl:param* Element

The `xsl:param` element works closely with its cousin, the `xsl:with-param` element, to produce results that come as close to variable value changing as is possible within the XSL framework. You can use `xsl:param` the exact same way you use `xsl:variable`. You can also replace the values of `xsl:param` elements using the `xsl:with-param` element, whereas you can't replace the values of the `xsl:variables` element.

You can see an example of how the `xsl:param` element works in the next section. The attributes used with the `xsl:param` element are listed in Table 15.18.

TABLE 15.18: `xsl:param` Element Attributes

Attribute	Required	Possible Values, Description
`name`	Yes	Name token is the name given to the variable.
`select`	No	An expression provides the value of the variable.

Using the *xsl:with-param* Element

The `xsl:with-param` element is used to reference an `xsl:param` element's value and insert new values as needed within a template. In the following example, an `<xsl:choose>` element is used to test whether or not an attribute is equal to a declared variable. Remember that the state of an XSL variable never changes. Rather, the variable's value is assigned to other elements (or not, depending on whether you end up using it):

```
<xsl:choose>
<xsl:when test="$color='red'">
     <xsl:call-template name="apples_oranges">
            <xsl:with-param name="fruit" expr="'apple'">
            <xsl:with-param name="season" expr="'spring'">
     </xsl:call-template>
</xsl:when>
```

```
<xsl:when test="$color='orange'">
     <xsl:call-template name="apples_oranges">
            <xsl:with-param name="fruit" expr="'orange'">
            <xsl:with-param name="season" expr="'winter'">
     </xsl:call-template>
</xsl:when>
<xsl:otherwise>
     <xsl:call-template name="text-template"/>
</xsl:otherwise>
</xsl:choose>

<xsl:template name="apples_oranges">
<xsl:variable name="color" expr="FRUITS/@color">
<xsl:param name="fruit" expr="'nectarines'">
<xsl:param name="season" expr="'all'">
<xsl:text>
Eat some <xsl:value-of select="$color"/>. You'll feel better.
</xsl:text>
</xsl:template>
```

In the preceding example, the value of the `xsl:variable` element (in the `apples-oranges` template) is extracted from a pattern matching process. The `FRUIT` element's `color` attribute in the source document being tested will have some color value and you can't change that color value once you find it in the source document. This is one big difference between XSL and programming languages. Rather than providing the ability to change the `FRUIT` element's property, XSL provides the ability to reference that property and produce more sophisticated result trees based on variable references.

After the `xsl:variable` is declared, two `xsl:params` are declared. The value of these won't change and the value of any objects in memory is unchanged. You're only performing a value switch based on the results of your test. This is a fairly important distinction from a programming standpoint. For our purposes here, it just means that if the value of the `FRUIT` element's `color` attribute is `red`, then, using the `xsl:param` element, a new reference is made based on the original `xsl:param` reference. If you look at the `name` attribute of the `xsl:param` element and the `name` attribute of the `xsl:param` element, you'll see that they're the same. That's the reference that makes it possible to insert the new node into the XSL result tree. You didn't change the variable's (the `xsl:param`) properties as you would in a procedural programming language. Rather, you used that variable's properties to establish a new reference and insert a node into your result tree. The attributes for the `xsl:with-param` element are listed in Table 15.19.

TABLE 15.19: `xsl:with-param` Element Attributes

Attribute	Required	Possible Values, Description
`name`	Yes	Name token is the name given to the variable.
`select`	No	An expression; provides the value of the variable.

Using Expressions

Chapter 14 looked at the way pattern matching uses a process similar to searching to make it possible for you to develop your result trees. Architecturally, the process is not quite that simple. A pattern is considered a subset of a larger group of *expressions* that are used for a variety of transformation purposes. These are expressed in the XPath language, which is a separate set of syntax rules governing XML node access.

Evaluating Expressions

Technically, an expression is set of conditions used to determine whether a node meets some criteria. If it does, the result is one of the following four possible data types:

1. A node set.
2. A number, which can be any floating-point number. If you flinch when you encounter mathematical terms, a floating-point number is basically a number with a decimal point in it, like `3.14` or `55.5555`. Specifically, XPath numbers are allowed any IEEE double-precision 64-bit format value.
3. A Boolean (true or false).
4. A string (in Unicode format).

Some specific uses for expressions include:

- Generating text into the result tree using the `xsl:value-of` element's `select` attribute

- Managing conditionals to process named nodes using the `test` attribute in the `xsl:if` and `xsl:when` elements
- Processing nodes from the source tree using the `xsl:apply-templates`, `xsl:for-each`, `xsl-sort`, and `xsl:copy-of` elements
- Using the `xsl:template` element to name patterns matched to the source tree using the `match` attribute
- Managing default variables or processing values using the `xsl:number`, `xsl:param`, and `xsl-variable` elements

When you're evaluating an expression, you are not strictly limited to the context node. More complex expressions evaluate by referencing the context in a number of additional ways. The simplest is the context node, but there are five possible uses in all:

1. The context node.
2. The context position and the context size (always both, and the integer representing the context position is never greater than the context size).
3. A set of XSLT functions (often referred to as a function library), which consists of a number of functions built into the XSLT language and which facilitate the expression evaluation process.
4. Variable bindings (derived from the way XSLT variable names map out to variable values).
5. The namespace declarations in scope.

Using Axis Identifiers

Axis identifiers are qualifiers that establish the relationship between nodes in a source document and your context node. They are the guideposts for a specific type of location paths called *bases* (plural for *basis*) used in selecting nodes for processing by certain elements and attribute value templates (attribute value templates will be explored in the next chapter). Axis identifiers help determine how to traverse the source tree to select nodes to satisfy your more complicated addressing needs. Table 15.20 provides a roundup of these identifiers, the most important of which is probably the `child` identifier, if only because it is the one used to obtain the children of the context node in the most basic way. The axis identifiers shown in Table 15.20 demonstrate the long version and provide a conceptual summary of each axis identifier. The syntax demonstrated throughout this chapter and the generally uses the abbreviated version of axis identifiers, rather than the long version shown in Table 15.20.

TIP

When considering axis-identifiers, and their relationship to your context node, remember that your context node is your current node, and that your current node, in a complex XSL document, may actually change. It may help to think of your context node as your "home" node, much like an `index.html` is a home page upon which are based the paths of other Web documents in determining relative link and `href` relationships.

TABLE 15.20: Axis Identifiers

Axis Identifier	Description
`ancestor`	Contains all ancestors of your context node, and indicates that the nodes are searched in reverse order within the source document.
`ancestors-or-self`	Contains all ancestors, plus the actual context node itself, and indicates that the nodes are searched in reverse order within the source document.
`attributes`	Contains all the attributes of the context node.
`children`	Contains the children of the context node, in order of their appearance within the source document.
`descendant`	Contains the descendants of the context node in order of their appearance within the source document.
`descendants-or-self`	Contains the descendants of the context node in order of their appearance within the source document, plus the context node itself.
`following`	Contains all nodes in the same document as the context node in the order of their appearance within the source document. These nodes all appear in document order after the context node, and do not include descendants, namespace nodes, or text nodes.
`following-siblings`	Contains the siblings that follow the context node in order within the source document, unless the context node is an attribute node or namespace node, in which case there is no match for the selection.

Continued on next page

TABLE 15.20 CONTINUED: Axis Identifiers

Axis Identifier	Description
`parent`	If the context node has a parent, this axis identifier identifies it. The parent of an attribute node and namespace node is the element that contains those nodes.
`preceding`	Contains all nodes in the same document as the context node in reverse order of their appearance within the source document, except for ancestors, namespace nodes and attribute nodes.
`preceding-siblings`	Contains the siblings of the context node that precede the context node itself, in reverse order of their appearance within the source document, unless the node is an attribute node or namespace node, in which case there is no match for the selection.
`self`	Contains only the current (context) node.

Axis identifiers are actually constructs of the XPath language, and are not directly encountered in `match` attributes. They are used by expressions, primarily by the `select` attribute of the following elements:

- `xsl:apply-templates`
- `xsl:for-each`
- `xsl:value-of`
- `xsl:variable`
- `xsl:param`
- `xsl:sort`
- `xsl:copy-of`

Most likely, you'll use abbreviated forms of axis-identifiers as shown throughout this chapter. XSL allows you to use operators as a form of shorthand so that you don't need to use the whole syntax as listed in Table 15.20. For example, the following `child` axis identifier:

```
xsl:template match=" child::ADVERTISEMENT"
```

becomes the following as an abbreviated location path:

```
xsl:template match="ADVERTISEMENT/TEXT"
```

Similarly:

```
xsl:template match="child::ADVERTISEMENT/from-children(TEXT)"
```

becomes the following as an abbreviated location path:

```
xsl:template match="ADVERTISEMENT/TEXT"
```

The colon pairs separate the axis identifier (on the left) from the node test (on the right). The colon pairs are used in expressions, thus allowing you to traverse the source tree in more powerful ways than pattern matching allows.

NOTE

One more reason not to be overly concerned with the syntactical details of axis identifiers is that XPath is still a moving target in terms of the Web. The abbreviations haven't changed, but the syntax of the actual axis identifiers has, and the syntax behind the more verbose axis identifiers may still change before the standards become finalized.

Using Abbreviations Using the location path `myelement/myotherelement` abbreviates the `child::myelement/child::myotherelement` location path. The `child` locator is the most common location path you'll encounter when developing basic XSL style sheets. It may be easier to think in terms of paths because the abbreviated syntax of location paths and path syntax used on the Web are similar:

```
http://www.myWeb.com/myParentDirectory/myChildDirectory/
myGrandchildDirectory.
```

In addition to the / character, which operates on the root of the tree, there are five abbreviations that work on four axes, as follows:

- // operates on descendents (the `descendent` axis).
- `.` operates on the context node (the `self` axis).
- `nodeName` operates on a child, or, if `nodeName` is replaced with *, works on all child elements (the `child` axis).
- `@nodeName` operates on an attribute, or if `@nodeName` is replaced with *, works on all attributes (the `attributes` axis).

Table 15.21 shows how the location path abbreviations work.

TABLE 15.21: Abbreviated Location Paths

Abbreviated Location Path Used with a Sample Element	Description
MYELEMENT	Selects all immediate MYELEMENT child elements
*	Selects all immediate child elements (not including character data) of the context node
*[last ()]	Selects the context node's last child
*/MYELEMENT	Selects all grandchild MYELEMENT elements
../MYELEMENT	Selects the MYELEMENT children of the parent element
MYELEMENT[@MYATTRIBUTE]	Selects all MYELEMENT child elements that have an attribute named MYATTRIBUTE
MYELEMENT[MYCHILDELEMENT]	Selects all child MYELEMENT elements that have a child MYCHILDELEMENT
MYELEMENT[@MYATTRIBUTE and not(@MYATTRIBUTE="GREEN")]	Selects all child MYELEMENT elements that have a MYATTRIBUTE attribute whose value is not "GREEN"
/*	Selects the outermost element of the document
//MYELEMENT	Selects all TITLE elements anywhere in the document
ancestor(MYELEMENT)	Selects the innermost containing MYELEMENT element
ancestor(MYELEMENT)/@MYATTRIBUTE	Selects the MYATTRIBUTE attribute of the most deeply nested containing MYELEMENT element
./@*	Selects all attributes of the current element

NOTE

How do axis identifiers fit into the selection process of the `xsl:apply-templates` element? The `<xsl:apply-templates/>` tag translates to `<xsl:apply-templates select="child::/*"`, which in abbreviated form looks like this `<xsl:apply-templates select="*"/>`. This selection process generates a context node list that contains all children of the context node. The template is then "applied" to each child member of this context node list. In this context, the pattern starts with the / character and the context node list contains all children of the root of the tree.

Using Node Tests Every axis has a node type. In addition to the node tests that can be created for axis identifiers, there are node tests for nodes that aren't elements or attributes, such as text nodes. For example, `MYELEMENT/text()` will select the text node children of the MYELEMENT node. Four node tests you'll encounter are included in Table 15.22.

TABLE 15.22: Node Tests

Node Test	Description
text()	Any text node
node()	Any type of node
comment()	Any comment node
pi()	Any processing instruction node

Using XSLT Predicates and Expression Operators

One subset of expressions, called *patterns*, is used to manage the selection process. Another subset of expressions is the *predicate*. A predicate typically extends the capability of a pattern match by filtering the pattern's selected nodes. Filtering will be explored in more detail in the section on functions, but one commonly used function returns the position of a node in a node list. The best way to understand how this works is to see it in action. Review the following XML document, to find out the position of a specific node in the node list:

```
<?xml version='1.0'?>
<?xml-stylesheet type="text/xsl" href="position2.xsl" ?>
<nodeTester type="referral">
  <function>
    <name>position() function</name>
  </function>
  <text> The position in the node list is:
   </text>
 </nodeTester>
```

To find out the node list position of an element, for instance the text element, you could develop a simple test using a predicate that takes advantage of one of XSLT's built-in functions as follows:

```
<?xml version='1.0'?>
<xsl:stylesheet xmlns:xsl="http://www.w3.org/1999/XSL/Transform">
     <xsl:output method="text" indent="no"/>
```

```
  <xsl:template match="nodeTester">
    <xsl:apply-templates/>
</xsl:template>
<xsl:template match="text"> The position in the node list is:
<xsl:value-of
         select="position()"/>
</xsl:template>
</xsl:stylesheet>
```

This results in the following result tree (output as text):

```
position() function

   The position in the node list is: 4
```

Using Expression Operators

The previous chapter discussed pattern matching and introduced a number of special characters called operators. Operators are also used in evaluating expressions within the context of a particular data type. You'll encounter them most often when using predicates and functions. The data-type operators used in expressions are shown in Table 15.23.

TABLE 15.23: XSL Expression Operators

Operator	Description
+	Used with numbers for addition
-	Used with numbers for subtraction
*	Used with numbers for multiplication
=	Equal to
!=	Not equal to
< (< when used in an attribute value)	Less than
<= (<= when used in an attribute value)	Less than or equal to
>	Greater than
>=	Greater than or equal to

TIP

Earlier this chapter introduced a special character called a variable reference (`$`). The variable reference is not an expression operator, but rather is used as a way to reference an XSL variable.

NOTE

How operators function syntactically within XPath statements was in flux at the time of this publication. Of particular concern was how brackets are used to nest expression predicate statements. For updates on this issue, visit **`http://www.w3.org/TR/xpath`**.

Some operators can also be called by name and are called operator names, as described in Table 15.24.

TABLE 15.24: Operator Names

Operator	Description
`and`	Logical `and`, meaning the combination of two selections
`or`	Logical `or`, meaning one or the other selection
`mod`	Modulus, which takes the remainder of two divided numbers
`div`	Division

XSL Functions

Sets of expressions that return values based on criteria stated within given parameters are known as XSL functions. They provide a means for expanding the way you create selections and allow you to develop very specific criteria for matches as you develop a result tree.

If you're a non-programmer, don't be scared off by programming in XSL. XSL functions help enhance the transformation process, generally by helping you refine search criteria with patterns. Functions in object-oriented languages, like Java or C++, have a much broader range of capabilities.

XSL functions use standard arguments within their syntax. Arguments are keywords within parentheses that are passed on as parameters. This means that the function may need some extra information to be processed. Arguments give you the chance to pass that information along. In a programming language, a function doesn't necessarily need to contain any specific parameters to work properly, but they do add functionality. The same is true with XSL functions: whether a function is required to take an argument depends on the function and its purpose. The functions available through XSLT and XPath are shown in Table 15.25. Note that some of these may be changed before the final W3C Recommendation is approved.

TABLE 15.25: XPath and XSLT Functions

Function	Syntax	Description
`Boolean()` function	`Boolean()` Node lists and result fragments return true if they're not empty, a string returns true if its length is not zero, and a number returns true if it is zero or `NaN` (which stands for Not a Number, which is nevertheless a distinct value that is a "result" of a floating point calculation, such as dividing by zero).	Converts the value within its argument to a Boolean.
`ceiling()` function	Returns the smallest integer less than the number named in the argument's parameter.	
`concat()` function	`concat(string, string...)`	Returns a concatenated value (joined together string values) of any number of strings in the argument.
`count()` function	`count()`	Returns the number of nodes in the node set named in the argument.
`current()` function	`current()`	Returns a node set whose only member is the current node.

Continued on next page

TABLE 15.25 CONTINUED: XPath and XSLT Functions

Function	Syntax	Description
`document()` function	`document("object" | node-set)`	Permits access of documents outside the original source document by returning either a document element (the root node) or a document fragment (specified as a string URI in the argument's first parameter, with the second parameter as the base string).
`floor()` function	`floor(number)`	Returns the largest integer closest to the number named in the argument's parameter.
`extension-element-available()` function	`extension-element-available(`*`ElementName`*`)`	Returns true if XSLT processor supports the element named as an extension element.
`extension-function-available()` function	`extension-function-available(`*`stringFunctionName`*`)` Where `stringFunctionName` is the name of the function you are testing against.	Searches the XSL patterns for a named function; generally used as part of Conditional, such as `xsl:test`.
`generate-id()` function	`generate-id(`*`string`*`)` Where `string` is a string consisting exclusively of ASCII text and which must begin with an alphabetic character.	Creates a string value to be used as a unique identifier.
`id()` function	`id(string)` `idref(1011)` The function returns an element by simply searching for an `id` whose value matches the parameter in the function (1011).	Returns a string value representing a node set's unique identifier by evaluating the string parameter and matching it against any node's containing that value as an `id`.
`key()` function	`key(string, scalarNodeSet)` Where string is a string naming the key (acquired from the `xsl:key` element's `name` attribute) and `scalarNodeSet` is a string value representing the NodeSet to be matched.	Returns a matching node set by retrieving the string value from the `name` attribute value of the `xsl:key` element named in the function's parameter.
`last()` function	`last()`	Selects the number of nodes in the context node list.

Continued on next page

TABLE 15.25 CONTINUED: XPath and XSLT Functions

Function	Syntax	Description
`local-part()`function	`local-part()`	Returns a string consisting of a first node's local name part.
`namespace()` function	`namespace()`	Selects the namespace in the first node of the argument node set.
`number()` function	`number(string | Boolean | nodeSet)` Where a named `string` value is converted to a number, `Boolean true` is converted to 1, `false` to 0, and a node set is converted to a string, then converted to a number. If there is no argument (no parameter within the parentheses), then the context node is returned.	Converts the value of the function's argument into a number.
`position()` function	`position()`	Returns a value based on the position of the context node within the context node list.
`name()` function	`name(stringNodeName)` Where `stringNodeName` represents the name of the node. The name must be a qualified name as defined by the XML 1 spec. If there is no argument, the function returns the context node.	Returns a string that represents the name of the first node in the argument.
`round()` function	`round(`*`number`*`)`	Returns the closest integer to the number contained in the argument. If two numbers can be returned, the even number wins.
`substring()` function	`substring(string, number, number)` Where `string` is the source string; the first `number` is the position in the source string of the first character in the string that starts the string fragment; the second `number` is the length of the target string (the substring). Note to JavaScripters: the first position in the string is not 0; it is 1. XSL does not begin indexing with 0.	Returns a specified string fragment, determined by a start and end point as named in the parameters.

Continued on next page

TABLE 15.25 CONTINUED: XPath and XSLT Functions

Function	Syntax	Description
`substring-before()` function	`substring-before(string, string)`	Returns the substring from the source string's beginning up to the first instance of the substring's appearance in the original source string.
`substring-after()` function	`substring-after(string, string)`	Returns the substring beginning from the source string's end up to the first instance of the substring's appearance in the original source string (beginning but not including the substring's first character).
`sum()` function	`sum(`*`number1, number2`*`)`	Returns the sum of the numbers named in the function argument's parameters.
`system-property()` function		Returns a string identifying various aspects of the system, such as the version number of the XSLT transformation used, and other relevant information (not yet defined at the time of this writing).

There are a number of functions that relate specifically to strings. Table 15.26 provides explanations of string functions available to XSLT processors.

TABLE 15.26: String Functions of Available XSLT Processors

Function Name	Syntax	Description
`concat()` function	`concat(`*`string1, string2, | OptionalString3...`*`)` Where the first two parameters are concatenated, as well as an optional third parameter (and fourth and fifth and so on).	Returns concatenated strings from the parameters within the argument (see the note that follows this section for an explanation of concatenation.
`contains()` function	`contains(`*`string1, string2`*`)`	Used to match same strings together, returns true if the first string within the argument is identical to the second string in the argument.

Continued on next page

TABLE 15.26 CONTINUED: String Functions of Available XSLT Processors

Function Name	Syntax	Description
`format-number()` function	`format-number(number, format-Pattern, OptionalLocale)` Where number is the number to be converted to a string, `formatPattern` is the pattern specified using a Java-based decimal class called the `DecimalFormat` class, which is defined in the JDK 1.1, and `OptionalLocale` is the notation used to describe valid localized characters as defined in JDK 1.1. This means some characters can have a special meaning within your search pattern, but for Java-related reasons these characters can't be either quotes or the currency sign.	Converts a number to a string using decimal formatting based on the Java programming language.
`normalize()` function	`normalize(string)`	Normalizes (strips leading and white space from a group of characters) the text contained within the argument.
`starts-with()` function	`starts-with(string1, string2)` Where `string1` is the parameter being tested against by the second parameter.	Tests to see if one string starts with a specific string, which itself is named in the second parameter of the function argument. If the test works the function returns true, otherwise it returns false.
`string()` function	`string(node-set | resultTree-Fragment | number | Boolean)` Where `node-set` returns a string value based on the first node in the tree, or an empty string if the node set is empty; `resultTreeFragment` returns a string of the nodes within the document fragment, and automatically concatenates the result as if the fragment were an original source tree node; `number` is converted to a string and concatenated automatically with a – character if the number is a negative number. If there is no argument, the context node is returned.	Converts the value contained within the argument to a string.

Continued on next page

TABLE 15.26 CONTINUED: String Functions of Available XSLT Processors

Function Name	Syntax	Description
`substring-before()` function	`substring-before(`*`string1`*`, `*`string2`*`)` Where **string1** contains the value to be evaluated, and **string2** contains the value of the string that defines the end of the substring (exclusive of the second string): `substring-before("mySubstring is cool", "cool")` Would return `mySubstring is`.	Returns a substring by evaluating the argument's first parameter against the second parameter. The substring that is searched for ends when the processor encounters the string contained in the second argument. A substring is simply a portion of a longer string. In the `string "This is my sentence", "This is my"` is a substring.
`substring-after()` function	`substring-after(`*`string1`*`, `*`string2`*`)` Where **string1** contains the value to be evaluated, and **string2** contains the value of the string that defines the end of the substring (exclusive of the second string): `substring-after("mySubstring is cool and so are you", "cool")` Would return `and so are you`.	Returns a substring by evaluating the argument's first parameter against the second parameter. The substring that is searched for begins when the processor encounters the string contained in the second argument.
`translate()` function	`translate(string1, string2, string3)`	Designed primarily for changing between upper- and lowercase.

NOTE

Concatenated strings are built from more than one string and JavaScript uses this procedure extensively. For example, in JavaScript, if you have two variables, `x` and `y`, each variable might contain the value of a string. If `x=this` and `y=string`, you would concatenate these two string variables with `x+y` and the result would be "this string." In XSL, you would use `${x}`, `${y}`. Concatenation, addition, and the use of the + operator make data typing very important. For example, in a scripting language, like JavaScript, you don't want the processing engine to mistake the + for a sum argument and add the values arithmetically. Rather, you want to add the values as strings, so that the result is `this string`. That's concatenation.

Learning about Extensions

Microsoft wanted to include a number of *extensions* to XSL in the release of IE5 to make up for some features it found lacking in XSL, in particular the handling of data type management. So Microsoft developed elements like the `xsl:eval` element that is used to evaluate data types and convert them as needed. However, at the time of IE5's release, there was no way to extend XSL. Microsoft's stated goal was to rework their XSL support to include extensibility added to the W3C Specification as the various drafts made their way to W3C Final Recommendation. The specification developers were able to develop syntax for adding this extensibility.

Extension Functions

Extensions are handled by two special functions called the `extension-element-available()` and the `extension-function-available()` function. These return true when the XSLT processor supports the element or function named in the string parameter, respectively.

The *xsl:fallback* Element

The `xsl:fallback` element contains a template for the XSLT processor to fall back on if it doesn't support the element named in the `extension-element-available()` element. Rather than issue an error, the XSLT processor uses the template named within the `xsl:fallback` element. This is a way to manage backward (and forward) compatibility issues.

You control the way your result tree is output by the `xsl:output` element. This element must be a top-level element, meaning that it must appear as a child of the `xsl:stylesheet` element or the `xsl:transform` element (synonymous with one another). You can find an example of how to use this element in the section describing the `xsl:text` element. The attributes for this element are listed in Table 15.27.

TABLE 15.27: `xsl:fallback` Attributes

Attribute	**Required?**	**Possible Values, Description**
`xml:space`	No	`default`, `preserve`; used to manage white space.

Learning about Formatting Objects

One formatting process involves formatting objects, which allow you to create display objects and insert them into the template as you would in HTML. One disadvantage to formatting objects is that IE5 and Netscape 5 do not support them, but formatting objects are supported in at least one new Web browser: InDelv from InDelv, Inc., of Edmonton, Canada. The W3C also devoted half of the official XSL Recommendation to formatting objects and there are plans to use formatting objects to develop documents that transition easily from Web to print (by converting formatting-object-centric files to `.pdf` files, the Portable Document Format developed by Adobe Systems, Inc.).

NOTE InDelv is available on the *Mastering XML* companion CD-ROM. InDelv is also available for download at `http://www.indelv.com/`.

Formatting objects allow you to create containers for styled formatting objects. You can manage the style of the formatting object in many ways as these objects are inserted into an XSL template in much the same way HTML is inserted.

WARNING The formatting object specifications were still in working draft stage when this book went to press. By contrast, the XSLT working draft had just become a W3C Proposed Recommendation when this book went to press. There was still a large amount of work to be done on formatting objects, so use caution when using this vocabulary.

Developing with Formatting Elements

Although formatting objects may result in containers, these containers (rectangles and spaces) are not themselves formatting objects. A formatting object can create an area (though not all do) that has traits in the broad sense. These traits are characteristics that help describe the area created by the formatting object, but they do not have any identifiable or programmable properties, because they aren't objects. Rather, objects are created when a formatting object is defined and placed into a container. What follows is a typical example of how a formatting object is inserted into a node:

```
<?xml version='1.0'?>
<xsl:stylesheet
xmlns:xsl=" http://www.w3.org/1999/XSL/Transform"
```

```
xmlns:fo="http://www.w3.org/1999/XSL/Format"
result-ns="fo">
<xsl:template match='/'>
     <fo:display-sequence
             start-indent='6pt'
             end-indent='6pt'
             font-size='18pt'
     font-family='sans-serif'
     >
<xsl:for-each select="advertisement">
<xsl:value-of select="text"/>
</xsl:for-each>
     </fo:display-sequence>
</xsl:template>
</xsl:stylesheet>
```

This syntax may be a bit different to you, so let's focus on what is familiar. First, take a look at the way the namespace is used. Rather than using the HTML 4 namespace, you can use a formatting object namespace. There is no guarantee an XSL processor will recognize that namespace. The InDelv browser was used to render the XML document associated with the preceding style sheet, because it can process the document and render the type as indicated in the style sheet. You could also process an XSL file that outputs formatting objects by using a processor like XT, then read the result file into another program that converts the file into a `.pdf` format.

Another familiar aspect of the preceding lines of code should be the template elements. If you recall how the HTML fragments are placed into the templates, you can see how this is the same with the formatting objects, but instead of inserting HTML, you insert the formatting objects.

You can isolate the same elements' preceding code by taking a different approach to template development. For example, take a look at the following lines of code and see if you can see what looks different:

```
<?xml version='1.0'?>
<xsl:stylesheet
<xsl:stylesheet xmlns:xsl="http://www.w3.org/1999/XSL/Transform"
xmlns:fo="http://www.w3.org/1999/XSL/Format"
     <xsl:template match="/">
     <fo:block
font-size="40pt"
background-color= "#ff6600"
```

```
border-color="#000033"
     start-indent="12pt">
          <xsl:apply-templates select="//text"/>
     </fo:block>
</xsl:template>
</xsl:stylesheet>
```

Although the `xsl:for-each` and `xsl:value-of` elements perform different functions than the `xsl:apply-templates` element, they're nested in similar ways because they tell the processor to insert specified elements into their containing elements. In the preceding code, the `xsl:apply-templates` element tells the processor to apply any templates that match any text elements that are descendants of the root node. The way location paths are used, as well as the `xsl:apply-template` element, can be confusing at first. The easiest way to learn about the relationship of various elements is by playing around with the attributes of each element. For example, try changing the operators in the `select` attribute. Or, add some templates to the one you see here and apply each one to a different block element. In the next chapter, you'll see a somewhat more complex style sheet in action that demonstrates how to use multiple templates in a style sheet. Figure 15.1 shows how the rendered document looks.

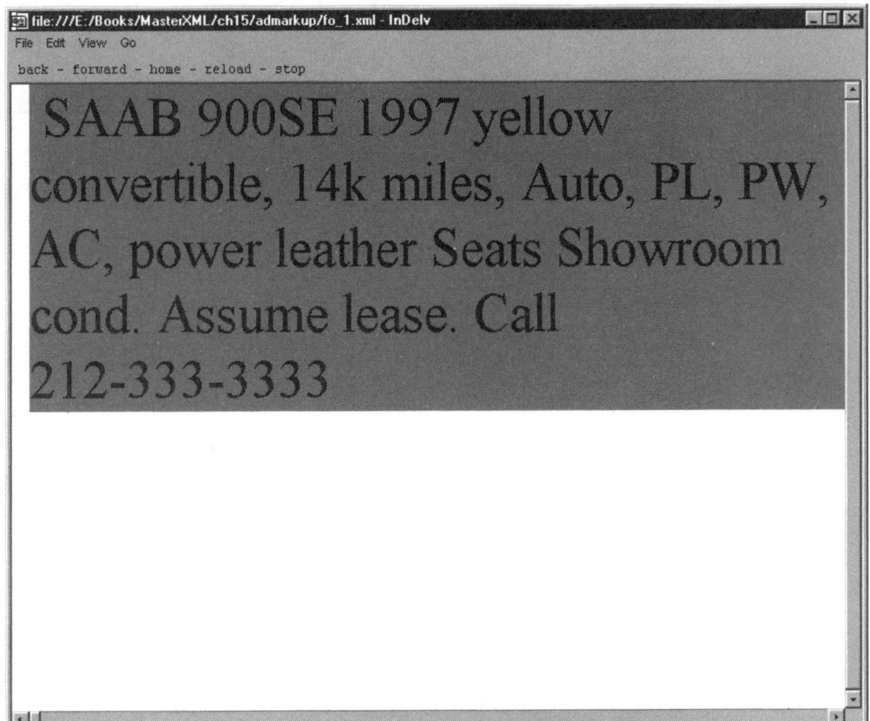

FIGURE 15.1: Formatting objects rendered in the InDelv browser

Examining Formatting Element Properties

If the properties associated with formatting objects are familiar to you, it's because many of them are based on the CSS model. Many are also based on the DSSSL-model, as is CSS. DSSSL is a large, complex style language used in the SGML world. Much of what you find in CSS and XSL is derived from that language.

In the next several sections we'll look at many of the properties associated with formatting objects by looking at CSS properties. Formatting object property categories are more localized as they are broken down, starting with such global objects as pages and working all the way down to the character level. These properties can generally be categorized as follows:

- Page management
- Block level (such as paragraphs)
- Inline

NOTE

Most of the major elements in this chapter appeared in the working draft for XSL published April 21, 1999 (xsl-19990421). Of all the XSL-related specifications, this was the least stable as this book went to press. It is possible that there will be substantial changes made to this extensive specification.

Note that the descriptions in the next several sections use attributes and properties somewhat interchangeably. This is because attributes are used to access an element's properties in code.

Page Management

The following elements manage page layout including the management of master pages that act as templates for other pages.

`fo:root` This is the top-level element for a formatting-object result tree. It doesn't generate any containing area itself, but is instead used to define the root level of the formatting-object tree. It can contain an `fo:layout-master-set` formatting object and one or more `fo:page-sequence` objects.

`fo:page-sequence` This element handles page layout management and master pages, including child elements (`fo:simple-page-master` and `fo:queue`). This flow object can manage the way both print and online pages are sequenced to make it easier to break large documents into more manageable chunks of information, such as chapters and part sections. As such, it doesn't create a containing area, but rather acts as a grouping agent for other objects. Available properties for this object are:

- `id, first-page-master, letter-value, digit-group-sep, n-digits-per-group, sequence-src, id, initial-page-number`

`fo:page-number` This element contains, in an inline area, the page number of a page. The available property for this object is:

- `id`

`fo:queue` This element is only allowed in a page-sequence element and this object contains information about how content flows within a document. Available properties for this object are:

- `id, queue-name`

`fo:layout-master-set` This element contains all the page masters used in a document.

`fo:simple-page-master` This element contains information about a master page, which is a template containing characteristics common to a group of pages. This element is always a child of the page-sequence element, and can never be nested within another flow object. There are four valid simple-page-masters (although more will be added to future specifications): `first`, `odd`, `even`, and `scrolling`. Some of the properties available for this element include:

- Common background properties

Block-Level Flow Objects

Page layout objects apply formatting to flow objects at the widest level. Next on the global formatting hierarchy are block level flow objects. These allow you to work with blocks of objects, such as groups of paragraphs and text, groups of images, etc.

`fo:display-sequence` This object indicates that a group of flow objects should inherit the same properties; it acts as a global formatting object to the objects assigned to it. You can only include block-level flow objects as child elements within this object. These elements are displayed in document order. Available attributes for this element include:

- `ID`
- Any attribute that can be applied to one of this element's child elements

fo:block This object denotes a block area whose height and width by default are determined by a combination of the containing area (such as an application window) and the number of lines of text within the block. This element should be used for formatting paragraphs, and can also be used for such other block-level type objects as titles, captions, and headlines. Content that exists *within* an `fo:block` element is called inline content, and thus contains elements such as `fo:inline-graphic` and `fo:inline-rule` elements.

Attributes available for this element include the following:

- Common absolute position properties
- Common aural properties
- Common border, padding, and margin properties
- Common font properties
- `color`
- `text-align`, `text-align-last`, `text-indent`
- `space-after` and `space-before`
- `visibility` and `z-index`
- `writing-mode`
- `wrap-option`
- `widows`, `hyphenation-keep`, `hyphenation-ladder-count`
- `line-height`, `line-height-shift-adjustment`, `last-line-end-indent`, `line-stacking-strategy`

fo:display-graphic This object represents a block-level container that manages a graphic object. No child formatting objects are available for this object. Some of the attributes available for this include the following:

- Common border and margin properties
- `ID`, `width`, `height`, `href`

fo:display-rule This object contains block-level information about an object holding a line (called a rule in the graphic arts industry). Some of the attributes available for this include the following:

- Common border and margin properties

- Common font properties
- Color properties
- Text alignment and indent properties
- `rule-thickness`, `id`, `color`, `text-align`, `href`

Block-Level Lists

You can also manage list blocks, which are block-level flow objects that contain lists.

`fo:list-block` These lists are block-level flow objects that contain lists, whose valid children `list-item` pairs are `list-item-label` and `list-item-body` flow objects. Some of the attributes available for this include the following:

- Common background properties
- Common font properties
- Common border properties
- Common padding and margin properties
- `break-before`, `break-after`
- `end-indent`, `start-indent`
- `space-after`, `space-before`, `keep`, `keep-with-next`, `keep-with-previous`

`fo:list-item` These lists manage the position and spacing (padding) of `list-item-label` and `list-item-body` flow objects within an `fo:list-block` object. The parent of a `list-item` flow object always contains an `fo:list-block` object. This element uses the same attributes as its parent, the `fo:list-block` element.

`fo:list-item-body` These lists manage the formatting properties of a list item, such as font styles, spacing between lines and paragraphs, and line breaks. This is different than `list-item`, which focuses on the placement of the `list-item` body.

`fo:list-item-label` These lists are used as a mechanism for supplying additional information about a list-item. As such, it is always a child element of the `list-item` to which it is applied. This element uses the same attributes as its parent, the `fo:list-block` element, and a few additional properties that did not have implementation support as this book went to press.

Managing Inline Areas

You can also manage inline areas. In modern page layout programs like Quark Xpress, PageMaker, and InDesign, it's possible to include a graphic *inline*. This means that the graphic flows with the text, rather than the other way around. Typically, text flows around a graphic, but not an inline graphic. In a desktop publishing program, an inline graphic will move along with the character it was inserted next to (see Figure 15.2).

FIGURE 15.2:

An inline graphic in Adobe PageMaker

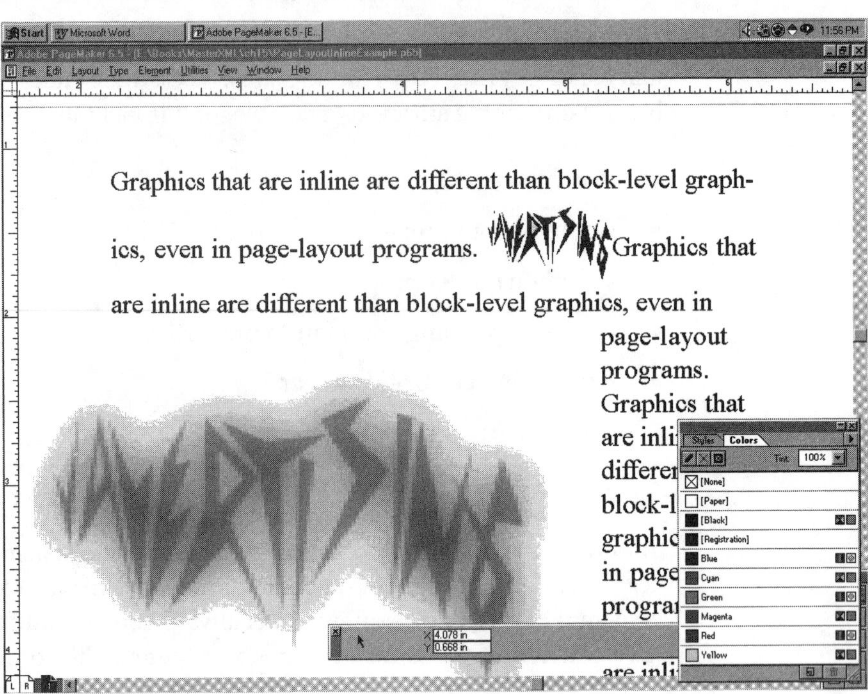

fo:inline-sequence This inline graphic is used to assign properties to a group of inline flow objects. Its only property is:

- `id`

fo:inline-graphic This represents the area occupied by an inline graphic. It is a generalized container used to name properties its child elements will inherit. Although it has no direct formatting properties of its own, you can assign formatting properties to it that will then be used by its child elements. It can have inline formatting objects or PCDATA as its children. The one attribute directly used by this element is:

- `ID`

`fo:inline-rule` This inline graphic represents an inline rule, inheriting properties from the inline area where the rule is used. Available properties include:

- Common border properties
- `ID`, `color`, `rule-thickness`, `length`

`fo:character` You can keep drilling down in specificity when developing flow objects. The `fo:character` element can be used to manage the formatting of specific characters. It overrides any previously applied formatting. Among the properties available to this element are:

- Common absolute position properties
- Common aural properties
- Common border, padding, and margin properties
- Common font properties
- `color`
- `text-align`, `text-align-last`, `text-indent`
- `line-height`, `line-height-shift-adjustment`

`fo:inline-included-container` This element is used to embed block-level objects in inline-level areas. These elements move with the general flow of the page inline like other inline elements do, but the objects they contain act like block level objects. The attributes used by this element are the same as those used by `fo:block`.

Understanding Formatting Data Types

The vocabulary for XSL formatting objects allows a number of data types that are listed in Table 15.28. Advanced users may want access to these descriptions when developing programs that manage XML documents and data types. However, you don't need to be a programmer to know that if, for example, you're preparing an annual report, it might be nice to show losses in red and gains or positive values in black. XSL allows you to do that by giving access to these data types.

TABLE 15.28: XSL Data Types

Data Type	Description
Boolean	A string containing a true or false values. Also the only valid string values.
Char	A Unicode character with no surrounding white space.
Color	A hexadecimal (such as `#000000` for black or `#FFFFFF` for white) or named color.
Country	A string representing a country in accordance with ISO 3166 country code.
Enumeration	XML `NMTOKEN` values enumerated into a list.
Font List	A white space delimited list of font names.
Font Name	A string representing a font name.
ID	String of characters conforming to `NMTOKEN` and that are unique within a given style sheet.
IDREF	String of characters conforming to `NMTOKEN` and that matches a specific `ID` within the style sheet.
Language	A string specifying the human language in accordance with either ISO 639 three-letter code or with `xml:lang` in the XML 1 specification (which of these would be used was not determined as this book went to press).
Name	String of characters conforming to `NMTOKEN`.
Percent	A signed real value representing a percentage.
Positive Integer	An unsigned integer (not including 0) consisting of digits in sequence.
Positive Length	A positive real number (not including 0) with a unit qualification.
Positive Real	A signed integer (not including 0) that can include an additional trailing character and trailing digits.
Signed Integer	A signed integer that can include the + or – and trailing digits.
Signed Length	A signed real number (meaning they can hold positive or negative values) with a unit qualification.
Signed Real	A signed integer that can include the + or – and trailing digits, in addition to a trailing character and trailing digits.
Space Specifier	A data type that can hold several kinds of data representing maximum, minimum, and optimum lengths, as well as conditional values and values that specify precedence.

Continued on next page

TABLE 15.28 CONTINUED: XSL Data Types

Data Type	Description
String	A sequence of one or more characters.
Unsigned Integer	An unsigned integer (including 0) consisting of digits in sequence.
Unsigned Length	An unsigned real number (meaning they can't hold positive or negative values, but can hold 0) with a unit qualification.
Unsigned Real	An unsigned integer that can include the + or – and trailing digits, in addition to a trailing character and trailing digits.
URI	A series of characters denoting a Uniform Resource Identifier.

Up Next

The W3C Specification for XSL is changing, so you'll want to view the latest syntax at `http://www.w3.org/TR/WD/xslt`. If you love playing around with code and script, you'll spend hours fooling around with this extremely hardy language. To learn more, check out the XSL Public List archives at `http://www.mulberrytech.com/xsl/xsl-list/archive/index.html`. In addition, use XT, which is very helpful for tracking down problems in your code and bouncing around ideas.

In the next chapter, you'll learn how to convert HTML to XML. Hopefully, by now you've already developed some of the habits you'll need for developing XML-compliant HTML. Now it's time for a step-by-step approach.

PART V

Converting to XML

CHAPTER

SIXTEEN

16

Converting from HTML to XML

- Why move from HTML to XML?
- What is an XHTML document?
- Differences between HTML 4 and XHTML 1
- The rules of XHTML

In this chapter, you will be introduced to the *Extensible Hypertext Markup Language* (XHTML). You might remember that XHTML was mentioned back in Chapter 1: "The Road to XML," which compared XML to SGML and HTML. As noted there, the intent of the XHTML language is to provide a clear and easily understandable transition path from HTML to XML that Web content developers can begin incorporating now.

Why Move to XML?

Why should you be motivated to move to XML? One big reason: extensibility. The current state of the Web is a patchwork of HTML, proprietary browser extensions, and more. Web developers are left with the choice of supporting only those elements defined in the W3C HTML Recommendations or alienating users of browsers that don't support the proprietary element sets they've chosen to use. Even worse is the task of creating multiple versions of a site so that each browser's unique element sets are incorporated.

XHTML, by its very name, is meant to be extensible. With its close relationship to XML, the process of adding a new element such as the infamous `<BLINK>` is a relatively trivial matter, especially as compared to the current state of HTML, which requires authors to create invalid documents.

This easy customization allows developers to create industry- or company-specific documents using unique elements that may not be of use elsewhere but that, when properly added to the DTD and used in a well-formed XHTML document, add significant value for that audience.

Even with all the new and exciting extensibility features, XHTML allows authors to retain the semantics present in HTML. Indeed, XHTML can be rendered in current HTML browsers with only a few minor considerations to backward compatibility. This electronic bridge from HTML to XML lets Web developers sharpen their skills and become fully prepared for the explosion of XML about to occur on the Web.

Portability is another good reason to switch to XHTML. The world is already seeing a significant increase in Internet access from devices other than the traditional desktop or laptop computer. Hand-held and palm PCs, PDAs, televisions, cell phones, pagers, telephones, and other devices are all accessing the Web at an ever-increasing rate. By some estimates, in the next two years, up to 75 percent of Web access will occur from these nontraditional platforms. PCs will actually be in the minority! HTML can't be rendered on all the new machines in use today, but well-formed and valid XHTML can.

What is an XHTML Document? The popular idea of what an HTML document is has moved away from the definition provided by the HTML Specifications. In part, this is because browsers try to correct for errors or other problems they encounter in documents. It's also because many authoring tools have failed to make HTML authors aware of the components that form the basis of good authoring practices but that the major browsers don't necessarily need, such as the Doctype definition.

What is or isn't an XHTML document is very narrowly defined in the W3C's XHTML Working Draft, which says:

A *Strictly Conforming* XHTML Document can only require that which is described as mandatory in the specification. That means it will meet each of these criteria:

1. It must validate against one of the three DTD found in Appendix A (of the XHTML Working Draft).
2. The root element of the document must be `<html>`.
3. The root element of the document must designate one of the three defined namespaces by using the xmlns attribute. The namespace designated must match that of the DTD that the document purports to validate against. The defined namespaces are:
    - `http://www.w3.org/Profiles/xhtml1-strict.dtd`
    - `http://www.w3.org/Profiles/xhtml1-transitional.dtd`
    - `http://www.w3.org/Profiles/xhtml1-frameset.dtd`
4. There must be a DOCTYPE declaration in the document prior to the root element. The public identifier included in the DOCTYPE declaration must reference one of the three DTD found in Appendix A [of the HTML Working Draft] using the respective Formal Public Identifier. The system identifier may be modified appropriately:

```
<!DOCTYPE
     html PUBLIC "-//W3C/DTD XHTML 1.0 Strict//EN"
                 "xhtml1-strict.dtd">
<!DOCTYPE
     html PUBLIC "-//W3C/DTD XHTML 1.0 Transitional//EN"
                 "xhtml1-transitional.dtd">
<!DOCTYPE
     html PUBLIC "-//W3C/DTD XHTML 1.0 Frameset//EN"
                 "xhtml1-frameset.dtd">
```

A Strictly Conforming XHTML Document can use the Internet Media Type text/html or text/html. When labeled as text/html, authors should take care to follow the guidelines provided in Appendix C of the XHTML Specification.

It's important that a user agent—which may be a traditional browser or access software for alternative devices—follow the XHTML Specification to the letter. Those that don't will run into serious trouble as the XHTML draft begins to incorporate modularization and profiling, both of which will be discussed in depth in Chapter 17: "Advanced XHTML."

Differences between HTML and XHTML

Though XHTML is designed in part to provide authors with a smooth transition from HTML to XML, there are still some XHTML requirements that are critical to the success of an XHTML document and are new to those who are used to the constraints of HTML.

As the complexity of HTML grew over the past few years, Netscape Navigator and Microsoft Internet Explorer, as well as other less popular browsers, began to try to interpret what a document author *meant* to do when there were errors present in an HTML file. Many times the programmers that worked on those programs were able to have the browser "guess" correctly.

An XML processor depends on authors having produced a solid structure for their documents. This is even more important than it is with HTML documents, because there isn't a set vocabulary for XML. A programming team can teach a browser every tag that can be found in an HTML document, but when document authors create their own tags in XML, the browser can't know the possibilities in advance. This makes it nearly impossible for the browser to second-guess or aid the author when errors occur.

While XHTML retains some of the semantics of HTML, it does require authors to be more careful with document construction. This is actually a good thing because authors know their documents will render as intended rather than in the browser's "best guess."

The next section goes into further detail on structurally complete documents and outlines several other key differences between HTML and XHTML.

Well-Formed Documents

For several years now, major browsers have been very forgiving of poorly written HTML documents. In fact, as mentioned in the previous section, a significant part of their code is devoted to error handling. Authors who have relied on such features in HTML will be very surprised when faced with XHTML documents, where the document being well-formed is a requirement for rendering success. While some may complain that this is overly restrictive, in the end, the benefits far outweigh the extra effort that must be made when the document is created. All conforming user agents will be able to render the document, and no presentation surprises will occur because of misguided error-handling attempts by the browsers.

The Rules of XHTML

To better understand the differences between HTML and XHTML, let's take a look at the basic rules governing XHTML and see how they compare to what has traditionally been done with HTML.

Nested Elements Must Be Closed

Nested elements have always been required to be closed in proper order. However, the forgiving nature of browsers has lead to some sloppy authoring habits. When authoring with XHTML, such constructs result in ill-formed documents that will be required to fail in an XHTML conforming user agent.

For example:

```
BAD:
<p><font face="arial">This sentence has <strong>three <em>improperly
nested</strong></em> tags.</p></font>
```

This is not well formed because the elements are closed out of order. Despite this, both of today's most popular browsers interpret the intent of the author and display the markup as intended, as seen in Figure 16.1.

FIGURE 16.1: Ill-formed HTML markup is still rendered as intended.

Were this markup presented to a conforming XHTML user agent, the document would fail to render because each element must be closed in reverse order of which it was opened. Nested elements are like a set of nesting mixing bowls and lids. The stack won't work properly if you try to put the lid—the closing tag—on a bowl after it's already inside another bowl with its lid on. The markup segment should actually appear as:

```
GOOD:
<p><font face="arial">This sentence has <strong>three <em>improperly
nested</em></strong> tags.</font></p>
```

This segment is well-formed and would be accepted by any conforming user agent.

End Tags Are No Longer Optional

In HTML 4, elements were either *containers* that had opening and closing tags and content contained in between, or they were *empty* elements, where the element itself stood alone. In many cases, the closing tags for nonempty elements were optional. The presence of another block level element implied the closing of the first. This was typically found with several paragraph blocks:

```
<P>The first paragraph is written here.
<P>Paragraph two begins here, implying the end to paragraph one.
```

Under HTML 4, this example was perfectly legal and valid. Under XHTML, it is considered ill formed because all elements must be complete.

XHTML is much stricter in requiring closing tags for *all* nonempty elements. Therefore, the two-paragraph passage must be written:

```
<P>The first paragraph is written here.</P>
<P>Paragraph two begins here, and no longer relies on an implied clo-
sure to paragraph one. </P>
```

Authors who develop XHTML documents by hand will, of course, need to pick up the habit of closing all tags, although authoring tools should provide automatic support for this practice soon.

Empty Elements Must Be Terminated

Empty elements are those that perform a function simply by their presence—they do not bound other content between an opening and closing tag. They can be tags without any attributes, such as <BR> and <HR>, or they can be complex tags such as those for images with four or five attributes:

```
<img src="picture.gif" height="100" width="100" border="0"
align="left">
```

In XHTML, each element must be terminated. With nonempty elements, that's done with the closing tag, such as </P>. An empty element, by definition, doesn't have a closing tag. Therefore, to terminate it, the forward slash (/) is inserted just prior to the closing angle bracket (>) character:

```
<br/> or
<img src="picture.gif" height="100" width="100" border="0"
align="left"/>
```

All Attribute Values Must Be Quoted

All attribute values under XHTML must now be quoted. Previously, values were only required to be quoted if they contained a URL or if they contained non-alphanumeric characters (that is, spaces, punctuation, the # character used for hex color codes, etc.). Best practices traditionally advised authors to quote all attributes, simply to prevent accidental errors when trying to remember when it is required and when it isn't. Under XHTML the dilemma is solved: all attributes must be quoted.

Attributes Cannot Be Minimized

HTML 4 allows some attributes values to be reduced, or *minimized*, to a Boolean representation. That is, the attribute is turned "on" simply by its presence in the element; it remains off if it doesn't appear. For example, authors can provide a default selection in form elements by inserting the Boolean attribute `checked`, as seen here.

```
<input type="radio" name="widget" value="yes" checked>
```

In XML, and consequently XHTML, attribute minimization is not supported. Therefore, the attribute name=value pair must be fully written. In the case of this form element, it would be written:

```
<input type="radio" name="widget" value="yes" checked="checked">
```

White Space in Attribute Values Is Compacted

HTML authors are undoubtedly familiar with fact that excess white space within CDATA content is compacted, as illustrated in the following markup sample and in Figures 16.2 and 16.3:

```
<P>     This paragraph began with 5 spaces, intended to provide an
"indented" first line.
..
```

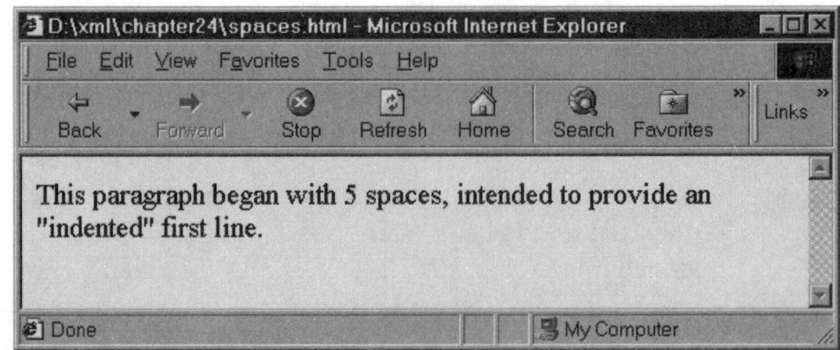

FIGURE 16.2: White space is compacted when rendered by Internet Explorer 5.

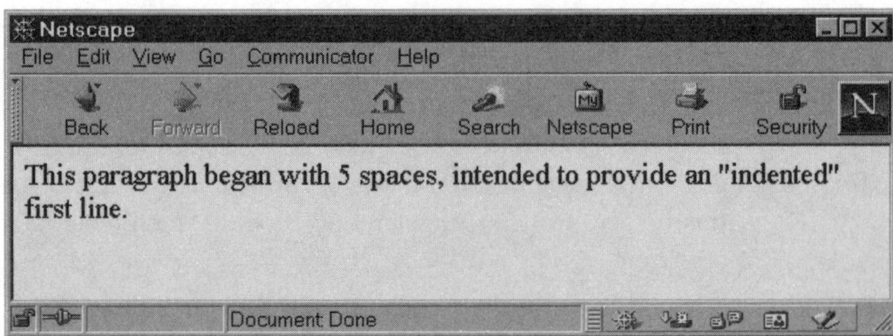

FIGURE 16.3: White space is also compacted by Netscape Navigator.

What's occurring here in HTML is multiple contiguous space or carriage return/line feed characters are being interpreted as a whole space or line feed unit, rather than as individual characters.

Under XHTML, this user agent behavior of having the white space compacted is required when dealing with the content of attribute values as well as elsewhere in the body of the document.

Script and Style Elements Are Wrapped in CDATA

The content and directives of script and style elements are supposed to be processed after the document itself has been delivered. Because this happens after the document is delivered, many character entities occur inside those elements. When an XML processor comes upon entities such as < or &, it will attempt to process them and expand them to their > and & form, which results in *Parsed Character Data* (PCDATA). To avoid having the XML processor operate on these entities, script and style element content needs to be wrapped in a CDATA section. For example:

```
<style>
<![CDATA[
…style sheet content…
]]>
</style>
```

This blocking of style or script content tells the XML parser to ignore the contents of that blocked container and allows the entities to pass through without being processed.

Element Exclusions Are Not Allowed

In SGML, as well as HTML, it is possible to forbid certain elements from appearing within other elements. For instance, a <FORM> element cannot appear inside another <FORM> element, and a <P> element cannot appear inside an <H1> element. These prohibitions are formally known as *exclusions*. Unfortunately, in XML it is not possible to write such exclusions into the DTD; therefore, they cannot be written in an XHTML DTD.

Despite this limitation, XHTML does recognize that certain elements should not be nested and provides a normative list of prohibited nesting scenarios. Table 16.1 outlines these rules.

TABLE 16.1: Elements That Cannot Be Nested in XHTML

Element	May Not Contain...
<a>	other <a> elements
<button>	button, fieldset, form, iframe, input, label, select, textarea
<form>	other <form> elements
<label>	other <label> elements
<pre>	big, img, object, small, sub, sup

XHTML Elements Are Case-Sensitive

A change that has sparked more fervent debates in HTML circles than any other aspect of the XHTML drafts is the case-sensitivity of elements.

XML recognizes differences in case, therefore it considers a <P> element to be different than a <p> element, whereas in HTML they are dealt with as one and the same. Since XHTML must be compliant with XML, a decision had to be made regarding case for HTML elements. Other applications of XML have taken a lowercase position on the subject, meaning that lowercase element names must be used, and the W3C Working Group charged with producing the XHTML Working Draft agreed that it would follow suit. Therefore, well-formed and valid XHTML documents must use lowercase element names.

Errata Handling

In any specification, minor items that need correction are inevitably found after publication. Such is the case with HTML 4. The W3C has collected a list of these issues, known as *errata*. The HTML 4 DTDs themselves have not been updated to reflect the acceptance of these changes, but they have been incorporated into the DTD for HTML 4 that is used as a basis for XHTML. Authors should be aware that the DTD documents will be different if compared side by side, and that the XHTML DTD reflects the current state of errata handling.

Porting HTML into XHTML

Any time you undertake the effort of converting existing content from one format to another, it can seem like a never-ending task. Two tools are currently available that can help speed up the process, the HTML Tidy Utility and HTML-Kit. When you see how useful they are, both of these may become a part of your regular document authoring war chest.

The HTML Tidy Utility

The HTML Tidy Utility is a tiny command-line program that helps Web authors tidy up their documents. It is published by the W3C and made available on their Web site. (The W3C publishes a number of software programs and modules under the Open Source philosophy. Open Source software is published with the source code available, and license is given to others to freely distribute it or incorporate it in other products, provided the original copyright statements are included. For more information about the Open Source movement, visit `http://www.open-source.org`.)

Dave Raggett, the author of HTML Tidy, originally wrote the utility to help catch errors in HTML documents. For instance, it can find missing closing tags or mismatched tags and organize HTML markup so that it's easy for humans to read.

With the introduction of XHTML, Raggett added the ability to turn valid HTML into well-formed XML. The resulting markup is also well-formed XHTML.

NOTE

The HTML Tidy Windows executable and the C source code for compiling on Unix systems can be found on the CD at the back of this book. It may also be downloaded in other formats from the W3C Web site at `http://www.w3.org/People/Raggett/tidy/`.

Tidy is a command line utility that is run from a DOS box in Windows. A number of formatting and output arguments are available (the full list can be accessed by executing `tidy -help`), though, for the purposes of this book, we'll use the options geared toward converting HTML to XML.

Listing 16.1 is the small HTML file seen earlier in this chapter that contains improperly nested elements, complete with a DOCTYPE declaration and other required HTML elements.

LISTING 16.1 `nesting.html`

```
<!DOCTYPE HTML PUBLIC "-//W3C//DTD HTML 4.0 Transitional//EN">
<html>
<head>
<title>Improperly Nested Tags</title>
</head>
<body>
<p><font face="Garamond">This sentence has <strong>three <em>improperly
nested</strong></em> tags.</p></font>
</body>
</html>
```

HTML Tidy will be run using the following syntax:

```
tidy -f errors.txt -asxml > new.html
```

The -f argument directs Tidy to write each error it encounters to a text file named errors.txt. The -asxml switch indicates the desired output: well-formed XML. Finally, the windows redirect option of > tells the system to write the new file to new.html.

Figure 16.4 displays an abbreviated copy of the error report as compiled into the errors.txt output file.

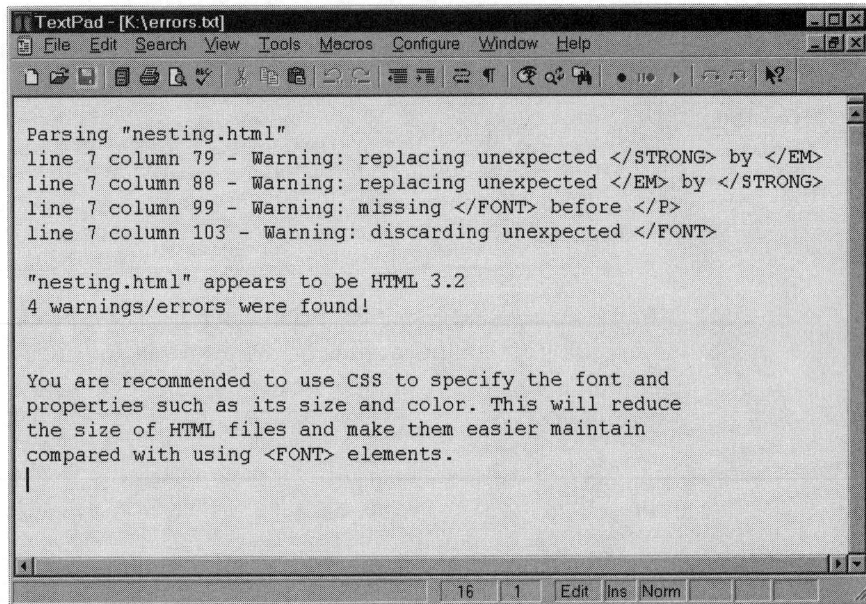

FIGURE 16.4: The error reporting produced by HTML Tidy

Listing 16.2 is the corrected version of nesting.html that we had Tidy output to new.html.

LISTING 16.2 **new.html**

```
<?xml version="1.0"?>
<!DOCTYPE HTML PUBLIC "-//W3C//DTD HTML 4.0 Transitional//EN">
<html>
<head>
<title>Improperly Nested Tags</title>
</head>
<body>
```

```
<p><font face="Garamond">This sentence has <strong>three <em>
improperly nested</em></strong> tags.</font></p>
</body>
</html>
```

Note that the first error encountered is reported at line 7, column 79, and involves an "unexpected" </strong> tag:

```
<strong>three <em>improperly nested</strong></em>
```

The </strong> tag was unexpected because Tidy is looking for the most recently opened element, <em>, to be closed first. To correct the error, it replaces </strong> with </em>, as indicated in the warning. At this point, the markup has two closing </em> tags, since the erroneous </strong> was replaced, but Tidy has not yet moved on to the next element, as seen here:

```
<strong>three <em>improperly nested</em></em>
```

Tidy now looks for either another element to be opened, or the next most recently element to be closed. In this case, it expects to find a closing </strong> but instead encounters that second </em>. Tidy corrects this in the second error warning, and the set of <strong> and <em> tags are now properly nested:

```
<strong>three <em>improperly nested</em></strong>
```

The final two warnings work much the same way:

```
line 7 column 99 - Warning: missing </FONT> before </P>
line 7 column 103 - Warning: discarding unexpected </FONT>
```

This markup has the closing </p> tag appear before the closing </font>:

```
<p><font face="Garamond">This sentence has <strong>three <em> improp-
erly nested</em></strong> tags.</p></font>
```

Since Tidy works one step at a time, it decides the closing </p> is unexpected and replaces it with a closing </font>. When it encounters an extra closing </font> next, it discards it and adds the closing </p> required to make the document well-formed.

HTML-Kit

HTML-Kit is an HTML editing tool that has incorporated the HTML Tidy Utility functionality. Authors who are more comfortable with graphical user interfaces may wish to use this version rather than the command-line version distributed by the W3C.

Operating HTML-Kit is quite simple. Your file doesn't have to be created using HTML-Kit; you only need to open it in the HTML-Kit before running the Tidy function. Figure 16.5 shows the short HTML 4 file used previously to illustrate improperly nested tags loaded in the HTML-Kit program.

FIGURE 16.5:

The HTML-Kit user interface

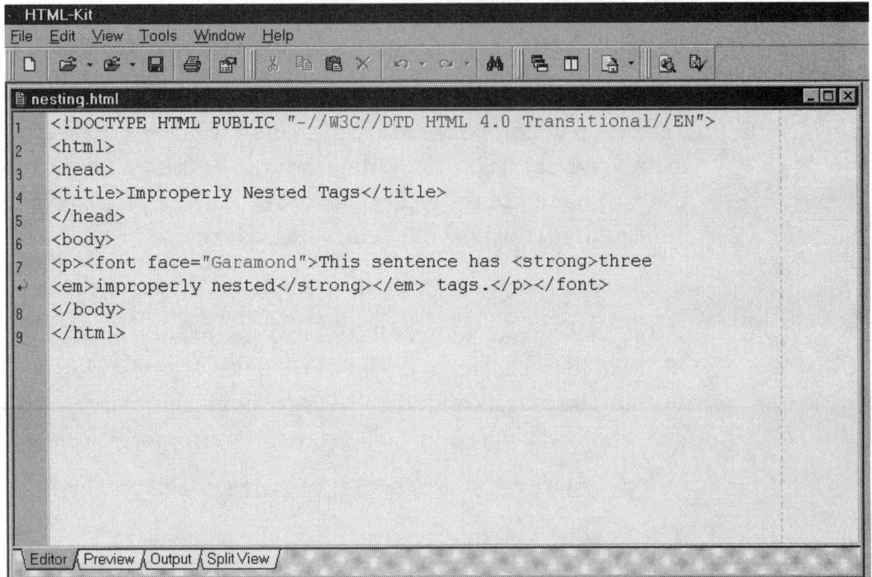

To perform the Tidy operation, simply choose the check icon shown below from the toolbar.

Alternatively, select Tools ➢ Check code using Tidy, or press the F9 key. HTML-Kit performs the check and writes the corrected output to a new window, which is displayed in split-screen mode next to the original version (see Figure 16.6).

The Messages Window is also opened that provides details on which corrections were made. The row where the error occurred, the character column, and a description of each change are included (see Figure 16.7).

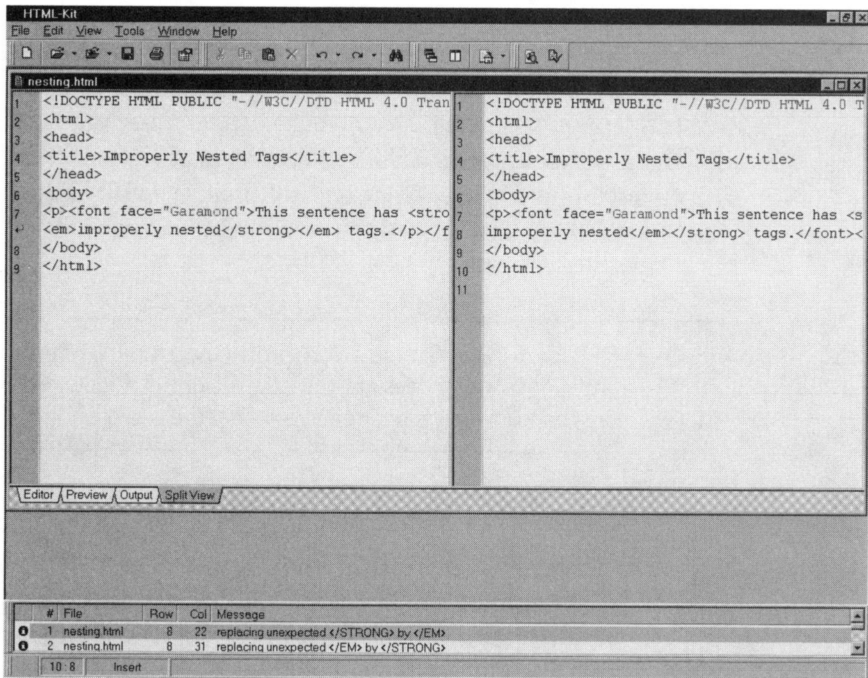

FIGURE 16.6:

The TIDY results are displayed in split-screen mode.

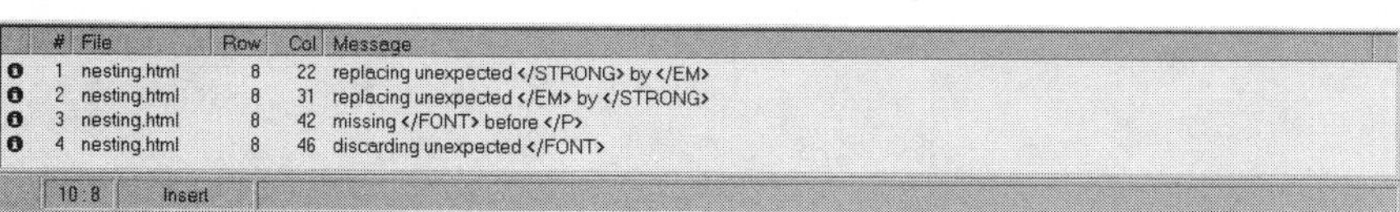

FIGURE 16.7:

The Messages Window provides correction details.

Designing XHTML Documents for Use in Current Web Browsers

A troublesome aspect of any new Web technology is that it often takes months (or even years) for that technology to be incorporated into existing tools. This is especially true with XML and XHTML and the Web browsers available on today's market.

The W3C HTML Working Group is acutely aware that early success of a new markup language is dependent on early adoption by the Web development community. Indeed, the entire idea behind XHTML was to present developers with a clear transitional path from HTML to XML. Toward that supportive goal, the HTML Working Group has published an informative set of authoring guidelines along with the current XHTML Working Draft. By following these eight points, authors should be able to successfully deliver XHTML content to browsers with functional capabilities compatible with those found in Microsoft Internet Explorer 5 and Netscape Navigator 4.5.

NOTE

An *informative* section in a W3C working draft or recommendation is presented as a suggestion. It does not carry the weight of a requirement. Those rules that *must* be followed are referred to as *normative* sections.

The eight points that make up the authoring guidelines are:

Empty elements must be terminated. XHTML requires empty elements to be terminated, as with `<br/>`. This construct confuses most current browsers, but it can be easily remedied by including a single space before the / terminator, as in `<br />`.

Nonempty elements without content are not allowed. There are times when a nonempty element such as a paragraph or title may not have any content. Despite this, those elements cannot be written in minimized form like empty elements. Therefore, the construct of `<title />` is incorrect, while `<title> </title>` is valid.

Avoid line breaks and white space in attribute values. Current browsers handle line breaks within elements (such as a long IMG tag) and extra white space inconsistently. Though the XHTML Working Draft requires extra white space to be compacted, that behavior is currently unpredictable.

Use both `lang` and `xml:lang` attributes when specifying the language of an element. Browser support for these attributes is inconsistent. By implementing both versions, you will maximize your chances of successful interpretation.

Use both `ID` and `name` attributes when identifying URI fragments. In XML, URIs that end with fragment identifiers (`#fragment`) refer not to an element with the attribute `name` of "fragment," but instead to an element with an ID attribute of "fragment." This is directly in conflict with the HTML usage of the name attribute. To remedy this, either avoid using fragmentary URI constructs, or provide both a name and ID attribute in the fragment anchor, e.g., <a id="fragment" name="fragment">.

Character encoding should appear in both the XML declaration and in a meta tag. Current Web browsers expect character encoding information to be presented in a meta tag, taking the form of: <meta http-equiv= "Content-type" content="'text/html; charset="EUC-JP"' /> for Japanese encoding, for example. This statement should appear in the <head> element of the document, and the encoding attribute should also appear in the XML declaration as: <?xml version="1.0" encoding="EUC-JP"?>.

Processing instructions may be rendered by some browsers. Currently, there isn't an elegant remedy for this situation. If at all possible, avoid using PIs in documents that will be viewed by existing Web browsers.

Up Next

In this chapter, we reviewed the basics of the Extensible Hypertext Markup Language (XHTML). You learned the differences between XHTML and HTML and how to create documents that retain the well-formed structure of XHTML and will still render properly on today's Web browsers.

The next chapter delves further into the XHTML Working Draft and introduces the extensible aspects of XHTML: modularization and document profiles.

CHAPTER

SEVENTEEN

17

Working with XHTML

- Modularizing XHTML
- Design goals for modularizing XHTML
- Defining modules
- Creating your own modules
- Document and client profiles for XHTML

The excitement surrounding XHTML comes not only from providing a clean transition between HTML and XML, but also from the customization available with the concept of modularization.

The Modularization of XHTML

As the *X* in its name implies, one of the key differences between HTML and XHTML is that it is *extensible*. The extensibility imagined by the W3C HTML Working Group, who is continuing to draft and refine this specification at the time of this writing, is not just a means to provide additional features to HTML. (If that were the idea, we wouldn't have to go much further than how elements such as `<blink>` and `<layer>` made their way into certain browsers). Instead, the extensibility in XHTML is intended to provide a standardized way of customizing XHTML to fit the needs of your documents or specific clients.

To provide that extensibility, XHTML is being defined in subsets of elements that can be combined and extended, allowing content developers, application programmers, and any others that need to create or output XHTML to make sure that their devices and environments are supported with the most economy of effort. That support can be maintained by carefully selecting the appropriate building blocks, or *modules*, for content, and by device manufacturers providing sufficient profile information about their clients and alerting the content developers as to which modules are supported by which devices.

Design Goals for Modularizing XHTML 1

The work to be done on modularizing XHTML 1 is truly the meat of the project put before the Working Group. The XHTML 1 specification outlined in Chapter 16: "Converting from HTML to XML" provided the migration path between HTML and XML. The next phases of the XHTML project provide the mechanisms for the extensibility of the Web for which developers have been clamoring.

In reviewing the stated needs of various user communities (individual developers, the educational community, corporate users, scientists, and more), five major design requirements were distilled:

- Granularity
- Composibility

- Compatibility
- Conformance
- Ease of Use

Each of these requirements is discussed in the following sections.

Granularity

Modules need to be flexible enough to provide a meaningful method of expressing content and capabilities. If you simply labeled the XHTML 1 Strict DTD a "module," it would not provide a solution for devices and environments for whom that set of elements and attributes is too much (or not enough!). At the same time, the modules should be substantial enough to promote interoperability. Granularity, in this case, refers to how limited each module is. The most granularity you could have would be to put each element in its own module, but that would get overwhelming very quickly. Instead, look for a suitable number and type of elements to group together into logical modules.

The approach of defining semantic modules—modules of logically related elements—is intended to facilitate both interoperability and sufficient granularity. Mechanisms for excluding elements and attributes as well as embracing individual elements and attributes in a "free-floating" format should cover all needs.

Composibility

As a basis for module composition, the framework must supply a means of collecting semantically related XHTML elements that at the same time closely approximate the semantics of HTML 4. The transformation between HTML 4 and XHTML 1 took place in the XHTML 1 Specification. The arrangement of semantic modules should mirror, as closely as possible, the semantic groupings found in the HTML 4 Recommendation.

The composition mechanisms must also allow for producing semantic modules made up of elements and attributes from other XML applications such as MathML, SMIL, and SVG. There must also be a means of grouping modules along preferences and profile lines as opposed to the semantics of the elements themselves.

Compatibility

As with all work produced by this group, the modularization process must strictly conform to the XML 1 Recommendation. Further, it needs to be compatible with both the XML Linking and XSL Specifications, as both of those techniques must be applicable to documents composed from modularized DTDs.

In order to retain the conformance with XML 1, the Working Group has chosen not to rely on specifications produced outside of the W3C (where conformance to XML is not necessarily required). They have also resolved that XHTML will be sufficiently expandable to allow incorporation of new W3C recommendations that impact XHTML.

Conformance

Authors must be able to determine whether their collected modules and the documents produced based on those collections are both well-formed and valid. The behavior of elements and attributes should be definable, as well as verifiable in the end product. It must be possible to identify a conforming compound document as a member of the XHTML document family.

In addition, user-defined modules created through the syntax to be provided in the specification cannot duplicate or contradict the element or parameter entity names defined in the official XHTML modules.

Ease of Use

The syntax framework resulting from the other four requirements must of course be relatively understandable. If only highly skilled programmers can perform modularization, it is unlikely that the widespread use scenarios envisioned will be realized. Technical issues may stand in the way of a true plug-and-play type environment, but the reasonably skilled Web developer should be able to compose modules after a moderate learning curve. Testing and validation of the combined modules must also be accessible to the general developer.

Breaking Down XHTML: Defining Modules

Within the XHTML 1 modularization effort, there are two major types of modules, *semantic modules* and *DTD modules*.

A *semantic module* is a group of related elements. (They are also sometimes referred to as *abstract* modules.) The ideas or means of expression the elements provide are logically similar. For instance, all elements that are related to lists are grouped together in the list semantic module, specifically: dir, dl, dt, dd, ol, ul, li, and menu.

A DTD module is a set of element types, a collection of attribute declarations, and a content model definition. Note that this doesn't specify a collection of *related* attribute declarations or a *corresponding* content model definition. By definition, a DTD module may contain an attribute list declaration that operates upon an element type other than the ones declared in that module. Additionally, a content model may be defined in a module and then be used by other modules or individual elements and attributes.

While this type of grouping may at first seem disorganized, it can be very powerful when specifying the needs of a specific community. If a custom scripting language were developed for WinCE-based devices, and it identified events that were unique to WinCE, developers might need to create an attribute list that recognized those event handlers in order to provide proper scripting for documents displayed on those devices. At the same time, global content model requirements could be defined, perhaps along with a new element or two. By allowing grouping by purpose rather than solely by semantics, developers can create a single portable module that meets the design requirements for compatibility and granularity defined earlier in this chapter.

Creating Your Own Modules

The skills you developed in Chapter 8: "Creating Your Own DTD" will help you to create your own modules that enhance and extend the abilities of XHTML. There are, however, a few restrictions placed on designers when working with the XHTML space: you must meet the module conformance criteria, and you must follow the naming rules.

Module Conformance

To be considered a conforming XHTML module, it must meet five distinct criteria:

1. The module must be created using one of the methods defined in the Building XHTML Modules specification. As of this writing, only XML-based DTDs have been defined. Future work will likely include an XML Schema-based mechanism and perhaps others.
2. The module must have a unique identifier that follows the naming rules defined in the specification, which are outlined in the next section.
3. When using XML DTDs to define the module, parameter entity names must have unique prefixes or other means of insulating themselves from the rest of the DTD.

4. The module must be sufficiently commented with descriptions of the syntactic and semantic requirements of the elements, attributes, and content models found within.
5. You cannot reuse element names defined by the W3C contrary to that original definition or that extend the original definition.

Naming Rules

To avoid collisions when processing XHTML document types composed of modules defined in more than one location, strict rules for names must be adhered to. Names will always be based on XML Formal Public Identifiers (FPIs).

NOTE

Though you may not think of them as FPIs, you're already familiar with them through HTML. The `<DOCTYPE>` tag uses a form of FPI with strings such as `-//W3C//DTD HTML 4.0//EN`.

Each *field* of the FPI is delimited by the double slash characters `//`. The first field in the HTML 4 Strict FPI is a hyphen (-), the second is W3C, the third is DTD HTML 4, and the last is EN. The same conventions occur within XHTML module names.

Four conditions must be met by each name:

1. The first field, which is used to identify the relationship of the resource to the formal standard, will be a hyphen (-) for privately created resources (such as one that you might write). If it is the result of a formal standard such as those published by ISO, the field value must be the formal reference identifier (e.g., ISO 10646:1990).
2. The second field is the name of the organization or individual responsible for maintaining the module. Though there isn't a registry available, you should choose this name carefully to avoid duplication of common names, i.e., MyModules would be a poor choice. WebGeekCommunications would be a unique choice if Ann Navarro were to define her own modules.
3. The third field must start with the string `ELEMENTS XHTML-`, with a unique identifier attached by the authoring organization, e.g., `ELEMENTS XHTML-WebGeek FormWidgets 1.0`, if Ann were to define extended functionality for form

controls. It is strongly recommended that version numbers be included in this string to allow for appropriate updating as new versions are published.

4. The last field identifies the language in which the module was developed. The EN seen in the HTML example identifies English.

Continuing with the idea of a FormWidgets module defined by WebGeek, the full FPI would be expressed as:

```
-//WebGeekCommunications//ELEMENTS XHTML-WebGeek FormWidgets 1.0//EN.
```

Combining Modules into a Singular Document Type

The mechanisms involved in combining modules into a new DTD have not yet been formally defined. As you learned previously, the process of creating DTDs is as much an art form as it is a science. The vision many authors have of modularization is something akin to Plug-and-Play, where there is a simple means to glue a bunch of modules together into a single DTD instance. In practice, however, modularization isn't nearly that simple. What makes a good DTD "good" also makes chopping it into pieces difficult.

Concrete examples and demonstrations of these techniques are likely to be included in the future output of the W3C HTML Working Group. We anticipate that the process of creating your own modular DTD will be considerably more onerous than writing your own XML documents, but that is to be expected. The average XML user won't be creating, enhancing, or modularizing DTDs. Instead, they'll be using DTDs provided by their companies or other organizations, with the IT staff having produced the DTDs and any required modules. Or, they may use DTDs built from modules that have been made publicly available by industry groups or other communities.

Document and Client Profiles for XHTML

Since modularization provides the flexibility of combining XHTML features by using the building blocks represented by modules, it follows that those same building blocks would be used to represent the content of a document set and also the capabilities of the client.

The Modularizing XHTML 1 Working Draft outlines a *framework for content negotiation* in which two or more devices, such as a client and a Web server, or a client, proxy server, and Web server, exchange information about what type of content has been requested, what the end-client capabilities are, and even any organizational restrictions that may be placed on content coming in through a proxy server. Figure 17.1 illustrates the paths between a three-device scenario.

FIGURE 17.1:

A unidirectional link between a sender and receiver through a proxy

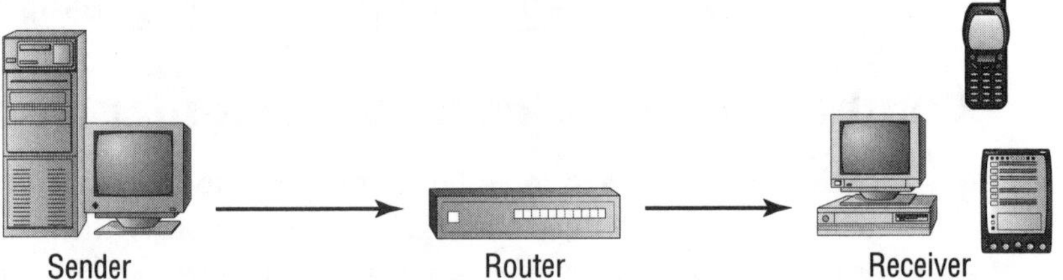

By no means do we envision that content negotiation be *required* of every client, Web server, proxy, or other device. Instead, these processes will be enhancements that may fine-tune content delivery. As of this writing, the W3C is considering forming a working group to deal with protocols for composite capabilities and preference profiles. The work that may be conducted in that group would certainly influence the outcome of the framework envisioned in the XHTML modularization draft. Indeed, it is likely that both working groups (CC/PP and HTML) will exchange ideas and conduct collaborative development in this area.

How Profiles May Be Expressed

A profile will end up containing more than a list of XHTML modules that are supported. Additional details will be described, such as what scripting languages are understood and what kind of style sheet support is available, as well as user or site preferences, security requirements, and a host of other issues that have not yet been enumerated.

The historical method of declaring profile properties is through the DTD. This approach fails on many fronts, for example, consider the underlying need of the emerging device market: small and mobile devices have limited memory and processing power. If we require them to be able to retrieve and/or read DTDs with every document, the load may be too great. Additionally, the expense involved in such access may multiply along with the increase in file size and bandwidth that such exchanges would require.

Therefore, a more generalized approach, which would be able to specify the following, is predicted:

- A vocabulary for designating features and feature sets
- An extension mechanism for the addition of new features
- A means to store preferences
- Methods for discovering interfeature dependencies
- Existing DTDs that are supported by the base feature sets
- Which XHTML modules are understood within the profile
- Whether any XHTML elements or attributes outside the stated modules are viable for use or are excluded

Because work is just beginning in this space, the syntax for specifying these details has not yet been formulated. The W3C Note that formed the basis of the CC/PP Working Group proposal uses RDF (see Chapter 25: "Using XML Applications" for more information), where suggestions have taken a mathematical relationship approach. Being that XHTML is based in XML, it is very likely that the final approach will embrace one or more of the current XML-related mechanisms, such as RDF, Schemas for XML, etc.

Fifteen specific functional requirements have, so far, been identified for the syntax to be developed. They include:

- Receiver and sender capabilities

  The syntax may:

  - Identify a collection of supported XHTML modules through a DTD
  - Identify XHTML modules by a name (e.g., public identifiers)
  - Indicate support for an XHTML module, yet specify individual elements and attributes from within that module that will not be supported
  - Assert support for individual elements or attributes that will be supported that are outside the specified modules
  - Allow statements of preferences between XHTML modules

    - Identify extended attribute value support for scripting languages, media types, or other needs
    - Allow statements of preferred attributes
- Additional sender capabilities

  The syntax may:

    - Indicate support for transformation of XHTML modules
    - Indicate possible transformation of elements and attributes
    - Provide for declaration of preferences regarding transformation
- Content capabilities (features)

  The syntax may:

    - Define a list of required XHTML modules through publication of a DTD
    - Simply identify required XHTML modules
    - Provide support for requiring individual elements and attributes outside of the stated supported XHTML modules
    - Provide for declaration of preferences for modules
    - Identify preferences pertaining to attributes

It is expected that the work on CC/PP will extend the syntax even further, providing greater granularity in preference statements and capabilities that are beyond the scope of XHTML.

Looking Forward with XHTML

As indicated earlier in this chapter, work on XHTML and its related components is ongoing. The current W3C Working Group tasked with writing the XHTML specification is chartered to run at least through late spring of 2000. The public working drafts indicate that the specifications we've seen so far are just the tip of the iceberg in extending HTML into the XML space. As major milestones in this work occur, pointers to the new specifications and supporting documents will be added to the supporting Web site for this book.

Up Next

In this chapter, you were introduced to the concept of modularizing the XHTML 1 Specification. You learned that each abstract module has its own namespace and DTD and may also have its DTD expressed as an XML Schema. You also learned that the mechanisms for gluing the DTDs and schemas together will be clarified in future work from the W3C HTML Working Group and that a means of describing document and client profiles will work in conjunction with modularization to provide a platform for content negotiation.

Next, you'll explore the tools used in XML development and browsing, starting with server and parser tools and then moving on to XML-enabled browsers and server processes.

PART VI

The XML Toolbox

CHAPTER

EIGHTEEN

18

XML Development Tools

- Using development tools
- Using IDEs to manage XML applications
- A look at some XML parsers
- Using IBM alphaWorks tools

It would be natural to believe that because XML is still in its nascent stages, development tools are somewhat hard to come by. There are, however, already a fairly large number of tools available. The number might seem surprising until you consider that XML comes from the SGML world, which has had years to develop software for an environment much more complex than XML.

Another reason tools are appearing so quickly is the marriage of XML with Java. Java is perfectly set up as a language partner with XML because of its object-oriented design, which makes managing XML node types a natural.

The amazing thing about the proliferation of tools appearing on the market is their stability, even in early beta stages. We tried Stylus, an XSL development tool while still in alpha stage. It didn't crash once, and it performed admirably. Its few quirks were implementation issues. The developers had simply not yet added undo capabilities, and the interface was still a bit raw. Such is the world of XML software development. The competition to get product to market is intense.

Development Tools

XML is all about development, and tools are emerging on a daily basis to help developers produce XML in a wide variety of situations. These range from enterprise-based XML development environments that connect to huge corporate databases to simple text editors with small footprints that simplify the markup development process. In this chapter we'll focus on development tools that you can try on machines with no server-side or database connections. Ultimately, XML may most often be deployed on servers to allow for the most dynamic interchange with clients, but there are numerous development tools to help you run XML on the client side. This chapter will introduce you to some of them. Be aware that new tools appear frequently in the XML world.

NOTE You can learn more about server-side tools in Chapter 20: "XML-Enabled Server Technologies."

One good source for keeping up with the latest tools is `http://www.xml.com`. The site run by Seybold Publications does a good job of keeping abreast of the latest trends in the industry as a whole, including the latest tools.

Editors

Editors allow you to input markup and save files as XML files. An editor can be as simple as Microsoft's XML Notepad, which is just a step above a simple text editor or as complex as XMetaL™ 1 from SoftQuad Software Inc., which validates XML documents against DTDs. One thing most of them have in common is a choice between a tree view and a source view. Many markup professionals like to toggle between the two. This is because working in the source view exposes all the tags to the markup author, making it easier to maintain control over the nuances of the markup they're working with. It's nice to have a chance to view the tree structure of an XML document, however, because proper structure plays such a key role in successful XML deployments. Figure 18.1 and Figure 18.2 show how the tree structure looks in two basic XML editors. As you can see, the concept is the same, but the view is different.

FIGURE 18.1: The XML Spy editor Interface

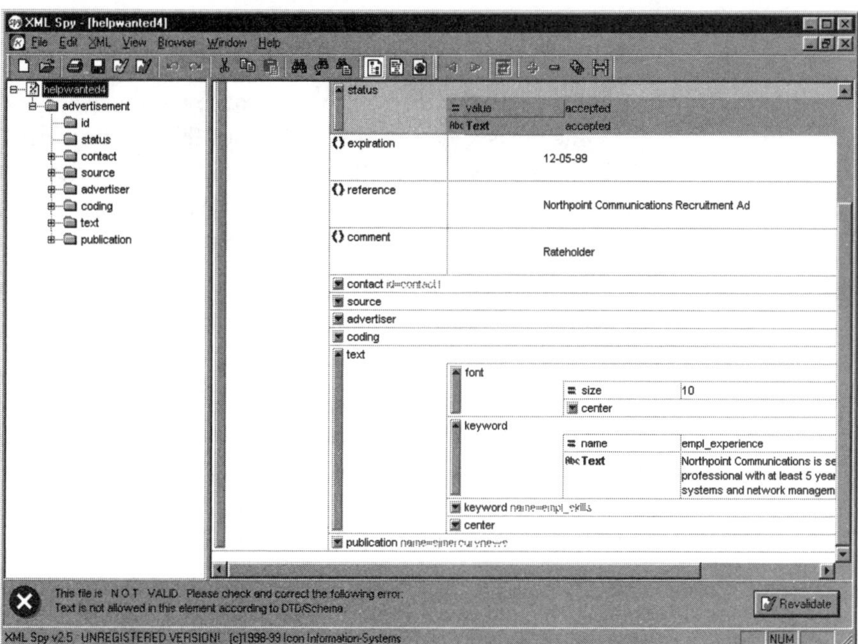

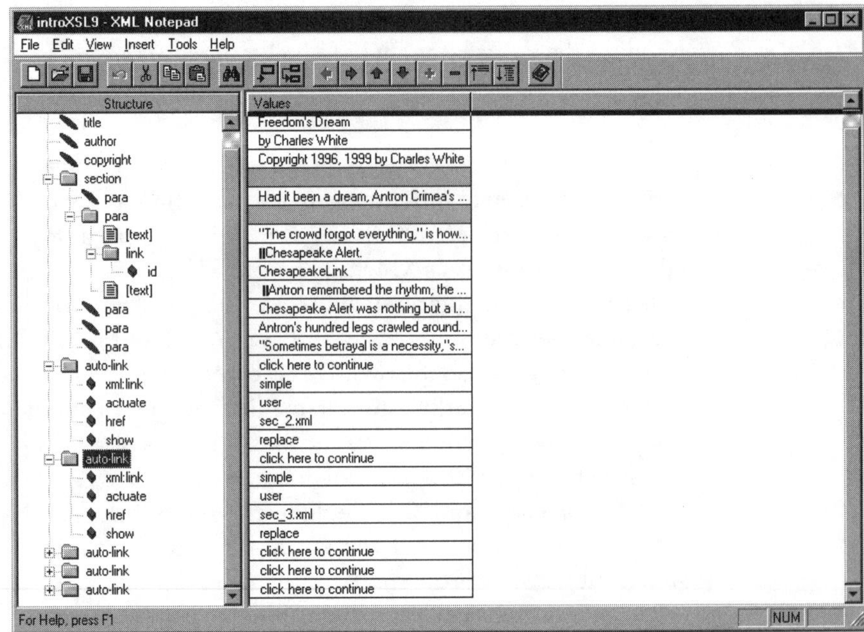

FIGURE 18.2:

The XML Notepad editor Interface

HomeSite 4

HomeSite by Allaire Corp. is an old standby in the HTML development community. HomeSite is a feature-rich text editor that has powerful search and replace capabilities, syntax highlighting, a CSS editing component, live preview, and many more features. In fact, even with all the XML editing tools out there, a good solid all-purpose text editor is an indispensable tool. For many developers, HomeSite is the one.

XMetaL 1

XMetaL 1 is the most comprehensive editor on the market, and remarkably, was also one of the first. The reason this seems remarkable is that the program is fairly full featured, with support for document validation and the Document Object Model (DOM). If you are an HTML professional who has worked with HoTMetal 5, an HTML editor from SoftQuad Software the interface of this program will be familiar to you. XMetal features the same user interface as HoTMetal Pro, including the buttons HoTMetal uses for element representation, which collapse and expand the tree as you toggle them. XMetaL features include:

- XML document validation against DTD.

- A rules set development tool that assists you in creating DTDs using rule sets, which are saved in an XMetaL proprietary format and matched against the XML document you are working on for validity.
- Support for the DOM that includes extensive documentation about each DOM interface that is included in the official recommended spec by the W3C.
- Support for scripting the DOM via JavaScript and VBScript.
- Support for COM.

One of the nicest features of XMetaL is the program's validation services. When you try to open a file that doesn't follow the rules associated with its DTD, it displays an error message describing what the problem is (See Figure 18.3).

FIGURE 18.3:

XMetaL displays an error message when there are validation problems

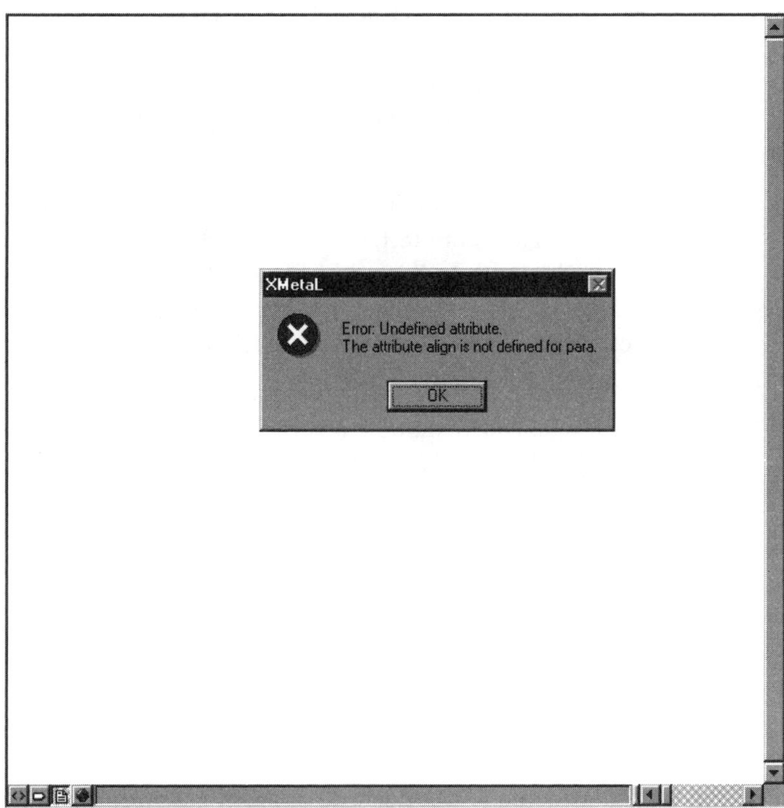

SoftQuad Software recently added James Clark, one of the driving forces behind XML development, to its management team. In addition to his substantial SGML background, Clark edited the latest XSLT Working Draft for the W3C, and developed some excellent Java-based parsing and transformation software (see descriptions of XT and XP later in this chapter). This bodes well for the future of SoftQuad's XML development software, so keep an eye on future versions of this product and other developments at this company on their Web site (`http://www.softquad.com`).

XML Spy 2.5

XML Spy 2.5 uses what its developers call an Enhanced Grid View to manage element/attribute creation. If you refer back to Figure 18.1, you can see that the left pane of the grid view window contains the tree structure in a hierarchical format that uses folder icons to represent elements. Within the right pane is an expanded tree structure where the actual editing takes place. Clicking an arrow next to an element name toggles the structure view of that element. If the view of the element's contents is collapsed, the view of the element's content expands when the arrow that corresponds to the element is clicked. If the view is expanded, the view collapses when the arrow is clicked.

XML Spy from Icon Information Systems also includes a validation service. Referring again to Figure 18.1, if you look at the bottom of the screen in the picture you'll see a circle with an X inside. This tells the document author the document is not valid, and tells where the problem area lies and highlights that area on the grid. You can then make changes and click on a button that revalidates the document.

This is a fairly lightweight program from the standpoint of disk space and memory usage, which makes it an excellent tool for whipping up XML documents quickly. The interface is easy to work with, and you can easily toggle to the text editor. The text editor includes syntax highlighting. You can find XML Spy at `http://www.xmlspy.com` or at `http://www.icon-is.com`.

XML Notepad

XML Notepad is a simple text editor from Microsoft that optionally validates an XML document against the XML DOM that runs in IE5. This object model is not the same as the DOM as defined by the W3C. IE5 runs on an object model whose basis is formed around the DOM but has a number of extensions to that model. You can create and edit XML documents in XML Notepad without using the validator.

If you refer back to Figure 18.2, you can see how the interface looks upon launch. The left panel makes it obvious where the root element is, so when you give that root element a name you know that this is the parent of every other element in the tree. You can change the type of content the node is, so if you mistakenly call a node an element when you really wanted it to be a text node, you simply go to the Tools menu and navigate to the Change submenu. This gives you the option of changing the node to a text node, an attribute node, or an element node.

XML Notepad also checks for well-formedness and validates against a DTD if there is one, but doesn't object if the XML file you open doesn't have an associated DTD.

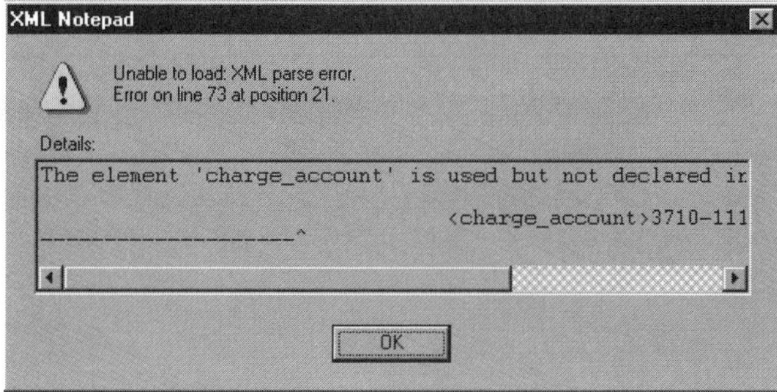

The version of XML Notepad that was evaluated for this book was a beta version and was available as a free download at `http://msdn.microsoft.com/xml/notepad/intro.asp` as this book went to press.

NOTE

The Microsoft developer's site has an extensive library of XML documentation, particularly as it applies to Microsoft products. You can visit the Microsoft XML Web site at `http://msdn.microsoft.com/xml/`.

Developing Schemas with XML Authority 1

Another editor, this one from Extensibility™, is called XML Authority 1. This editing program specializes in schema and DTD development, and provides a very useful tool if you've already begun producing XML documents or have legacy files you expect to convert to XML but have no DTDs or schemas for them. XML Authority will read an imported XML document and instantly create a DTD for you. The program evaluates the various elements and attributes in an XML document and develops a set of rules based on the way the document was written.

NOTE For a review of the differences between schemas as implemented in IE5 and the standards being developed by the W3C, see Chapter 19: "XML-Enabled Browsers."

This feature alone can be a major time saver, because, although it's likely you'll want to make some changes to the final DTD, the program provides an excellent starting point with a core group of definitions. Of course, if you want to simply build a DTD or schema from scratch, XML Authority provides an excellent interface for doing so. Look at Figure 18.4 for a view of the program's Graphical User Interface (GUI).

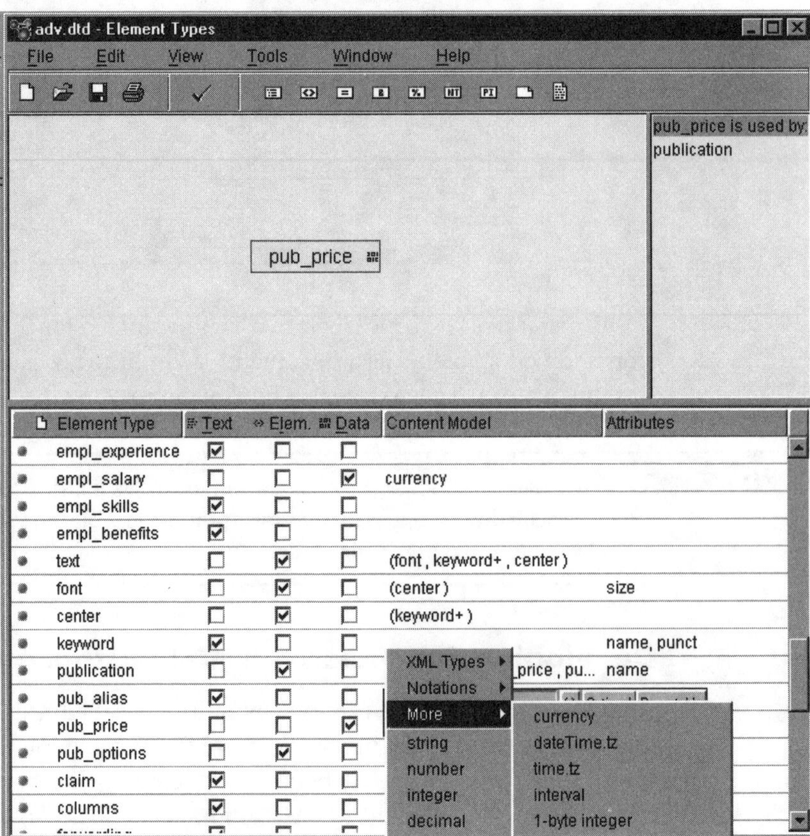

FIGURE 18.4: The XML Authority GUI

From the GUI, you can export the DTD (the native file format for the program is a `dtd` file) as a schema document that conforms to the May 6, 1999 W3C Schema recommendation issued by the W3C. When you do that, you get a `DOCTYPE` declaration that looks like this:

```
<!DOCTYPE schema PUBLIC "-//W3C//DTD XMLSCHEMA 19990506//EN
"http://www.w3.org/1999/05/06-xmlschema-1/structures.dtd">
```

You can also export the schema to a document that conforms to the IE5 data subset, which is the schema IE5 uses to manage the data schema definition supported by Microsoft. Microsoft's schema definition interpreter was built before the final recommendation was complete, but this XML Authority makes it simple to work from the same document to create a standards-based schema as well as one that works in IE5. Microsoft has made public pronouncements that they will support the standard in future versions of Internet Explorer.

In fact, you can export your DTD to a number of different file formats, including:

- Schema Definition Language files (with a `.xsd` extension; this is the standard as defined by the W3C group).
- XML Data files (with a `.xdl` extension; this is the subset supported by IE5).
- SOX files (with a `.sox` extension; this supports an earlier W3C note on schemas, NOTE-SOX-19980930).
- DCD files (with a `.dcd` extension; this supports Resource Description Framework (RDF) format data files, in accordance with the W3C RDF Model and Syntax Specification. See `http://www.w3.org/TR/REC-rdf-syntax/`.
- DDML files (with a `.dml` extension; this supports DDML format data files, a logical data markup definition found `at http://www.w3.org/TR/NOTE-ddml`.
- BIZ TALK files (with a `.biz` extension.)
- XML (with a `.xml` extension; the program exports a sample document from the rules you define DTD file).

XML Authority's user interface provides an easy way to manage the most important processes of schema development by creating menu-based drop down lists in the editing panel that help you choose element and attribute types, along with their appropriate content models. This includes the various data types supported through the two main data schema resources available on the Internet, the W3C model as represented by the specification at `http://www.w3.org/1999/05/06-xmlschema-2/datatypes.dtd`, and the Microsoft datatype schema.

All in all, you'll find XML Authority an extremely helpful tool for developing schemas. The program comes with good documentation, including extremely helpful descriptions about the use, limitations, and advantages of using schemas in your XML application development. You can download a free 10-day trial at `http://www.extensibility.com/`.

Developing Style Sheets with Stylus

Stylus, from Transformis, is an XSL style sheet editor that provides a real-time preview of the result tree. The ability to see a result tree is an important consideration when learning how to develop XSL documents. One of the great things about XT, a Java-based XSL processor, is the way it outputs the result tree to either a file or to the Java terminal display. As this book went to press, Stylus did not support previewing XSL Formatting Objects (FOs), which is page description markup for XML documents , but the developers said they were looking into ways to make that happen, perhaps by integrating `.PDF` viewing capabilities.

As this book was being written, Stylus was still in alpha development. The program was quite stable for such an early version, partly because the developers focused on making sure the implemented features of the program were stable.

When you launch Stylus, the program presents a dual-dialog box that asks you to open an XML source document and an associated style sheet. If no style sheet exists, the dialog box contains an option for creating a new style sheet.

You then have several options for developing your style sheets. You can use the source view to work in the XSL document and input text directly. Or, you can choose a specific element from the XML source in the right panel and create a style sheet template for it in the panel underneath, which is a text editor with Help Tooltips that you can scroll to for help with finishing tags.

After you select one of these options you can then create several style sheet templates for all the elements in the source XML document that you're developing. Stylus is a good program for developing templates because not only can you see the result tree in real time, but you also can see how the XML source document looks without needing to associate the style sheet within the XML source document. Stylus even highlights the portion of the result tree that comes from your specific template. (see Figure 18.5). Stylus does this automatically when it generates the preview file. Stylus uses the IE5 XSL processor to display XML files that use XSL transformations.

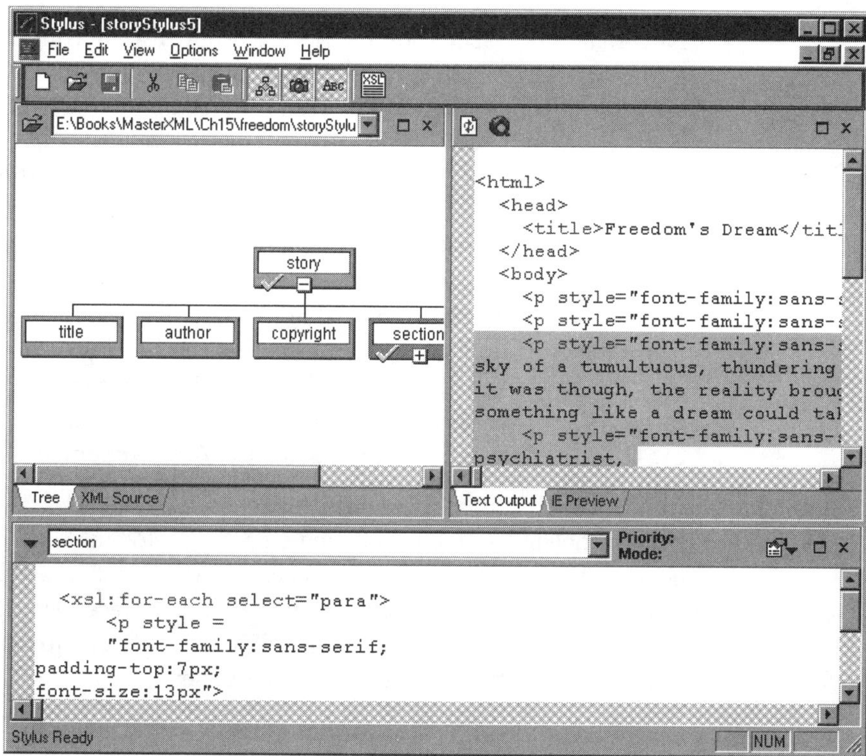

FIGURE 18.5: The Stylus user interface

Developing XML on the Mac

Unfortunately, developing XML on the Mac is not a simple proposition, unless you're using Mac OSX (Mac's Operating System 10), which runs from a Unix-based Kernel and is thus capable of running Java command line tools. This is an important consideration for hard-core programmers because so many experimental XML technologies use Java from the command line. Theoretically, there are tools that you can use to get Java to run on a Mac by mimicking the command line (for example, JBindery, which comes with the MRJ Java runtime), but getting a Java file to execute can still be a nightmare. Of course, if you are using Mac OSX, the question is moot. One option would be to go ahead and get OSX, and if you're not ready to have it running as your machine's main OS, deploy it separately (you don't need to sacrifice your System 8.*x* to run OSX, as long as you run it on a different drive or a partitioned drive).

Running XT on the Mac

Now that we've issued some serious warnings about running Java-based programs on the Mac, it's time for a quick walk through on how to run an example application. XT, a program you'll learn more about in Chapter 14: "Introducing XSL," is a Java-based tool written by James Clark for transforming XML into XSL files. XT comes as a jar file, which is similar in format to the zip compression scheme used in Windows. Jar is used to group a number of Java class files, often including the main class file that executes a Java program, and compresses them into one easily portable file. The following instructions will work on any number of Jar files, if you keep in mind that the parameters for running them will be different for different kinds of software. Again, even if you follow along closely, you may still have trouble running XT on your Mac, but we did test these instructions on a G3 using the MRJ 2.1SDK (the Apple Java software development kit). You can download the MRJ 2.1 SDK at `http://developer.apple.com/java/text/download.html`.

The problem lies in the fact that you're trying to build Java command lines using a GUI. The program you use to do this, JBindery, will issue the command lines for you, but you need to fill the fields in the user interface correctly in JBindery in order for the process to work correctly. It will help if you refer to the following command line structure James Clark has on his XT page:

```
java -Dcom.jclark.xsl.sax.parser=your-sax-driver com.jclark.xsl.sax.Driver
source stylesheet result
```

The preceding command line parameters are those that would be used in a traditional Java runtime environment using command lines.

TIP

Don't know what a command line is? Have you ever seen the MS-DOS interface that appears when Windows is not in session? You see a dark screen with a `C:\>` prompt (assuming you're running off a C drive). When you enter text you can tell MS-DOS to do something, such as list a directory's contents: `C:\>dir`. You can also tell it to execute a program, and include parameters with the command, which in turn provide some additional information about the program, such as which files to run. Java also includes a similar command line program that does essentially the same thing.

The following directions will compare the GUI stuff with the corresponding commands one would normally use in a command line environment.

1. When you launch JBindery, you're presented with a screen with six icons on the left and a series of text fields on the right. Clicking on the top icon reveals the fields you use to create your "command line" setup. The top-most field is called `Class name`. Here you should input `com.jclark.xsl.sax.Driver`. This corresponds to the command of the same name in the XT command line, and is the name of the main class file. The field below that is called `Optional parameters`. Here, you should input the file names at the end of the above command line: `source style sheet result`. If you download XT, you might want to input the information based on the XT sample files: `slidesTest.xml slides2.xsl slidesOut.xml`. Do it just like that, without any commas. Below the `optional parameters` fields are a `redirect stdout` drop down menu and a `redirect stdin` drop down menu. Leave the `redirect stdin` field alone, but for the `redirect stdout` you should name a file with a name like `test.out`. This text file will troubleshoot any problems you're having (by receiving any error codes from XT), and should be empty if all is well. This first set of fields also has a `Save Settings` option, which is of course a good idea. That way, you can save the program as an applet that will run with the same parameters whenever you double click, eliminating the need to redo this whole process over and over again.
2. Next, set up the class path that would normally be a first step. You manage this procedure with the next icon on the left, the `classpath` icon. This is actually pretty easy in JBindery. You just use the dialog box that is revealed on the right when the classpath icon is clicked to browse for any jar files you think you'll be using. It's easiest to put in all the jar files you anticipate using, including XPSAX (required Jar files for running XT). It's also easiest to put the XT jar files in the same folder as JBindery so as not to deal with any other classpath issues for now.
3. The next icon on the left is the properties icon. This is a somewhat confusing interface, but your goal is to mimic the properties shown first in the XT command line we listed at the beginning of this section:

   ```
   -Dcom.jclark.xsl.sax.parser=your-sax-driver
   ```
4. You'll see three fields on the right hand side of the dialog box after clicking the properties icon. Ignore the top field. It will fill in automatically when you

fill in the two fields below it. In the left field, input `jclark.xsl.sax.parser`. In the right field, input `com.jclark.xml.sax.Driver`. You can put whatever SAX driver you want, but XT will need a SAX driver of some kind, and if you don't know exactly which one to use, this one will work fine.

Other Mac XML Tools

Within the OS 8.*x* environment, the most comprehensive suite of XML development tools available for the Mac as this book was going to press are Emilé 1 and XPublish 2 Alpha from Media Design in•Progress. The company develops Mac-only editing tools and a server side tool. The editing components of these development tools include a tag palette that tells you what elements are available. The programs make a determination by reading the DTD indicated in your working file. The editors provide validation services, but, unlike some validating editors, they let you work in the file even if the file doesn't validate.

The major difference between the two editors, XPublish and Emilé, is that XPublish is used for publishing XML documents to HTML so that other browsers can read the documents. The program helps you set up the file according to one of three DTDs: The Transitional, the Strict, and the Frameset HTML 4 DTDs. As this book went to press, there was not yet any direct built-in DTD for XHTML, but the program has customization features that make it possible to include the DTD yourself. Emilé is designed for direct XML document authoring, and in that sense resembles most of the editors available for the PC, except that it doesn't have a tree display. Instead, you get the palette view of all your tags, and a constant source view of your document with syntax highlighting. When you click on the palette to select a tag, a Help Tooltip appears with a detailed description of the type of content that is allowed within the selected element, what attributes are available to it, and what children exist within the document's tree structure.

The bottom line on Mac XML development is that vendor support may not be strong enough for applications running on OS 8.*x*. Most vendors will likely focus their attention on OSX for two reasons. The main reason is that OSX is designed as server software and is based on the much-ballyhooed NeXTStep operating system from NeXT Software, which has a substantial and devoted following. It's not likely that developers will want to pour a many resources into what is truly an antiquated operating system such as OS 8.*x*. Without true multithreaded tasking, OS 8.*x* will always offer poor Java support, and Apple is destined to replace the operating system with something that will be much more state-of-the-art. This doesn't mean, however, that the Mac isn't an excellent XML development environment, in fact if you're working in OSX it's quite the contrary. If your organization already has a heavy Mac commitment, don't abandon ship just yet, because OSX offers substantial server-side capabilities that you'll want to keep an eye on.

Using IDEs to Manage XML Applications

An Integrated Development Environment (IDE) is a set of software modules that are "integrated" into a comprehensive suite of tools that support one another in the development of a project. They're often used as development applications for computer languages such as C++ or Java. In those scenarios, IDEs typically consist of a compiler, a text editor with syntax highlighting, and a component manager for dropping components into the text editor and setting the component's properties. It may also include one or several additional modules, such as a class browser that displays inheritance and property information of a particular class or language object that you might want to include in a software build.

XML is ripe for this kind of software. Think of all the schemas and vocabularies already in existence in the XML world. You may want an IDE to help you manage all or some of the many vocabularies and schemas out there. Many server-side tools are IDEs, but there is plenty of opportunity for client-side tools, as well (client-side meaning, in this case, tools that don't require real-time server side or access to live database connections in order to function). It's a nascent industry, but it is bound to grow quickly over the next several months.

Imagine the powerful tool you could have in your hands if you bundled XML Authority and Stylus (two of the applications discussed previously in this chapter) together in one package, and included a validation-aware XML editor with it. That is generally how IDEs work. You'll begin to see them come onto the market very soon, if industry history is any guide.

LivePage Enterprise 2

LivePage Enterprise 2 from LivePage Corp. is a comprehensive XML development suite consisting of three principal components. The architecture is similar to many other development environments, although rather than setting up everything in dockable panels, like most IDEs do, each LivePage component operates independently and doesn't dock to other components. The three principal components of LivePage are:

- The LivePage Manager, which is the main workhorse of the application and provides access to Web page authoring and site maintenance/development.
- LivePage Administrator, which is the tool that the systems operator, administrator, or Webmaster uses to manage user access permissions and the actual Web site itself (including the database side of the environment).
- LivePage ContentServer, which operates with your site server and services pages from an environment's database.

LivePage Enterprise falls within the realm of what is termed by some "middleware," a somewhat nebulous term because it is defined differently depending upon whom you talk to. Rather than suggest a definition that can be considered definitive, for our purposes we'll consider middleware as being software that helps facilitate communication between a server and client using, in this case, XML. Figure 18.6 provides a screen shot of all the LivePage Enterprise component windows open at one time.

Database professionals will be especially comfortable with the user interface of LivePage. In fact, much of its power derives from its data-binding capability. The IDE includes an embedded database engine (Sybase SQL Anywhere) that acts as the default engine, but you can tie it to a number of other databases the program supports. These include Sybase Adaptive Server Anywhere, Sybase SQL Server, Oracle SQL 7, Watson SQL, IBM DB2, and Microsoft SQL Server.

The IDE operates with a rather convoluted set of rules that you need to configure in order to develop XML files. Not only do you need a DTD you need to declare—at a minimum—a root element in the database program's native DCL format. However, once you get it up and running, it includes some powerful search capabilities that make it possible to query for specific element content. You can also create your own query templates within the program's Document Type Rules (DTR) file. The template names then appear as a drop down list in the database program's Manager Query dialog.

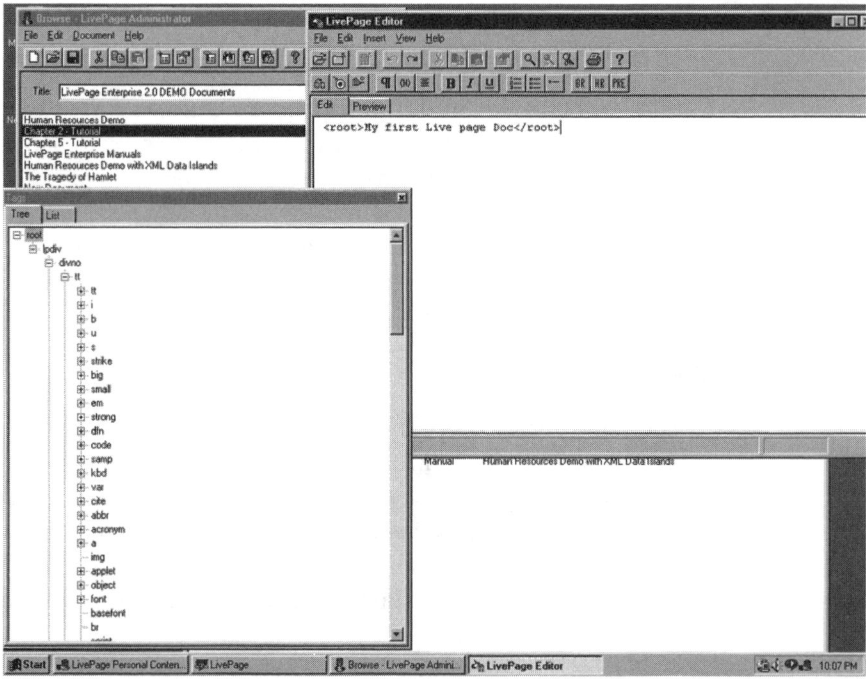

FIGURE 18.6: The LivePage user interface

Building the Perfect IDE

So far there aren't a great number of IDEs available for XML, but by looking at some of the tools available in this chapter you can begin to think about what to look for in an IDE. Your wish list is likely to include an XSL style tool, like Stylus, and a Schema editor, like XML Authority. A good validating editor is important, too, and should provide the option of opening a file that doesn't require a DTD or schema to be associated with it. You might even want to see a component that outputs FOs as PDF files, or displays them in real time in some way, perhaps to be interpreted and output for CD-ROMs or on the Internet. Of course, there are numerous server-side issues to look at too, but you shouldn't need to purchase server-side solutions to develop XML applications. If indeed you are looking at server side solutions, you'll have a completely different set of criteria to examine anyway, which is why we've devoted a chapter to that, as well.

Parsers

Parsers are programs that are dedicated to parsing an XML document. They are often incorporated into larger programs, such as is the case with Mozilla, which uses James Clark's Expat. They can usually be used as stand-alone programs. In those cases, they are often run from a command line interface because they were designed when XML was still in its infancy and subject to change. They are excellent resources for programmers because they often provide access to class libraries, thus enabling you to design your own software around them.

Expat

The expat parser, formerly known as xmltok, is the parsing engine written in C that is used to run the Mozilla XML parser. It is one of many contributions to the XML community made by James Clark. You can use its libraries under either the Mozilla Public License Version 1.1 or the GNU General Public License, or you can contact the program's author directly to negotiate a different license. You can download it at `http://www.jclark.com/xml/expat.html`.

XP and XT

There are two parsing agents that developers swear by, both written by James Clark. XP is a Java-based XML validating parser, and XT is an XSL processor. They're both written in Java, and can be used in Java programs aiming for a broader reach. An example of this is the InDelv browser (`http://www.indelv.com`). InDelv is a Web browser that can read XSL formatting objects and uses the XT transformation engine to transform the source tree into a result tree before displaying the formatting object-based result tree (see Chapter 14: "Displaying XML: Introducing XSL," for a more detailed description of formatting objects).

SAX

Simple API for XML (SAX) was developed as a community effort by members of a public mailing list (XML-DEV). SAX is an API that takes an event-based approach to XML parsing. The W3C's DOM is an API that you can also you use to work with XML documents, but it is based on the tree of an XML document. SAX, on the other hand, is based on events. This means that rather than going from node to node to report on the XML document (root element to child element to grandchild element, etc.), it goes from event to event (start of document to start of element tag to text characters). The bottom line on SAX is that many XML parsers use its interface as part of their own parsing routine. You can download it at `http://www.megginson.com/SAX/`. In fact, this is the reason we included SAX in this section of the book. Technically, SAX is not itself a parser. Instead, it is an API (Application Programming Interface) that others who want to build parsers use in their parsing software.

Other Parsers

There are several other parsers available on the Internet. Some were developed when XML was still in a W3C Working Draft, and some may still be in a state of flux. The names of the parsers and their locations are as follows:

- SAX for Python from Lars Marius Garshol (`http://www.stud.ifi.uio.no/~larsga/download/python/xml/saxlib.html`), a Python version of SAX.
- Silfide's SXP (`http://www.loria.fr/projets/XSilfide/EN/sxp/`) a client-server XML distribution system.
- Project X, Sun Microsystems, Inc. is a Java-based parser with XML 1 and SAX conformance, plus support for the DOM (Specification 1). It can be found at `http://developer.java.sun.com/developer/products/xml/`.
- XML Parser for Java, Oracle Corporation (`http://technet.oracle.com/`).
- Tim Bray's Lark (`http://www.textuality.com/Lark/`).
- XML Parser by Dan Connolly (`http://www.w3.org/XML/9705/hacking`), an early XML parsing application.
- XTL, from Vivid Creations (`http://www.vivid-creations.com/`), a COM object for processing XML.
- SAXON from Michael Kay (`http://home.iclweb.com/icl2/mhkay/saxon.html`), a multi-featured interface that includes support for XSL and some extensions to XSL for more full-featured transformations.
- IBM's XML parser (see the next section on IBM alphaWorks).

IBM alphaWorks Tools

A couple of years ago IBM launched a massive developer's corner in their portion of the Web world called IBM alphaWorks (`http://www.alphaworks.ibm.com`). What is especially intriguing about this site is that there are literally hundreds of free downloads of test bed software programs that explore the most recent changes in software technology. This includes extensive libraries of Java and, of course, XML tools. The XML tools, in fact, are all Java-based tools that are either designed to be included as components in larger applications or used as stand-alone tools for your development efforts. Table 18.1 lists these tools and their functions. The alphaWorks Web site also lists all the tools, but you need to click each tool to view a description of it, so we've included this table to make it easier to decide which you're really interested in using. By the time you read this, some of these tools may no longer be available, and some new tools will be available not shown on this list. Many of them will most likely be updated in some way. And all of them are free.

TABLE 18.1: IBM alphaWorks Tools and Their Functions

Tool	Function
Bean Markup Language (BML)	A markup language and compiler that can be used to wire Java Beans to XML via Java or the JavaScript or NetRexx scripting languages.
Data Descriptors by Example	A Java component library that enables the user to automatically build DTDs from well-formed XML documents.
DataCraft	Provides a method, using Java, of describing and querying the data structure of relational databases using RDF and XML.
Dynamic XML for Java	Creates Java servlets that bind annotations to XML documents.
LotusXSL	A Java-based XML transformation processor that transforms XSL documents into result trees.
PatML	A pattern-matching tool for XML documents consisting of three Java beans that can be deployed in larger programming applications.
RDF for XML	An RDF processor that can read and query RDF structures and writing them to XML.
Speech Markup Language	A browser that interprets the Speech Markup Language, an XML-based markup language created by IBM for conversation-based communication process.
TaskGuide Viewer	A Java-based tool for creating wizards (application components that guide users through tasks).

Continued on next page

TABLE 18.1 CONTINUED: IBM alphaWorks Tools and Their Functions

Tool	Function
TeXML	A program that transforms XML documents into TeX documents. The XML source must first be transformed using XSL into a document that conforms to the TexXML DTD.
XEENA	Builds a palette of elements based on a source DTD that guides the user into inserting appropriate nodes in the order dictated by the governing DTD. This tool is Java-based.
XML BeanMaker	Creates a Java Bean interface class from the root element defined in a DTD and inner classes that correspond to elements and attributes.
XML Diff and Merge Tool	A Java-based tool that compares the differences between two different XML documents and allows you to merge the two documents into one by managing, rejecting and allowing for specific differences between the documents.
XML EditorMaker	A Java-based program that builds a lightweight XML editor based on a source DTD document.
XML Enabler	A Java-based program that reads the User-Agent field of an HTTP header and chooses an XSL style sheet (based on a site administrator's parameters) to send to an installed LotusXSL processor, which creates a result tree. XML Enabler then sends the result tree to the client. This technology enables all XML documents to be returned to any client browser, regardless of whether a client browser supports XML parsing.
XML for C++	A validating parser for C++ environments.
XML Parser for Java	A validating parser for Java environments.
XML Productivity Kit for Java	This is a general Java-based productivity kit for building e-commerce applications using Java.
XML Security Suite	A suite of security tools for XML based encryption.
XML Translator Generator	Translates XML documents into other XML documents that have different DTDs. The tool can also generate XML documents out of HTML documents.
XML TreeDiff	A set of Java Beans used to manage DOM tree differentials.
XML Viewer	A Java-based XML viewing application that provides several viewing modes, including source and tree views, along with DTD source views.
Xplorer	Allows you to search XML files based on such criteria as PIs, element and attribute names, etc., and then runs any valid document through XML Viewer.

Figure 18.7 shows the user interface of one of these XML tools, XEENA, that helps users build XML documents based on DTDs.

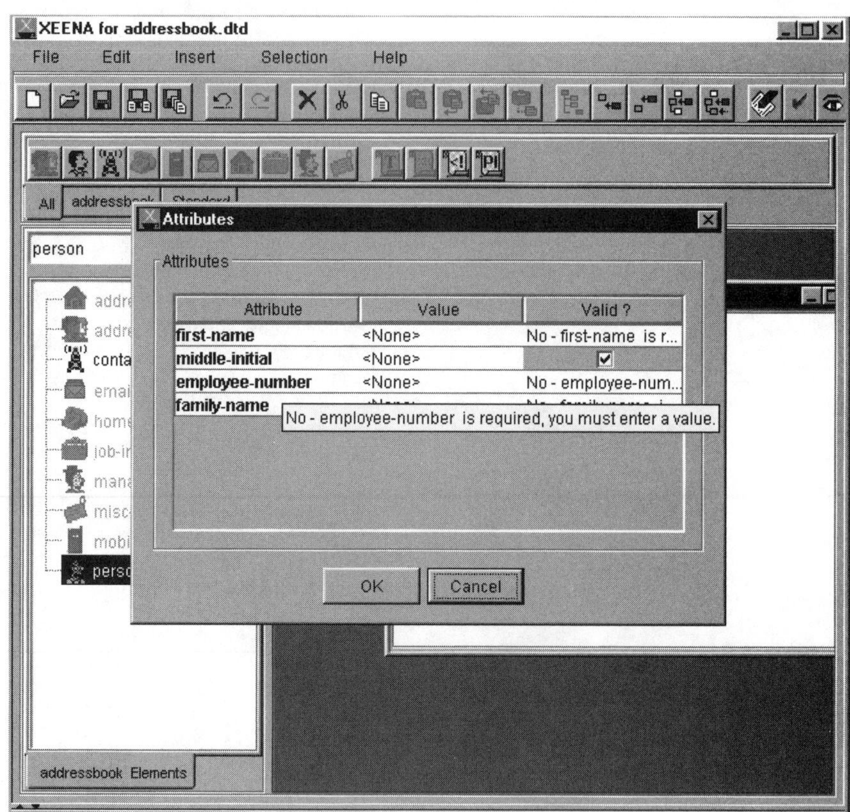

FIGURE 18.7:

Building a document with XEENA

Other Tools

There are numerous, hundreds actually, of other tools out there you may want to take a look at while developing XML. These range from small conversion utilities like FOP to software you're already familiar with, such as Microsoft Access which doesn't officially have XML support, but can be used to develop databases for later use with XML. We'll lead off with a look at a tool from a major publishing software developer, Quark, Inc.

avenue.quark

QuarkXpress is a longtime favorite in the professional publishing industry. It's a program that allows you to create publications and make them ready for press. It is found in places like magazine publishing companies, advertising agencies, newspapers, and other publishing-related organizations. The advent of XML has invoked a natural question among veteran QuarkXpress users: Wouldn't it be nice if QuarkXpress offered some way to export a QuarkXpress document to XML?

NOTE

A Quark Xtension is a plug-in type of program that can be developed by third party software developers to extend the capabilities of QuarkXpress. avenue .quark happens to be an extension that was developed by Quark. The company, along with a number of third party developers, sells a large number of extensions. You can find more information on Quark Xtensions at `http://www.quark.com/products/xtensions/download.html`.

Attempts to create XML-friendly extensions have been made. Challenger XT by HexMac is an innovative extension (called a Quark Xtension in trademark parlance) that allows you to create a DTD from a QuarkXpress document, then export an XML file from the QuarkXpress document based on the DTD you create. The extension was really almost ahead of its time. It came out shortly after the XML 1 Recommendation, so the program is now about due for a new release. Its biggest drawback is that to convert QuarkXpress layout objects to XML, you have to manually select them. Although it wasn't a perfect solution, Challenger XT was a start.

avenue.quark takes the process of working with XML files considerably further by providing a comprehensive mapping solution that maps QuarkXpress objects such as style sheets, text boxes, and picture boxes to XML elements. The program, in pre-release as this book went to press, shows the potential to have the type of impact QuarkXpress itself had on the publishing world when it was released.

What follows is not a comprehensive tutorial on avenue.quark. Instead, because it is such a new product, we can only give you a brief glimpse into what a user can expect to encounter when using it. In a production environment, it's unlikely the graphic designer or desktop publisher will use avenue.quark. Most likely, the actual conversion process will be handled by someone else, perhaps someone in IT. Large organizations may have individuals dedicated solely to the conversion process. Whatever the case, a typical avenue.quark session might go something like this:

1. You create or choose a DTD to use with the QuarkXpress document you wish to convert. The early pre-release version of avenue.quark requires a

DTD. This looks to be a design goal of the software, so you'll need to consider this when the conversion process begins.

2. Open the QuarkXpress document you want converted to XML.
3. Open avenue.quark by following this sequence of menu commands:
   - File+New+XML
   - Then you can develop a tagging rule set from the resulting palette.
   - You use a tagging rule set to map QuarkXpress style sheets to specific XML elements, or specific font styles to XML elements.
   - Thus if you have a QuarkXpress style sheet named Headline, you can map it out to an XML element (you can map it to any element in the DTD that makes sense) such as head or headline.
4. Create a new XML document from the avenue.quark palette (that was opened in step 3) and choose the tagging rule set you wish to use with the document.
5. Tag the new XML document by dragging the QuarkXpress objects you want to tag from the QuarkXpress document to the avenue.quark XML window.
6. Save the XML document (Mac users, be sure to use that `.xml` extension at the end of the file name – `myXMLfile.xml`).

avenue.quark is actually the first of what should be a number of Web-related, and possibly, XML-related software solutions from Quark. For the latest developments, check out `http://www.quark.com`.

FOP

FOP is a Java component that examines the result tree from an XSL file and converts it into a Portable Document Format (PDF) file. A PDF file is a file format developed by Adobe Systems that has become popular for a variety of specialized documents (like IRS manuals). The reason it's possible to create PDF files from XSL result trees is that PDF files are themselves sequences of objects. If you were to examine the architecture behind PDF files, you'd find that one central aspect underlying their structure is that although it is based on a random access type of hierarchy, there is one root object which can be found near the end of the file. The root object is always present.

You access objects through a table in any order you specify, meaning that when a program such as Adobe Acrobat Reader reads a PDF file, the file is not read in sequential order, but randomly. This keeps the processing time shorter, and access to all the file's objects makes it a perfect target for XSL processing using Java. In fact, Adobe thought enough of the promise that it announced a $90,000 "bounty" for anyone who could successfully create a PDF converter using XSL (the reward was later withdrawn for legal reasons).

NOTE For a detailed description on how to run FOP, look for the sidebar titled *Using FOP, an XSL to PDF converter* in Chapter 15: "Displaying XML: Advanced XSL."

At the time this book was being written FOP was still in alpha development. The tool is free and is being written by James Tauber. You can download both the program and the source code for free at `http://www.jtauber.com/fop/`.

Even though the program is in Alpha development, it works, as long as your XSL is not too complex. This program shows the tremendous potential available with XML and Java.

Database Tools

It wouldn't be appropriate to discuss XML tools without mentioning the database world. Database development environments are beyond the scope of this book, but much of the power of XML will be fueled by databases. We won't get into a discussion in this chapter about the various database languages available, or the merits of each one. Chances are, your organization will be basing database design decisions around a number of goals and implementations, and XML will be one part of that. Even more likely, your organization already has an investment in a database, so the question will center around how to integrate that database into your XML application development plans.

There is a general tendency among many to assume that Microsoft Access has support for XML. To a limited degree this is true, but database implementations aren't really as simple as opening up a Microsoft Access document and exporting it as XML (as anyone who has labored through a database development project will tell you). Managing your database and its relationship with XML on the server side is unavoidable. We'll explore these issues further in Chapter 20: "XML-Enabled Server Technologies."

NOTE

For a look at database integration in a real world environment, take a look at Chapter 27: "Using XML for Business to Business Data Integration: A webMethods Case Study."

Using XML with RealAudio

RealAudio Networks has established a solid foothold in the Web arena with its RealAudio and RealVideo line of streaming media products. RealAudio has been a big SMIL booster since the markup language's inception. The company has introduced a number of development products suitable for many different kinds of budgets. The least expensive, RealSlideShow and the Real G2 Producer Kit, are both free. On the other side of the spectrum, you can purchase the Real Producer G2 Pro for $449. There's not much you can do with the Real Producer Pro that you can't do with the Real G2 Producer Kit, except save lots and lots of time. That, of course, means the product pays for itself instantly if you're doing any amount of multimedia development using this technology.

RealSlideShow

So far, the tools we've seen within the XML development community are fairly labor intensive as far as the document developer is concerned. Even those tools with extended GUIs, such as XMetaL and Stylus, require a significant amount of knowledge on the part of the developer using the tool. Not so with RealAudio's RealSlideShow, a free tool for developing SMIL documents. RealSlideShow has a simple drag and drop interface that allows you to create "slide shows" viewable in the newest version of RealAudio's Real Player. The user interface is so simple it will take minutes to learn. You'll then have a legitimate multimedia file up in minutes.

To create a file, all you do is drop image or sound files (or record sound files from a CD) onto the user interface. Just in case someone new to the program doesn't know where to start, the program offers a small hint (Figure 18.8).

The resulting SMIL documents created with RealSlideShow are not particularly complex. The program generates a sound and slide multimedia presentation, and a basic timeline for managing time sequences. If you're comfortable with SMIL markup, of course, you can go in and edit your own files after the program generates the files onto your hard drive (by clicking generate). The program collects all the files you've added to the presentation and generates the SMIL document. A typical SMIL document produced by RealSlideShow looks similar to the code shown in Listing 18.1.

FIGURE 18.8:

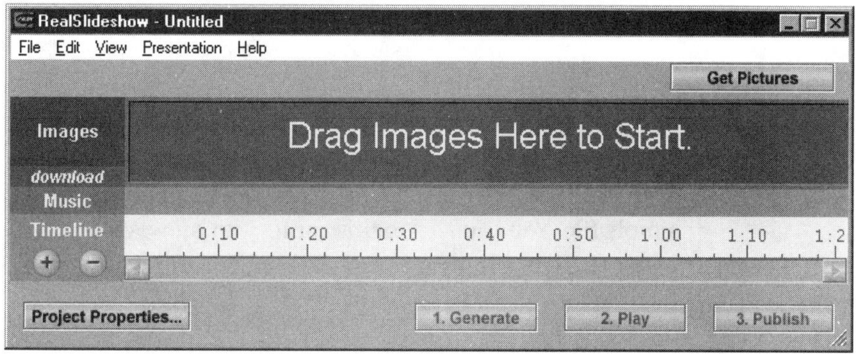

RealSlideShow tells you how to start

LISTING 18.1 A SMIL document generated by RealSlideShow

```
<smil>
    <head>
        <meta name="title" content="Javertising: Advertising for
        the Next Generation." />
        <meta name="author" content="Chuck White" />
        <meta name="copyright" content="©1999 Javertising" />
        <meta name="keywords" content="Javertising Demo" />
        <meta name="description" content="A demo" />
        <meta name="robots" content="all" />
        <meta name="pics-label" content='(PICS-1.1 "http://www
        .classify.org/safesurf" labels comment "Real
        Slideshow 6.0.0.315 Windows" ratings (SS~~000 1))'/>
        <meta name="file_id" content="63e0d799-b9e8-1cbf-aaca-
        79fd6f958268" />
        <layout type="text/smil-basic-layout">
                <root-layout width="320" height="240" background-
        color="black"/>
                <region id="pix_region" left="0" top="0" width="320"
        height="240" z-index="1" />
        </layout>
    </head>
    <body>
        <par>
                <seq>
                        <text src="javertising.rt"
    region="pix_region"/>
                        <img src="javertising.rp"
```

```
region="pix_region" fill="freeze"/>
                </seq>
                <audio src="javertising.rm"/>
            </par>
</body>
</smil>
```

You can see in Listing 18.1 that the file RealSlideShow generates is a fairly simple file. You can add to this content if you wish, by merely altering the text file using SMIL markup. You can see how the content the code generates looks in RealPlayer.

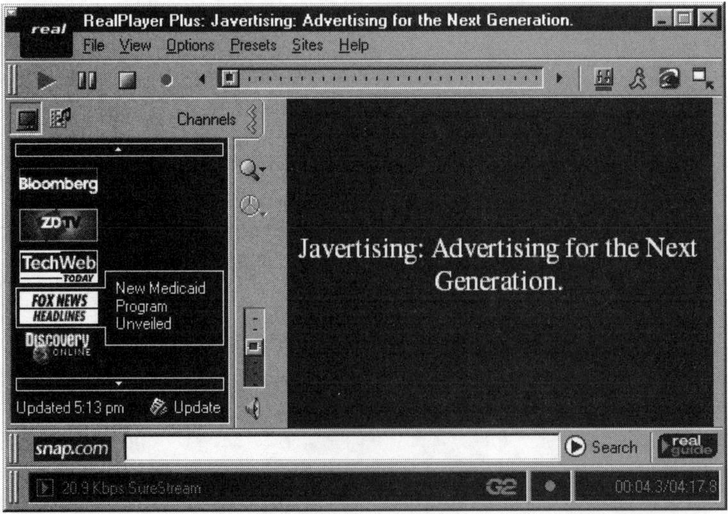

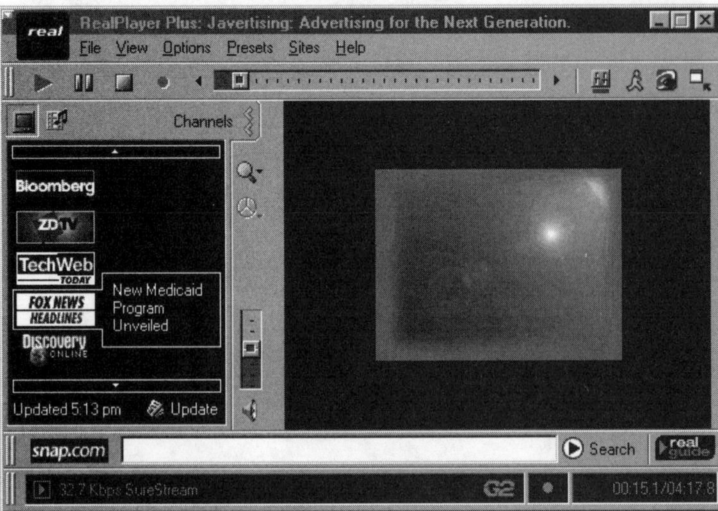

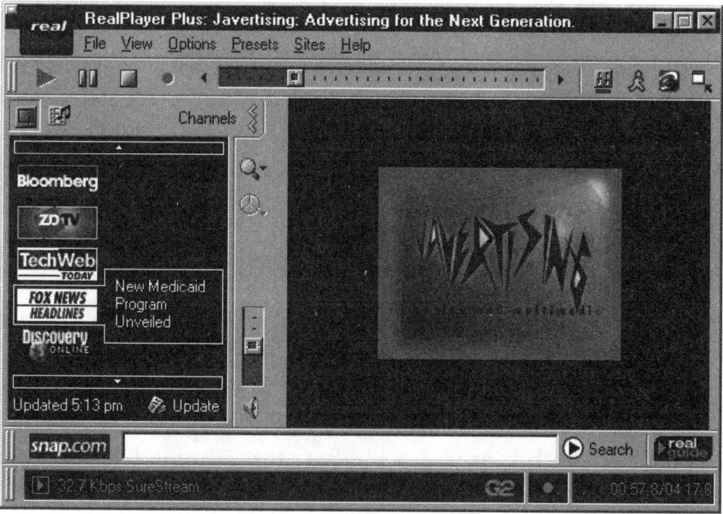

The first screen is generated by a small XML-based text file called `javertising.rt`. The `rt` extension is the file extension for the Real `text file` format. This file is just another text file with some special markup (XML-based but designed for play by RealPlayer):

```
<window
     type="generic"
     bgcolor="black"
     duration="11.547"
     width="320"
     height="240"
>

<pos y="96"/>
<font size="+2" color="white">
<center>
Javertising: Advertising for the Next Generation.
</center>
</font>
</window>
```

If you want to create more sophisticated multimedia presentation, then you can take things a step further with the Real G2 Producer Kit, available for download at `http://www.real.com`. This is a very well documented developer's kit that answers just about any question that might arise while developing multimedia for RealPlayers.

Real G2 Producer Kit

The Real G2 Producer kit consists of a comprehensive documentation of multimedia development for RealPlayers and a wizard-based application for creating SMIL documents. It's a good idea to download the Producer Kit if only to familiarize yourself with the markup languages used by RealPlayers. The documentation covers a wide range of areas, including:

- Cross-platform and cross-browser compatibility issues
- Full documentation of all RealText and RealPix markup tags. You can think of RealText and RealPix as RealNetwork extensions to the SMIL markup language, just as HTML+Time is considered by Microsoft to be an extension of SMIL. You can use RealText and RealPix together or separately, as well as with RealAudio. For the most current documentation and a detailed description on how to incorporate these presentational markup languages into your multimedia presentation, go to `http://service.real.com/help/library/index.html`.

Table 18.2 and Table 18.3 show some of the elements available in RealText and RealPix, respectively. Keep in mind that these tables are not comprehensive or definitive lists of available elements.

TABLE 18.2 RealText Elements

Element	Attributes/Values	Description
`<a >...</a>`	`href ="command | mailto:xxx@xxx.com | url"` target = "_player | browser"	Hyperlink element that links to either a URL or opens a mail client. The **target** attribute is required if used in conjunction with the **command** attribute, otherwise it is optional. When the value is **_real**, a new stream is opened in RealPlayer. When the value is **_browser**, the new stream is opened in a browser. The **command** attribute executes a RealPlayer command.
`<b>...</b>`	NA	Bolds text.

Continued on next page

TABLE 18.2 CONTINUED: RealText Elements

Element	Attributes/Values	Description
` `	NA	Adds a line break, except for TickerTape and Marquee, in which case the cursor moves to the far right edge of the window. Notice the closing slash mark. For compatibility with HTML, you would need to add a space: ` `
`<center>...</center>`	NA	Centers text.
`<clear/>`	NA	Clears text so that new text can appear based on synchronization settings; any pre-existing text will not clear if its time has not elapsed as set by the `time` element.

`<font>...</font>`	`bgcolor="Hexadecimal color description | white | silver | gray | black | yellow | fuchsia | red | maroon | lime | olive | green | purple | aqua | teal | blue | navy" "charset = "us-ascii | x-sjis | gb2312 | big5"`where `xsjis` is the Kanji and Osaka font character set, `gb2312` is the character set for Simplified Chinese, and `big5` is the character set for Traditional Chinese.
	`color="Hexadecimal color description | white | silver | gray | black | yellow | fuchsia | red | maroon | lime | olive | green | purple | aqua | teal | blue | navy"`
	`face = "aFontFace"size="2 | -1 | +0 | +1 | +2 | +3 | +4; or 1 | 2 | 3 | 4 | 5 | 6 | 7"`
		Describes the font characteristics of the font used in the text of the presentation. The default character set is US-ASCII, regardless of the character set of the client. This means folks in Beijing will not be able to read your text if you don't specify the correct character set. And if you do specify that character set, clients whose default character set is `us-ascii` won't be able to decipher it.

`<hr/>`	NA	Sets two spaces between lines.
`<i>...</i>`	NA	Italicizes text.

Continued on next page

TABLE 18.2 CONTINUED: RealText Elements

Element	Attributes/Values	Description
`<li>...</li>`	NA	Performs same action as the **` `** tag set, and is supported primarily for compatibility reasons.
`<ol>...</ol>`	NA	Not the same as an HTML ordered list, this tag is supported for compatibility with HTML, but only indents the text.
`<p>...</p>`	NA	Adds two lines between lines of text, except for TickerTape and Marquee, in which case the cursor moves to the far right edge of the window.
`<pos x="pixels"/>`	x="pixels" y="pixels"	Positions text horizontally or vertically when the scroll rate and crawl rate are 0.
`<pre>...</pre>`	NA	Same as HTML **`pre`** element; used to preserve spacing characteristics using Courier as the typeface.
`<required>... </required>`	NA	When the stream delivery encounters problems, text contained within this element will be sent to the player at all costs, even if the presentation needs to be paused.
`<s>...</s>`	(none)	Strikethrough element, like the HTML **s** element.
`<time begin="dd: hh:mm:ss.xyz"/>`	`begin="dd:hh:mm:ss:xyz"` `end ="dd:hh:mm:ss:xyz"`	A synchronization setting that denotes when text should appear and disappear from the presentation window.
`<time end="dd: hh:mm:ss.xyz"/>`	(none)	Sets time when text disappears.
`<tl [color= "color"]> ...</tl>`	`color ="Hexadecimal color description | white | silver | gray | black | yellow | fuchsia | red | maroon | lime | olive | green | purple | aqua | teal | blue | navy""`	Used to display text at the bottom of a TickerTape.

Continued on next page

TABLE 18.2 CONTINUED: RealText Elements

Element	Attributes/Values	Description
`<tu [color= "color"]> ...</tu>`	`color ="Hexadecimal color description | white | silver | gray | black | yellow | fuchsia | red | maroon | lime | olive | green | purple | aqua | teal | blue | navy""`	Used to display text at the top of a TickerTape.
`<u>...</u>`	NA	Underlines text.
`<ul>...</ul>`	NA	Indents text.

`window`	`bgcolor="color"`
	Default is `white`, except for tickertape windows, which default to `black`.
	`crawlrate="pixel/second"`
	Crawl rate is how fast the text moves horizontally; default is `0`, except for tickertape and marquee windows, which default to `20`.
	`duration="dd:hh:mm:ss.xyz"`
	Default is 60 seconds.
	`extraspaces="use|ignore"`
	`height="pixels"`
	Default is 120 pixels for all but the tickertape and marquee windows, which are 30.
	`link="color"`
	`loop="true|false"`
	`scrollrate="pixels per second"`
	This determines how fast text moves vertically. Default is `0`, except for `scrollingnews` windows, which default to `10`.
	`type="generic | tickertape | scrollingnews | marquee | teleprompter"`
	The default value is `generic`.
	`underline_hyperlinks="true|false"`
	`width="pixels"`
	Default is 320 pixels for all but the tickertape and marquee windows, which are 500 pixels.
	`wordwrap="true|false"`
		Sets the window properties using a number of attributes, all of which are optional. If you don't set an attribute, the player will default to each attribute's default.

TABLE 18.3: RealPix Elements

Element	Attributes/Values	Description
<imfl>...</imfl>	none	This is the root tag of a RealPix presentation. This is the only RealPix element with an end tag.
<head/>	aspect = "true | false" author="string" bitrate="bitsPerSecond" duration="TimeInSeconds" height="pixelHeight" maxfps="number of Frames"time in seconds" preroll ="time in seconds" timeformat="dd:hh:mm:ss.xyz" This attribute is required. title="name of presentation" url="valid URL" width="width in pixel units" This attribute is required.	Provides a description of header information. Always follows the <imfl>...</imfl> tags.
<image/>	handle="number" Similar to ID attribute in other markup environments, this attribute acts as a unique number for the image for easy reference by effects. This attribute is required. name = "pathName" where **pathName** is the image path relative to the actual RealPix file (as in **pathName.jpg**). This attribute is required.	Added after the **<head/>** tag, there must be one **image** element for every image in the presentation. Any series of one or more images is included in the markup immediately following the **head** element.
<fill/>	color="Hexadecimal color description | white | silver | gray | black | yellow | fuchsia | red | maroon | lime | olive | green | purple | aqua | teal | blue | navy" This attribute is required. dsth ="Height in pixels." (**dsth** is short for destination rectangle height) dstw ="Width in pixels" (**dstw** is short for destination rectangle width). dstx ="X coordinate in pixels" Location of the left top corner of the rectangle along the x axis (**dstx** is short for destination rectangle x coordinate). dsty ="Y coordinate in pixels" Location of the left top corner of the rectangle along the y axis (**dsyx** is short for destination rectangle x coordinate). start="Time in seconds" from the start of the RealPix track that the fill takes place. This attribute is required.	Creates a rectangle in the presentation.

Continued on next page

TABLE 18.3 CONTINUED: RealPix Elements

Element	Attributes/Values	Description

<fadein/>	`aspect ="true or false"`
	`dsth ="Height in pixels."`
	`dstw ="Width in pixels"`
	`dstx ="X coordinate in pixels"`
	Location of the left top corner of the rectangle along the x axis.
	`dsty ="Y coordinate in pixels"`
	Location of the left top corner of the rectangle along the y axis
	`start = "Time in seconds"` from the start of the RealPix track that the effect begins to takes place.
	This attribute is required
	`target = "Target image handle."`
	(refer to the **handle** attribute of the **head** element at the beginning of this table)
	This attribute is required.
	`url="valid URL"`
		This is a transition filter that allows one image to transition itself by fading into the presentation. You could, for example, fade in from a solid white to the image over a specified amount of time.

<fadeout>	`aspect = "true | false"`
	`color="Hexadecimal color description | white | silver | gray | black | yellow | fuchsia | red | maroon | lime | olive | green | purple | aqua | teal | blue | navy"`
	`This is a required attribute.`
	This attribute is required.
	`dsth ="Height in pixels."`
	`dstw ="Width in pixels"`
	`dstx ="X coordinate in pixels"`
	Location of the left top corner of the destination rectangle along the x axis.
	`dsty ="Y coordinate in pixels"`
	Location of the left top corner of the destination rectangle along the y axis
	`duration="number of seconds"`– total time for the transition to complete.
	This attribute is required.
	`maxfps="number of maximum frames"` per second allowed for effect" (Include as last attribute.)
	`start = "time in seconds"` from the start of the RealPix track that the transition effect begins to takes place.
	This attribute is required.
		This is a transition filter that allows one image to transition itself by fading into the presentation. You could, for example, fade out from a solid white to the image over a specified amount of time.

Continued on next page

TABLE 18.3 CONTINUED: RealPix Elements

Element	Attributes/Values	Description

<crossfade/>	`aspect = "true | false"`
	`dsth ="Height in pixels."`
	`dstw ="Width in pixels"`
	`srcw="source rectangle width in pixels"`
	`srcx="source rectangle X coordinate in pixels"`
	`srcy="source rectangle Y coordinate in pixels"`
	`start = "time in seconds"` from the start of the RealPix track that the crossfade effect begins to takes place.
	This attribute is required
	`target = "Target image handle."` (refer to the handle attribute of the head element)
	This attribute is required.
	`url="valid URL"`
		A transition element used to change from one image to another.

<wipe/>	`aspect = "true | false"`
	`dsth ="Height in pixels."`
	`dstw ="Width in pixels"`
	`srcw="source rectangle width in pixels"`
	`srcx="source rectangle X coordinate in pixels"`
	`srcy="source rectangle Y coordinate in pixels"`
	`start = "time in seconds"` from the start of the RealPix track that the crossfade effect begins to takes place. This attribute is required.
	`target = "Target image handle."` (refer to the handle attribute of the head element). This attribute is required.
	`type = "normal | push"` `normal` means the new image covers current, `push` means the current image is pushed out. This attribute is required.
	`url="valid URL"`
	`direction="up | down | left | right"` Direction of the wipe.
		Transitioning element that covers an image or wipes it away.

<viewchange/>	`aspect = "true | false"`
	`dsth ="Height in pixels."`
	`dstw ="Width in pixels"`
	`srcw="source rectangle width in pixels"`
	`srcx="source rectangle X coordinate in pixels"`
	`srcy="source rectangle Y coordinate in pixels"`
	`start = "time in seconds"` from the start of the RealPix track that the crossfade effect begins to takes place. This attribute is required.
		Defines panning and zooming effects.

The Real G2 Producer Kit also includes another free SMIL development tool called a SMIL Wizard, which walks you through the process of creating

SMIL-based multimedia productions. You can use the tool to set up the framework, then edit the code using a text editor if you want to customize it in some way. Figures 18.9 and 18.10 show what the SMIL Wizard interface looks like.

FIGURE 18.9:

The SMIL Wizard opening dialog box

FIGURE 18.10:

Selecting source files in the SMIL Wizard interleaf

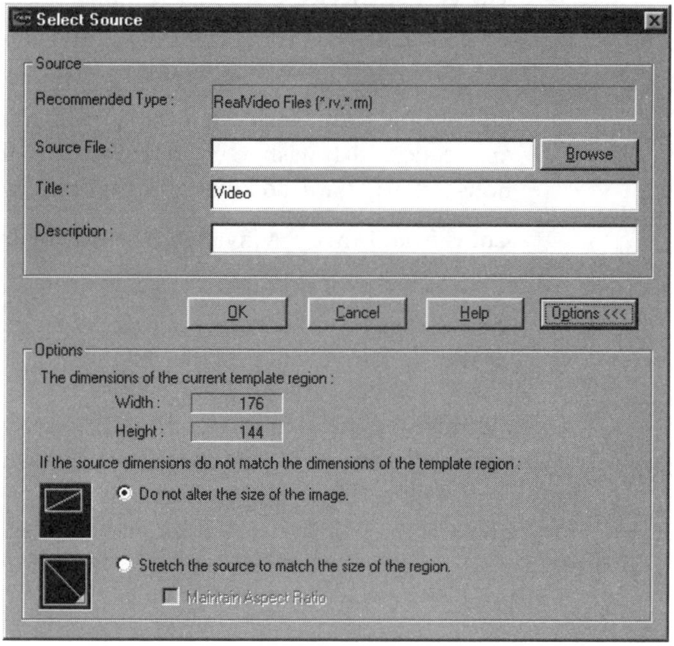

Interleaf

Interleaf has been used in workgroup publishing for many years for large documentation projects. It has always had features important to large scale publishing projects, such as revision management and workflow tools that seamlessly operate within networks containing UNIX and PC workgroups, as well as powerful cross-referencing, file conversion and indexing capabilities.

From an XML standpoint, of course, the most important file conversion capabilities center on the fact that the program can convert between XML, SGML, PDF, Postscript, WorldView, and ASCII formats. You can find out more information about Interleaf at `http://www.interleaf.com`.

Additional Tools of Interest

As we mentioned earlier, there are hundreds of tools available for XML development. As you become more familiar with XML, you'll discover more and more each day. Here's a look at just a few you can find on the Internet:

The W3C's SiRPAC An RDF compiler. You can go to the URL and paste in some RDF, and the Web page will return a view of the RDF graph (`http://www.w3.org/RDF/Implementations/SiRPAC`).

DOM SDK from Docuverse A software development kit for Java-based applications that wish to use both SAX and the W3C DOM Recommendations (`http://www.docuverse.com/domsdk/index.html`).

Coins from JXML A JavaBeans connector and XML processing implementation (`http://www.jxml.com/coins/`).

Weasel from WebEasy A Java servlet technology for XML (`http://www.webeasy.com/products/weasel.htm`).

Of course, there are many more out there. Basically, no matter what you need, you can probably find it. We're hoping the lists we've provided will help you track some of them down. Happy hunting!

Up Next

In this chapter we tried to introduce a number of tools to you so that you can develop XML and go in any direction you might be able to think of. Most of these tools are client-based from the standpoint that you don't need to run them off a server to get the most out of them. There is one very important category of truly client-based XML products we did not cover in this chapter, however. XML-capable browsers will require an entirely separate chapter. That's what you'll learn about next.

CHAPTER

NINETEEN

XML-Enabled Browsers

- Introducing the Document Object Model
- Using InDelv, an XSL FO browser
- Using XML and Internet Explorer
- Using XML and Netscape Navigator
- Creating your own browser interface using Mozilla

XML support has taken an interesting turn as browser developers commit themselves to supporting standards. In the old days, browser developers improved upon a standard, HTML, which was considered insufficient in many areas. Major vendors, responding to demands from developers who wanted to build more appealing and dynamic Web sites, added their own tags to the HTML markup language. Things got very messy. Meanwhile, the W3C, the international group overseeing the Web standardization process, seemed almost helpless. They were, pardon the pun, on the verge of becoming a non-entity.

What's different today is that these same vendors are struggling to keep up with this same standards group. New recommendations and working drafts are flying fast off the W3C Web pages, and only a portion of them are supported.

Netscape is trying desperately to implement XSL, but as this book was being written the browser had thus far been relegated to XML/CSS support. However, the driving force behind the new Netscape, Mozilla.org, has created such a simple, ingenious plan for managing the development of the next generation of Netscape it's hard to believe they won't accomplish their goals. The new Mozilla browser (we'll be calling it Netscape and Mozilla interchangeably in this chapter) supports X-Link and XML using CSS and/or an HTML namespace, as well as RDF (Resource Description Framework). But Netscape's support for XML goes beyond just reading and writing files over the Web. The user interface is actually built using XML and CSS, which means you can alter the way the browser looks if you're willing to dig into the code and make some changes. This is a stated goal of Mozilla as an open source project.

Remarkably, even Microsoft has been unable to muster its substantial resources to adopt all the standards available. There is no support for XLink, for example, nor has the company made much of an effort to embrace RDF, although that's likely to change. The company has no plans to support XSL formatting objects, even though it is likely to be a standard by the time this book is released and it would be a perfect complement for the vector markup languages.

The InDelv browser supports XSL formatting objects, but doesn't read HTML files. This limits InDelv's usefulness for the time being, although the next release should support XHTML.

This chapter will look at XML browser support. Hopefully, you can get an idea what to expect as you begin to explore the wide range of possibilities today's browsers offer the XML enthusiast.

Introducing the Document Object Model

To master the way browsers work, it helps to develop an understanding of the Document Object Model (DOM). For a long time, the term document object model was a generic term because it had different meanings to different people (and browser makers).

It all started when Netscape introduced JavaScript into its browser. The earliest versions of JavaScript included a core document object model with key constructs that included windows, the document instance, and forms. JavaScript has undergone several stages of enhancement since then. Today it is often referred to as ECMAScript, which is a reference to the European organization that has standardized the language.

NOTE ECMAScript is roughly equivalent to JavaScript 1.2.

An object is some entity (not in the XML sense but in a generic sense) that can be acted upon in some way. The window object, for example, can be opened through the use of a simple line of script:

```
window.open()
```

`Window` is the object and `open()` is a method that acts upon that object, in this case, opening it. The extent to which you can manage these kinds of object depends upon the browser you are working in. When IE4 was released, Microsoft introduced a huge library of objects to its browser that were accessible to scripting languages like JavaScript (called JScript by Microsoft because it contained so many extensions to the original language) and VBScript (a scripting language based on Visual Basic syntax).

With IE5, Microsoft extended the object model further by adding a huge library of additional objects, properties, and methods. A property is akin to an XML (and HTML) attribute. It acts as a modifier to the object. An object, whether it's a window, a link, or a word, can be blue, and the IE5 library allows you to describe this. The code fragment below is a JScript function that can be used to change the color of a word:

```
<span id="thisWord" onmouseover="thisWord
.style.color='blue'">Word</span>
```

Introducing the DOM Specification

The World Wide Web Consortium (W3C), the international body that issues Web-based standards and specifications papers released an official specification for the DOM in October, 1998. The specification can be found at `http://www.w3.org/TR/REC-DOM-Level-1/`. To see a W3C Working Draft of the next generation DOM, you can go to `http://www.w3.org/TR/WD-DOM-Level-2`, but be warned that it is not a stable document and you should not do any production work based on its syntax. The specifications transformed the document object model from a generic and loosely defined set of different models into one DOM. This doesn't mean the others went away. IE5 still has a library of objects and associated properties and methods that are considerably more extensive than what the DOM provides. These are now considered extensions to the DOM.

NOTE

Further references to actions of scripting and programming languages on the DOM will be called `procedures`. This is just our way of applying a broader stroke to the notion of these languages' interaction with DOM. The specifics of how Java and JavaScript interact with the DOM actually contain differences. These differences are clearly spelled out in the specification.

DOM Level-1 is a stable document, and it can be used in production environments. In the context of this chapter, you'll encounter DOM descriptions as they pertain to XML, although there are specific HTML interfaces that are included in the specification. Level-1 describes a set of node interfaces that make it possible for scripting languages and other programming languages to access the nodes of a document. DOM Level-1 describes several types of nodes. These can be accessed in different ways, depending on the node.

Why is the DOM important? Well, it's not unless you want to access a browser's functionality (or the functionality of an XML document within the scope of another environment, like a Java program). If you do want to engage in that type of functionality, it's a good idea to take a look at the core structure of the DOM. This involves understanding the different types of nodes that are described in the DOM, and a few of their more important properties and methods.

Node

This is the base class from which all other nodes (except for NodeList and NamedNodeMap nodes) are derived. This node is used to describe a class of objects called nodes, all of which fall within this class. This node contains several important properties. Each node type (except for NodeList and NamedNodeMap nodes) inherit these properties:

nodeName This is a string that maps out to the name of the node.

nodeValue This is a string that describes the data contained in the node.

attributes This is a NameNodeMap collection that contains all attributes of a given node.

parentNode This property represents a given node's parent node.

firstChild This property represents a given node's first child within a given node's NodeList collection, with the index value of `0` representing the first in the list.

lastChild This property represents a given node's last child within a given node's NodeList collection, with the index value of `0` representing the first in the list.

childNode This property is a NodeList that contains a collection of all of a node's children.

previousSibling This property describes a given node's position in the node list relative to another node with a common parent when the given node occurs after the node sharing the parent in document order. In other words, two elements might be nested within the same parent element. The first that appears in document order is the `previousSibling` of the next appearing element, assuming there are no other nodes.

nextSibling This property describes a given node's position in the node list relative to another node with a common parent when the given node occurs before the node sharing the parent in document order. In other words, two elements might be nested within the same parent element. The second that appears in document order is the `nextSibling` of the element that appears before it in document order, assuming there are no other nodes.

ownerDocument This property represents the document instance within the DOM tree structure.

nodeType This is an unsigned short integer that represents the type of node.

Table 19.1 shows how these values map to each node type.

TABLE 19.1: NodeType Property Values

Node	NodeType
Element	1
Attribute	2
Text	3
CDATASection	4
EntityReference	5
Entity	6
ProcessingInstruction	7
Comment	8
Document	9
DocumentType	10
DocumentFragment	11
Notation	12

Each node type (except for NodeList and NamedNodeMap nodes) also inherits a number of methods. These methods can then be incorporated into script to manipulate nodes:

`insertBefore(newChild, referencedChild)` A method that inserts a new child node before an existing child node; there must really be a child node, and inserting the new child must not result in non-well-formed XML markup.

`replaceChild(newChild, oldChild)` A method that replaces an old child from a node lists' list of child nodes and replaces it with another.

`removeChild(oldChild)` A method that removes an old child from a node lists' list of child nodes; an error is thrown if there is no old child.

appendChild(newChild) A method that inserts a new child to a list of child nodes.

hasChildNodes() A method that returns true if a node has children, false if not.

cloneNode() A method that generates a copy of a given node.

Character Data

This node class is not directly accessible, but instead acts as a base class for the properties and methods of *text*, *CDATA section*, and *comment nodes*. Its properties include:

data This property describes text contained in any node that can inherit properties from the character data class.

length This is a property that names the number of characters (in integers) of a given text string.

In addition to these properties, the character data class contains a number of methods:

substringData(offsetIntegerValue, CountIntegerValue) This method counts the number of characters beginning at the `offsetIntegerValue` and ending by the named `CountIntegerValue`. If you're familiar with scripting, this is a basic JavaScript-like substring function.

appendData(appendStringValue) This method appends a string to an existing string in a node.

insertData(offsetUnsignedLongInteger, newStringValue) This method inserts a new string into an existing string of text at a given index location (named by the `offsetUnsignedLongInteger` argument).

deleteData(offsetValue, countValue) This method deletes string data from a string.

replaceData(offsetValue, countValue, dataValue) This method replaces string data.

Document

The *document node* is the document instance of an XML document. Don't confuse this with the root element, because they're different things. From the Document node you can create other nodes and insert them in the tree using a procedure. The main property of this node is the `documentElement`, which represents the document instance. The most important methods available to this node are the `createElement()` and `createDocumentFragment()` methods. The `createElement()` method creates an element node. It has one parameter, the name of the element tag that should be given the element. The `createDocumentFragment()` method creates a new document fragment node. An example of this node being accessed in IE5 might look like this:

```
alert(myXMLdoc.documentElement.attributes.item(0).nodeValue)
```

The preceding line of code would find the first instance of an attribute value within a root element, and return it to an alert window.

Element

This node represents an *element*. Like other nodes, it inherits all the properties and methods of the node class. Its only property is the `tagName` property, which is a string that describes the tag name of the element. This node has several methods native to it, including `getAttribute(name)`, `setAttribute(name, value)`, `removeAttribute(name)`, `getAttributeNode(name)`, `removeAttributeNode(oldAttribute)`, `setAttributeNode(newAttribute)`, and `getElementsByTagName(name)`.

You'll see the latter used often within the user interface JavaScript files of the new Mozilla (described later in this chapter) browser if you look around the JavaScript source files in the Mozilla builds.

DocumentType

Currently, this node represents the `ENTITY` and `NOTATION` declarations from a DTD. This will be expanded on in future iterations of the DOM spec.

NodeList

This node is a collection of child nodes and contains information about its number of children. Some nodes can't have children, so this node in those cases doesn't exist. The NodeList is the main navigational highway for traversing an XML document using the DOM. The key behind this navigation is the `item()` method, whose parameter is the index value that is used to ascertain a node's position in a node list. The `length` property provides information about the number of children in the NodeList.

NamedNodeMap

This node is a collection of child nodes that also contain information about attribute nodes. The `length` property provides information about the number of children in the NamedNodeMap collection. The `item()` method uses an index value in its argument that is used to ascertain a node's position in a NamedNodeMap collection.

Entity

This node results from a DTD's `ENTITY` declaration, whose properties (notation name, public id, etc.) in turn result in attribute nodes.

EntityReference

This node is the result of an entity that is referenced in a document instance. In other words, it isn't a result of the `ENTITY` declaration of a DTD, but the reference to that declaration that gets made in the document itself.

Notation

This node is a result of the `NOTATION` declaration in a DTD.

Text

This node is character data contained by an element. It inherits properties and methods from the character data node class.

Attribute

This node is the representation of attributes in an element or defined in entity or notation node declarations. Most of the operations involving the attribute node are actually performed by the element node's methods. This node contains:

`name` property This string represents the name of the given attribute.

`value` property Represents the value of the node.

`specified` property Is `true` if the attribute was present in the document before being loaded into an XML parser.

CDATASection

This node is the representation of CDATA sections.

ProcessingInstruction

This node is a representation of a processing instruction.

Comment

This node is a representation of a comment.

Document Fragment

This node is a representation of a document instance's partial tree, which can then be used to insert additional nodes. Each of these nodes is accessible through a `nodeType` property, which is common to all nodes.

Using InDelv, an XSL FO Browser

The InDelv browser, from InDelv, Inc. is written in Java. It's sole purpose is to browse XML documents that have been transformed into XSL formatting objects. The browser was still in Alpha development at the time of this writing, but the program looks promising as a Formatting Objects browser (see Figure 19.1 to see how it looked in Alpha).

Early Alpha versions of the browser did not have support for the DOM or scripting. It did offer support for X-Link, and most of its examples were based on X-Link linking mechanisms and parent style sheets. You can download InDelv at `http://www.indelv.com`.

FIGURE 19.1:

The InDelv browser can view XSL Formatting Objects

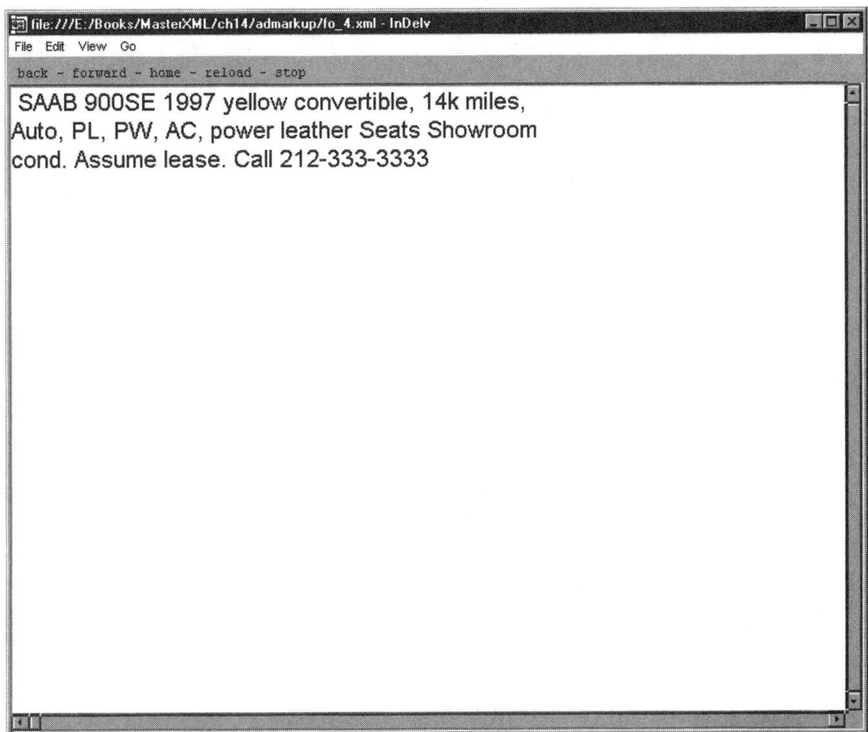

Using XML and Internet Explorer

When you open an XML file in IE5, the browser reveals either a tree view of the XML document, a page rendered via CSS, or a page rendered from an HTML result tree created by XSL. The tree view is the default XML style sheet that IE5 applies automatically to every XML document that doesn't have another style sheet linked to it. The result is a collapsible tree structure like that shown in Figure 19.2. For this reason, IE5 is a great free tool for learning XML.

FIGURE 19.2:

An XML tree structure in IE5

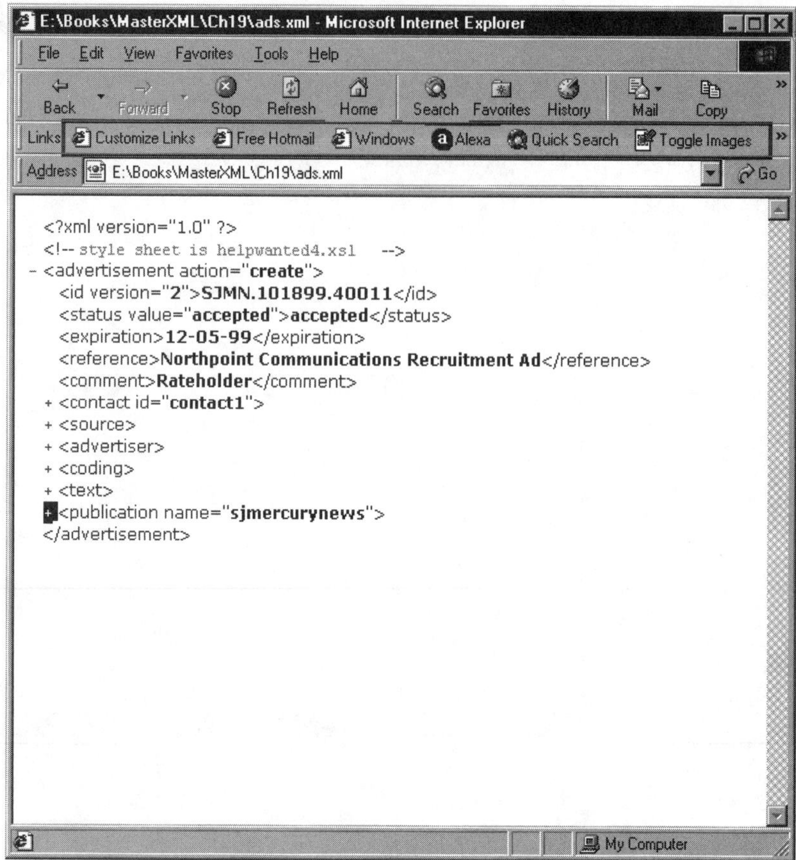

Although XML support in IE5 is extensive, it is not perfect, at least as far as XML developers are concerned. Rather than engage in this debate, let's just take a look at how Internet Explorer handles XML. In many ways, IE5 could almost be considered XML Internet Explorer 1. It's a first version. It isn't perfect, but it is a very nice start. IE5 supports the following XML implementations:

- Direct browsing of XML using a default XSL style sheet.
- Support for an early working draft of XSL (Extensible Style Sheets).
- Support for schemas (but a Microsoft variety, not the W3C spec) and extended data types.
- Support for XML-based client-side data binding.

Using XSL in Internet Explorer

There are plenty of things to worry about if you're developing XSL style sheets for Internet Explorer, because there are tons of incompatibility issues between the Microsoft version of XSL and the final recommendations coming out of the W3C. The first thing you'll need to do is make sure you're using the correct namespace. You'll then need to resolve the dilemma surrounding unsupported elements.

Getting Around IE5 Namespace Issues

You can get thrown off when developing XML if you don't use the correct namespace. Internet Explorer requires that you use specific namespaces for XSL style sheets and for schema development.

Using the IE5 XSL Namespace According to Microsoft documentation, you need to use the following namespace for your XSL style sheets:

```
<xsl:stylesheet xmlns:xsl="http://www.w3.org/TR/WD-xsl">
```

However, at the time of this writing a newer implementation of the XSL spec had been issued by the W3C, and after this book is published there may be another. Unfortunately, that namespace doesn't mesh with the Microsoft namespace. The official namespace for XSL as implemented according to the W3C spec as this book went to press is:

```
xmlns:xsl="http://www.w3.org/1999/XSL/Transform"
```

The Microsoft processor recognizes a specific W3C working draft. The XSL style sheet language is broken into two parts. IE5 supports Section 2 (Tree Construction) (the December 18th 1998 Working Draft). It can be found at `http://www.w3.org/TR/1998/WD-xsl-19981216.html`.

What exactly does all this mean? The key thing to remember about namespaces is that they are just mechanisms that help the processor know which XSL implementation to use when processing the style sheets. If the processor doesn't support that implementation, it won't recognize the namespace and your style sheets won't work correctly. The processor either has built-in processing support for a namespace or it doesn't. So if you use the XSL namespace for the official spec (`xmlns:xsl="http://www.w3.org/XSL/Transform/1.0"`), it won't work for IE5. The processor just doesn't recognize the namespace, so it can't do anything with it. It doesn't understand the underlying vocabulary, or how the elements associated with the prefixes that are identified with the namespace are defined.

This can be confusing, so think for a moment about how browsers read HTML files. Some can handle style sheets, some can't. On a certain conceptual level, it's the same thing. Browsers that can't handle style sheets don't recognize the CSS specification, even though you're doing everything correctly when you add your link to them.

Using an HTML Namespace In Internet Explorer, you don't have to use the `xsl:stylesheet` element as your root element when developing XSL style sheets. Instead you can create an XML document that uses an HTML element as its root element and declares a namespace within the root element. From that point on you just build an XML document using HTML elements, and add the style sheet elements to the parts of the HTML you want to use for displaying various parts of the source tree:

```
<?xml version="1.0"?>
<html xmlns:xsl="http://www.w3.org/tr/wd-xsl">
     <body style="font-family:arial, helvetica, sans-serif;
font-size:12px; background-color:#ffffff">
             <img src="mylogo.gif"/>
     <br/>
<table>
<tr>
<td >
<a href="http://www.javertising.com">Home Page</a>
</td>
<td>

     <xsl:for-each select="myElement">
             <div style="background-color:black; color:white;
     padding:7px">
             <span style="font-weight:900; color:white;">
<Some results here - could be any number of things, including text, or
more result elements, or even functions.>
                             </span>
             </div>
     </xsl:for-each>
</td>
</tr>
</table>
     </body>
</html>
```

The key aspect to this is the `html` root element. Did you notice the way the `img` element was handled? It included a closing tag. IE5 will interpret this kind of tag correctly.

The namespace issue isn't as big as it might seem. That is, unless you're using XSL elements that either are Microsoft extensions (in other words, they made them up and didn't worry too much about whether they would be included as part of a final spec), or standard elements not supported by IE5. Unfortunately, there are plenty of both.

Coping with Unsupported Elements

The easiest way to grasp the element support issue is to just take a look at the elements Microsoft's IE5 supports. Table 19.1 shows the elements the IE5 processor supports, and whether or not those elements are included in the W3C specifications.

Element	Included in W3C XSL Recommendations?
`xsl:apply-templates`	Yes
`xsl:attribute`	Yes, but in IE5 there are no attribute value templates (curly braces in attribute values), such as `<img src="{$myVariable}/myElement."` Variables (indicated by a preceding `$` operator) are not recognized either, so this whole statement would really be a mess in IE5.
`xsl:choose`	Yes
`xsl:comment`	Yes
`xsl:copy`	Yes
`xsl:element`	Yes, but in IE5, prefixes aren't allowable unless they can be resolved according to the namespace in effect at the time the element is encountered by the processor.
`xsl:eval`	No. In IE5, this element evaluates a statement to evaluate data types, with an optional language attribute specifying the language used (JScript is the default).
`xsl:for-each`	Yes
`xsl:if`	Yes
`xsl:otherwise`	Yes
`xsl:pi`	Yes
`xsl:script`	No. This element allows you to create global variables and script extensions for use in IE5. Includes an optional language attribute specifying the language used (JScript is the default).

Continued on next page

Element	Included in W3C XSL Recommendations?
xsl:stylesheet	Yes
xsl:template	Yes
xsl:value-of	Yes. IE5 does not support any of the following: name(), constant(), and arg() functions. You can use variables in script, however, and IE5 has an extensive object model with which to manage nodes.
xsl:when	Yes

As for the elements in the W3C Recommendations that are not supported by IE5, any XSL element you don't see in Table 19.1 is not supported by IE5, and will not work. The most important of these are probably the `xsl:variable` and `xsl:param` elements.

Using Schemas in IE5

Data types allowed in DTD-validated XML documents are fairly limited (entities, enumerations, name tokens, ids, idrefs, notations, and strings). Therefore, some proposals were developed to enhance the data typing available to XML developers so that data types like integers, floats (numbers with floating decimal points) dates, and other specific data types could be accessed and used easily within XML documents.

Microsoft has been a driving force behind these proposals, but the initial draft of the data typing and schema proposals the company introduced to the W3C were not adopted in the same format they were submitted. Significant changes were made, particularly to the way schemas are structured (the data type proposals are fairly close).

The schema elements Microsoft uses can be seen in Table 19.2. These are quite different than the schema elements that can be found in the W3C proposals.

NOTE The W3C recommendation (in Working Draft as this book went to press) can be found at `http://www.w3.org/TR/xmlschema-1/`). It is actually broken down into two different vocabularies. This URL references the XML Schema Part 1: Structures spec, which references the XML Schema Part 2: Datatypes (`http://www.w3.org/TR/xmlschema-2/`) spec in its entirety (using a parameter entity in its DTD to do so).

Using IE5 Schema Namespaces

When developing schemas for IE5, the same thing holds true for schemas that holds true for XSL. You need to use the proper namespace. The IE5 processor will not recognize the namespace used for XML Schema Part 1 or Part 2. Instead, you need to use the following two namespaces (the first namespace sets up the structure, the second provides access to data typing facilities):

```
xmlns = "urn:schemas-microsoft-com:xml-data"
xmlns:dt = "urn:schemas-microsoft-com:datatypes"
```

TABLE 19.2: IE5 Schema Elements

Element	Description
Attribute	Used to name attribute types available to the ElementType element.
AttributeType	Used to define the attribute type available to the Schema element.
datatype	Names a datatype available to the ElementType and AttributeType elements. The datatypes available are shown in Table 19.3, and go far beyond the primitive data types available to Document Type Definitions.
description	Used to provide descriptions about ElementType or AttributeType elements.
element	References a previously declared element.
ElementType	Acts as a declaration describing the element types that are available to the Schema element
group	Groups content.
Schema	The root element of a schema.

Data types can be described much more completely in a schema than by using DTDs. Take a look at how the element `pub_price` is declared in the following DTD fragment:

```
<!ELEMENT pub_price (#PCDATA)>
```

Now, look at that same element as declared in the schema:

```
<ElementType name = "pub_price" content = "textOnly" dt:type =
"fixed.14.4"/>
```

The difference lies in the `dt:type` attribute, which in this case has a value of `fixed.14.4`. In other words, it is a currency data type. What follows is a list of data types supported by IE5.

Data Types Supported by IE5

`string` (pcdata)	number (a number with no limit on digits, with an optional leading sign, exponent and fractions, and with U.S. English-style syntax)	`int` (a number with no limit on digits, with an optional leading sign, exponent and fractions, and with U.S. English-style syntax, stored in memory as a 32 bit binary)	`float` (a number with no limit on digits, with an optional leading sign, exponent and fractions, and with U.S. English-style syntax, stored in memory as 64 bit IEEE 488)
`fixed.14.4` (a number no more than 14 digits to the left of the decimal and no more than 4 digits to the right.	`Boolean` (1 or 0)	`dateTime.iso8601` (date in ISO 8601 format, containing year, month, hour, minute, second, and nanosecond)	`dateTime .iso8601tz` (date in ISO 8601 format, containing year, month, hour, minute, second, nanosecond, and zone)
`date.iso8601` (date in iso8601 format)	`time.iso8601` (time in iso8601 format)	`time.iso8601tz` (time in iso8601 format with zone)	`i1` (number, with optional sign, no fractions or exponent stored in memory as an 8 bit binary)
`i2` (number, with optional sign, no fractions or exponent stored in memory as a 16 bit binary)	`i4` (number, with optional sign, no fractions or exponent stored in memory as a 32 bit binary)	`i8` (number, with optional sign, no fractions or exponent stored in memory as a 64 bit binary)	`ui1` (An unsigned number having no fractions or exponent, stored in memory as an 8 bit number)

Continued on next page

Data Types Supported by IE5

`ui2` (An unsigned number having no fractions or exponent, stored in memory as an 16 bit number)	`ui4` (An unsigned number having no fractions or exponent, stored in memory as an 32 bit number)	`ui8` (An unsigned number having no fractions or exponent, stored in memory as an 64 bit number)	`r4` a number with no limit on digits, with an optional leading sign, exponent and fractions, and with U.S. English-style syntax, stored in memory as an IEE488 4 byte float)
`r8` (a number with no limit on digits, with an optional leading sign, exponent and fractions, and with U.S. English-style syntax, stored in memory as an n IEE488 8 byte float)	`float.IEEE.754.32` (a number with no limit on digits, with an optional leading sign, exponent and fractions, and with U.S. English-style syntax, stored in memory as an n IEE754 4 byte float)	`float.IEEE.754.64` (a number with no limit on digits, with an optional leading sign, exponent and fractions, and with U.S. English-style syntax, stored in memory as an n IEE754 8 byte float)	`uuid` (Hexadecimal octet digits stored in memory as 128-bytes Unix UUID structure
`uri` (uniform resource identifier)	`bin.hex` (hexadecimal octet digits)	`char` (string stored in memory as Unicode 16 bit characters)	`string.ansi` (ascii text)

Using the DOM in IE5

IE5 includes extensive support for the DOM, as well as another extensive library of additional objects that extend the capabilities of the DOM. IE5 object model support for XML is split in two. One part of the object model is direct support for the DOM and its interfaces. The other consists of the Microsoft extensions to the DOM. Using any of these is risky unless you're sure everyone who accesses any code using these extensions will be running IE5. The document instance, and therefore the base node class as well as all of Microsoft's extensions to the DOM can be accessed when an XML document is instantiated in the browser. An XML document is instantiated in one of four ways:

- IE5 can directly read any file with a `.xml` or `.xsl` extension to the file name. IE5 parses the document, then applies its own default XSL style sheet to the document so that the document is rendered as a collapsible tree in the browser.
- You can add a data island, which is an XML document fragment, directly into your HTML code.
- You can load an XML document into the browser. IE5's XML support derives from an ActiveX object, which means you can create a variable and name the newly loaded document instance as the value of your new variable.
- Load the XML document as a data source using Microsoft data binding technology.

When adding data islands to an IE5 document, all you do is add it to the HTML:

```
<html>
<body>
<xml id="myXML">
<rootElement>
    <element/>
</rootElement>
</xml>
</body>
</html>
```

Then you can access the document instance by declaring a variable and instantiating it with the document instance, referenced by the `xml` element's data island's `id` attribute:

```
var myDocInstance = myXML;
var myRootElement = myXML.documentElement;
```

With those two lines of code, you have instantiated your document instance and your root element. You could also have loaded an external XML document instead. You start by instantiating the XML ActiveX object:

```
var myXML= new ActiveXObject("microsoft.XMLDOM")
```

Generally, you'll then want to use a special property used on IE5-loaded XML documents that prevents asynchronous loading:

```
myXML.async=false
```

Then you load the document itself:

```
myXML.load("http:www.myDomain.com/myXMLDoc.xml")
```

One additional option is to load a data source using IE5's DSO, another ActiveX control:

```
<XML ID=xmlData src="myXML.xml"></XML>
<TABLE DATASRC="#xmlData">
  <THEAD><TH>NAME</TH><TH>HEADING</TH></THEAD>
  <TR>
    <TD><SPAN DATAFLD="information1"></SPAN></TD>
    <TD><SPAN DATAFLD="information2"></SPAN></TD>
  </TR>
</TABLE>
```

In the proceeding code the DATASRC attribute of the TABLE element is identified by the unique identifier that identifies the XML document (ID=xmlData). This "binds" the data from the XML source into the table cells. The DATAFLD attribute in the SPAN element accomplishes this because this attribute value maps out to an element of the same name in the XML document. So the source document has an information1 and information2 element and each are then accessed and their data inserted into the table.

Using XML and Netscape Navigator

Netscape Navigator 4 does not support XML. However, the Mozilla community, which is a dedicated and on some levels a loosely organized group of developers responsible for the next implementation of Netscape Navigator, is a vibrant one. Although there has always been a devoted Netscape following, the Mozilla community was given a huge boost when Netscape Communications released the Mozilla source code to the public. The Mozilla source code is the uncompiled code that makes Netscape run. Its availability within an open source environment means it is available for anyone to tinker with as they please within the constraints of the open source license. The result is the Mozilla community, which has a home base at http://www.mozilla.org. The Mozilla community is a loosely organized group because if you decide to develop using the source code, that really makes you a member of the community. Nevertheless, there is a core group that really drives the process, and decides on implementation issues that must be adhered to by the community. What makes the group so vibrant is the evangelism behind much of their work, the volunteerism that drives much of the code development, and the community-based process that creates excitement among a diverse range of talent.

Looking at the Mozilla XML Strategy

The Mozilla effort on XML browsing capabilities has taken a completely different approach than that of IE5. Rather than trying to drive the standards process, the Mozilla community has organized its efforts around attaining standards compatibility.

In addition, the underlying architecture is much different and much more accessible from a number of angles. The browser relies on CSS for displaying XML, but there are plans within the Mozilla community to support XSL as well.

Learning about Standards Compatibility Efforts in Mozilla

As this book went to press, the Mozilla browsing engines' most stable build was capable of rendering XML documents using CSS, XML-link, and elements that use the HTML namespace. You can also use CSS with any XML element. Plans are underway for enabling browser viewing of XML pages using XSL.

Browsing an XML Document Using CSS

Those of you who have worked extensively with CSS and HTML and tried to figure out how to develop compatible Web pages that work well in both Netscape and IE5 are going to need to sit down before reading the next line. Generally, any CSS1 code you use with XML will work in both IE5 and Mozilla (Netscape) *without any changes*. No browser redirects, no `if else` JavaScript statements. The code flat out works in both browsers (assuming Navigator 5 continues its current course). However, support for CSS2 appears to be better in Mozilla than IE5. Mozilla uses the newer selection properties to a much greater extent in the actual interface of the browser. It also can read documents linked to CSS2 style sheets.

Understanding the Mozilla Architecture

The Mozilla code, which will be the core API behind the next rendition of Netscape Communicator, is at its core something you can use yourself to make your own browser. In other words, if you're a Java programmer and you can't wait for

Netscape 5, you can make your own. The underlying structure as it relates to XML browsing revolves around four areas:

- The RDF, which is used to provide access to data descriptions throughout the Internet.
- James Clark's expat XML parsing engine, which can be accessed by any Netscape module.
- The DOM as defined for XML by the W3C. The DOM is accessible to any plug-in and JavaScript.
- XUL (pronounced "zool," which is short for XML-based User Interface Language; this is an XML-based markup language that uses HTML 4 and CSS to describe the Mozilla user interface (soon to migrate to XHTML/CSS).
- A large number of core JavaScript files that work with the DOM and XUL files to complete the user interface.

Understanding the Relationship between RDF and Mozilla

RDF architecture is based on a graph that is created by the connection between nodes and properties. The nodes can be any URI or string value. The property consists of URIs that consist of a vocabulary as defined by a schema and the associated namespace. The following is an example appearing in Mozilla documentation on RDF (`http://www.mozilla.org/rdf/doc/`) written by Netscape's Chris Waterson:

```
<?xml version="1.0"?>
<RDF:RDF xmlns:RDF="http://www.w3.org/TR/WD-rdf-syntax"
                    xmlns:NS="http://somecompany.com/RDF#">
<RDF:Description RDF:ID="#foo">
     <NS:title>babulach</NS:title>
     <NS:pointer>
            <RDF:Description RDF:ID="#bar">
                   <NS:title>bilch</NS:title>
            </RDF:Description>
     </NS:pointer>
</RDF:Description>
</RDF:RDF>
```

The graph for the above fragment looks as follows:

```
(x.rdf#foo)
     |
     +---[NS:title]-->("babulach")
     |
     +--[NS:pointer]->(x.rdf#bar)-+
                                  |
      ("bilch")<---[NS:title]---+
```

That graph can then become serialized, which basically means that you've implemented data sources that can talk to the graph model. To get a better look at an RDF document consider the following lines of code, used to access cataloged resources within the Dublin Core, which is a domain that manages registries for metadata:

```
<r:RDF xmlns:r="http://www.w3.org/1999/02/22-rdf-syntax-ns#"
     xmlns:d="http://purl.org/dc/elements/1.0/"
     xmlns="http://directory.mozilla.org/rdf#">
<Topic about="Arts/Books">
     <catid>1</catid>
     <narrow resource="http://www.amazon.com/"/>
     <narrow resource="http://www.barnesandnoble.com/"/>
     <narrow resource="http://www.borders.com/"/>
     <narrow resource="http://dir.yahoo.com/Arts/Humanities/Litera-
     ture/"/>
     <narrow resource="http://www.cnn.com/books/"/>
</Topic>
```

This is just a small snippet from a much larger document, which can then be accessed and manipulated using DOM interfaces. The Mozilla browser build contains many such RDF files on the client, which end up in directories on the hard drive upon installation. RDF documents on the Internet can also be accessed. The browser accesses these RDF documents and displays them using CSS after an RDF document has been converted into a tree by a component that builds the tree beginning with a root element. This root element is based on the first object that comes into the stream from the RDF document (hence the term serialized RDF). Generally, a transformation process of some kind generates this tree for communication with the Netscape layout component, but the exact architecture behind this transformation process was not yet finished as this was being written. XSL is expected to be a major conduit for expressing these transformations, which would remove some of the difficulty currently encountered in developing the transformation from RDF to a tree using the Netscape layout component.

Netscape Navigator, then, is a series of components that talk to each other and access a variety of resources and style sheets to present a graphical user interface and to deliver content. It uses JavaScript extensively to manage events that once were managed by classes within an executable. This description makes it all sound so simple, but the truth is, the Mozilla community has been struggling to create a reliable means for making the RDF tree conversion process clean and stable for some time. Many Mozilla developers are counting on XSL, with its transformation capabilities, to ease the burden.

Understanding How Mozilla Implements the DOM

Many of the working parts of Mozilla are invoked by JavaScript files that work with the DOM. Take a look at the following snippet, which, if you refer to the DOM documentation, reveals quite a bit:

```
function toggle_open_close() {

  var sidebar = document.getElementById('sidebarframe');
  var grippy = document.getElementById('grippy');

  if (is_sidebar_open)
  {
    // Close it
    sidebar.setAttribute('style','width: 0px');
    sidebar.setAttribute('src','about:blank');

    grippy.setAttribute('open','');

    is_sidebar_open = false;
  }
  else
  {
    // Open it
    sidebar.setAttribute('style', 'width:' + sidebar_width + 'px');
    sidebar.setAttribute('src',   sidebar_uri);

    grippy.setAttribute('open','true');

    is_sidebar_open = true;
  }

  try {
      // Save new open/close state in prefs
      if (prefs) {
        prefs.SetBoolPref(sidebar_pref + '.open', is_sidebar_open);
      }
```

```
}
catch (ex) {
   dump("failed to set the sidebar pref\n");
}
```

In the preceding code, methods that act on the DOM are highlighted in bold face. You can see that Mozilla relies on two methods in this particular code fragment. This is only a small fragment of a much larger amount of code that is included with the build. There are hundreds of JavaScript files used with the Mozilla build, each using a part of the DOM.

Understanding XUL

By now you've seen how the user interface of Mozilla is being built in a way that really does make it accessible to anyone with some programming skills (or, depending on what you're trying to accomplish, substantial programming skills). XUL, or the XML-based User Interface Language, makes at least parts of Mozilla accessible to anyone with a text editor and decent HTML/CSS skills. In fact, the Mozilla.org Web site (`http://www.mozilla.org`) has an interesting mission statement on its XUL developer table of contents page: "We will make UIs as easy to build as Web pages, and we will make applications easier to write and to customize along the way."

Building XUL-Based Windows and Widgets To develop XUL user interface widgets, you develop an XML file just like you've been learning to do throughout the book, starting with your XML processing instruction, then with a link to a default style sheet using another processing instruction. Then you declare the HTML namespace. Most likely, this will change by the time you read this to an XHTML namespace, if the XHTML has reached recommendation status (it was in working draft stage at press time). So the beginning of your code will look something like this:

```
<?xml version="1.0"?>
<?xml-stylesheet href="xul.css" type="text/css"?>
<!DOCTYPE window>
<window xmlns:html="http://www.w3.org/TR/REC-html40"
     xmlns="http://www.mozilla.org/keymaster/gatekeeper/there.is
     .only.xul">
```

Notice the reference to the style sheet `xul.css` in the preceding code? This is the default style sheet Mozilla uses to build the interface. A portion of this style sheet is shown in Listing 19.1

LISTING 19.1 Part of the Mozilla `xul.css` Style Sheet

```
box {
     display: block;
}
box[debug] box {
     border: 5px solid blue;
     margin: 1px;
     padding: 1px;
}
box[debug] box[align="vertical"] {
     border: 5px solid red;
}
spring {
     display: block;
}

box[debug] spring {
     background-color: green;
}

toolbar {
     display:block;
     background-color: #CCCCCC;
     border-bottom: solid darkGray 1px;
     border-top: solid white 1px;
     border-left: solid white 1px;
     border-right: solid darkGray 1px;
     font: 10pt sans-serif;
     min-height: 20px;
}

toolbar[collapsed="true"] {
     display:none;
}
toolbar[hidden="true"] {
     display:none;
}

toolbox {
            background-color:darkgray;
            display: block;
}
```

You can find the entire `xul.css` style sheet at `MozillaRootDirectory/res/samples/xul.css` on your hard drive (Mozilla Root Directory is whatever your Netscape 5 directory is called). Each Mozilla component generally has its own style sheet. You can experiment by making backups of the original `.xul` and `.css` files and altering them. You may get nasty, unexpected results, but the worst that can happen is you'll have to reinstall Netscape, which isn't such a huge deal anymore.

Looking at XUL Elements

There are a large number of elements that come with the XUL model. Eventually, Mozilla should have an official DTD for XUL, but for now you need to rely on the documentation on the Mozilla Web site to build your browser skin. A description of a few of the more important elements follows.

Window Element The `window` element is the root XUL element, where you declare any namespaces you are using. If you are only using the XUL namespace, there's no need to add prefixes, but many XML authors believe it is always better to include a prefix with namespaces to cut down on confusion. The syntax basically looks like this:

```
<xul:window
     xmlns:html="http://www.w3.org/TR/REC-html40"
     xmlns:xul ="http://www.mozilla.org/keymaster/gatekeeper/there.is
     .only.xul"
     title = "Dialog creation sample">
```

The next step is to actually make the window happen. This is done through script (see JavaScript extensions a bit later in this section for a closer look at how this is done). You can either build the window right in the element itself using the `html` namespace:

```
<html:script>
<![CDATA [
your script here
]]>
</html:script>
```

Or, you can link to an outside resource:

```
<html:script language="javascript" src="myWindow.js">
     </html:script>
```

From this point on, you can use any number of html elements and CSS style sheet rules to create your user interface. There are also a number of other XUL elements you can use in support of the `window` element.

Menubar Element This is the root element for a menu bar. It can contain menu elements as children. They can contain several menus nested within the main menu bar.

The most recent builds of Mozilla did not support style sheets for any of the menu elements, including `menu`, `menubar`, `menuitem`, and `separator`. The reason is that Mozilla developers anticipate too many problems at the operating system level if style sheets are supported, so they justifiably don't want to deal with that level of unpredictability. There are no attributes with this element. If the XUL document isn't opened as a top-level window then any `menubar` elements are ignored by Mozilla.

Menu Element This element is the child of the `menubar` element and contains a list of menu items (see `menuitem`) in sequential order, and, optionally, can consist of submenus. Valid attributes are `name`, `disabled`, and `icon`. The `name` attribute is the display name of the menu. The following is an example of the menu element in action, from Mozilla documentation:

```
<menu name="File" shortcut="f"/>
     <menuitem name="New..." shortcut="n" key="newKey"/>
     <menuitem name="Close" shortcut="c" key="closeKey"/>
     <separator/>
     <menuitem name="Save" shortcut="s" key="saveKey"/>
     <menuitem name="Save As..." shortcut="a" key="saveAsKey"/>
     <separator/>
     <menuitem name="Exit" shortcut="x" key="exitKey"/>
</menu>
```

Menuitem Element This element is a child of the `menu` element. It consists of a name to be displayed represented by text, and can be enabled or disabled, and checked or unchecked, and can have shortcut keys. The `menuitem` element also has a `name` attribute, which displays the name of the menu item.

Separator Element This element specifies a dividing horizontal line that doesn't actually do anything other than act as a way to separate one menu item from another.

Toolbox Element The `toolbox` element is a wrapper for the `toolbar` element. You can style the `toolbox` element using two CSS extensions, the `:toolbox-normal` and `:tool-box-rollover` pseudo elements. The `:toolbox-normal` pseudo-element is used to describe the look of the toolbar when there is no activity, and the `:toolbox-rollover` pseudo element is used to describe the look of the toolbox when a user rolls a mouseover the toolbox.

Toolbar Element This is an element used to specify a strip of controls called widgets that can be displayed horizontally or vertically using the `align` attribute. The plan is for the `align` attribute to be replaced by a CSS property, but the most recent implementation of Mozilla continued to use `align`. Values for the `align` attribute can be either `horizontal` or vertical. They are supposed to support drag and drop, but as of this writing they did not yet do so. An example of a toolbox and toolbar element might look something like this:

```
<toolbox>
     <toolbar id="myToolBar">
            <html:button>DoIt</html:button>
     </toolbar>
     <toolbar id="CoolToolBar">
            <html:img src="myCoolIcon.gif"/>Your Name: <html:input/>
     </toolbar>
</toolbox>
```

You might want to add some style to the toolbox, as well:

```
:toolbox-normal {
     background-color: #ffffcc;
     background-image: url("TooCool.gif");
     background-repeat: no-repeat;
     color: darkGray;
     border-bottom: solid darkGray 1px;
     border-top: solid darkGray 1px;
     border-left: solid black 1px;
     border-right: solid black 1px;;
}
```

The `toolbar` element includes an attribute called `collapsed`, which can be set to true both in the XUL document or dynamically through script. See Figures 19.3 and 19.4 to see how this looks and works in the browser. You can also access and manage the toolbar using standard CSS and script: `myToolbar.style.display = none`.

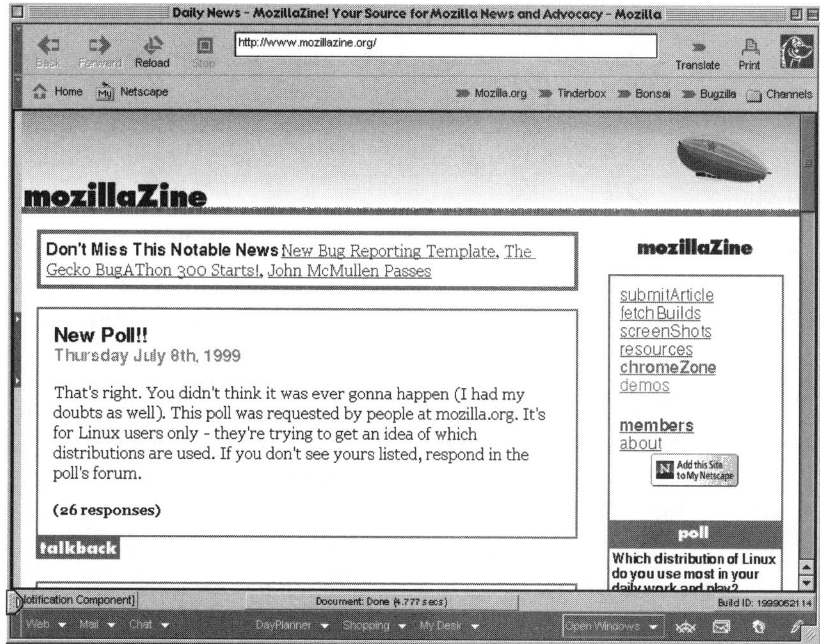

FIGURE 19.3:

The toolbar element collapsed

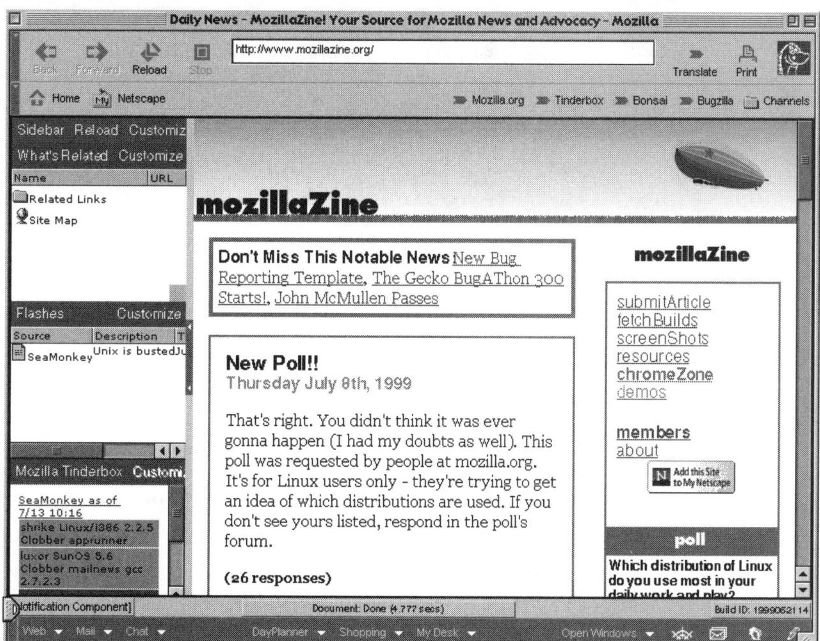

FIGURE 19.4:

The toolbar element not collapsed

Titledbutton Element You can use the `titledbutton` element to add a button to the XUL document. The button can contain one single image and one single text string. The image can be added using either the element's `src` attribute (a URI string) or with a CSS class selector:

```
<titledbutton src="myImage.gif">
```

Or

```
.mytitledbutton { list-style-image: url("myImage.gif")}
```

The preceding line of code adds style to the following element because it applies to the `class` attribute belonging to the `titledbutton` element in the line of code that appears before it.

Tree Element The `tree` element actually includes a number of sub-elements that mimic the behavior of HTML table elements. You can map the similarities according to Table 19.4, which compares a table element with its counterpart in the tree class.

TABLE 19.4 Comparing Table and Tree Elements

Table	Tree
table	tree
caption	treecaption
colgroup	treecolgroup
col	treecol
thead	treehead
tbody	treechildren, treeitem
tfoot	treefoot
tr	treerow
td	treecell

Tabcontrol Element The `tabcontrol` element makes it possible to create tab panels that can be clicked on by users to hide and show panels. This is one of a number of widgets available to Mozilla UI developers. The `tabcontrol` element acts as a declaration mechanism. Then, you add additional elements to build your tab control widget. You can provide alignment control using the `align` attribute to make the control align vertically or horizontally (using values of `horizontal` or `vertical` in the `align` attribute).

Tabbox Element The `tabbox` element is used to manage a group of `tab` elements. You can provide alignment control using the `align` attribute to make the `tabbox` align vertically or horizontally (using values of `horizontal` or `vertical` in the `align` attribute).

Tab Element The `tab` element is a child of the `tabbox` element. It contains content that helps identify its purpose in life. The following is a typical set of elements using the `tabcontrol` element as a root element for a tab widget:

```
<tabcontrol align="vertical">
     <tabbox align="horizontal">
            <tab>myTab</tab>
            <tab>yourTab</tab>

</tabcontrol>
```

Tabpanel Element There's more to the development of a tab widget than creating a `tabbox` element. To finish your tab control box, you will want to create a `tabpanel` element, which is the element that represents the object that is revealed when a tab is clicked on. In the preceding line of code (under the description of the `tab` element), when the tab `myTab` is clicked, a tab panel is revealed. Take a look at the following code:

```
     <tabpanel flex="100%">
            <titledbutton value="myView"/>
            <titledbutton value="yourView"/>
</tabpanel>
```

Now, take a look at the complete widget:

```
<tabcontrol align="vertical">
     <tabbox align="horizontal">
            <tab>myTab</tab>
            <tab>yourTab</tab>
</tabbox>
<tabpanel flex="100%">
            <titledbutton value="myView"/>
            <titledbutton value="yourView"/>
</tabpanel>
</tabcontrol>
```

When the user clicks the tab `myTab`, the view `myView` is revealed. Similarly, when the user clicks the tab `yourTab`, the view `yourView` is revealed.

Progress Meter Element You can even customize the look of the progress meter, which is the bar that displays the status of a download, using the `progressmeter` element. You can use a CSS color property to color the bar in its default `normal` mode (using the attribute value pair `mode="normal"`).

Altering the Look of Mozilla

Armed with what you now know, it's time to tackle the basic Mozilla navigator interface, and change it a bit. First you'll change a few pictures and the word "Home" (next to the original "home" button) to "Advance." Customizing the Mozilla interface for your own needs can be as easy as changing an image specified in the style sheet associated with `navigator.xul` file (the style sheet is called `navigator.css`):

```
titledbutton#home-button {
list-style-image:url(resource:/res/toolbar/logoButton.gif);
}
```

Then you need to go through the entities in the XUL document's document definition until you find the entity that corresponds to the button label you need. The XUL document is fairly long, so you perform a search operation using the MacIntosh BBEdit text-editing program. The code fragment that follows is a tiny portion of the document type definition in the XUL file. The text in the `homeButton.label` entity is changed to read "Advance" instead of "Home." The result in Figure 19.5 isn't art, but it works.

```
<!- Toolbar items ->
<!ENTITY  homeButton.label "Advance">
<!ENTITY  netscapeButton.label "Netscape">
<!ENTITY  bugzillaButton.label "Bugzilla">
<!ENTITY  tinderboxButton.label "Tinderbox">
```

Everything on the tool bar can be changed. It is just a matter of finding out which parts of the XUL (and which XUL document) to use.

FIGURE 19.5:

A customized navigator interface

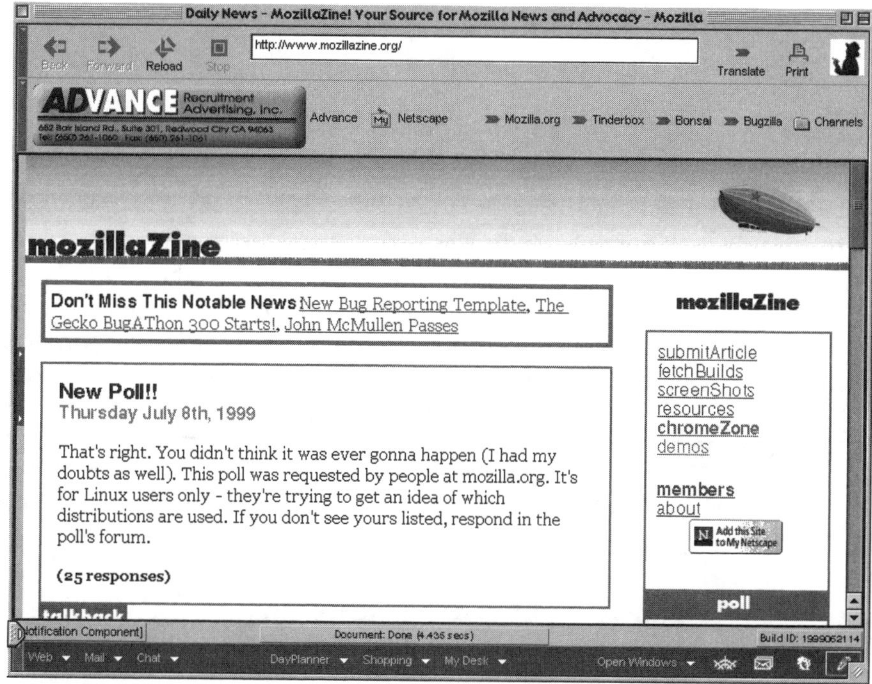

Accessing XUL Objects in Script

You can access the DOM from script within XUL, just as you can in HTML. Only this time, you're actually implementing changes in the user interface, rather than documents read by the browser. The Mozilla `navigator.xul` document, for example, contains a link to a JavaScript document that drives much of the event management process:

```
<html:script language="javascript" src="navigator.js">
     </html:script>
```

The XUL document object acts like the HTML document object, and thus has access to that object's attributes and methods. The most important of these is the `getElementByID()` method. This method retrieves an element named within the method's parameters. You'll see this method used throughout Mozilla XUL code, such as the lines of code below that come from the `navigator.js` file:

```
function RefreshUrlbar()
    {
    //Refresh the urlbar bar
    document.getElementById('urlbar').value = window
    .frames[0].frames[1].location.href;
```

Quite a bit of the source code you look at, at least in early renditions of Mozilla, include script that is placed in an element without CDATA sections, so you want to be careful about emulating this kind of code development when developing your own script implementations. You should always wrap your script in CDATA to prevent the XML from being ruined by the JavaScript.

NOTE

XUL development criteria is subject to change. You can find current documentation on XUL at `http://www.mozilla.org/xpfe/xptoolkit/index.html`.

Using JavaScript Extensions

In order to implement some features that make XUL documents accessible to markup and script developers, Mozilla decided to add a few windows-based extensions to the JavaScript DOM.

One of those extensions is an added parameter to the `window.open()` method. This is a well known method within the JavaScript world used to open a new browser window. This is accomplished through the use of parameters, which are passed using parentheses. Traditionally, the `window.open()` method syntax has looked like this:

```
window.open(URL, windowName, [windowFeatures])
```

In JavaScript documentation, the parameters in the brackets are optional. The `windowFeatures` optional parameter is actually a list of comma delimited features that describe the window structure. This allows you to include or not include things like a status bar or menu bar, and lets you open a new browser window at a specified size. The JavaScript extension for XUL adds one additional feature called `chrome`. This feature will disable the traditional action of the `window()` method, which is to open a new browser window. Instead, when using the `chrome` feature in the parameter list, the new window is not within the browser interface, but instead becomes the new browser interface. A new "skin" is applied, replacing the older skin. Mozilla calls this skin "chrome," hence the name for this feature.

You can go one step further, and build an array from parameters by using the `window.openDialog()` method. This is quite similar to the `window.open()` method, except it builds an array automatically from its parameters list and applies them automatically to a property called `arguments`. The new window then can provide access to this property, which gives it additional flexibility with event management.

A new property, called `window.content`, can be used as a shortcut for managing information normally found in the `iframe` element's `type` attribute:

```
window.content.location.href= "http://www.mydomain.com"
```

Up Next

You've now had a chance to look at XML tools (in the previous chapter) and XML browsers. Much of what you've seen so far is all on the client end. Much of the action, if not most, regarding XML, will be on the server end. The next chapter will look at XML-enabled servers, and how you can fit them into your development plans.

CHAPTER

TWENTY

20

XML-Enabled Servers and Server Technologies

- What is a server?
- How servers can be XML-enabled
- An overview of two XML-enabled servers
- XML server technologies: ULCP and ICE

So far, we've concentrated on XML as a document creation language. We've looked at how elements and attributes are defined; how entire DTDs or schemas are developed; and the tools to create documents, DTDs, and schemas, and we've even discussed XML-enabled browsers.

But XML isn't just about documents. Data can be stored in XML fragments, and XML can be used to bring together data from disparate sources and merge it into a single presentation. To do this, however, you need the help of XML-enabled servers and XML server technologies.

What Is a Server?

Before we can begin to talk about XML-enabled servers or server technologies, let's take a step backward and discuss what a server is, exactly.

When people talk about "servers," there are two major distinctions that can be made:

- The actual computer (hardware) that performs server functions

or

- A software program that performs server functions

The hardware version of a server is pretty straightforward. It's a computer. A computer that holds all of a company's sales documents, product literature, and other data files may be referred to as a *file server*. Its purpose is to be a repository of data. The resources of another computer may be reserved to manage printing functions for a large workgroup.

Software programs can also be labeled as servers. For instance, Microsoft's Internet Information Server (IIS), a popular Web server program, is a software-based server. The computer it resides on may perform many functions, but the IIS program performs the function of accepting and responding to requests for data on the Internet, which makes it a Web server.

What Makes a Server XML-Enabled?

So we have two types of servers: pieces of hardware that perform basic functions in the client-server computing model and software-based servers that perform specific functions in managing or distributing information. Where does XML fit in?

The market has yet to agree on exactly what an XML-enabled server is, but several generalizations can be made here. An XML-enabled server is one that

- Stores or manages XML documents
- Parses XML
- Generates XML as part of an output task
- Can transform XML to other formats

Many XML-enabled servers on the market today are tied into publishing and content-management systems. Later in this chapter, you will be introduced to two of the most successful products available right now, UCLP and ICE.

Dynamic Web Publishing with DynaBase

One XML-enabled server that's popular with the network-computing crowd is eBusiness Technologies' DynaBase, which is touted as a dynamic Web publishing system.

Dynamic Web publishing is a label placed on the model of storing information in its native components, then bringing it together from those disparate places at the time of publication. For instance, a corporate annual report will often contain data that is natively stored in or retrieved by query from a database, image files, spread sheets, existing marketing materials, and new content developed specifically for the report.

Rather than requiring a staff member to manually compile the information, using a layout tool such as Microsoft Word or Publisher, Quark XPress, or others, and then producing the final copy, a dynamic publishing system automates the process of bringing these pieces together and composing the end product.

But it's more than just automated publishing. That same annual report that is sent out to major shareholders in a slick, glossy-paper presentation also needs to be placed on the company Web site. Normally, this means that same staff member, or a second staff member with special skills, is required to retrieve that content again and this time produce an HTML version suitable for the Web site. Using a dynamic publishing system, the output format is managed by the server; the same staff member that creates the glossy print version can also select a Web-based output, and the system will create both versions, optimized for each of their own special needs.

DynaBase Components

The DynaBase publishing system has six major components: the Web Manager, Web Author, Command Line Interface, Data Server, Web Developer, and the Web Server plug-in. Let's take a quick look at each of these.

The Web Manager

Many content management tasks are handled through the Web Manager component, shown in Figure 20.1. It provides a graphical interface for access to the Data Server component. The screens will look familiar if you've used other integrated development environments (IDEs) such as Microsoft's Visual InterDev or Allaire's Cold Fusion Studio.

FIGURE 20.1:

DynaBase Web Manager graphical user interface

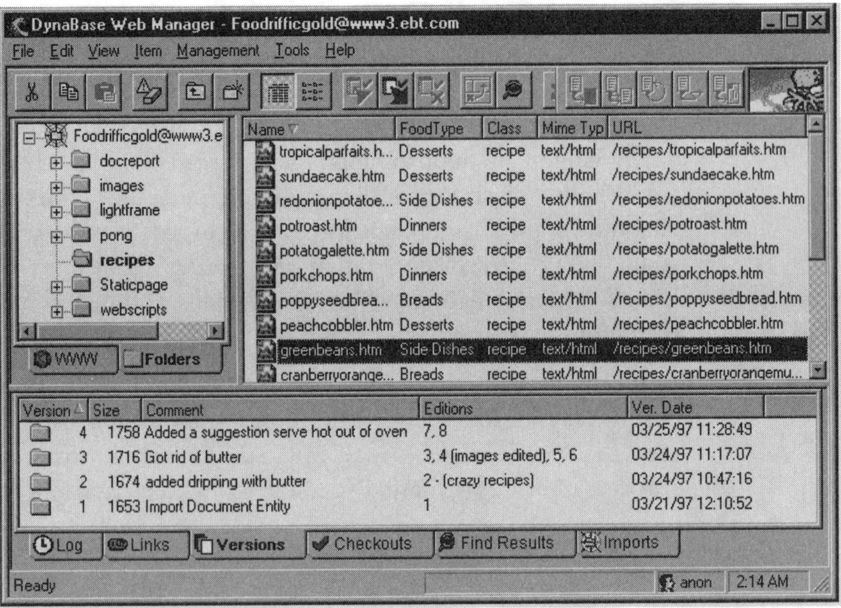

The left-hand pane displays the resources you have at your disposal, both locally in folders and on the Web. The right-hand pane provides file-level detail. Traditional Windows metaphors such as drag-and-drop work between panes, allowing you to easily move data around from within the IDE. The lower pane provides version control information, check-in/check-out status, team and workflow management tools, and permissions controls.

Web Author

The DynaBase system is designed specifically to allow users to launch any authoring environment they wish. However, Web Author, an integrated authoring application, is included in the package. This Java-based client is designed to leverage the use of remote content contributions without regard to platform standardization. Staff may run the application on Windows, Macintosh, or Unix platforms without conflict.

Command Line Interface

The DynaBase Command Line Interface (CLI) extends the power of the Web Manager interface. Developers can customize existing applications and integrate back-end systems to work directly with the DynaBase servers through the CLI, which acts as a simple API (application programming interface).

For example, server tasks such as cron jobs can be scheduled to open a connection to the server, check out specific items, perform maintenance or routine updates, check the items back in, and close the server connection. By using the CLI, these processes can be integrated directly into these third-party applications with no need for staff to be on hand to use the traditional interface.

DynaBase CLI and the ICE Protocol

An interesting note is that the CLI is based on ICE, the Information and Content Exchange protocol jointly developed by Adobe Systems, CNET, Microsoft, Sun Microsystems, and Vignette Corporation. Intended for use by content aggregators or syndicates, it allows for machine processing of publication negotiations across distributed data sources. Schedules for delivery of data, known as *payloads*, can be automatically negotiated between systems.

Continued on next page

For instance, if you published a local community portal and wanted to provide technical news that related to companies in your area, you might build a syndicate relationship with CNET. Using ICE, CNET could automatically deliver content to be stored in your data repositories. That data would then be available for the DynaBase CLI to further manipulate according to your internal publishing practices.

More details on ICE are available later in this chapter.

Data Server

The Data Server acts as the repository for all Web components in the DynaBase environment. It provides version control and secure storage for nearly a dozen media formats, including (of course) HTML and XML, graphics, video, sound, Perl scripts, Java applets, Microsoft Office documents, and more. The Data Server has a built-in database known as ObjectStore, which provides transaction control mechanisms, mirroring, replication, and backup options.

Web Developer

The Web Developer component provides the framework used for content delivery. Touted as "intelligent page-scripting," it uses a cross-platform scripting language that is similar to Visual Basic. The scripts are actually compiled, providing for faster deployment in high-traffic situations.

The scripting environment supports access to documents through the Document Object Model (DOM), full-text searching capabilities, ODBC connectors for databases, access to Web request and response objects, and component-based document assembly techniques.

Web Server Plug-In

The scripts compiled using the Web Developer component are instantiated through the Web Server plug-in. It acts as an application server, dynamically generating pages on demand.

Current Implementations

DynaBase enjoys current commercial buy-in, with several prominent Web sites that are published using its dynamic publishing model. For example, Hearst New Media automated the content management for a recently developed Web site, `homearts.com`, a conglomerate of several print publications such as *Good Housekeeping*, *Redbook*, and *Cosmopolitan*.

eBusiness Technologies claims additional major customers for DynaBase, including investment bank Adams, Harkness, and Hill; publishing house Houghton Mifflin; LifetimeTV; and SGI.

Enhydra Java/XML Application Server

Another XML-enabled server, the Enhydra Application Server, takes a platform-independent approach by using the Java programming language. One of its unique features is that it is an *open source* project, meaning not only is the application server available for use, but you can also obtain the source code to those programs.

From the viewpoint of XML-enabled servers, Enhydra acts as a "server of applications," meaning that it enables the instantiation of other applications and serves them out to the end client through a traditional Web server such as Apache or Netscape. When needed, Enhydra can also communicate with the client Web browser directly through HTTP requests. This means that it is capable of retrieving XML-source and using a Java-based parser and processor for presentation and output.

The Enhydra project was undertaken in response to developer demand for a rapid development system that was both scalable and reusable. By working in Java, Java classes can be developed and managed for reuse from project to project yet still retain the flexibility needed to meet individual client needs.

Enhydra Components

Like DynaBase, Enhydra has six major components: the Application Framework, Multiserver, XMLC, JDDI, DODS, and App Wizard.

Application Framework

Development of Enhydra applications centers around the Application Framework, a *servlet* (server side applet or application) runtime environment that manages the common services necessary to support N-tier applications. This could mean database connectivity, session-state data, authentication services, and more.

Multiserver

The Multiserver acts as a manager for the other servlets that comprise the Enhydra system, including the Application Framework servlet. Multiserver provides debugging and monitoring support at the system level.

XMLC

XMLC, Enhydra's integrated XML Compiler, was created to help both the designer and the developer manage the transition between application logic and the presentation layer in a Web site or application.

XMLC views HTML files as XML documents, internally recomposing them into a hierarchical view of Java classes. Designers don't need to become Java programmers; they only need manage the ID attributes assigned to the dynamic content that developers will provide. XMLC then manages the transition.

JDDI

The Java Dynamic Data Interchange (JDDI) provides a server-side solution to dynamic HTML. A current drawback of much of the dynamic content on the Web is the interoperability issues found between today's popular Web browsers. By creating the dynamic aspects of the presentation in Java, developers and designers no longer have to create two separate presentations using the disparate methods supported by either browser. JDDI is fully integrated into the Application Framework.

DODS

The Enhydra Data Object Design Studio (DODS) takes the mystery out of working between your applications and relational database content. Easy-to-use dialogs (see Figure 20.2) walk the user through the process of setting up data-layer classes. DODS generates the Java source code to be used within the Application Framework.

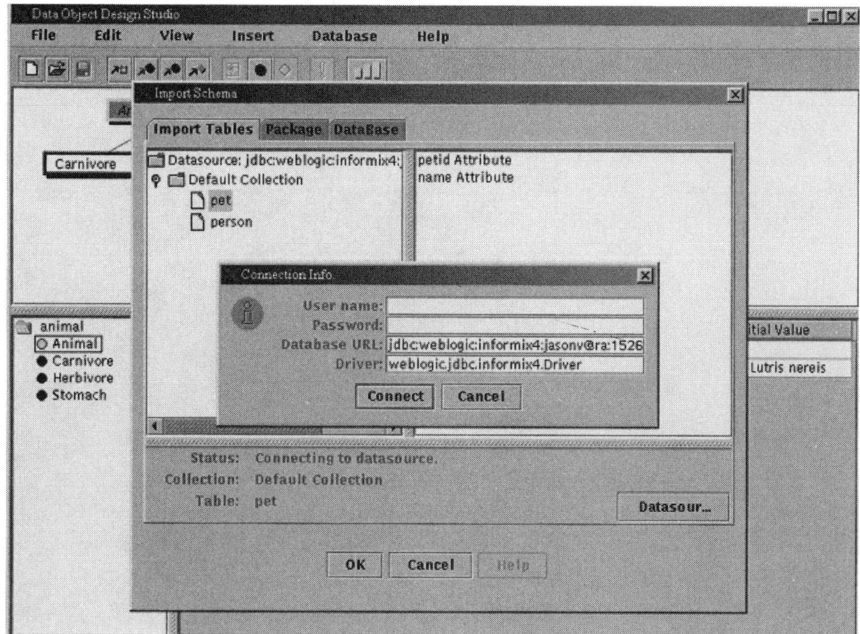

FIGURE 20.2:

The Enhydra DODS (Data Object Design Studio)

App Wizard

A rapid application development tool, the Enhydra App Wizard allows the developer to quickly generate a new source tree for a simple Enhydra Web application. Dialogs step the user through each piece of information necessary to instantiate the application environment.

Current Implementations

Several entertaining demonstration applications, such as the photo-realistic calculator applet seen in Figure 20.3, are available on the Enhydra Web site, complete with source code. Visit `http://www.enhydra.org` for more details.

FIGURE 20.3: An Enhydra Web application

XML Server Technologies

XML server technologies differ from XML-enabled servers in that they aren't full server applications in and of themselves but are technologies that work at the server level using XML. In this section, we'll look at two XML server technologies that were first presented as submissions to the W3C, where they now reside as a Note. A W3C Note carries no endorsement or assurance of adoption by the Consortium; instead, it is a means of providing the information to Consortium member-companies for review and discussion.

SAIC/Bellcore: Universal Commerce Language and Protocol (UCLP) and the MISTI Application

On January 20, 1999, Science Applications International Corporation (SAIC/Bellcore) submitted the Universal Commerce Language and Protocol (UCLP) specification to the W3C for consideration. As with most submissions, the W3C acknowledged the submission and published it on their Web site as a Note.

UCLP is designed as an XML-compliant schema for authoring metadata that will facilitate locating and extracting information located across the Internet. While similar in scope to RDF (Resource Description Framework), UCLP is intended to provide a base level of datatyping that may be extended as necessary for industry-specific applications and granularity needs.

Implementing UCLP

A UCLP-compliant document has the same structure as an HTML document. In fact, the UCLP tags are intermixed within the body of the HTML page. This coexistence is possible when user agents comply with the requirements of processing HTML documents, which are to ignore what you don't understand. Therefore, the presence of foreign elements won't harm the HTML document.

The following code sample represents a basic document that uses an educational domain-tagging schema:

```
<HTML>
<HEAD>
<TITLE>Central College Course Catalog: Introduction to Computer
   Sciences</TITLE>
</HEAD>
<BODY>
<UC domain="Catalog" version="Spring 99" class="Undergraduate"
   status="current">
<H1 align=center>CS101: Introduction to Computer Sciences</H1>
<table border="1">
<tr>
```

```
<th>Course Number</th>
<th>Course Title</th>
<th>Instructor</th>
<th>Meeting Day</th>
<th>Time</th>
<th>Location</th>
</tr>
<tr>
<td>CS101</td>
<UC_ID name="Course Number" value="CS101"/>
<td>Introduction to Computer Sciences</td>
<UC_ID name="Course Title" value="Introduction to Computer
   Sciences"/>
<td>Jason Abromovitz</td>
<UC_ID name="Instructor" value="Jason Abromovitz"/>
<td>Tu-Th</td>
<UC_ID name="Meeting Day" value="Tu-Th"/>
<td>11:00-12:30</td>
<UC_ID name="Time" value="11:00-12:30"/>
<td>Gates Hall Room 110</td>
<UC_ID name="Location" value="Gates Hall Room 110"/>
</tr>
</table>

<P>Introduction to Computer Sciences is a survey course designed to
   give students an overview of potential careers and areas of study
   available in the computer sciences department here at Central College.
   It is a required course for all freshmen.
<UC_FEAT name="Type" value="survey"/>
<UC_FEAT name="Required" value="All students"/>
<UC_FEAT name="Transferrable" value="Yes"/>

</BODY>
</HTML>
```

The display of this document would be the same as it would on any XML/HTML compliant user agent, as seen in Figure 20.4.

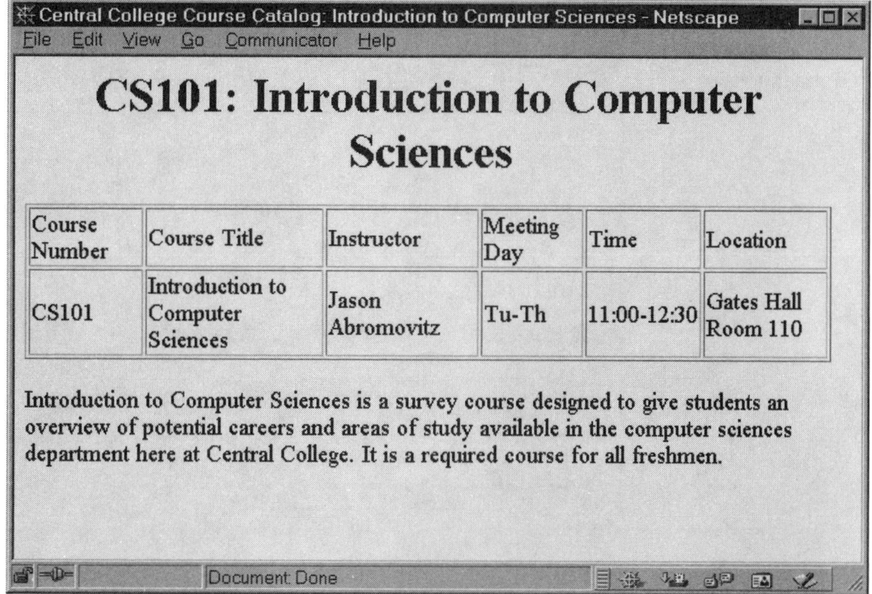

FIGURE 20.4: UCLP documents render as traditional XML/HTML documents

One of the UCLP tags found in this document is UC_FEAT, which describes a domain-specific feature for the information in the document—in this case, the fact that the course is a survey class, required of all students, and eligible for transfer to other educational institutions.

The UC_ID tag identifies discrete chunks of information that may be used in the extraction of data. For example, a UCLP-compliant system could be asked to search the Internet for college courses that are transferable survey courses.

UCLP Applications

SAIC has developed a tag generator for UCLP known as MISTI. This tool assists implementers in creating valid instances of parameter and feature names in accordance with the rules set forth in their domain-specific ontologies. Information about MISTI, including a download of the standalone generator, and the ontology database can be found online at `http://misti.apo.saic.com/pagegen.htm`. An online tutorial for using the MISTI system is also provided (see Figure 20.5).

FIGURE 20.5:

The online MISTI tutorial for UCLP page generation

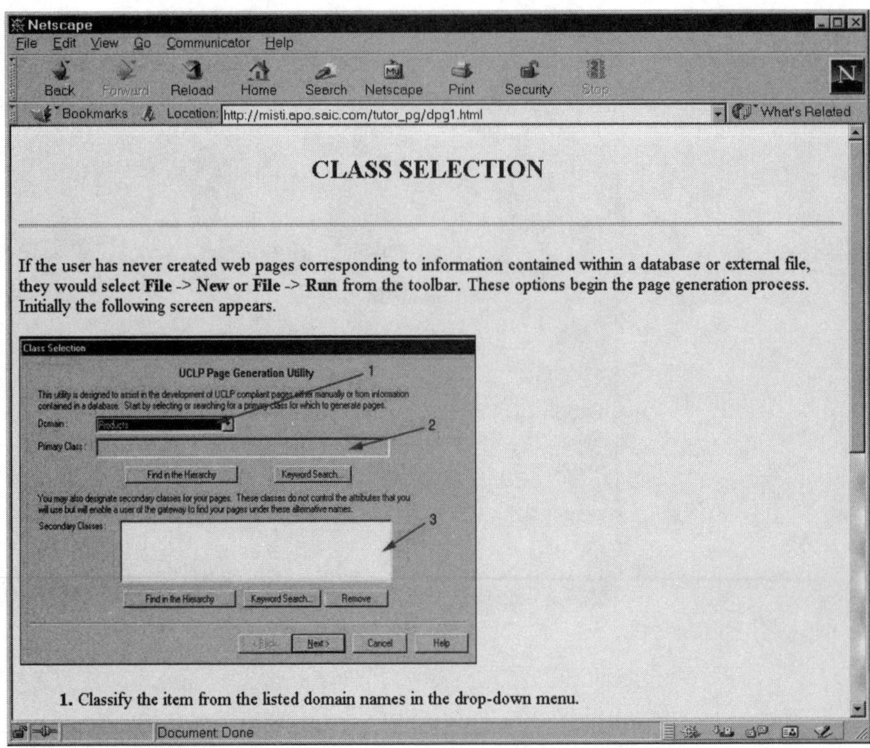

The Future of UCLP

UCLP highlights the need for domain-specific vocabularies and methods of data extraction and aggregation. The W3C Recommendation for RDF parallels many of the goals of UCLP. It's not clear at this time whether UCLP should be reformulated as an RDF Schema or if it has additional usage that would be limited by that scope.

Adobe Systems Inc., et al: The Information and Content Exchange Protocol (ICE)

Another recent submission to the W3C is known as the Information and Content Exchange Protocol (ICE). This XML application was developed by W3C members Adobe Systems Inc., CNET Inc., Microsoft Corporation, Sun Microsystems Inc., and Vignette Corporation. It is intended for use by content aggregators or syndicates to streamline and automate content exchange and reuse.

NOTE

The full text of the ICE protocol proposal may be found on the W3C's Web site at `http://www.w3.org/TR/NOTE-ice`.

Two major areas of concern for major syndicates like CNET, many news organizations, and portal sites needed to be addressed:

- Before successfully sharing and reusing information, both parties involved in the transaction need a common vocabulary.
- Before successfully transferring any data and managing the relationship, both ends need a common protocol and management model.

The ICE authoring group noted that the first requirement was already being successfully addressed in the work undertaken in part by the W3C and in part by industry-specific organizations. For instance, the W3C has developed MathML, an XML-based markup language used to describe mathematical expressions. Other groups are working on vocabularies for chemical markup, health care needs, music, and more.

The ICE protocol builds upon this existing work and provides the second half of this aggregator equation: a means to manage the relationships between parties. Seven goals were stated at the beginning of the ICE development process:

- ICE shall be straightforwardly usable over the Internet.
- ICE shall support a wide variety of applications and not constrain data formats.
- ICE shall conform to a specific XML syntax.

- The ICE requirements shall constrain the ICE process to practical and implementable mechanisms.
- ICE shall be open for future unknown uses.
- Compactness of representation in ICE is of minimal importance. Note: This is a statement about low-level encoding methodology, i.e., the use of XML in general and the particular choice of tag and attribute names in particular.
- ICE shall keep protocol and packaging overhead to a minimum. Note: This is a statement about protocol overhead in the sense of round trips, complexity, and other high-level performance effects. It is not a contradiction of the previous point. The design of ICE achieves its performance objectives by optimizing the high-level design of the protocol flow and state management, not by micro-optimizing the spelling of individual packets.

It should be noted that ICE differs from other document-based applications in that it describes a *protocol*, not just an XML-based DTD. Even so, it retains the element/attribute markup model established for XML.

Implementing ICE

In any system that requires consistent implementations across multiple participants, constraints must be placed on either the expression of content or the structural form that content may take. Two design goals for ICE address constraints are as follows:

- ICE shall support a wide variety of applications and not constrain data formats.
- The ICE requirements shall constrain the ICE process to practical and implementable mechanisms.

At first glance, these goals may seem contradictory, but actually, they complement each other. The domain the ICE authoring group used to illustrate this point is the production and sharing of banner ads. For successful collaboration between content partners, what constitutes a banner ad must be defined. Rules could be developed that dictate the file format (GIF vs. JPG) and physical dimensions expressed in pixels.

Note that while these rules can be viewed as constraints, they do not conflict with either of the design goals. Defining a common format for banner ads does fit with the idea of supporting a wide variety of applications, and it also passes the test of a solution to a practical and implementable mechanism.

Defining the Syndicate/Subscriber Relationship

Organizations that produce content and make that content available for republication or repurposing are known as *syndicates*. For example, in traditional print media, the Associated Press (AP) is a syndicate. Newspapers that print stories provided by AP subscribe to the service and are granted license to use stories in a specific manner.

The same syndicate/subscriber relationship exists in many forms on the Web. The content may be news stories, as with AP, but it may also be data such as stock quotes, weather forecasts, customized maps, movie or theater reviews, or public event calendars.

ICE enters into the syndicate/subscriber scenario after a business relationship has been firmly established, meaning that any contractual, payment, and organizational issues have been handled. On the technical end, the subscriber is given access to specific offers from the syndicate's catalog of subscription offerings. In other words, a Miami-based Web portal may wish to purchase news stories from a news syndicate by subscribing to the South Florida offer in their catalog of target markets.

The syndicate's technical staff creates an account on the ICE server for the new subscriber, providing the subscribing organization with a URL to be used for ICE communication and any authentication parameters required to establish communication. The subscriber's staff then logs the new subscription on their ICE server and makes the initial connection with the syndicate's ICE server. Any additional details to be determined (such as delivery times or protocol parameters) are set at this point, and automatic communication between ICE servers is ready to begin.

The Future of ICE

Once the initial communication between ICE servers is established, delivery of content from syndicate to subscriber may be fully automated. The ICE protocol defines the process by which new ICE *payloads*, or collections of subscribed data, are announced, delivered, and confirmed. Error handling is built into the system as well, allowing a subscriber to indicate that a problem occurred during transport or to notify the syndicate that an expected delivery did not occur.

Event logs are stored on both ICE servers to assist in problem analysis and performance debugging. Either party can initiate a request for log exchange, as well as generate text messages that would be delivered by the ICE server to a human user for handling.

The possibilities for automated data exchange using ICE appear to be endless. By using an XML-based format for ICE payloads and processing instructions, the authoring group has positioned this technology well for adoption across large industry groups and the Web community in general. The technical requirements of running an ICE server on both ends may initially limit its usefulness to large corporations, but smaller users may find ISPs or other services that will provide access to an ICE server on a collective basis.

Up Next

In this chapter, we reviewed what functions a server performs and how a server may be XML-enabled. Two popular servers were overviewed: the DynaBase dynamic publishing system and the Enhydra Java/XML Application Server. A related concept, XML server technology, was introduced with an overview of two such technologies: the ULCP proposal and the ICE project. Many more exciting entries to this arena can be found (see Chapters 27 and 28 for some more examples), illustrating the great flexibility XML brings into the server application and technology space.

Next, we'll dive further into the Java world and explore in more detail how Java and scripting languages can work side by side with XML. You'll see how Java is uniquely suited to working with XML, and you'll be introduced to a freely available XML parser to put to use.

CHAPTER

TWENTY-ONE

21

XML and Java

- Java in the XML application architecture
- Java on the client side, server side, and as middleware
- XML parsing with Java across open networks
- Examining parsers: Ælfred and XJParser

It's been said that XML gives Java something to do. Indeed, it may be that XML will become the driving force behind Java, now that the language has stopped being an object of media hype and become a tool for practical software-development projects. As cute animation applets fade from the scene, serious tools will take their place. Java is the best tool around for writing platform-flexible, network-centric applications with elaborate feature sets. For one thing, Java servlets are attracting quite a following. Integrating XML parsing capability into a Java servlet is a highly efficient means of parsing on the server side.

The relationship between Java and XML is very fluid, technically speaking. Even as the specifications that define both XML and Java evolve, other specifications, meant to serve as bridges between the two languages, are appearing. One of the most important of these is the Simple API for XML (SAX). A sort of *de facto* standard—not the product of any particular specification body—SAX provides a set of guidelines for the interfaces parser developers should provide to programmers. SAX applies to all languages, not just Java.

Why rely on Java for XML jobs when so many other tools exist? It's possible to develop XML parsers and display engines in C and C++, and to write XML tools more quickly in languages like Perl and JavaScript. But only Java provides the combination of network-centricity, text processing power and security features that constitutes an ideal environment for picking apart and displaying XML documents. Let's start with Java's native suitability for creating programs that make references to resources across the Internet or smaller networks.

Why XML Needs Java

The difference between XML and a traditional database management system (DBMS) is that XML documents are meant to be portable. They're supposed to be on the Internet—or another network—as super-simple files that are available to all or at least some multi-member community, for access and use.

The thing is, when you have a super-simple file format—XML files are just text files with some special character sequences stuck into them—you have a special kind of architecture. This architecture dictates that the client—the person or, more typically, the piece of software that accesses the XML file—must handle much of the processing responsibility. In contrast, a traditional DBMS puts most of the data-preparation responsibility on the server side. The client or user—again, a person or a piece of software—sends a query to the DBMS, which interprets it and returns the relevant information, usually formatted as a table, the contents of a graphical user interface form, or an HTML page. The software that runs the database does most of the work.

XML files are stupid. They can't do anything. They just sit there, waiting for people to access them. When a client or user does access a particular XML file, all the client gets is a string of text—character data with tags organized in a particular way. There's no way to impose a query upon an XML file directly. If you want to squint at a string of XML data until you locate the data you need, you can, but that's hardly the way to run a railroad.

There's not even an integral way to display XML files attractively. Sure, you can tie style sheets to XML documents and run the assembly through a browser that understands such systems, but it's the browser that does all the work in that equation. The XML file continues to just sit there and be available for download.

If you're going to build applications that center on XML data, you must understand what these programs need to do in order to carry out their work.

Understanding XML Application Architecture

Every program starts with a set of specifications—a customer or user declares that he or she wants a piece of software that does something in particular. In the event that a user wants to see some sort of results that are based upon information extracted from an XML file that's accessed across a network, you can divide the functioning of your application (or at least the XML-centric part of it) into the following four sequential steps:

1. Retrieving the data.
2. Parsing the data.
3. Processing the data.
4. Presenting the data.

Retrieving the Data

To retrieve the data users request the XML files must be accessed and read wherever they are located on the network. In some situations the data drawn from the file must be transmitted securely to the client computer.

Parsing the Data

After the data is drawn from the XML file it must be examined and then assigned relevant variables for the next step. This is called parsing.

Processing the Data

The parsed data must then be processed to supply the user with the information he or she needs. To do this data is run through an appropriate computational processes, for instance, a user might want to know the total number of accidents that occurred in a company's finance and accounting departments last year. The computational process extracts the numerical values—two representing the number of accidents in accounting and three representing the number of accidents in finance—and adds them together to provide the answer to the user.

Presenting the Data

After the data has been retrieve, parsed, and processed, the results must be formatted attractively and presented to the user in such a way that he or she can manipulate them as needed. This format will vary from organization to organization.

In some situations, the data won't be presented to a human being at all. Rather, it will be formatted for communication with and use by another piece of software, which may or may not eventually be presented to a person. Regardless of whether the information is made human-readable, it's always formatted for presentation in some manner or another.

Java in the XML Application Architecture

As it turns out, Java is a competent tool for all the tasks you need to perform in building an XML application. It's good at parsing, processing, and displaying data, and also is simply excellent at accessing files across a network.

Java, the File-Getter

You'd be hard-pressed to find a programming language that exceeds Java's capability to access resources in a networked environment. There's no more need for concern about accessing a remote file than there is about accessing a local resource. In fact, it's sometimes easier to access resources from a distant URL.

The keys to Java's performance as a file-getter are the classes in the `java.net` package (classes are, to put it simply, Java programs). These classes enable the programmer to open a URL, read what's there, and assign those contents to a data structure. Java can deal with streams of data, so it's possible to start dealing with really long XML files before they've completely downloaded. It's also possible to assign a download job to an independent thread, so as not to tie up other processes while the file comes across the network.

TIP

Java also features a number of security-related classes that exist to make it difficult for bad guys to read what travels over a network connection. You can either implement the connection itself securely, or use some sort of public-key encryption scheme to garble the data before it's sent and unscramble it when it's reached its proper destination. It's true that other languages can do this, too, but Java makes the implementation easier on the programmer.

Java, the Parser

Java, as a full-fledged programming language, has considerable capacity to muck around with strings of text. You can use methods of the string object (procedures you can perform on strings, which are sequences of characters) to do dozens of things with strings, including:

- Extracting a substring from a larger string
- Converting a string to a series of pieces and dividing the string at a particular delimiter.
- Chopping the end off of a string.
- Attaching two or more strings together.
- Adjusting the case of characters in a string.
- Replacing substrings with other strings.

And those are just string methods. The latest version of Java includes the `javax.swing.text.html.parser.Parser` object, to which you can specify a DTD and then direct it to an XML file to parse. After the raw XML data is parsed, additional formatting might be needed in order to bring the data into compliance with the requirements of the program being used.

Java, the Processor

This one's a no-brainer. As a full-fledged programming language, Java has the power to do any calculation or processing operation you can think of (or at least any that's possible in any computer language). In those situations for which Java isn't the best tool for a particular type of calculation or processing, it's relatively easy to build references from a Java program to a non-Java resource that can handle the job.

Java, the Displayer

Java also has the capacity to create full-featured user interfaces—far more elaborate than the ones you could create with the HTML form elements available to you in a browser. Plus, Java supports a complete suite of text-formatting and graphics tools. Therefore, if you want to make some data you've extracted from an XML file as attractive as possible, Java has the fonts and other formatting tools you need. What's more, if you plan to "display" your data to another piece of software, Java makes it easy to do that as well.

Examining Parsers

As you might expect, a certain amount of work is done with XML parsers written in Java. It's reasonable to assume that most Java developers will incorporate someone else's pre-written parser into their own code, rather than sweat through the development of their own parsing tools.

This section is an introductory survey. We'll take a look two products currently in development and distribution:

- Ælfred 1.2 from Microstar Software Ltd. is a complete package of Java classes that provides some excellent tools for parsing and processing XML—and, perhaps eventually, SGML—data.

- XJParser from DataChannel Inc. is oriented toward the server side of the client-server system and provides XML data validation against DTD and schemas. Java Project X, from Sun Microsystems, is the name applied to Sun's diverse collection of Java technologies that pertain to XML. These include a set of Java APIs that may someday be incorporated into the standard Java distribution and two kinds of XML parsers, one validating and one non-validating. At present, Java Project X is a "technology release," which means it's official, but not supported like the other Java tools from Sun.
- XML Parser for Java from IBM is widely used and received praise from *Java Report Magazine* in that publication's February 1999 issue. A collection of Java classes that you're free to import and refer to, XML Parser for Java adheres closely to the W3C's XML 1 specification.

Here, we'll use Ælfred for illustration purposes. It does a good job of showing what XML parsers do—the others accomplish pretty much the same thing, with varying degrees of programming ease and processing speed. For quite a bit of technical information about how these parsers stack up competitively, check out David Brownell's test page at `http://home.pacbell.net/david-b/xml/`.

Ælfred

Generally regarded as the best of the client-side XML parsing tools, Microstar's Ælfred provides a powerful XML parsing API in a compact package that's suitable for downloading as part of an applet.

TIP

Ælfred is freely downloadable, complete with source code. Go to `http://www.microstar.com/downloadform-a.html` to download the Zip file that contains everything you need.

Ælfred's makers have put together a demonstration of what their product can do. The demo takes the form of an applet that reads in an XML document from a known URL (in this case, an XML version of John Donne's *Elegy XIX: To His Mistress Going to Bed*) and a DTD from another known URL. It then looks at the XML file and separates the wheat from the chaff, so to speak—it generates output that clearly states what the content of the document is, and how each piece of the content is tagged as an XML element. Take a look at the Ælfred demonstration applet yourself at `http://www.microstar.com/aelfred/browser-test.html`. Figure 21.1 shows what this applet looks like when it runs.

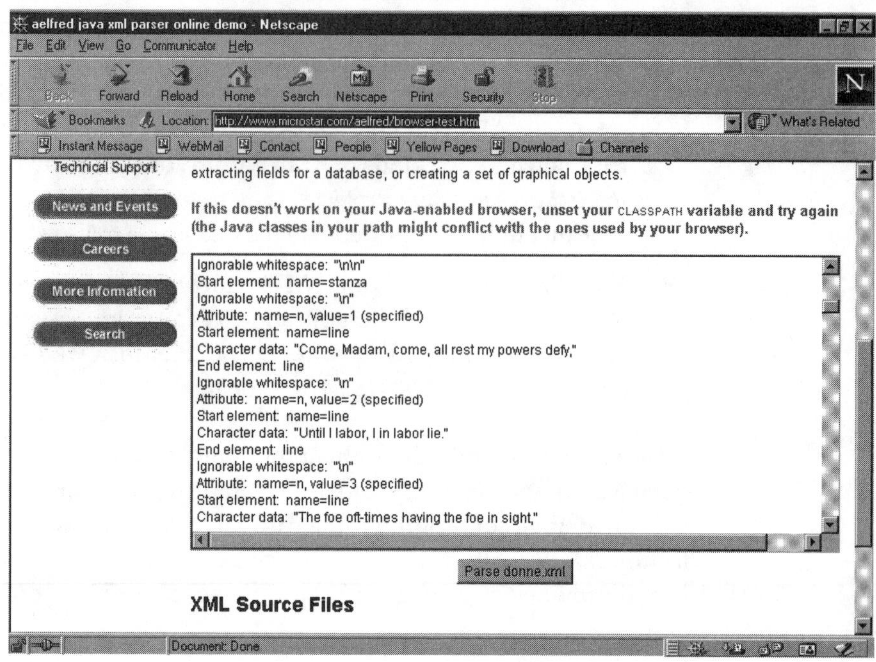

FIGURE 21.1: Ælfred from Microstar Software Ltd.—presented here as an applet—picks out XML tags from an XML file. It's able to identify the bits of information tagged in a particular way.

The Files

This Ælfred system demo operates upon an XML document (`donne.xml`) that is encoded under a simple DTD (`poem.dtd`). There's no style sheet needed here, because Ælfred and its associated applet handle the parsing and display operations.

LISTING 21.1 donne.xml

```
<?xml version="1.0" encoding="UTF-8" standalone="no"?>

<!DOCTYPE poem PUBLIC "-//Megginson//DTD Simple Poem//EN" "poem.dtd">

<poem>

<front>
<title>Elegy XIX: To His Mistress Going to Bed</title>
<author>John Donne, d.1631</author>
<revision-history>
```

```
<item>1997-12-08: XML markup added by David Megginson,
dmeggins@microstar.com</item>
</revision-history>
</front>

<body>

<stanza>
<line n="1">Come, Madam, come, all rest my powers defy,</line>
<line n="2">Until I labor, I in labor lie.</line>
<line n="3">The foe oft-times having the foe in sight,</line>
<line n="4">Is tir'd with standing though he never fight.</line>
<line n="5">Off with that girdle, like heaven's Zone glittering,</line>
<line n="6">But a far fairer world encompassing.</line>
<line n="7">Unpin that spangled breastplate which you wear,</line>
<line n="8">That th'eyes of busy fools may be stopt there.</line>
<line n="9">Unlace your self, for that harmonious chime,</line>
<line n="10">Tells me from you, that now it is bed time.</line>
<line n="11">Off with that happy busk, which I envie,</line>
<line n="12">That still can be, and still can stand so nigh.</line>
<line n="13">Your gown going off, such beautious state reveals,</line>
<line n="14">As when from flow'ry meads th'hills shadow steals.</line>
<line n="15">Off with that wiry Coronet and show</line>
<line n="16">The hairy diadem which on you doth grow:</line>
<line n="17">Now off with those shoes, and then softly tread</line>
<line n="18">In this, love's hallow'd temple, this soft bed.</line>
<line n="19">In such white robes, heaven's Angels us'd to be</line>
<line n="20">Receiv'd by men: thou Angel bringst with thee?</line>
<line n="21">A heaven like Mahomet's Paradice, and though</line>
<line n="22">Ill spirits walk in white, we eas'ly know,</line>
<line n="23">By this these Angels from an evil sprite,</line>
<line n="24">Those set our hairs, but these our flesh upright.</line>
</stanza>

<stanza>
<line n="25">License my roving hands, and let them go,</line>
<line n="26">Behind, before, above, between, below.</line>
<line n="27">O my America! my new-found-land,</line>
<line n="28">My kingdom, safeliest when with one man man'd,</line>
<line n="29">My mine of precious stones: my emperie,</line>
<line n="30">How blest am I in this discovering thee!</line>
<line n="31">To enter in these bonds, is to be free;</line>
```

```
<line n="32">Then where my hand is set, my seal shall be.</line>
</stanza>

<stanza>
<line n="33">Full nakedness! All joys are due to thee,</line>
<line n="34">As souls unbodied, bodies uncloth'd must be,</line>
<line n="35">To taste whole joyes. Gems which you women use</line>
<line n="36">Are like Atlanta's balls, cast in mens views,</line>
<line n="37">That when a fool's eye lighteth on a gem,</line>
<line n="38">His earthly soul may covet theirs, not them:</line>
<line n="39">Like pictures or like books gay coverings made</line>
<line n="40">For lay-men, are all women thus array'd.</line>
<line n="41">Themselves are mystick books, which only wee</line>
<line n="42">(Whom their imputed grace will dignify)</line>
<line n="43">Must see rever'd. Then since that I may know;</line>
<line n="44">As liberally, as to a midwife show</line>
<line n="45">Thyself: cast all, yea, this white linen hence,</line>
<line n="46">There is no penance due to innocence.</line>
</stanza>

<stanza>
<line n="47">To teach thee I am naked first; why than,</line>
<line n="48">What needst thou have more covering then a man?</line>
</stanza>
</body>

</poem>
```

LISTING 21.2 **poem.dtd**

```
<?xml encoding="UTF-8"?>
<!--
**********************************************************
poem.dtd - a simple poetry DTD
Written by David Megginson <dmeggins@microstar.com>
**********************************************************
-->

<!-- Inline mixed content -->
<!ENTITY % inline "#PCDATA|emphasis">

<!-- The whole poem -->
<!ELEMENT poem (front, body)>
```

```
<!-- The front matter -->
<!ELEMENT front (title, author, revision-history)>

<!-- The poem's title -->
<!ELEMENT title (%inline;)*>

<!-- The poem's author(s) -->
<!ELEMENT author (%inline;)*>

<!-- The revision history of the electronic text -->
<!ELEMENT revision-history (item+)>

<!-- An item in the revision history -->
<!ELEMENT item (%inline;)*>

<!-- The main body of the poem -->
<!ELEMENT body (stanza|line)+>

<!-- Lines grouped into a stanza -->
<!ELEMENT stanza (line)+>

<!-- A single metrical line -->
<!ELEMENT line (%inline;)*>
<!ATTLIST line
  n CDATA #IMPLIED>

<!-- An emphasised phrase -->
<!ELEMENT emphasis (%inline;)*>

<!-- end of DTD -->
```

What Ælfred Does

You can use the Ælfred API to parse XML files and identify particular elements, such as strings that are tagged a certain way. Here's how the Ælfred demo applet provides information on some code lines from the XML document:

```
Attribute:  name=n, value=7 (specified)
Start element:  name=line
Character data:  "Unpin that spangled breastplate which you wear,"
End element:  line
Ignorable whitespace:  "\n"
Attribute:  name=n, value=8 (specified)
```

```
Start element:  name=line
Character data:  "That th'eyes of busy fools may be stopt there."
End element:  line
```

Microstar's choice of English poetry is interesting, but instead more important is what the API has enabled them to do in this applet. Each element is clearly labeled with start and end points, and character data is labeled as such. The applet used calls on the Ælfred API to generate this list of information.

Java Project X

Java Project X incorporates technologies that integrate Java with XML. Chief among these pieces of software are two XML parsers, one validating and one non-validating. The other elements of the Java Project X API include classes for editing existing XML-formatted text and writing new strings of XML-formatted text. Sun's XML parsers, particularly the non-validating one, are reputed to be quite fast—though the performance of any parser depends on specific conditions. In many cases, the speed contest seems to be a horse race between Sun's parsers and IBM's XML Parser for Java.

TIP

You'll find Sun's documentation of Java Project X, including a free download link, on their Web site at `http://developer.java.sun.com/developer/products/xml/`.

XJParser

Designed with server-side processing in mind, XJParser from DataChannel Inc. provides a complete suite of XML validation and parsing utilities. It's a reliable, high-speed tool kit for handling many XML transactions. It has a considerable contingent of followers among those who participate in XML programming discussion groups.

XJParser includes capacity to handle eXtensible Style Language (XSL) documents, making it possible for you to take XML text, pick out the information you need, apply formatting information to the resulting string and put out something that's ready for rendering in a Web browser. For what it's worth, a variation of XJParser provides Microsoft IE5 with its XML functionality.

TIP

DataChannel hypes XJParser on its Web site at `http://www.datachannel.com/products/xjparser.html` (you can download the information in Adobe Acrobat format there). If you prefer, you can download XJParser, free of charge, elsewhere on DataChannel's Web site (`http://xdev.datachannel.com/downloads/xjparser/`).

XML Parser for Java

IBM's XML Parser for Java runs on any platform for which there is a Java Virtual Machine that complies with the Java 1.1 or 1.2 ("Java 2") standard. It doesn't run under Java 1.

XML Parser for Java (XML4J, as it is sometimes called) has an interface that allows you to take a string of XML-formatted text, pick the XML tags out of it and use those tags as your keys for extracting the tagged information. It separates you from the need to deal with the text string directly—there's no need to fool with the text string directly. What's more, XML Parser for Java supports the XML Namespaces standard.

TIP

IBM provides all the details of XML Parser for Java, including a link for free download, at `http://www.alphaworks.ibm.com/aw.nsf/xmltechnology/xml+parser+for+java`. There's also an excellent, detailed technical discussion of the software at `http://www.alphaworks.ibm.com/aw.nsf/discussion?ReadForm&/forum/xmlforjava.nsf/discussion?createdocument`.

Regular Expressions in Java

The term regular expression throws some people for a loop. Indeed, the title of the definitive book on the subject, Jeffrey E. F. Freidl's *Mastering Regular Expressions* (O'Reilly, 1997), sounds like the title of a book for people trying to learn the colloquialisms of a language, such as "Hey, man, how is it going?" But in this case, regular expressions refer to a structured way of specifying sequences of characters. For example:

```
/<.*>/
```

This is a regular expression (or **regexp**) that specifies an open angle bracket (<) followed by any number of other characters, followed by a closed angle bracket (>). Doesn't that sound handy? It is, though it's easy to run into trouble with tag languages and regular expressions. Here's the reason why. Say you have a string of XML data that looks like the contents of this line:

```
<BIRD> <BEAK> Long </BEAK> <TOES> 3 </TOES> </BIRD>
```

You decide to parse that string by applying the previous regular expression (`/<.*>/`) to it in order to get the tags. You expect to get six hits, as follows:

- `<BIRD>`
- `<BEAK>`
- `</BEAK>`
- `<TOES>`
- `</TOES>`
- `</BIRD>`

Instead of the expected six, you get only one hit as follows:

```
<BIRD> <BEAK> Long </BEAK> <TOES> 3 </TOES> </BIRD>
```

Do you see why? The whole string matches the regular expression because it begins with a <, contains a bunch of other characters, and ends with a >. The regular expression is satisfied with that match, which isn't what you want. This actually is a pretty tough **regexp** problem to solve—more challenging than is worthwhile in most situations. For this reason, regular expressions usually are combined with string-manipulation methods.

TIP

Surprisingly, Java does not support regular expressions natively. You must import a special library to use them. One of the most highly regarded **regexp** libraries for Java is OROMatcher™, developed and published by Original Reusable Objects, Inc. Check out the company and the product at **http://www.oroinc.com**.

Summary

In this chapter, you've seen what an application needs to do in order to incorporate XML files into its collection of computing resources. You now know that an XML-aware application is in large part a parser, which also has responsibility for accessing files, processing their contents, and displaying results. XML applications also must be able to provide an intelligent and powerful user interface that provides the user with the tools he or she needs. Java excels at all of these jobs and is very well suited to the construction of XML applications. You even got an introduction to Ælfred and XJParser, two ready-built tools you can use to provide your applications with XML capability.

Up Next

In the next chapter, we'll take a look at the JavaScript language as an alternative to Java for building client-side applications for managing the display of XML documents and the individual pieces of data they contain. Although Java is superior to JavaScript in terms of network operations and general richness of features, it's harder to learn and as a consequence, there's a smaller body of people who know how to do advanced work in Java. More people know JavaScript, and it's not a bad tool for developing simpler kinds of XML display and parsing tools.

CHAPTER

TWENTY-TWO

22

Extracting XML Data with JavaScript

- Switching JavaScript among multiple XML documents
- Listing XML elements
- Extracting XML tags from strings of XML data
- Client-side scripting working with server-side pre-processing
- Converting XML data into HTML data using JavaScript for older non-XML-aware browsers
- XML manipulation and display applications

EXtensible Markup Language (XML) is, at its core, a means by which to represent a collection of data—a database—as a highly portable text file. XML tags define pieces of data and their relationships to one another. These tags and the data they characterize are stored in plain-text files with a special filename extension, that is easily accessed by programs on a given computer or passed across a network from one machine to another.

As you've seen, it's also possible to make modifications to XML files in order to make them suitable for human consumption. That is to say, it's possible to teach a machine to look at the nested XML tags and their contents and translate it all into a presentation that makes immediate visual sense. You can use Cascading Style Sheets (CSS) or eXtensible Style Language (XSL) to tell a browser—one capable of understanding the references— how to format the various pieces of data in the XML file.

If you think about it, these means of making XML files human-readable are pretty clunky. Sure, CSS and XSL have considerable capacity to make XML data look pretty. But if we've all learned anything on the Web during the past five years, it's that pretty doesn't cut it. The best sites are those that present plenty of data and enable their visitors to do many different things with it.

But XSL and CSS provide no means of futzing—manipulating—the data and no built-in scripting language with the power that JavaScript, Jscript, and VBScript provide to plain old HTML. It's certainly possible—even easy—to do this on the server side with PerlScript, Java servlets, and other types of programs, but many Web developers regard server-side programming as a nuisance to be avoided wherever possible. Many more people can write scripts for browsers than know Perl, Java, or C. In addition, client-side programming has the advantage of reducing network traffic and server load. There's no need to send a request across the network and make the server do something every time a user decides they want to change the contents of the browser window.

What's needed is a way to combine the computing power of client-side scripting languages with the data-definition power of XML. That's what this chapter is about. Here, you'll find out about some ways to leverage your existing knowledge of JavaScript to better present XML data to the people who view your pages. This is exciting stuff that has a lot to do with how to deal with data on the Web in coming years, both as publishers and as surfers. Let's get going!

Switching among XML Documents

One of the first lessons you learned as you began to explore JavaScript probably had to do with frames, and JavaScript's capacity to manipulate the contents of one frame independently of another frame in the same browser window. You may use this capacity of JavaScript for a variety of purposes. It's often used to provide navigation tools, or to provide a way for users to use one frame as a place to enter values to be used in a calculation, the results of which appear in another frame.

Many people don't know this, but it's possible to display an HTML document in one frame and an XML document in another. Although you can't refer to the XML document from the HTML document and manipulate its contents directly, you can provide controls in one frame that determine which of several XML documents are displayed in the other frame. This provides users with a familiar interface in the form of standard HTML user interface elements (buttons, selection lists, check boxes, and so on) with which to control the display of several XML files. Users appreciate a consistent interface. Such interfaces enable them to quickly find the data they need and provide a certain level of comfort in a data-rich environment that can be alienating.

What the Document Chooser Does

The program written for this exercise—the Document Chooser—consists of two standard HTML files and two XML files. Each of the XML files, in turn, has an associated Document Type Definition (DTD) document and CSS.

- The first of the standard HTML documents, `index.html`, is a frameset master document that defines a display that includes two frames.
- The second HTML document, encoded on the CD-ROM and discussed here as `docChooser.html`, contains a form containing two standard user interface components: a selection list and a button. The selection list enumerates the XML files available for display and allows users to choose from among them; the button is a trigger that implements the choice.
- The two XML documents contain two different kinds of data, each associated with a DTD that defines data relationships and a CSS that dictates cosmetic matters. One of the XML files, `countryList.xml`, contains a list of facts about various countries around the world. The other XML file, `playerList.xml`, contains some statistics about Major League Baseball players.

All these add up to an application that surfers can use to choose between geography data and baseball data. Figure 22.1 shows how the application looks when loaded by Microsoft Internet Explorer 5 (IE5).

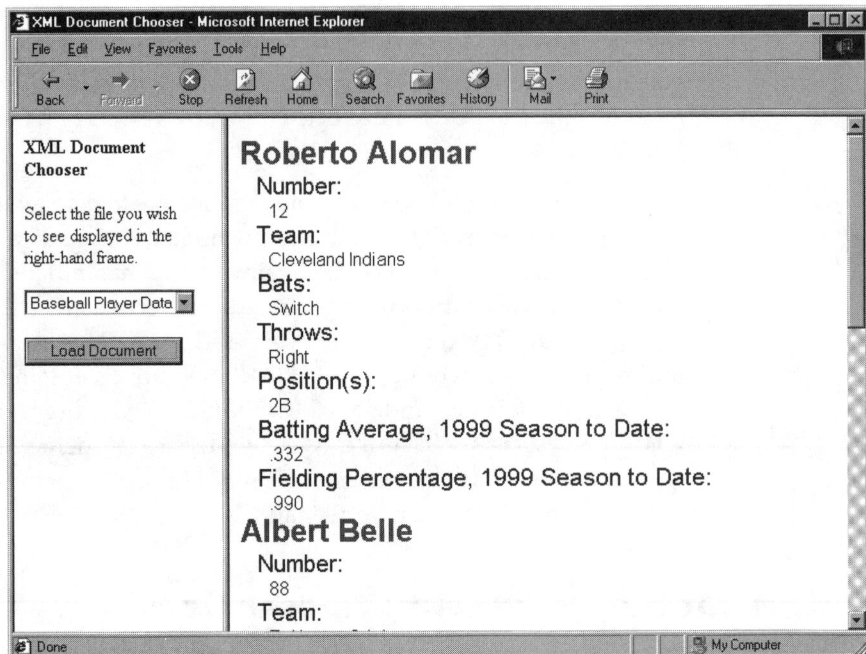

FIGURE 22.1: The Document Chooser application allows you to select which of several XML documents are displayed.

The Files

Here are listings of the files used in the Document Chooser application. There are eight files listed as follows:

`playerList.xml` An XML document that lists information about baseball players

`playerList.dtd` An XML DTD that defines the structure of `playerList.xml`

`playerList.css` A CSS that explains how `playerList.xml` is to be rendered in a browser

`countryList.xml` An XML document that lists information about some of the world's countries

countryList.dtd An XML DTD that defines the structure of countryList.xml

countryList.css A cascading style sheet that explains how countryList.xml is to be rendered in a browser

index.html The over-arching frame-definition document

docChooser.html The HTML document that contains all the interesting JavaScript code

LISTING 22.1 **playerList.xml**

```
<?xml version="1.0"?>
<?xml:stylesheet href="playerList.css" type="text/css"?>
<!DOCTYPE playerCollection SYSTEM "playerList.dtd">
<playerList>
     <player>
        <name>Roberto Alomar</name>
        <label>Number:</label>
        <number> 12 </number>
        <label>Team:</label>
        <team>Cleveland Indians</team>
        <label>Bats:</label>
        <bats> Switch </bats>
        <label>Throws:</label>
        <throws> Right </throws>
        <label>Position(s):</label>
        <position>2B</position>
        <label>Batting Average, 1999 Season to Date:</label>
        <battingAverage> .332 </battingAverage>
        <label>Fielding Percentage, 1999 Season to Date:</label>
        <fieldingPercentage> .990 </fieldingPercentage>
    </player>
    <player>
        <name>Albert Belle</name>
        <label>Number:</label>
        <number> 88 </number>
    <label>Team:</label>
    <team>Baltimore Orioles</team>
    <label>Bats:</label>
    <bats> Right </bats>
    <label>Throws:</label>
```

```
      <throws> Right </throws>
   <label>Position(s):</label>
      <position> LF </position>
      <position> RF </position>
      <position> DH </position>
      <label>Batting Average, 1999 Season to Date:</label>
   <battingAverage> .277 </battingAverage>
      <label>Fielding Percentage, 1999 Season to Date:</label>
   <fieldingPercentage> .978 </fieldingPercentage>
   </player>
   <player>
      <name>Jose Cabrera</name>
      <label>Number:</label>
      <number> 51 </number>
      <label>Team:</label>
      <team>Houston Astros</team>
      <label>Bats:</label>
      <bats> Right </bats>
      <label>Throws:</label>
      <throws> Right </throws>
      <label>Position:</label>
      <position> P </position>
      <label>Earned Run Average, 1999 Season to Date:</label>
      <ERA> 4.26 </ERA>
      <label>Batting Average, 1999 Season to Date:</label><battingAv-
   erage> .000 </battingAverage>
      <label>Fielding Percentage, 1999 Season to Date:</label>
   <fieldingPercentage> 1.000 </fieldingPercentage>
   </player>
</playerList>
```

LISTING 22.2 **playerList.dtd**

```
<!ELEMENT playerList (player+)>
<!ELEMENT player (
     name,
     number,
     team,
     bats,
     throws,
     position+,
     ERA?,
```

```
        battingAverage,
        fieldingPercentage
)
>
<!ELEMENT name (#PCDATA)>
<!ELEMENT number (#PCDATA)>
<!ELEMENT team (#PCDATA)>
<!ELEMENT bats (#PCDATA)>
<!ELEMENT throws (#PCDATA)>
<!ELEMENT position (#PCDATA)>
<!ELEMENT ERA (#PCDATA)>
<!ELEMENT battingAverage (#PCDATA)>
<!ELEMENT fieldingPercentage (#PCDATA)>
```

LISTING 22.3 **playerList.css**

```
name  {
display: block;
font-family: Arial, Helvetica;
font-weight: bold;
font-size: 20pt;
color: "red";
}
number, team, bats, throws, position, ERA, battingAverage, fieldingPer-
     centage {
margin-left: 25;
display: block;
font-family: Arial, Helvetica;
font-size: 12pt;
color: "black";
}
label  {
margin-left: 15;
display: block;
font-family: Arial, Helvetica;
font-size: 16pt;
color: "blue";
}
```

LISTING 22.4 **countryList.xml**

```
<?xml version="1.0"?>
<?xml:stylesheet href="countryList.css" type="text/css"?>
```

```
<!DOCTYPE countryCollection SYSTEM "countryList.dtd">
<countryList>
     <country>
        <officialName>United States of America</officialName>
        <label>Common Names:</label>
        <commonName>United States</commonName>
        <commonName>U.S.</commonName>
        <label>Capital:</label>
        <capital>Washington, D.C.</capital>
        <label>Major Cities:</label>
        <majorCity> Los Angeles </majorCity>
        <majorCity> New York </majorCity>
        <majorCity> Chicago </majorCity>
        <majorCity> Dallas </majorCity>
        <label>Bordering Bodies of Water:</label>
        <borderingBodyOfWater> Atlantic Ocean </borderingBodyOfWater>
     <borderingBodyOfWater> Pacific Ocean </borderingBodyOfWater>
        <borderingBodyOfWater> Gulf of Mexico </borderingBodyOfWater>
        <label>Bordering Countries:</label>
        <borderingCountry> Canada </borderingCountry>
        <borderingCountry> Mexico </borderingCountry>
     </country>
     <country>
        <officialName> Japan </officialName>
        <label>Common Names:</label>
        <commonName> Japan </commonName>
        <label>Capital:</label>
        <capital>Tokyo</capital>
        <label>Major Cities:</label>
        <majorCity> Nagoya </majorCity>
        <majorCity> Osaka </majorCity>
        <majorCity> Kobe </majorCity>
        <label>Bordering Bodies of Water:</label>
        <borderingBodyOfWater> Sea of Japan </borderingBodyOfWater>
        <borderingBodyOfWater> Pacific Ocean </borderingBodyOfWater>
     </country>
     <country>
        <officialName> Republic of Kenya </officialName>
        <label>Common Names:</label>
        <commonName> Kenya </commonName>
        <label>Capital:</label>
        <capital> Nairobi </capital>
        <label>Major Cities:</label>
        <majorCity> Mombasa </majorCity>
```

```
        <majorCity> Lamu </majorCity>
        <majorCity> Malindi </majorCity>
        <majorCity> Kisumu </majorCity>
        <label>Bordering Bodies of Water:</label>
        <borderingBodyOfWater> Indian Ocean </borderingBodyOfWater>
    </country>
</countryList>
```

LISTING 22.5 countryList.dtd

```
    <!ELEMENT countryList (country+)>
    <!ELEMENT country (
        officialName,
        label,
        commonName*,
        label,
        capital,
        label,
        majorCity*,
(
(borderingBodyOfWater+, borderingCountry+)
| (borderingCountry+)
| (borderingBodyOfWater+)
)
    )>
    <!ELEMENT officialName (#PCDATA)>
    <!ELEMENT commonName (#PCDATA)>
    <!ELEMENT capital (#PCDATA)>
    <!ELEMENT majorCity (#PCDATA)>
    <!ELEMENT borderingBodyOfWater (#PCDATA)>
    <!ELEMENT borderingCountry (#PCDATA)>
    <!ELEMENT label (#PCDATA)>
```

LISTING 22.6 countryList.css

```
officialName  {
display: block;
font-family: Arial, Helvetica;
font-weight: bold;
font-size: 20pt;
color: "black";
}
```

```
commonName, capital, majorCity, borderingBodyOfWater, borderingCountry
{
margin-left: 25;
display: block;
font-family: Arial, Helvetica;
font-size: 12pt;
color: "red";
}
label  {
margin-left: 15;
display: block;
font-family: Arial, Helvetica;
font-size: 16pt;
color: "blue";
}
```

LISTING 22.7 index.html

```
<!DOCTYPE HTML PUBLIC "-//W3C//DTD HTML 4.0 Transitional//EN">
<html>
<head>
    <title>XML File Selector</title>
</head>
<frameset COLS="25%,75%">
<frame name="leftFrame" src="docChooser.html">
<frame name="rightFrame" src="">
</frameset>
</html>
```

LISTING 22.8 docChooser.html

```
<!DOCTYPE HTML PUBLIC "-//W3C//DTD HTML 4.0 Transitional//EN">
<html>
<head>
<script language="JavaScript">
function loadFile ()
     {
     var filename
     var selectionValue
     selectionValue = document.forms[0].selectList.selectedIndex
     filename = document.forms[0].selectList
        .options[selectionValue].value
     parent.rightFrame.location = filename
```

```
    }
</script>
</head>
<body>
<H4>XML File Chooser</H4>
<P>Select the file you wish to see displayed in the right-hand frame.
<FORM NAME="selectForm">
<P>
<SELECT NAME="selectList">
<OPTION VALUE="countryList/countryList.xml"> Country Data
<OPTION VALUE="playerList/playerList.xml"> Baseball Player Data
</SELECT>
<P>
<INPUT TYPE="BUTTON" VALUE="Load Document" onClick="loadFile()">
</FORM>
</body>
</html>
```

What's Going On in the Document Chooser

The basic idea of the Document Chooser is that there's a two-framed browser window. The right frame contains an XML document; the left frame contains user interface elements with which you can chose from among available XML documents. The document you choose on the left is displayed on the right.

The button in Document Chooser is defined by this line:

```
<INPUT TYPE="BUTTON" VALUE="Load Document" onClick="loadFile()">
```

The `onClick` event handler calls the `loadFile()` function, which then looks at the selection list (by examining the `selectedIndex` property of the list), and then determines which of the options is selected and extracts the `value` property of the selected option.

As it happens, the value properties of the options are set equal to strings that define relative URLs—the locations of the two XML files in their respective subdirectories. The program plugs these values into this statement:

```
parent.rightFrame.location = filename
```

The contents of the right frame are then adjusted accordingly.

Listing XML Elements

Any program that will be extracting XML information must be able to identify and extract XML tags. The program you'll write in this section does exactly that with JavaScript. It examines a string of XML-delimited text and identifies the XML tags that appear in it. It then makes a list of all unique XML tags and writes them to the browser window for users to examine.

Standing alone this program lacks much immediate practical value, but the code contained here performs a function that will prove useful in any XML-centric JavaScript application. You'll be able to build all kinds of applications upon this base. Truth be told, Tag Lister is not a complete client-side solution. It can't be, because a characteristic of JavaScript programs—a limitation or a security feature, depending upon how you look at it—is that they can't open files at a particular URL and perform operations on their contents. For that reason, you'll see that this program incorporates a workaround that requires some server-side activity. Really, all you need to implement is a straightforward server-side include (SSI). Regardless of that necessity, the load this program places on the server is far less than that imposed by a similarly functional application based on back-and-forth Common Gateway Interface (CGI) activity.

What Tag Lister Does

Tag Lister consists of a single HTML file with a lot of embedded JavaScript. If you prefer, you can isolate most of the JavaScript code in a JavaScript library (`.js`) file and refer to it via a <SCRIPT> tag with a SRC attribute. Figure 22.2 shows what Tag Lister looks like when running in Microsoft Internet Explorer.

FIGURE 22.2:

The Tag Lister application looks at a string of XML data and presents a list of the XML elements it contains.

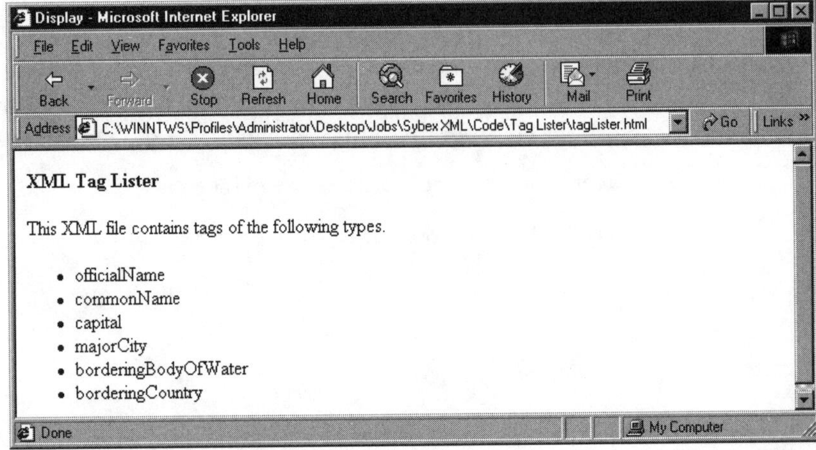

The File

There's only one file involved in Tag Lister. It's called `tagLister.html` and appears in this chapter's Tag Lister subdirectory on the companion CD-ROM.

LISTING 22.9 `tagLister.html`

```
<!DOCTYPE HTML PUBLIC "-//W3C//DTD HTML 4.0 Transitional//EN">
<html>
<head>
     <title>Display</title>
<script LANGUAGE="JavaScript">
/*The global variable containing the XML string we'll examine. Nor
   mally, global variables are to be avoided. But here, it's the
   easiest way to approach the problem, since it would be easy to
   have a server-side script include the contents of the XML file as
   a single line here. */

gXMLString = " <officialName> United States of America </officialName>
   <commonName> United States </commonName> <commonName> U.S. </com-
   monName> <capital> Washington, D.C. </capital> <majorCity> Los
   Angeles </majorCity>   <majorCity> New York </majorCity>
   <majorCity> Chicago </majorCity> <majorCity> Dallas </majorCity>
     <borderingBodyOfWater> Atlantic Ocean </borderingBodyOfWater>
     <borderingBodyOfWater> Pacific Ocean </borderingBodyOfWater>
     <borderingBodyOfWater> Gulf of Mexico </borderingBodyOfWater>
     <borderingCountry> Canada </borderingCountry>
     <borderingCountry> Mexico </borderingCountry>"
function findTagsPresent()
     {
     var arrayOfPieces = new Array()
     arrayOfPieces = gXMLString.split(" ")
     numberOfPieces = arrayOfPieces.length
     var tagsPresent = new Array()
     var tagsPresentCounter
     tagsPresentCounter = 0
     for (i=0; i<numberOfPieces; i++)
        {
        if ((arrayOfPieces[i].indexOf("<") == 0) &&
     (arrayOfPieces[i].indexOf(">") == (arrayOfPieces[i].length-1)) &&
     (arrayOfPieces[i].indexOf("</") == -1))
           // If that's the case, then we've found an opening tag.
           {
           var arrayLength
```

```
            arrayLength = tagsPresent.length
            var foundIt
            foundIt = false
            for (j=0; j<arrayLength; j++)
               {
                  if (tagsPresent[j] == arrayOfPieces[i])
                     {
                     foundIt = true
                     break
                     }
               }
            if (foundIt != true)
              //And if that's the case, it's not already in tagsPresent

               {

               tagsPresent[tagsPresentCounter] = arrayOfPieces[i]
               tagsPresentCounter++
               }
            }
         }
      return tagsPresent
      }
   function writeListOfTagsPresent()
      {
      var listOfTags
      listOfTags = findTagsPresent()
      listLength = listOfTags.length
      document.write("<UL>")
      for (i=0; i<listLength; i++)
         {
         document.write("<LI>")
         var tagStringLength
         tagStringLength = listOfTags[i].length
         var strippedTagString
         strippedTagString = listOfTags[i].substring(1,
         (tagStringLength-1))
         document.write(strippedTagString)
         }
      document.write("</UL>")
      }
   </script>
   </head>
   <body>
```

```
<H4>XML Tag Lister</H4>
<P>This XML file contains tags of the following types.
<SCRIPT LANGUAGE="JavaScript">
writeListOfTagsPresent()
</SCRIPT>
</body>
</html>
```

What's Going On in Tag Lister

There are four distinct operations that must happen in Tag Lister:

- A server-side program must insert the XML string into the file.
- XML tags must be identified in the XML string.
- Only one of each kind of XML tag must be assembled into a list of tags.
- The list must be written to the browser window.

Let's take a look at how each of these operations is done.

The Server's Job

This solution does not operate entirely on the client side because of JavaScript's inability to read data from files in any way. That would be the ideal way to get XML data into this document, but it's not possible.

The workaround this Tag Lister uses requires a bit of intervention on the server side. The idea is that when this document is put together by the server and sent out to the browser, the assembly program (Perl, PHP, LiveScript, or whatever) must insert a single line in the code. In this case, it's best to operate as though this line of code was inserted as a server-side include (SSI):

```
gXMLString = " <officialName> United States of America </officialName>
   <commonName> United States </commonName> <commonName> U.S. </common
   Name> <capital> Washington, D.C. </capital> <majorCity> Los Angeles
   </majorCity> <majorCity> New York </majorCity> <majorCity> Chicago
   </majorCity> <majorCity> Dallas </majorCity> <borderingBodyOfWater>
   Atlantic Ocean </borderingBodyOfWater> <borderingBodyOfWater> Pacific
   Ocean </borderingBodyOfWater> <borderingBodyOfWater> Gulf of Mexico
   </borderingBodyOfWater> <borderingCountry> Canada </borderingCountry>
   <borderingCountry> Mexico </borderingCountry>"
```

This code is a section of an XML document, strung together as one big string, surrounded by quotes and preceded by a JavaScript assignment statement (`gXMLString=`). That's the only line the server needs to insert in order for Tag Lister to work. You may wonder what all those spaces are for. There's a space at the beginning of the long string and spaces before and after each of the XML tags in the string (except the concluding one). Those spaces exist to support the method Tag Lister uses to parse the string. Ideally, they wouldn't be necessary, as they're not required by the XML specification (a server-side program reading from an XML file would have to insert the spaces). The solution presented by Tag Lister requires them and so imposes a bit of extra server processing overhead.

Finding Opening Tags

One of the first things that happen when `tagLister.html` loads is that the JavaScript interpreter makes a call to `writeListOfTagsPresent()`. True enough, this function writes the list of tags present in the XML string—more on that in a minute—but first it has to figure out what tags exist in the string. It delegates that task to another function, `findTagsPresent()`.

That function, `findTagsPresent()`, takes the huge XML string and breaks it up, like this:

```
arrayOfPieces = gXMLString.split(" ")
```

NOTE The `String.split()` method divides a string into the elements of an array, using the contents of the parentheses as a delimiter (that's why the XML string must contain spaces). The delimeters are deleted by `String.split()`—they're not anywhere in the resultant array.

The `findTagsPresent()` loops through the array of XML string pieces and applies an `if` statement to each element in order to identify the elements that are opening XML tags (there's no reason to search for closing tags, too). The `if` statement looks like this:

```
if ((arrayOfPieces[i].indexOf("<") == 0) &&
   (arrayOfPieces[i].indexOf(">") == (arrayOfPieces[i].length-1)) &&
   (arrayOfPieces[i].indexOf("</") == -1))
```

The statement has three parts. The three conditions, all of which must be met in order for the array element to be recognized as an opening tag, are as follows:

- `(arrayOfPieces[i].indexOf("<") == 0)`. The first character is a "<" character.
- `(arrayOfPieces[i].indexOf(">") == (arrayOfPieces[i].length-1)`. The last character is a ">" character.

- `(arrayOfPieces[i].indexOf("</") == -1)`. The sequence "</" does not appear anywhere in the element.

If all three of the preceding conditions are true, then the loop has found an opening XML element, but is it a new opening element?

Verifying the Uniqueness of Tags

After identifying an XML opening tag, the execution of `findTagsPresent()` drops into another loop that compares the newly found tag to what's already in the `tagsPresent` array. Again, it does the comparison with a `for` loop.

This time, the variable `j` indexes the loop, because it's already inside a loop indexed by `i`. One by one, the loop compares the elements of `tagsPresent` to `arrayOfPieces[i]`, which is the string that was earlier identified as an opening XML tag. If the new string is found to match one of the elements in `tagsPresent`, the Boolean variable `foundIt` becomes `true`, execution breaks out of the loop, and the next element of the XML string is investigated.

However, if a match is never found, the program concludes that a new tag has been found. It adds the new element to the `tagsPresent` array and `tagsPresentCounter` is incremented. The `i`-indexed loop then proceeds to the next piece of the XML string.

Writing the Tags to the Document

When `findTagsPresent()` returns its array of unique XML tags, `writeListOfTagsPresent()` proceeds to loop through the array and write each element to the document as elements in an unordered list. But first, it strips the "<" and "/>" character sequences from the strings.

The trick to that operation is another method of the String object—`String.substring`. Here's the relevant line:

```
strippedTagString = listOfTags[i].substring(1, (tagStringLength-1))
```

TIP

The `String.substring` method works by taking a string and picking a substring from it based on character index values. The first index value is the start of the substring; the second index value defines its end. Characters in a string are indexed starting with zero. Furthermore, the character designated by the first index value is included in the resultant substring. The character designated by the second index value is not.

Selecting XML Elements to Display

You can put Tag Lister to use by making it a utility function in a larger program that allows you to tailor the display of an XML document. Say you knew what kind of information is in a document. You could then choose portions of that information to display on an *a la carte* basis. This would make the difference between a huge document and a smaller, better-tailored document. This section shows how to put Tag Lister to practical use in that way.

The program covered in this section, Display Controller, takes a string containing data formatted as a series of XML elements (the illustration uses a subset of the `countryList.xml` data used in the Document Chooser application). It identifies the elements contained in the string and presents them as a list of tags, each adjacent to a familiar HTML checkbox element in one frame of a two-frame browser window. Display Controller asks which of the elements users wish to see. Users then check each of the elements they wants to see displayed, click a trigger button, and the JavaScript program picks out the desired elements, formats them with HTML tags, and sends the resulting document to the other frame for display.

The advantage of Display Controller is that users may be faced with an enormous amount of data in an XML document, only a small amount of which they care about at a given time. Rather than make users scroll through a long list of unimportant data—however nicely formatted—this application allows users to pick out only those elements that meet their current needs. In effect, this program provides the human XML user to derive some of the same benefits from the language's structured formatting as are already enjoyed by computer program users (i.e. specifying the data you want, clicking the trigger, and there you go). Information provided, problem solved—and without a million trips to the server for trivial parsing jobs.

One of the side benefits of the Display Controller is that it translates XML data into HTML data, which means it and the output it creates may be interpreted and displayed accurately by older browsers that have no idea of what XML is or how to display it.

What Display Controller Does

Display Controller consists of two files, one trivial and one rather elaborate. Here they are:

- `index.html` is a *frameset master* document that defines the frames displayed in the browser window. It sets up two vertical frames, the left one containing the HTML (and JavaScript) document that appears next in this list; the other (occupying most of the window) initially blank and later filled with XML-derived data.

- The other document is the big one. Called `controller.html`, this file contains the user interface for selecting which elements are to be displayed, as well as a trigger button that's used to create or change the displayed XML-derived data.

You can encapsulate most of `controller.html` in an independent JavaScript library file (a `.js` file) if you like—the JavaScript and HTML appear together here for purposes of illustration.

When you load `index.html` in your browser, you see something like what appears in Figure 22.3.

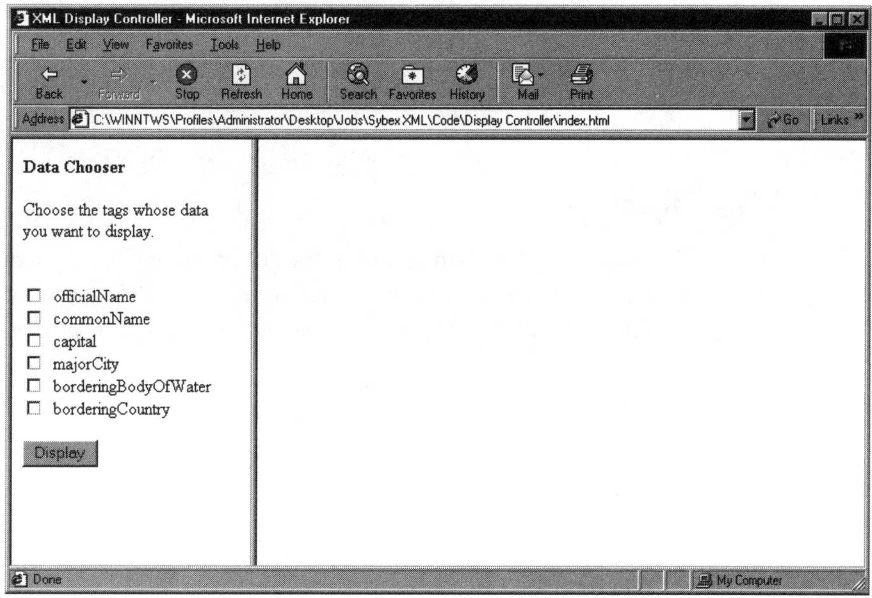

FIGURE 22.3:

This is what Display Controller looks like when you initially load it. Note the XML element names listed in the left-hand frame.

Then, when you choose some tags and click the Display button, you see a display like the one in Figure 22.4.

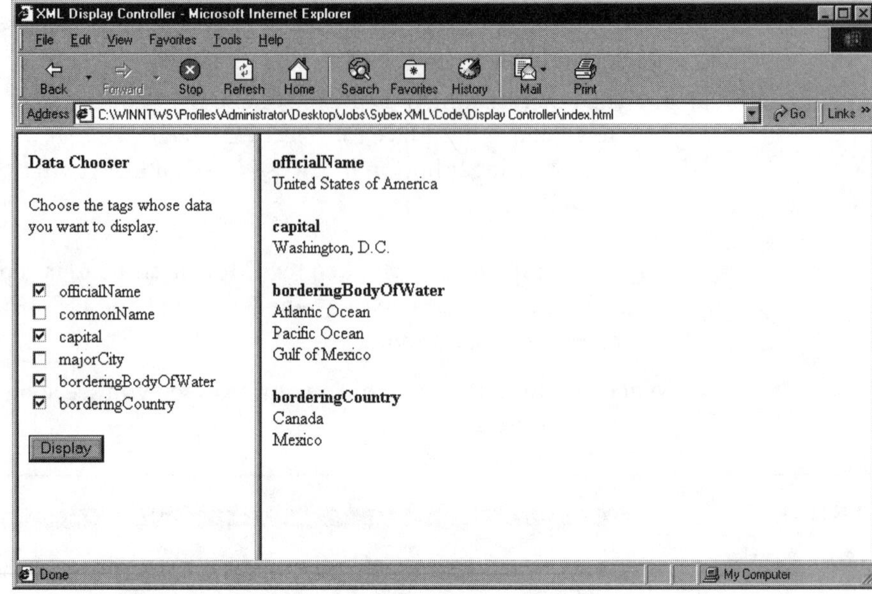

FIGURE 22.4:

This is what Display Controller looks like after you've chosen some XML elements from the list and clicked the Display button. You're free to select more check boxes and uncheck others to alter the displayed data.

The Files

The following are listings of the files used in the Display Controller application. There are two. The file `index.html` is a frame-definition document. The other file, `controller.html`, is where all the interesting XML-parsing JavaScript is.

LISTING 22.10 `index.html`

```
<!DOCTYPE HTML PUBLIC "-//W3C//DTD HTML 4.0 Transitional//EN">
<html>
<head>
    <title>XML Display Controller</title>
</head>
<frameset COLS="25%,75%">
<frame name="leftFrame" src="controller.html">
<frame name="rightFrame" src="">
</frameset>
</html>
```

LISTING 22.11 controller.html

```
<!DOCTYPE HTML PUBLIC "-//W3C//DTD HTML 4.0 Transitional//EN">
<html>
<head>
<script LANGUAGE="JavaScript">
/*
The global variable containing the XML string we'll examine. Normally,
     global variables are to be avoided. But here, it's the easiest way
     to approach the problem, since it would be easy to have a server-
     side script include the contents of the XML file as a single line
     here.
*/
gXMLString = " <officialName> United States of America </officialName>
     <commonName> United States </commonName> <commonName> U.S. </com-
     monName> <capital> Washington, D.C. </capital> <majorCity> Los
     Angeles </majorCity> <majorCity> New York </majorCity> <majorCity>
     Chicago </majorCity> <majorCity> Dallas </majorCity> <bordering-
     BodyOfWater> Atlantic Ocean </borderingBodyOfWater> <borderingBody-
     OfWater> Pacific Ocean </borderingBodyOfWater> <borderingBodyOfWater>
     Gulf of Mexico </borderingBodyOfWater> <borderingCountry> Canada
     </borderingCountry> <borderingCountry> Mexico </borderingCountry>"
function findTagsPresent()
     {
     var arrayOfPieces = new Array()
     arrayOfPieces = gXMLString.split(" ")
     numberOfPieces = arrayOfPieces.length
     var tagsPresent = new Array()
     var tagsPresentCounter
     tagsPresentCounter = 0
     for (i=0; i<numberOfPieces; i++)
        {
        if ((arrayOfPieces[i].indexOf("<") == 0) &&
     (arrayOfPieces[i].indexOf(">") == (arrayOfPieces[i].length-1)) &&
     (arrayOfPieces[i].indexOf("</") == -1))
           // If that's the case, then we've found an opening tag.
           {
           var arrayLength
           arrayLength = tagsPresent.length
           var foundIt
           foundIt = false
           for (j=0; j<arrayLength; j++)
              {
```

```
                    if (tagsPresent[j] == arrayOfPieces[i])
                      {
                      foundIt = true
                      break
                      }
                  }
                if (foundIt != true)
                  //And if that's the case, it's not already in tagsPresent
                  {
                  tagsPresent[tagsPresentCounter] = arrayOfPieces[i]
                  tagsPresentCounter++
                  }
                }
              }
            return tagsPresent
            }
        function writeListOfTagsPresentWithCheckboxes()
            {
            var listOfTags
            listOfTags = findTagsPresent()
            var listLength
            listLength = listOfTags.length
            var numberOfCheckBoxes
            numberOfCheckBoxes = 0
            for (i=0; i<listLength; i++)
              {
              var tagStringLength
              tagStringLength = listOfTags[i].length
              var strippedTagString
              strippedTagString = listOfTags[i].substring(1,
            (tagStringLength-1))
              document.write("<BR>")
              document.write("<INPUT TYPE='checkbox' NAME='box" + i + "'
            VALUE='" + strippedTagString + "'>  ")
              document.write(strippedTagString)
              numberOfCheckBoxes++
              }

            document.write("<P>")
            document.write("<INPUT TYPE='button' value='Display' onClick='dis
              playSelectedXMLData(" + numberOfCheckBoxes + ")'>")
            }
```

```
function contentsTaggedThisWay(tagString)
     {
     var arrayOfPieces = new Array()
     arrayOfPieces = gXMLString.split(" ")
     var numberOfPieces
     numberOfPieces = arrayOfPieces.length
     var taggedData
     taggedData = ""
     var i
     i = 0
     while (i<numberOfPieces)
        {
        if (arrayOfPieces[i] == ("<" + tagString + ">"))
           {
           var foundEndTag
           taggedData += "<BR>"
           foundEndTag = false
           var j
           j = 1
           while (!(foundEndTag))
              {
              if (arrayOfPieces[(i + j)] == ("</" + tagString + ">"))
                 {
                 foundEndTag = true
                 }
                    else
                       {
                       taggedData += arrayOfPieces[(i + j)]
                       taggedData += " "
                       j++
                       }
              }
           }
        i++
        }
     return taggedData
     }

function displaySelectedXMLData(numberOfBoxes)
     {
     var stringToWrite
     stringToWrite = ""
```

```
        parent.rightFrame.location.reload()
        stringToWrite = "<HTML> <HEAD> </HEAD> <BODY>"
        var i
        i=0
        while (i<numberOfBoxes)
           {
           currentBoxName = "box" + i
           if (document.selectionForm.elements[currentBoxName].checked)
              {
              stringToWrite += "<P><B>" + document.selectionForm.ele-
        ments[currentBoxName].value + "</B>"
              stringToWrite += contentsTaggedThisWay(document.selection-
        Form.elements[currentBoxName].value)
              }
           i++
           }
        stringToWrite += "</BODY> </HTML>"
        parent.rightFrame.document.write(stringToWrite)
        }
</script>
</head>
<body>
<H4>Data Chooser</H4>
<P>Choose the tags whose data you want to display.
<FORM NAME="selectionForm">
<SCRIPT LANGUAGE="JavaScript">
writeListOfTagsPresentWithCheckboxes()
</SCRIPT>
<P>
</FORM>
</body>
</html>
```

What's Going On in Display Controller

There's a whole lot going on in Display Controller. In summary:

- The server must insert a properly formatted XML string into the HTML/JavaScript document.
- The unique elements must be identified and written as an HTML form that includes check boxes and a trigger button.

- There must be a mechanism that reacts to a click of the trigger button. This mechanism must be able to identify which of the check boxes are selected at the time of the trigger click, then go back to the XML string and pick out pieces of data that are tagged that way. Those pieces must then be formatted as HTML and written to the right-hand frame of the browser window.

There are some shortcomings to Display Controller that you'll be able to identify and may want to try to correct. Let's look at the processes individually.

The Server's Job

As is the case with Tag Lister, Display Controller requires the server to insert a carefully formatted line of XML-tagged text into the document. In this case, the line the server supposedly inserted is:

```
gXMLString = " <officialName> United States of America </officialName>
    <commonName> United States </commonName> <commonName> U.S. </com-
    monName> <capital> Washington, D.C. </capital> <majorCity> Los
    Angeles </majorCity> <majorCity> New York </majorCity> <majorCity>
    Chicago </majorCity> <majorCity> Dallas </majorCity> <bordering-
    BodyOfWater> Atlantic Ocean </borderingBodyOfWater> <bordering-
    BodyOfWater> Pacific Ocean </borderingBodyOfWater> <borderingBody-
    OfWater> Gulf of Mexico </borderingBodyOfWater> <borderingCountry>
    Canada </borderingCountry> <borderingCountry> Mexico </bordering-
    Country>"
```

Again, the quotes and spaces are important.

In point of fact, the integration of server-side processing into this application may be a good thing. It enables you to do coarse XML parsing on the server side and leave fine display adjustments for JavaScript to perform on the client side. In this case, you can assume that some other form—one that interacted with the server—enabled users to select the United States from a list of countries for which data were available. Now, it's up to this JavaScript program to enable users to parse the United States data further, without needing to refer to any server resources.

Listing the Elements and Writing the Form

Very little straight HTML gets written to the browser window—just the heading, the instructions, and the opening and closing form tags. The most important parts of the Display Controller interface—the check boxes and the trigger button—are written by a function called `writeListOfTagsPresentWithCheckboxes()`.

This function has several duties to perform before it can carry out its interface-writing job. It must examine the XML string, identify the opening XML tags it contains, and make a list that contains exactly one copy of each element. It must then take that list and format it as a series of HTML check boxes in a form, then follow that list of labeled check boxes with a trigger button.

The process of preparing and writing the list of labeled check boxes is largely identical to the process described in the section of this chapter on Tag Lister. Refer back to that for an explanation of how the list is compiled and written.

The differences have to do with the checkbox elements themselves. Each check box is written to the page with this line:

```
document.write("<INPUT TYPE='checkbox' NAME='box" + i + "' VALUE='"
+ strippedTagString + "'>  ")
```

The neat thing about that line is the `NAME` attribute that's written into the HTML. Each box has a unique `NAME` attribute; the names take the form of `boxi`, where `i` is a number zero or greater. Each check box's HTML definition also includes a `VALUE` attribute that's set equal to `strippedTagString`, which is (as was the case in Tag Lister) the name of a unique XML element in the XML string, without the opening "<" and closing ">" characters.

Reacting to the Trigger Button

The Display Controller user interface has successfully written to the left-hand frame of the browser window. Now, it's important to allow users to check as many or as few check boxes as they wish, then click the trigger button to parse and format the XML string properly for display in the right-hand frame. Checking and unchecking boxes is easy enough, and an event handler is attached to the display button to trigger a response to a user click there.

The event handler calls the `displaySelectedXMLElements()` function, sending the number of check boxes in the form as a parameter (this stems from the names given to the check boxes by the loop that wrote them).

One of the first things this function does is reset the right-hand frame to its original state (which is to say, blank). Here's how that's done:

```
parent.rightFrame.location.reload()
```

That resets the right frame to the contents it had when its parent, `index.html`, was loaded.

The function also sets up a string called stringToWrite. Since this is what's eventually written to the right-hand frame, it's initially endowed with opening HTML tags—the usual boilerplate.

Then, execution drops into a while loop with which the set of check boxes in the left-hand frame is examined. Once it's in the loop, the first thing the program does is reconstruct a checkbox name using the counter, i. It adds i to the word box, giving us (in the first iteration, anyway) box0.

The loop uses that name to examine a particular check box in the list, using this statement:

```
if (document.selectionForm.elements[currentBoxName].checked)
```

That statement is true if the current check box contains a check. If that's not the case—if the check box is not checked—the index i is incremented and the loop investigates the next check box. On the other hand, if the statement is true and, therefore, the check box in question does contain a check, some extra work is done.

Specifically, stringToWrite has a heading appended to it—the heading is just the name of the XML element specified by the current check box, formatted with a <P> tag and <B>...</B> tags. Here's the line that does that:

```
stringToWrite += "<P><B>" + document.selectionForm.elements[currentBox
   Name].value + "</B>"
```

Below that header, we want to list all bits of data in the XML string that are defined by such tags. That involves a call to another function, contentsTaggedThisWay(), whose returned value is appended to stringToWrite. Here's the call:

```
stringToWrite += contentsTaggedThisWay(document.selectionForm.elements
   [currentBoxName].value)
```

In the contentsTaggedThisWay() line of code, you'll see a whole lot of string and array manipulation, some of which you've seen before. As in Tag Lister and earlier in Display Controller, contentsTaggedThisWay() breaks the XML string into a series of array elements with the String.split() method, keyed on spaces. contentsTaggedThisWay() then examines those array elements to see if they match the tag name set to it by displaySelectedXMLElements().

The comparison process uses a pair of nested while loops, each containing an if statement. The outermost while loop runs through the elements in arrayOfPieces, which is the array that resulted from splitting the big XML string at the spaces. The first thing it does with each piece is determine whether it's an opening tag. Here's the test:

```
if (arrayOfPieces[i] == ("<" + tagString + ">"))
```

If that's true—if an opening tag has been found—the program sets up a nested `while` loop, indexed by the variable `j`. It also adds an HTML <BR> tag to `taggedData`, the string that contains the list of data marked with the relevant tags (and which, eventually, the function returns).

The `j`-indexed `while` loop starts with `j` equal to `1`, and checks to see whether `arrayOfPieces` element `i+j` is a matching closing tag. The test looks like this:

```
if (arrayOfPieces[(i + j)] == ("</" + tagString + ">"))
```

If it is, the internal `while` loop breaks (as a result of `foundEndTag` becoming `true`) and the external `while` loop proceeds to investigate the next element in `arrayOfPieces`. If the if statement above doesn't find a closing tag, whatever it does find is appended to `taggedData`.

TIP

Note that an extra space also is appended to `taggedData` at this point. That's to allow for multi-word tagged data, such as `Los Angeles`. The spaces between those words get cut out by `String.split`, too.

Eventually, `contentsTaggedThisWay()` returns a string containing data extracted from the XML string, delimited with line-breaking <BR> tags. `displaySelectedXMLElements()` appends this string to `stringToWrite`, which ultimately—after all the check boxes have been investigated and the tags denoted by the checked ones run through `contentsTaggedThisWay()`—is written to the right-hand frame.

Users are free to check or uncheck the boxes they chose and then click the trigger button to see the chosen data displayed. The program can handle this.

What's Wrong with Display Controller

There's plenty the matter with Display Controller. For one thing, it's dependent upon having spaces in the XML string. The spaces must be created and patched into place on the server side, taking up valuable processing cycles there. A better version of this program would use a different method—probably something that involved the `String.substring()` method—to extract the tags without relying upon extra server-side pre-processing of the included XML string.

Second, this program has no capacity to deal with nested XML elements. Although it doesn't matter in this example, it's not any sort of stretch to imagine a situation in which a pair of matched XML tags contains another pair of matched XML tags. The `<capital>`...`</capital>` tags might contain `<mayor>`...`</mayor>` tags or something. Such a situation would break this program in its present form.

Third, the program won't work with blind (single-part) XML tags. It depends upon getting tags in pairs. Blind XML tags are legal under the XML specification and may be included in a DTD. A program like this ought to be able to deal with them.

Summary

A great deal of JavaScript's client-side processing power was brought to bear on XML problems in this chapter. Three programs were created—one that used a JavaScript-powered HTML interface to switch among XML documents, another that extracted a list of tags from an XML string, and a third that enabled the user to manipulate the display of XML data in something approximating real time. Along the way, processing textual data with JavaScript was discussed as well as a bit about how server-side routines can combine forces with client-side processing.

Up Next

Part VII: *XML Applications* introduces you to the structure and function of XML, including the Channel Definition Format and many of the most useful XML applications. Chapter 23: "Standards, Applications, and Vocabularies" dissects the complicated framework of standards and the organizations that determine and enforce them.

PART VII

XML Applications

CHAPTER

TWENTY-THREE

23

Standards, Applications, and Vocabularies

- What are standards?
- Which organizations are standards bodies?
- How do standards bodies create standards?
- De facto standards
- What are applications and vocabularies and how do they differ?

Part I introduced the terms standards, applications, and vocabularies and subsequent chapters have made liberal use of them. But what do they really mean? And what are the differences between them? This chapter examines the specific meanings of these terms within the context of XML.

Standards and Standards Bodies

What is a standard? A *standard* is generally perceived as a specification, which is controlled, and under the jurisdiction of an appropriate *standards body*. But what is an appropriate standards body? Are *accredited standards bodies* the only organizations that can change a *specification* into a *standard*? And what are the names of these organizations?

According to the Web site of the International Organization for Standardization (ISO), the following are accredited international standards granting bodies:

- American National Standards Institute (ANSI)
- Association for Information and Image Management (AIIM)
- Data Interchange Standards Association (DISA)
- European Telecommunications Standards Institute (ETSI)
- International Federation for Information Processing (IFIP)

It seems, then, that these bodies are the only ones recognized as producing real standards. Or are they? If you check out the standards bodies' Web sites, some of these are affiliated with standards granting bodies and some are actual granters of standards. Furthermore, this list is not comprehensive. Another place to look is the Web site of the European Commission's Open Information Interchange *(OII).* The OII lists more Standards Organizations. It uses the word "formal" to mean accredited:

- European Broadcasting Union (EBU)
- European Board for EDIFACT Standardization (EBES)
- ICT Standards Board (ICTSB)

- International Electrotechnical Commission (IEC) Web Server
- ISO/IEC JTC1 SC24Computer graphics (ISO subcommittee)
- International Telecommunication Union (ITU)
- National Institute for Science and Technology (NIST)

NOTE This list only contains organizations not listed by ISO.

You may have noticed by now that the World Wide Web Consortium (W3C), the Internet Engineering Task Force (IETF), and a number of other organizations that the Internet community views as standards bodies are not on either list. Does this mean we've been making a mistake all this time? The OII refers to organizations, such as the W3C, as *Consortia.* However, it lists them under the heading International and Regional Standards Organizations. If you are beginning to feel confused, you are not alone. In fact, if you were to engage in exhaustive research you would find a number of different lists. Also you'll find that not all standards-related sites even differentiate between *accredited* or *formal* standards bodies and *informal* standards bodies like consortia.

It appears then, that the technology world at large regards both accredited standards bodies and informal standards bodies as being able to turn specifications into what are commonly referred to as standards. In other words even the most respected resource Web sites, with the exceptions of the consortia themselves, use *standard* and *recommendation* almost synonymously.

NOTE Note that the informal standards bodies themselves make the distinction between approved recommendation and formal standard. See the W3C Process Document, `http://www.w3.org/Consortium/Process/`.

The following is a list of consortia that are often referred to as standards bodies. You may be surprised to see names that you thought belonged to formal standards granting bodies.

- European Committee on Standardization (CEN)
- International Commission on Illumination (CIE)

- Digital Audio-Visual Council
- European Telecommunications Standards Institute (ETSI)
- European Association for the Co-ordination of Consumer Representation in Standardization (ANEC)
- Internet Engineering Task Force (IETF)
- International Federation for Information Processing (IFIP) Gopher
- The Unicode Consortium
- Open Applications Group (OAG)
- Object Management Group
- World Wide Web Consortium (W3C)

The Standards Bodies

Because this chapter focuses on standards and standards bodies, it seems fitting to describe the most relevant bodies and their processes in some detail. (This section builds on the overview in Chapter 2: "Getting Acquainted with XML") The following section includes information extracted directly from the appropriate sites in addition to commentary.

International Organization for Standardization (ISO)

As described on the ISO Web site `http://www.iso.ch/`, international standardization began in the electrotechnical field when the International Electrotechnical Commission (IEC) was created in 1906. The International Federation of the National Standardizing Associations (ISA), set up in 1926, continued this work. Following a meeting in London in 1946, delegates from 25 countries created a new international organization for industrial standards. The new organization, ISO, began to function officially on February 23, 1947. The first ISO standard was published in 1951 with the title, "Standard reference temperature for industrial length measurement."

What Is ISO? ISO is a worldwide federation of national standards bodies from approximately 130 countries. As described on the ISO Web site, the mission of ISO "is to promote the development of standardization and related activities in the world with a view to facilitating the international exchange of goods and services, and to develop cooperation in the spheres of intellectual, scientific, technological, and economic activity." Its members and revenues from the sale of ISO standards and other publications fund ISO.

The ISO Web site provides an additional definition of standards:

> "Standards are documented agreements containing technical specifications or other precise criteria to be used consistently as rules, guidelines, or definitions of characteristics, to ensure that materials, products, processes, and services are fit for their purpose."

ISO has a huge amount of technical work going on at all times all over the world. Approximately 2,850 technical committees, subcommittees, and working groups that contain more than 30,000 participating members meet each year. The productivity is enormous! "To date, ISO's work has resulted in more than 12,000 International Standards, representing more than 300,000 printed pages in English and French." Terminology is often provided in other languages as well.

NOTE ISO has produced standards such as ISO 8879:1986. Standardized General Markup Language (SGML) XML is a subset of SGML and therefore would not exist if SGML had not come first.

World Wide Web Consortium (W3C)

As you may know, the W3C was established in October 1994 in collaboration with *Conseil European pour la Recherche Nucleaire,* (CERN) now known as The European Laboratory for Particle Physics with support from the United States Defense Advanced Research Project Agency (DARPA), and the European Commission. According to the W3C Web site, its goal was "to facilitate the development of common protocols to enhance the interoperability of the World Wide Web." The W3C is jointly hosted by the Massachusetts Institute of Technology (MIT) Library of Computer Science, the Institut National de Recherche en Informatique et en Automatique (INRIA) in Europe, and the Keio University Shonan Fujisawa Campus in Japan.

Services provided by the Consortium include:

- A repository of information about the World Wide Web and all of its activities including working groups.
- Reference code implementations of prototype and sample applications to demonstrate use of new technology.

The W3C is designed to be vendor neutral and makes every attempt to be so. However, one must always consider that in the W3C as in all consortia, some member companies are able to participate in multiple working groups. Thus they are sometimes able to exert more influence than smaller companies—although this is not always true. The W3C is a unique organization; the passionate commitment of the people working for the W3C is evident in the breadth and volume of the work that has already been completed.

European Commission's Open Information Interchange

On its Web site, the European Commission's Open Information Interchange (OII) describes itself as providing a service "to all market actors—including standards and specification developers, product and service providers, and end-users of these products and services—with an overview of existing and emerging standards and industry specifications designed to facilitate the exchange of information in electronic form." The following description of the *raison d'être* for standards appears on the OII Web site:

> "Standards are a pillar for the Information Society. Within the European Union there is a consensus that the information infrastructure which underpins the Information Society must be characterized by the interconnectivity of networks and the interoperability of services. In recent years, there has been a rapid increase in the number of industry consortia in the development of specifications, outside the formal standardization processes. This list provides reference information on some of the major organizations who are actively engaged in standards/specifications development today at a European level and/or with a global impact."

The Standards Process

How does the standards process compare between accredited standards granting bodies and informal ones, such as the W3C? There are some small differences between accredited standards granting bodies and industry consortiums in terms of the consensus requirements for approval of standards or recommendations. Also, the submission processes are somewhat different. However, over all, the processes are quite similar. One common perception is that industry consortia may be able to push specifications through the recommendation process more rapidly than accredited standards bodies can approve standards because of the structure and procedures of those bodies. However, that's not always true. For instance, ISO has implemented the *Fast Track* procedures, allowing members to advance "existing national or other approved standards more quickly through the process."

NOTE

One difference between the W3C and ISO is that ISO Standards must be purchased, but W3C Recommendations are freely available for implementation.

Let's look at how ISO standards are developed and then compare that process to the W3C process.

The ISO Standards Process

As described on the ISO Web site and by ISO members, there are three main phases to the ISO standards process. First an industry sector communicates a need for a standard in a particular area to a national member body. Then the national member body proposes the new work item (standard) to ISO as a whole. When ISO recognizes the need formally, a *working group* is formed to define the technical scope of the future standard.

The specific progress happens as follows. The *new work item* proposal must be approved by the participating members of the *technical committee* to which the item is presented. At least five members must agree to take an active role in the development of the standard. During its life cycle, the new work item will take on several designations including: *working draft*, *committee draft*, *draft international standard*, and *final draft international standard*.

After a new work item has been approved, it is either assigned to an existing *subcommittee* of a technical committee or a new subcommittee is created. The subcommittee may set up a specific working group for the new work item. Those who participate in these working group sessions are referred to as individual experts.

When the working draft is completed and approved by the working group, it is then forwarded to the parent subcommittee. The resulting document, a committee draft, is then balloted by the subcommittee members. The ballot process may go smoothly or there may be concerns and issues raised through comments and negative votes.

The comments and negative ballots must be resolved (either in meetings or via correspondence). The project leader oversees all of the changes. Unanimity is not required, but all comments are considered. It may be necessary to prepare another committee draft and ballot it. After the required number of votes is achieved, the CD is registered at ISO headquarters as a *draft international standard.*

The draft international standard is sent to each member of the technical committee for review and ballot. After the vote closes and assuming that the required number of affirmatives was obtained, a ballot report and the final draft standard are registered with the ISO Central Secretariat as a final draft international standard. It is circulated again to technical committee members for a final two-month ballot. ISO publishes the approved international standard following the close of the last ballot.

Next, one of the national standards bodies that make up the ISO membership—AFNOR, ANSI, BSI, CSBTS, DIN, SIS, and so on—takes the major responsibility for administrating a standards committee. The ISO Central Secretariat in Geneva ensures the flow of documentation, clarifies technical points with secretariats and chairmen, and manages the progression of the draft standard through the voting and publishing process. Although the greater part of ISO technical work is done by correspondence, there are, on average, a dozen ISO meetings taking place somewhere in the world every working day of the year.

The W3C Standards Process

Understanding the organization of the W3C is the first step in learning the standards process. You learned about this process in Chapter 2. This chapter will delve more deeply into all the aspects of the process.

Organization of the W3C

The W3C Activities are divided into the following three domains:

Technology & Society This domain's charter is to understand the social impact of the Web and to reach out to affected communities. The metadata activity falls formally under this domain and it includes Resource Description Framework (RDF), a metadata structural framework, XML Digital Signatures, and the Platform for Privacy Preferences Project.

User Interface This domain's charter is improving the technology that allows users effectively to perceive and express information. This domain includes Hypertext Markup Language (HTML), Style Sheets (CSS, XSL), the Document Object Model (DOM), Multimedia, Math, Graphics (SVG), Voice Browser, Internationalization, and Mobile Access.

Architecture Domain This Domain's goal is to enhance the infrastructure of the Web and increase its automation. It includes HTTP, HTTP-NG, Television and the Web, Web Characterization, Jigsaw, a new Java-based, object-oriented Web server, and XML, the technology covered in this book.

Dan Connolly, who leads the XML Activity, describes the architecture domain as follows:

> "The challenge is to find the right mix of reliability and flexibility and the right mix of tried-and-true techniques with novel but promising ideas."

From Submission to Recommendation: Developing Standards

NOTE See `http://www.w3.org/Consortium/Process/` for the complete document. The following description contains summarized information from that document and direct quotes. However, the entire document is of considerable length and should be read thoroughly before making a submission to the W3C.

Submission The first stage in the process is typically a *submission* from one or more W3C member companies or an Advisory Committee representative. The submission package must only be sent by one of the submitting members. The e-mail submission package is sent to submissions@w3.org.

When a submission is received by the W3C a *validation* e-mail message is sent to the submitter meaning that the submission was complete and has been accepted as a submission. A submission can also be rejected if it is deemed to be outside the scope of the W3C or if it is not submitted in HTML according to the template provided.

The W3C must then *acknowledge* the submission within one to four weeks. The *acknowledgment* always contains some commentary about the submission, which could be positive or negative. After the acknowledgment, the documents in the submission may be published on theW3C Web site as a *note*.

Making a submission is not always a positive experience for a member company or an industry consortium. If the submission receives unfavorable commentary, it can negatively affect its progress. This might happen because the specification has been submitted before it is actually ready, for instance.

Notes A *note* is merely a dated, public record of an idea, comment, or document. Notes do not imply a commitment on the part of the W3C.

According to the *process document* published by the W3C (see `http://www.w3.org/Consortium/Process/`) notes can be:

- Documents that are part of an acknowledged *submission request*.
- Used to encapsulate a document that is not published by W3C or to refer to a version of a WC document that was published on a particular date, rather than the current version.
- To document ongoing work in a W3C Working Group that is not part of a draft that would be targeted at becoming a recommendation.

The status field of a note indicates whether or not any W3C resources have been applied to the submission.

Working Groups and Drafts In some cases, W3C member companies are eager for the W3C to pursue work on topics they submit. In these cases, if the W3C decides that the proposal is critical to one of its *activities* as defined within the three domains, (as in the XML Activity), it may create a W3C Working Group to explore the proposal. The *working group* may then develop various *drafts*.

Typically the working group releases a number of working drafts which are published on the W3C Web site. A considerable amount of excitement in the industry usually accompanies each one of these releases. For instance, the initial release of the first draft from the XML Schema Working Group caused quite a stir because they completed this critical work so rapidly.

NOTE

It is important to note that all documents that are published by the W3C have to be approved by the director. The purpose is not to hold documents up or to capriciously cancel them. Rather it is to ensure that someone who is responsible for the entire organization sees every official document before it is released to the public.

Proposed Recommendation At some point the working group comes to consensus (hopefully) and decides to turn the current draft into a proposed recommendation. Before they do that, however, the working group must issue a "last call" for comments.

NOTE

When a working group issues a "last call" for comment, all documents must contain a statement about how the technology relates to international standards and to other relevant standards activities. If you refer back to Chapter 2 you will see that while ease of localization was not mentioned as one of the design goals for XML, it was a key issue throughout the process according to Tim Bray in his Annotated Version of the XML Specification `http://www.xml.com`.

When the last call period is over, the working draft still doesn't become a proposed recommendation until the director of the W3C Advisory Committee proposes it to the advisory committee for review. At this point the working draft document is given a new name to clearly indicate its status.

Recommendation All of the members of the advisory committee must reach consensus on the *proposed recommendation* before it can become a *recommendation*. After the advisory committee completes their vote, the fate of the proposed recommendation is entirely up to the director. After the director makes a decision the working draft document may be:

- Issued as a recommendation.
- Issued as a recommendation with minor changes indicated.
- Returned to the working group for modification.
- Abandoned and removed from the W3C agenda.

The first two options are the most likely. However, in the case of Resource Description Framework (RDF) Schemas did not move from proposed recommendation to recommendation because datatypes are decided by the XML Schema Working Group. In this case, the W3C determined that modifications needed to be made to avoid conflict between the working groups and the resulting specifications.

Other Standards Bodies

ISO and the W3C are the two organizations that are most related to XML standards. However, other key related technologies are developed in the Internet Engineering Task Force (IETF), such as World Wide Web Distributed Authoring and Versioning (webdav) which is an extension to HTTP that allows authoring and versioning across the Web. See `http://www.ietf.org/html.charters/webdav-charter.html` for more information.

Defining Standards

Now that you know a specification is definitely a standard when it's been approved by a formal standards body. But what about the informal standards bodies, such as W3C and IETF? Are all specifications that reach the recommendation stage considered standards?

For example, MathML is a W3C Recommendation. Does that make it a *standard*? By the definitions we have developed in this chapter it is not a *formal* standard. In fact, W3C Process Document clearly states that "a W3C Recommendation can be submitted to a formal standards body like ISO if desired." However, because the purpose of standards is to promote easy interoperability and interchange of information, specifications that are recommended by recognized informal standards bodies are, for all intents and purposes, standards.

Vocabularies

What are vocabularies? Chapter 2 introduced the idea of XML being a *family of standards*. The extended XML family also includes a large number of *cousins*. A cousin can be defined as a group of elements and commonly understood semantics that are appropriate for a particular vertical application—such as magazine publishing—or horizontal application—such as e-commerce. The XML industry calls these commonly understood elements and semantics *vocabularies*. The industry often equates vocabularies with DTDs or schemas. For example, a vocabulary could be:

- Very tiny, or very large, for vertical industries such as aerospace or semi-conductors
- General purpose or very specific. A general purpose DTD might be one that facilitates e-commerce. A specific one again might be one of the vertical industry DTDs.
- A formal or informal standard
- An industry or individual company initiative

Our opinion is that for XML to be useful, each industry must define and agree to use a common set of definitions. Already several organizations have been working to define these market-segment or function-specific definitions and several more organizations are in the process of forming. Two examples of such organizations are Information Content and Exchange (ICE) and Publishing Requirements for Industry Standard Metadata (PRISM), which are both industry standard initiatives hosted by GCARI, the research and development arm of the Graphics Communications Association, a vendor-neutral consortium.

Many individual companies have developed vocabularies to support their own products and have then made them public in the hopes that they will be widely adopted and become industry or function-specific standards. An example might be Web Distributed Data Exchange (WDDX), which has been developed by Allaire.

So, you ask, vocabularies and standards are not mutually exclusive? That's right. XML is a standard but only the syntax has been standardized. XML is in fact a language that can be used to create all kinds of vocabularies and applications. If a vocabulary or application goes through the standards process at a recognized standards body, it is a standard. Vocabularies sometimes describe the content of an XML document, sometimes the *metadata*, and sometimes both. *Metadata* is data about data. In other words, it describes the document but does not tell you what is actually written in the document. For instance, metadata about a magazine article might include the publication name and date, the number of images in the article, the photographers of those images, all the other publications those images have appeared in, and all of the secondary rights and permissions associated with them. Metadata about a magazine article could also include classification information that describes what the article is about but those specific words may never appear in the actual article.

NOTE

Metadata is critical to integrating XML into print processes, site management, asset management, channels, and other process-to-process communication. It is also the key to making search engines work because it is unlikely that all of the content on the Web will be tagged in XML.

Examples of XML Vocabularies

As discussed at the beginning of this chapter, there are a mind-boggling number of XML vocabularies that have already been developed and even more are in the process of being developed. It's possible to imagine that at some point there may be a small XML vocabulary to describe almost every kind of content or transaction. Many are listed on the W3C Web site (`http://www.w3c.org`) and it will also be possible to find industry-specific standards in repositories like BizTalk.org (`http://www.BizTalk.org`) and XML.org (`www.oasis-open.org/`).

Below are a few examples of XML vocabularies that you may not be familiar with and that will show the range of uses for XML. These vocabularies are described on Robin Cover's page on the Oasis Web site (`http://www.oasis-open.org/cover`).

- Financial Product Markup Language (FpML™) jointly created by J.P. Morgan & Co. Inc. and PricewaterhouseCoopers LLP is expected to become the standard for the derivatives industry in the rapidly growing field of electronic commerce. FpML™ is an XML vocabulary that "enables the integration of a range of services, from Internet-based electronic dealing and confirmations to the risk analysis of client portfolios." More information about FpML™ is available at `http://www.fpml.org/`.
- The Advanced Television Standards Committee Digital TV Applications Software Environments (ATSC/DASE) group has published a specification for a Broadcast HyperText Markup Language (BHTML) which is actually an XML vocabulary. It adds attributes for standardizing multimedia object descriptions using the Synchronized Multimedia Integration Language (SMIL) `SWITCH` option and introducing an `EVENT` element to manage the actions to be taken when certain conditions are encountered. It also contains "properties for defining 3D effects, controlling the volume of audio presentations, and for clipping and overflowing image areas." More information about SMIL is available at `http://www.w3.org/TR/REC-smil/`.
- FlixML is a vocabulary created to describe B movies. The author of the vocabulary says it was created for fun and to provide a tutorial on how to build an XML document. More information about FlixML is available at `http://www.flixml.org/flixml_build.html`.
- VoxML is a vocabulary described as "The Markup Language for Voice Applications." It was developed by Motorola in an effort to develop a broadly supported platform for voice applications "just as HTML provides for Web based applications." VoxML technology provides an application interface in the form of dialogues. "Navigation and input is produced via speech recognition of end-user's voice and output is produced via text-to-speech technology or recorded audio samples." More information about VoxML is available at `http://www.voxml.com`.

- NVML is a vocabulary for describing the navigation of information. As described in the specification, NVML is designed to be used by mobile information appliances such as smart phones with capability of Internet access, Personal Digital Assistants (PDAs) equipped with Global Positioning System (GPS), and car navigation systems. As described on the Navigation Markup Language (NVML) Web site `http://www.w3.org/TR/NVML`.
- Real Estate Transaction Standard (RETS) is an open standard for exchanging real estate transaction information. It consists of a transaction specification and a standard DTD. RETS is being implemented by many real estate industry leaders in their next generation of real estate information systems. More information is available at `http://RETS-WG.ORG`.
- Another related real estate application using XML is OpenMLS which is a Web-based real estate listing management system. See `http://www.openmls.com/` for a search engine and an interesting and dynamic integration of XML into the management system.

Weather Observation Markup Format (OMF)

Another interesting XML vocabulary is Weather Observation Markup Format (OMF) used to encode weather observation reports. It has been incorporated into a software application. Weather information is critical to all of us at one time or another, but it is something we take very much for granted. Thus we chose the OMF to provide an example which is pertinent to everyone.

According to the W3C Web site, the markup system is in actual use today "to distribute up-to-the-hour annotated weather observations and advisories." The following scenario describes the implementation of OMF.

The Business Problem Weather observations are reported in a variety of formats. Unfortunately, these formats are rather unsuitable for providing observation information if requested for a particular area of interest. These formats are unsuitable because:

- The weather reports refer to observation stations only by their call signs or what is known as "block-IDs." Neither the observation station's location nor its full name is given. To interpret the information every receiver of the reports is supposed to have a current copy of a *Master Station Library*, which contains the information about the stations. This process of interpreting the observation station call-signs and block-IDs is well suited for organizations that require massive feeds of weather information, but it doesn't work very well for clients only interested in weather reports for a relatively small area. If the description of an observation station were carried along with its report as an *annotation* it would be much more useful to these clients.

- The standard weather reports do not carry a complete timestamp. This makes the raw reports unsuitable for archival storage, record keeping, and trend processing as there is no means to benchmark the reports chronologically.
- *Derived* quantities such as cloud ceiling, flight conditions, or humidity are not easily computed from the weather reports on the client side. If the server computed the most popular derived parameters and provided them along with the raw report data the information would be much more usable.

Desired Solution The purpose of OMF is the annotation of weather reports. The goal is to deliver the reports without any interference, but with the addition of station information (location, name, etc.), and a few derived parameters.

Structure of an OMF Document The following description of OMF structure includes technical terms associated with weather data. It is beyond the scope of this chapter to define all these terms but the intent of the elements is clear.

OMF contains the following elements:

Reports Reports define a group of weather observations.

METAR A single METAR report.

SPECI A single SPECI report.

UAR A combined Rawinsonde and Pibal Observation report.

BTSC Ocean profile data (temperature, salinity, current, etc.).

SYN A surface synoptic report from a land or sea station.

Advisories Advisories define a collection of weather hazard warnings.

SIGMET SIGnificant METeorological information.

Forecasts Forecasts define a set of weather predictions.

TAF Terminal Aerodrome Forecasts.

OMF Basic Attributes The following OMF attributes provide basic annotation information about the weather reports. These attributes may (and often must) be present in appropriate elements that describe the reports.

`TStamp`

Time Stamp

`TRange`

Time Interval

`LatLon`

Specification of a point on the globe

`LatLons`

Specification of a sequence of points on the globe

`BBox`

Bounding box, which tells the latitudinal and the longitudinal spans of an area of the globe

`BId`

Block ID of a weather observation station

`SName`

Call sign and the full name of a weather observation station

`Elev`

Elevation relative to the sea level, in meters

OMF Example: How the Vocabulary Is Used This following is an example of a weather report document that is provided by the specification:

```
<!DOCTYPE OMF SYSTEM "http://zowie.metnet.navy.mil/~spawar/JMV-TNG/
XML/OMF.dtd">
<Reports TStamp="888965153">
<METAR TStamp="888965153" LatLon="36.58, -121.85" BId="724915"
    SName="KMRY, MONTEREY PENINSULA" Elev="77" Vis="80500"
    Ceiling="INF">
```

```
KMRY 032245Z 29007KT 50SM SKC 15/03 A3003</METAR>
<SPECI TStamp="888966299" LatLon="36.97, -86.42" BId="746716"
     SName="KBWG, BOWLING GREEN" Elev="167" Vis="12880" Ceiling="2400">
KBWG 032304Z VRB05KT 8SM BKN024 OVC035 04/01 A2990 RMK A02</SPECI>
<METAR TStamp="888968939" LatLon="37.00, -101.9" BId="724604"
     SName="KEHA, ELKHART (AWOS)" Elev="1099">
KEHA 032348Z AUTO 08004KT 15/M10 RMK A01 PK WND 06 000
T01501099</METAR>
<METAR TStamp="888967859" LatLon="36.67, -4.48" BId="84820"
     SName="LEMG, MALAGA (CIV/MIL)" Elev="7" Vis="4000" Ceiling="INF">
LEMG 2330Z 31006KT 4000 BR FEW008 08/07 Q1027 NOSIG</METAR>
</Reports>
```


When an updated OMF document is created, the new information is merged with the information already contained in the local database. Specifically, the expired weather observations are purged, and a new report from an observation station replaces the old one.

Applications

What is an application and how is it different from a vocabulary? *Vocabulary* and *application* seem to be used interchangeably and the distinction between them is difficult to make. Let's examine some of the ways that *application* is used to make the difference clear.

The word *application* can be used in many different ways. In the introduction to the XML 1 Specification, application is defined as follows: "XML is an application profile or restricted form of SGML, the Standard Generalized Markup Language." It is also defined in the introduction as follows:

> "It is assumed that an XML processor is doing its work on behalf of another module, called the *application*."

You can see that even in the same section of the specification the word is used differently. Two common usages of application are:

- To mean a software application
- To mean an implementation; actually applying a particular technology in a real world setting

In this chapter "XML Application" describes a situation where XML has been applied but it is more than just a vocabulary. It definitely *includes* a vocabulary—maybe the DTD or schema as well—and also has some defined rules/behaviors and characteristics written in XML.

NOTE

Some in the industry define a vocabulary as a simple list of elements and attributes without a DTD or XML schema. To them *XML application* means the combination of elements and attributes with a DTD or schema.

Examples of XML Applications

You have already learned about one of the best examples of an XML application—eXtensible Style Language (XSL) which is completely written in XML (now XSLT).

Another example of an XML application is Scalable Vector Graphics (SVG). As described on the W3C Web site (`http://www.w3.org/Graphics/SVG/`), SVG is "an XML-based language for describing the rendering of two-dimensional graphics objects.

Locating Standards, Applications, and Vocabularies

At this point in *Mastering XML*, we have described many standards, applications, and vocabularies in use and new ones that are being developed at a dizzying speed. All these options are great, but how do you find them?

This issue is critical for XML to be successful. If developers can't find out if standards and vocabularies have already been developed, they will develop new and different ones to do the same things using different terminology. This compromises transparent interoperability.

At the time of writing there are at least two organizations developing repositories for XML vocabularies and applications: XML.org, (`http://www.xml.org/`)

under the auspices of OASIS and BizTalk, a Microsoft initiative (`http://www.biztalk.org`). If these repositories are successful, they—and others like them—will be definitive sources for formal and informal XML DTDs, Schemas, and vocabularies that may not have a DTD or schema associated with them.

Up Next

In this chapter you have learned more about the definitions of particular terms—standards, applications and vocabularies. You have also gained insight into the standards bodies and how the standards are actually created.

The next chapter examines Channel Definition Format including implementation, and the benefits of using channels. In addition, structuring channels with CDF Files, advanced channel options, and design tips are covered.

CHAPTER

TWENTY-FOUR

24

A Closer Look at the Channel Definition Format

- Implementing Channel Definition Format (CDF)
- The benefits of using channels
- Structuring channels with CDF files
- Advanced channel options
- Microsoft's CDF Generator software
- Design tips for channels

In this chapter, we will begin to explore current implementations of XML found on the Web. One of the very first to garner media attention was Microsoft's Channel Definition Format (CDF), which was the basis of the Active Channel concept introduced with Internet Explorer 4 (IE4).

Active Channels have blurred the lines between the desktop and the Web by providing single-click access to Web-generated content and the invisible (to the user) updates of channel content. The success of Active Content rests with its tight integration into IE4, which has the unfortunate result of limiting its usefulness to those users who choose IE4 as their browsing platform. Despite this limitation, CDF provides the new XML author with an avenue for testing their new skills in an easy to implement format.

Implementing CDF

Implementing channels on a Web site can be quickly accomplished by either using tools such as Microsoft's CDF Generator (see the section "Microsoft's CDF Generator" later in this chapter) or writing the code by hand. In this section, you will take a look at the benefits of using channels and walk step-by-step through the process of creating channel code and other supporting objects.

Developer Benefits

Developers and site owners can benefit from implementing Active Channels in several key ways:

- The subscription mechanism provides you with a voluntarily captive audience. Channels can offer special insider sales on retail sites or subscriber-only hints and tips from a support-forum site.
- Implementation of a channel is only nominally different than implementation of a traditional Web page. Nearly all of the content that can be presented in a regular HTML file can be displayed in an Active Channel. The only constraints involve the offline-browsing mode, which may introduce difficulties for some Java applets or ActiveX controls.
- Active Channels retain the visual branding you've worked hard to achieve on your primary site. Developer-provided logos populate the user's Channel

Pane, which lists all of the channels the user has subscribed to, the Favorites menu found in both IE4 and the Windows Start Menu, and the Active Desktop Channel Bar if the user has the Active Desktop option installed on their system.

Subscriber Benefits

Subscribers benefit from easy access to selected information. Many users find channels easier to access and manage than favorites or bookmarks because of the hierarchical structure presented in the Channel Pane. Additionally, the content is updated for them automatically. They can know at a glance when new data arrives rather than having to schedule time to surf to a Web site and hunt for new information. This sort of convenience is definitely the motivating factor that drives new subscriptions.

Channel Structure: The CDF File

The structure of the channel is defined in a single file, the CDF file. It works somewhat like HTML files that use frames, where you have a single document that contains the frameset, which points out the documents that contain the actual content. Similarly, a CDF file contains descriptive information and pointers to content and navigation. The code shown here is a complete CDF file, which this section goes over step-by-step.

```
<?xml version="1.0"?>
<CHANNEL HREF="http://www.citrusgrove.com/community/events.html">
<ABSTRACT>This channel is used to provide weekly updates to the Citrus
   Grove community calendar.</ABSTRACT>
<TITLE>Citrus Grove Community Calendar</TITLE>
<LOGO HREF="http://www.citrusgrove.com/community/images/grove.ico"
   STYLE="icon" />
<LOGO HREF="http://www.citrusgrove.com/community/images/grove-s.gif"
   STYLE="image" />
<LOGO HREF="http://www.citrusgrove.com/community/images/grove-w.gif"
   STYLE="image-wide" />
<ITEM HREF="http://www.citrusgrove.com/community/city/">
   <ABSTRACT>City of Citrus Grove Public Meeting Schedule</ABSTRACT>
   <TITLE>City of Citrus Grove Public Meeting Schedule</TITLE>
</ITEM>
<ITEM HREF="http://www.citrusgrove.com/community/movies/">
   <ABSTRACT>Movie schedules for each of the three Cineplexes in
   town</ABSTRACT>
```

```
    <TITLE>This Week's Movie Times</TITLE>
</ITEM>
<ITEM HREF="http://www.citrusgrove.com/community/schools/">
    <ABSTRACT>Weekly school lunch menus for Orange Elementary, Lemon
    Grove Middle School, and Citrus High School</ABSTRACT>
<TITLE>Weekly School Lunch Menus</TITLE>
</ITEM>
</CHANNEL>
```

The CDF File: Element by Element

As with all XML files, the CDF file must begin with an XML document header.

```
<?xml version="1.0"?>
```

Note that a DOCTYPE element isn't present to identify a DTD for use in this document. Microsoft has chosen not to provide a DTD for use with CDF, though an author may of course create one of their own.

WARNING Remember that an XML document that does not use a DTD cannot be valid—it can only be well formed.

The root element for a CDF file is the CHANNEL element.

```
<CHANNEL HREF="http://www.citrusgrove.com/community/events.html">
```

In this instance, the root element takes only one attribute, an HREF for the URI of the primary HTML document for the channel. This URI should always be written in fully qualified form.

Additional descriptive information and support graphics are provided for the channel, but the content is contained with new elements, rather than as attributes to the CHANNEL element. The first of these is the channel ABSTRACT element. The abstract contains a description of the channel's overall content or purpose.

```
<ABSTRACT>This channel is used to provide weekly updates to the Citrus
Grove community calendar.</ABSTRACT>
```

Next comes the familiar document TITLE element:

```
<TITLE>Citrus Grove Community Calendar</TITLE>
```

The final required elements for the CDF file are references to three graphic entities:

```
<LOGO HREF="http://www.citrusgrove.com/community/images/grove.ico"
   STYLE="icon" />
```

```
<LOGO HREF="http://www.citrusgrove.com/community/images/grove-s.gif"
   STYLE="image" />
<LOGO HREF="http://www.citrusgrove.com/community/images/grove-w.gif"
   STYLE="image-wide" />
```

Each Active Channel requires three unique graphics to be used in identifying that channel to users. A 16x16 GIF or ICO file is used to identify the channel on the submenus for Favorites within IE4 and the Windows Start menu (see Figure 24.1). An 80x32-pixel GIF image is used in the Active Desktop Channel bar, as seen in Figure 24.2, if the user has the Active Desktop option in place. The final 194x32-pixel GIF image is known as the wide logo, which is used to identify your channel in the Channel Pane that holds logos for every channel to which the user is subscribed (see Figure 24.3).

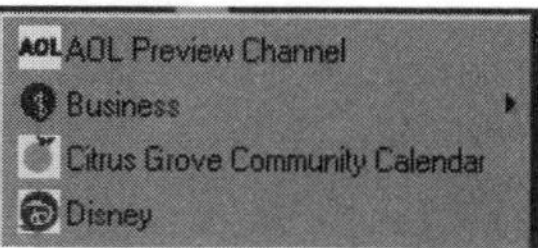

FIGURE 24.1:

The Channel ICO file as it appears in the Windows Start menu hierarchy

FIGURE 24.2:

The 80×32-pixel GIF image in the Active Desktop Channel bar

FIGURE 24.3:

Subscribed channels and their wide logos in the Channel Pane

At this point, these items comprise the sum of the required elements to create a CDF file. If you were to stop here, your CDF file would appear like the following:

```
<?xml version="1.0"?>
<CHANNEL HREF="http://www.citrusgrove.com/community/events.html">
<ABSTRACT>This channel is used to provide weekly updates to the Citrus
   Grove community calendar.</ABSTRACT>
<TITLE>Citrus Grove Community Calendar</TITLE>
<LOGO HREF="http://www.citrusgrove.com/community/images/grove.ico"
   STYLE="icon" />
<LOGO HREF="http://www.citrusgrove.com/community/images/grove-s.gif"
   STYLE="image" />
<LOGO HREF="http://www.citrusgrove.com/community/images/grove-w.gif"
   STYLE="image-wide" />
</CHANNEL>
```

Adding Subpages to the CDF File

Our sample channel for the Citrus Grove Community Calendar contains links to several subpages. To incorporate this, we need the new CDF element ITEM.

An ITEM element contains two additional elements: ABSTRACT and TITLE. As when they appeared in the primary CHANNEL block, these elements provide additional information about the content linked in the ITEM—in this case, an HTML subpage. Syntactically, these attributes are the same as they were in the CHANNEL block, with ITEM assuming the HREF attribute for the HTML file URI.

```
<ITEM HREF="http://www.citrusgrove.com/community/city/">
   <ABSTRACT>City of Citrus Grove Public Meeting Schedule</ABSTRACT>
```

```
    <TITLE>City of Citrus Grove Public Meeting Schedule</TITLE>
  </ITEM>
```

The abstract text should be a short description of the page and will appear as a subentry in the Channel Bar listing for your channel. The title content will be rendered as a ToolTip when the entry is viewed in the Channel Pane (see Figures 24.4 and 24.5).

FIGURE 24.4:

ITEM content visible in the Channel Bar listings

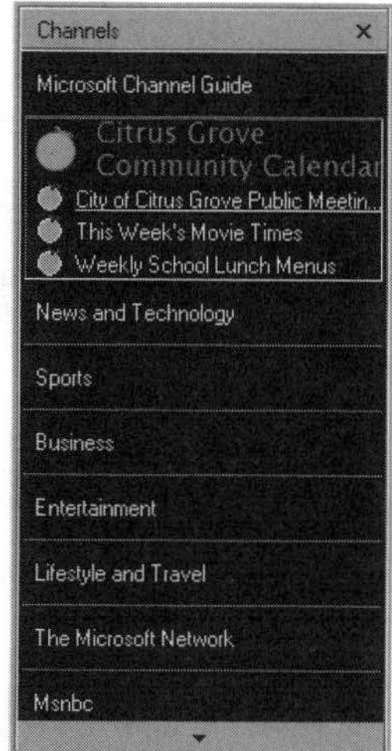

FIGURE 24.5:

TITLE rendered as a ToolTip in the Channel Pane

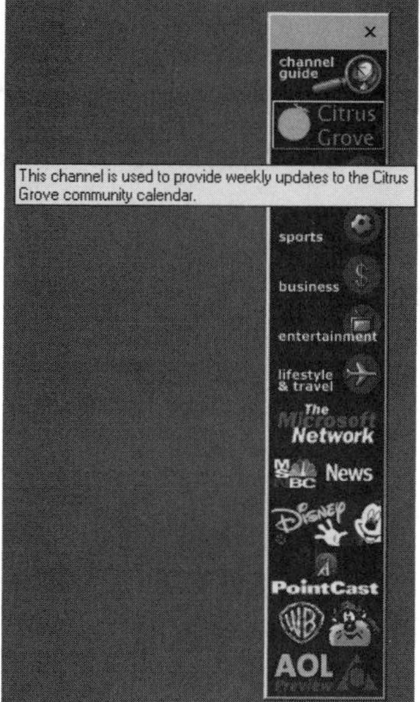

Additional ITEM elements are added to the CDF file until all the major subpages you wish to include have been incorporated, and the file ends with the closing </CHANNEL> tag. The completed CDF file is shown in Listing 24.1.

LISTING 24.1 citrusgrove.cdf

```
<?xml version="1.0"?>
<CHANNEL HREF="http://www.citrusgrove.com/community/events.html">
<ABSTRACT>This channel is used to provide weekly updates to the Citrus
   Grove community calendar.</ABSTRACT>
<TITLE>Citrus Grove Community Calendar</TITLE>
<LOGO HREF="http://www.citrusgrove.com/community/images/grove.ico"
   STYLE="icon" />
<LOGO HREF="http://www.citrusgrove.com/community/images/grove-s.gif"
   STYLE="image" />
<LOGO HREF="http://www.citrusgrove.com/community/images/grove-w.gif"
   STYLE="image-wide" />
<ITEM HREF="http://www.citrusgrove.com/community/city/">
   <ABSTRACT>City of Citrus Grove Public Meeting Schedule</ABSTRACT>
   <TITLE>City of Citrus Grove Public Meeting Schedule</TITLE>
</ITEM>
<ITEM HREF="http://www.citrusgrove.com/community/movies/">
   <ABSTRACT>Movie schedules for each of the three Cineplexes in
   town</ABSTRACT>
<TITLE>This Week's Movie Times</TITLE>
</ITEM>
<ITEM HREF="http://www.citrusgrove.com/community/schools/">
   <ABSTRACT>Weekly school lunch menus for Orange Elementary, Lemon
   Grove Middle School, and Citrus High School</ABSTRACT>
<TITLE>Weekly School Lunch Menus</TITLE>
</ITEM>
</CHANNEL>
```

The last item required to prepare your channel for visitors is a means for them to subscribe to it. Microsoft has created a recognizable image that may be used for this purpose, which is shown here:

NOTE

While anyone may use the Add Active Channel logo provided by Microsoft, they do require you to accept the terms of license for that image, known as the Active Channel Logo Agreement. A form is provided at `http://www.microsoft.com/sbnmember/ielogo/default.asp`.

The subscription link is a simple anchor element on your regular Web page:

```
<A HREF="http://www.citrusgrove.com/community/citrusgrove.cdf"> <IMG
SRC="http://www.citrusgrove.com/community/addChan.gif"> Subscribe to
the Citrus Grove Community Calendar Channel!</A>
```

Your channel is now ready for action.

Advanced Channel Options

The basic channel you just developed is only a start. Channels can grow to encompass just as much information as a large Web site, or they can act as vehicles for the delivery of additional Active content.

Subchannels

Navigation within a channel presentation is just as important as navigation within a traditional Web site. Users need to be able to find their way around the site without getting lost, and information must be readily accessible.

Web sites help guide users through the site hierarchy by providing links to major site subsections from every page. Channels build navigation systems from the Channel Pane. Major subsections are structured with nested `<CHANNEL>` elements instead of using multiple `<ITEM>` elements.

Continuing with the Citrus Grove Community Calendar channel, say that the theater owners have asked for some additional space to do promotions and provide other movie-related information. To create a subchannel for movie times, rearrange the CDF file as follows:

```
<?xml version="1.0"?>
<CHANNEL HREF="http://www.citrusgrove.com/community/events.html">
```

```
<ABSTRACT>This channel is used to provide weekly updates to the Citrus
  Grove community calendar.</ABSTRACT>
<TITLE>Citrus Grove Community Calendar</TITLE>
<LOGO HREF="http://www.citrusgrove.com/community/images/grove.ico"
  STYLE="icon" />
<LOGO HREF="http://www.citrusgrove.com/community/images/grove-s.gif"
  STYLE="image" />
<LOGO HREF="http://www.citrusgrove.com/community/images/grove-w.gif"
  STYLE="image-wide" />
    <CHANNEL HREF="http://www.citrusgrove.com/community/movies/index
    .html">
    <ABSTRACT>Movie schedules for each of the three Cineplexes in
    town</ABSTRACT>
    <TITLE>Citrus Grove Movie Houses</TITLE>

        <ITEM HREF="http://www.citrusgrove.com/community/movies/cin-
        ema6.html">
        <ABSTRACT>Citrus Grove Cinema 6 Theatre Information</ABSTRACT>
        <TITLE>Citrus Grove Cinema 6</TITLE>
        </ITEM>
        <ITEM HREF="http://www.citrusgrove.com/community/movies/
        orange10.html">
        <ABSTRACT>Orange 10 Theatre Information</ABSTRACT>
        <TITLE>Orange 10 Theatre - Downtown Citrus Grove</TITLE>
        </ITEM>
        <ITEM HREF="http://www.citrusgrove.com/community/movies/
        grove8.html">
        <ABSTRACT>The Grove 8 Theatre Information</ABSTRACT>
        <TITLE>Citrus Grove's Original Multiplex - The Grove 8</TITLE>
        </ITEM>
    </CHANNEL>
<ITEM HREF="http://www.citrusgrove.com/community/city/">
  <ABSTRACT>City of Citrus Grove Public Meeting Schedule</ABSTRACT>
  <TITLE>City of Citrus Grove Public Meeting Schedule</TITLE>
</ITEM>
</ITEM>
<ITEM HREF="http://www.citrusgrove.com/community/schools/">
  <ABSTRACT>Weekly school lunch menus for Orange Elementary, Lemon
  Grove Middle School, and Citrus High School</ABSTRACT>
<TITLE>Weekly School Lunch Menus</TITLE>
</ITEM>
</CHANNEL>
```

Whether the subchannels appear first in your channel hierarchy or elsewhere isn't mandated by CDF, but choosing a consistent approach will help your visitors get around the site without unnecessary confusion. Figures 24.6 and 24.7 illustrate a view of the Channel Pane with the subchannel expanded and without.

FIGURE 24.6:

An unexpanded channel hierarchy with subchannels present

FIGURE 24.7:

Subchannels expanded in the Channel Pane

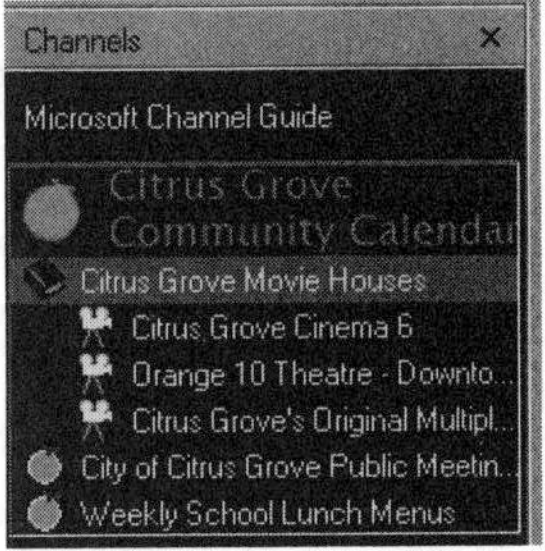

By default, Internet Explorer will use the Book icon (as shown below), which is familiar to most Windows users from its appearance in Windows Help files, to denote a subchannel.

You do, however, have the option to replace the Book icon with the icon of your choice by including a <LOGO> element and corresponding icon file for the subchannel:

```
<CHANNEL HREF="http://www.citrusgrove.com/community/movies/index.html">
<ABSTRACT>Movie schedules for each of the three Cineplexes in
   town</ABSTRACT>
<TITLE>Citrus Grove Movie Houses</TITLE>
<LOGO IMG SRC="http://www.citrusgrove.com/community/movies/movies.ico"
   STYLE="icon" />
…channel content…
</CHANNEL>
```

TIP

You can also change the image used for individual items by inserting a LOGO element within each ITEM.

Updating and Scheduling Options

One of the key features of Channels is the content developer's ability to regularly send the subscriber new information after the initial subscription request without any proactive effort on the subscriber's part. Users enjoy not having to chase down new information, and Channel owners have fully qualified and interested audiences for their material or offers. It's definitely a "win-win" situation.

Adding scheduling tasks to a channel requires a new element block: <SCHEDULE>. The schedule block contains elements that detail which day of the week or at what interval expressed in days (every two days, every third day, etc.) updates should occur on, what time updates should start, and, if an update interval is selected, when that update window should close. These options allow you to conserve your available bandwidth during peak need times and schedule updates in a broad enough time span so that they won't overtax the servers.

A schedule block is only implemented once per CDF file, and it's done in the primary channel block. All subchannels and items will update on the same schedule.

The markup for the schedule block appears as follows:

```
<SCHEDULE STARTDATE="1999-06-01">
    <INTERVALTIME DAY="3" />
    <EARLIESTTIME HOUR="0" />
    <LATESTTIME HOUR="6" />
    </SCHEDULE>
```

This block indicates that updates are available beginning June 1, 1999, and that updates should be performed every three days, any time between midnight and 6 A.M. All times in the update block are based on the subscriber's local time, unless an absolute time zone is applied. To do that, you would add a TIMEZONE attribute to the SCHEDULE element:

```
<SCHEDULE STARTDATE="1999-06-01" TIMEZONE="-0500">
```

The TIMEZONE value is written in hours relative to Greenwich Mean Time (GMT). In this example, the time zone in use is Eastern Standard Time in the United States, which is five hours earlier than GMT. If the absolute time were written from the French point of view, it would be expressed as "+0100", because France is one hour ahead of GMT.

Notifying Users of Updated Content

Once new content is available for your channel, users must be notified that it is there so they can access it—whether or not the update was done automatically. Two methods are available: creating a *gleam* on the channel's icon in the Channel Bar or sending an e-mail to the subscriber.

The gleam on a channel icon, as seen in Figure 24.8, visually notifies the user that new content has been made available. The channel developer initiates that gleam by updating the channel's CDF file. IE4 recognizes the change in the CDF file's date/time stamp and will create the change in the image.

FIGURE 24.8:

The upper-left corner of the Channel Bar icon gleams when new content is available.

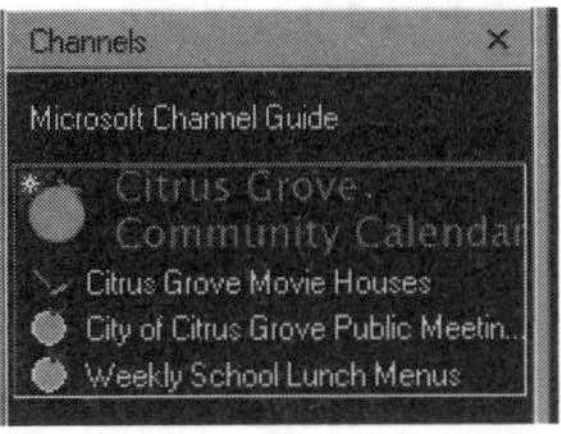

TIP

The CDF file doesn't have to have new and substantial content to generate the gleam on the Channel Bar icon. A change as insignificant as adding a space is enough to update the file and trigger the gleam.

The second method of notifying users involves sending them e-mail. This option is only available on a fully voluntary opt-in basis when the user subscribes to your channel (see Figure 24.9).

FIGURE 24.9:

Subscribers can opt-in to e-mail notifications of new channel content.

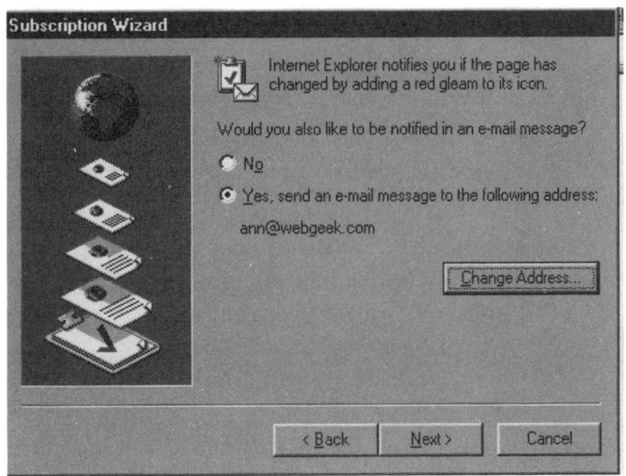

How Much Information Should Be Updated?

Along with specifying when a channel should be updated, the developer needs to dictate *how much* content will be updated. Automated updates are performed through a process called *crawling*, where every item in a channel is read and, if it's allowed, where the links in each page are followed. To control just how far links will be followed, the LEVEL attribute is set in the CHANNEL or ITEM element:

```
<CHANNEL HREF="http://www.citrusgrove.com/community/events.html"
LEVEL="1">
```

This usage indicates that the update process should follow links on each page, but go no further—in other words, traverse just one level past the starting page. The default value for LEVEL is "0", meaning no links will be followed. This is true even when the LEVEL attribute does not appear in the CHANNEL or ITEM element.

WARNING

Be careful when setting the LEVEL value past 1. Many pages have links to outside Web sites, and you may find yourself sending content updates from deep within someone else's Web site—not something your subscribers are likely to appreciate.

The Usage Element

Channels can be used to deliver content that goes beyond the traditional HTML files and graphics. Active Desktop items (where content is delivered immediately to the user's screen), Channel Screen Savers, and the strategic preloading of content files are all accomplished through the <USAGE> element. This element takes a single attribute VALUE, which announces what type of additional content is being delivered.

Desktop Items

A Desktop item allows the developer to place content directly on a user's Windows Desktop. This CDF implementation requires a CDF file separate from any other Channel content your site may have. Typically, Desktop items are used to deliver information that is time-critical in nature: news headlines, stock quotes, and any other use that requires up-to-the-minute data. That's not to say that a Desktop item couldn't be used to handle Citrus Grove's Community Calendar, but doing so would take up precious desktop screen real estate that not many users would be willing to surrender for something that's only updated once or twice a week.

When implementing a Desktop item, a new element block is introduced: the USAGE element. Usage defines parameters for the Desktop item, including what type of data will be transmitted (HTML, Java applet, etc.), the size of the item, and whether it can be resized by the user.

A simple Desktop item CDF file is shown here:

```
<?XML version="1.0"?>
<CHANNEL>
<SCHEDULE STARTDATE="1999-06-01">
   <INTERVALTIME DAY="1" />
   <EARLIESTTIME HOUR="0" />
   <LATESTTIME HOUR="6" />
</SCHEDULE>
<ITEM HREF="http://www.citrusgrove.com/littleleague/scores.html"
   PRECACHE="yes">
<TITLE>Citrus Grove Little League Desktop Item</TITLE>
<USAGE VALUE="DesktopComponent">
   <OPENAS VALUE="HTML" />
   <HEIGHT VALUE="150" />
   <WIDTH VALUE="200" />
<CANRESIZE VALUE="NO" />
</USAGE>
</ITEM>
</CHANNEL>
```

The USAGE element OPENAS indicates that the content you'll be sending is an HTML file, and it should be displayed accordingly. The HEIGHT and WIDTH parameters set the size of the item on the desktop, and the CANRESIZE value of "NO" results in the user not being able to change the size of the Desktop item (though it may be moved around the desktop as any other item can be).

Microsoft has provided developers with a graphic to alert users that they may add your Active Desktop content to their system, as shown here. It's quite similar to the Add Active Channel graphic, and it is subject to a similar licensing agreement (which may be found at http://www.microsoft.com/sbnmember/ielogo/default.asp).

After each game, the league's statistics coordinator updates the `scores.html` file, which automatically delivers the day's game scores to interested family members.

Active Technology and Dialup Accounts

A nagging implementation problem for Active Technologies is the fact that optimal performance relies on the subscriber having a full-time Internet connection. Most home users don't leave their systems on 24 hours a day, let alone leave them connected to the Internet all the time. Therefore, any Channels or Active Desktop items they may be subscribed to may not be able to update at the times set by the developer in the CDF files. In these instances, Internet Explorer will queue an update to occur the next time that the user is online.

However, reengaging the update schedule isn't always that simple. Several major failure points exist, including:

- Users may have a tendency to cancel an update that starts immediately after they log on to the Internet, as it can usurp bandwidth that they want to use for checking e-mail or a quick visit to information portals on the Web.
- Updates are set by default only to occur when a system is idle. If a user begins work immediately after logging on, the update will be suspended. Once the system is idle again, the update resumes—but only for content missed the first time. If additional content has meanwhile been updated, the user won't get that new content until the *next* update window.
- Active Desktop items may go blank when a system is restarted, or a "navigation canceled" message may be displayed. There is currently no mechanism for jump-starting the item once this occurs.

Screen Savers

Through CDF, content developers may provide HTML files for users to implement as screen savers. If a subscriber has downloaded more than one screen-saver file, they will be rotated at an interval that can be set by the user. To provide this option, the screen-saver item must be offered in the top-level channel block, and another USAGE value must be introduced:

```
<ITEM HREF="http://www.citrusgrove.com/community/screen.html" PRE-
CACHE="yes">
<USAGE VALUE="ScreenSaver"></USAGE>
</ITEM>
```

Note the use of the PRECACHE attribute in the ITEM element. This indicates that the HTML file should be sent ahead to the user's system before display, so it is available for Windows to adopt as part of the new screen-saver choices.

Should this be the first Channel Screen Saver the user has downloaded, the user will be prompted in a dialog box to choose between keeping their current screen saver or replacing it with the Channel Screen Saver. Once accepted, the behavior of the screen saver can be modified as can any other screen saver through the Screen Saver Properties dialog found in the Windows Control Panel (see Figure 24.10).

FIGURE 24.10:

Channel Screen Saver properties may be adjusted through the Screen Saver Properties dialog.

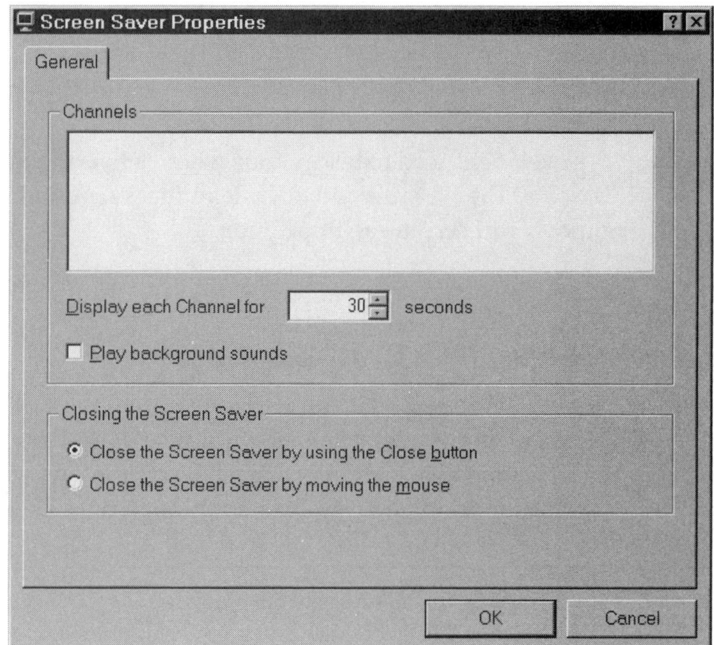

Precaching for Offline Access

In addition to the precaching of Channel Screen Saver files, there will be other times when optimal performance of your channel will require the user to have access to additional files such as sound files or program objects. This is especially critical when a channel is used in offline mode.

The USAGE element can be used to precache those items on the subscriber's system by setting the value to "NONE":

```
<ITEM HREF="http://www.citrusgrove.com/community/movies/movietune.wav">
   <USAGE VALUE="NONE"></USAGE>
   </ITEM>
```

This way, the sound file will be downloaded to the user and can be accessed any time it is found in an associated HTML file being viewed offline. Should multiple items need to be precached, an entire subchannel can be sent by created a USAGE block:

```
<CHANNEL>
<USAGE VALUE="NONE">
     …multiple ITEM elements…
</USAGE>
</CHANNEL>
```

Developers need to be cautious when delivering precached files to their subscribers. The file sizes and download times required should remain small, or the process will become an imposition.

Microsoft's CDF Generator

Microsoft has provided a handy utility to help create CDF files. It operates as a combination editor and Wizard, allowing the user to either write directly to a new file or be guided step-by-step through the CDF creation process.

NOTE

The CDF Generator is available both on the CD included with this book and for download through Microsoft's SiteBuilder Network at `http://www.microsoft.com/sitebuilder/`.

The first CDF Generator Wizard screen (see Figure 24.11) collects data about the channel itself: the HREF value for the primary HTML file, the BASE URL, and the fully qualified URL of the CDF file (referred to as SELF).

The second dialog requests TITLE and ABSTRACT data and provides an option for generating log entries for views on the main channel document (see Figure 24.12).

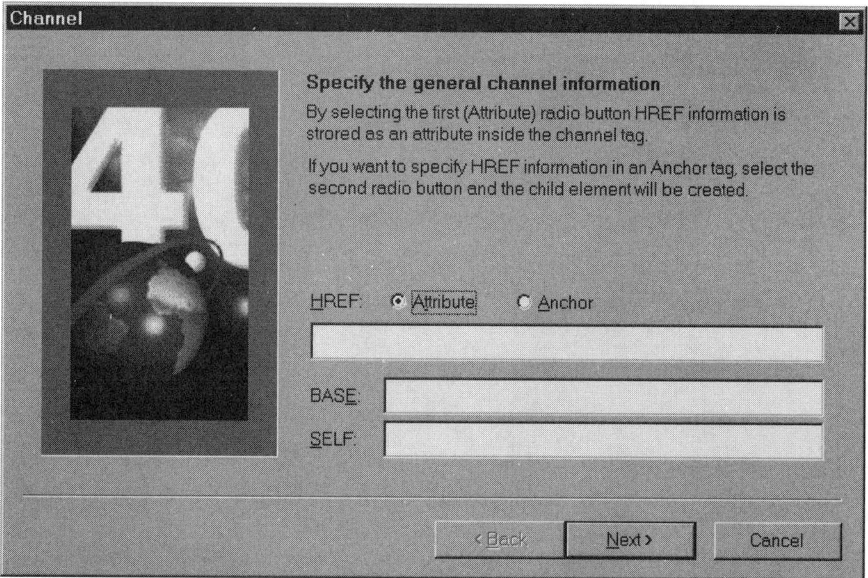

FIGURE 24.11: Collecting channel data with the CDF Generator Wizard

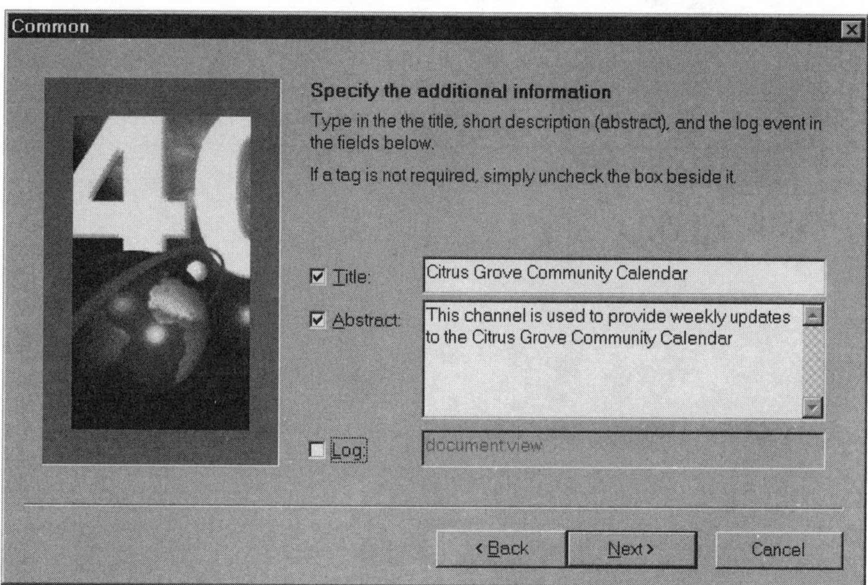

FIGURE 24.12: Describing the channel

Next, each of the three logos—the 16x16 icon file, the 80x32 Channel Bar GIF, and the larger 194x32-wide logo—to be used in the channel are identified (see Figure 24.13).

FIGURE 24.13:

Required logos are identified.

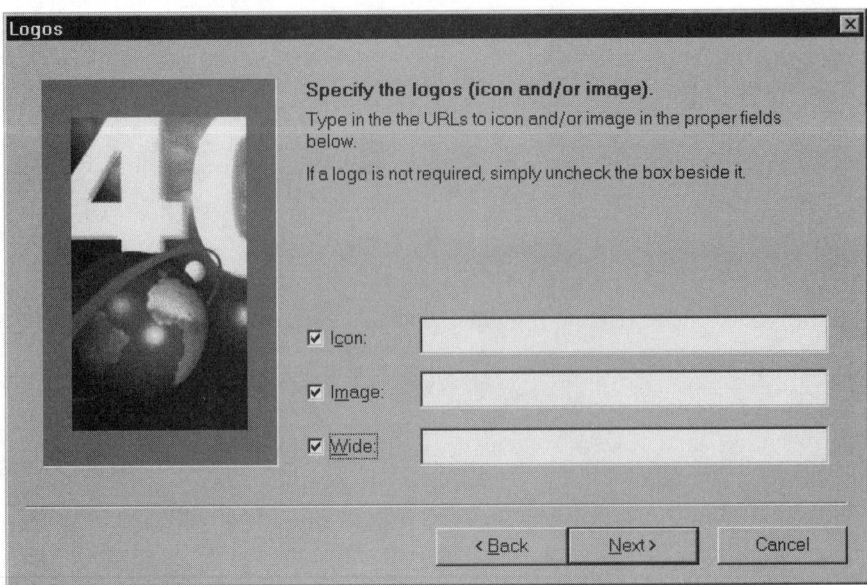

The fourth Wizard screen, shown in Figure 24.14, identifies each of the scheduling options available, including start and end dates, time zone offsets, and interval definitions. You are not required to complete each item, just those you wish to incorporate.

FIGURE 24.14:

A complete set of scheduling options is provided.

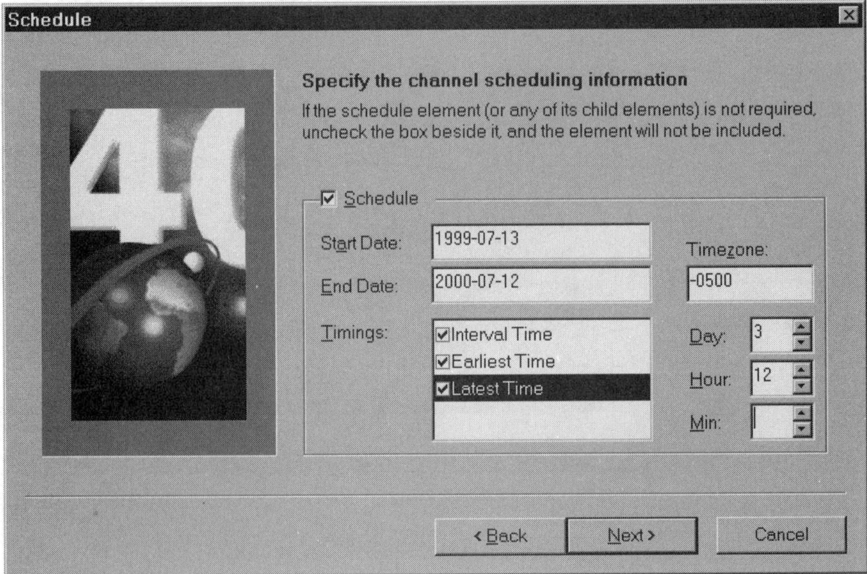

The final input screen provides advanced options for logging subscriber accesses. Logging is not required, but should you choose to implement it, you would set the target URL, the logging scope, and purge times here (see Figure 24.15).

FIGURE 24.15:

Logging options for your channel

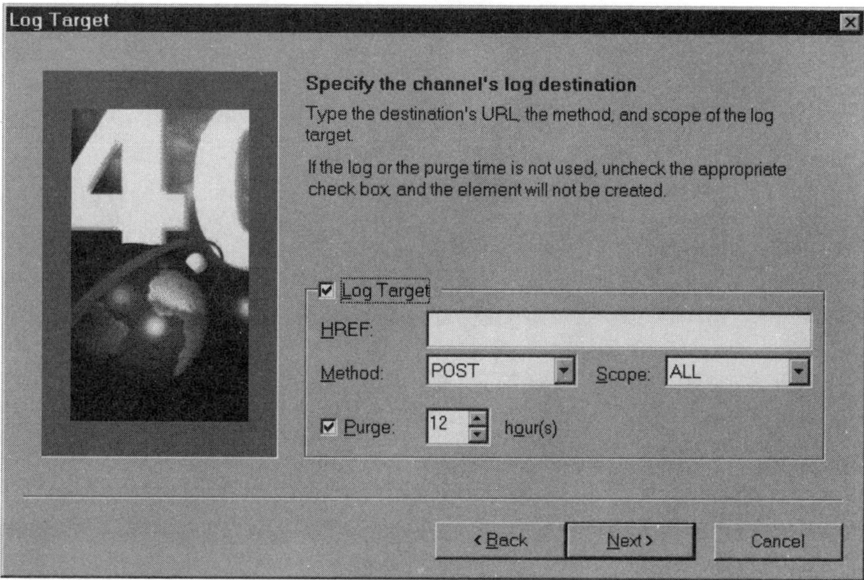

The Wizard then gives you a final opportunity to edit the results of your choices (see Figure 24.16). You can either type directly in the text area window, or you can use the dialog's back button to change options in the previous screens.

Additional editing can be performed on the CDF file once the Wizard has completed its task (see Figure 24.17). The left-hand pane of the editor—referred to as the *tree pane*—now contains a visual hierarchy to the channel's contents. The right-hand pane, known as the *code pane*, contains the code associated with each tree item.

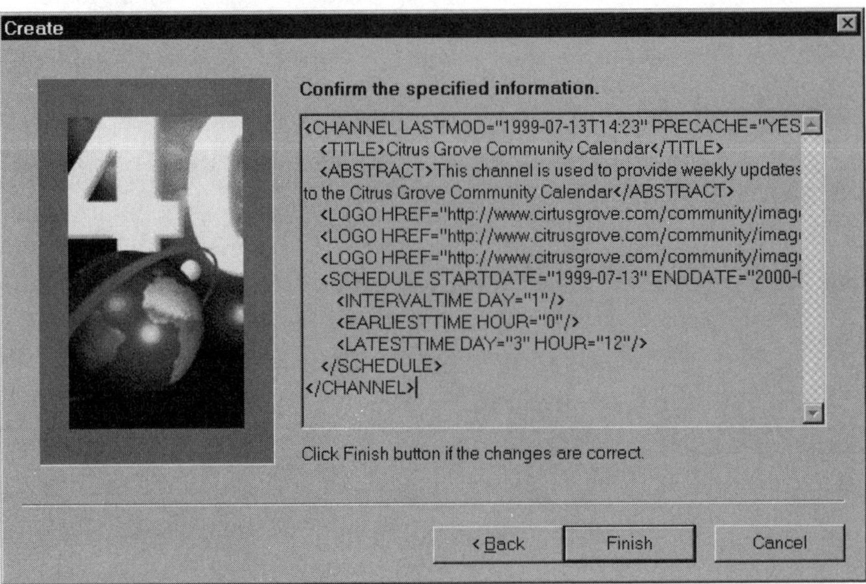

FIGURE 24.16:

Confirming the final output

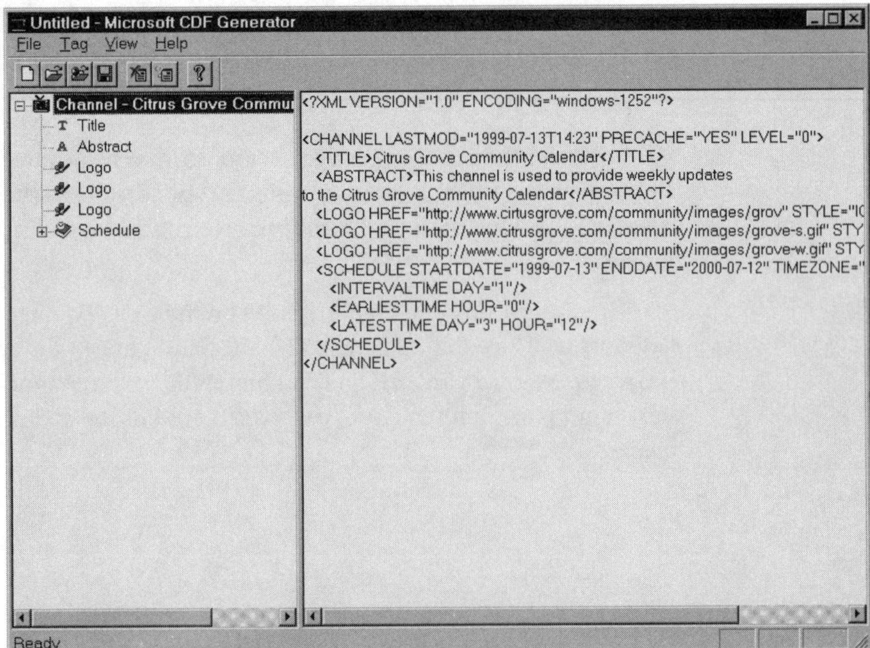

FIGURE 24.17:

The CDF Generator's output into the editor

You add `ITEM`s and any required subchannels from the primary editor interface. To do so, follow these steps:

1. Select the Channel by clicking it in the tree pane.
2. Choose the Tag menu ➢ New ➢ Item or Channel.
3. Complete the information for the Item in the Wizard screens, as with the generation of the original CDF file.
4. Review the new content in the final text area, and choose Finish to send the new item to the editor.

The item now appears in the tree pane, and the associated code is found in the proper place within the CDF file displayed in the code pane.

Design Tips for Channels

While Active Channels are similar to traditional Web sites in that they use HTML files, graphics, and other elements found on the Web, subscribers interact with them in slightly different ways. To maximize the value of your channel, keep these concepts in mind during the development process:

- Channels have a unique navigation scheme. The Channel Pane provides instant access to the hierarchy of items and subchannels.
- Recognize that your channel is a stand-alone delivery vehicle. Don't assume that users of your Web site are necessarily subscribers to your channel, and vice-versa. Critical content should be provided to users in both places.
- Currency is vital. Users will subscribe to channels for quick and easy access to changing information.
- Keep updates manageable—for Active Channels, update them no more than once a day but at least once a week. Consider using an Active Desktop item if up-to-the-minute information is required.
- Time your channels' update schedule for when your audience is likely to be online. Is it business related? Schedule it during the day when your audience is likely to be at the office. Is it an entertainment- or family-oriented channel? Consider scheduling it on evenings and weekends.

- Use update intervals whenever possible. The server load remains well balanced, and your subscribers aren't frustrated by slow response during updates.
- Keep updates small. No one likes to sit through megabytes worth of downloads. For larger items, provide a link so that the user can initiate the download, rather than sending large files to the subscriber during updates.

Up Next

In this chapter, you discovered how easy it can be to integrate XML into your Web site using Active Channels. Microsoft's Channel Definition Format is XML 1–compatible. It allows you to provide customized content, which is automatically updated on a schedule you set, to subscribers.

Next, you'll learn about using other XML applications that enhance the user experience. Each of the four applications featured in the next chapter is a specification developed by the W3C. Highlighting applications that are based on standards allows us to introduce you to techniques that have proven market need and acceptance. We'll take a look at using math on the Web with MathML, synchronized multimedia with SMIL, a system for standardized resource description with RDF, and a mechanism for addressing privacy issues with P3P.

CHAPTER

TWENTY-FIVE

Using XML Applications

- MathML: Math and formula on the Web
- SMIL: Synchronized multimedia without proprietary encoding
- RDF: Describing Web resources
- P3P: Protecting user privacy with XML

So far, we've focused primarily on building documents with XML. While it's true that a considerable number of users will utilize it only in that manner, there are many additional uses of XML that can expand your experience on the Web or enhance interoperability between systems. In this chapter, we'll look at four specifications from the W3C: MathML, SMIL, RDF, and P3P. They all share a common thread: they are applications of XML, and they enhance the user experience.

Mathematical Calculations on the Web: The MathML Specification

With the introduction of HTML, document authors were able to publish text-based content and its inherent structure on the Web. Early on, many users found it difficult, if not impossible, to express mathematical equations or even simple numerical expressions such as exponents using the text processing tools that HTML provided.

Bringing Math to the Web: The Problem Space

The inability of HTML to natively support the intricate level of typesetting that has been the evolving standard for mathematical expression over hundreds of years has hampered the ability of scientists to fully realize the potential of the Web for distributed information exchange. The fonts, character spacing, and line spacing used for math are subtly different than those used in prose text. Anyone who's taken an algebra course is likely to remember the ubiquitous × variable. It's not simply an italicized letter x, which would be *x*, it's a distinct font that is standard in mathematical publishing.

More complex representations suffer from HTML's inability to adjust seemingly simple issues such as changing the baseline of an equation inline in a sentence or properly placing superscripts. These items could be presented as GIF images, which can help the presentation within the equation or expression itself, but the placement within the surrounding prose is still problematic when you try to align an image at the appropriate baseline.

Beyond issues of placement within prose, using images to represent mathematical concepts is less than desirable because the content of those images cannot be readily imported into other applications or even retrieved using cut and paste—they remain static images. The use of images also complicates searching (how can you find *x=36* in an image?) and proper indexing of the data contained within the images.

The Basic Structure of MathML

MathML belongs to a set of markup languages known as *applications of XML*. That is, it is a unique implementation of XML that has been given its own name rather than a whole different markup language. Because it is XML, MathML follows the same basic rules as XML does: it must be well-formed, it can be checked for validity, and the elements, attributes, entities, and so forth are all formed according to the rules laid out in the XML specification. Those rules are not repeated in MathML—you might say they are considered "understood." What makes MathML unique is the rules and syntax supplied above and beyond those of XML.

The MathML-specific features can be divided into two groups: those that further constrict child elements and those that further constrict attribute values.

MathML Arguments

As noted previously, XML does not have the capacity to place constraints on child elements other than order of appearance. In mathematical situations, an equation might require a specific number of child elements or a certain semantic importance applied to a child element. To differentiate between a child element that has no non-XML features and those carrying MathML-specific constraints, the MathML specification labels the special child elements as *arguments*.

Authoring MathML

Because of its inherent complexity of structure, it is not expected that many people will attempt to hand-author MathML as they will HTML, XHTML, and even XML. Instead, equation editors and other software products will be used to create the formulae and equations desired, and the output will then be saved in MathML format.

Consider the relatively basic equation of the Pythagorean theorem:

$$a^2 + b^2 = c^2$$

Written as a MathML expression, the source appears as:

```
<math>
  <msup>
    <msup>
      <mrow>
        <msup>
          <mi>a</mi>
          <mrow>
            <mn>2</mn>
            <mi></mi>
          </mrow>
        </msup>
        <mo>+</mo>
        <msup>
          <mi>b</mi>
          <mn>2</mn>
        </msup>
        <mo>=</mo>
        <msup>
          <mi>c</mi>
          <mn>2</mn>
        </msup>
        <msup>
          <none/>
          <none/>
        </msup>
      </mrow>
      <none/>
    </msup>
    <none/>
  </msup>
</math>
```

It's easy to imagine how cumbersome authoring complex formulae could be. To that end, powerful existing mathematical software programs such as Mathematica are adding support for MathML and dedicated MathML applications are being developed, as well as plug-ins or additional features for existing Web editors. Two of these programs, WebEQ and Amaya, are highlighted here.

WebEQ

WebEQ, from Geometry Technologies, Inc., is a suite of Java applets that provide authoring and editing tools for MathML. The basic interface consists of an Equation

Editor, which has the look and feel of a standard text editor, and a symbol palette, which provides a set of the most often used mathematical symbols that cannot be readily reproduced on the keyboard (see Figure 25.1).

FIGURE 25.1:

The WebEQ Equation Editor and symbol palette

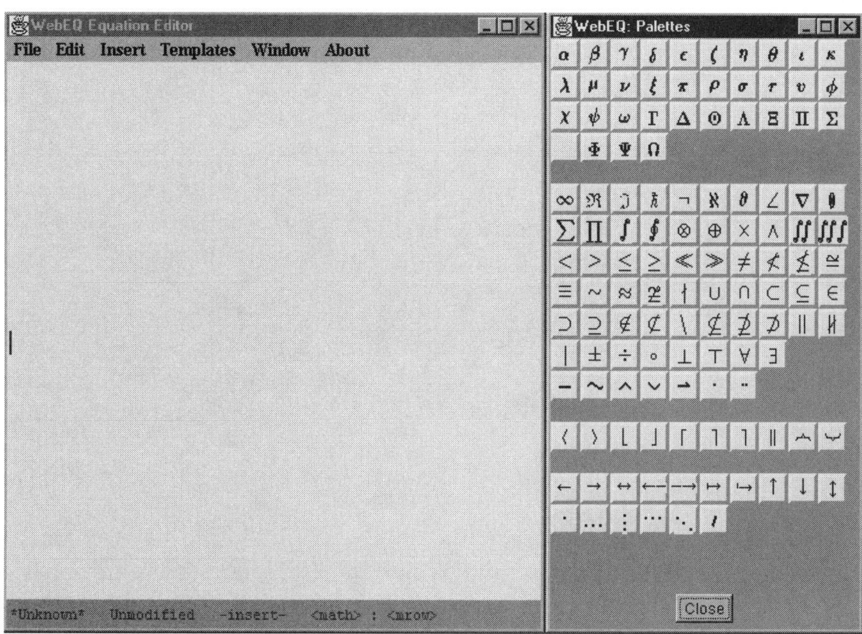

Highly detailed styling options are provided in the Attributes Editor, shown in Figure 25.2, including font choices, super- and subscript placement, line heights and widths, row placement, and more.

The Equation Editor applet has three primary output methods: you may save your work as a Java applet, convert it to a JPEG or PNG graphics file, or export the MathML source to the Windows clipboard for use in another application.

TIP

If you create both a graphic and MathML source for your equation, you can provide links to the image view for people who aren't using a MathML-capable browser but who are viewing your documents that include MathML source.

The makers of WebEQ have also created plug-ins that enable Netscape Navigator 4 or Internet Explorer 4 (IE4) (or higher) to view the applet output of WebEQ. The free add-ons, as well as a trial version of the WebEQ editor, are available for download from the Geometry Technologies Web site at `http://www.webeq.com`.

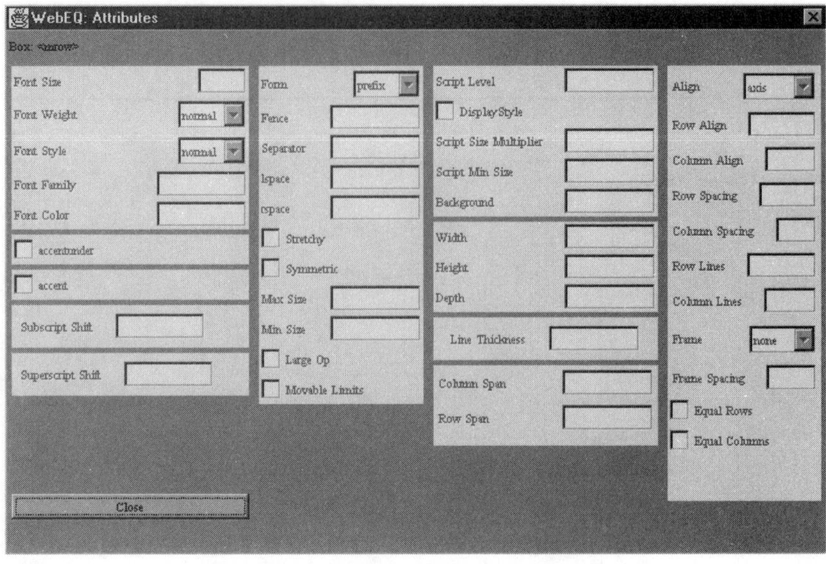

FIGURE 25.2:

A full array of style options is available from the WebEQ Attributes Editor.

Amaya

The Amaya program is both an editor and a fully functional Web browser. Created by W3C staff as a test-bed for new technologies, Amaya has support for both displaying and editing MathML. The editor interface is similar to that of the WebEQ product, though the math palette may be less intuitive for those who don't work with mathematical expressions on a daily basis (see Figure 25.3).

FIGURE 25.3:

Amaya's math palette uses visual representations of expressions.

It is, however, very flexible to use; it provides not only the palette, but extensive menu options (see Figure 25.4) and keyboard shortcuts, as well as the option to transform existing text characters into proper math presentation.

FIGURE 25.4:

Amaya doesn't limit users to a palette for expression selection.

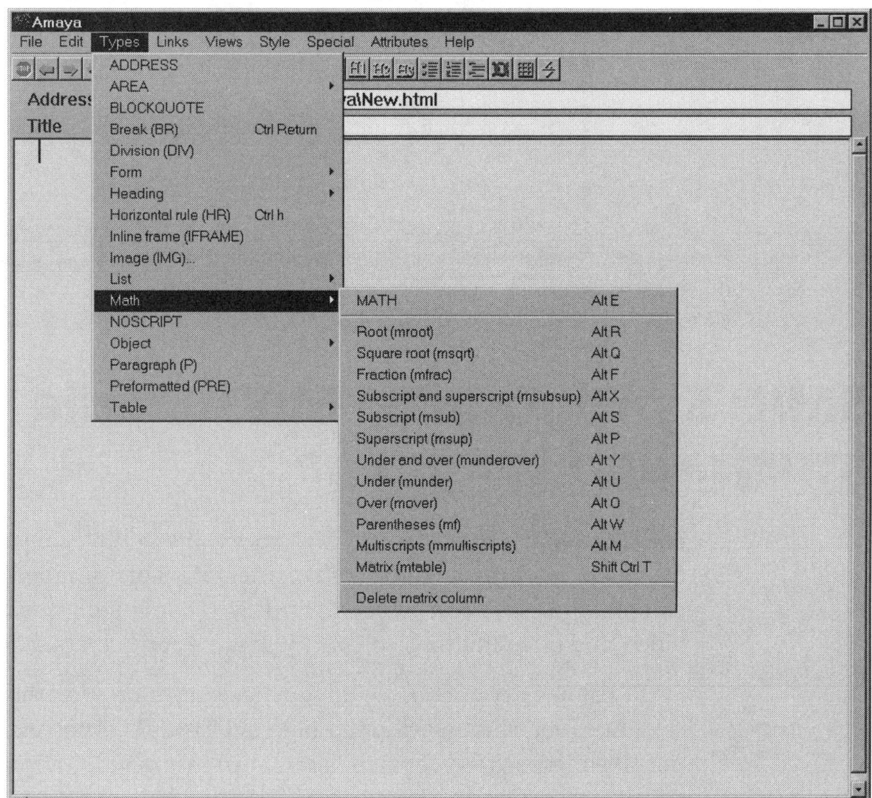

The most exciting aspect of using Amaya is the ability to immediately see your MathML rendered in the browser (see Figure 25.5). The Amaya software makes public MathML publishing a reality today.

TIP

Amaya is available for download from the W3C Web site, at `http://www.w3.org/Amaya/User/BinDist.html`. It is available in PC Linux, Sparc /Solaris, AIX, OSF/1, and Windows (NT and 95/98) executables. As an Open Source project, the source code is also available for those who wish to compile a version for another platform.

FIGURE 25.5:

The Pythagorean Theorem rendered properly in the Amaya Web browser

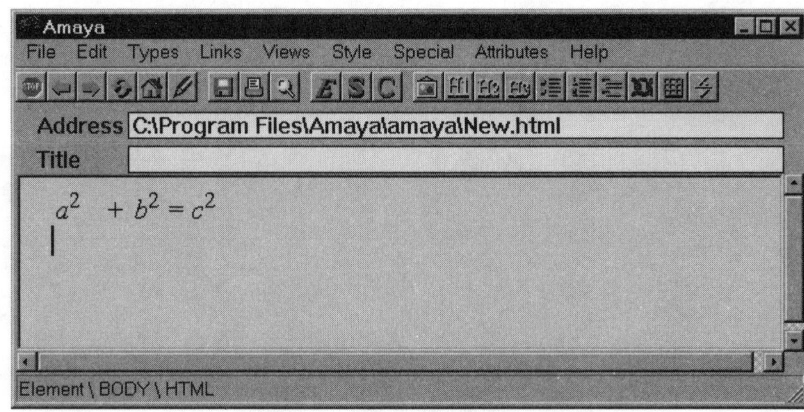

SMIL: Synchronized Multimedia Integration Language

SMIL, the W3C's Synchronized Multimedia Integration Language, is a fully XML 1 compliant markup language for the integration of multimedia objects into a synchronized presentation. In other words, you can combine text, still images, audio, video, and other multimedia content in nearly any combination imaginable.

The complexity of SMIL is in the synchronization of all the elements in your presentation. For those used to working in CD-ROM or television or video production, the ideas will be very similar: for instance, a video stream is cued to start after a five-second display of a still image with music.

Of course, SMIL documents don't necessarily have to be that complex. A simple slide show presentation, formerly only available using animated GIFs or through fairly complicated scripting, can be easily composed using SMIL.

Creating a Slide Show in SMIL

A simple SMIL document, such as the slide show you'll be creating here, can easily be done by hand using a plain text editor. As with all XML documents, it must begin with the XML and DOCTYPE declarations:

```
<?xml version="1.0" encoding="ISO-8859-1"?>
<!DOCTYPE smil PUBLIC "-//W3C//DTD SMIL 1.0//EN"
"http://www.w3.org/TR/REC-smil/SMIL10.dtd">
```

The public identifier and corresponding URL used here are provided by the W3C.

The root element for all SMIL documents is, not surprisingly, <smil>. Next is a <head> element that operates like the <head> found in HTML documents. It is specifically used to store document information that is not related to the temporal aspects of the display. Those aspects are stored as metadata in any desired number of meta elements or, if they pertain to the general layout of the document, in a <layout> element, as shown here:

```
<smil>
  <head>
    <layout>
      <root-layout id="pictures-" title="Amsterdam" width="300"
height="300"/>
      <region id="pictures" title="Amsterdam" width="300" height="300"
fit="meet"/>
    </layout>
  </head>
```

The root-layout element, a child element to layout, determines the size of the viewport used to present the document. (This element actually operates on the root element of the document, <smil>, hence the name root-layout.)

The second child element of layout is a region. The region determines the size and placement of the content for your slide show. As you'll only have the one region containing the photographs, the size of the region and the size of the root layout are the same. If, however, you were to add text captions or other media that needed to share screen space with the photos, the size of the pictures region would be modified accordingly.

The body element contains the remainder of the slide show document:

```
<body>
      <seq dur="indefinite" repeat="indefinite">
        <img src="waag.jpg"
             dur="3s"/>
        <img src="stairs2.jpg"
             dur="3s"/>
        <img src="stairs.jpg"
             dur="3s"/>
        <img src="vault.jpg"
             dur="3s"/>
         <img src="street.jpg"
             dur="3s"/>
        <img src="fokkin.jpg"
             dur="3s"/>
```

```
            <img src="pub.jpg"
                 dur="3s"/>
            <img src="canal.jpg"
                 dur="3s"/>
         <img src="central.jpg"
                      dur="3s"/>
       </seq>
   </body>
 </smil>
```

The sequence element is what sets up the timing or temporal aspect of the display. In this case, you have a sequence of images that will be rotated in the viewport. The attributes for `dur` (duration) and `repeat` govern how long the display may run and how many times it will repeat. Since you've set those attribute values to indefinite, the slide show will continue to run through the sequence until the display is proactively paused, stopped by the user within the SMIL player, or the player is closed.

TIP

The individual image durations are set in seconds of display. While each duration in the above example is the same amount of time, it isn't required that this be so. Take care, however, not to create a jerky feeling when the time periods shift.

The final result can be seen in Figure 25.6, using the GRiNS media player developed by CWI, the Dutch national computer science research center.

FIGURE 25.6:

The slide show as seen in the viewport of the GRiNS SMIL player

The GRiNS tool also provides an enhanced editing environment for SMIL documents. It provides templates for common SMIL presentations such as slide shows; an extended slide show that incorporates captions, music, and other objects; and a default "empty" document (see Figure 25.7).

FIGURE 25.7:

The GRiNS editor user interface

Untitled1 - GRiNS Editor
File Edit Play Tools Navigate View Window Help
Structure View (Untitled1)
Title
picture_1
pictures
picture_2
pictures
picture_3

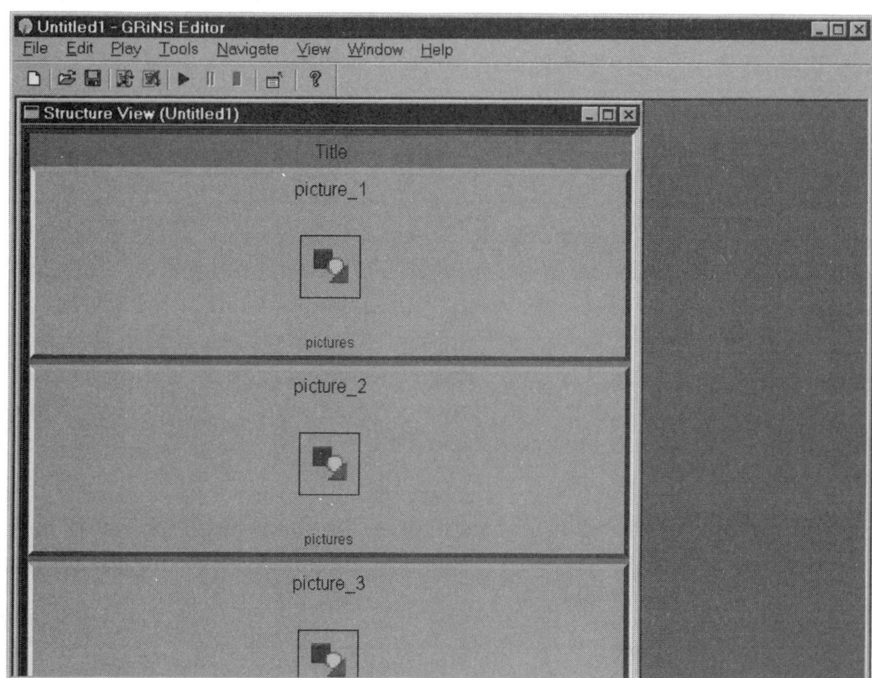

Additional dialog boxes allow the author to set nearly every potential variable for the object selected in the template (see Figure 25.8).

FIGURE 25.8:

Additional details selected through dialogs

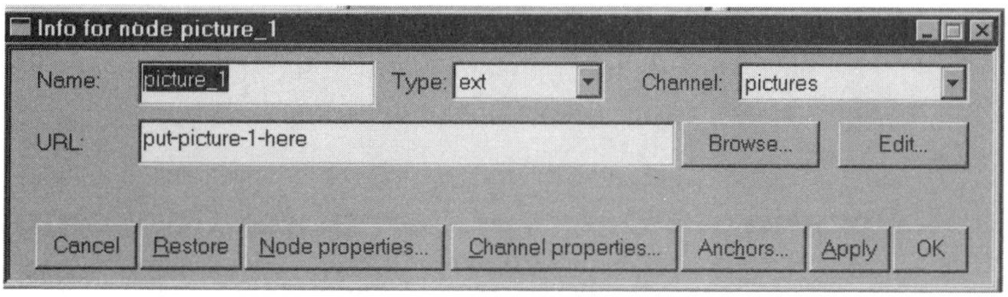

Info for node picture_1
Name: picture_1
Type: ext
Channel: pictures
URL: put-picture-1-here
Browse...
Edit...
Cancel
Restore
Node properties...
Channel properties...
Anchors...
Apply
OK

While SMIL documents certainly can be composed by hand, authoring tools such as GRiNS will likely be the predominate method of creating SMIL-based multimedia displays.

TIP GRiNS may be found online at `http://www.oratrix.com/GRiNS/`.

RDF: Resource Description Framework

The Internet has often been described as a vast electronic library. Servers could be likened to shelves or topical sections, with the sites or individual files found on the Web being like individual books. Unlike libraries, however, which have the Dewey Decimal System, the Internet does not have a universal classification scheme. Certainly, it has URIs that uniquely identify resources, but those identifiers don't supply any universally understandable meta information about the resource that they represent.

Using Dewey, a library visitor looking for a book on religion could quickly discover that they need to go to the shelves holding books in the 200–299 range. On the Web, however, the URL and its corresponding IP address have no such logical groupings.

Beyond the relatively simple task of locating resources, the Web suffers from a lack of information that can be *understood* by a machine. At first, that might sound absurd since the entire Web is based on data stored on computers. But that only means that data is machine-*readable*, not necessarily understandable. Consider a telephone number. In the U.S., local phone numbers consist of a three-digit prefix followed by the four-digit local number, e.g., 555-1234. Humans recognize such a string of digits as a telephone number from the context surrounding it. A computer, however, only knows that it's a string containing three numerals, a character, and four more numerals. That is, it can read the data, but it doesn't understand what it means beyond that it's a string.

Organizing Data for Computer Consumption

To allow computers to catalog and process data in a more intelligent manner, engineers have been testing ways of describing or labeling files and data objects. If a standard description or labeling method were adhered to, then, as with libraries and the Dewey Decimal System, computers would be able to understand more about the resources they are handling.

Toward this end, the W3C created the Resource Description Framework (RDF). RDF provides an environment for processing metadata. We've previously defined metadata as data about data, or descriptions. These descriptions contain the data that needs to be understood by the computer. Using a standard method for processing this metadata allows applications to be programmed with an understanding of an expected description language, as well as the syntax and transports involved that will allow applications to exchange information without worrying about interoperability.

NOTE

The W3C's RDF Model and Syntax Recommendation specifically mentions three major communities that provided instrumental influence to the outcome of the specification: the library community (as you might expect), the "structured documents" community (SGML, XML), and the "knowledge representation" (KR) communities. Working with such disparate groups from the beginning has given RDF a great start on being accepted and implemented.

Three Basic Components

The data model for RDF includes three basic components:

Resources Anything that is to be described by RDF is called a resource. All resources can be referred to through a URI.

Properties The specific traits of the resource that are being described. If you were a resource, one of your properties would be your eye color.

Statements An expression that includes a reference to a resource, along with a property for that resource and that property's value.

Rather than needing to refer to the "value of the property of that resource," RDF has created a basic grammar. Consider the following sentence:

Linda is the Webmaster for `http://www.soccergal.com`.

The resource in that statement is the Web site `http://www.soccergal.com`. It may then be referred to as the *subject* of the statement. The property that is being defined is the Webmaster for that site, which becomes the *predicate*. Finally, the *object* of that predicate (the value of the property) is Linda.

TIP

If the grammar metaphor gives you horrible flashbacks to eighth-grade English class, don't worry too much. In most basic RDF statements it's easy to pick out the properties, values, and resources without having to refer to them in this manner.

If you prefer a flow-chart type system, RDF statements are also frequently represented as diagrams of nodes and arcs. The nodes, drawn as ovals, represent the resources. Objects that are string literals, like the name "Linda" in the sample sentence, are drawn as rectangular nodes. The arc between the two represents the property (see Figure 25.9).

FIGURE 25.9:

A sample RDF statement represented in a nodes and arcs diagram

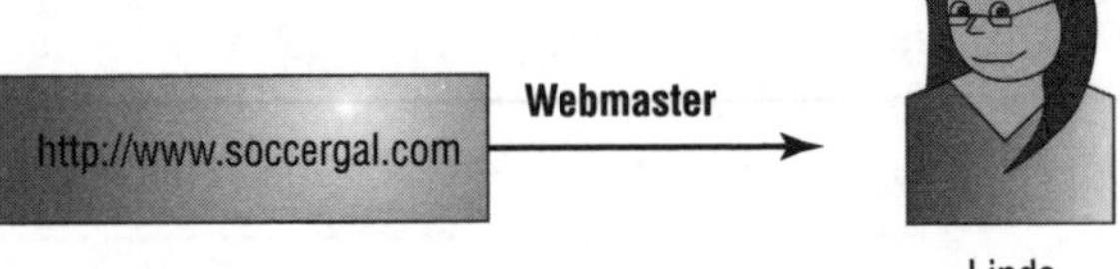

RDF Syntax

So far, we've discussed the abstract ideas behind properties and resources. To be able to use these ideas in a document, you need appropriate syntax. RDF, like all of the other applications in this chapter, uses XML as a framework for its own syntax.

NOTE

It should be noted that RDF also relies on the namespaces in the XML specification to properly bind properties to the schemas that define them.

The RDF namespace property defines the element `Description`. The child element, which is the property being defined, must either be defined in the local DTD or schema, or have an appropriate namespace reference to the schema that does define it. In this case, assume the namespace being used is that of the current document and that both the current namespace and the RDF namespace have previously been declared. The RDF statement, written in XML syntax, then becomes:

```
<rdf:RDF>
    <rdf:Description about="http://www.soccergal.com ">
      <Webmaster>Linda</Webmaster>
    </rdf:Description>
  </rdf:RDF>
```

Online Resources for RDF

There are several useful resources for RDF that can be found online. An extensive list of examples, articles, and RDF implementations can be found at the W3C RDF Web page at `http://www.w3.org/RDF/`.

One of the most useful sites is the Reggie Metadata Editor from the Distributed Systems Technology Centre. Reggie, at `http://www.metadata.net/dstc/`, is a Java applet that allows you to select a schema (including one of your own), identify a resource you wish to describe (such as a Web site), and then interactively edit the metadata. Reggie then compiles it into the format you choose—options are available for HTML metadata, RDF, and others.

Figure 25.10 shows the initial Reggie user interface. Choose from one of the default schemas or enter the URL for one you created yourself or that you have permission to use from another site, as shown in the figure. Then initialize the editor itself by clicking the Go! button (see Figure 25.11).

After entering data in the desired descriptive fields, choose RDF as the output format by using the Select a Syntax drop-down menu. Figure 25.12 displays a preview of the editor output.

FIGURE 25.10:

Start by choosing a schema and identifying the resource Reggie should describe.

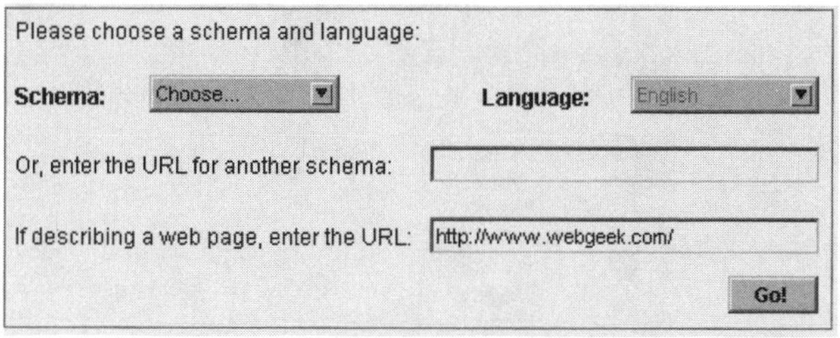

FIGURE 25.11:

Reggie's editor prompts the user for descriptions of each element in the chosen resource.

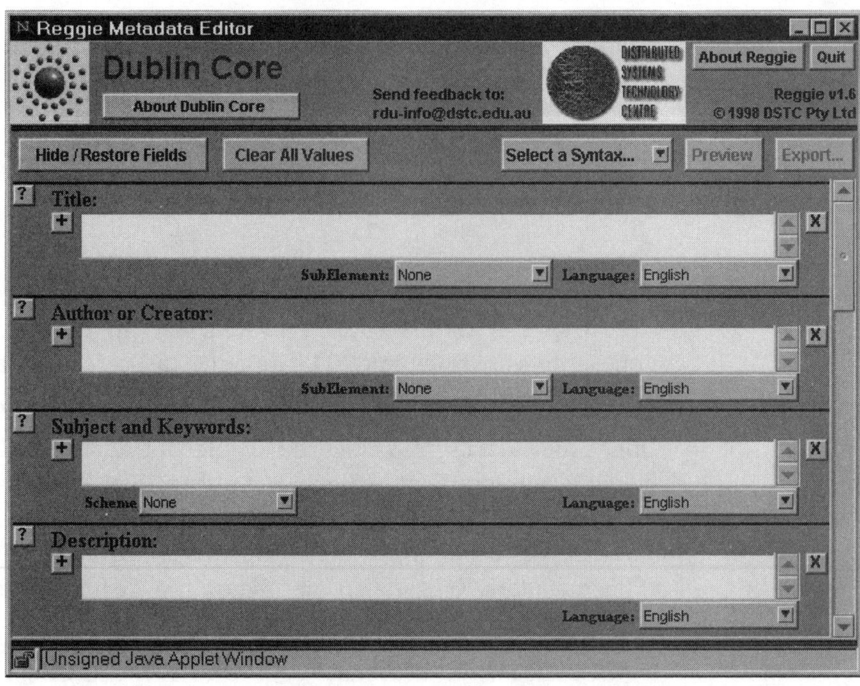

FIGURE 25.12:

Users may preview the Reggie editor output before exporting the final data.

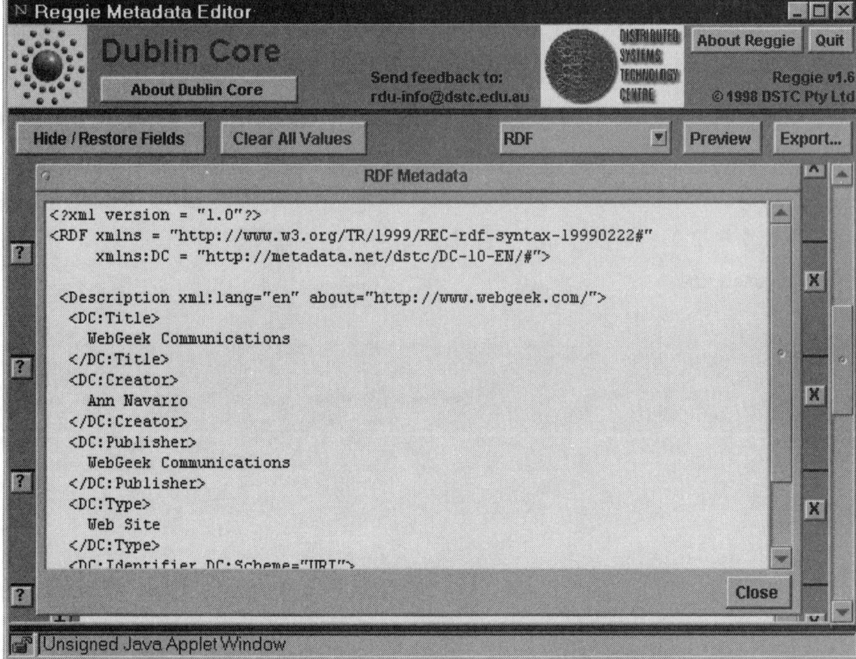

P3P: Platform for Privacy Preferences Syntax Specification

As the Web grows, we as a society are performing more and more functions online, from daily correspondence to banking and bill-paying to game playing to shopping for electronics and computer equipment and even cars and real estate. As the value of these transactions increases, concerns for privacy grow beyond that of the standard "will they send me junk mail?" concern of paper-advertising days.

To allay those fears, the W3C began work on the Platform for Privacy Preferences, or P3P. P3P defines an RDF/XML syntax for automated exchanges between user agents (Web browsers, proxy servers, etc.) and *services*. Services are most often Web sites, but they may be any application that collects user information or makes statements about the privacy of user information.

The first step in such an exchange occurs when the user enters their preferences in a Web browser or other user agent. Instead of only asking for a name and e-mail address as do many current installation routines, browsers that are P3P-compliant might also allow the user to set parameters about when it might be given to a service.

For instance, you may not generally mind submitting your e-mail address to a site when you download a software program. However, you probably do wish to know how the owner of that site will use your name and e-mail address. Ideally, the browser will let you set the level at which you prefer to be notified about software updates and information, giving you choices such as "always," "never," "only if no sales messages are sent," "only for information surrounding this transaction," "only when purchasing products or services," or some other choice from a group of default selections for your e-mail address.

When first visiting a service that uses P3P, they send the browser a *proposal* that details what type of information they wish to collect from you, and how they intend to use it. If their proposal matches your preferences—say you've elected to give your e-mail address for a download, and that's all the service requires for one—then your access to the service will continue without interruption or you ever being outwardly aware that the exchange took place (see Figure 25.13).

If, however, the proposal exceeds the permissible uses you've stated in your preferences, one of two events would take place: the service will send an amended proposal automatically, or the browser will prompt you for a decision regarding that service.

FIGURE 25.13:

When preferences and proposals match, access continues transparently.

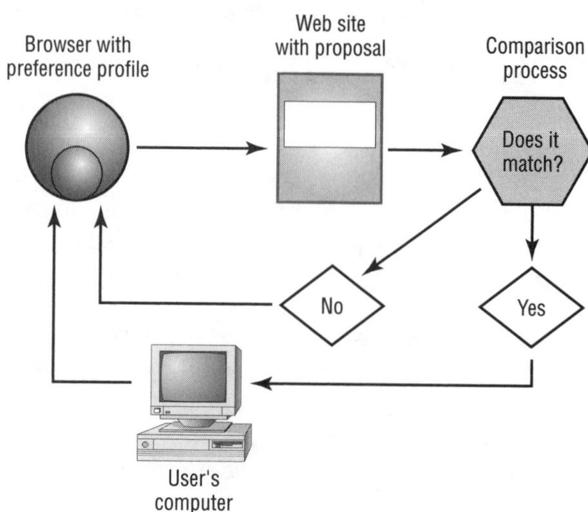

What's Covered by Privacy Preferences

When dealing with issues of privacy, you're dealing with more than just name, address, telephone number, and credit card details. P3P can help users manage how tracking of their habits and behavior within a site can be collected and used as well.

The P3P specification defines 10 distinct categories of data, as follows:

Physical contact information A user's home or business address, telephone number, fax number, etc.

Online contact information Primarily an e-mail address.

Unique identifiers A means of identifying a specific individual. This may be a government-issued ID such as a U.S. social security number, a driver's license number, or any other unique label given to a distinct individual.

Financial account numbers Credit card numbers, checking account numbers, or other numbers tied directly to a financial resource (brokerage accounts, etc.).

Computer information Which browser and operating system is being used, what IP address the user accessed from, etc.

Navigation and click-stream data What pages a user visited, how long they stayed, etc. (this is data that can be obtained through most Web server logs).

Interactive data What portions of a site a user proactively engaged. May include purchases, queries, or other calculations.

Demographic and socioeconomic data Basic marketing information such as age, gender, education level, income, family size.

Preference data A user's specific tastes (as opposed to P3P preferences), e.g., do they prefer romantic comedies to action movies?

Content Copies of specific information entered by the user, such as postings to a message board, copies of e-mail queries, etc.

How Information May Be Used

Now that a common vocabulary for information types is available, services can describe their intended uses for this data. P3P provides six potential-use scenarios:

Completion and support of current activity Information is necessary to complete a transaction, e.g., a physical address that is required to ship merchandise being purchased.

Web site and system administration Information may only be used in the process of maintaining and servicing the Web site and the computer it resides on. For example, if a Web page is reported to crash some users' browsers, the user agent data may be used to determine which browser is having a problem with site content.

Customization of site to individuals Data is necessary to provide information. For example, a news site may offer local weather updates and need the user's zip code or other locale-defining data to provide correct information.

Research and development Information is used in aggregate to enhance the Web site or service offerings. For example, if the hit count for a specific page seems unduly low, the service owner may create a more obvious link to it from their main page. No individually identifying information is used in this scenario.

Contacting of visitors for marketing of services or products Just as it sounds, the service wants to use information to make sales contacts with the user at a later date.

Other uses Uses not defined in the other five categories. If a service declares that it will use data for "other" purposes, a human-readable explanation of those purposes is required.

In addition to the purposes declared in these six types, an additional statement is required by P3P that reinforces whether data is used in a manner that could potentially be personally identifiable. For instance, if a collection of IP addresses were kept as a record of "users," that information could potentially identify individuals. While many users access the Web through a pool of IP addresses reserved by their ISP, many more users have fixed IP addresses assigned to their companies and perhaps even to their individual machine. This additional statement of identifying use is therefore important.

Who Has Access to This Information?

Not only must a privacy policy state how information will be used, it must also cover who will have access to the information collected. If you've ever subscribed to a magazine or made a catalog purchase, you may have received an increased volume of similar postal mail and realized that your name and address were sold or rented to other companies.

To that end, four distinct categories of information users have been established in the P3P specification. Those are:

Ourselves and/or our agents The service provider or others whom they may hire to perform the previously stated task. For example, a drop shipper may be given a postal address in order to complete the shipment of your merchandise order.

Organizations following our practices The service provider may share your information with other providers who have the same policies. For example, two universities that have the same privacy statements may exchange information about students' educational history.

Organizations following different practices The original service provider may share your information with providers of different services. The secondary providers are still accountable to the original provider, but they may treat the information in differing manners. For example, a magazine publisher may share information with their advertisers, who in turn may solicit your purchase of products featured in the magazine.

Unrelated third parties or public forums Providers whose practices aren't known or who may make user data publicly available in a directory or other public-use manner.

User Management of Collected Data

Finally, service providers must disclose whether a user can see the information being collected about them and how any errors or concerns may be addressed. Details on how long data is retained and whether any *assuring party* watches over the provider's policies are also disclosed. An assuring party is a third-party organization that service providers may subscribe to. Essentially, they are self-regulatory bodies. By becoming a member, the service provider pledges to behave in the manner declared in the assuring party's privacy policies and grants the assuring party the right to revoke membership and/or take other action against them if violations occur.

Consumers are used to being able to work with third-party organizations such as the Better Business Bureau and consumer affairs departments of local governments. Knowing that someone else is also watching over a service provider can be reassuring to consumers.

Up Next

In this chapter, you looked at four different implementations of XML in other W3C specifications. These uses demonstrate the flexibility inherent in the Extensible Markup Language and perhaps will have inspired you to envision even more uses for XML in the future.

In the next part, *Using XML in the Real World*, you'll find five chapters that provide detailed examples from companies that have already successfully implemented XML into their business methods. This insight into the processes others have gone through may serve as the basis for your own integration of XML in your workplace.

PART VIII

Using XML to Solve Real Business Problems

CHAPTER

TWENTY-SIX

26

Introduction to Real World Examples

- Do real world XML implementations exist?
- How is XML used in the real world?
- Summary

It would be very difficult for you to have read this far and not be caught up in the spell of XML. The story of XML's history has definitely been a page-turner. You've learned about suggested design methodologies, XML Schema construction, the building blocks of XML, how to construct XML documents, and how to convert HTML to XML. Furthermore, you've been exposed to some of the tool groups and many of the specialized XML vocabularies.

"OK," you say. "Now I'm ready to learn about real implementations. What do people actually use XML for?

Do Real World XML Implementations Exist?

Although XML V1 has been a W3C Recommendation for more than a year and a half, and has enjoyed substantial exposure in the press and in the developer community, many people still ask if XML is really there yet. They aren't asking if it's possible to construct XML DTDs or use XML parsers. They want to know if XML is mature enough to be used for mission critical applications. Can companies create business applications based on XML, even though pieces like XSL, XML Schemas, Xlink, and XPointer are only partially complete? Are the tools ready enough to accomplish business solutions?

One cannot answer a blanket yes to all these questions. Some aspects of XML are more ready for prime time than others. Also, prime time doesn't always mean the same thing, depending on a company's culture and track record for taking advantage of new enabling technologies.

Chapters 27-30 are case studies that demonstrate uses of XML in the business world. Each presents a specific business problem, the solution, and its dependence on XML. In some cases, the solution is fully formed and already implemented, as in Chapter 29: "Using XML for Content Repurposing and Dynamic Content Delivery," the sophisticated document management application developed at Dell Computer. In other cases, the XML design is mostly complete but the implementation is still in progress, like Chapter 30: "Using XML for School Interoperability Framework." However, in all cases, it's clear how XML-based systems provide—or will provide—the enabling technology to make the whole solution operative.

This chapter examines two possible models for these implementations and describes which model various functional aspects fit into. In this context, it also presents short examples of how XML-based solutions can enable cost-effective and efficient business solutions.

How Is XML Used in the Real World?

First, let's go back and review what XML is good for. In Chapter 2: "Getting Acquainted with XML," we looked at the business drivers for XML. We will examine those again in this chapter, in the context of the business models.

XML for Documents or Data in the Real World: Does It Matter?

Chapter 2 briefly introduced the concept of *document centric* and *data centric* applications. Now we'll discuss how these phrases relate to real world applications.

Models are sometimes useful for applying *context* or explaining a concept. The following models help in understanding XML applications.

Some folks believe that in the beginning there was light and after that came Standard Generalized Markup Language (SGML). Perhaps that account of evolution is not completely accurate, but the important point is that the development of SGML certainly preceded XML by many years.

The initial incentive behind SGML (actually GML, its predecessor) was to provide a way to separate structure and presentation—or to create an *abstraction* of the data. Charles Goldfarb, the inventor of SGML, describes it this way:

> "The principle of separating document description from application function makes it possible to describe the attributes common to all documents of the same type…[The] availability of such 'type descriptions' could add new function to the text processing system…A generalized markup language then would permit full information about a document to be preserved, regardless of the way the document is used or represented."

SGML is all about documents. GML initially looked at legal documents and SGML built on that use and added technical manuals and reference publishing. Up to the time of SGML, the process of updating huge manuals and keeping track of all the places that certain sections were used was time consuming, cumbersome, and practically impossible, much like managing some Web sites today. By providing a means to break a document down into components, SGML made it possible to manage documents and document fragments, and also to deliver them in any presentation format.

As an example of what SGML delivers, a large aerospace manufacturer sells the same planes to different airlines. All the airlines use the same manuals for the planes, but each airline has critical policy sections and safety procedures that are different. Using SGML, the sections that change are identified and only the appropriate ones are printed—or delivered online—for each airline. When the manufacturer develops a new plane it uses some of the same parts that other planes use but many are different. The sections of the manual that are still valid can be reused, because they can be identified and extracted as separate pieces of information—without any formatting characteristics—and combined into new documents automatically with SGML.

XML can be used for exactly the same kinds of applications although some features of SGML will not be available. In fact, any implementation that requires management of document components in order to retrieve, reuse, and recombine data objects is a perfect use for XML.

The point of all of this is in the definition of *document.* In the example above the end result (the document) is a presentation perceived by humans.

You could describe the following process of creating and delivering documents as the traditional publishing model:

- Information is authored (or converted from some other source) by a person.
- Information is then delivered on the appropriate medium and presented with the appropriate presentation format through the use of style sheets.
- The information is then stored.
- Often today, the information is also managed in some way by a document/content/media asset management system so that some of the content can be reused from the repository or repositories in subsequent documents.

This is called a *document centric* application.

As most of the members of the original XML Working Group had backgrounds in SGML and had been developing document systems in the traditional sense, it's no surprise the abstract of the specification in Chapter 2 appeared to be very *document centric.*

Today, the picture is somewhat different. A representative of Chrystal Software, a leading XML vendor of document management software, describes it as

> "a fundamental shift away from the traditional use of documents and files to thinking about a document as a container into which various pieces of data are combined or 'poured' as required. This kind of document may be stored for an extended period of time, or it may exist only as long as a person interacts with it. The kinds of data that are poured into this container may be text, images, and audio clips and so on that we identify with traditional publishing. But they may also be numeric data drawn from various databases."

Rather than a document being a synonym for a story, book, magazine article, and so on, a document in the *data centric* world is transitory. A document may last only as long as one transaction and may be viewed only by software programs. Documents may be generated by a software program for another software program or may be a compilation of various pieces of information, such as text, numbers, or charts that are viewed on a single Web page. Figure 26.1 is an example of this is a very non-traditional model referred to as a multitiered architecture model.

FIGURE 26.1:

Multitier architecture for data centric applications

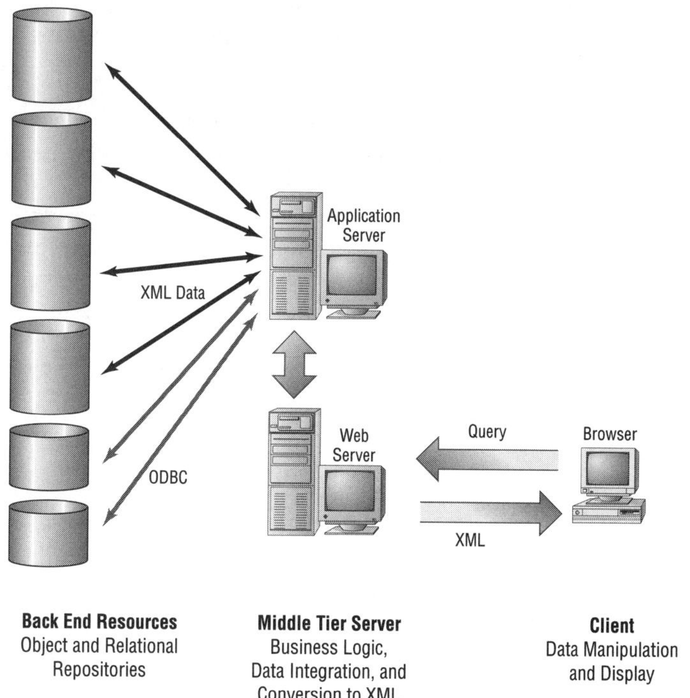

Unlike the traditional publishing model where the application begins with creation (or conversion) of data on the client, the multiple-tier architecture model begins with a query. The query goes from the client to the middle-tier application server, which then communicates with the back-end resources that are usually repositories of some kind, although they could be flat files as well. Naturally the data was created at some point, but the emphasis is on data acquisition rather than authoring.

The middle tier is where the business logic or, you could say, the *intelligence* of the application, resides. Based on that business logic, the server communicates with back-end resources and acquires specific data.

According to Figure 26.1, the data is acquired in two formats and probably from two types of repositories. The XML data could come from either an object or a relational database. Typically, the relational data would be in the proprietary format of the source relational database. Servers may have a translation engine built-in to translate the proprietary data, or alternatively they call an outside translation engine.

NOTE Most major relational database vendors are in the process of adding an XML layer that will provide data transformation on-the-fly.

The middle-tier application server consults its business logic to determine how to combine the small XML documents (sometimes referred to as snippets) into one larger document that corresponds to the client's query.

Once all the XML documents are assembled according to the business logic, the document is sent to the client for display and post processing.

NOTE Depending on your definition of *document* the combined chunks of XML data are referred to as document fragments or XML documents.

Message Oriented Middleware

The programs that act between other software programs are often referred to as middleware. In this case, we are discussing a particular kind of middleware called Message-Oriented-Middleware (MOM). Previously, MOM applications lived in a very separate world from traditional document applications; they were MRPs, Database, finance, and Supply Chain applications. Now as application categories have begun to overlap it is becoming a fairly common term.

Matching Functions to Business Models

With the traditional publishing model and the multi-tier application model in mind, let's look at the following functions and see if they are data or document centric:

Media-independent publishing This is document centric.

Search and retrieval of precise data using element names and Metadata Both data and document centric applications require this function.

Post processing Usually data centric.

Component/media management This function is generally used for document centric applications.

Web site management This can be either or both depending on what aspects of the Web site are being managed—content, statistics, and load balancing.

Event-driven database interaction The actual function is data centric but the usage could be either.

Interapplication communication Again, the actual function is data centric but applications can include both models.

Data aggregation The function of combining disparate pieces of XML data into one XML document is data centric, but the data being combined could result in a presentational document.

Electronic Commerce E-commerce applications are usually regarded as data centric. Although they often include information from catalogs, which is made up of text and images, the document that they present is a page that is created on the fly and lives only for one view.

Real World Scenarios

Today, we are starting to see data and document centric models being combined for different parts of a single application. However, it is still very useful to consider if the application is primarily data or document centric when choosing tools. Different tools are definitely optimized for either presentation-oriented or MOM functions.

The following scenarios illustrate how data centric and document centric aspects can be used and combined in applications. These scenarios are not descriptions of existing implementations, although parts of each scenario are in actual operation. Rather these scenarios are examples of the types of business solutions you will be able to construct with XML-enabled software when the key related specifications become XML Recommendations, and some of the tools, particularly data aggregation tools, become more sophisticated. The importance of these examples is that they illustrate business challenges related to the bottom line.

Electronic Commerce Scenario

It is very easy to understand how XML can be used for document markup to enhance retrieval and reuse of data. However, one of the reasons XML has caught on is its applicability to e-commerce. When all parts of a commerce system understand and interchange the same data format, performance and functionality will improve.

The Business Problem

A large testing equipment manufacturer has bought about 10,000 pogo pins per week from the same supplier for ten years. Since expanding its facilities, the manufacturer has found that its regular supplier is unable to provide the additional 6,000 pogo pins needed for the expanded capacity.

In a non-XML enabled system to find a new supplier, someone in purchasing will sort through all of the different suppliers' catalogs to compare prices and then call each company to determine available inventory. Finally, an order will be placed electronically, but first someone will need to find the guide for how to set up the order.

Scenario: An XML-Enabled System

The manufacturer's purchasing manager, John Casehammer, has everything under control. He clicks on a special icon on his desktop and is connected to a form where he can specify pogo pins. The search results are returned as a table on a single Web page. The table shows all of the suppliers who carry pogo pins, their prices (and volume discounts), delivery options (and pricing), and existing inventory.

John can sort this list according to any of the cells in the table. If price is critical, he can sort suppliers by price so the least expensive supplier is easiest to find. If volume is the priority, he can sort by that criterion, and so on.

Once John determines what he wants to buy he can initiate the order—provided that he has the appropriate signing authority that the application requires. As soon as he selects the manufacturer, a purchase order (PO) is created and automatically translated into the supplier's automated PO format. The PO already has all the critical data filled in, including data about John's company (account number, John as the contact, preferred shipping methods, etc.). The order is then passed automatically into the supplier's internal order-tracking database to be fulfilled.

John's system saves the day. He gets a big raise and lives happily ever after.

Analysis

John's system is a data centric electronic commerce application based on the multitier application model. Although the data is integrated into a single document that is presented in human readable form, it is not persistent—the document lasts only as long as it stays on the screen. Once another action is initiated, that document is gone. Furthermore, the major functions of the application are software talking to software, rather than software producing documents for people to read and store.

John's system combines many of functions of XML:

- Search and retrieval of precise data using element names and Metadata.
- Post processing.
- Accessibility. (This is not stated explicitly, but the assumption is that it has been considered.)
- Event-driven database interaction.
- Interapplication communication.
- Data aggregation.

To make John's application work, you need a client that can interpret, sort, and render XML. You also need to create the appropriate XML forms and XSL and/or CSS templates.

You also need an application server with business logic built into the middle tier that is able to:

- Query various kinds of databases with a tool that searches within elements to retrieve precise information.

- Activate sophisticated conversion technology to translate the retrieved data into XML and vice versa—either built-in or via an external middleware engine that provides that functionality. (Unless the data is already in XML which is pretty unlikely for this kind of data.) There are also some vocabularies that make this task easier depending on the type of data being transferred. For instance, no matter what middleware package a particular vendor uses on their Web site, there is a Web Distributed Data Exchange (WDDX) module that can make vendor's proprietary cost, quantity, or other types of data available in XML.
- Integrate the XML snippets it received back into one XML document (based on the appropriate style sheet), that is sent to the client. Integrating XML snippets is not trivial because each will probably be based on different schema. This function could also use some assistance from a middleware vocabulary like WDDX. Integrating the snippets of data from various vendors is easier using WDDX, because modules can translate the XML into objects native to whatever programming language you are using.

For this system to work all of the products need to be really fast! For example, a performance goal might be that updates be at least five to ten times as fast as the airline sites are today. All of the transactions would require the consistent use of an XML vocabulary (or vocabularies) that contains a predictable set of known elements—in other words, an industry standard XML vocabulary.

NOTE

You could get around the performance issue in part by creating the integrated catalog in advance. By polling the various suppliers' Web sites at specified intervals the client only sends a request for an update on a specific item when the user chooses a product, which improves response time. To set up such an integrated catalog it is necessary to have an accepted standard vocabulary for updating.

This may all sound like a lot of blue sky but there are server tools and client tools in use today that include some of these features, and vendors are racing to provide more. Although it's true that this particular scenario requires a considerable amount of scripting, this will diminish over time, as more middleware becomes available. Nate Zelnick, a journalist at *InternetWorld* described this type of scenario as follows:

> "This type of scenario demonstrates how XML can be used as the lingua franca for structured data within a particular industry or group of related businesses even if they make no arrangements to coordinate their systems ahead of time. This makes it possible

for the Internet to act as a conduit for complex business transactions without requiring complex, time-consuming and expensive re-engineering of information systems. It also brings the same level of flexibility in commerce that the Web brought in the presentation of information to unknown users."

NOTE The previous scenario example is loosely based on a scenario created for the Microsoft XML Web site (`http://www.microsoft.com/xml`).

Personalized Market Monitoring

One of the most exciting ways that XML-based systems can increase personal productivity is through personalized publishing. A business problem that faces many of us today and a solution using XML are described in the following scenario.

The Business Problem

Once upon a time—just a few years ago—many of us complained that we never had enough information. Now we have way too much. Some might say, "Not too much. Just not the right information."

Of course, the right information may be sitting on our desks, or in one of the online newsletters we subscribe to, or in an archive, somewhere, if only we had time to look. How many of us recognize ourselves in this scenario?

Many companies subscribe to online market reports tailored to match personal/company profiles. These profiles provide some filtering, but often they deliver articles that are off topic and miss out on key pieces of information. Furthermore, we don't necessarily want to read through whole articles. Ideally, reports combine sections of articles with charts and graphs from other articles, for instance, and with investment and economic predictions that all relate to the specific topic in which we're interested.

Scenario

When Nancy enters her office every morning there is a report on her desktop that may reorder her priorities for the day. Nancy is an investment advisor currently tracking two companies in the health care industry that both are about to launch initial public offerings (IPO) of their stock. She needs to advise one of her corporate clients whether they should invest in one company or the other—in this scenario they don't want to invest in both. The corporate client also wants to sell shares of stock they own in another company to maximize their investment in one of the health care firms and Nancy must advise them as to the right moment to sell those shares.

The rumor mill says that both offerings of stock will skyrocket the first day of trading on the market. The relevant financial indicators also point in the same direction because both companies have recently developed new products that are hot. Still, Nancy doesn't want to take any chances.

Nancy has analyzed the financial history of both companies, but there are many other factors that can affect the stock price. Consequently, the daily report that potentially reorders her day is actually two reports; one for each health care company she tracks. Each report includes pertinent sections from articles printed the previous day about the specific areas of the health care industry that are relevant to each company. The reports also include information about the overall economy, factors that might influence investor enthusiasm including information from all of the major world markets. The information is presented in tables and graphs that Nancy can manipulate to see multiple views of the same data. The report also incorporates political information that might affect investor confidence. All of this information is integrated into a few Web pages that she can review rapidly.

Analysis

Nancy's scenario is both document and data centric. The final result is an online document formatted using appropriate XSL style sheets, so this scenario fits the publishing model. Also, search and retrieval of precise data using element names and Metadata plays a critical role. These functions fit into either document or data centric applications, but here their role is document centric. In this situation, XML enables the integration and delivery of extremely meaningful, up-to-date, on-demand data. It also makes data retrieval much more precise, as searching can be specified to take place within elements/document fragments rather on whole documents as in traditional file-based document management system.

However, most of the other functions in Nancy's scenario are the same as those in John's purchasing/manufacturing scenario. The *data centric* aspects are as follows:

- Post processing occurs when Nancy manipulates the data in the tables, charts, and graphs in the report.

- Event-driven database interaction and interapplication communication occurs when the application queries databases that contain the financial data and other content that is delivered in the report. This is all based on the business logic built into the middle tier server.
- It's likely that the image and possibly news content is stored in a media asset management system and that the other kinds of data each have their own database and all are proprietary. However, they can all export to XML via a built-in transformation engine or one that they call to accomplish this task.
- The application also must perform data aggregation of the small XML snippets to combine them into one XML document. Then it must deliver this content and present it using style sheets. This is very tricky because the data constantly changes and therefore the mapping can't be hardwired. XML is used as the means of communicating between these data sources, enabling intelligent information to be delivered directly to the browser desktop of the end-user.

Summary

In this chapter you have learned about document centric applications that concentrate on presenting information to humans. Often this information is kept and stored in some kind of archive, although it is not required.

You have also learned that data centric applications focus on software-to-software communication and typically produce XML documents that are either never read by humans or are read but are immediately and automatically discarded.

Sophisticated XML applications usually combine aspects of both types of application. When you are choosing software tools, it's very important to consider the design goals for manipulation and presentation of documents or for interapplicaton communication.

This chapter also reviewed some types of business challenges that are solved by XML-enabled application systems.

Now it is time to move on to actual designs and implementations. The chapters that follow in Part VIII: "Using XML to Solve Real Business Problems" present examples of how XML is being used in the real world today.

CHAPTER TWENTY-SEVEN

Using XML for Business-to-Business Data Integration: A webMethods Case Study

- Dun & Bradstreet's business problem
- Dun & Bradstreet's Global Access solution
- webMethods's B2B Integration Server
- How XML is used by Global Access
- The Global Access toolkit
- XML development tips

CRAIG MCQUEEN is a principal consultant at Sage Information Consultants, Inc. His role at Sage is guiding clients through the adoption of Internet technologies. Recently, he led an e-commerce implementation of Site Server at a major consumer electronics company. In addition to his contributions to *Mastering XML*, Craig is a contributing author to *XML Applications* and *Professional Site Server 3*. He also writes monthly articles for *ASPToday.com* and *ActiveWeb Developer*. Craig holds a Master of Science degree from the University of Toronto, where he specialized in Human-Computer Interaction.

The initial draft of the XML specification, first presented at the November 1996 SGML Conference in Boston, has progressed from being a W3C Working Draft to a W3C Recommendation. Since then many parsers have been written and there has been much speculation in the XML community as to how many great applications will be built using XML. There has been talk in the media and the industry that XML will save the Web and organize it into a more structured source of information.

Many tools are available for working with XML and some products are now XML-enabled. However, there are still not many solutions being built that use XML as a foundation for solving problems. In this case study, you will see how XML enabled Dun & Bradstreet to solve a business problem, transform the way they do business, create new opportunities, and open markets.

This chapter assumes you have an understanding of XML, and specifically of a DTD. You also should have a general understanding of a tiered-architecture and the HTTP protocol.

You'll see how XML can be used as the glue to pull together a number of disparate systems. You also will see how webMethods's B2B Integration Server can shorten the development time of XML applications. Finally, you will take away some hints on real-world XML development from the team that built the solution you are about to see.

Note that this case study is not meant as a guide to using the solution presented, but rather is a demonstration of how XML was a key component in solving a business problem.

About Dun & Bradstreet

Dun & Bradstreet (D&B) is in the business of providing information about other businesses. This includes business-to-business credit, marketing, purchasing, receivables, management, and decision-support services.

D&B Customers use D&B information to build relationships with their customers, suppliers, and business partners and to make informed business decisions. Some examples of decisions that a customer might use D&B information to help reach a determination include:

- Assessing credit and risk
- Assessing a supplier's overall financial and operational performance
- Thoroughly understanding the current status of key suppliers as well as their future outlook
- Knowledge of newsworthy events relating to suppliers culled from hundreds of nationwide news sources

One of D&B's marketing messages is that they strive for quality—in other words, accurate and complete information. D&B's goal is to provide fast and fresh information for their customers. To provide that information D&B maintains one of the world's largest business information databases (they claim it is *the* largest). The database holds information about businesses around the globe, including more than 53.8 million companies in 200 countries; there are up to 1,500 data elements for any given company. D&B obtains this information from many diverse sources, including:

- Federal bankruptcy filings
- The office of the United States secretary of state
- Public utility companies
- The United States Postal Service
- More than 2,500 state filing agencies
- Daily newspapers, publications, and electronic news services

Hundreds of millions of pieces of data, ranging from trade styles to trade experiences to financial statements, are integrated every day into one file through the use of D&B's proprietary business identifier, the D-U-N-S® Number. The Data Universal Numbering System (D-U-N-S) is D&B's standard for tracking the world's businesses and is used by D&B customers to obtain information and services. The unique nine-digit code is also used in Electronic Data Interchange (EDI) and global electronic commerce transactions.

D&B's customers purchase information from D&B because it helps them to run their businesses more profitably. The more useful D&B can make information to customers, the more those customers are willing to pay, which in turn increases D&B's revenue. One way to make the information more useful is to allow customers to automatically integrate or embed D&B information into the their business processes.

The Business Problem: Extending Reach without Increasing Complexity

The value D&B provides its customers is in gathering information from many diverse sources and making it available in a timely fashion. As D&B gathers information from an increasing number and variety of global sources, they needed a way to adapt to different systems quickly and easily.

At the same time, D&B wanted to make information available to its customers as easily as possible, thus reducing barriers for existing and potential customers. D&B also wanted to increase the value of its information by making it available in a format integrated with a customer's existing business processes.

The solution for D&B had to integrate information from diverse sources and make it available in an easy-to-work-with format and on an easily accessible platform. In the past, D&B dedicated resources to developing systems for customers to use D&B data, but D&B wanted to shift this role to customers both to allow them more flexibility in building solutions and to save D&B the expense of building solutions for each customer.

The Solution: XML as the Great Enabler

To deliver on their dedication to quality, D&B chose XML as a significant part of their solution. Fortunately their timing was right, because at the time XML 1 was already an official W3C Recommendation.

NOTE

XML 1 being an official W3C Recommendation meant that XML's technical issues had been worked out and the specification would not change until the next official version.

Most companies have access to the Internet, which provided the common platform across which D&B could deliver information. Because XML is an open specification, it is easy for customers to build applications; D&B also provided an XML toolkit to further ease development.

A common thread to the problems D&B faced was normalizing data to a workable and accessible format. Choosing an XML solution aligned many protocols, platforms, hosts, and structures for D&B and allowed D&B to make their business global. As a D&B product manager said, "XML is the great enabler."

D&B began building most of the application in-house without any third party products. However, in an effort to cut development time, they decided to use a product called B2B from webMethods because B2B had much of the functionality required by D&B.

About webMethods

Founded in 1996, webMethods (`http://www.webmethods.com`) is a vendor of XML-based solutions for business-to-business integration. Their mission is to "enable companies to link their applications and enterprises via the Internet as easily and effectively as the Web browser has linked people and information." The goal of their products is to automate and integrate information transfer over the Web. Specifically, their products enable real-time data exchange between XML and HTML documents.

webMethods believes that XML is the new EDI. EDI is the standardized way to exchange forms between computer systems for business use. XML, because it offers substantial benefits over traditional data interchange, is easier to deploy, easier to understand, and can be adopted much more rapidly than EDI solutions.

webMethods's server product is called B2B. It is designed to enable organizations with legacy applications and diverse data to enter into the Internet marketplace. It does this by converting diverse protocols and platforms to a common language—XML. It was these features that led D&B to select B2B as the solution for their data integration problem.

The B2B Solution

The B2B solution is comprised of three components. The B2B Developer and B2B Integration Server are tools for building the application and interface and facilitating the flow of information. To facilitate integrating data from many sources, including databases, Enterprise Resource Planning (ERP) applications, and EDI systems, webMethods developed a technology called the Web Interface Definition Language (WIDL).

WIDL

WIDL is an XML application that simply consists of a DTD. The DTD defines an interface definition language that takes an existing data structure and attributes context to it, making it available to an application. WIDL can extract data from an HTML page and convert it to XML, thus separating the data from its presentation. Details of WIDL are covered later in this chapter.

B2B Developer

B2B Developer is a set of visual tools used by developers to assist in creating applications and data access interfaces. B2B Developer uses WIDL to set the context of data. That data can then be mapped to other Application Programming Interfaces (APIs). B2B Developer also provides server administration tools, testing tools, and client-side code generation.

B2B Integration Server

The B2B Integration Server coordinates and facilitates information flow between applications and Web sites. Data can be exchanged between intercorporate applications and Web sites and B2B allows applications to access other applications across the Internet. It also permits applications to access data embedded in Web pages.

The B2B Integration Server is a central integration point to enable internal and external applications to communicate transparently. Companies can encapsulate business services that their business partners can automatically access. XML is used for exchanging data between applications and legacy data sources. An example of its use is shown in Figure 27.1. The B2B Integration Server obtains data from various sources, integrates it, and presents it to a user via the Internet.

FIGURE 27.1:

A solution using webMethods B2B Integration Server

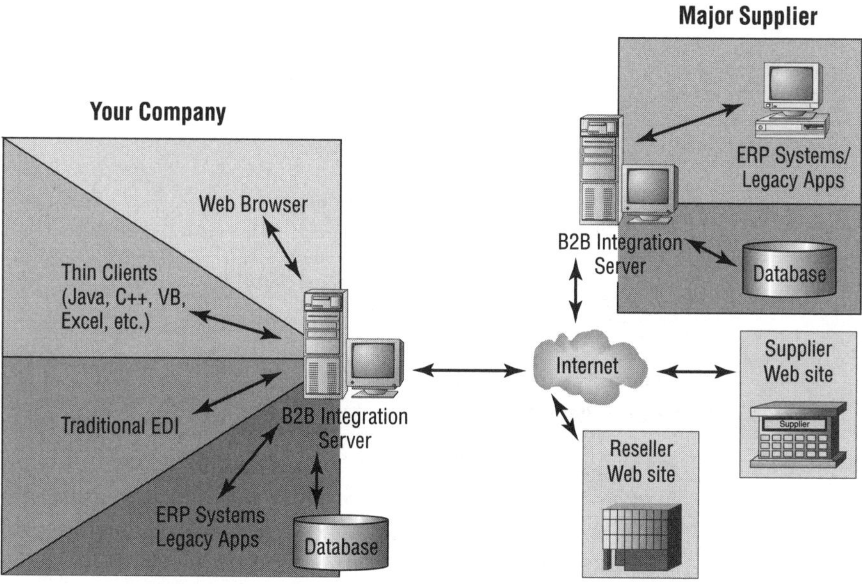

The solution in Figure 27.1 uses XML as a key part of the solution, which allows Hypertext Transfer Protocol (HTTP) to be used as the transport for XML documents. HTTP powers all the Web sites on the Internet and using HTTP insures that the XML data can move through firewalls without requiring modification.

The B2B Integration Server also has a security manager and XML middleware that automates the communication of all XML tagged data. These two components enable real-time monitoring to both ensure efficiency and increase security.

The security manager can also protect data using Secure Sockets Layer (SSL) and RSA Data Security Inc.'s standard public/private key authentication and encryption mechanisms. This process not only encrypts the data, but also confirms that the data comes from a trusted source.

The Final Product: D&B Global Access

The solution devised by D&B to provide customers with global data products was branded Global Access. Global Access was designed so that customers could easily integrate D&B information into their work processes. The design goals included the following criteria:

- A standard, easy-to-use interface
- Options for customization
- Easy system integration
- Flexibility
- Minimal customer development costs

Over time, D&B anticipates migrating their own existing products to the Global Access platform and D&B software applications will use the Global Access platform to gain access to D&B data and reports.

Through Global Access D&B customers have new data products available to them and they will be able to integrate D&B information into their work processes easily because Global Access uses industry standard Internet technologies. Customers can download D&B information data via their corporate intranet, Win32 application, Web browser or any other container environment.

The Global Access project has the following four main components:

A component-based toolkit The component-based toolkit is used by D&B, customers, software vendors, and system integrators and includes software to assist with integrating D&B information into their systems. This offloads development work from D&B and gives customers the flexibility to use the information according to their specific needs.

New global data products As a leading provider of business-critical information, D&B continually adapts to the global marketplace and strives to continue offering new Global Access data products based on a consistent set of data elements from worldwide databases.

Standard data definition language It is important that D&B ensure their data is easily accessible and useable, and to accomplish this goal, D&B chose XML as its transaction and data definition language. Other major software vendors such as IBM, Microsoft, and SAP are also integrating XML into their product lines with the hope that XML-enabled applications will allow for easy exchanges of information and thus streamline business processes.

Customizable user interface The Global Access project aims to deploy a new, highly customizable user interface for accessing D&B products in a single, consistent way.

The Global Access Platform

The Global Access platform is a multitiered platform—data tier, middle tier, and client tier. Each tier has defined responsibilities and roles. The data tier contains the sources for all D&B information and there are many different systems and platforms participating.

The middle tier is responsible for integrating the different data sources contained in the data tier. The middle tier is driven by the webMethods B2B Integration Server. This tier not only integrates the data but also looks after other business functions, such as tracking requests for billing purposes and collecting data for auditing. The middle tier is also the server to the client tier.

The client tier can take many different forms—it could be an application server, a Visual Basic program, or even a Web browser if the XML support is rich enough. The client tier talks to the B2B server using XML, which is why there is such a variety for options for the client tier.

How XML Is Used in Global Access

The D&B Global Access platform uses XML on a number of different levels. XML is an integral part of the B2B Integration Server used in the Global Access solution. B2B uses Web Interface Definition Language (WIDL) to gather information from various sources and make it available through an API. An XML application, the Global Access Data Exchange (DGX), is used as the interface between the Global Access client and the Global Access server.

WIDL

The founders of webMethods realized that a method of abstracting data out of Web pages was key to enabling integration of many different organizations' data. At the time of this realization, XML had been submitted as a draft to the W3C as a standard for exchanging information between different platforms. One of its design goals was that "XML be straightforwardly usable over the Internet." An XML application that described how to obtain information from Web pages and make it available through an API seemed to be the solution for webMethods and thus, WIDL was born.

WIDL is an XML application that implements a service-based architecture for integrating data and applications over the World Wide Web. The WIDL specification has evolved from its original conception into two separate DTDs, WIDL-SPEC and WIDL-MAPPING. The current version of the B2B product uses these two XML applications. WIDL is a key aspect of the B2B Integration Server.

NOTE

WIDL was submitted to the W3C in September 1997 as a W3C Note. This means the specification is publicly available but it does not mean there are currently any W3C resources allocated to it. Details of the specification can be viewed at `http://www.w3.org/TR/NOTE-widl`. The specification contains the original WIDL DTD and a detailed description of each of the elements.

WIDL Specification The WIDL Specification DTD (WIDL-SPEC) is used to create XML documents that describe an application interface abstractly. This is similar to an Interface Definition Language (IDL). However, because it is an XML application, it is an IDL with a well-known syntax rather than one specific to a compiler vendor. The WIDL Specification is listed below:

```
<!ELEMENT WIDL-SPEC (METHOD | RECORD)+
<!ATTLIST WIDL-SPEC
     NAME CDATA #REQUIRED
     VERSION CDATA #FIXED "3.2"
     COMMENT CDATA #IMPLIED
<!ELEMENT METHOD EMPTY
<!ATTLIST METHOD
     NAME CDATA #REQUIRED
     INPUT CDATA #IMPLIED
     OUTPUT CDATA #IMPLIED
     COMMENT CDATA #IMPLIED
<!ELEMENT RECORD (VALUE | RECORDREF)+
<!ATTLIST RECORD
     NAME CDATA #REQUIRED
     COMMENT CDATA #IMPLIED
<!ELEMENT VALUE EMPTY
<!ATTLIST VALUE
     NAME CDATA #REQUIRED
     DIM (0 | 1 | 2) "0"
     TYPE CDATA "STRING"
     COMMENT CDATA #IMPLIED
<!ELEMENT RECORDREF EMPTY
```

```
<!ATTLIST RECORDREF
     NAME CDATA #REQUIRED
     DIM (0 | 1 | 2) "0"
     RECORD CDATA #REQUIRED
     COMMENT CDATA #IMPLIED
```

A WIDL-SPEC document names the interface and lists the services associated with the interface. An interface can have methods with input and output parameters. An interface can also have records associated with it. A record is similar to structures in C+ or collections and arrays in Visual Basic.

The interface described by the WIDL-SPEC document hides the implementation details. This means that two completely different applications could provide the same functionality as long as they conform to the interface.

WIDL Mapping The WIDL-Mapping DTD (WIDL-MAPPING) is used to create documents that describe how to map between HTML or XML pages and a WIDL specification. WIDL mappings abstract the underlying document format (HTML or XML) and network protocol as a set of services. The developer can then interact with the Web through program functions and procedures.

A WIDL-Mapping document consists of three sections: header, input binding, and output binding. This is a fairly large DTD; take a look at it and then we will discuss the major sections.

```
<!ELEMENT WIDL-MAPPING (SERVICE | INPUT-BINDING
     | OUTPUT-BINDING)+ >
<!ATTLIST WIDL-MAPPING
NAME CDATA #REQUIRED
VERSION CDATA #FIXED "3.2"
BASEURL CDATA #IMPLIED
DEFAULT-CONTENT (WOM | CONSTANT) "WOM"
COMMENT CDATA #IMPLIED >
<!ELEMENT SERVICE EMPTY >
<!ATTLIST SERVICE
NAME CDATA #REQUIRED
INPUT CDATA #IMPLIED
OUTPUT CDATA #IMPLIED
URL CDATA #REQUIRED
METHOD (GET | POST) "GET"
AUTHUSER CDATA #IMPLIED
AUTHPASS CDATA #IMPLIED
SOURCE CDATA #IMPLIED
TIMEOUT CDATA #IMPLIED
```

```
RETRIES CDATA #IMPLIED
COMMENT CDATA #IMPLIED >
<!ELEMENT INPUT-BINDING (VALUE)+ >
<!ATTLIST INPUT-BINDING
NAME CDATA #REQUIRED
COMMENT CDATA #IMPLIED >
<!ELEMENT OUTPUT-BINDING (CONDITION | REGION | VALUE
     | BINDINGREF)+ >
<!ATTLIST OUTPUT-BINDING
NAME CDATA #REQUIRED
COMMENT CDATA #IMPLIED >
<!ELEMENT VALUE (#PCDATA) >
<!ATTLIST VALUE
NAME CDATA #REQUIRED
DIM (0 | 1 | 2) "0"
TYPE CDATA "STRING"
CONTENT (WOM | CONSTANT) #IMPLIED
FORMNAME CDATA #IMPLIED
USAGE (DEFAULT | HEADER | INTERNAL) "DEFAULT"
NULLOK (TRUE | FALSE) "FALSE"
COMMENT CDATA #IMPLIED >
<!ELEMENT BINDINGREF (#PCDATA) >
<!ATTLIST BINDINGREF
NAME CDATA #REQUIRED
DIM (0 | 1 | 2) "0"
BINDING CDATA #REQUIRED
CONTENT (WOM) #IMPLIED
FORMNAME CDATA #IMPLIED
USAGE (DEFAULT | HEADER | INTERNAL) "DEFAULT"
NULLOK (TRUE | FALSE) "FALSE"
COMMENT CDATA #IMPLIED >
<!ELEMENT CONDITION (REFERENCE?, REASONREF?) >
<!ATTLIST CONDITION
TYPE (SUCCESS | FAILURE | RETRY) "SUCCESS"
MATCH CDATA #IMPLIED
WAIT CDATA #IMPLIED
MASK CDATA #IMPLIED
REBIND CDATA #IMPLIED
SERVICE CDATA #IMPLIED
REASONTEXT CDATA #IMPLIED
RETRIES CDATA #IMPLIED
COMMENT CDATA #IMPLIED >
```

```
<!ELEMENT REGION (START?, END?) >
<!ATTLIST REGION
NAME CDATA #REQUIRED
START CDATA #REQUIRED
END CDATA #REQUIRED
NULLOK CDATA #IMPLIED
COMMENT CDATA #IMPLIED >
<!ELEMENT REFERENCE (#PCDATA) >
<!ATTLIST REFERENCE
CONTENT (WOM) "WOM" >
<!ELEMENT REASONREF (#PCDATA) >
<!ATTLIST REASONREF
CONTENT (WOM) "WOM" >
<!ELEMENT START (#PCDATA) >
<!ATTLIST START
INCLUDE (TRUE | FALSE) "TRUE"
CONTENT (WOM) "WOM" >
<!ELEMENT END (#PCDATA) >
<!ATTLIST END
INCLUDE (TRUE | FALSE) "TRUE"
CONTENT (WOM) "WOM" >
```

Header The header, defined within the <SERVICE> block, defines the name of the service, the binding it uses, and identifies the URL of the Web pages from which it extracts information. Here is an example that specifies a service for obtaining the precipitation forecast:

```
<SERVICE NAME="WeatherNetwork_GetPrecipitation"
INPUT="WeatherNetwork _GetPrecipitationInput"
OUTPUT="WeatherNetwork _GetPrecipitationOutput"
METHOD="GET"
URL="http://someserver.weathernetwork.com/query.asp"
SOURCE="http://someserver.weathernetwork.com/"/>
```

Input Binding The Input Binding defines the input requirements of the service and associates those inputs with the corresponding elements within the Web document. Continuing the example, input to the service is the city and country for which the forecast is desired.

```
<INPUT-BINDING NAME="WeatherNetwork_GetPrecipitationInput">
<VALUE NAME="City" FORMNAME="city" USAGE="DEFAULT"/>
<VALUE NAME="Country" FORMNAME="country" USAGE="DEFAULT">v1</VALUE>
</INPUT-BINDING>
```

Output Binding The Output Binding specifies the output that the service produces and associates each output variable with an object. In the example, the output is bound to the first cell in the second table of the Web page.

```
<OUTPUT-BINDING NAME="WeatherNetwork_GetPrecipitationOutput">
<VALUE NAME="TodaysAmount" USAGE="DEFAULT" VALUEONLY="TRUE">
Doc.table[1].td[1].text</VALUE>
</OUTPUT-BINDING>
```

Note that the output value is referenced using the webMethods Object Model (WOM) which is discussed next.

WOM WOM is used for mapping data from Web documents. When an XML or HTML document is parsed by webMethods, it is made accessible to the developer through the WOM. XML and HTML elements are converted to arrays of document objects and the element attributes become object properties. Any text within the start and end tag of an element becomes the text property of that document object.

An example of referring to an object within a parsed document is `doc.p[2].txt`, which would return the text of the third paragraph element. A range of elements can be returned as well. For instance, `doc.li[1-4].src` would return the HTML or XML source of the second through fifth LI elements.

Regular expressions are also supported for extracting elements from within a document. For example, the object reference `doc.p[/webMethods/]` would select all paragraphs within the document containing the word "webMethods."

webMethods required an object model to represent an HTML document before the W3C DOM was a specification. The WOM and the W3C DOM function have similar ways to access object and similar properties on each object.

Using DGX for Custom Applications

If customers decide to write their own applications to access D&B data they can use Global Access Data Exchange (DGX), which is an XML application. DGX looks after the messaging and transaction portion of the Global Access platform. DGX is composed of a set of records, each record designed to represent a transaction type between a Global Access Server and a client.

Each transaction includes a request and a response. Therefore DGX records come in pairs—one for the request and one for the response. A typical DGX transaction consists of a DGX request record sent to a server asking data on a particular company and a DGX response record containing the data to be delivered to the client.

Before delving into DGX, it is important to understand OFX. CheckFree, Intuit, and Microsoft created the Open Financial Exchange (OFX) standard in early 1997 for exchanging financial data between financial institutions, businesses, and the consumer via the Internet. OFX was designed to be open in nature because its goal is to exchange data between diverse platforms. Because financial information is sensitive, security and reliability of data was a high concern with the design of OFX. For these reasons, authentication and transactional support were built into the OFX model.

NOTE

For information about the OFX specification, see the web site `http://www.ofx.net/`. It contains the specification and the companies involved in the OFX standard.

In many ways, D&B data is similar to financial data. D&B must authenticate the user requesting the data and each request must be uniquely identified. In addition, a request may require the participation of multiple databases, which requires transactional support. Thus D&B used the OFX standard as a model for DGX. In fact, you will see that many of the tags even have the same name and meaning. One of the main differences is that OFX is still an SGML application whereas DGX is an XML application.

A DGX document consists of records, aggregates, and elements. Each DGX record can contain elements and/or aggregates. An element is a single piece of data, such as a date or username. An aggregate is a collection of related elements used to describe a more complex structure, such as a lookup request or a data product.

As mentioned, transactions must be uniquely identified within DGX. This is done through the use of two elements. The `<TRNUID>` element is assigned by a Global Access client to uniquely identify an element. Every DGX record has a TRNUID except a Signon Request and a Signon Response. The server will echo the TRNUID so the client can match a response with a request.

The `<SRVTID>` is the server transaction identifier. Again, this is a unique identifier except this time it is assigned by the server. An example of its use is as a confirmation number of a transaction.

Message Levels Like OFX, DGX is a five-layer model. The OFX specification defines the following model:

Tags	Level	Description
<OFX>	1	Top level
<xxxMSGSRQVn>,<...RS>	2	Message set and version
<yyySYNCRQ>, <...RS>	3	Synchronization wrappers
<yyyTRNRQ>, <...RS>	4	Transaction wrappers
<yyyRQ>	5	Specific requests and responses

where xxx is a message set, yyy is a message, RQ is a request, and RS is a response. A sample D&B Signon Response looks as follows:

Tags	Level	Description
<DGX>	1	Top level
<SIGNONMSGSRSV1>	2	Message set and version
<001SYNCRS>	3	Synchronization wrappers
<0001TRNRS>	4	Transaction wrappers
<SONRS>	5	Specific response

This example for a Signon Response starts with a DGX block at level 1. There is one <DGX> block per transaction. The second level contains either a request or a response. For instance, a client passes <SIGNONMSGSRQV1> to request a Signon and the server responds with <SIGNONMSGSRSV1>.

Level 3 in the OFX specification is for synchronization. It is currently not supported in DGX.

Level 4 in OFX wraps its contents as a message (i.e. a unit of work). It refers to a request-response pair and the status codes associated with the response. Level 4 is also not currently supported in DGX.

Level 5 has the details about each specific message. The supported messages in DGX are:

- Profile
- Lookup
- Product Availability
- Data

Below you'll find an example request-response that shows how these details fit together.

Message Example This example shows a request for a user profile and a response.

Request The client prepares the request by creating a DGX document. First an XML header is given to specify the XML version and the character encoding being used. The DTD for the document also is provided.

```
<?xml version="1.0" encoding="UTF-8" ?>
<!DOCTYPE DGX SYSTEM "DGX.dtd" >
```

Next, the document is started:

```
<DGX>
```

The user must be authenticated before any transaction can take place so a Signon Request comes next:

```
<SIGNONMSGSRQV1>
<SONRQ>
```

The Signon Request includes the date, username, and password. The tags <APPID> and <APPVER> identify the client application making the request; in this case it is the computer program Marlow 0.2. The organization of the user making the request and the desired language are also specified.

```
<DTCLIENT>050398</DTCLIENT>
<USERID>111</USERID>
<USERPASS>111</USERPASS>
<APPID>MARLOW</APPID>
<APPVER>0.2</APPVER>
```

```
<FI>
<ORG>DUNandBRADSTREET</ORG>
</FI>
<LANGUAGE>EN</LANGUAGE>
</SONRQ>
</SIGNONMSGSRQV1>
```

After the Signon Request is defined, a credit application request message is specified.

```
<CREDITMSGRQV1>
<CREDITRQ>
```

The specific request is set, which in this case is a Profile Request. The user number for the profile request is defined.

```
<PROFILERQ>
<USR_ID>111</USR_ID>
</PROFILERQ>
</CREDITRQ>
</CREDITMSGRQV1>
</DGX>
```

Finally, all the end tags are included and the DGX request document is complete. At this point, the document would be sent to the Global Access server, most likely via the HTTP protocol.

Response If the request is successfully processed, a DGX response is generated. As with the DGX request, the DGX response has the XML version and character encoding. The DGX DTD is also specified.

```
<?xml version="1.0" encoding="UTF-8" ?>
<!DOCTYPE DGX SYSTEM "DGX.dtd" >
```

The DGX and the credit message response start tags are set.

```
<DGX>
<CREDITMSGSRSV1>
<CREDITRS>
```

Next, the success or failure of the request can be determined from the <CODE> element. A value of '0' indicates success. A failure is shown in a later section.

```
<STATUS>
<CODE>0</CODE>
```

```
<SEVERITY>0</SEVERITY>
</STATUS>
```

The <PROFILERS> section contains the details of the response.

```
<PROFILERS>
<USR_ID>111111</USR_ID>
```

The <USR_CUST> section contains basic information about a Global Access customer. Address, phone number, and contact information are the default information if no user-specific data is supplied.

```
<USR_CUST>
<SUBR_NBR>999999999</SUBR_NBR>
<DUNS_NBR>022666150</DUNS_NBR>
<DELV_CO_NME>Kuhns Jewelers</DELV_CO_NME>
<DELV_ADR_LNE_1>345 Main Street</DELV_ADR_LNE_1>
<DELV_CITY>Salisbury</DELV_CITY>
<DELV_RGN>MD</DELV_RGN>
<DELV_POST_CD>10017</DELV_POST_CD>
<DELV_CTAC_PH_AREA_CD>301</DELV_CTAC_PH_AREA_CD>
<DELV_CTAC_PH_NBR>5559999</DELV_CTAC_PH_NBR>
</USR_CUST>
```

For each D&B customer, there must be at least one employee or representative defined. This information is given in the <USR> section.

```
<USR>
<DB_USR_ID>111111</DB_USR_ID>
<DEFU_ENDR>Susan Purnell</DEFU_ENDR>
<USR_NME>Susan Purnell</USR_NME>
<LAST_CTAC_DT>19980826</LAST_CTAC_DT>
</USR>
```

Finally, the end tags are given.

```
</PROFILERS>
</CREDITRS>
</CREDITMSGSRSV1>
</DGX>
```

The great thing about the data being returned as an XML document is that XSL can be applied to either render it as HTML or rearrange it. It is easy to imagine D&B partners taking a DGX response and branding it themselves by applying XSL to it. Perhaps the D&B partner is adding some value to the D&B data and reselling it to their own customers. In this case, it can be customized for each customer by applying a different XSL style sheet to the DGX document.

Error Handling A <STATUS> aggregate is included in every DGX response. It contains error codes and messages generated by the server. If the STATUS field in the HTTP response header is `100 Continue`, a Global Access client should display the text in the <CODE> and <MESSAGE> elements. If the text for the <CODE> element is not 0, then the server did not process the requested record. If the server rejects a request, the text in the <MESSAGE> element will describe why the request was rejected and how to correct the situation. The following is an example of a response to a credit application request that failed:

```
<CREDITMSGRSV1>
<CREDITRS>
<STATUS>
<CODE>41</CODE>
<SEVERITY>4</SEVERITY>
<MESSAGE>No companies match your criteria</MESSAGE>
</STATUS>
<SRVTID>987654322</SRVTID>
<LOOKUPRS>
</LOOKUPRS>
</CREDITRS>
```

As you can see, a non-zero status code is given along with an error message.

Comments You may have noticed a few things about DGX. First, authentication and error reporting are performed within the DGX document, not as part of the document transport. HTTP has authentication and error reporting built right into the protocol, so it almost seems that there is an overlap in responsibilities. The probable reason DGX evolved this way is that DGX is based on OFX, which is an SGML application. SGML is more protocol-independent, therefore it requires authentication and status reporting within the SGML application.

You may have also noticed that there are no attributes used in a DGX document other than the standard XML attributes. Even since SGML came into being, there has been much discussion of when to use attributes and when to use elements. The designers of OFX must have been in the use elements camp. The good thing is, D&B maintained consistency when designing DGX, as DGX also does not have any attributes.

The Global Access Toolkit

An alternative to using DGX to interact with the Global Access server is to use the Global Access Toolkit, which provides easy access to D&B information. The toolkit is component-based in that it consists of a number of objects with properties and methods (see Figure 27.2). The toolkit is available in a COM-based version and a Java version for Windows and Unix. Because both COM and Java have similar object model paradigms (they support properties, methods, and interfaces but not multiple inheritance), the Global Access Toolkit object model can be built with both languages while keeping the same API.

FIGURE 27.2:

Global Access Toolkit object model

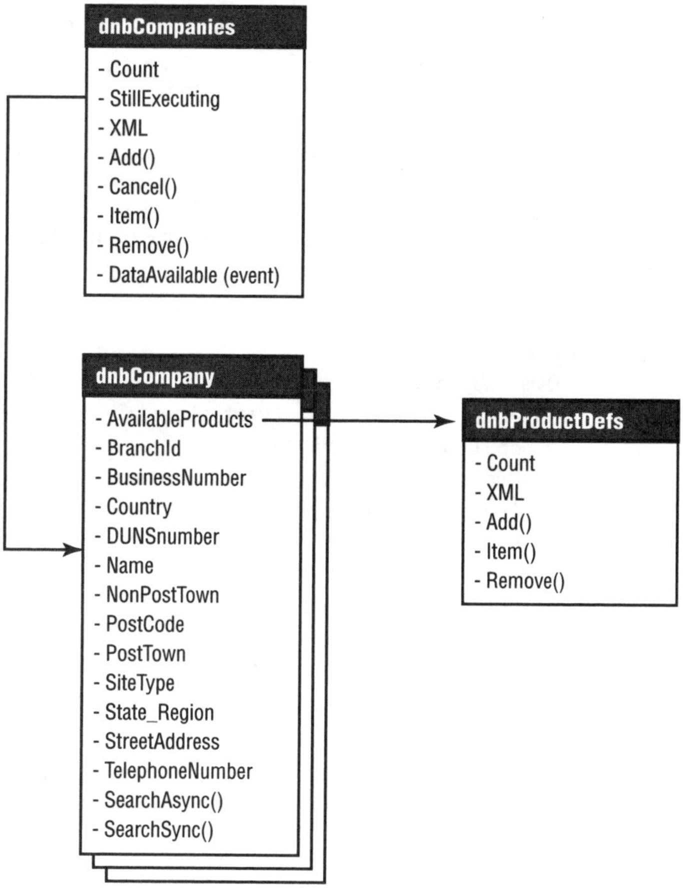

By using the Global Access Toolkit, the developer does not need to know any XML. The toolkit generates and consumes XML for the developer. Developers also can rely on the toolkit to look after the network communication instead of needing to send and receive DGX documents themselves. Developers can focus on solving the problem of integrating D&B data into their organization's business process.

The objects with the toolkit are used for all tasks within a D&B transaction, including authenticating the user, preparing a request, and retrieving results. For instance, to log on from a Microsoft Active Server Page using the `Login()` method of the user object, the following VBScript would be used:

```
Dim  objToolKit
Dim  objUser
objToolKit = Server.CreateObject( "dnb.dnbToolkit" )
objUser = toolKit.User
objUser.ID = "juser"
objUser.Password = "password"
toolKit.Url = "https://theserver.dnb.com/scriptdirectory"
```

If the user is properly authenticated, `objUser.Login()` would return true. At that point you can then find a company using the following code:

```
Dim  objPrototype
Dim  lMaxResults
Dim  objCompanies
Dim  objCompany
objPrototype = Server.CreateObject( "dnb.dnbCompany")
' populate search fields
objPrototype.Name = "Northern Telecom" objPrototype.State_Region = "ON"
objPrototype.Country = "CA"
lMaxResults = 25    ' limit search results
' run the search
objCompanies = oPrototype.SearchSync(lMaxResults)
' iterate over results
For Each objCompany In objCompanies
   Response.Write objCompany.TelephoneNumber
Next
```

This code would prepare a request to find all the Northern Telecom records in Ontario and then iterate over the results to display all the phone numbers.

Making Global Access Secure

In establishing a security plan for Global Access, developers focused on four issues: authentication, authorization, encryption, and auditing.

Authentication is determining if the client is who they say they are and DGX has authentication built in. A username and password are placed inside the DGX document and the server uses this information to authenticate the client.

Authorization is the process of assigning rights and privileges to a client once they have been authenticated. Much of this responsibility is usually placed on the middle tier, which in this case is the B2B Integration Server. The rights assigned would be related to which users have access to which transactions.

The great thing about XML is that it is a clear-text, human-readable format, which makes it easy to use in development and to debug. However, these features make it difficult to secure transactions. For example, the username and password are sent as clear-text in the DGX document, meaning that anyone who listened in on the network communication between the Global Access client and server could obtain the username and password, along with all the data requested by the client. This is why it is important to encrypt the DGX exchange so that is it not intelligible outside of the client and server. SSL is used on top of HTTP to encrypt the data in the Global Access platform.

Finally, if there are breaches of security, it is important to be able to detect and trace them. Therefore auditing is an important part of the security plan. Auditing is the process of recording all the transaction that take place and perhaps running jobs against the transaction to detect anomalies. Again, the middle tier—the B2B Integration Server—handles this job.

Releasing Global Access

D&B is planning three major releases for Global Access:

- Version 1 went live on December 23, 1998. It meets the initial needs of worldwide D&B Global customers with sophisticated systems and specific data needs. It is running on two Web servers and two application servers with the Windows NT operating system. For a large packet of data, the response time is about 12 seconds.

- Version 2 will add functionality suiting the requirements of middle-market customers needing a more user-friendly interface and a broader range of products and services.
- Version 3 will add functionality for all customers, including the retail/ consumer mass market, with a highly intuitive interface and a credit card purchase facility.

D&B customers can use their existing systems to access D&B information for the immediate future. They can begin to use the new data products and data integration capabilities of Global Access as D&B releases them.

Major corporations mostly use Global Access at this point. However, as new releases are made, Global Access will be available to a broader range of customers.

XML Development Tips

The Dun & Bradstreet development team for Global Access was asked if they had tips for people creating XML applications.

One of the foremost comments was "decide on your DTD early and put them under change control." This way all developers are working towards the same DTD. If someone needs to make a change there is a process in place. The change control process should involve consultation with other developers. This way they can voice their concerns in the event that a change might adversely affect their existing code.

Along the same lines, information that cannot be included in a DTD should be documented near the beginning of the project and put under change control. Examples include data types and domain ranges for content.

Finally, the developers suggested that when designing DTD, one should take an object-oriented approach. An XML document can be modeled after a business object, similar to component software classes. If an object-oriented approach is taken, it is easier to map the XML document to a software class that implements the business logic to process the document.

Summary

There have been many hopes and promises that XML will make the Internet a great business tool, yet not many solutions have reached prominence. D & B needed to integrate many sources of data and make them easily available to customers. The solution, Global Access, uses XML throughout its platform. Global Access not only saves them money, but also opens up new business opportunities and markets. The speed with which the project was built and deployed can be attributed to webMethods's B2B product. As XML solves more business problems and people see the value in products like B2B, XML's use will flourish.

CHAPTER TWENTY-EIGHT

WDDX: An Allaire Case Study

- The business problem: transparent data transfer and integration
- Enter WDDX
- What does WDDX look like?
- WDDX in real life: background and resources
- A look inside WDDX
- WDDX lessons

JOEL MUELLER is senior developer at Creative Internet Solutions, the Web application development arm of Control Data, where he does extensive work with both Allaire ColdFusion and Microsoft Active Server Pages.

Web Distributed Data Exchange (WDDX) is a pragmatic approach to the problem of exchanging common data structures between various programming environments and operating systems. This chapter uses a scenario of a hypothetical business problem to find out what WDDX is best suited for, and when a developer might choose WDDX over straight XML. We'll also take a look at some sample code used to generate the WDDX in the scenario.

The Business Problem: Transparent Data Transfer and Integration

Imagine for a moment that your company has just merged with another company, and it's your job to make the two companies' intranets work together. That's the sort of thing you do for a living, so you're not too worried. Naturally, though, there are complications. First, your company's intranet was built using Allaire ColdFusion. Your new sister company's intranet, however, was constructed with Microsoft Active Server Pages (ASP). This is not an insurmountable hurdle; most companies would simply pick the more advanced intranet, the one that uses the company-standard programming environment, or simply the intranet of the purchasing company and convert the data from the other intranet to make it part of the chosen intranet. However, for political reasons the two groups' intranets will remain separate for the time being. The network administrators wouldn't give you access through the firewall if you were the CEO, so you can't access the database behind the other group's intranet directly. Your job is to get the two intranets exchanging data with one another, right now.

What do you do? Instead of despairing, you recall that XML makes an excellent data exchange format. Why? The plain-text format of XML makes it operating system– and programming environment–independent. It also lends itself to a wide variety of transmission methods. Of greatest interest to you is the fact that XML data can be sent over FTP or even HTTP connections—ports that are likely to already be open between the two companies' firewalls. If you need secure transactions, you can use SSL encryption when sending the data over HTTP.

But you're not out of the woods yet. Before you can use XML to share data between the two systems, you have to find a good generic XML parser for both programming environments (in this case ASP and ColdFusion). You then must negotiate an XML dialect for storing the data you need to transmit. There is such a wide variety of things you need to communicate that you'll probably need to come up with (and agree upon) several DTDs.

When you've done all this, code must be written in both ASP and ColdFusion to get the data from the local data store, convert it to a format compatible with the DTD you've agreed on, and transmit it to the other system. Likewise, you must be able to decode the XML data and convert it to a structure native to your programming environment so that you can manipulate it or save it to a database as appropriate. All of this code must be written to the XML Document Object Model (DOM). The DOM is very flexible and powerful, but it is perhaps not ideal for manipulating tabular data. It is syntax oriented with no concept of data types. The XML Data specification has the notion of simple data types, but not complex data types such as arrays, associative arrays, and tabular recordsets. Therefore, in order to perform this task using raw XML, you must write custom code to handle both the encoding and decoding of the data you need to transfer between the two systems.

This is certainly feasible, but not exactly fast. What would really make your life easier would be a way to take a complex data structure in the ASP system (an array or maybe an ADO recordset) and convert this structure to XML in a single step. Then, once it's been transmitted, you could, in a single step, convert the XML data to a data structure in ColdFusion equivalent to the original ASP structure. Manipulating the data would become easy and you wouldn't need to bother with DTD and such.

Enter WDDX

Good news! Everything described in this not-exactly-far-fetched scenario is already possible today. It can be accomplished through open and extensible XML-based technology called WDDX. What is WDDX? At its core, WDDX is a dialect of XML that is designed to easily represent data structures common to most programming environments (things like simple data types, arrays, recordsets, and structures—also known as associative arrays or dictionaries). WDDX is focused on solving a particular problem: application-to-application data exchange where the syntax of the XML encoding does not matter.

There's more to WDDX than the DTD, however. One of the main focuses of WDDX is ease of use, and to that end there are WDDX modules for many major programming environments. The purposes of these modules are to handle conversion of native data types to a WDDX packet (a process called *serialization*) and the conversion of a WDDX packet back to native data types (a process called *deserialization*). WDDX modules already exist for the following programming environments, with more on the way:

- JavaScript 1.*x*
- ColdFusion 4.*x*
- COM
- Perl
- Java
- PHP

The COM implementation is usable from any environment that supports COM, such as Active Server Pages, Visual Basic, C++, Delphi, and PowerBuilder. All of these implementations provide single-step conversion from native data types to WDDX and back, without requiring any knowledge of XML on the programmer's part.

NOTE

You can find all of the WDDX modules mentioned, plus reference material and examples, in the WDDX SDK, available at `http://www.wddx.org`.

Does this mean that WDDX is only good for sharing data between disparate systems? Not at all. WDDX can be used for a variety of tasks without leaving your own system. You can use the JavaScript implementation of WDDX to provide the data storage that allows offline browser-based data entry—simply create some HTML files that accept user input and save it in WDDX format to the local file system. These HTML files can then send all of the input data to the server at once the next time the user is on-line. Or perhaps you're storing data about an object in a structure (or associative array, or whatever term you like) and you want to store this structure in a format that's quickly retrievable, and you don't require searching on this data. With WDDX, you can simply serialize this object into XML, and store the XML string in your database. Another use would be a case where you need some sort of structured storage on your Web site, but for some reason an actual database would be overkill.

WDDX was originated by Allaire Corporation (`http://www.allaire.com`) and first appeared in their ColdFusion 4 product. It has since been released to Web community as an open specification, although at this time it has not been submitted to the W3C as a potential standard. You can find out more about WDDX by visiting `http://www.wddx.org`, where you can find the volunteer-maintained WDDX SDK as well as white papers and discussion groups on WDDX.

What Does WDDX Look Like?

This is all well and good, but what, you may ask, does WDDX look like? As any discussion of WDDX would be meaningless without examining the code that generated the WDDX, let's return to the intranet scenario and examine a template in the ASP-based intranet. This page is designed to retrieve staff information from the database and present it in WDDX format, so the ColdFusion-based intranet can call this template whenever it needs an up-to-date staff listing. For simplicity's sake, a hard-coded recordset is substituted for the database code.

```
<%
    Option Explicit
    ' Build a recordset of the staff and their positions
    Dim objStaff
    Set objStaff = Server.CreateObject("WDDX.Recordset.1")
    objStaff.addColumn("FirstName")
    objStaff.addColumn("LastName")
    objStaff.addColumn("Position")
    objStaff.addRows(4)
    objStaff.setField 1, "FirstName", "Jeff"
    objStaff.setField 1, "LastName", "White"
    objStaff.setField 1, "Position", "Intern"
    objStaff.setField 2, "FirstName", "Marjorie"
    objStaff.setField 2, "LastName", "Green"
    objStaff.setField 2, "Position", "Programmer"
    objStaff.setField 3, "FirstName", "Burt"
    objStaff.setField 3, "LastName", "Gringlesby"
    objStaff.setField 3, "Position", "Programmer"
    objStaff.setField 4, "FirstName", "Reginald"
    objStaff.setField 4, "LastName", "Blotchet-Halls"
    objStaff.setField 4, "Position", "Manager"
    ' Create an instance of the WDDX Serializer COM object
    Dim objSerializer, strWDDX
    Set objSerializer = Server.CreateObject("WDDX.Serializer.1")
```

```
        strWDDX = objSerializer.serialize(objStaff)
        ' Output WDDX to client
        Response.ContentType = "text/xml"
        Response.Write(strWDDX)
%>
```

Here is what the output of this code looks like:

```
<wddxPacket version="0.9">
       <header />
<data>
     <recordset rowCount="4" fieldNames="FirstName,LastName,Position">
     <field name="FirstName">
       <string>Jeff</string>
       <string>Marjorie</string>
       <string>Burt</string>
       <string>Reginald</string>
  </field>
     <field name="LastName">
       <string>White</string>
       <string>Green</string>
       <string>Gringlesby</string>
       <string>Blotchet-Halls</string>
</field>
     <field name="Position">
       <string>Intern</string>
       <string>Programmer</string>
       <string>Programmer</string>
       <string>Manager</string>
</field>
</recordset>
</data>
</wddxPacket>
```

As you can see, this WDDX data is well formed XML, of a fairly easy-to-read format. Even an untrained eye can tell pretty quickly that when this data is deserialized in any programming environment, it will create a recordset of four rows with the field names `FirstName`, `LastName`, and `Position`.

For the sake of completeness, let's examine the ColdFusion code required in the ColdFusion intranet to read this data:

```
<!-- Get WDDX data -->
<CFHTTP URL="http://URL_TO_ASP_INTRANET_TEMPLATE"
     METHOD="GET"
```

```
    RESOLVEURL="false">
<!-- Deserialize WDDX into native recordset -->
<CFWDDX ACTION="WDDX2CFML"
    INPUT="#CFHTTP.FileContent#"
    OUTPUT="objStaff">
```

There are several important things to note here. The first is perhaps the most obvious: ColdFusion is a very different programming environment from Active Server Pages. Yet, a recordset created in ASP is used without doing much work at all. The second thing to notice is that the conversion to ColdFusion was done with a grand total of two commands: one to get the WDDX and another to convert it into a native format. From this point, you can do whatever you like with this recordset—display it, loop through the data and insert it into a database, and so on.

WDDX in Real Life: Background and Resources

It should come as no surprise that Allaire, the creators of WDDX, use WDDX in their own Web site. Specifically, they use it to expose the data behind their Developer's Exchange. The Developer's Exchange is a Web resource for ColdFusion programmers to browse and download user-created extensions to ColdFusion, or to upload their own contributions.

NOTE The Developer's Exchange Web site is located at `http://www.allaire.com/developer/gallery.cfm`.

Figure 28.1 shows what the Developer's Exchange looks like when users access it through the typical HTML interface. Content is divided into four main categories: Custom Tags, Applications, Visual Tools, and Web Content. Users can browse and search the content and download individual items.

There is another way to access this information; a special template one can call returns the same data as the HTML view, but it returns it in WDDX format. The URL to this page is: `http://www.allaire.com/developer/gallery/remote.cfm`.

This template takes two arguments on the URL—the object ID that you want to retrieve and the number of child objects to return for that object. Each major category and subcategory is an object, so if you wanted to retrieve the WDDX data for the VTOM Scripts subcategory of the Visual Tools category and show only the first five scripts, you would call this URL: `http://www.allaire.com/developer/gallery/remote.cfm?ID=6790&tags=2`.

FIGURE 28.1:

The HTML view of the Allaire Developer's Exchange

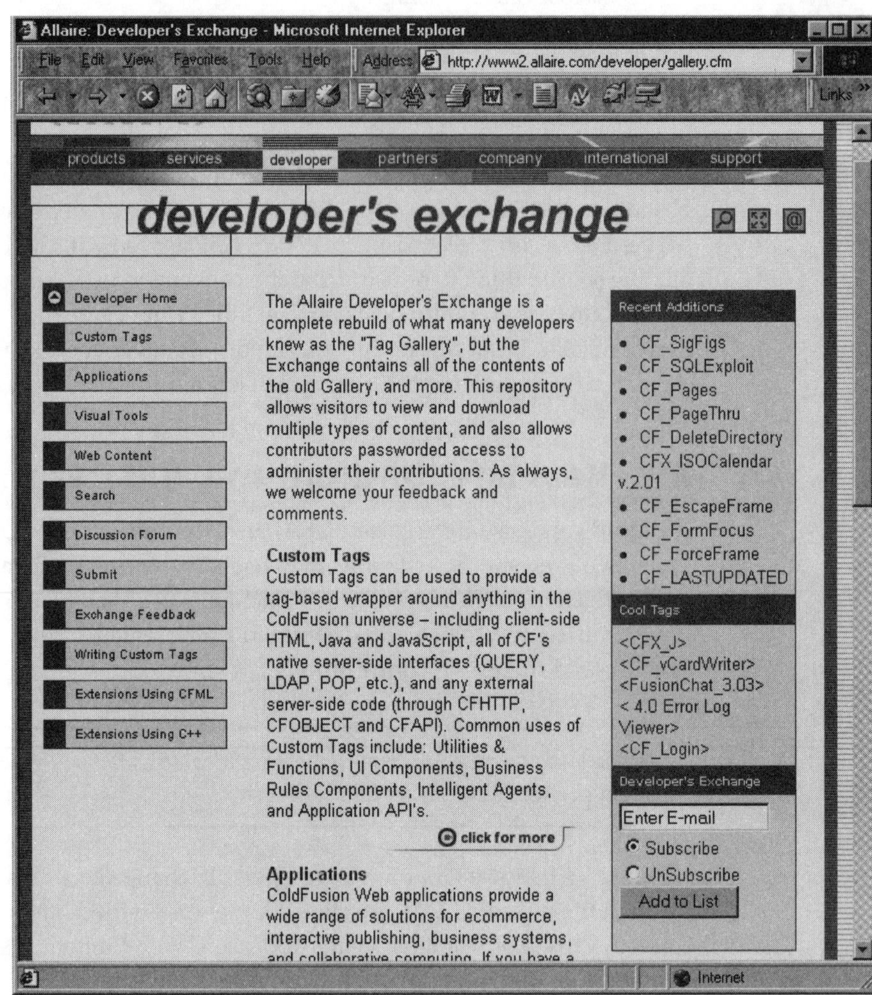

The WDDX data you get back from this URL looks like this:

```
<wddxPacket version="0.9">
  <header />
<data>
<recordset rowCount="2" fieldNames="WDDXOBJECT">
<field name="WDDXOBJECT">
  <string><wddxPacket version='0.9'><header></header><data><struct><var
name='HITS'><string>10</string></var><var
```

```
name='STATUS'><string>1</string></var><var
name='PAYMENT_TYPE'><string>Freeware</string></var><var
name='LICENSE_URL'><string>None</string></var><var
name='MODIFIED'><string>1999-04-23 11:57:43</string></var><var
name='EXAMPLE'><string> </string></var><var
name='FILE_NAME'><string>saveas.zip</string></var><var
name='PRICE'><string>0.00</string></var><var
name='DESCRIPTION'><string>Like the name says: saves a copy of a file
to a different name. Why use this instead of Save As? Because this one
leaves you with two open documents: the original and the
copy.</string></var><var
name='USERID'><string>754275</string></var><var
name='OBJECTID'><string>7331</string></var><var
name='TYPEID'><string>29</string></var><var
name='COMPANY'><string>Alive! Online</string></var><var
name='EMAIL'><string>bradford@aliveonline.com</string></var><var
name='COOL_TAGS'><string>0</string></var><var
name='AUTHOR'><string>Christopher Bradford</string></var><var
name='URL'><string>http://www.aliveonline.com/homesite/index
.html</string></var><var
name='PARENT'><string>6790,6799</string></var><var
name='NAME'><string>Save a copy</string></var><var
name='DOWNLOAD_URL'><string> </string></var><var
name='DOWNLOADS'><string>136</string></var><var
name='DATE'><string>1998-10-22
13:32:14</string></var></struct></data></wddxPacket></string>
  <string><wddxPacket version='0.9'><header></header><data><struct><var
name='HITS'><string>4</string></var><var
name='STATUS'><string>1</string></var><var
name='PAYMENT_TYPE'><string>Freeware</string></var><var
name='LICENSE_URL'><string>None</string></var><var
name='MODIFIED'><string>1999-04-23 12:06:12</string></var><var
name='EXAMPLE'><string> </string></var><var
name='FILE_NAME'><string>stripoutertags.zip</string></var><var
name='PRICE'><string>0.00</string></var><var
name='DESCRIPTION'><string>Use this script to strip outer tags from a
selection.</string></var><var
name='USERID'><string>754275</string></var><var
name='OBJECTID'><string>7351</string></var><var
name='TYPEID'><string>29</string></var><var
name='COMPANY'><string>Alive! Online</string></var><var
```

```
name='EMAIL'><string>bradford@aliveonline.com</string></var><var
name='COOL_TAGS'><string>0</string></var><var
name='AUTHOR'><string>Christopher Bradford</string></var><var
name='URL'><string>http://www.aliveonline.com/homesite/index
.html</string></var><var
name='PARENT'><string>6790,6799</string></var><var
name='NAME'><string>Strip outer tags</string></var><var name='DOWN-
LOAD_URL'><string> </string></var><var
name='DOWNLOADS'><string>64</string></var><var
name='DATE'><string>1998-10-22
14:25:49</string></var></struct></data></wddxPacket></string>
</field>
</recordset>
</data>
</wddxPacket>
```


A careful examination of this WDDX packet will show that it is a recordset of two rows. Each row contains another WDDX packet, a structure containing all the data for a particular object.

This information is all one needs to start building a custom application that uses Developer's Exchange data. One such application, from Creative Internet Solutions, is a tool for Allaire's HomeSite and ColdFusion Studio editors that eases the download and installation of VTOM Scripts, which are basically extended macros that enhance the editors. This tool gets a list of all the available VTOM scripts from Allaire's site, determines which ones are already installed, and presents the user with a list of not-yet-installed scripts. The user can then pick one or more to install, and the tool handles downloading, unpacking, and creating toolbar buttons for the user.

Figure 28.2 shows an example of what this script installation tool looks like, using the WDDX data from the Developer's Exchange that we examined earlier. If you are a HomeSite or ColdFusion Studio user, you can find this tool in the WDDX SDK available at `http://www.wddx.org`.

NOTE

For another example of a utility that uses the Developer's Exchange data remotely, check out Catouzer's remote browsing tool: `http://synergy.catouzer.com/devcenter/index.htm`.

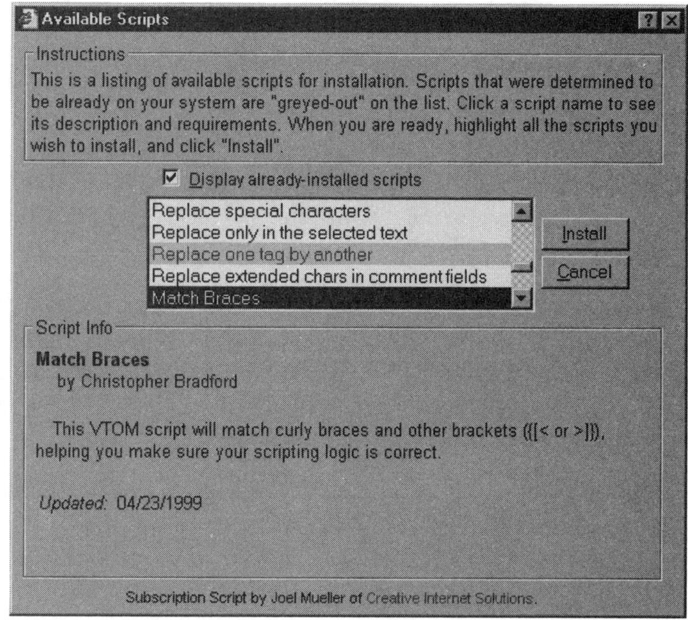

FIGURE 28.2:

The Script Installation Tool, using WDDX data behind the scenes

How WDDX Enhances Browser Support for XML

There has been a lot of talk recently about browser support for XML. Debates have gone back and forth: Is the XML implementation in IE5 truly standards compliant? Will Netscape 5 ever come out? When it does, will the same XML work the same way in both version 5 browsers? What about older browsers?

If you're like many Web developers, you've held off on doing any sort of browser-based XML implementation because of these very questions. WDDX may be just the solution you've been looking for.

Because WDDX has already been implemented in JavaScript 1.*x*, it is compatible with the majority of the browsers in use today, although its usefulness may be limited in non-DHTML browsers.

Continued on next page

This opens up some very intriguing options as Simeon Simeonov, creator of WDDX, notes:

"Despite their ever-increasing capabilities, browsers have been limited by the fact that HTTP is a flat text-based protocol/format and as such they make it very difficult to deliver complex structured data to the client. Niclaus Wirth, the inventor of Pascal, said, '*Algorithms+data structures=programs.* This is the same as *processing+data=applications.*' Well, browsers can do all the processing they want, but they can't get any good data. I say they are data-starved. WDDX changes things completely because now arbitrarily complex data packets can be exchanged between browsers and servers. This means that Web applications don't need to make a request to the server for every single operation. WDDX+script+DHTML can lead to a new level of browser-based applications, especially as structured data can be delivered behind the scenes via either a COM object, a hidden applet, or even a hidden frame. This has huge implications for the scalability of Web applications and the power of their UI's. Also, as both Java and JavaScript are supported these applications can be delivered on thin clients."

A Look Inside WDDX

At this point, it's worthwhile to talk about the database structure behind the Developer's Exchange, as it's different from others you may have encountered. Also, it has some interesting concepts.

First, an object's attendant properties (such as name, description, author, last modified, etc.) are not stored in separate fields in the database unless they need to be searched. Instead, a structure containing all of the properties for an item is serialized as a WDDX packet, which is stored in a text field in the database along with a primary key containing the object ID. This makes item retrieval very fast, as any query becomes as simple as selecting one field from one row of one table. WDDX deserialization time is negligible, except perhaps for extremely large bodies of data.

That's all very well if you always know exactly what items you wish to retrieve from the database, but what if, for example, you needed all of the items updated since the first of the month? All the database knows about your object is a bunch of text—it can't tell that one of the WDDX-encoded properties happens to be a date. The solution is a separate table that is only used for searching. This table contains an object ID, an attribute name (or possibly an attribute ID from a table listing possible attributes), and the value. Allaire uses an administrative tool for defining attributes of a new object, and what their data types are, so that they can automatically place attributes marked as searchable into this table. When you need to search, you have only to scan this search table for the object IDs that have a particular attribute that matches particular criteria.

Summary

If one had to pick a single word to describe WDDX, it would be pragmatic. WDDX is a practical, working solution for sharing data between disparate operating systems, databases, and programming environments. Although WDDX may or may not be the ultimate way to share this sort of data, it works now, and it will get the job done, and it is flexible enough to accommodate future standards.

Other proposed standards and technologies, notably BizTalk, a Microsoft repository and framework and Information Content and Exchange (ICE) are emerging that are perceived as competing with WDDX. However, this does not mean you should wait to work with WDDX until you understand all the vocabulary structures perfectly. One beauty of XML is that it's very easy to transform XML from one format to another format. That's what XSL is all about. If you built a Web site that exposed data to the outside world in WDDX format, and a year later your client changed to accepting data only in BizTalk format, all that (in theory) you would need to do is to make an XSLT style sheet to convert your WDDX packets to BizTalk XML. Another aspect of this issue is that ICE is in fact a communications protocol, whereas WDDX is a data-encoding format. This means that WDDX and ICE can be used successfully together for the syndication of structured data.

One colleague recently asked how they could use LDAP with XML, as they'd heard so much about XML recently. This is perhaps the wrong question; rather they should have asked how to use XML with LDAP? In other words, XML—and by extension WDDX—is not necessarily about changing how you do things; it's about making what you already need to do easier to accomplish.

In this light, examine your business needs. If you find that they include sharing data between nominally incompatible systems, or making data available to other businesses over the Internet, or any of the other uses discussed in this chapter, consider using WDDX as your solution.

CHAPTER TWENTY-NINE

Content Management with XML: A Dell Case Study

- Dell and XML
- XML, HTML, SQL, and Internet Information Architecture
- Composition and Reuse
- Putting the Page Together
- Composition Example

DAVID BROOKE majored in physics before working as a schoolteacher around the beginning of the personal computing revolution. His interest in making computing easier and more accessible led him to take up technical writing role at Seiko Epson Corporation, where he played a key role in pioneering the use of DTP in Epson's Japanese and United Kingdom offices.

After six years with Dell's European marketing team, specializing in mobile computing, David is the founding member of Dell's EMEA (Europe, Middle East, and Africa) Internet team, established in fall 1996. For the last year has led a project to create and implement an XML-based content-management system for the many Dell EMEA Web sites.

David is married with three computer-mad teenage children, and a house full of musical instruments of all shapes and sizes! In September 1999, David will become an ordained minister of the Church of England, and it remains to be seen where his publishing interests will resurface. Watch out for church bulletins, schedules, rotas, and prayer lists maintained in XML.

STEVE SAXON has been a software developer since the CP/M days, but it was the Apple Macintosh's predecessor—the Apple Lisa—that made him want to do it as a career. The Lisa influenced his first major project, a desktop publishing program for the Atari 800 back in the mid-'80's.

When Windows 3 came out he taught himself C++ and Windows, then spent the years that followed developing a few successful shareware programs for progressively more and more complex applications. Before joining Dell he developed a showroom system for French car manufacturer Renault which was rolled out to more than 90 percent of the United Kingdom's dealer network. Also during this time he was a member of Borland's TeamB, a group of volunteers who used their free time to provide online assistance to users of Borland's products.

Since joining Dell in 1998 Steve has been technical architect on Dell's XML-based content publishing project. He brought his own propeller hat for the top of his monitor.

Steve is married and has two mad cats, although the nature of his work doesn't allow him to see them much. He loves Japan and all things Japanese but isn't able to go there as much as he'd like, and makes do with his little Japanese garden at home.

In line with Dell's global commitment to the Internet, the Dell EMEA (Europe, Middle East, and Africa) Online group was founded in 1996 and quickly established itself as the European e-commerce leader. The EMEA online team is based at Dell's European offices in Bracknell, United Kingdom, and works together with local teams in each of the 18 countries it serves to drive Dell's Internet business forward.

Dell EMEA conducts more than $3.5 million a day of business over the Internet across the region. It also provides a wealth of information on products and services, and a full range of online service and support information. In addition to its well-known public sites, Dell also provides a customized online experience for more than 1,500 of its top EMEA customers through the Premier™ pages program.

In February 1999, Dell EMEA relaunched its family of Web sites using an XML-based content management system developed in-house. The team had defined ambitious requirements for a next-generation publishing system to support the hypergrowth it was experiencing, and quickly recognized the potential of XML as the basis for their system. With the core of the system in place, the Dell team is delighted with the flexibility it has given them and excited about the next steps.

Following is our story of why we chose an XML-based solution and how we implemented it. The first section describes the business challenges—the problems we had to solve and the challenges we faced. The second section describes our actual implementation.

How Dell Got Started with XML: Defining the Business Problem

Early in 1998, the content team in charge of the Dell EMEA Web sites began work on a vision for a next-generation publishing system that would support the organization's growth and act as the platform for future innovation. The project grew out of the recognition that conventional HTML publishing processes simply weren't scaleable in the way we needed. From the user perspective, the Internet was the perfect match with the Dell Direct Model, but from the maintenance perspective it was labor-intensive and demanding.

Dell's EMEA business spans a wide variety of languages and cultures, and the Internet represents a tremendous opportunity to kick Dell's business into high gear in every single market. We were determined to push ahead and deliver the best possible customer experience on the Internet—for all our EMEA customers. That required a flexible system of publishing that would empower the entire business to deal direct with customers via the Internet.

As we set out to define that publishing system, we didn't start by looking at technology options. We began by looking at several classes of business problems that the system would need to address. These are some of the things we thought about.

How the Internet Challenged the Organization

The Internet changes everything. It changes the way we relate to our customers, it changes the way we work as individuals, and it changes the way we work as a team. Michael Dell has written at length about the impact of the Internet on Dell in his recent book, *Direct from Dell*, and one of the most powerful points to emerge is his view of change as opportunity—especially when the organization is in hyper-growth. The Dell attitude to change is to dive in headfirst. Change is opportunity, and the Dell way is to create change, not just to react to it.

Traditional HTML publishing processes work against change for a variety of reasons. The first group of reasons is organizational, and includes skill-set issues and ownership issues.

Skill-Set Issues

It goes without saying that Internet technology is advancing at an astounding pace, and demanding ever-deeper and broader levels of technical knowledge. Michael Dell's "Know the Net" campaign has ensured that everybody at Dell eats, breathes, and sleeps the Internet, but it is still fundamentally important to allow everyone to play to his or her strengths.

Product managers, marketing communication managers, and Internet specialists have specific skill sets to contribute, and need to be empowered to work as a team, instead of being forced to become experts in each other's fields. With new Internet technologies emerging all the time, matching the publishing paradigm to specific skill sets was a priority.

Ownership Issues

The Internet also challenges the organization because it defies classification. Even on a clearly e-commerce–oriented Web site, the boundaries between advertising, marketing collateral, and merchandising are blurred. To ensure that content stays fresh and up-to-date, every piece of information, and preferably each page, needs to have a clear owner. However, in reality, each page could contain information contributed by several different groups in the organization.

With these types of challenges, getting content to market rapidly requires extraordinary cross-functional execution. Once again, the page-oriented HTML paradigm is the root of the problem.

Empowering the Organization

HTML publishing is great for getting a good idea to market fast. As Michael Dell has pointed out in his book, the real value is in "being out in front with the best version of a good idea, not the twenty-eighth guy to show with a good Web site—no matter how good it is."

The real challenge is to provide ways for an organization to innovate in this way, so that it is always one step ahead, but to do it in a way that is rapidly scaleable to a multi-lingual implementation, and can be easily maintained and adapted. There's even more leverage if the publishing paradigm allows great ideas to be shared across segments, countries, and regions. Although great for one-off projects, page-by-page HTML publishing works against this kind of wide-ranging and aggressive leadership.

Achieving Globalization, Localization, and Personalization

There's no getting away from it—the Internet industry is captivated with personalization. As the Internet becomes more and more clearly commercial, personalization has become the means to refine the end-user experience and deliver targeted information. With personalization—we are told—both the customer and the supplier benefit.

At Dell we firmly believe that personalization is a key contributor to a great online customer experience. But from a global perspective there's another issue that needs attention, and has far more impact on the user experience for the majority of our users: localization.

High-quality localization means translating content into the appropriate language and catering to local character sets and writing systems, including right-to-left and top-to-bottom. It means taking into account aesthetic and cultural considerations. It means ensuring the information provided takes into account organizational differences, trading regulations, pricing differences, and legal differences.

The Internet has completely leveled the playing field between small and large companies, and it is breaking down geographical barriers. Ironically, it is still dominated by English-language content. For a global organization, high-quality localization is the biggest single opportunity to differentiate on the Internet, and the publishing systems we use need to make support for localization a top priority.

Resolving Fundamental Internet Tensions

In many ways the Internet is like an awkward adolescent—growing at an alarming pace, and in search of identity. It is fantastically creative, but fraught with tensions. To get the most out of the Internet and make good strategic decisions, it is important to understand those tensions and work with them. We want to highlight just three that we took into account in our planning.

Creativity vs. Uniformity and Ease-of-Use

Although Microsoft Windows has provided a greater level of consistency and usability in commercial software applications than ever before, the Internet has been the catalyst for an explosion of creativity in interactive applications. This contrast is one of the first big tensions on the Internet.

Freedom of expression is part of the essence of the Internet, and every content publisher fiercely protects the right to be creative. If browsing is fun, all kinds of flaws can be forgiven and word travels—you have a great Web site. At the same time, Web sites with a clear, simple, consistent interface also provide a satisfying experience for users with a job to do, and easy-to-use sites draw visitors back again and again.

Striking the right balance between creativity and ease-of-use can make a huge difference to the success of a site. That requires publishing tools that allow the freedom to experiment creatively, while also providing easy mechanisms for repeating a winning formula.

Commerce vs. Content

The Internet is home to both purists and pragmatists. For purists, the overt commercialization of the Web is a betrayal of all that they stand for. The Web is about open information sharing, not commercial interests. The groundswell of support for the open-source community shows how strongly this kind of view can be held. For pragmatists, the Web was just made for commerce, and their motivation for rich content is to support the sale.

In a sense, both positions are true, and the implication for companies like Dell is that server-side Web applications and content must be smoothly integrated. The experience must be user directed, but at the same time the site must communicate a coherent message and eliminate unnecessary steps for the purchaser. Publishing and Internet applications are often separated from each other—they need to converge.

Proprietary Needs vs. Open Standards

One of the most obvious aspects of the Internet is the pace of progress, and the way that benchmark applications and standards get out of synch with each other. The success of the Internet ultimately depends on open standards and interoperability, yet the pace of innovation is driven by proprietary developments. Arguably this will never change. Once again, the purists and the pragmatists come face to face.

As a technology leader, Dell is absolutely committed to standards, but equally committed to innovation. Standards are the right platform for long-term solutions, which is exactly what we need from a publishing system. At the same time, we must follow our instincts and leverage new technology where we can see clear advantages.

In *Direct from Dell,* Michael Dell proposes that success "comes from being willing to challenge conventional wisdom and having the courage to follow our convictions." That was our inspiration as we chose XML as a solution to our content management challenge.

Diving Headfirst into XML

At the same time we were examining the business requirements that would drive our publishing system choices, we also were taking a look at emerging technologies and software solutions. All the talk was about content management using SQL databases and personalization engines, but very early in our research process we hit upon XML, and we were extremely excited by what we discovered.

Dell had been among the first to deliver a channel for Microsoft Internet Explorer 4 (IE4) using the CDF format developed by Microsoft. This quite naturally led us into an exploration of the XML technology behind it. At the time, we were looking for ways to quickly update the visual look and feel of the site, and we had tried out a few techniques for the Dell channel that decoupled data maintenance and made it easier. We followed that with some early experiments with the IE4 XML/XSL support, and that gave us the feeling that we were onto something big. In a matter of hours, we were quickly able to define a custom data format for product specifications and reproduce pages from our site in numerous different visual identities.

At the time, XML was close to reaching final recommendation, and XSL was still at the proposal stage, so we knew there was a long way to go before there would be a complete family of XML-related specifications from the W3C. But we were convinced that XML was going to play a big part in the Internet's future. Over the coming months, we researched XML heavily, and at the same time investigated a variety of heavyweight integrated publishing solutions. As we looked at each one, the flexibility and simplicity of XML gave us a benchmark by which to measure them.

By the time we had completed our business analysis and our review of the market, it was clear—XML was the way to go for Dell. In the next section, we'll examine some of the technical reasons why XML and XSL held such a strong appeal for us. But first, let's review the business issues.

How XML Addresses the Organization's Needs

We'll be discussing the problem of the page paradigm in more detail later in this chapter, but as far as the skill-set issues, ownership issues, and empowerment issues were concerned, XML looked like a winner. The clear ability to separate out the tasks of data maintenance from formatting was perfect for matching tasks to skills and enabling everyone to participate in the Dell Web site. At the same time, we could see how it would enable us to handle the matrix of ownership that existed across the site. We also saw tremendous opportunities for creating scaleable campaigns and exciting content that could be maintained quickly, easily, and cost-effectively.

How XML Helps Alleviate Internet Tensions

If the Internet is adolescent in character, XML is in its infancy, yet the potential for it to stand in the gap until they both reach maturity is tremendous. XML lays down standards that are tighter and clearer than anything we have seen on the Internet thus far, but at the same time it is, by definition, eXtensible. Though XML was explicitly made to support innovation and freedom of expression, it also provides a natural way of establishing data standards across industries and markets without dictating look and feel. The beauty of it is that even where there isn't 100 percent agreement, translating from one form of XML to another is fast and simple!

When it comes to the tension between applications and content, XML again bridges the gap. We'll look at data versus documents later in this chapter, but it is worth saying right away that no matter where the XML comes from, an XML-based Web site can publish it. Application data and traditional content can share a common vocabulary, and a common technology base—XML. We were sold.

HTML, SQL, XML, and Internet Information Architecture

In this section we want to share some of the things we have learned about the way we were creating our site in the past, and the opportunities for leveraging XML. This will prepare the ground for a more thorough discussion of how we look at document composition and the role XML plays in that process, followed by examples of how that can work in practice.

The HTML Problem

HTML is great, but when it comes to running a large-scale Web site it presents real problems. We need HTML to express creativity and describe the user experience, but as a way of describing the data behind a Web site so that it can be reused and manipulated, HTML doesn't make the grade. However hard the standard setters try, it simply isn't possible to reverse the trend toward using HTML tags for visual effect.

HTML: Too Rigid and Too Flexible

One aspect of the problem is that HTML is both too rigid and too flexible. Another is the conflict, inefficiency, and duplication inherent in a page-oriented publishing paradigm. Let's look at both of these problems. What do we mean by too rigid and too flexible?

It is too flexible in the sense that browsers only loosely enforce the SGML definition of HTML. They tolerate badly written documents and do their best to present them as intended. Browser idiosyncrasies and unique features are too numerous to count, and achieving cross-browser compatibility is a time-consuming affair. If the content of a page is to be treated as data with any integrity, this kind of looseness can't be tolerated.

On the other hand, HTML is too rigid in two ways. The first is that there is no formalized method for extending HTML in specific applications, and in a sense there are already too many tags in the language. The addition of custom tags by Netscape and Microsoft to achieve specific effects was widely condemned, at the same time the abuse of the existing tags in the service of tightly controlled formatting became the norm.

The second way in which HTML is too rigid is, quite simply, the impossibility of separating format and content in a meaningful way. It is true that with CSS you can radically alter the way page elements are presented, but a table is still a table and a list is still a list. More importantly, a page is still a page, and that is the problem we want to look at next.

Breaking the Page Paradigm

When you browse a Web site, you experience it as a set of pages. True, with dynamic HTML those pages might have application-like functionality built into them, but there will still be a sequence of screens or pages. In the conventional HTML paradigm, authors prepare pages or they program ASP or CGI scripts that map closely to pages, perhaps pulling in a set of data from a database on the fly. Databases may be used for repetitive tabular data on the site, or to store data submitted via a form, but for everything else, pages are hard-coded.

As highlighted earlier, the data owned by any one part of an organization will span many pages, while at the same time any one page may incorporate data from many groups. Two things can happen: either the page structure ends up being modified to mirror the internal structure of the organization rather than the information needs of users, or the organization has to build processes to handle the matrix of ownership. In the second case, it isn't always clear who owns the pages, and they may not be maintained properly.

The bottom line is that although we still work in a page-oriented publishing paradigm, there will be conflict, inefficiency, and duplication. The Internet will fail to live up to its promises. Information owners need to be able to maintain their data easily without combing the site for every instance of data relating to their domain, and without worrying about formatting issues. Site designers need to be able to set presentational standards that will be consistently applied across the site without worrying about the data they are dealing with. In other words, the page paradigm has to be broken!

The SQL Problem

The answer to the HTML problems, according to some content management suppliers, is to break down the site into HTML/ASP templates and a set of SQL tables. That way you can isolate look and feel, easily manage the data, and enable yourself to publish far more data. That's great, and for a long time on the Dell site we have used Microsoft SQL Server in a number of areas for exactly this purpose. It is fast, highly scalable, robust, and the data is held in a completely media-neutral format.

If the majority of your site is highly consistent in format (for example, you may have thousands of news articles, classified advertisements, or product specifications), and you don't have the challenges of providing localized content to a variety of markets, then SQL might be the right answer. However, in many cases where this technique is used, much secondary data is incorporated in the templates, and localization and maintainability are lost.

If you are determined, you can model the structure of most classes of Web content using SQL. However, the more complex the page type, the more tables, keys, and joins it requires and the more performance suffers. What's more, the more difficult to the initial design, the more difficult it is to adapt later. If you want flexibility of design and ease of reuse, SQL rapidly shows its limitations and XML shows its strength.

Understanding XML Properly

Having looked at the problems of HTML and SQL in the context of content management, we now need to look at how we can model a Web site using XML. However, it is important to first deal with a handful of issues that we at Dell feel very strongly about.

XML Data vs. XML Documents

There has been a tremendous amount of debate about how XML documents will be formatted and browsed, and an equal amount of discussion about XML as data. These discussions have created the impression that there are two classes of XML applications: document applications, in which XML represents a page and just needs formatting, and data applications in which the XML describes a message exchanged behind the scenes. We believe that this is an artificial distinction based on a faulty understanding of XML.

If you think of XML purely as a document language with clearer markup than HTML, and your primary concern is with formatting and browsing XML documents, then you are stuck in the page paradigm and are missing out on more than half of XML's potential. In fact, we would go so far as to say that if all you have done is move from HTML to XML documents that map one-to-one to on-screen elements, you have largely wasted your time and effort. Likewise, if you think of XML only as a behind-the-scenes data description language for application messaging, you are again narrowing your view.

The reality is that all XML documents are data, and all XML data messages are documents or document fragments. There are times when you want to query documents for information contained in them, especially as you develop interactive DHTML applications, and the strict markup of XML makes the queries both possible and meaningful in a way that HTML could not support. There are also times when you want to display application messages as documents for editing, approval, and so on.

NOTE

Refer back to Chapter 25: "Using XML Applications" for more discussion of whether XML is for *data* or *documents*.

In the system we have built at Dell, we use XML to level the playing field between all sources of data—static and dynamic. Application messages and data documents are treated identically and can be handled with the full power of the system. They can be merged into the same document. One can be transformed into the other. And so on.

Data-Backed Web Sites vs. Data-Driven Web Sites: The Template Approach

When XML is applied properly to Web site design, there is a big difference from the template-driven approach. Templates basically consist of fixed (or slowly changing) content with slots to be filled from a regularly updated database or even a live data source. SQL databases are great for storing the things you want to place in the slots, even if they contain some markup (preferably XML markup). This is what we call a data-backed site.

XML (in tandem with XSL) puts control in the hands of the data author. The recursive processing of the data document by the style sheet means that the data structure is the primary driver of the document assembly process, not a script or a template. In the system we have at Dell, we still have a kind of template, but it is at a very high level, and completely empty. There is no fixed content at all. This is what we call a data-driven site.

XML Is Not a Replacement for HTML

This cannot be said often enough, so we will say it again: *XML is not a replacement for HTML*. The idea that XML is a short- to medium-term replacement for HTML is related to the data/document confusion we have already outlined. It asks XML to do things it wasn't made for, and it fails to recognize the strengths of HTML.

HTML is the lingua franca of Internet browsers, and provides a rich set of formatting possibilities. With the re-casting of HTML 4 as an application of XML rather than SGML (the proposed XHTML standard), HTML should gain a new lease on life as the premier XML document output vocabulary for mainstream browsing.

Other XML-compliant vocabularies will emerge for other classes of devices. For example, Wireless Markup Language (WML) is already available on one model of mobile phone and is likely to establish itself quickly as the HTML equivalent for phones and pagers. Both WML and HTML are, or are about to become, vocabularies for specific XML applications. Neither of them is made obsolete by XML; they are both enabled by the underlying XML standards.

Will XML Be Delivered to Browsers?

Will XML be browsed directly? Yes, it will. In certain applications and certain browsers, it makes sense to deliver XML directly and apply styling and script behaviors on the client side. The DOM of the XML is far more consistent and easier to manipulate than the HTML DOM, and a combination of XSL formatting and CSS can achieve excellent results. However, the bottom line is that when delivering XML in place of HTML, there are no pre-built styles—everything must be done by hand.

The most likely scenario for the time being is that XML will initially be deployed most heavily on Web servers, and that the server will combine and convert XML data sources into HTML documents, WML card decks, VoxML dialogues, or whatever predefined XML vocabulary is tailored to the particular client. If XML is delivered to the browser at all, it will most often be as part of a document (as with Microsoft IE5 Data Islands), or when an object, such as a Java applet or ActiveX control, accesses a server-side data source that provides XML (whether it is a static document, a script, or a database).

Is XML Ready for Prime Time?

Despite all the enthusiasm, but we often hear people asking whether XML is really ready for prime time. After all, there are numerous different XML-related specifications under consideration by the W3C, and only the XML 1 proposal itself and one or two others have reached the ultimate status of the W3C Recommendation. Doubters point to the fact that key proposals such as XML Schemas, XSL, and XML query languages are far from completion. All that notwithstanding, our answer to this question is that XML is absolutely ready for prime time.

The XML 1 recommendation, DOM level 1 recommendation, and XML Namespaces provide a firm platform for application development, and DTD provides a good basis to begin formalizing vocabularies. Yes, schemas will add a great deal, and the final version of XSL will lead to many generic tools becoming available. As soon as they are finalized, we will be building them into our applications. But the reality is that it is possible to get started now, with no risk, and the benefits are there, even without those final specifications in place.

XML Data Analysis and Information Engineering: Tips from the Front Line

For anyone accustomed to writing long documents, or who is practiced in the art of using the outliner tools in Microsoft Office applications, structuring XML should be easy to learn. However, there are a number of pitfalls—we know, we fell into the pits!

For anyone who has worked primarily with HTML, a big adjustment may be needed. SQL database designers will also need to make a significant mental adjustment. XML documents are more like software objects than traditional documents. They don't run from top to bottom, they are hierarchical and structured. If you just open an editor and start writing, all sorts of problems can arise. If you start by thinking about pages on your site, the process is doomed.

We found that the number one tip for XML data design was to draw out the design before ever opening up an editor. XML documents are more like software objects than traditional documents. They don't run from top to bottom, they are hierarchical and structured. If you just open an editor and start writing, all sorts of problems can arise. Here are some tips we gleaned from our experiences in learning and working with XML.

Outside-In vs. Tree Structure

Draw out the proposed data structure rather like a family tree. There will be one thing at the top of the tree, and the whole structure will hang from there. When you transfer the tree structure into the editor later, the root of the tree becomes an opening tag at the top and a closing tag at the bottom of the document. To understand the tree structure, you need to think from the outside in when you look at the XML in the editor.

TIP

That's hard to do at the beginning while you are inventing the data structure design, but it becomes easier with practice!

The following is an example of tags in a tree structure, which illustrates the point:

```
[<a>
     <b>
               <c>
               </c>
               <c>
               </c>
</b>
<b>
               <d>
               </d>
               <d>
               </d>
     </b>
</a>]
```

This is equivalent to a tree hierarchy in Figure 29.1.

FIGURE 29.1:

An example of a tree structure hierarchy

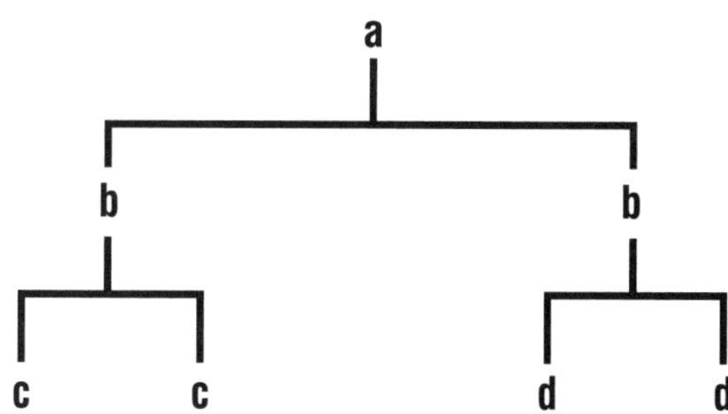

Hierarchical Thinking vs. Linear Thinking

Because of the way most people naturally write, it is easy to fall into a linear mode of thinking, proceeding from the top to the bottom of a document. Word processors encourage this. Word processor documents are typically created as a series of paragraphs separated by headings, not as chapters that contain a title and some sections, sections that consist of a title and some paragraphs, and so on. The styles you use in your document create a sense of hierarchy visually, but the underlying data is actually more of a flat list of document components. Even worse, there are no rules to say, "Hey, you can't put a picture there," or "You must have two or more items in your list."

The real purpose of the XML document structure is to describe the data and its relationships. It is easy to describe the data very richly indeed, but in doing so you can end up discarding important data about the relationships between items. Items of data that are truly cousins to each other can end up sitting under the same parent. That's why it is so important to have a defined tree structure and to stick with it.

People often worry about elements that don't seem to do anything but group other elements. These can often be the most important parts of the whole document, as they express important relationships between the data. It is easy to flatten out a document later when transforming or styling it, but you can't add back in something that wasn't there in the first place.

Anticipate the Future

One of the worst pitfalls is to start out modeling the simplest case, with a minimal data set. It is far better to really stretch the model to see where it breaks down. For example, if you decide to express an item of data as an attribute to keep the model simple, but you discover later that you want to break it down into a finer structure, you will need to convert it into an element. This type of action makes the process becomes much more painful than it needs to be. Use test cases, look for exceptions that break the model, and dream big dreams.

Take the user's perspective with *user-centered design*. When designing a data structure, ask yourself who the users will be. It is very easy to fall into the trap of structuring the data around the needs or work patterns of the data provider, rather than the data consumers. Identify all the possible users. Ask yourself how they would want to interrogate and manipulate the data. Ask yourself what they would want to know, as well as what you want to tell them.

Technological Aspects of Managing Content with XML

Now that we have thoroughly examined the business challenges that got us started with XML, the second half of this chapter looks at the technical issues. In particular, it reviews some of the principles that guided our implementation, describes how we made key technology decisions, and illustrates some important techniques for using XML in content management.

Composition: The Key to Separating Form from Content

One of the main wins that a content management system provides is in the separation of form from content; that is, the ability to separate the data in its rawest form from the final presentation. At Dell we realized early on that we needed to separate our data from our presentation—ruthlessly! Without this clear separation, it is difficult to support a large amount of content, as all parts of the business are constantly changing and this needs to be reflected and updated in a timely fashion.

In this section we will look at some of the ways separation can be achieved, go on to cover some of the pitfalls, and finish by covering some of the standards that can help support us.

The Need for Composition

If you've ever had to manage a large Web site, you know some of the problems you face maintaining content. Let's quickly cover a few of the big ones.

- Chances are your site has frequently changing content, such as press releases, special offers.
- Your site may also have product information. Although this may not change often, a single product may have tens or hundreds of pages, which all need to live together.
- In order to keep your site looking fresh you may change it periodically. How long will it take you to change each of your pages? This kind of mass change happens even to the largest sites, and can cost millions of dollars to make the transition, what with all of the changes to layout, images, and script-code.

- If that wasn't enough, every January 1st you need to update every page which shows a copyright year. If it takes you a minute to each one, a medium sized site of 5,000 pages would take more than 80 hours to update—that's more than 10 days!
- In order to keep the site consistent it is preferable to have a team of professional designers look after the look and navigation of the site. This team then needs to keep in close touch with the various product groups, marketing, and legal departments, each of which wants input into the content of the site.
- This last point gives us the beginnings of a solution to the broader problem of managing large amounts of content—delegation. If you can delegate the maintenance of content out to the person who owns that content, the whole site content will scale far better. The design team will then only need concentrate on the issues around presentation.

To understand the whole point of composition, let's look straight into a page from the Dell Europe Web site that illustrates composition in practice (Figure 29.2).

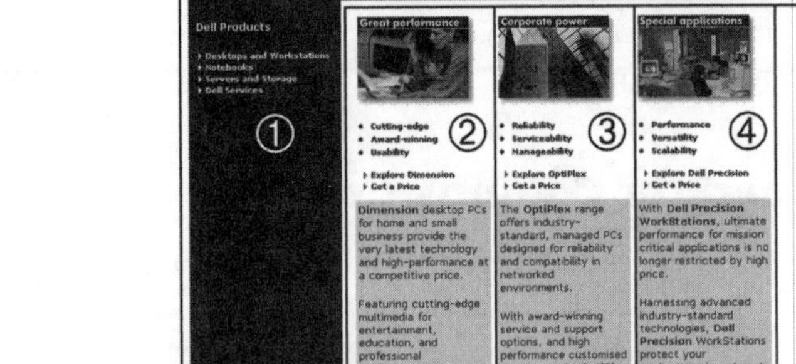

FIGURE 29.2: Composition in practice

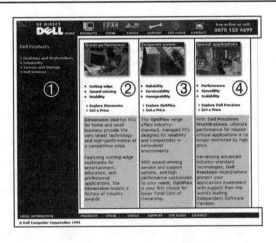

In this example, four groups broadly own the page. The design team owns the navigation and page structure (1), and the product managers for the respective products own the content for each of the three products being described (2, 3, and 4). From here, each of the product managers could be issued a template to submit their content in the required format and from there the maintenance becomes fairly trivial.

The key point to bear in mind is that there are at least four documents, all stored in XML, and all being maintained separately—one controlling the navigation on this page, and three for branding messages (one for each product).

Turning the XML into documents that can be passed to a browser will involve passing them through a style sheet, which acts as a template controlling how the final page is constructed. As you will see in the next section, the breakdown of the page into a number of documents requires additional functionality, as neither of the two common style sheet technologies (XSL and CSS) support collating of data from multiple documents.

Before tackling this, there is one important benefit of composition that we should cover—reuse. Traditional Web sites are built from static HTML pages, each of them self-contained. Using a content management system, you can build pages up from components as shown above. A useful spin-off from this is the ability to rework the same content for use over several pages. This improves consistency, while at the same time reducing the amount of content that requires management.

Compare the page shown in Figure 29.3 to the previous example (see Figure 29.2). Notice how the first two paragraphs of text describing Dell's Precision Workstation are the same on the two pages. This text is shared from the same Precision branding document, and only needs to be maintained in one place.

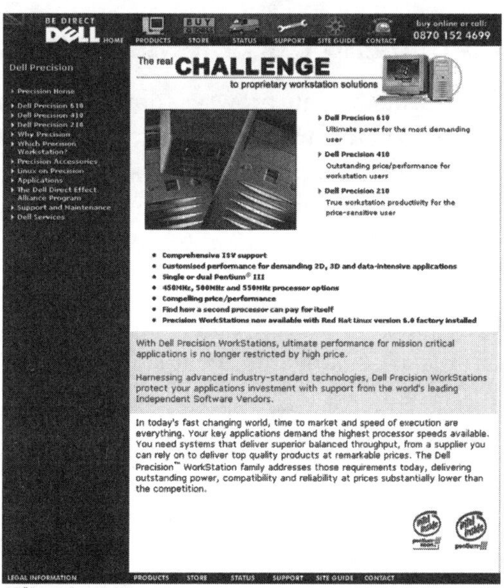

FIGURE 29.3:

Dell's Precision Worksheet

Putting the Page Together

Now that it's decided that page composition is the way to go, we will look here at how to put pages together, and some of the issues you need to confront along the way. We will also address for the first time the issues of client- vs. server-side processing and the issue of browser compatibility.

Table 29.1 shows the main technologies available to solve the various problems of composing pages and producing final documents in HTML that a browser can understand.

TABLE 29.1: Composition Challenges

Problem	Supporting Technologies
Composing a document on the client	IE5
Composing a document on the server	ASP, ISAPI, CGI
Transforming the XML document into HTML	XSL, CSS

We will now go through each of the problem areas and expand on the different technology choices.

Composing Documents on the Client Side

At present, the only browser supporting client-side XML processing out of the box is Microsoft IE5, which introduced a feature called XML Data Islands that provides an extremely simple way to get started with XML. With Data Islands, an HTML document can contain any number of XML documents in any vocabulary, including raw XML data and XSL style sheets.

The sample scripts provided on the *Mastering XML* companion CD to accompany this case study are all composed client side using IE5, and use XML Data Islands to demonstrate client-side composition.

The main problem with performing composition on the client side is the issue of compatibility, as this solution is currently only available using one browser. On other browsers client-side processing requires the use of custom scripting code to access an XML parser written in Java or ActiveX, such as the IBM alphaWorks parser.

TABLE 29.2: Pros and Cons of Composition on the Client- vs. Server-Side

Pros	Cons
Easy to try things out.	Only available in IE5, without the use of third-party libraries.
Client-side caching can greatly reduce traffic between client and server, as the navigation parts typically don't change between pages.	As the client is asking for structured XML data, it is trivially easy for someone to syndicate your content and change the presentation, at which point you have lost control of the branding.
As all transformations occur on the client side, server-side load is negligible, which helps page delivery performance.	Users with slower PCs may get a poor experience of your site as their machine may be pushed to the limit rendering your content.
The transformation can be done using either XSL or CSS.	Requires an XSL-enabled browser.

Composing Documents on the Server Side

In an intranet or extranet environment you may be able to dictate which browsers support access to your site. On the broader Internet, this is typically not an available option available and content needs to work in all of the common browsers, which typically means rendering the document on the server side and passing back HTML to the client.

Bear in mind that these server environments are generic platforms. That is to say that, at present, none supports XML directly. In order to manipulate and transform XML you are going to need to make use of the DOM API. Thankfully, performing XSL transforms typically involves nothing more than using the DOM to open a data document and a style sheet (typically single calls to the DOM), then making a third DOM call to perform the transform.

As performance was important to Dell, we ruled out Java for server-side processing fairly early. This eliminated a number of options, and left us looking closely at Microsoft's work for IE5.

To use Microsoft's XML API you must install IE5 on the server, so that you get `MSXML.DLL` and all of its dependencies installed correctly. Microsoft's DOM API conforms closely to the DOM Level 1 W3C Recommendation.

Outside a client-side browser environment, there is no access to CSS. There is a DOM Level 2 Working Draft in progress with the W3C that includes CSS transforms, but at the time of writing MSXML does not support this. Consequently, we need to use XSL to transform XML documents. We will come back to the use of XSL in the section on transforming the XML document into HTML later in this chapter. At Dell, we looked at the common technologies available for rendering on the server.

ASP Active Server Pages (ASP) is a server technology built into Microsoft's Web server Internet Information Server (IIS). Developing pages using ASP involves producing an ASP script containing embedded HTML markup, mixed in with blocks of ASP control code. This control code can contain scripting code in JavaScript or Microsoft's VBScript.

TABLE 29.3: Pros and Cons of Using ASP

Pros	Cons
Relatively easy to try things out	DOM is a fairly low-level interface, so there is a learning curve involved.
Can be maintained by any reasonably experienced ASP developer	Coding DOM manipulations requires a lot of complex script at a high performance cost. Also, with the amount of script required, it is easy to reach a state where the code is almost as hard to maintain as the original site was!

ISAPI and CGI Internet Server API (ISAPI) and Common Gateway Interface (CGI) are technologies for running compiled code on the server, the main difference being that ISAPI technology is based on the use of DLLs in Windows, whereas CGI invokes external applications. ISAPI is supported by Microsoft's Internet Information Server, and by the Apache Web server.

As both of these technologies use compiled code, the performance is much better than interpreted ASP script code. The main downside is that, being compiled code, these solutions require the use of a compiled language such as C, C++, Java, or Visual Basic.

TABLE 29.4: Pros and Cons of ISAPI vs. CGI

Pros	Cons
Best performance	The code is more difficult to change, as it requires compiling and deploying new binary code. Also, developers that can produce ISAPI or CGI applications are harder to come by than ASP developers.

Packaging XML Capabilities Using DOM and COM

If you only have a few C++, Java, or Visual Basic developers available to you, another method is to develop a COM object that packages up the key DOM functionality you need. You can then develop the site with ASP and make use of this COM component across your site.

Transforming the XML Document into HTML

We have already talked about the use of XSL and CSS to produce final rendered documents. In this section we will go into this in greater detail.

It is worth noting that Microsoft IE5 supports a style sheet processing instruction at the top of the XML data documents that allows a default view to be defined for the contained data. This style sheet can either be an XSL style sheet or in Microsoft's flavor of CSS.

XSL EXtensible Style sheet Language (XSL) is actually a misnomer in two ways. First of all, it isn't actually directly extensible at all! It is only extensible in the sense that it allows you to create a set of style sheet templates to match the tags you defined in your XML vocabulary, indirectly supporting the extensibility of XML. Secondly it is a misnomer because it isn't only a style sheet language. XSL can be used to transform XML for many purposes, only one of which is styling it. At least it is definitely a language!

At the time of this writing XSL is a W3C Working Draft with the W3C, and has not reached final Recommendation as yet. Microsoft's implementation of XSL, as supplied in IE5, is modeled on the December 1998 XSL working draft, but differs in some areas. The two most significant are: the lack of support for formatting objects, which makes up a large portion of the working draft; and in the lack of support for Attribute Value Templates, which provide a way to easily set attribute values based on the result of a query and can be used for doing joins.

Still, Microsoft has done a good job up until now of interpreting the outcome of the standards process, and in our opinion has kept a firm sense of what is actually needed to get the most of out of the technology despite the incomplete state of the W3C Specification.

In our experience at Dell, we have found XSL capable of expressing most of the data relationships we threw at it. The main limitation we found when producing

HTML output is in the output of client-side script code. Quite often when writing script, you will need to perform comparisons using the < and > characters. However, these are reserved characters in XML, so in order to output them properly, it is necessary to wrap the blocks of script code within CDATA blocks that tell the XML parser to skip over the contents. This generally makes your data look ugly and your script code harder to maintain.

The pros and cons of using XSL are listed as follows:

Pros	Cons
Uses an XML-based syntax.	XSL style sheets sacrifice human readability for machine readability.
Supported transformation of XML from one form to another.	As the input document and style sheet are both well-formed XML, the output will be well formed XML too. This means single HTML tags such a ` ` will come out as ` `, which may blow up in some browsers. Similarly some HTML tags need closing, and if empty, will not generate the correct output, for example you would get `<TD/>` when you need `<TD></TD>`.
Gives the best level of support for XML documents, as it was designed to do this from day one.	The specification is still only a working draft and subject to change. Most implementations have extrapolated anyone the variations because the spec is not final because of different WD versions to solve some of the problems in the specification, leading to differing non-standard implementations.
Supports a broad range of matching and transformation constructs.	The syntax is a little esoteric and the learning curve is quite steep as a result.
	Outputting script code is tricky because of the need for wrapping them inside CDATA block.
	The style sheet cannot be parameterized, say based on settings from a URL, except by modifying the style sheet XML document on the fly, which isn't very elegant.
	Tools support is still pretty thin on the ground.

CSS Cascading Style Sheets (CSS) have been around for a few years now. They were first provided in basic form in IE3 and Netscape Navigator 4. Since this time, adoption has been fairly limited, not least because of the major differences in the level of support between different browsers. Even now, the W3C is working on CSS2, although most browser vendors have yet to implement the original CSS1 fully.

CSS is literally only a style sheet language, not a full-blown transformation language like XSL. This means that you will get out what you put in, and as such you will need to use it in conjunction with XSL to reduce and transform the data and then CSS to style it. As XSL is capable of styling too (adding style is in itself a type of transformation), this makes use of CSS rather burdensome.

Finally, Microsoft IE5 is currently the only environment to use CSS with XML. Until CSS2 achieves broad support, it is unlikely that use of CSS will make much of an inroad into the world of content management.

The pros and cons of using CSS are listed as follows:

Pros	Cons
Simple, easy to read text-based syntax.	Only suitable for styling, not for transformation.
CSS is well established and understood with broad tools support.	CSS+XML is still fairly new, and support is limited to display in the Microsoft IE5 browser, which rules out its use on the server.
	Only a styling syntax. Cannot filter or transform the input document as XSL does.

What Are Dell's Criteria?

At Dell, one of our major goals was to ensure that customers had the best possible experience when visiting our site. This meant our primary concern was for browser compatibility, which in turn meant all transformations had to happen on the server so that the browser would only see HTML.

CSS was ruled out because of lack of either server-side support or means for transforming data. XSL, though new and unfinished, provided the best combination of features, in that it supports styling, transformations, and most importantly, works in a server environment.

As for the choice of side-by-side environments, for a content-management system we suggest avoiding widespread ASP deployment because of the problems of scaling large amounts of DOM code. Although Sun Microsystems has made a commitment to XML along with several Java-based XML parsers and XSL processors, in the author's experience the best, most scalable platforms are dedicated ISAPI solutions, again probably implemented in C or C++ rather than Java or Visual Basic. If ASP is unavoidable, look to put as much core (i.e. shared) functionality into a COM object or suite of objects that provides some abstraction to the low level DOM APIs, as this will ensure that your ASP code is at least maintainable once you go beyond a few scripts.

Another Point about Standards XML provides great methods for content management. Data is held in easily managed text documents rather than in any number of disparate databases, so that tools are really easy to develop and deploy. Putting control of content back into the hands of the people who own it will cut days from the deployment times and reduce workloads, as users can make their own changes to content and see the effects for themselves, rather than going through an endless revision process.

There is of course a catch: XML is new, and as such some of the standards that support it are also new, or still incomplete. Support is also a problem for some of the newer technologies.

It seems that regardless of what happens in the next few years, the area of content management is likely to involve threading a course through any number of new or incomplete standards. With many bright minds focused on this area, we can expect a great deal more neat ideas and compelling products in this arena. In Table 29.5 we've summarized the current state of the technologies and standards discussed here.

TABLE 29.5: Summary of Technologies and Standards

Technology	Standards Position	Support
XML 1	W3C Recommendation (10th February 1998)	Many implementations, both client and server side. Some editors available. Some database support, particularly from object oriented database vendors.
XSL 1	W3C Working Draft (16th December 1998)	Incomplete. Few good implementations. Few tools.

Continued on next page

TABLE 29.5 CONTINUED: Summary of Technologies and Standards

Technology	Standards Position	Support
CSS1	W3C Recommendation (17th December 1996, revised January 11, 1999)	Well understood. Broad, though patchy browser support. Little or no server-side support.
CSS2	W3C Recommendation (12th May 1998)	Little or no support at present either on the client or server.
ASP, ISAPI	Microsoft proprietary. Some minor cosmetic changes expected in IIS 5	Well understood. Broad support, particularly through Microsoft tools such as Visual InterDev.
CGI	Unlikely to change in the near future.	Well understood. Supported by most if not all Web servers on all platforms.

A Composition Example

To demonstrate some of the ideas behind composition from multiple XML data files, let's take a simple example page using a tab metaphor that shows some basic product information from Dell's current line of desktop systems.

TIP

This example uses client-side processing as the simplest way to demonstrate composition using multiple XML sources and XSL style sheets. As described earlier, we strongly recommend using server-side processing in real-life scenarios.

The final output of this page is shown in Figure 29.4.

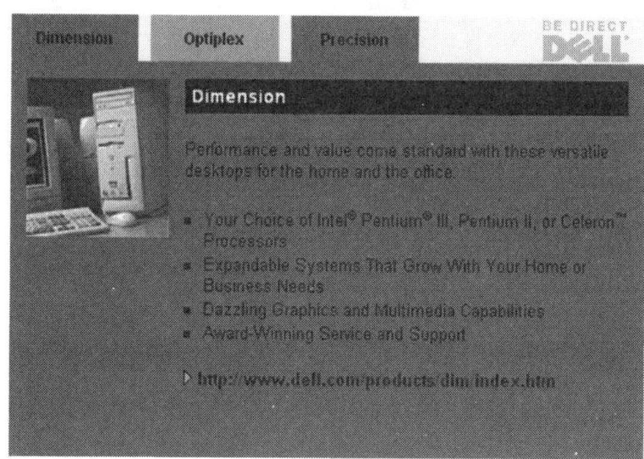

FIGURE 29.4: The final output

The page in Figure 29.4 uses some of the features of IE5 to provide a rich viewing experience. Such features as absolute positioned <DIV> elements and z-ordering mean that all three tabs are in memory and held as tabs—switching between pages is then only a matter of deciding which page should be on top.

A traditionally created HTML page might have implemented this by placing lots of HTML code directly into the <DIV> tags, or, for cross browser support, resorted to implementing each of the pages as a separate HTML page with server round trips. For this example we have a fairly small HTML file that contains <SPAN> tags for the tabs and <DIV> tags for the pages. Together with some XML data islands and some script that glues it all together, using XSL to convert the raw XML data into something the browser can present.

The Data

Figure 29.3 contains three XML data files—one for each page. It also has two XSL style sheets, one of which renders the tabs and the other that renders the panel associated with the tab. Taking this approach we were able to simple create a small, reusable framework with very little effort.

Before leaping into the XSL and the script that brings it all together, let's take a look at the actual data for one of these pages. The XML below is the entire data file for the first of the three pages—the data on the dimension range.

```
<product>
    <brand name="Dimension" color="#F06050" homepage="http://www
    .dell.com/products/dim/index.htm">
    <message>Performance and value come standard with these versatile
    desktops for the home and the office.</message>
    <sellingpoints>
    <point>Your Choice of Intel<reg/> Pentium<reg/> III, Pentium II,
    or Celeron<tm/> Processors</point>
        <point>Expandable Systems That Grow With Your Home or Business
    Needs</point>
        <point>Dazzling Graphics and Multimedia Capabilities</point>
    <point>Award-Winning Service and Support</point>
    </sellingpoints>
    </brand>
    <images>
    <thumbnail>dimension.jpg</thumbnail>
    </images>
</product>
```

Each of the three files in previous example contains a single product. Each product has a brand definition, which defines the name, standard brand color, and home page location. Within the brand is the standard branding message (in the `<message>` tag), and a block of selling points.

In addition to the branding information, there is an `<images>` section that contains images associated with the product, though in this case only a thumbnail is available.

It is worth pointing out that this file clearly only contains data, and no presentation. There is nothing here that says how it should appear on a Web page. Of course, we know that the branding color should be used in some places. And the selling points might be displayed as bullet points, though they could equally well be simple rows of text in a table, or not displayed at all.

Handling Special Characters Using XML Tags

You may have noticed that we have handled the need for registered trademark and trademark symbols using XML tags. Of course you could code these values into your document using the appropriate character encoding, but first of all you need to remember that the encoding for the registered trademark character ® is `®` (HTML entity references such as `®` are not available in XML unless you define them in a DTD). Secondly, some fonts such as those in Eastern Europe do not support this character (as it isn't part of the ISO-8859-2 character set), so in those countries you need to display it as (R). By handling this case using XML markup you only need a separate style sheet for these cases, not an entirely separate set of all of our data documents.

The Presentation

For the presentation, we just wanted something simple. The brand name will be used to define the text on the tag, and also the highlighted title displayed on the panel. The brand color will define the color of the tab and associated panel. The home page will appear as a link on the panel and also as a link from the thumbnail. Each of the selling points will appear as a bullet within the panel. The thumbnail image will appear on the left-hand side.

TIP

As previously mentioned, this example necessitated two XSL style sheets—one for the tab and a second for the actual panel. When composing a document with a number of flows like this, you can expect to have one XSL style sheet per flow, as XSL doesn't yet support processing data from multiple sources, or for multiple targets.

The two style sheets, called `tab.xsl` and `page.xsl`, contain the rules that build up the tab and panel sections, respectively.

The Tab Style Sheet

Let's start by looking at `tab.xsl`, as this is the simpler of the two:

```
<xsl:stylesheet xmlns:xsl="uri:xsl">
     <xsl:template match="product">
     <SPAN ONCLICK="tabClick()">
         <xsl:attribute name="style">
                     font: 12 'Arial';
                     font-weight: bold;
                     background-color: <xsl:value-of
                     select="brand/@color" />;
                     border: 20px;
                     width: 100px;
                     height: 30px;
                     cursor: hand;
                     text-align: center;
                     padding: 10px, 10px, 10px, 10px;
                 </xsl:attribute>
     <xsl:value-of select="brand/@name" />
     </SPAN>
</xsl:template>
</xsl:stylesheet>
```

You will notice straight away that this style sheet isn't very large. Look closer and you'll notice that really all it is doing is acting on the `<product>` tag, and using it to output an HTML `<SPAN>` tag. This `<SPAN>` tag is given a CSS style that defines the font and various padding options. The background color for the `<SPAN>` is taken from the color associated with the brand by using an `<xsl:value-of>` clause. Finally, the text to place on the tab is taken from the name associated with the brand. From this, you can quickly see that we have a nice scalable approach to the way the tabs are handled.

The Page Style Sheet

Lets move on now to look at how the page itself is handled by looking at the `page.xsl` style sheet:

```
<xsl:stylesheet xmlns:xsl="uri:xsl">
     <xsl:template match="product">
     <SPAN>
         <xsl:attribute name="style">
                     background-color: <xsl:value-of
                 select="brand/@color" />;
                     border: 20px;
                         width: 500px;
                     height: 300px;
                     text-align: left;
                     padding: 10px, 10px, 10px, 10px;
         </xsl:attribute>
         <xsl:apply-templates select=".">
                 <xsl:template match="textNode()"><xsl:value-of
             /></xsl:template>
                 <xsl:template match="reg">
                     <SUP><FONT SIZE="-1">&#174;</FONT></SUP>
                 </xsl:template>
                 <xsl:template match="tm">
                     <SUP><FONT SIZE="-1">&#8482;</FONT></SUP>
                 </xsl:template>
     <xsl:template match="copy">
         &#169;
         </xsl:template>
         <xsl:template match="keyword">
                     <B><xsl:apply-templates /></B>
                     </xsl:template>
                     <xsl:template match="product">
                             <xsl:apply-templates select="brand" />
                     </xsl:template>
                     <xsl:template match="product[images/thumbnail]">
                             <TABLE WIDTH="100%" BORDER="0">
                                     <TR>
                                             <!-- first column -->
                             <TD WIDTH="120" VALIGN="TOP">
                                     <IMG BORDER="0">
                                             <xsl:attribute name="src">
```

```
                        <xsl:value-of
                    select="images/thumbnail" />
                        </xsl:attribute>
                            </IMG>
                        </TD>
                    <!-- second column -->
                    <TD VALIGN="TOP">
                    <xsl:apply-templates
                select="brand" />
                    </TD>
                    </TR>
                </TABLE>
            </xsl:template>
        <xsl:template match="brand">
            <P style="font-size: 14; font-weight:
    bold; background-color: #000000; color: #FFFFFF;
    padding: 5px, 5px, 5px, 5px">
            <xsl:value-of select="@name" />
        </P>
            <xsl:apply-templates select="message" />
        <xsl:apply-templates select="sellingpoints"
    />
        <xsl:apply-templates select="@homepage" />
    </xsl:template>
    <xsl:template match="message">
        <P><xsl:apply-templates /></P>
    </xsl:template>
    <xsl:template match="sellingpoints">
        <UL STYLE="margin-left: 15; list-style-type:
square">
        <xsl:for-each select="point">
                <LI><xsl:apply-templates /></LI>
                </xsl:for-each>
        </UL>
    </xsl:template>
    <xsl:template match="brand/@homepage">
        <P><A STYLE="color: #000000; font-weight:
    bold; text-decoration: none">
        <xsl:attribute name="href">
        <xsl:value-of select="@homepage" />
        </xsl:attribute>
```

```
                                <IMG SRC="yellow.gif" WIDTH="7" HEIGHT="11"
                        BORDER="0" />
                                <xsl:value-of select="@homepage" />
                                </A>
                                </P>
                        </xsl:template>
            </xsl:apply-templates>
        </SPAN>
        </xsl:template>
</xsl:stylesheet>
```

Straight away you will notice that this style sheet is much larger than `tab.xsl`, but on closer inspection, it actually isn't that complicated.

It starts off just like `tab.xsl` by matching on the `<product>` in the data. As with the tab, this is used to output an HTML `<SPAN>` tag with a style that size, padding and color of the page. The color is once again taken from the color attribute associated with the brand, making the page the same color as the tab. This is a good example of reuse of data, as we now only have to maintain our brand color in the once place—in the data file associated with the brand.

Having set up the `<SPAN>` we then use `<xsl:apply-templates>` to drill down further into the data. In this case the syntax `<xsl:apply-templates select=".">` was used. This means "apply the following templates to myself," and allows us to limit the scope of the templates that follow to that element and its children, rather than making everything global.

Let's quickly go over some of the templates being used here:

- The `textNode()` template is used to convert text within the data into text in the output. Notice the way that this whole template is done in one line rather than expanded out. This prevents unwanted white space from appearing in the output.

```
<xsl:template match="textNode()"><xsl:value-of /></xsl:template>
```

- The `reg`, `tm`, and `copy` templates are used to output ®, ™, and © symbols respectively. We want the first two displayed as superscripts and in a smaller font, so the use of XML to output these symbols allows us to do that here.

```
<xsl:template match="reg">
    <SUP><FONT SIZE="-1">&#174;</FONT></SUP>
```

```
</xsl:template>
<xsl:template match="tm">
     <SUP><FONT SIZE="-1">&#8482;</FONT></SUP>
</xsl:template>
<xsl:template match="copy">
     &#169;
</xsl:template>
```

- Because we used `<xsl:apply-templates select=".">` meaning "apply the following templates to myself," we will hit the `<product>` element in the data again. There are actually two rules matching the `<product>` element. The first simply matches the element by itself and simply drills down into the brand data. In this simple case we will simply get the branding information filling up the page, with no image displayed.

```
<xsl:template match="product">
<xsl:apply-templates select="brand" />
</xsl:template>
```

- The second rule appears below the first (and is therefore checked first due to XSL's bottom-to-top evaluating sequence). This rule says "match a product element which has a thumbnail within its images." In this case we create a two-column table, with the image in the first column and the branding information in the second column. Notice that the `<xsl-apply-templates>` in the second column is identical to that used in the first `<product>` rule where no image was available.

```
<xsl:template match="product[images/thumbnail]">
     <TABLE WIDTH="100%" BORDER="0">
     <TR>
         <!-- first column -->
         <TD WIDTH="120" VALIGN="TOP">
                    <IMG BORDER="0">
                           <xsl:attribute name="src">
                              <xsl:value-of select="images/thumbnail" />
                           </xsl:attribute>
                    </IMG>
               </TD>
                    <!-- second column -->
               <TD VALIGN="TOP">
               <xsl:apply-templates select="brand" />
```

```
            </TD>
        </TR>
        </TABLE>
</xsl:template>
```

- The rule matching the brand is fairly straightforward. It throws out the name of the brand (which will be the same as the text on the tab, as they are both taken from the name attribute on the `<brand>` element within the data—a second example of reuse). Below the brand name, the standard brand message is displayed, followed by the selling points and finally the home page link.

```
<xsl:template match="brand">
      <P style="font-size: 14; font-weight: bold; background-color:
      #000000; color: #FFFFFF; padding: 5px, 5px, 5px, 5px">
      <xsl:value-of select="@name" />
      </P>
      <xsl:apply-templates select="message" />
      <xsl:apply-templates select="sellingpoints" />
      <xsl:apply-templates select="@homepage" />
</xsl:template>
```

- The brand message is a simple paragraph, but because it may include copyright symbols or other formatting, we must use `<xsl:apply-templates>` to output it, rather than `<xsl:value-of>`, which would only output the text.

```
<xsl:template match="message">
      <P><xsl:apply-templates /></P>
</xsl:template>
```

- The selling points are displayed as a series of bullet points. A CSS style attribute is used on the <UL> tag to prevent the bullets from being indented (the default behavior in HTML) and to output a square bullet.

```
<xsl:template match="sellingpoints">
      <UL STYLE="margin-left: 15; list-style-type: square">
      <xsl:for-each select="point">
          <LI><xsl:apply-templates /></LI>
      </xsl:for-each>
      </UL>
</xsl:template>
```

- Finally, the following template handles the home page link. The link itself is displayed in bold, with a yellow arrow to the left of it. The key thing to bear in mind for this particular link is that the data merely said "this is my home page" and the decision on the formatting was made entirely by the style sheet.

```
<xsl:template match="brand/@homepage">
    <P><A STYLE="color: #000000; font-weight: bold; text-decoration:
    none">
    <xsl:attribute name="href">
        <xsl:value-of />
    </xsl:attribute>
    <IMG SRC="yellow.gif" WIDTH="7" HEIGHT="11" BORDER="0" />
    <xsl:value-of />
    </A>
    </P>
</xsl:template>
```

The HTML Glue

We can't end our discussion on client-side composition without looking at the HTML that glues it all together. The HTML code contains three major sections:

- The outline structure of the document, which defines the positioning of the tabs and pages relative to each other.
- The definition of the XML data islands for the data and style sheets.
- The script code that uses the data islands to populate the tabs and pages, and which also handles the switching between pages.

Let's look at each of these in turn.

The Document Outline Structure

A number of <DIV> and <SPAN> blocks provide the basic structure of the document.

```
<DIV ID="above">
    <SPAN ID="tab1"></SPAN>
    <SPAN ID="tab2" STYLE="position:relative; left:10"></SPAN>
    <SPAN ID="tab3" STYLE="position:relative; left:20"></SPAN>
    <SPAN STYLE="position:absolute; left:425">
    <A HREF="http://www.dell.com/"><IMG SRC="WATER.GIF"
    BORDER="0"></A>
```

```
    </SPAN><BR>
</DIV>
<DIV ID="page1" STYLE="z-index: 2; position:absolute"></DIV>
<DIV ID="page2" STYLE="z-index: 1; position:absolute"></DIV>
<DIV ID="page3" STYLE="z-index: 0; position:absolute"></DIV>
<DIV ID="below" STYLE="position:absolute; top:310">
</DIV>
```

At the top is a <DIV> called above that contains the spans for each of the tabs and a fourth one for the Dell logo, which links to the Dell home page.

Below this are three <DIV> blocks, one per page. Each of these is defined as using absolute positioning, and has a default z-order. Using absolute positioning will cause each of the <DIV> blocks to be positioned over each other. The z-order is used to determine which page appears on top. By changing the z-order we can give the appearance of changing pages by simply bring the required <DIV> to the top of the stack.

Finally we have a <DIV> called below. Although this <DIV> is currently empty, you can cut and paste the <SPAN> tags from the above block into this block to have the tabs appear below the page rather than above. This <DIV> has a top position of and the page <DIV> blocks are 300 pixels high.

Defining the XML Data Islands

The XML data islands are defined as follows:

```
<XML ID="tabstyle" SRC="tab.xsl"></XML>
<XML ID="pagestyle" SRC="page.xsl"></XML>
<XML ID="doc1" SRC="dimension.xml"></XML>
<XML ID="doc2" SRC="optiplex.xml"></XML>
<XML ID="doc3" SRC="precision.xml"></XML>
```

XML data islands are a new feature in Microsoft IE5. They are defined by using an <XML> tag, and either giving it a `src` attribute as shown here, or by placing the XML data inline between the <XML> and </XML> tags.

The meaning of the code here should be fairly obvious. The first two data islands load the two XSL style sheets described earlier. The last three are for the page data itself.

You may like to experiment with rearranging the ID or `src` attributes on these three data islands. The first tab has an `ID` of `doc1`, the second `doc2`, and so on. By changing these around you can control which data appears in which order. For example, to change the tab order to Precision, Dimension, Optiplex you would change the data islands as follows:

```
<XML ID="doc1" SRC="precision.xml"></XML>
     <XML ID="doc2" SRC="dimension.xml"></XML>
     <XML ID="doc3" SRC="optiplex.xml"></XML>
```

It's All Done with Smoke and Mirrors

Well, actually, there's a small piece of script code that does the magic here. There are two parts to the script code. The first populates the tab <SPAN> and page <DIV> blocks by using the XSL style sheets to transform the data. This is done using a simple DOM method. DOM is easily accessible in IE5 because the Data Island is simply holding on to a DOM document that can then be drilled into using the DOM API.

```
<SCRIPT LANGUAGE="JavaScript">
     function OnLoad() {
             PopulateTab( tab1, page1, doc1 );
             PopulateTab( tab2, page2, doc2 );
             PopulateTab( tab3, page3, doc3 );
}
     function PopulateTab( tab, page, doc ) {
             var docRoot = doc.documentElement;
                     tab.innerHTML = docRoot.transformNode( tabstyle.doc-
     umentElement );
                     page.innerHTML = docRoot.transformNode( pagestyle
     .documentElement );
     }
     // other functions
</SCRIPT>
```

The PopulateTab() method defined here is used to perform the XSL transformations for the tab and page blocks. It is called three times, once for each page, from the OnLoad() method. OnLoad() is called from an onload event defined on the <BODY> tag of the HTML document. This method is called when the <BODY> has finished loading (at which point all of the data islands will have loaded too).

```
<BODY ONLOAD="OnLoad()" TOPMARGIN="10">
```

The three parameters passed to PopulateTab() are the ID of the tab's <SPAN>, the ID of the page's <DIV> and the ID of the XML data island that contains the data for that tab/page.

NOTE In DOM terminology, **documentElement** is the root element of the document. The **transformNode** API is use to perform an XSL transformation, and takes the root of an XSL document as its single parameter.

Flipping between Tabs

There are several ways to handle this but we chose a fairly simple method. Although not pretty, it is easy to understand and extend.

```
function tabClick() {
     id = window.event.srcElement.parentElement.id;
     page1.style.zIndex = ( id == "tab1") ? 1 : 0;
     page2.style.zIndex = ( id == "tab2") ? 1 : 0;
     page3.style.zIndex = ( id == "tab3") ? 1 : 0;
}
```

The tabClick() method uses IE's event model to find the ID of the tag that fired the event and called the method. The z-order of the <DIV> corresponding the chosen tab is then set to 1, with the others set to 0. The <DIV> with the highest z-order will displayed on top of the others, and allows us to flip between pages without needing a server round trip.

Future Proofing

In content management, you can never fully anticipate what your users will want to do. Your use of XML and XSL will constrain them (and you) to an extent, and that in it will force you to be more consistent in your approach. Inevitably though, you will need to have some tricks up your sleeve to allow the content to be more varied, to keep your users happy, and to keep your site interesting and fresh.

Obviously, if you are going to keep the data in a maintainable form, you need to ensure that all similar data is in a similar format. That's not to say you can't make it flexible.

Even the simple example here has some flexibility built into its XSL style sheets:

- The tab and panel share the same color, as defined in the XML data. The tab name is shared in the same way.
- Although all three pages presented here have a home page link, this can be removed from the XML data, and the page will simple not display it, or the arrow that is shown next to it.
- If no `<thumbnail>` image is supplied, the text and bullet points are expanded to take up the full width of the panel.

Summary

In discussing how Dell has applied XML to deliver content through its Web site, we hope it's clear how *XML is not a replacement for HTML.* (There, we said it again.)

XML is a great way to store data in a way your organization can digest and manage it. HTML is the way to get that data to your conventional browser users in a compelling and highly visual way. Using the two in tandem as described can empower your data owners, and free up your designers to focus on making your site world class, rather than spending their time maintaining other people's content.

The XML Advantage: Why We Chose XML

Our experience has been that it has been possible to model the entire content of the Dell EMEA Web sites using a small set of XML vocabularies for different classes of documents. The transition from HTML to XML has been smooth and straightforward. We now have datasets by product line and by segment, with clear ownership, and these are combined into the pages published on the site by the content-management system we devised.

We also have special datasets to express rapidly changing data such as the news links on home pages, or the special offers that are created daily. We have vocabularies to support longer documents such as white papers or legal documents. Each vocabulary is clear and simple, and data maintenance has been made far easier than ever before.

The conversion to XML has brought greater consistency to the site and reduced classic HTML defects to zero. It has also made us think carefully through the site architecture, making it easier to use. Site look and feel is now managed through a small number of XSL style sheet components that enforce visual standards, and remove the repetitive grind of formatting page after page of almost identical content in different languages.

Rather than the painful process of working with heavily marked-up HTML, language translation has now been reduced to a straightforward matter of translating the XML data documents, making the process simple and foolproof. And because the data structures drive the output, if we have more material in one language than another, it is automatically accommodated with no work required by an HTML programmer.

Whichever way we look at it, XML has been a big winner for Dell.

CHAPTER

THIRTY

30

XML for Sharing Information within a School Framework: The SIF Case Study

- Introducing Schools Interoperability Framework (SIF)
- The business problem SIF addresses
- What are the SIF components?
- How does SIF work?
- Inside individual components

This case study is somewhat different from the others in this section. SIF is an initiative in progress. It is in the early stages of prototype development in the Minnesota and New York school systems. SIF has not yet been deployed as a real-world solution. However, because the key vendors of education software are involved in the initiative and it has received a tremendous amount of interest from several school systems, it is likely that it will be used in the real world as the standard develops.

The reason this SIF case study has been included in this section is that it presents a view of how XML-based solutions can benefit one of the most important systems of our culture—one that affects all of us.

In this case study we will explore how XML can be used in a very exciting way to improve the way schools function. It provides the conduit for schools to exchange critical information among departments within the school and between schools and the district office.

LINDA BURMAN is president of L.A. Burman Associates, a consulting company providing services to the XML industry including: strategic business/market development, industry and tools analysis, training, journalism, freelance writing, and leadership of industry XML initiatives, such as the development of new vocabularies.

Prior to founding her own company, Burman was Director of Worldwide Marketing at SoftQuad International and before that the Publishing Evangelist at Apple Computer.

Burman chairs the Publishing Requirements for Industry Standard Metadata (PRISM) Working Group, a new XML Metadata initiative hosted by the GCA Research Institute (GCARI). She also teaches an XML course at the University of Toronto and is an active member of the Organization for the Advancement of Structured Information Standards (OASIS), which includes XML.ORG, and the GCA Independent Consultants Consortium of the Graphics Communications Association (GCA).

She also sits on the advisory board for the day care program of the Baycrest Centre for Geriatric Care and in a previous life she taught English Literature and theater.

Introducing Schools Interoperability Framework

Schools Interoperability Framework (SIF) is an education industry initiative to develop a standard XML vocabulary and other specifications, which will allow multiple applications to interoperate and exchange many kinds of data within an educational environment. In this case study *schools* refers to kindergarten through grade twelve. *Interoperability* refers to the interchange of data between and among many different software packages. *Framework*, not surprisingly, refers to the entire system—both process and software—that supports these capabilities.

NOTE The official SIF motto is: "A blueprint for educational software interoperability and data access."

Figure 30.1 demonstrates how SIF will hook previously disparate systems together into one framework so that data can be easily transferred. It is intended as a visual representation of the concept, not as an actual diagram.

FIGURE 30.1:

Interoperability framework

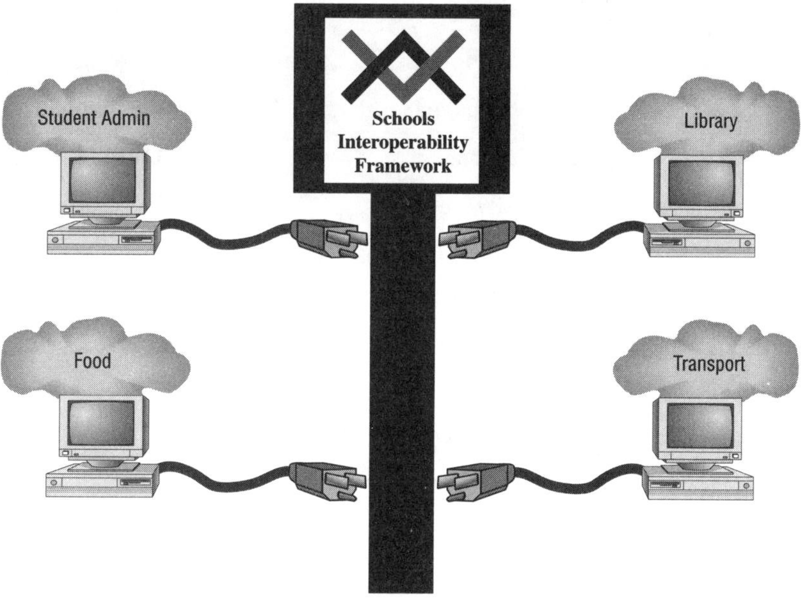

NOTE

SIF is an initiative in progress. The architecture will remain constant but it is important to note that the specifications that appear in this chapter may change as pilot systems reveal new requirements. To keep up to date on the SIF initiative, check into `http://www.schoolsinterop.org`.

Participating SIF Organizations (at the Time of Writing)

Anoka Hennepin School District
Chancery Software
Computer Curriculum Corporation
Creighton Manning
dataTech Systems
DP Consultants
Follett Software
Jackson Corporation
Jostens Learning Corporation
Laidlaw Education Services
Learning Tools International
Microsoft Corporation
Misty City Software
National Computer Systems (NCS)
Netel Educational Systems
Nichols Advanced Technologies
Olympia Computing Company
Oracle Corporation
Parlant Technology
PCS Revenue Control
Pentamation Enterprises
PeopleSoft
PhoneMaster
SNAP Systems
SRB International
The Administrative Assistants
TRO Learning
Vision Associates
Winnebago Software
SAP Public Sector & Education

Why SIF Was Created: The Business Problem for the Education Industry

Over the past few years there have been enormous technological advances in most schools. In most cases, student enrollment, attendance, and grade data is now generated and stored electronically. Many teachers use instructional software to assist in teaching basic skills.

However, all these educational applications are isolated from each other. Each is highly specialized for one particular task, and there is no easy way to share data with any other application. Each application uses a different format and in many cases a proprietary database. Also, as no standard data format is being used, special scripts must be written before there can be any data interaction between the current systems. These scripts are required to transform extracted data into a format that the other program's database understands. It's true that most vendors provide an Application Programming Interface (API) to allow access to the data. However, APIs are often proprietary and require specialized knowledge. In addition, each time any piece of software is upgraded, the scripts must be rewritten. This is a time-consuming and costly operation because the resources to accomplish these tasks may not be available within the particular educational system.

In some cases, two vendors collaborate to provide a consistent data interface. For instance, a school might use a student administration application that manages demographics, attendance, and grade data. It also has a library management application that uses the demographic information. The vendors for each of these applications could build a layer that provides a common interface and write scripts to translate the data, point to point. However, if a third application is added that also needs access to the demographics data, this solution is no longer useful. The problem compounds as other applications are added each with a different interface and proprietary data format.

Further compounding the problem is the fact that applications exist for only one hardware platform. Thus the same information must be keyed into each different application—sometimes multiple times. This labor-intensive task not only wastes time, but also introduces the possibility of errors with each additional keystroke. Furthermore, subsequent changes, such as a new address or phone number also must be keyed into multiple locations. This demands that someone track which applications use which data and thus personnel spend a huge amount of time entering, maintaining, and managing redundant data.

Schools might be able to cope with these workload problems if they had large administrative staffs. However, like many other industries, budget cuts to education have resulted in fewer, not more, full-time administrators, and therefore teachers end up doing a great deal of this work. School administrators are in an analogous situation; instead of developing strategies for the next millennium, they focus on data management. In addition, data reporting is costly and inefficient because it is impossible to use existing reporting tools to gather information from multiple applications.

Therefore, it is impossible for schools to leverage the valuable analysis and decision support information that is locked in their *data tombs.* Thus the school's ability to take advantage of funding opportunities and to improve the process of education may be affected.

> **"Schools are a huge business that is subject to conflicting and changing local, state and federal requirements. Data mining is important for controlling costs and time, meeting reporting deadlines, applying for grants...If data is not readily available, real dollars have to be spent on people time to compile it."**
>
> *—Chuck Rosengard, Manager Information Systems & Technology, Kern High School District, Bakersfield, Calif.*

XML to the Rescue

What the schools need is a platform-neutral, application-neutral, data interchange format that can be accessed, interpreted, and rendered by a consistent, *standard* client interface. Enter XML.

XML is a format-independent, platform- and application-neutral language. Therefore, as long as all the software applications in the system support the XML vocabulary defined by SIF data can be seamlessly exchanged between applications. Similarly, a standard browser with XML support can be used to access each application. With SIF and XML-enabled software, schools can choose "best of breed" applications for each individual area knowing that they will interoperate. They not only can use applications they're familiar with, but also create flexible, more powerful solutions by plugging in new modules, possibly from other vendors. No longer does even a slight change to the configuration break the data transfer links between two applications. With an intermediary format like XML, each application can maintain its own formats as long as it easily and accurately transforms the data into and from XML.

Additionally, XML provides the ability to integrate data from multiple sources. This capability really does make data mining and data analysis possible. What does data mining and data analysis mean for schools, you may ask?

The reporting software that many schools use today is not designed to access multiple databases and to integrate the data into one report. For instance, although it would be highly desirable to determine which teachers need to take a course in a given year to qualify for the next salary level, it is impossible to run an ad-hoc query to produce such a report. With SIF and XML-enabled systems, such a report could be run which would automatically send reminders to teachers. This would increase morale, avoid possible union disputes, and give teachers more time to spend on kids.

Another way data mining and analysis is very useful is for predictive analysis. With integrated information about demographics, schools can accurately predict, for instance, when student populations will increase or decrease and when the particular makeup of the student population will change significantly. This allows school districts to properly plan for new facilities, new services, and so on. Another application of data analysis is to find interesting patterns in the collected data. For example, the internal and external factors that affect a student's performance in school could be analyzed.

NOTE

Microsoft IE5 and DocZilla, built on Mozilla by CITEC, (see `http://www.citec.fi` for more information) both support XML and certain aspects of XSL. At the time of writing, Netscape Navigator does not have equivalent XML support although Netscape has announced that it will be included in the next version of Navigator. See `http://www.netscape.com` for the latest information.

Why Schools Need XML-Based Solutions

"Solutions that adhere to a common data format will have a major competitive edge in comparison to those that do not. When I am looking at competing applications, I will choose those which simplify daily tasks such as integrating student data and mining data, transforming it into information."

—Chuck Rosengard, Manager Information Systems & Technology, Kern High School District, Bakersfield, Calif.

Rosengard's comment addresses a very real issue for schools. Schools are no longer fully funded and they must apply for grants based on need, which in turn must be substantiated by data. For example, a district that can accurately report the number of handicapped students—all handicaps including physical, cognitive and so on—may qualify for additional funding. Schools require tools that make data gathering from multiple sources possible; not to mention efficient. An integrated solution based on XML with the right components can supply these tools. Furthermore, with Internet connectivity and an XML-enabled browser, administrators can view these reports on their desktops.

The SIF Components

To understand the SIF initiative, it's important to look at its parts and pieces. SIF can be described in terms of *components*. There are two types of components in the SIF initiative. First, are the software applications. The goal of the SIF initiative is to get these applications talking to each other via SIF and XML and to make them accessible from a consistent, standard browser interface. The second type is the components of the actual framework, which consist of groups of people.

SIF Software Components

Schools use a number of different software applications today that can be integrated into SIF. Some of the common applications include:

- Student administration software
- Curriculum management software
- Grade book software
- Interactive voice response software
- Library management software
- Cafeteria management software
- Human resources and financial software
- Transportation management software
- Reporting and data management/warehousing software

Another software component that is being created by the SIF initiative is the underlying architecture.

SIF Framework Components

The SIF Framework includes ten components that in many cases correspond to the software application components. Those SIF Framework components are represented as working groups that are developing the specifications of a particular piece of the whole vocabulary. SIF initiative also refers to groups of people as components.

The framework includes groups that provide a feedback mechanism called Customer Involvement Requirements. They include groups such as education associations, district technology coordinators, and state level organizations.

SIF has a large and ever-increasing number of companies and associations among its membership. Each member sits on one or more component work groups which are charged with defining the objects and events of each different component and making them interoperable, and also with defining portions of the common vocabulary that relate directly to individual functional areas. When functional areas overlap, the component work groups must agree on a common solution.

The component work groups more or less match up with the various SIF software components as follows:

Grade Book Information Working Group This group defines the data related to student grade books.

Library Services Working Group This working group has identified the need for a single new object called Library Patron Status which will communicate the current library status of a given student or teacher.

Data Warehousing Working Group This group's task is to determine the types of data management and warehousing possible once SIF is put into practice. It provides feedback to other groups that are defining data objects that will be used for data reporting and analysis.

Curriculum Management Working Group The charter of this group is to develop the objects and events related to state frameworks, learning resources, and curriculum management.

Customer Involvement Requirements Working Group This group is made up of representatives from schools, school districts, and state level organizations and is responsible for evangelizing SIF awareness and gathering feedback from the education community.

Human Resources and Financials Information Working Group This group is tasked with defining the data objects for human resources and financials. The initial scope will describe teachers only.

Food Services Working Group This working group has identified the need for a single new object called Student Meal which will communicate the current meal status of a given student.

Student Information Working Group This group's task is to define the objects and events needed to exchange student information with other applications. Library, transportation, and food services are examples of applications that need the same student data. The information that is defined by this group includes:

Student Personal Information Student demographics, contact, and other personal data.

Student School Enrollment All data related to student school enrollment.

Student Course Enrollment The courses in which students have enrolled.

Student Assessment Information Standardized student test data.

Student Health Information Student medical and health data.

Student Discipline Student discipline data.

School Information General data about the school.

Transportation and Geographic Information Working Group This group has the opportunity to supply some unique elements to the geographic component of the transportation system. These elements will be very valuable for locating data and events in space and will permit a wide range of data analysis. Like the other components, the transportation system is made up of objects and events.

Data Warehousing Working Group The responsibility of this group is to investigate the reporting and data warehousing capabilities that are possible, and provide feedback into the other groups that are defining the data that will be used for reporting purposes and analysis.

Infrastructure Working Group This group produces the *Infrastructure Definition*, the component that defines the messaging protocol that the different applications must use to interoperate. This group is critical to the framework because without the messages, the data and event objects can't be sent from one application to another. This group is also responsible for developing the Implementation Specification, a vendor-neutral specification for building the middleware that the software applications use to exchange data.

The section "Exploring the Framework Component Specifications" later in the chapter explores some of the actual specifications in detail.

Describing SIF Functionality

This section provides an overview of the functional operation of the SIF initiative—an understanding of how all the pieces interoperate. It does not, however, explain in total detail how every aspect of SIF is implemented due to space restrictions.

A good place to begin looking at functionality is with the SIF goals for each implementation. A SIF implementation must enable different applications to exchange data efficiently, reliably, and securely.

The following section examines some of the implications of the following objectives:

Efficiency Efficiency implies that the SIF implementation must support real-time data exchange—in addition to batch data exchange—between different applications. It also must scale well.

Reliability Reliability implies that when an application sends out a message to a destined receiver, the delivery is guaranteed; messages will arrive at the receiver in the same order as they are sent, and each message will only be delivered once.

Security Security has three aspects. Each message that is sent to SIF must be encrypted and authenticated to restrict access to designated applications. For example, an application designed for students should not be allowed to request personal information for teachers.

NOTE Each of these aspects is defined in considerable detail in the *Implementation Specification*, which will be available on the public SIF Web site, `http://www.schoolsinterop.com`. Because this specification is in progress, examples have been derived directly from the specification.

The Pieces and Parts That SIF Uses

The main idea behind SIF, and the key to making it work, is a common XML data vocabulary used by the SIF messaging protocol and describing all of the objects. Just supporting basic XML is not enough. For all the applications to understand one another and to exchange data transparently, the same vocabulary must be used. The two most important parts of the SIF XML vocabulary are *messages*, which describe the interaction protocol, and *objects*, which the messages send. An *object* can be either a *data object* or an *event object*. Event objects act on data objects.

The Implementation Specification documents all of the functional aspects of SIF including the message protocol. It also contains other functional information that may interest you such as the type of communications used by SIF (asynchronous in this case), the Security model, and the Customization possibilities. However, these are not described in this chapter because it focuses on the aspects of SIF that are directly related to XML.

The SIF Data Model

At the time of writing, the SIF data model is still in development. The parts that exist are the specifications from each of the working groups that describe the individual elements that make up the various objects and events, and the actual XML DTD(s). The data model describes the structure of the XML documents, which make up the event and data objects and the SIF messages. A breakdown of the two main components—messages and objects—as defined in the following data model.

Data Objects Data objects are schemas that define the semantics of information that can be managed by one or multiple applications. For example, StudentPersonal, StudentSchoolEnrollment, and School are data objects. Each object is represented with XML elements and attributes.

Event Objects Event objects, or simply events, represent changes to the information that are defined in the data objects. Typically, there are one or multiple events that can act on each data object and all of the elements it contains. For example, Student Add/Delete/Change events are actions that can happen to the StudentPersonal data object. StudentSchoolEnrollment Add/Delete/Change is for the StudentSchoolEnrollment object and School Add/Delete/Change event is for School object and so forth.

Messages Data and event objects must be contained in SIF messages (which are also defined using XML) before they can be exchanged between applications. In other words, messages can be regarded as "wrappers," a term often used when discussing communications protocols.

Some of the message types are as follows:

```
K12Event:  used to broadcast events to interested listeners and it is
also used to deliver events
K12Request:  used by one application to explicitly query  another and
to request certain data
K12Response:  the response that has to be sent to the query
K12Ack:  general purpose Acknowledge message for handshaking
```

Event Reporting

SIF uses a publishing and subscription model. Events are published or reported by any application. In other words when a student record is updated, the appropriate events—Add, Delete, or Change—are published. Applications that have indicated that they want to be notified every time such an event occurs are subscribers. When applications publish events, the delivery of the messages to the subscribing applications is guaranteed. This process is called *event reporting*. Each application must subscribe to events that it is interested in receiving. In other words, a student might change his or her address and applications like Library Services, Food Services, and Transportation Services might subscribe to that event.

Data Provision

SIF also uses a request and response model. Each application can claim to be a provider of certain data objects. The process by which application advertises itself as the provider of certain data objects is called *provision*.

When an application requests information about an object, SIF will identify the provider of the object and send the request to the provider application. The provider application can then either fulfill the request or reply with a message indicating it is unable to provide the information to the requesting application. SIF knows who the providers are because they have *registered* themselves as providers of certain objects.

SIF Architecture and Implementation

The following discussion will provide an overview of the SIF Architecture. It is beyond the scope of this chapter to discuss the architecture and implementation in detail, but some knowledge of the architecture is very useful for understanding how the XML documents (objects and messages) are used.

The architecture of SIF is a distributed networking system that is based on *agents* and a middle-tier server called the *Zone Integration Server* (*ZIS*) that provides data integration services according to the business logic or rules defined by each school district. These rules are completely determined by the school district and are not pre-set in any way.

Agents are created by each software application and they act as interfaces for the application to the ZIS. In other words, applications do not talk to each other directly but rather connect to the ZIS, which acts as the intermediary. So the agents actually provide data, subscribe to events, publish events, request data, and respond to requests although conceptually it is the application.

The ZIS is the integration point for all the agents in the framework. The ZIS understands all the messages described in the *SIF Message Specification*. The SIF messages (used by agents) perform the various operations described previously such as *provision*, *subscription*, *event report*, *request*, and *response*.

The Role of Agents in Implementation

In the previous section "SIF Functionality" you learned about the functional aspects of SIF. In this section, you will learn how the agents use those functional aspects to carry out the SIF interapplication communication.

Providing and Requesting Data Each application must advertise what data objects it provides. The message that the application uses for advertising data objects is `K12Provide`, one of the messages in the Infrastructure Specification, which is described in more detail in the next section.

Applications do their advertising via their *agent(s)*. Agents deliver messages to the local ZIS, store them in the *Provider database table*. Agents can also pass them on to another ZIS if necessary. An agent registers an application as a provider with the message `K12Provide`. Applications only need to do that once unless they increase or decrease the list of provided data objects.

This process is required for the request and response mechanism to work. When requests come in, the ZIS has the information about which agents to forward them to. The ZIS also keeps track of which agents the responses should go to. The agents then deliver the messages (and the contained objects) to their applications.

Updating Information Agents receive updates by subscribing to particular event objects using the message `K12Subscribe`. The same mechanism is used for event subscription as for data provision. The ZIS stores subscription information in the subscriber database table.

The updating process itself is called event reporting, as described previously. The way it works is that an agent detects that a data element has changed in any SIF-defined data object. It then reports that information to the ZIS. The ZIS informs the agents who have subscribed to that event and so the update is accomplished.

Exchanging Data When an application needs data, its agent makes a request by submitting a `K12Request` message to the ZIS. The ZIS knows which agents can provide the requested data object(s) because they previously advertised which objects they provide. Therefore the ZIS passes the query (the request for data) to the appropriate agent which then delivers it to its application. The response is provided in a `K12Response` message, which includes the requested information. An agent can also send a message saying that it can't provide the information and the `K12Response` may include a reason.

Validating Messages The specification recommends that each message receiver validate any incoming message to ensure that it is a valid SIF message. Message validation will be done with the most current XML DTD or XML Schema. The SIF Implementation Specification advises that each agent and ZIS should specify the version of the SIF Message Specification that they support in the same way that they would do it for other specifications.

Key Aspects of SIF Architecture and Implementation

Communications, Security Requirements, InterZone Communication, the Data Integration Agent for Complex Requests, and Administration are all described in considerable detail in the SIF Specification to ensure that software developers can create successful SIF applications. Once more it is important to note that these specifications are in flux. Therefore, it is critical to consult the Web site for the most current information about how to build SIF applications. The Web site will also have the most current list of vendors who are developing applications for SIF, which is important information for integration. Figure 30.2 represents the way the SIF architecture works.

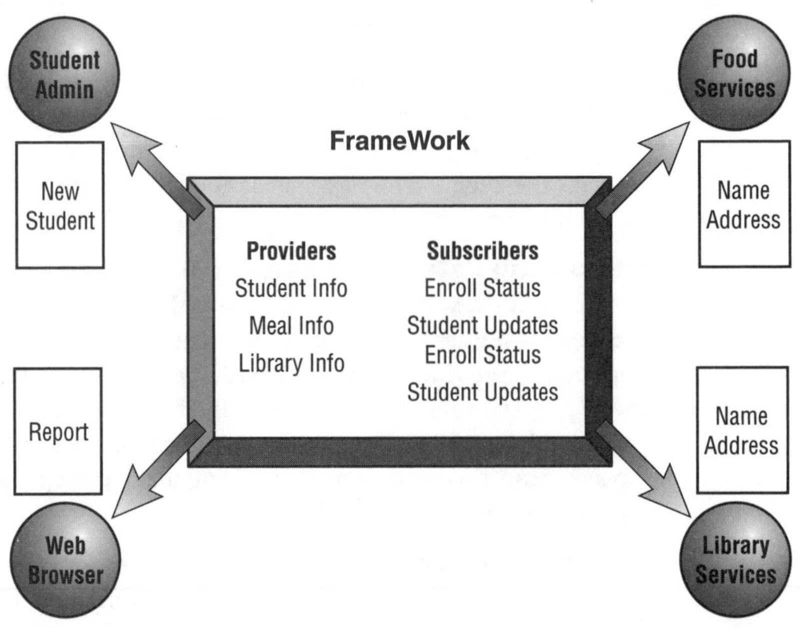

FIGURE 30.2: A conceptual description of the workings of SIF Architecture

Exploring Framework Component Specifications

This section will look at the innards of three SIF components: the *Curriculum Management Working Group*, the *Transportation and Geographic Information Working Group*, and the *Infrastructure Working Group*. The specifications for each will be examined in some detail to demonstrate the use of XML in SIF.

NOTE Please note that all of these specifications are in progress and will most likely change somewhat from the descriptions here. To view the most current information available, please see `http://www.schoolsinterop.org`.

Curriculum Management Working Group

The Curriculum Management Working Group is developing a specification for the data objects and events related to state frameworks, learning resources, and curriculum management. The initial activities of the Curriculum Management Group focus on the data model for lessons, learning resources, and assessments. These objects and events can be used in many diverse ways as demonstrated by the following examples:

- Running any type of courseware under any courseware management system.
- Automated access to courseware using source and purchase information.
- Analysis of lesson requirements to find gaps in available resources.

The data objects in the data model for curriculum management are:

```
LessonInfo
AssessmentInfo
Learning ResourceInfo
Learning ResoucreResult
ResourceSourceInfo
```

Figure 30.3 is called a structure diagram and, as you might suspect, it describes the structure of the LessonInfo Object. This diagram provides a visual view of the LessonInfo element in the DTD. You can see that it is possible to include a substantial amount of very specific data about specific lessons. The diagram makes it easy to see the element structure, which attributes are required and so on. With the data from the LessonInfo Object, various school boards will be better able to schedule special kinds of classes, short courses and so on.

At present the Curriculum Management Data Model does not contain any event objects and it is still unknown if they will be required.

Transportation and Geographic Information Working Group

This group has the opportunity to supply some valuable data unique to the transportation system. Some of this is geographic information that has never been captured before. This information will be invaluable for wide range of data analysis that will result in better planning of the transportation system, less waste of time and resources and thus more savings for the school system. It will also provide information about student demographics—for instance what the density of students is at any given distance from any given bus stop or from any given school.

FIGURE 30.3:

A LessonInfoObject

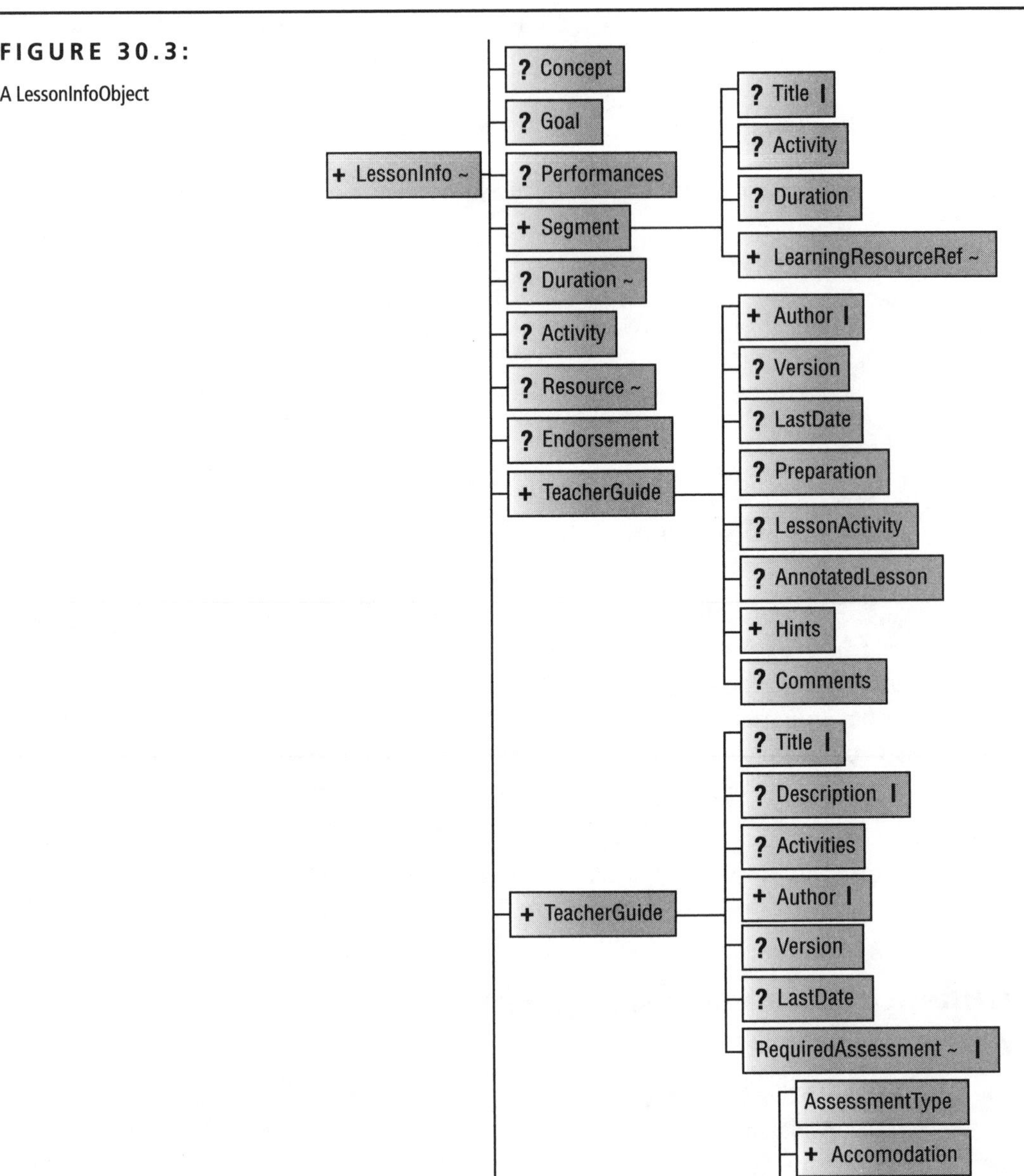

Data Model for Transportation Information System

This group defines only one data object, which contains a number of elements. The only events it includes are changes to the student transformation object.

Student Transportation Information Object The structure diagram for the Student Transportation Information Object is shown in Figure 30.4. The unique data that was referred to previously will be contained in the "Walkto-StopDist" and the "HometoSchoolDist." You can also see that the object includes information about "Special Accommodations," which refer to possible handicaps that students may have. Because this information can be related to bus and route numbers it will allow the school system to plan appropriately for special accessibility requirements.

FIGURE 30.4:

Student Transportation Information Object

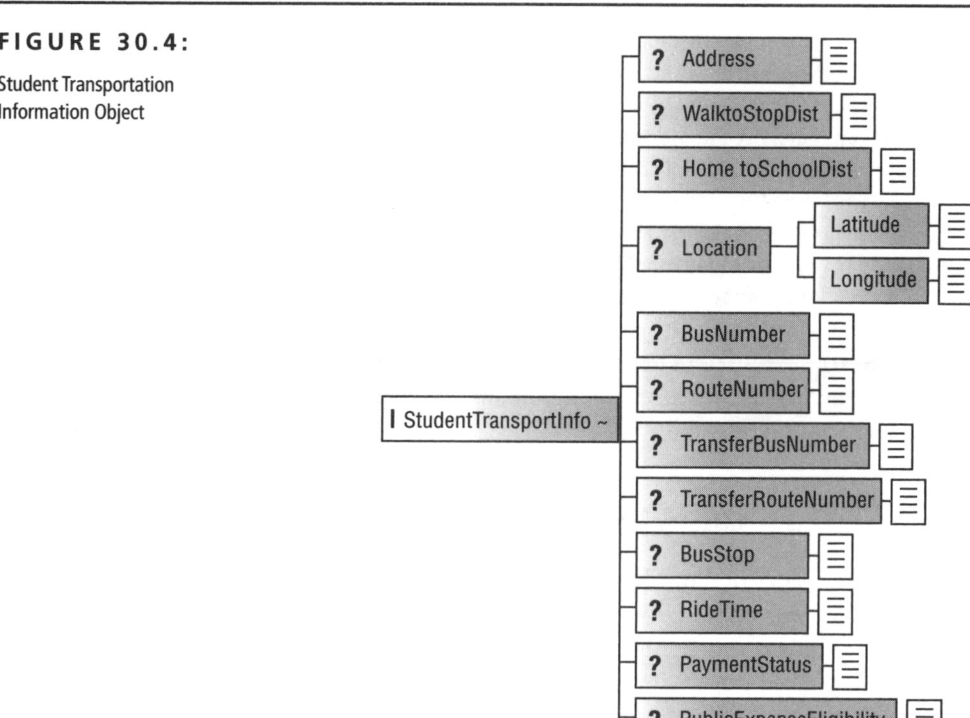

Listing 30.1 is an example of the XML code that would represent a Student Transport Info Object. As you can see, the student who is being referenced here requires a wheelchair.

LISTING 30.1 An Example of a Student Transport Info Object

```
StudentTransportInfo StudentRefId="349" Location="Pickup">
<Address>
    <Street>….</Street>
             <City>…</City>
    ….
</Address>
<WalkToStopDist Units="Miles" >1.2</WalkToStopDist>
<HomeToSchoolDist Units="Miles">5.8</HomeToSchoolDist>
<Location>
<Latitude>79.548445</Latitude>
<Longitude>41.7699657</Longitude>
</Location>
<BusNumber>50</BusNumber >
<RouteNumber>687</RouteNumber>
<TransferBusNumber>51</TransferBusNumber>
<TransferRouteNumber>688</TransferRouteNumber>
<BusStop>Elm St @ Pine Ave</BusStop>
<RideTime>40</RideTime>
<PublicExpenseEligibility>Yes</PublicExpenseEligibility>
<SpecialAccomodations>Wheelchair</SpecialAccomodations>
</StudentTransportInfo>
```

Student Transportation Information Events The only Events in the Student Transportation Information data model include any changes to this student transportation information.

Infrastructure Working Group

The Infrastructure Working Group is responsible for defining the messages that carry data objects and event objects from one application to the other via the application's agent(s). Messages are not data or event objects, but they contain data and event objects inside them. The message type tells the receiving application (Agent) what kind of data/event objects it is carrying.

NOTE

From an implementation point of view, it is important to keep in mind that the applications are not exchanging messages directly but are receiving/sending them (and so on) by means of their agents and the ZIS.

Infrastructure Data Model

The Infrastructure Data Model defines the SIF messages that are used by all the applications participating in SIF. They are defined in XML. Some of these messages were discussed earlier in the chapter in the "SIF Functionality" section but they are described here in more detail. The message types and their definitions follow:

K12Event: Used to broadcast events to interested listener and to deliver events to appropriate application (Agents).

K12Request: Used by one application to explicitly query data from another application (via the Agents).

K12Response: Defines the response that has to be sent to the query.

K12Register: Registers the message sender to the ZIS.

K12Provide/K12UnProvide: Used by applications to register/unregister themselves as the Provider of a particular type of data object.

K12Subscribe/K12UnSubscribe: Used by an application to register/unregister itself as the listener/Subscriber of a particular event.

K12Ack: General purpose *Acknowledge* message for handshaking within the communications protocol. (SIF is designed to support multiple network protocols like TCP, HTTP, MSMQ, or any other protocol that is chosen by the message vendor.)

The Infrastructure Data Model defines messages not data objects and specific events. However, the elements that make up the SIF messages *are* part of the data model. Some examples of the elements are described as follows.

The section that follows provides some examples of the SIF message types and the elements they're made up of. It does not include all the message types listed previously because the goal of this chapter is to provide an understanding of how XML can be used by an initiative like SIF, rather than to teach you everything about SIF. However, if you are interested in using SIF or learning more about it, you will find the information on the Web site very useful.

We will begin with the Header element because it is common to all the SIF message types.

Header The structure model for the common Header element is shown in Figure 30.5.

FIGURE 30.5:
SIF Message Header

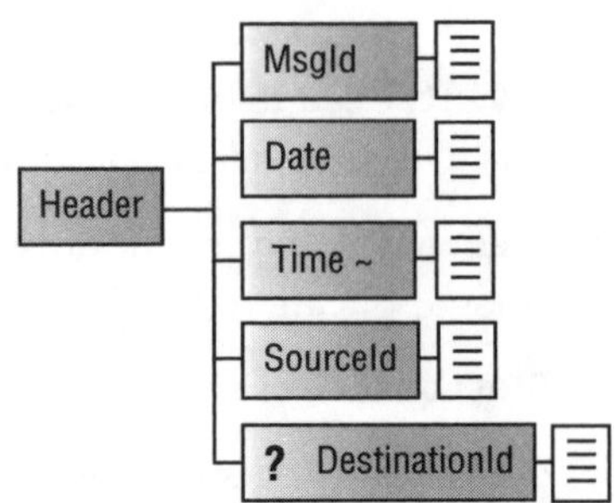

Contained within the Header are:

MsgId Provides a unique identifier so that the message can be tracked. This identifier is actually supplied by the application's agent or by the ZIS.

Date and Time Tells when the message is sent.

SourceId The unique identifier of the sender of the message.

DestinationId The unique identifier of the destination of the message. As you can see from Figure 30.5, this element is optional.

Two samples of Header elements follow:

```
<Header>
   <MsgId>101</MsgId>
   <Date>19990218</Date>
   <Time Zone = " GMT-08:00">20:39:12</Time>
   <SourceId>ABC_Corp.Agent</SourceId>
   </Header>
<Header>
   <MsgId>102</MsgId>
   <Date>19990311</Date>
   <Time Zone = " GMT-08:00">08:20:09</Time>
   <SourceId>ABC_Corp.Agent</SourceId>
   <DestinationId>XYZ_Corp.Agent</DestinationId>
</Header>
```

SIF Message Types The **K12Event** is used to deliver and broadcast event objects. As you learned earlier, events represent changes to the data objects.

Following is an example of a K12Event that updates (changes) the phone number in an existing StudentPersonal object (record). The new number (data) will automatically replace the existing number (data). This example could also be used to change the name and address in the same record.

```
<Event ObjectName="StudentPersonal" Action="Change">
<StudentPersonal RefId = "1234">
            <Name>...</Name>
<Address>...</Address>
<PhoneNumber>
            AreaCode>416</AreaCode>
                   <Number>699-7198<AreaCode>
                   <Ext/>
</PhoneNumber>

</StudentPersonal

</Event>
```

K12Request and K12Response Two very important messages are K12Request and K12Response. They are used to request information (data objects) from other applications (agents) and to return the data in response to the specific queries.

For example, the following query element (which is one of the elements in the K12Request) indicates that the elements Name and Address are requested from the *StudentPersonal* object.

```
<Query>
<Object Type = "StudentPersonal">
            <Element>Name</Element>
            <Element>Address</Element>
</Object>
</Query>
```

NOTE The element can be expressed in XSL syntax, representing the path of the element within the specified object. Element attributes can also be expressed in XSL syntax.

To give you an idea of how the K12Request message works and what the XML code might look like for a given request, the following example has been created. The actual request is to select the first name, last name, and ID of all the students whose ID is not 10233 and whose first name is Alicia, and also whose teacher ID is A-203.

```
<K12Request>
<Header>…</Header>
<Query>
            <Object Type = "StudentPersonal" RefId="1234">
                   <Element>Name/FirstName</Element>
                   <Element>Name/LastName</Element>
                   <Element>Id</Element>
            </Object>
            <Conditions Type = "And">
                   <Condition>
                          <Element>StudentPersonal/@Id</Element>
                          <Operator>NE</Operator>
                          <Value>10233</Value>
                   </Condition>
                   <Condition>
                          <Element>
StudentPersonal/Name/FirstName
</Element>
                          <Operator>EQ</Operator>
                          <Value>Alicia</Value>
                   </Condition>
                   <Condition>
                          <Element>StudentGrade/Teacher/@Id</Element>
                          <Operator>EQ</Operator>
                          <Value>A-203</Value>
                   </Condition>
            </Conditions>
</Query>
</K12Request>
```

K12Response K12Response is used to respond to a K12Request message. The following is an example of a K12Response that involves the StudentTransportation-Info, discussed previously in this chapter.

The following Student Transportation Information Event will be launched when the student's bus number is updated in the system.

```
<K12Event>
<Header>
…..
</Header>
<EventData>
     <Event Object Name="StudentTransportInfo" Action="Change">
<StudentTransportInfo StudentRefId=="349" Location="Pickup" >
                    <BusNumber>99</BusNumber>
                    </StudentTransportInfo>
             </Event>
     </EventData>
</K12Event>
```

NOTE The SIF Developer Web site and SIF members provided information for this chapter.

Summary

SIF tackles a real and critical business problem that directly affects the education industry and therefore indirectly affects all of us—as parents and as taxpayers. The fact that the disparate software applications used by school systems cannot easily talk to each other and therefore exchange data, is an expensive problem. Resources that could be better used elsewhere are spent keying in data that could be made available automatically. Also, the fact that each of the software applications operates separately limits the functionality of the whole system. Data that could be analyzed for planning, writing grants, and improving services and programs, for instance, is not being captured or is buried in data tombs.

The SIF initiative shows that creating a framework that leverages XML (and related XML technologies) can address this major business challenge. If implemented correctly, SIF will provide the functionality to schools to forecast accurately, to analyze data to produce better programs, and much more. The description of the various aspects of SIF presented in this chapter gives you an idea of how SIF will accomplish these goals. As SIF continues to gain momentum, these specifications will be enhanced and refined as they are put into practice in real world situations.

APPENDIX A

Extensible Style Sheet Language Formatting Properties

A

The tables contained within this appendix provide the possible values for each formatting property listed in the left-hand column. Where indicated in the XSL Specification, a simple BNF (Backus-Naur Form) notation may be used. Comma-delimited lists are lists of individual choices.

As the XSL Specification is not yet a full W3C Recommendation, these properties and values are subject to change. Watch the W3C Web site for news when XSL becomes a W3C Proposed Recommendation and then a full recommendation.

Common Absolute Positioning Properties

Value	Description
static	Default value. Left and top properties are not applicable.
relative	Position is first calculated within the normal flow, then calculated again offset from the original placement.
absolute	Each of the left, right, top, and bottom property values are specifically set. The box is no longer part of the normal flow; therefore, it will not impact later siblings.
fixed	Uses the absolute model but takes position in terms of a secondary reference point, e.g., the distinct values for left, right, top, and bottom are set, but the overall box position may be gauged as 100 pixels from another box.

Common Aural Properties

Property	Value
azimuth	<angle>	left-side	far-left	left	center-left	center	center-right	right	far-right	right-side	behind	leftwards	rightwards
cue	<'cue-before'>	<'cue-after'>
cue-after	<uri>	none
cue-before	<uri>	none
elevation	<angle>	below	level	above	higher	lower

Continued on next page

<table>
<tr><th>Property</th><th>Value</th></tr>
<tr><td>pause</td><td><time> | <percentage> | {1,2}</td></tr>
<tr><td>pause-after</td><td><time> | <percentage></td></tr>
<tr><td>pause-before</td><td><time> | <percentage></td></tr>
<tr><td>pitch</td><td><frequency> | x-low | low | medium | high | x-high</td></tr>
<tr><td>pitch-range</td><td><number></td></tr>
<tr><td>play-during</td><td><uri> mix? repeat? | auto | none</td></tr>
<tr><td>richness</td><td><number></td></tr>
<tr><td>speak</td><td>normal | none | spell-out</td></tr>
<tr><td>speak-header</td><td>once | always</td></tr>
<tr><td>speak-numeral</td><td>digits | continuous</td></tr>
<tr><td>speak-punctuation</td><td>code | none</td></tr>
<tr><td>speech-rate</td><td><number> | x-slow | slow | medium | fast | x-fast | faster | slower</td></tr>
<tr><td>stress</td><td><number></td></tr>
<tr><td>voice-family</td><td>[[<specific-voice> | <generic-voice>],]* [<specific-voice> | <generic-voice>]</td></tr>
<tr><td>volume</td><td><number> | <percentage> | silent | x-soft | soft | medium | loud | x-loud</td></tr>
</table>

Common Border, Padding, and Background Properties

<table>
<tr><th>Property</th><th>Value</th></tr>
<tr><td>background</td><td><background-color> || <background-image> || <background-repeat> || <background-attachment> || <background-position></td></tr>
<tr><td>background-attachment</td><td>scroll (default), fixed</td></tr>
<tr><td>background-color</td><td>transparent (default), <color></td></tr>
<tr><td>background-image</td><td>none (default), <uri></td></tr>
</table>

Continued on next page

Property	Value
background-repeat	repeat (default), repeat-x, repeat-y, no-repeat
background-position	[<percentage> | <length>] {1,2} | [[top | center | bottom] || [left | center | right]]
border-before-color	transparent, <color>
border-before-style	none (default), hidden, dotted, dashed, solid, double, groove, ridge, inset, outset
border-before-width	medium (default), thin, thick, unsigned length
border-after-color	transparent, <color>
border-after-style	none (default), hidden, dotted, dashed, solid, double, groove, ridge, inset, outset
border-after-width	medium (default), thin, thick, unsigned length
border-start-color	transparent, <color>
border-start-style	none (default), hidden, dotted, dashed, solid, double, groove, ridge, inset, outset
border-start-width	medium (default), thin, thick, unsigned length
border-end-color	transparent, <color>
border-end-style	none (default), hidden, dotted, dashed, solid, double, groove, ridge, inset, outset
border-end-width	medium (default), thin, thick, unsigned length
border-top-color	transparent, <color>
border-top-style	none (default), hidden, dotted, dashed, solid, double, groove, ridge, inset, outset
border-top-width	medium (default), thin, thick, unsigned length
border-bottom-color	transparent, <color>
border-bottom-style	none (default), hidden, dotted, dashed, solid, double, groove, ridge, inset, outset
border-bottom-width	medium (default), thin, thick, unsigned length
border-left-color	transparent, <color>
border-left-style	none (default), hidden, dotted, dashed, solid, double, groove, ridge, inset, outset
border-left-width	medium (default), thin, thick, unsigned length
border-right-color	transparent, <color>
border-right-style	none (default), hidden, dotted, dashed, solid, double, groove, ridge, inset, outset

Continued on next page

<table>
<tr><th>Property</th><th>Value</th></tr>
<tr><td>border-right-width</td><td>medium (default), thin, thick, unsigned length</td></tr>
<tr><td>border</td><td><'border-top-width'> || <'border-style'> || <color></td></tr>
<tr><td>border-top</td><td><'border-top-width'> || <'border-style'> || <color></td></tr>
<tr><td>border-bottom</td><td><'border-top-width'> || <'border-style'> || <color></td></tr>
<tr><td>border-left</td><td><'border-top-width'> || <'border-style'> || <color></td></tr>
<tr><td>border-right</td><td><'border-top-width'> || <'border-style'> || <color></td></tr>
<tr><td>border-color</td><td><color></td></tr>
<tr><td>border-style</td><td>none (default), hidden, dotted, dashed, solid, double, groove, ridge, inset, outset</td></tr>
<tr><td>border-width</td><td>medium (default), thin, thick, unsigned length</td></tr>
<tr><td>padding-before</td><td>unsigned length (default 0.0pt)</td></tr>
<tr><td>padding-after</td><td>unsigned length (default 0.0pt)</td></tr>
<tr><td>padding-start</td><td>unsigned length (default 0.0pt)</td></tr>
<tr><td>padding-end</td><td>unsigned length (default 0.0pt)</td></tr>
<tr><td>padding-top</td><td>unsigned length (default 0.0pt)</td></tr>
<tr><td>padding-bottom</td><td>unsigned length (default 0.0pt)</td></tr>
<tr><td>padding-left</td><td>unsigned length (default 0.0pt)</td></tr>
<tr><td>padding-right</td><td>unsigned length (default 0.0pt)</td></tr>
<tr><td>padding</td><td><padding-width> {1,4}</td></tr>
</table>

Common Font Properties

<table>
<tr><th>Property</th><th>Value</th></tr>
<tr><td>font</td><td>[[<'font-style'> || <'font-variant'> || <'font-weight'>]? <'font-size'> [/ <'line-height'>]? <'font-family'>] | caption | icon | menu | message-box | small-caption | status-bar</td></tr>
<tr><td>font-family</td><td>[<family-name> | <generic-family>],]* [<family-name> | <generic-family></td></tr>
</table>

Continued on next page

<table>
<tr><th>Property</th><th>Value</th></tr>
<tr><td>font-size</td><td><absolute-size> | <relative-size> | <length> | <percentage></td></tr>
<tr><td>font-stretch</td><td>ultra-condensed, extra-condensed, condensed, semi-condensed, normal (default), semi-expanded, expanded, extra-expanded, ultra-expanded, wider, narrower</td></tr>
<tr><td>font-size-adjust</td><td>none (default), positive real value</td></tr>
<tr><td>font-style</td><td>normal (default), oblique, italic</td></tr>
<tr><td>font-variant</td><td>normal (default), small-caps</td></tr>
<tr><td>font-weight</td><td>normal, bold, bolder, lighter</td></tr>
</table>

Common Hyphenation Properties

Property	Value
country	none (default), use-document
hyphenate	Boolean true/false (false = default)
hyphenation-char	character
hyphenation-remain-char-count	positive integer value
language	none (default), use-document
script	none (default), use-document, string

Common Keeps and Breaks Properties

Property	Value
break-after	auto (default), column, page, even-page, odd-page
break-before	auto (default), column, page, even-page, odd-page
keep-with-next	Boolean true/false (false = default)
keep-with-previous	Boolean true/false (false = default)

Common Margin Properties—Block

Property	Value
margin-top	auto, unsigned length (defaults to 0.0pt), percentage
margin-bottom	auto, unsigned length (defaults to 0.0pt), percentage
margin-left	auto, unsigned length (defaults to 0.0pt), percentage
margin-right	auto, unsigned length (defaults to 0.0pt), percentage
margin	any valid padding-width statement
space-before	valid space specification
space-after	valid space specification
start-indent	signed length (default 0.0pt)
end-indent	signed length

Common Margin Properties—Inline

Property	Value
space-end	valid space specification
space-start	valid space specification

Pagination and Layout Properties

Property	Value
column-count	positive integer
column-gap	signed integer
extent	unsigned length

Continued on next page

Property	Value
flow-name	name
initial-page-number	unsigned integer
page-master-blank-even	name
page-master-even	name
page-master-first	name
page-master-last-even	name
page-master-last-odd	name
page-master-name	name
page-master-odd	name
page-master-repeating	name
page-height	auto (default), indefinite, unsigned length
page-width	auto (default), indefinite, unsigned length
precedence	Boolean true/false (true = default)

Table Properties

Property	Value
caption-side	before (default), after, start, end, top, bottom, left, right
table-layout	fixed, auto (default)
border-collapse	collapse (default), separate
border-spacing	positive length
empty-cells	show (default), hide
table-width	<length> | <percentage> | auto
table-height	<length> | <percentage> | auto

Continued on next page

Property	Value
table-omit-middle-footer	yes, no (default)
column-number	positive integer
n-columns-spanned	positive integer (default = 1)
n-rows-spanned	positive integer (default = 1)
column-width	unsigned length
n-columns-repeated	positive integer (default =1)
caption-width	<length> | <percentage> | auto
row-height	<length> | <percentage> | auto
may-break-after-row	yes, no (default)
may-break-before-row	yes, no (default)
ends-row	yes, no (default)
starts-row	yes, no (default)
cell-height	<length> | <percentage> | auto

Character Properties

Property	Value
character	string
letter-spacing	normal | <length>
word-spacing	normal | <length>
text-decoration	none | [underline || overline || line-through || blink]
text-shadow	none | [<color> || <length <length <length>?,]* [<color> || <length> <length> <length>?]
text-transform	none (default), capitalize, uppercase, lowercase

Rule Properties

Property	Value
rule-orientation	escapement (default), horizontal, line-progression, vertical
rule-style	none (default)
rule-thickness	unsigned length (default = 1.0pt)
length	auto (default), unsigned length

Page-Related Properties

Property	Value
page-break-inside	auto, avoid
orphans	unsigned integer value (default = 2)
widows	unsigned integer value (default = 2)

Horizontal Float-Related Properties

Property	Value
float	left, right, none (default)
clear	left, right, both, none (default)

Properties for Links

Property	Value
external-destination	URI
internal-destination	IDREF value

Continued on next page

Property	Value
show-destination	replace (default), new
indicate-destination	Boolean value (default = false)
space-above-destination-start	unsigned length
space-above-destination-block	unsigned length
auto-restore	Boolean value (default = true)
initial	Boolean value (default = true)
name	name
title	string
switch-to	#preceding, #following, #any (default), or name list
state	DOM state (or event)

Miscellaneous Properties

Property	Value
clip	auto, a_shape
color	<color> (any valid color specification)
direction	ltr, rtl, btt, ttb
font-height-override-after	use-font-metrics (default), signed length
font-height-override-before	use-font-metrics (default), signed length
href	none, URI
hyphenation-keep	column, none, page, spread
hyphenation-ladder-count	none (default), unsigned integer value
id	ID
inhibit-line-breaks	Boolean value (default = false)

Continued on next page

Property	Value
last-line-end-indent	signed length
line-height-shift-adjustment	consider-shifts, disregard-shifts
line-height	normal I <length> I <number> I <percentage>
line-stacking-strategy	line-height (default), font-height, max-height
min-width	<length> I <percentage>
max-width	<length> I <percentage>
height	<length> I <percentage> I auto
min-height	<length> I <percentage>
max-height	<length> I <percentage>
overflow	visible (default), hidden, scroll, auto
ref-id	IDREF value
provisional-label-separation	unsigned length (default = 6.0pt)
provisional-distance-between-starts	unsigned length (default = 24.0pt)
space-between-list-rows	minimum, maximum, optimum, precedence, conditionality
reference-orientation	0 (default), 90, 180, 270, -90, -180, -270
scale	positive real value
score-spaces	Boolean value (default = false)
size	<length>{1,2} I auto I landscape I portrait
span	none (default), all
width	<length> I <percentage> I auto
text-align	start (default), centered, end, justified, page-inside, page-outside
text-align-last	relative (default), start, end, justified
text-indent	signed length
vertical-align	baseline I middle I sub I super I text-top I text-bottom I <percentage> I <length> I top I bottom

Continued on next page

Property	Value
visibility	visible, hidden, collapse
wrap-option	no-wrap, wrap (default)
white-space-treatment	preserve (default), collapse, ignore
writing-mode	use-page-writing-mode, lr-tb, rl-tb, tb-rl, tb-lr, bt-lr, bt-rl, lr-bt, rl-bt, lr-alternating-rl-bt, lr-alternating-rl-tb, lr-inverting-rl-bt, lr-inverting-rl-tb, tb-rl-in-rl-pairs
z-index	auto, signed integer value

APPENDIX B

Semantic Modules Defined in Modularization of XHTML

The Modularization of XHTML Working Draft has identified 22 semantic modules that will be supported in XHTML. Among those are several semantic groupings of modules as outlined in this appendix. Each table presents the elements, each element's supported attributes, and the minimal content model for each element. See Chapter 3: "Creating XML Documents" for a review of the Extended Backus Naur Form (EBNF) notation used in the Minimal Content Model column.

Before we define the modules themselves, however, we will review the attribute types available in XHTML and define the collections of attribute sets that can abbreviate the element definitions.

TABLE B.1: Attribute Types Used in the Modules

Attribute Type	Definition
CDATA	character data
ID	an identifier that is unique within the document
IDREF	a reference to an ID
NAME	a name that is unique within the document
NMTOKEN	a name composed of CDATA characters but no white space
NMTOKENS	multiple names composed of CDATA characters separated by white space (a space-delimited list)
PCDATA	parsed character data

TABLE B.2: Attribute Collections Defined

Collection Name	Member Attributes
Core	class (NMTOKEN), id (ID), title (CDATA)
Internationalization (I18n)	dir ("rtol" | "ltor"), xml:lang (NMTOKEN)
Events	onclick, ondblclick, onmousedown, onmouseup, onmouseover, onmousemove, onmouseout, onkeypress, onkeydown, onkeyup
Style	style (CDATA)
Common	Core+Events+Internationalization+Style

Basic Modules

These modules must be present in any document type that purports to be a conforming member of the XHTML family.

Structure Module

Elements	Attributes	Minimal Content Model
body	common	(PCDATA I Flow)*
div	common	(Heading I Block I List)*
head	I18n, profile	title
html	I18n, version, xmlns	head, body
span	common	(PCDATA I Inline)*
title	I18n	PCDATA

Basic Text Module

Elements	Attributes	Minimal Content Model
abbr	common	(PCDATA I Inline)*
acronym	common	(PCDATA I Inline)*
address	common	(PCDATA I Inline)*
blockquote	common, cite	(PCDATA I Heading I Block)*
br	core	EMPTY
cite	common	(PCDATA I Inline)*
code	common	(PCDATA I Inline)*
dfn	common	(PCDATA I Inline)*
em	common	(PCDATA I Inline)*
h1	common	(PCDATA I Inline)*
h2	common	(PCDATA I Inline)*

Continued on next page

Elements	Attributes	Minimal Content Model
h3	common	(PCDATA | Inline)*
h4	common	(PCDATA | Inline)*
h5	common	(PCDATA | Inline)*
h6	common	(PCDATA | Inline)*
kbd	common	(PCDATA | Inline)*
p	common	(PCDATA | Inline)*
pre	common	(PCDATA | Inline)*
q	common	(PCDATA | Inline)*
samp	common	(PCDATA | Inline)*
strong	common	(PCDATA | Inline)*
var	common	(PCDATA | Inline)*

Hypertext Module

Elements	Attributes	Minimal Content Model
a	common, charset, href, hreflang, rel, rev, type	(PCDATA | Inline – a)*

List Module

Elements	Attributes	Minimal Content Model
dl	common	(dt | dd)+
dt	common	(PCDATA | Inline)*
dd	common	(PCDATA | Inline)*
ol	common	li+
ul	common	li+
li	common	(PCDATA | Inline)*

With the definition of this module, we've also defined a new set list that has its own minimal content model of (dl | ol | ul)+, which is then added to the Flow content set within the Basic Text Module.

Content Model Sets Several of the minimal content model entries in these tables make reference to sets, such as "heading" or "flow." These sets are defined as:

Set	Member Elements
Heading	h1 I h2 I h3 I h4 I h5 I h6
Block	address I blockquote I p I pre
Inline	abbr I acronym I br I cite I code I dfn I em I kbd I q I samp I strong I var
Flow	Heading I Block I Inline

Additional Modules

These modules may be combined with the core modules and/or custom modules in any manner desired to create new document types.

Applet Module

Elements	Attributes	Minimal Content Model
applet	core, alt, archive, code, codebase, height, name, object, width	param?
param	id (ID), name (CDATA), type, value, valuetype	EMPTY

When the Applet Module is present, the applet element is included in the Inline Content set for the Basic Text Module.

Text Extension Modules

TABLE B.3: Presentation Module

Elements	Attributes	Minimal Content Model
b	common	(PCDATA I Inline)*
big	common	(PCDATA I Inline)*
hr	common	EMPTY
i	common	(PCDATA I Inline)*
small	common	(PCDATA I Inline)*
sub	common	(PCDATA I Inline)*
sup	common	(PCDATA I Inline)*
tt	common	(PCDATA I Inline)*

When this module is present, hr becomes a part of the Block content set, and the remaining elements of this module are included in the Inline content set for the Basic Text Module.

TABLE B.4: Edit Module

Elements	Attributes	Minimal Content Model
del	common	(PCDATA I Inline)*
ins	common	(PCDATA I Inline)*

Del and ins are added to the Inline content set when this module is used.

TABLE B.5: BDO module

Elements	Attributes	Minimal Content Model
bdo	common	(PCDATA I Inline)*

The bdo element is added to the Inline content set when the BDO Module is included.

Forms Modules Two modules have been created to handle forms functions. The first, the Basic Forms Module, provides for features found in HTML 3.2—namely, the basic form functionality. The larger Forms Module includes elements that enhance accessibility for forms. The intent is not to subvert the accessibility features of HTML 4 Forms in any way, but to provide a base set of form functionality that lightweight devices can still handle.

TABLE B.6: Basic Forms Module

<table>
<tr><th>Elements</th><th>Attributes</th><th>Minimal Content Model</th></tr>
<tr><td>form</td><td>common, action, method, enctype</td><td>Heading | Block – form</td></tr>
<tr><td>input</td><td>common, checked, maxlength, name, size, src, type, value</td><td>EMPTY</td></tr>
<tr><td>select</td><td>common, multiple, name, size</td><td>option+</td></tr>
<tr><td>option</td><td>common, selected, value</td><td>Inline*</td></tr>
<tr><td>textarea</td><td>common, columns, name, rows</td><td>PCDATA*</td></tr>
</table>

Two sets are referenced in this module:

<table>
<tr><th>Set</th><th>Member Elements</th></tr>
<tr><td>Form</td><td>form</td></tr>
<tr><td>Formctrl</td><td>input | select | textarea</td></tr>
</table>

TABLE B.7: Forms Module

<table>
<tr><th>Elements</th><th>Attributes</th><th>Minimal Content Model</th></tr>
<tr><td>form</td><td>common, accept, accept-charset, action, method, enctype</td><td>(Heading | block – form | fieldset)+</td></tr>
<tr><td>input</td><td>common, accept, accesskey, alt, checked, disabled, maxlength, name, readonly, size, src, tabindex, type, value</td><td>EMPTY</td></tr>
<tr><td>select</td><td>common, disabled, multiple, name, size, tabindex</td><td>(optgroup | option)+</td></tr>
</table>

Continued on next page

TABLE B.7 CONTINUED: Forms Module

Elements	Attributes	Minimal Content Model
option	common, disabled, label, selected, value	PCDATA
textarea	common, accesskey, columns, disabled, name, readonly, rows, tabindex	PCDATA
button	common, accesskey, disabled, name, tabindex, type, value	(PCDATA I Heading I List I Block – Form I Inline – Formctrl)*
fieldset	common	(PCDATA I legend I Flow)*
label	common, accesskey, for	(PCDATA I Inline – label)*
legend	common, accesskey	(PCDATA I Inline)+
optgroup	common, disabled, label	option+

The larger Forms Module also has two sets labeled as Form and Formctrl. Note that the sets have expanded membership based on their presence in this larger module vs. the pared down sets for the Basic Forms Module.

Set	Member Elements
Form	form I fieldset
Formctrl	input I select I textarea I label I button

NOTE

With both modules, the Form content set is added to the Block content set. Additionally, the Formctrl content set is included in the Inline content set. When form functionality will be included in your document type, you can include only one of the forms modules, not both. Choose which one to include based on the elements required in your document instance.

Tables Modules Table functionality has also been split up into two modules. The Basic Tables Module covers rudimentary functionality appropriate for limited capability devices or user agents, and the larger Tables Module carries over most features found in HTML 4.

TABLE B.8: Basic Tables Module

Elements	Attributes	Minimal Content Model
caption	common	(PCDATA I Inline)*
table	common, border, cellpadding, cellspacing, summary, width	caption?, tr+
td	common, abbr, align, axis, colspan, headers, rowspan, scope, valign	(PCDATA I Flow)*
th	common, abbr, align, axis, colspan, headers, rowspan, scope, valign	(PCDATA I Flow)*
tr	common, align, valign	(th I td)+

TABLE B.9: Tables Module

Elements	Attributes	Minimal Content Model
caption	common	(PCDATA I Inline)*
table	common, border, cellpadding, cellspacing, datapage-size, frame, rules, summary, width	caption?, (col* I colgroup*), ((thead?, tfoot?, tbody+) I (tr+))
td	common, abbr, align, axis, colspan, headers, rowspan, scope, valign	(PCDATA I Inline)*
th	common, abbr, align, axis, colspan, headers, rowspan, scope, valign	(PCDATA I Inline)*
tr	common, align, valign	(td I th)+
col	common, align, span, valign, width	EMPTY
colgroup	common, align, span, valign, width	col*
tbody	common, align, valign	tr+
thead	common, align, valign	tr+
tfoot	common, align, valign	tr+

In both instances, the table element is added to the Block content set when either table module is present.

Image Module

Elements	Attributes	Minimal Content Model
img	common, alt, height, ismap, longdesc, src, usemap, width	EMPTY

The `img` element is incorporated in the Inline content set when this module is present.

Image Map Module

NOTE In this module and several modules to come, the attribute sets of elements introduced in the core module set are extended by their presence in these new modules. To indicate where this occurs, the element has the "&" character appended to its name, such as **a&** to indicate an extended attribute set for the **a** element. The element name itself, of course, remains just **a**.

Elements	Attributes	Minimal Content Model
a&	coords, shape	n/a
area	common, accesskey, alt, coords, href, nohref, shape, tabindex	EMPTY
map	common, name	((Heading I Block) I area)+

Object Module

Elements	Attributes	Minimal Content Model
object	common, archive, classid, codebase, codetype, data, declare, height, standby, tabindex, type, usemap, width	(PCDATA I Flow I param)*
param	id, type, value, valuetype	EMPTY

When this module appears, the object element is included in the Inline content set.

Intrinsic Events

Elements	Attributes	Notes
a&	onblur, onfocus	
area&	onblur, onfocus	When the Image Map Module is present
form&	onreset, onsubmit	When the Basic Forms or Forms Module is present
body&	onload, onunload	
label&	onblur, onfocus	When the Forms Module is present
input&	onblur, onchange, onfocus, onselect	When the Basic Forms or Forms Module is present
select&	onblur, onchange, onfocus	When the Basic Forms or Forms Module is present
textarea&	onblur, onchange, onfocus, onselect	When the Basic Forms or Forms Module is present
button&	onblur, onfocus	When the Forms Module is present

Metainformation Module

Elements	Attributes	Minimal Content Model
meta	18n, content, http-equiv, name, schem	EMPTY

Scripting Module

Elements	Attributes	Minimal Content Model
noscript	common	(Heading I List I Block)+
script	charset, defer, src, type	PCDATA

The script and noscript elements are added to the Block content set when this module is used.

Style Sheet Module

Elements	Attributes	Minimal Content Model
style	I18n, media, title, type	PCDATA

The Block content set is updated to include style when this module is present.

Link Module

Elements	Attributes	Minimal Content Model
link	common, charset, href, hreflang, media, rel, rev, type	EMPTY

The link element is added to the content model of the head element, as it appears in the Structure Module, when this module is utilized.

Base Module

TIP Note that this module shouldn't be confused with the Core Modules; it instead refers to the base element.

Elements	Attributes	Minimal Content Model
base	href	EMPTY

The base element is added to the content model of the head element, as it appears in the Structure Module, when this module is utilized.

IFrame Module

Elements	Attributes	Minimal Content Model
iframe	core, frameborder, height, longdesc, marginheight, marginwidth, scrolling, src, width	Flow

When used, the iframe element is included in the Block content set.

INDEX

Note to the Reader: Page numbers in **bold** indicate the principal discussion of a topic or the definition of a term. Page numbers in *italic* indicate illustrations.

SYMBOLS

A

B

C

D

E

F

G

H

I

J

K

L

M

N

O

P

Q

R

S

T

U

V

W

X

PRAISE FROM OUR READERS

Mastering HTML 4

"This is THE book!! If you can't find what you are looking for or learn HTML from this book, then there is no hope. This is the most comprehensive HTML book I have ever seen! Well worth the money and time to read it!"

Martha Rich, Arkansas

"Fantastic, Comprehensive, Easy-to-Read! I've thumbed through, and read thoroughly, many HTML books, but this one just grabs your brain, rattles out your neurons and implants the goodies you need to slam-dunk a great Web site. The authors provide an easy-to-read format with just the right amount of examples and details that won't leave you asking more questions or bore you with too many arcane details."

Sabrina Hanley, North Carolina

Mastering XML

"Got XML questions? This book has the answers. For implementers: detailed tips and techniques used by the experts. For XML users: clear explanations of the XML family of standards and XML applications. For managers: case studies of successful XML implementations. This book deserves a place on your bookshelf."

Eric Freese, Director of Consulting Services, ISOGEN International Corp., http://www.isogen.com

"Mastering XML provides a solid introduction to the concepts essential for mastering, and applying, XML. Navarro, White, and Burman offer details on various XML vocabularies, which are critical elements of any XML effort."

Laura Walker, Executive Director, OASIS, http://www.oasis-open.org/, http://xml.org

IBM ALPHAWORKS LICENSE AGREEMENT

Please read this IBM alphaWorks license agreement (called the "Agreement") carefully. Your use of the software or any related documentation (called the "Software") indicates your acceptance of the following terms and conditions. If you do not agree to these terms and conditions, you may not install or use the Software.

Notice: The Software that is made available through the alphaWorks project is not generally available software. It has not undergone complete testing and may contain errors. It may not function properly and is subject to change or withdrawal at any time. No support or maintenance is provided with the Software. Do not install this software if you are not accustomed to using experimental software.

The alphaWorks Software is made available without charge in the experimental stage in order to allow you to evaluate the Software in its developmental stage. We encourage your feedback and suggestions.

1. Ownership and License

The Software is owned by International Business Machines Corporation or one of its subsidiaries ("IBM") and is copyrighted and licensed, not sold.

IBM grants you a non-exclusive, non-transferable license to download the Software and use it only for your personal, non-commercial and lawful end use. Implied licenses are negated.

You may copy the Software for backup only. You may not: 1) merge, distribute (for free or for sale) or sublicense the Software; 2) reverse assemble, reverse compile, or otherwise translate the Software.

2. Term and Termination

This Agreement will terminate ninety (90) days after the date on which you receive the Software. Upon such termination you will delete or destroy all copies of the Software.

3. Warranty Disclaimer and Limitation of Liability

IBM licenses the Software to you on an "as is" basis, without warranty of any kind. IBM hereby expressly disclaims all warranties or conditions, either express or implied, including, but not limited to, the implied warranties or conditions of merchantability and fitness for a particular purpose. You are solely responsible for determining the appropriateness of using this Software and assume all risks associated with the use of this Software, including but not limited to the risks of program errors, damage to or loss of data, programs or equipment, and unavailability or interruption of operations. Some jurisdictions do not allow for the exclusion or limitation of implied warranties, so the above limitations or exclusions may not apply to you.

IBM will not be liable for any direct damages or for any special, incidental, or indirect damages or for any economic consequential damages (including lost profits or savings), even if IBM has been advised of the possibility of such damages. IBM will not be liable for the loss of, or damage to, your records or data, or any damages claimed by you based on a third party claim. Some jurisdictions do not allow for the exclusion or limitation of incidental or consequential damages, so the above limitations or exclusions may not apply to you.

4. License Rights

You hereby grant to IBM an irrevocable license under all intellectual property rights (including copyright) to use, copy, distribute, sublicense, display, perform and prepare derivative works based upon any feedback, including materials, fixes, error corrections, enhancements, suggestions and the like that you provide to IBM.

5. General

This Agreement is governed by the laws of the State of New York.

This Agreement is the only understanding and agreement we have regarding your use of the Software. It supersedes all other communications, understandings or agreements we may have had prior to this Agreement.

WHAT'S ON THE CD

The *Mastering™ XML* CD is packed with popular XML tools that will help you in parsing, browsing, developing, and more. The list below describes each tool available on the enclosed companion CD.

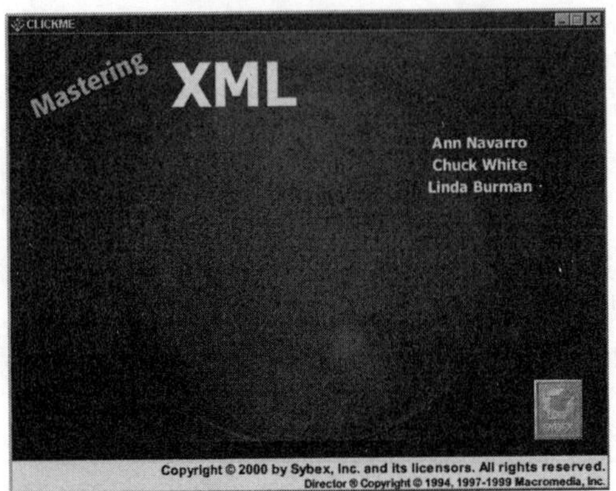

Source Code—A comprehensive listing of XML code taken directly from the book.

IBM Alphaworks Tools Suite—A series of Java-based XML software packages that provide early adopters access to IBM's emerging "alpha code" technologies. The suite includes LotusXSL, Xplorer, XML EditorMaker, and XML Security Suite.

HTML Tidy Utility (W3C)—A utility from W3C for cleaning up HTML markup.

Near & Far Designer—A DTD creation/management tool from Microstar that doesn't require you to have prior knowledge of the language syntax.

Visual XML—Written in Java, a tool from Pierre Morel that enables you to create and modify DTD and XML documents.

XML Client—A Java-based Web browser from InDelv that browses XML files with XSL style sheets and the formatting object namespace. Includes a free XML/XSL browser and supports CSS for HTML content.

XML Spy 2.5—An XML authoring and development tool from Icon that supports customizable work environment options, XML namespaces, limited DTD validation, and XML schema functionality.

XMetal 1—A highly customizable XML authoring tool from SoftQuad that is easy to use and shields you from the complexities of XML.

XT—An implementation of XSL transformations in Java from James Clark that is a must for XSL validation and processing.

XP—A non-validating XML parser written in Java from James Clark.

SAX—A standard interface for event-based XML parsing from James Clark.

FOP—A print formatter from James Tauber that reads formatting objects trees and converts them to PDF documents.

XMLNotepad—A simple prototyping application for HTML authors from Microsoft that enables building and editing of small sets of XML-based data.

Mozilla/Netscape—The most recent Web browser from Netscape.

Internet Explorer 5—The latest version of Microsoft's Web browser.

XML Authority—A graphical design tool from Extensibility that helps you create and manage XML schemas.